Writing Arguments

A Rhetoric with Readings

JOHN D. RAMAGE

ARIZONA STATE UNIVERSITY

JOHN C. BEAN

SEATTLE UNIVERSITY

ALLYN AND BACON

Boston   London   Toronto   Sydney   Tokyo   Singapore

Editor: Eben Ludlow
Production Supervisor: Anthony VenGraitis
Production Manager: Nick Sklitsis
Text Designer: Anne Flanagan
Cover Designer: Susan Paradise

Library of Congress Cataloging-in-Publication Data
Ramage, John D.
    Writing arguments: a rhetoric with readings / John D. Ramage,
John C. Bean. — 3rd ed.
        p.   cm.
    Includes index.
    ISBN 0-02-398145-8
    1. English language — Rhetoric.   2. Persuasion (Rhetoric)
3. College readers. I. Bean, John C.   II. Title.
PE 1431.R33   1995b
808'.042—dc20   94–4903
                                                          CIP

Acknowledgments begin on page 756, which constitutes a continuation of the
copyright page.

Printed in the United States of America
10 9 8 7 6 5 4   99 98 97

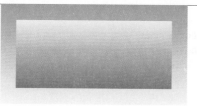

Preface

Overview

The success of the second edition of *Writing Arguments: A Rhetoric with Readings* has encouraged us to retain the text's strengths in this third edition while making judicious changes to enhance the text's clarity, comprehensiveness, and usefulness in the classroom. To enhance the text's flexibility, *Writing Arguments* is available for the first time in both a regular edition with an anthology of arguments and in a brief edition without the anthology.

Our primary purpose in both versions is to integrate a comprehensive study of argument with a process approach to writing. The text treats arguments as a means of personal discovery and clarification, as well as a means of persuading audiences. In both its treatment of argumentation and its approach to teaching writing, the text is rooted in current research and theory. *Writing Arguments* has been used successfully at the freshman level and in more advanced courses devoted solely to argument.

The third edition retains the following successful features from the second edition: The text has an extensive treatment of invention that includes use of the Toulmin system of analyzing arguments combined with use of the enthymeme as a discovery and shaping tool. To aid invention, it also has explanations of *logos, pathos,* and *ethos,* and a major section treating five categories of claims. It focuses on both the reading and the writing of arguments and also includes a copious treatment of the research paper, including two student examples—one using the MLA system and one using the APA system. Among the book's distinguishing features are numerous "For Class Discussion" exercises designed for collaborative groups, a full sequence of writing assignments, and an extensive appendix on working in groups. The third edition contains seventeen student essays of varied length and complexity as well as fifty-six professional essays aimed at producing discussion, analysis, and debate.

Improvements in the Third Edition

Based on recommendations from many users of the second edition at both four-year and two-year institutions, we have substantially strengthened the text through the following additions and changes.

- Extensive revision of Chapters 1 and 2 to create higher levels of student interest. In Chapter 1, a student's petition to waive an algebra requirement replaces the Montana Technology Board discussion, while in Chapter 2, the timely issue of illegitimacy and single-parenthood replaces the Brandt/Kannar debate on the exclusionary rule. (The single-parenthood issue is developed further in the anthology section.)

- Extensive rewriting of Chapter 5 to make the Toulmin system more teachable. Chapter 5 now includes clearer, more detailed explanations of Toulmin's system. There are also many new examples focusing on reading-based arguments, as well as personal experience arguments.

- General tightening, streamlining, and updating throughout. Judicious pruning and combining, as well as consistent updating of readings and examples, make the third edition more lively and relevant to student interests.

- Substantial revision of Part V, the anthology section. The third edition contains six new issues and thirty-two new essays including a complete updating of the readings on global warming. The third edition also includes a greater variety of argument types. Specifically added are several longer, research-based arguments that show students the contribution that serious scholarship can make to the study of public issues. Taken from reflective public affairs magazines or from academic journals, these essays in their documented use of evidence and their scrutiny of differing points of view, better illustrate in-depth argumentation than do typical op-ed articles. Examples of these research-based pieces include the widely cited Lee Robins study of drug usage among returning Vietnam veterans, Wallace Broecker's "Global Warming on Trial," or Barbara Dafoe Whitehead's *Atlantic* article on the decline of the two-parent family.

Our Approaches to Argumentation

Our interest in argumentation grows out of our interest in the relationship between writing and thinking. When writing arguments, writers are forced to lay bare their thinking processes in an unparalleled way. In an effort to engage students in the kinds of critical thinking that argument demands, we draw on four major approaches to argumentation:

- **The enthymeme as a rhetorical and logical structure.** This concept, especially useful for beginning writers, helps students "nutshell" an argument as a claim with one or several supporting *because* clauses. It also helps them see how real-world arguments are rooted in probabilistic assumptions granted by the audience rather than in universal and unchanging principles.

- **Toulmin's system of analyzing arguments.** Toulmin's system helps students see the complete, implicit structure that underlies an enthymeme and develop appropriate grounds and backing to support the claim. It also highlights the rhetorical, social, and dialectical nature of argument.

- **The three classical types of appeal—logos, ethos, and pathos.** These concepts help students place their arguments in a rhetorical context focusing on audience-based appeals; they also help students create an effective voice and style.

- **Stasis theory on categories of claims.** This approach stresses the heuristic value of learning different patterns of support for different categories of claims and often leads students to make surprisingly rich and full arguments.

Throughout the text these approaches are integrated and synthesized into generative tools for both producing and analyzing arguments.

Structure of the Text

The text has five main parts plus three appendixes. Part I gives an overview of argumentation. These first three chapters present our philosophy of argument, showing how argument helps writers clarify their own thinking. Throughout we link the process of arguing—articulating issue questions, formulating propositions, examining opposing arguments, and creating structures of supporting reasons and evidence—with the processes of reading and writing.

Part II examines the principles of argument. Chapters 4 through 6 show that the core of an argument is a claim with reasons. These reasons are often stated as enthymemes, the unstated premise of which must sometimes be brought to the surface and supported. Discussion of Toulmin logic shows students how to discover both the stated and unstated premises of their arguments and to provide structures of reasons and evidence to support them. Chapters 7 and 8 focus on the rhetorical context of arguments. These chapters discuss the writer's relationship with an audience, particularly with finding audience-based reasons, with using *pathos* and *ethos* effectively and responsibly, and with accommodating or refuting opposing views.

Part III discusses five different categories of argument: definitional arguments (X is/is not a Y), causal arguments (X causes/does not cause Y), resemblance arguments (X is/is not like Y), evaluation arguments (X is/is not a good Y), and proposal arguments (we should/should not do X). These chapters introduce students to two recurring strategies of argument that cut across the different category types: *Criteria-match* arguing in which the writer establishes criteria for a Y and argues that X meets those criteria, and causal arguing in which the writer shows that X can be linked to Y in a *causal* chain. The last chapter of Part III deals with the special complexities of moral arguments.

Part IV shows students how to incorporate research into their arguments. It explains how writers use sources, with a special focus on the skills of summary, paraphrase, and judicious quotation. Unlike standard treatments of the research paper, our discussion explains to students how the writer's meaning and purpose control the selection and shaping of source materials. Part IV explains both the MLA and the APA documentation system, which are illustrated by two student examples of researched arguments.

The appendixes provide important supplemental information useful for courses in argument. Appendix 1 gives an overview of informal fallacies. Appendix 2 discusses some uses and abuses of statistics in argument. Finally, Appendix 3, adapted from our textbook *Form and Surprise in Composition: Writing and Thinking Across the Curriculum* (Macmillan 1986), shows students how to get the most out of collaborative groups in an argument class. It also provides a sequence of collaborative tasks that will help students learn to peer-critique their classmates' arguments in progress. The numerous "For Class Discussion" exercises within the text provide additional tasks for group collaboration.

Finally, the anthology section provides a selection of professional arguments covering eleven provocative issues. The anthology begins with four issues treated, for pedagogical purposes, as sharply contrasted pro/con pairs. The remaining issues are treated in greater depth through inclusion of a wide spectrum of views suggesting the subtlety and complexity of arguments in the real world. Additionally, throughout the rhetoric section of the text we have included several dozen additional arguments—both student and professional—that illustrate the strategies under discussion. Two of the issues raised in the rhetoric section (illegitimacy and single-parenthood from Chapter 2 and the mentally ill homeless in Chapters 10 and 14 are treated more fully in the anthology).

Writing Assignments

The text provides a variety of sequenced writing assignments, including expressive tasks for discovering and exploring arguments, "microthemes" for practicing basic argumentative moves (for example, supporting a reason with statistical evidence), cases, and numerous other assignments calling for complete arguments. Thus, the text provides instructors with a wealth of options for writing assignments on which to build a coherent course.

Acknowledgments

We are happy for this opportunity to give public thanks to the scholars, teachers, and students who have influenced our approach to composition and argument. We give special thanks to Peter Ross of the University of the District of Columbia for suggesting and helping compile the "quick check" Works Cited and Reference lists for easy comparison of MLA and APA bibliographic formats (pp. 412-19). We also thank the following reviewers who gave us unusually helpful and cogent advice on this revision: Thomas Blues, University of Kentucky; Mary Lou Cutrera, Louisiana State University; James P. Farrelly, The University of Dayton; Christine Farris, Indiana University; Christy Friend, University of Texas at Austin; Rebecca Innocent, Southern Methodist University; Charles Kostelnick, Iowa State University; Joe Law, Texas Christian University; Renée H. Major, Louisiana State University; William Peirce, Prince George's Community College; Stephen Wilhoit, The University of Dayton; and Linda Woodson, University of Texas at San Antonio.

We would also like to thank our editor Eben Ludlow, whose unflagging good humor and faith in our approach to both composition and argument have kept us writing and revising for the better part of seven years. Eben called forth this book and kept it going. For that we are grateful.

Finally, we especially thank our families. To Kathleen Ramage and Rosalie (Kit) Bean, thanks for the professional help and encouragement. Kathy Ramage's many years' experience in teaching argumentation has shaped our ideas in numerous ways. And Kit Bean's background in library science has influenced our approach to research writing throughout Part IV. Moreover, we are especially grateful for Kit's advice in the section of Chapter 17 explaining the MLA and APA documentation systems. We would also like to thank Chris Ramage and Stephen and Andrew Bean for their invaluable assistance in library research, helping us determine issues that would interest college students, and tracking down leads for the professional readings throughout the text. And to Sarah Bean, thanks for taping six hundred tearsheets.

JDR
JCB

Brief Contents

PART I
Overview of an Argument   1

1   ARGUMENT: An Introduction   2
2   READING ARGUMENTS   24
3   WRITING ARGUMENTS   60

PART II
Principles of Argument   85

4   THE CORE OF AN ARGUMENT: A Claim with Reasons   86
5   THE LOGICAL STRUCTURE OF ARGUMENTS   98
6   EVIDENCE IN ARGUMENT   118
7   MOVING YOUR AUDIENCE: Audience-Based Reasons, *Ethos,* and *Pathos*   140
8   ACCOMMODATING YOUR AUDIENCE: Treating Opposing Views   166

PART III
Arguments in Depth: Five Categories of Claims   193

9   USING THE CATEGORIES OF CLAIMS TO GENERATE IDEAS   194
10   DEFINITION ARGUMENTS: X Is/Is Not a Y   202
11   CAUSAL ARGUMENTS: X Causes/Does Not Cause Y   234
12   RESEMBLANCE ARGUMENTS: X Is/Is Not Like Y   270
13   EVALUATION ARGUMENTS: X Is/Is Not a Good Y   288
14   PROPOSAL ARGUMENTS: "We Should/Should Not Do X"   312
15   ETHICAL ARGUMENTS   352

PART IV
Writing From Sources: The Argument as a Formal Research Paper   369

16   UNLOCKING THE LIBRARY: Finding and Selecting Sources   370
17   USING AND DOCUMENTING SOURCES   388

APPENDIXES   430

APPENDIX 1   Logical Fallacies   431
APPENDIX 2   Statistical Traps in Arguments   444
APPENDIX 3   The Writing Community: Working in Groups   452

PART V:
An Anthology of Arguments 471

Overview of the Anthology 471

Guide Questions for the Analysis and Evaluation of Arguments 473

Newcomers to our Shores: Should the United States Place a Moratorium on Immigration? 475

Dan Stein. "Timeout: The United States Needs a Moratorium on Immigration" 475

Frank Sharry. "Immigrants Help Make America Strong" 478

Guns and Public Safety: Should the Federal Government Enact Strict Controls on the Ownership of Handguns? 481

Molly Ivins. "2000 Million Guns—Let's Not Make It Any Worse" 481

Dave Kopel. "Why Good People Own Guns: Better Safe Than Sorry" 483

Mercy Killing and the Right-to-die: Can Active Euthanasia be a Moral Good? 487

William F. May. "Rising to the Occasion of Our Death" 487

Daniel C. Maguire. "Death by Choice: Who Should Decide?" 489

The Distribution of Wealth: What Responsibility Do the Rich Have for the Poor? 494

Garrett Hardin. "Lifeboat Ethics: The Case against Helping the Poor" 494

Peter Singer. "Rich and Poor" 504

Civil Disobedience: Is Refusal to Obey Laws Ever a Positive Good? 513

Martin Luther King, Jr. "Letter from Birmingham Jail" in Response to "Public Statement by Eight Alabama Clergymen" 513

Lewis H. Van Dusen, Jr. "Civil Disobedience: Destroyer of Democracy" 527

Plato. From The Crito 533

Political Correctness and Diversity: Freedom of Speech at What Cost? 538

Nat Hentoff. "'Speech Codes' on the Campus" 538

John Leo. "The Politics of Feelings" 544

Judith Martin and Gunther Stent. "Say the Right Thing—or Else" 546

Katherine T. Bartlett. "Some Factual Correctness about Political Correctness" 547

Barbara Ehrenreich. "Teach Diversity with a Smile" 550

The Legalization of Drugs: Would America Be Better Off or Worse Off If Drugs Were Legalized? 552

"The Federal Drugstore: An interview with Michael S. Gazzaniga 552

Walter Wink. "Biting the Bullet: The Case for Legalizing Drugs" 563

Richard J. Dennis. "The Economics of Legalizing Drugs" 569

James Q. Wilson. "Against the Legalization of Drugs" 579

Lee N. Robins, Darlene H. Davis, and Donald W. Goodwin. "Drug Use by U.S. Army Enlisted Men in Vietnam: A Follow-Up on Their Return Home" 593

Sexual Harassment: When Is Offensiveness a Civil Offense? 612

Stephanie Riger. "Gender Dilemmas in Sexual Harassment Policies and Procedures" 612

Naomi Munson. "Harassment Blues" 629

Erica Jong. "Fear of Flirting" 633

Gretchen Morgenson. "Watch That Leer, Stifle That Joke" 637

Susan Crawford. "A Wink Here, a Leer There: It's Costly" 641

Martha Chamallas. "Universal Truth and Multiple Perspectives: Controversies on Sexual Harassment" 643

Global Warming: How Serious Is the Greenhouse Effect? What Should Be Done about It? 648

Wallace S. Broecker. "Global Warming on Trial" 648

Jeremy Leggett. "Global Warming: The Worst Case" 656

S. Fred Singer. "Warming Theories Need Warning Label" 663

R. Monastersky. "Signs of Global Warming Found in Ice" 670

Dixy Lee Ray. "Global Warming: A Skeptic's View" 672

"Dissent on Warming" 674

Mental Asylums versus Community Care: What Should Be Done about the Mentally Ill Homeless? 676

Paul S. Appelbaum. "Crazy in the Streets" 676

Jonathan Kozol. " Are the Homeless Crazy?" 687

Steven Vanderstaay. "The Homeless Mentally Ill" 691

E. Fuller Torrey. "Who Goes Homeless?" 701

Illegitimacy, Single Parenthood, and Welfare Reform: Should the Government Enact Policies to Strengthen the Traditional Family? If So, How? 708

Dan Quayle. "Restoring Basic Values: Strengthening the Family" 708

Katha Pollitt. "Why I Hate 'Family Values' (Let Me Count the Ways)" 714

Elija Anderson. "Abolishing Welfare Won't Stop Poverty, Illegitimacy" 721

Barbara Dafoe Whitehead. "Dan Quayle Was Right" 723

INDEX 761

Detailed Contents

PART I

Overview of Argument   1

1   ARGUMENT: An Introduction   2

The Difference Between Persuasion and Argument   3

Initial Definition of Argument   6

Clarification or Victory? The Debate Between Socrates and Callicles   8

What Is Truth? The Place of Argument in Contemporary Life   10

A Successful Process of Argumentation: The Well-Functioning Committee   13

"Petition to Waive the University Math Requirement"—Gordon Adams (student)   17

CONCLUSION: What Happens when the Arguing Process Fails   21

2   READING ARGUMENTS   24

Why Reading Arguments Is Important for Writers of Argument   24

Suggestions for Improving Your Reading Process   24

Strategies for Reading Arguments: An Overview   26

Strategy 1:   Reading as a Believer   26

"The Coming White Underclass"—Charles Murray   27

    Summary Writing as a Way of Reading to Believe   32

    Incorporating Summaries into Your Own Writing   37

Strategy 2:   Reading as a Doubter   39

Strategy 3:   Analyzing Why Disputants Disagree   41

  Disagreement about Facts or Truth   41

  Disagreement about Definitions   42

  Disagreement about Appropriate Analogies   42

  Disagreement about Values, Beliefs, or Assumptions   43

"Letter to the Editor" in Response to Charles Murray
—Patricia Bucalo   44

"Letter to the Editor" in Response to Charles Murray
—Pamela J. Maraldo   45

Excerpt from "New Cultural Conscience Shifts the Welfare Debate"
—John Leo   46

"Wrong Way to Reform Welfare"—Dorothy Gilliam   47

  Writing Analysis of a Pro/Con Controversy   49

"An Analysis of the Sources of Disagreement between Murray and Gilliam"
(A Sample Analysis Essay)   49

Strategy 4:   Evaluating the Conflicting Positions   51

Joining an Argument: A Brief Case Study   52

"To Save Their Daughter from Leukemia, Abe and Mary Ayala Conceived a
Plan—and a Baby"—from People magazine   53

"We Have Children for All Sorts of Reasons, and Now One Is Made to
Save Her Sibling"—Ellen Goodman   56

3   WRITING ARGUMENTS   60

A Brief Description of Writers' Process   61

Strategies For Improving Your Writing Processes   62

Using Expressive Writing for Discovery and Exploration   64

  Freewriting   64

  Idea-mapping   65

  Playing the Believing and Doubting Game   66

  Brainstorming for Pro and Con "Because Clauses"   69

Shaping Your Argument: The Power of Tree Diagrams   70

A Case Study: Sandra's Argument   75

"Was it Morally Wrong for the Ayalas to Conceive a Child to Act as a Bone-
marrow Donor for Their Older Daughter?"—Sandra Nelson (student)   75

Using Expressive Writing to Discover and Explore Ideas: Two Sets of
Exploratory Tasks   77

  Set 1:   Starting Points   77

  Set 2:   Exploration and Rehearsal   79

Writing Assignments For Part I   81

PART II

Principles of Argument 85

4   THE CORE OF AN ARGUMENT: A Claim with
Reasons   86

The Rhetorical Triangle   86

Issue Questions as the Origins of Argument   87

Difference between an Issue Question and an Information Question   88

The Difference between a Genuine Argument and a
Pseudo-argument   90

Pseudo-arguments: Fanatics and Skeptics   90

Another Source of Pseudo-arguments: Lack of Shared Assumptions   91

FRAME OF AN ARGUMENT: A CLAIM SUPPORTED BY
REASONS   93

What Is a Reason?   93

Advantages of Expressing Reasons in "Because" Statements   94

Application of This Chapter's Principles to Your Own Writing   96

5   THE LOGICAL STRUCTURE OF ARGUMENTS   98

Overview to *Logos:* What Do We Mean by the "Logical Structure" of an
Argument?   98

Adopting a Language for Describing Arguments: The Toulmin
System   102

Using Toulmin's Schema to Determine a Strategy of Support   108

Creating Support: Using Evidence/Chains of Reasons for Grounds and
Backing   110

Evidence as Support   110

Chain of Reasons as Support   114

Conclusion   116

6   EVIDENCE IN ARGUMENT   118

Using Evidence from Personal Experience   118

Using Personal Experience Data   119

Using Personal Observations   119

Using Evidence from Interviews, Surveys, and Questionnaires   120

Conducting Interviews   120

Using Surveys or Questionnaires   121

Using Evidence from Reading: The Art of Library Research   122
    Seeking Clarity: Library Research as an Analysis of a Conversation   122
    Coping with Uncertainty: When the Experts Disagree   125
Writing Your Own Argument: Using Evidence Persuasively   127
    When Possible, Select Your Data from Sources Your Reader Trusts   127
    Increase Persuasiveness of Factual Data by Ensuring Recency, Representativeness, and Sufficiency   128
    In Citing Evidence, Distinguish Fact from Inference or Opinion   129
    To Use Evidence Persuasively, Position It Effectively   129
    Conclusion   131

Writing Assignments For Chapters 4–6   131
"Choose Life"—Dao Do (student)   138

7   MOVING YOUR AUDIENCE: Audience-Based Reasons
    Ethos, and *Pathos*   140

Starting from Your Readers' Beliefs: The Power of Audience-based Reasons   140
    Difference between Writer- and Audience-based Reasons   141
    Finding Audience-based Reasons: Asking Questions about Your Audience   145
Ethos and *Pathos* as Persuasive Appeals: An Overview   147
How to Create an Effective *Ethos:* The Appeal to Credibility   149
    Create Credibility by Being Knowledgeable about Your Issue   150
    Create Credibility by Demonstrating Fairness   150
    Create Credibility by Building a Bridge to Your Audience   150
How to Create *Pathos:* The Appeal to Emotions   150
    Appeal to Emotions by Using Concrete Language   151
    Appeal to Emotions by Using Examples and Illustrations   152
    Appeal to Emotions through Appropriate Word Choice, Metaphors, and Analogies   154
    Appeal to Emotions through Sensitivity to Your Audience's Values   157
Applying This Chapter's Principles to Your Own Writing: Where Should You Reveal Your Thesis?   157
    Standard Form Arguments   158
    Delayed Thesis Arguments   159
"Minneapolis Pornography Ordinance"—Ellen Goodman   160
CONCLUSION   165

8   ACCOMMODATING YOUR AUDIENCE: Treating
     Opposing Views   166

Opening Exercise: A Controversy In First-Year Composition   166
One Sided Verses Two-Sided Arguments   169
Beginning a Two-Sided Argument: Summarize Opposing Views   170
Response Strategy 1:   Rebuttal of Opposing Views   171
    Using the Toulmin Schema to Find a Strategy for Rebuttal   172
    Ways to Rebut Evidence   176
    Anticipating Adversarial Views throughout Your Essay   178
Response Strategy 2:   Concession to Opposing Views   178
Response Strategy 3:   Conciliatory or Rogerian Approach to Opposing
Views   179
Chapter Summary   183
Application of Principles from Parts I and II to Your Own Writing   183
    General Checklist for Evaluating Drafts   183

Writing Assignments for Chapters 5, 7 and 8   185
"Abstract Versus Representational Art" (student essay)   *186*
"Letter to Beth Downey" (student essay)   *189*

PART III

■

Arguments in Depth: Five Categories of Claims   193

9   USING THE CATEGORIES OF CLAIM TO
     GENERATE IDEAS   194

What Is a Truth Argument?   195
What Is a Values Argument?   196
A Three-Step Strategy for Discovering Audience-based Reasons   196
    An Argument from Definition or Principle   197
    An Argument from Consequence   198
    An Argument from Resemblance   199

10   DEFINITION ARGUMENTS: X Is/Is Not A Y   202
The Special Nature of a Definitional Issue   203

Writing Assignment for Chapter 10   Extended Definition/Borderline Case: Is This X a Y?   204

The Criteria-Match Structure of Definitional Arguments   205

Conceptual Problems of Definition   207

Language as a Way of Ordering the World   207

Why Can't We Just Look in the Dictionary?   207

Definitions and the Rule of Justice: At What Point Does X Quit Being a Y?   208

Conducting a Criteria-Match Argument   210

Defining the Y Term (Establishing Criteria For Y)   210

Aristotelian Definition   210

Effect of Rhetorical Context on Aristotelian Definitions   212

Operational Definitions   213

Conducting the Match Part of a Definitional Argument   214

Writing Your Definitional Argument   214

Starting Points: Finding a Definitional Controversy   215

Exploration Stage I: Developing Criteria for Your Y Term   216

Exploration Stage II: Exploring Your Match Argument   218

Writing the Discovery Draft—A Possible Organizational Structure for Your Essay   219

Revision Stage   219

Conditions for Rebuttal: Testing a Definitional Argument   221

Attacking the Criteria   221

Attacking the Match   222

Sample Arguments   224

"Oncore, Obscenity, and the Liquor Control Board"
—Kathy Sullivan (student)   224
A series of photographs in a gay bar should not be considered obscene because they do not violate the community standards of the patrons of the bar, because they do not appeal to prurient interests, because children are not apt to be exposed to them, and because they promote an important social purpose of safe sex to prevent AIDS.

"How to Save the Homeless Mentally Ill"—Charles Krauthammer   226
The United States should rebuild its system of asylums to care for the mentally ill homeless, who need to be involuntarily institutionalized if necessary. The criteria permitting involuntary institutionalization must be broadened, claims Krauthammer, to include the conditions of being degraded or made helpless by mental illness.

11   CAUSAL ARGUMENTS: X Causes/Does Not Cause Y   234

The Frequency of Causal Arguments   235

The Nature of Causal Arguing   236

Describing the Logical Structure of a Causal Argument: Because Clauses and the Toulmin Schema   238

Writing Assignment For Chapter 11:   An Argument Involving "Surprising" Or "Disputed" Causes   240

Three Methods for Arguing that One Event Causes Another   241

First Method: Explain the Causal Mechanism Directly   242

Second Method: Use Various Inductive Methods to Establish a High Probability of a Causal Link   244

Third Method: Argue by Analogy or Precedent   247

Glossary of Terms Encountered in Causal Arguments   248

Writing Your Causal Argument   251

The Starting Point: Finding a Causal Issue   251

Make a List of People's Unusual Likes and Dislikes   251

Make Lists of Trends and Other Puzzling Phenomena   251

Exploration Stage   252

Writing the Discovery Draft: Typical Ways of Organizing a Causal Argument   252

Revision: Seeing Your Argument Afresh   253

Conditions For Rebuttal: Critiquing Causal Arguments   254

If You Described Each Link in a Causal Chain, Would Skeptics Point out Weaknesses in Any of the Links?   254

If Your Argument Is Based on a Scientific Experiment, Could Skeptics Question the Validity of the Experiment?   254

If You Have Used Correlation Data, Could Skeptics Argue that the Correlation Is Much Weaker than You Claim or that You Haven't Sufficiently Demonstrated Causality?   255

If You Have Used an Analogy Argument, Could Skeptics Point out Disanalogies?   255

Could a Skeptic Cast Doubt on Your Argument by Reordering Your Priority of Causes?   256

Sample Arguments   256

"The Warming of the World"—Carl Sagan   256
A global catastrophe is inevitable unless the world's nations act cooperatively to combat the greenhouse effect.

"What Drugs I Take Is None of Your Business—The Consequences of Drug Testing"—Mary Lou Torpey (student)   261
A sufferer from narcolepsy, Mary Lou Torpey shows how mandatory drug testing may lead to job discrimination against persons with chronic diseases treatable with controlled substance drugs.

"Why Married Mothers Work"—Victor Fuchs   263
Rejecting the hypothesis that the increase in the number of working mothers has been caused primarily by feminism, by affirmative action, or by economic necessity, Fuchs proposes a different causal hypothesis: More mothers work because of increased wages and increased numbers of jobs in the service sector of the economy.

"Students Who Push Burgers"—Walter S. Minot   267
> What is wrong with American education? Although many critics blame drugs or
> television or the decline of the family, perhaps the chief cause is the desire of teenagers
> to hold part-time jobs.

12   RESEMBLANCE ARGUMENTS: X Is/Is Not Like Y   270

The Difference Between Resemblance Arguments And
Definition Arguments   271

Assignment Options for Chapter 12   273

First Type of Resemblance Argument: Arguments by Analogy   274
  Using Undeveloped Analogies   274
  Using Extended Analogies   275

Second Type Of Resemblance Argument: Arguments by Precedent   277

Writing Your Resemblance Argument   280

Conditions For Rebuttal: Testing a Resemblance Argument   280
  Will My Audience Say I Am Trying to Prove Too Much with My Analogy or
  Precedent?   280
  Will My Audience Point Out Disanalogies in My Resemblance Argument?   281
  Will My Audience Propose a Counteranalogy?   282

Sample Argument   284

From Against Our Will: Men, Women and Rape
—Susan Brownmiller   284
> Feminist writer Susan Brownmiller argues that pornography is analogous to racist
> propaganda. Liberals need to fight the degrading and dehumanizing images of women in
> pornography just as they have fought the racism implicit in Little Black Sambo or the
> Frito Bandido.

13   EVALUATION ARGUMENTS: X Is/Is Not a Good Y   288

Writing Assignment For Chapter 13:   Evaluate A "Controversial" X   290

Criteria-Match Structure of Evaluation Arguments   290

General Strategy for Evaluation Arguments   292
  The Problem of Standards: What's Normal or What's Ideal?   293
  The Problem of Mitigating Circumstances   293
  The Problem of Choosing between Two Goods and Two Bads   294
  The Problem of Seductive Empirical Measures   294
  The Problem of Cost   294

How to Determine Criteria for Your Argument   295
  Step 1:   Determine the Category in Which the Object Being Evaluated
  Belongs   295

Step 2:   Determine the Purpose or Function of This Class   296

Step 3:   Determine Criteria Based on the Purposes or Function of the Class to Which X Belongs   296

Step 4:   Give Relative Weightings to the Criteria   297

Determining Whether X Meets The Criteria   297

Writing Your Evaluation Argument   300

Starting Point: Finding and Exploring an Evaluation Issue   300

Writing a Discovery Draft: Some Suggestions for Organizing Your Evaluation Argument Revision   300

Conditions For Rebuttal: Testing Your Evaluation Argument   301

Will My Audience Accept My Criteria?   301

Are My Criteria Based on the "Smallest Applicable Class" for X?   301

Will Readers Accept My General Weighting of Criteria?   301

Will Readers Question My Standard of Reference?   302

Will Readers Criticize My Use of Empirical Measures?   302

Will Readers Accept My Criteria but Reject My Match Argument?   302

Sample Arguments   303

"Tarnished Image of Academy Awards Hasn't Dulled World's Appetite for This Flawed Farce"—William Arnold   304
Film critic William Arnold gives five reasons why the annual Academy Awards are "just about the most flawed, tarnished, infuriating, and downright perverse awards system ever devised."

"The Mandatory Motorcycle-Helmet Law is Bad Law"—Bill C. Healy (student)   307
Despite the state's belief that motorcycle-helmet laws reduce injuries and save lives, such laws are bad because statistics show they do not reduce injuries, because they often make motorcycle riding more dangerous rather than less dangerous, and because they infringe on individual rights without sufficient justification.

"Beauty Pageant Fallacies"—Debra Goodwin (student)   309
Beauty pageants harm society by damaging women's self-esteem, by reducing women to pornographic objects, and by exploiting women through stereotyping of female sexuality and devaluing older women.

14 PROPOSAL ARGUMENTS: "We Should/Should Not Do X"   312

The Nature of Proposal Arguments   313

The General Structure and Strategy Of Proposal Arguments   314

Special Requirements of Proposal Arguments   314

Adding "Presence" to Your Argument   314

Overcoming the Natural Conservatism of People   316

The Difficulty of Predicting Future Consequences   316

The Problem of Evaluating Consequences   316

Writing Assignment For Chapter 14:   Options for Proposal
Arguments   317

Developing a Proposal Argument   319

Convincing Your Readers That a Problem Exists   319

Showing the Specifics of Your Proposal   320

The Justification: Convincing Your Reader That Your Proposal Should Be
Enacted   320

Touching the Right Pressure Points   322

Using the "Stock Issues" Strategy to Develop a Proposal Argument   322

Using the Toulmin Schema to Develop a Proposal Argument   323

Writing The Proposal Argument   326

Starting Points: Finding a Proposal Issue   326

Exploration Stage   327

Writing the Discovery Draft: Some Ways to Organize a Proposal Argument   327

Revision Stage   328

Conditions for Rebuttal: Testing Your Proposal Argument   328

Will My Audience Deny That My Problem Is Really a Problem?   329

Will My Audience Doubt the Effectiveness of My Solution?   329

Will My Audience Think My Proposal Costs Too Much?   330

Will My Audience Suggest Counterproposals?   330

Sample Arguments   332

*"A Proposal to Restructure the Washington State High School Dance and
Drill Team Association Competition"—Karen Kartes (student)*   332
Annual state competition for high school dance and drill teams in Washington, claims
Karen Kartes, mixes different talent levels and genres of teams, produces animosity among
participants, confuses viewers, and places stress on judges. In this practical proposal,
Kartes offers two possible solutions.

*"What Should Be Done about the Mentally Ill Homeless?"
—Stephen Bean (student)*   339
Opposing Charles Krauthammer's proposal for massive rebuilding of the nation's mental
asylums, Stephen Bean argues that homelessness among the mentally ill is primarily a
social and economic problem rather than a psychiatric problem and that the mentally ill
homeless would be better served through community-based care.

15   ETHICAL ARGUMENTS   352

Special Difficulties of Ethical Arguments   352

An Overview of Major Ethical Systems   354

Naive Egoism   355

Consequences as the Grounds of Ethics   356

Principles as the Grounds of Ethics   357

The Two Systems Compared   357

Some Compromise Positions between Consequences and Principles   358

Developing an Ethical Argument   359

Testing Ethical Arguments   361

"The Ones Who Walk away from Omelas"—Ursula Le Guin   362
*The happiness of the mythical city of Omelas depends on the misery of one unfortunate
child. There is nothing the people can do. "If the child were brought into the sunlight . . . ,
in that day and hour all the prosperity and beauty and delight of Omelas would wither
and be destroyed. These are the terms."*

PART IV

■

Writing from Sources: The Argument as a Formal Research Paper   369

16   UNLOCKING THE LIBRARY: Finding and Selecting Sources   370

Formulating a Research Question   371

Searching for a Research Question: Exploring Your Interests   372

Another Means of Searching for a Research Question: Browsing the
Library   373

Locating Library Materials   374

Using the Card Catalog   374

Using Periodical and Newspaper Indexes   376

The Most Important Indexes   377

How to Use Periodical Indexes   379

Using Computer Searches   381

Using Other Library Sources   385

Beyond the Library   386

Using Your Sources: Sitting Down to Read   386

17   USING AND DOCUMENTING SOURCES   388

Clarifying Your Own Thinking: The Case of Lynnea   388

Developing a Good System of Note Taking   390

Incorporating Sources into Your Argument: Some General
Principles   390

"Reading, Writing, and (Ugh!) You Know What"—Science '86   391

Citing Information   391

Summarizing an Argument: Different Contexts Demand Different
Summaries   392

Article Summaries as a Note-Taking Tool   394

Paraphrasing Portions of an Argument   394

Quoting   394

Incorporating Sources into Your Argument: Technical Advice on
Summarizing, Paraphrasing, and Quoting   395

"The Case for Torture"—Michael Levin   395
*Although most people think of torture as an outdated, barbaric practice, under certain
conditions torture is not "merely permissible but morally mandatory."*

Summary   398

Paraphrase   398

Block Quotation   398

Inserted Quotation   399

Shortening or Modifying Quotations   399

Using Quotations within Quotations   400

An Extended Illustration: Martha's Argument   401

Signaling Directions: The Use of Attributive Tags   402

Avoiding Plagiarism   403

Note Taking to Avoid Plagiarism   404

Documenting Your Sources   404

When to Cite Sources   404

What Format to Use   404

Overview of the MLA and APA Systems of Documentation   405

Feature 1: Place a Complete Bibliographic List at the End of the Text   405

Form for Entries in "Works Cited" (MLA) and "References" (APA)   408

General Format for Books   408

General Format for Articles   413

Miscellaneous Materials   416

Conclusion   417

Example of a Student Research Paper as an Argument (APA style)   418

*"Women Police Officers: Should Size and Strength Be Criteria for Patrol
Duty?"—Lynnea Clark*   418
*Examining available data on women police officers, student writer Lynnea Clark concludes
that police departments should establish rigorous strength and size requirements for police
on patrol.*

APPENDIXES   430

Appendix 1   **Logical Fallacies**   430

The Problem of Conclusiveness in an Argument   430

An Overview of Informal Fallacies   431

Fallacies of *Pathos*   432 / Argument to the People (Appeal to Stirring Symbols) 432 / Appeal to Ignorance (Presenting Evidence the Audience Can't Examine) 433 / Appeal to Irrational Premises (Appealing to Reasons That May Have No Basis in Logic)   433 / Provincialism (Appealing to the Belief That the Known Is Always Better Than the Unknown)   433 / Red Herring (Shifting the Audience's Attention from a Crucial Issue to an Irrelevant One)   434

Fallacies of *Ethos*   434 / Appeal to False Authority (Appealing to the Authority of a Popular Person Rather than a Knowledgeable One)   434 / Appeal to the Person/*Ad Hominem* (Attacking the Character of the Arguer Rather than the Argument Itself)   435 / Strawperson (Greatly Oversimplifying an Opponent's Argument to Make It Easier to Refute or Ridicule)   436

Fallacies of *Logos*   437 / Begging the Question (Supporting a Claim with a Reason That Is Really a Restatement of the Claim in Different Words)   437 / Complex Question (Confronting the Opponent with a Question That Will Put Her in a Bad Light No Matter How She Responds)   438 / False Dilemma/ Either–Or (Oversimplifying a Complex Issue So That Only Two Choices Appear Possible)   438 / Equivocation (Using to Your Advantage at Least Two Different Definitions of the Same Term in the Same Argument)   438 / Confusing Correlation for Cause/*Post Hoc, Ergo Propter Hoc* / (After This, Therefore because of This) (Assuming That Event X Causes Event Y because Event X Preceded Event Y)   439 / Slippery Slope   439 / Hasty Generalization (Making a Broad Generalization on the Basis of Too Little Evidence)   440 / Faulty Analogy (Claiming That because X Resembles Y in One Regard, X Will Resemble Y in All Regards)   441 / *Non Sequitur* (Making a Claim That Doesn't Follow Logically from the Premises, or Supporting a Claim With Irrelevant Premises)   441

Appendix 2   **Statistical Traps in Arguments**   444

Making Numbers Meaningful: Charts, Tables, and Graphs   445

Interpreting Graphs   446

Number Traps to Avoid   449

Appendix 3   **The Writing Community: Working in Groups**   452

From Conflict to Consensus: How to Get the Most out of the Writing Community   452

Avoiding Bad Habits of Group Behavior   453

The Value of Group Work for Writers   453

Forming Writing Communities: Skills and Roles   455

   Working in Groups of Five to Seven People   455

   Working in Pairs   458

A Several-Days' Group Project: Defining "Good Argumentative
Writing"   459

   "Good Writing and Computers for Today's Modern American Youth of
   America"   461 / "Bloody Ice"   462 / "RSS Should Not Provide
   Dorm Room Carpets"   464 / "Sterling Hall Dorm Food"   465 /
   "ROTC Courses Should Not Get College Credit"   466 / "Legalization of
   Prostitution?"   467

A Classroom Debate   469

PART V

■

An Anthology of Arguments   471

Overview Of The Anthology   471

Guide Questions For The Analysis And Evaluation Of Arguments   473

   Questions for Analyzing and Evaluating a Conversation   473

   Questions for Analyzing and Evaluating an Individual Argument   474

**Newcomers to Our Shores: Should the United States Place a Moratorium
on Immigration?**   475

*Dan Stein. "Timeout: The United States Needs a Moratorium on
Immigration"*   475

   *Dan Stein argues that the recent influx of immigrants into the United States exceeds our
   ability to assimilate them into mainstream culture and prevents our developing policies to
   stop illegal immigration.*

Frank Sharry. "Immigrants Help Make America Strong"   478

   *"Immigrants help make America strong," claims Sharry, because of their family values,
   their love of freedom, and their work ethic.*

**Guns and Public Safety: Should the Federal Government Enact Strict
Controls on the Ownership of Handguns?**   481

*Molly Ivins. "Two Hundred Million Guns—Let's Not Make It
Any Worse"*   481

   *"[W]hen one confronts a large, hairy problem," says syndicated columnist Molly Ivins, "it
   is always useful to follow the First Rule of Holes: When you're in one, quit digging." To
   keep the mess of street violence from getting worse, Ivins believes we should "ban the sale
   of all handguns and assault rifles."*

Dave Kopel. "Why Good People Own Guns: Better Safe Than Sorry"   483

   *Ordinary citizens need handguns for protection, argues criminologist Dave Kopel,
   Research Director of the Independence Institute in Denver, Colorado, and author of an*

award-winning book on foreign gun control, The Samurai, the Mountie and the Cowboy. *"If a criminal attacks, it is almost certain that a police officer will not be there to help. Until this fundamental reality changes, tens of millions of Americans are going to hold onto their guns, no matter what."*

Mercy Killing and the Right to Die: Can Active Euthanasia Be a Moral Good?   487

William F. May. "Rising to the Occasion of Our Death"   487
   Legalizing active euthanasia to eliminate suffering may blind us to the value of suffering. "The community . . . may need its aged and dependent, its sick and its dying, and the virtues they sometimes evince."

Daniel C. Maguire. "Death by Choice: Who Should Decide?"   489
   Writing before recent court decisions brought these issues to full national consciousness, Catholic theologian Daniel Maguire asks whether any decision to end life can be a moral good. Using the cases of a hydrocephalic boy and a severely deformed infant girl, Maguire argues that it can. He remains in a quandary, however, about who should decide.

The Distribution of Wealth: What Responsibility Do the Rich Have for the Poor?   494

Garrett Hardin. "Lifeboat Ethics: The Case Against Helping the Poor"   494
   Hardin argues that rich nations are like lifeboats and that impoverished people are like swimmers in the sea clamoring to climb aboard the lifeboat. If we allow all the swimmers to come aboar.d, the lifeboat sinks. "Complete justice; complete catastrophe."

Peter Singer. "Rich and Poor"   504
   We have a moral obligation to help those living in "absolute poverty." "Helping is not, as conventionally thought, a charitable act which is praiseworthy to do, but not wrong to omit; it is something that everyone ought to do."

Civil Disobedience: Is Refusal to Obey Laws Ever a Positive Good?   513

Martin Luther King, Jr. "Letters from Birmingham Jail" in Response to "Public Statement by Eight Alabama Clergymen"   513
   On April 12, 1963, eight Alabama clergymen signed a public statement urging "outsiders" to halt the racial demonstrations they had instigated. Writing from the Birmingham jail, Martin Luther King, Jr., gives a compelling justification for his actions. "I am in Birmingham because injustice is here."

Lewis H. Van Dusen, Jr. "Civil Disobedience: Destroyer of Democracy"   527
   Attorney Lewis H. Van Dusen, Jr., a Rhodes scholar and graduate of Harvard Law School, distinguishes between "conscientious disobedience"— in which one willingly accepts punishment in order to make a moral protest—and active group disobedience aimed at changing laws. "[C]ivil disobedience [e.g., the kind practiced by Martin Luther King, Jr.], whatever the ethical rationalization, is still an assault on our democratic society, an affront to our legal order and an attack on our constitutional government."

Plato. From The Crito   533
Socrates, who was himself ill-served by the state, here argues in favor of a citizen's absolute obligation to obey the rules of the state. He has been unjustly sentenced to die, and his friend Crito urges him to escape from prison. Socrates declines on ethical grounds.

Political Correctness and Diversity: Freedom of Speech at What Cost?   538

Nat Hentoff. "'Speech Codes' on the Campus"   538
Civil libertarian Nat Hentoff reviews various campus attempts to write speech codes that don't imperil free speech and finds them all wanting.

John Leo. "The Politics of Feelings"   544
Columnist Leo attacks the notion that we can write codes that protect people from "feeling" that they have been harassed or intimidated. Feelings are ineffably personal, he argues, and to privilege feelings inevitably diminishes the force of communal standards.

Judith Martin and Gunther Stent. "Say the Right Thing—or Else"   546
Etiquette columnist Judith Martin ("Miss Manners") and scientist Gunther Stent argue that universities are within their rights to restrict free speech—just as every other major American institution, including the Supreme Court does—to maintain their sense of civility.

Katherine T. Bartlett. "Some Factual Correctness about Political Correctness"   547
Law professor Bartlett argues that PC critics have misrepresented the nature of the debate. They assume that they represent the "natural" (because customary) view of the issue, whereas their opponents argue for merely "political" ends.

Barbara Ehrenreich. "Teach Diversity with a Smile"   550
Writer Ehrenreich chides both sides of the PC debate for their humorless partisanship. Acceptance of multiculturalism, points out Ehrenreich, will be a boon to both critics and defendants of monocultural values.

The Legalization of Drugs: Would America Be Better Off or Worse Off If Drugs Were Legalized?   552

"The Federal Drugstore." An interview with Michael S. Gazzaniga   552
In this interview, Michael S. Gazzaniga, professor of neuroscience at Dartmouth Medical School, provides a scientific perspective on drug use and abuse. Gazzaniga's own stance is a scientifically cautious belief that the benefits of legalizing drugs outweigh the costs.

Walter Wink. "Biting the Bullet: The Case for Legalizing Drugs"   563
Theologian Walter Wink examines the arguments for and against legalization of drugs and concludes that it is wrong to fight evil with evil. "Legalization offers a nonviolent, non-reactive, creative alternative that will let the drug menace collapse of its own deadly weight."

Richard J. Dennis. "The Economics of Legalizing Drugs"   569
Conducting a cost/benefits analysis of drug legalization, Dennis concludes that "[t]o the pragmatist, the choice is clear: legalization is the best bet." It seems doubtful that making most drugs legal would significantly increase the number of addicts but certain that it would reduce crime and save society money.

James Q. Wilson. "Against the Legalization of Drugs"   579
Noted professor and former member of the National Council for Drug Abuse Prevention, James Q. Wilson compares contemporary arguments for cocaine legalization to earlier

arguments for heroin legalization. Focusing on the disquieting consequences, he rejects drug legalization as costly and dehumanizing, leading to huge increases in crime, addiction, and violence.

Lee N. Robins, Darlene H. Davis, and Donald W. Goodwin. "Drug Use by U.S. Army Enlisted Men in Vietnam: A Follow-Up on Their Return Home"   593

This frequently cited research study has been interpreted in different ways (see the conflicting interpretations by Gazzaniga and Wilson in this section). "The results of this study indicate that, contrary to conventional belief, the occasional use of narcotics without becoming addicted appears possible even for men who have previously been dependent on narcotics."

Sexual Harassment: When Is Offensiveness Civil Offense?   612

Stephanie Riger. "Gender Dilemmas in Sexual Harassment Policies and Procedures"   612

Psychology professor Riger analyzes reasons for the paucity of sexual harassment complaints. She concludes that a gender bias is built into the way sexual harassment policies are written.

Naomi Munson. "Harassment Blues"   629

Munson questions present definitions of sexual harassment and confusion between harassing remarks and innuendo. The writer blames "feminist rage" for much of the failure to distinguish between harassment and normal insensitivity in the workplace.

Erica Jong. "Fear of Flirting"   633

Erica Jong, while deploring the actions of many recently noted sexual harassers, argues for more tolerance toward a special class of harassers who can't "bring [their] intellect and [their] emotions into the same century, " who support women's issues with their heads but can't find it in their hearts to quit trying to exploit them.

Gretchen Morgenson. "Watch That Leer, Stifle That Joke"   637

Forbes writer Morgenson argues that "the alleged increase in sexual harassment [is] more a product of propaganda from self-interested parties," than from substantive cases.

Susan Crawford. "A Wink Here, a Leer There: It's Costly"   641

Attorney Susan Crawford offers a pragmatic defense of sexual harassment laws based on lost employee work time, inefficient use of the work day, and costly lawsuits growing out of sexual harassment issues.

Martha Chamallas. "Universal Truth and Multiple Perspectives: Controversies on Sexual Harassment"   643

Law professor Chamallas argues that the burden of proof in sex discrimination cases ought not to be on the putative victim but on the accuser; antidiscrimination laws, she contends, ought to take "the victim's perspective."

Global Warming: How Serious Is the Greenhouse Effect? What Should Be Done about It?   648

Wallace S. Broecker. "Global Warming on Trial"   648

Atmospheric scientist Wallace Broecker examines the historical development of theories about global warming and attempts to reach a balanced judgment. Imagining a mock trial between advocates and skeptics in the greenhouse debate, Broecker believes that "each side would have difficulty proving its case." Nonetheless, he arrives at a sobering conclusion: The real enemy to our planet is the population explosion.

Jeremy Leggett. "Global Warming: The Worst Case"   656
Jeremy Leggett, director of science in Greenpeace International's Atmosphere and Energy Campaign, outlines a worst-case scenario in which the greenhouse effect creates a positive feedback loop resulting in calamitous global warming. "In evaluating military threats throughout history, policy response has been predicated on a worst-case analysis. The standard military yardstick must also apply to environmental security."

S. Fred Singer. "Warming Theories Need Warning Label"   663
S. Fred Singer, director of the Washington-based Science and Environmental Policy Project (SEPP) and professor of environmental sciences at the University of Virginia in Charlottesville, believes that the risk of global warming is not as dire as environmental activists claim. Raising doubts about computer modeling and about the reliability of current data, Singer points to major uncertainties in greenhouse theory. "Does it make sense to waste $1000 billion a year on what is still a phantom threat when there are so many pressing—and real—problems in need of resources?"

R. Monastersky. "Signs of Global Warming Found in Ice"   670
In this brief article appearing in Science News, Monastersky presents evidence for global warming based on melting of glacial ice. It is not clear, however, that the warming is caused by greenhouse gases.

Dixy Lee Ray. "Global Warming: A Skeptic's View"   672
Dixy Lee Ray, former chair of the Atomic Energy Commission and former governor of the state of Washington, has long been skeptical of global warming theories. Here she points to some homely evidence against global warming—the latest hardiness zone maps used by farmers and gardeners to predict frosts. These maps show that the frost zone in the United States is moving south, not north.

"Dissent on Warming"   674
In late 1991, the Science and Environmental Policy Project (SEPP) circulated this statement to three hundred scientists in the United States. Within several months it had been signed by more than fifty scientists from a wide range of institutions, including MIT, Yale, Woods Hole, and the University of Virginia.

Mental Asylums versus Community Care: What Should Be Done about the Mentally Ill Homeless?   676

Paul S. Appelbaum. "Crazy in the Streets"   676
A professor of psychiatry outlines the history of deinstitutionalization of the mentally ill and calls for its reversal. "Far from impinging on their autonomy, treatment of [the psychotic homeless], even coercive treatment, would not only hold out some hope of mitigating their condition but might simultaneously increase their capacity for more sophisticated autonomous choices."

Jonathan Kozol. "Are the Homeless Crazy?"   687
The author of Rachel and Her Children offers a social and economic explanation of homelessness among the mentally ill. "The notion that the homeless are largely psychotics who belong in institutions, rather than victims of displacement at the hands of enterprising realtors, spares us from the need to offer realistic solutions to the deep and widening extremes of wealth and poverty in the United States."

Steven Vanderstaay. "The Homeless Mentally Ill"   691
Freelance writer Steven Vanderstaay spent many months living among the homeless and recording their stories. In his book Street Lives: An Oral History of Homeless

Americans, *Vanderstaay interweaves homeless persons' own stories with his own interpretive commentary based on research in the literature on homelessness. The following reading is extracted from Vanderstaay's chapter on the mentally ill homeless.*

E. Fuller Torrey. *"Who Goes Homeless?"* 701
Dr. E. Fuller Torrey, a clinical and research psychiatrist and volunteer worker in a clinic for homeless mentally ill women, places the problems of the mentally ill homeless within the larger context of general homelessness. He claims that the solutions to homelessness are known. "The mystery no longer is what to do, but rather why we do not do it."

Illegitimacy, Single Parenthood, and Welfare Reform: Should the Government Enact Policies to Strengthen the Traditional Family? If So, How? 708

Dan Quayle. *"Restoring Basic Values: Strengthening the Family"* 708
Former Vice President Dan Quayle, in a speech given during his last year in office, offers a wide-ranging analysis of American social ills that led up to the LA riots of 1992. In particular, Quayle is concerned with a "poverty of values" and the dissolution of the two-parent family. His criticism of sitcom heroine Murphy Brown's decision to have a child out of wedlock and raise it herself captured the national imagination and sparked a major debate.

Katha Pollitt. *"Why I Hate 'Family Values' (Let Me Count the Ways)"* 714
Writer Katha Pollitt argues that sitcom anchor Murphy Brown's decision to have a child is defensible and unlikely to influence welfare recipients to follow suit. Pollitt pans conservative critics of Brown for using vague, contradictory, and outmoded notions of "family values" to coerce married parents into remaining in unhappy marriages.

Elija Anderson. *"Abolishing Welfare Won't Stop Poverty, Illegitimacy"* 721
Sociologist Elija Anderson argues against abolishing welfare as an answer to the problem of a growing "underclass." According to Anderson, the prospect of increased welfare benefits does not motivate poor women to have more children. Anderson instead attributes the growing number of single mothers to underlying economic problems.

Barbara Dafoe Whitehead. *"Dan Quayle Was Right"* 723
Social scientist Barbara Dafoe Whitehead, responding to the furor created by Dan Quayle's critique of Murphy Brown, argues that the dissolution of the two-parent family has harmed many children, not to mention the very social fabric of the nation. Whitehead particularly laments the shift from a concern for children's welfare to a concern for adult happiness.

ACKNOWLEDGMENTS 756
INDEX 761

PART I

Overview of Argument

□

Argument:
An Introduction

Consider the following scenario:

STAGE 1:   You are a student representative on a new university task force to revise your institution's General Studies requirements. Your university president has charged the task force to create a new core curriculum emphasizing active learning and critical thinking and giving students from all majors a more coherent foundation of courses in liberal learning. Your task force examines core curricula at other universities and begins vigorous discussions about the goals of a revised curriculum and the best methods of achieving them.

STAGE 2:   After months of research and discussion, your task force formulates a preliminary proposal, which you take to the faculty senate for feedback from the wider university community. Your chairperson gives a formal speech outlining the proposal and presenting your task force's "best reasons" for adopting it. After the presentation, faculty senators raise objections: There aren't enough humanities faculty to teach all the wonderful courses you've devised; your plan to reduce class sizes is financially naive; business and engineering students can't possibly take all these core courses and still meet the requirements of their national accreditation agencies; you've underemphasized math and science. Why don't you require foreign languages? What about computer literacy? Frustrated but undaunted, your task force returns to the drawing board to revise its proposal in the face of these objections.

STAGE 3:   Many months later your task force forges a new proposal that wins widespread faculty support if certain conditions are met: (1) the administration must agree to fund a reduction in class sizes in several key courses; (2) the schools of Business and Engineering must accommodate the new core by slightly reducing the number of required courses in their majors; and (3) faculty development money must be found to train core faculty in the teaching of critical thinking and active learning. Members of your task force write arguments aimed at persuading key decision makers in the university to accept the new proposal, provide needed resources, and make necessary concessions. Another task force member writes a grant proposal for faculty development funds.

STAGE 4:   The new core curriculum has been approved by the faculty and adequately funded by the administration. You go to the admissions officer to explain the new curriculum so she can properly explain it to prospective students. She listens carefully, taking notes. At the end of your explanation, she smiles and promises to send you her presentation of the material in the new recruiting brochure. A month or so later, the slick, four-color brochure arrives in your box. It features an attractive young couple, sitting under a tree, huddled over a paper they are apparently drafting. The accompanying copy proclaims that the "active learning" incorporated in the university's new core curriculum means "having a close working relationship with your classmates." Another picture, touting close relationship with faculty, shows four students, each from a different ethnic background, gathered around an attentive professor. The new "core" of required courses, meanwhile, is touted not because it makes learning more coherent, but because it makes it easier to plan your schedule.

THE DIFFERENCE BETWEEN PERSUASION AND ARGUMENT

At the outset of this text, we need to distinguish between two important activities that are frequently mistaken for each other, *persuasion* and *argument*. Persuasion is concerned primarily with influencing the way people think or act, whereas argument is concerned with discovering and conveying our best judgments about the truth of things through an appeal to reason. All arguments involve persuasion, but all persuasive acts do not involve arguments. The distinction between the two terms, although fuzzy, is important because the two words imply different relationships between writer and audience as well as different purposes. Sometimes you write arguments with only minimal attention to persuasion; at other times, persuasion is foremost in your mind.

In the preceding scenario, Stages 1 and 2 illustrate argument aimed primarily at truth-seeking rather than persuasion. In Stage 1, the task force attempts through dialogue to arrive at the best decisions about a core curriculum. They raise issues, look at evidence, make comparisons, ask questions, play devil's advocate, imagine different consequences. In such a dialogue, participants reasonably assess the merits of different points of view with the aim of making the best decision possible. As we will see throughout this text, such exploratory and clarifying dialogues provide a model for the kind of thinking good writers go through in the process of composing an argument.

Stage 1 can be seen as argument-in-process. In Stage 2, your chair must go before the faculty senate to deliver a final product, a carefully planned oral argument that shows the senators "good reasons" for changing the curriculum. At this point, your chair's goal isn't to win immediate approval for this proposal, but to share the task force's thinking with particular attention to the reasons the task force prefers the kind of curriculum it has developed. Of course, she hopes that these are persuasive reasons and that the general direction of the proposal will be seen favorably, but she will be satisfied if the presentation creates interest in a revised core curriculum and prepares the way for the development of an improved proposal. The objections raised by the senators, although discouraging at the time, stimulate creative rethinking when the committee returns to argument-in-process during subsequent meetings.

The third stage once again involves argument as formal product, but this time persuasion *is* the foremost concern. The task force has developed a widely approved curricular plan to which it is firmly committed. Its goal now is (1) to persuade the administration to fund reduced class sizes, (2) to persuade the faculties of Business and Engineering to modify the requirements for the major in those fields, and (3) to persuade a granting agency to fund faculty development workshops in critical thinking and active learning. Persuasive arguments must now be formulated for each of these different audiences and purposes. Consider, for example, the difficulty of persuading the administration to reduce class sizes. No single document will suffice because different key administrators may require different kinds of arguments with different reasons and different structures. An academic administrator, for example, might be swayed by the argument that small classes lead to better student learning. A business-side administrator, however, might be more swayed by a bottom-line economic argument: Smaller class sizes will lead to higher retention of students or to greater alumni or legislative support among those who want to see less emphasis on research and greater attention to undergraduate education. Persuasive arguments, in other words, are tailored to their audience by appealing to that audience's values and beliefs. Whenever a change of audience means a change of values and beliefs, then the argument must be restructured accordingly.

In the fourth stage, persuasion and argument begin to drift apart. The brochure is still making and supporting a claim, but unlike the sorts of argumentative/persuasive strategies carried on in Stages 1, 2, and 3, this one, in adopting techniques from advertising, is moving toward what we might call *propaganda*. Consider, for example, the picture of the young couple apparently working together on a draft for an essay. Many people will have difficulty recognizing that this picture is part of the brochure's message, that it contributes to a claim. But what is that claim? The explicit claim is that the core curriculum promotes active learning, which in turn promotes the forming of friendships. But there is a submerged, unstated claim also: "Come to our university to find romance" (or, as the next picture claims, "Come to our university to make friends with interesting, diverse people").

Like many advertisements, the brochure relies on hidden rather than explicit claims. Instead of coming right out and announcing that the new core curriculum will improve both your love life and your social life (and then using rational evidence rather than psychological suggestion), the brochure merely suggests this possibility through visual imagery. The brochure associates active learning with friendship without providing reasons or evidence for the association, thereby shutting off further dialogue. You aren't really invited to ask, Is there really an equal mix of all those ethnic minorities? Will I ever gather in such a happy group of four around a friendly professor? Will I find romance through active learning? The Admissions Office thus pushes the arguments developed in Stages 1, 2, and 3 toward propaganda by relying on visual suggestion rather than evidence, by appealing to the audience's subconscious desires for romance and friendship, and by ignoring the major critical reasons for the importance of the new curriculum.

To sum up, all arguments are concerned with persuasion, but not all attempts at persuasion are arguments. Outside the realm of argument are all those persuasive acts that we have called propaganda: most advertising, much political speech (unfortunately), psychologically sophisticated sales techniques, and numerous other attempts at influencing human behavior through subterfuge, psychology, threat, or reward.

This book is not concerned with propaganda, but only with those acts of persuasion that are arguments. In some arguments the persuasive element itself is minimal: The writer focuses primarily on using argument to think through the complexity of an issue and to seek truth (what we might call argument with a referential or truth-seeking aim). At other times, the persuasive element is paramount: The writer, confident in the truth and rightness of his or her claim, concentrates on swaying an audience (what we might call argument with a persuasive aim). In our view, the value of referential or truth-seeking argument lies in its power to deepen and complicate our understanding of the world and help us to defend ourselves against the many propagandistic forces in our culture. The value of argument with a persuasive aim is its ability to help social groups make decisions in a rational and humane way without resorting to violence or to other assertions of raw power for which propaganda is always a tool. When persuasion becomes separated from truth-seeking, when it manipulates others and violates the dignity of opposing views—in short, when it moves from argument to propaganda—then persuasion becomes raw and dangerous power.

In the rest of this chapter we will examine various meanings of argument and explore the differences between argument and persuasion in more depth.

INITIAL DEFINITION OF ARGUMENT

To help us define argument, let's turn from the heady realm of higher education to a more humble but universal situation, one often associated with arguing: the conflict between parents and children over rules. All of us have probably engaged in that occasional parent–child skirmish. Some of us have had the dubious pleasure of being on both sides of the issue. In what way and in what circumstances do these conflicts constitute arguments?

Consider the following dialogue:

YOUNG PERSON (racing for the front door while putting coat on):   "Bye, guys. See you later."

PARENTS (in unison):   "Whoa! What time are you planning on coming home?"

YOUNG PERSON (coolly, hand still on doorknob):   "I'm sure we discussed this earlier. I'll be home around 2 A.M." (The second sentence, spoken very rapidly, is barely audible.)

PARENTS (with clenched jaws after exchange of puzzled looks):   "We did *not* discuss this earlier and you're *not* staying out 'til two in the morning. You'll be home at twelve."

At this point in the exchange, we have a disagreement but not, we would claim, an argument. A disagreement involves the exchange of two or more antagonistic assertions without any attempt to provide reasons for them. The key to whether or not a disagreement can become an argument is how the participants go about defending their assertions. If the dialogue never gets past the "Yes-you-will/No-I-won't" stage, it either remains a disagreement or turns into a fight, depending on how much heat and volume the participants generate.

Let us say, however, that the dialogue takes the following turn:

YOUNG PERSON (tragically):   "But I'm *sixteen years old!*"

Now we've got an argument. Not, to be sure, a particularly well-developed or cogent one, but an argument all the same. It's now an argument because one of the combatants has offered a reason for her assertion. Her choice of curfew is satisfactory, she says, *because* she is sixteen years old, an argument that depends on the unstated assumption that sixteen-year-olds are old enough to make decisions about such matters.

The parents can now respond in one of several ways that will either advance the argument or turn it back into a disagreement. They can simply invoke parental authority ("I don't care—you're still coming home at twelve"), in which case argument ceases, or they can provide a reason for their own position ("You will be home at twelve because we pay the bills around here"), in which case the argument takes a new turn. But enough is enough. We'll leave this little domestic tiff before Young Person has a chance to invoke her major piece of empirical evidence ("But all my friends are allowed to stay out 'til two") and the parents respond with theirs ("But we certainly never stayed out that late when we were your age").

So far we've established two necessary conditions that must be met before we're willing to call something an argument: (1) a set of two or more conflicting assertions and (2) the attempt to resolve the conflict through an appeal to reason.

But a good argument demands more. For the argument to be effective, an arguer is obligated to clarify and support the reasons presented. For example, "But I'm sixteen years old!" is not yet a clear support for the assertion "I should be allowed to set my own curfew." On the surface, Young Person's argument seems absurd. Her parents, of all people, know precisely how old she is. What makes it an argument is the unstated assumption behind her reason—all sixteen-year-olds are old enough to set their own curfews. What Young Person needs to do now is to defend that assumption.* In doing so, she must anticipate the sorts of questions the assumption will raise in the minds of the parents: What is the legal status of sixteen-year-olds? How psychologically mature, as opposed to chronologically mature, is Young Person? What is the actual track record of Young Person in being responsible? and so forth. Each of these questions will force Young Person to reexamine and clarify her assumptions about the proper degree of autonomy for sixteen-year-olds. And her response to those questions should in turn force the parents to reexamine their assumptions about the dependence of sixteen-year-olds on parental guidance and wisdom. (Likewise, the parents will need to show why "paying the bills around here" automatically gives them the right to set Young Person's curfew.)

In arguing, then, we often find ourselves in the uncomfortable position of being forced to clarify our reasoning and thus of having to justify ideas we had always comfortably assumed. Doing so can be a frustrating and humbling experience. Here we are encountering one of the earliest senses of the term *to argue*, which is "to clarify." An argument, according to one of the first definitions of the word, was "the naked setting forth of ideas." We still see this sense of the term when people read through an essay and say, "As I understand it, your argument here is. . . ." The argument is the core of the essay, which can be abstracted out and "set forth nakedly." In addition, when philosophers translate complex statements into the formal code of logic, they do so to reveal the "argument" at the core. Thus, a logician might translate Young Person's justification into something like this:

All sixteen-year-olds are old enough to stay out until 2:00 A.M.

I am a sixteen-year-old.

Therefore, I am old enough to stay out until 2:00 A.M.

---

* Later in this text (Chapter 5) we call this assumption a warrant.

Likewise, they might show the parents' argument this way:

Whoever pays the bills in the household has a right to set the rules.

The parents do pay the bills in the household.

Therefore, the parents have the right to set the rules.

Setting forth the argument in this fashion allows us to focus on the logical structure of the arguments. To our way of thinking, neither Young Person nor the parents have yet created a strong argument for their positions since we would take issue with the first statement in both of these three-statement structures.

Thus, in our view, any argument worth its salt should eventually lead toward clarification of the issue rather than increasing obscurity. Our emphasis on argument as clarification is an expression of our own assumptions about the function of argument. Although we are concerned with teaching people how to write persuasive arguments, we are more concerned with teaching them how to write arguments that advance understanding—their own understanding as much as their audience's or opponents' understanding. Thus, we think it may be more important for Young Person and the parents to work out a mutual understanding of the relationship between teenage maturity and parental responsibility than it is for either side to win the midnight versus 2 A.M. debate.

CLARIFICATION OR VICTORY? THE DEBATE BETWEEN SOCRATES AND CALLICLES

The issue we've just raised—whether the purpose of argument is clarification or victory—is one of the oldest in the field of argumentation. One of the first great debates on the subject occurs in Plato's dialogue *The Gorgias*, in which the philosopher Socrates takes on the rhetorician Callicles.

By way of background to the dispute, Socrates was a great philosopher known to us today primarily through the dialogues of his student Plato, who depicted Socrates in debates with various antagonists and friends. Socrates' goal in these debates was to try to rid the world of error. In dialogue after dialogue, Socrates vanquishes error by skillfully leading people through a series of questions that force them to recognize the inconsistency and implausibility of their beliefs. He was a sort of intellectual judo master who takes opponents' arguments the way they want to go until they suddenly fall over.

Callicles, on the other hand, is a shadowy figure in history. We know him only through his exchange with Socrates. But he's immediately recognizable to philosophers as a representative of the Sophists, a group of teachers who taught ancient Athenians how to be "successful," much as authors of contemporary self-help books offer to teach us how to make more money, be better looking, and look out for Number One. The Sophists were a favorite, if elusive, target of both Socrates and Plato. Indeed, opposition to the Sophists' self-centered, utilitarian approach to life is at the core of Platonic philosophy. Now let's look at the dialogue.

Early in the debate, Socrates is clearly in control. He easily—too easily as it turns out—wins a couple of preliminary rounds against some less determined Sophists before confronting Callicles. But in the long and arduous debate that follows, it's not at all clear that Socrates wins. In fact, one of the points being made in *The Gorgias* seems to be that philosophers committed to discovering truth may occasionally have to sacrifice winning the debate. If Callicles doesn't necessarily win the argument, he certainly gives pause to idealists, who like to see the purpose of argument as truth for its own sake. Although Plato makes an eloquent case for enlightenment as the goal of argument, he may well contribute to the demise of this noble principle if he should happen to lose. Unfortunately, it appears that Socrates can't win the argument without sinning against the very principle he's defending.

The effectiveness of Callicles as a debater lies in his refusal to allow Socrates *any* assumptions. In response to Socrates' concern for virtue and justice, Callicles responds sneeringly that such concepts are mere conventions, invented by the weak to protect themselves from the strong. In Callicles' world, "might makes right." And the function of argument in such a world is to extend the freedom and power of the arguer, not to arrive at some arbitrary notion of truth or justice. Indeed, the power to decide what's "true and just" belongs to the winner of the debate. For Callicles, a truth that never wins is no truth at all because it will soon disappear. In sum, Callicles, like a modern-day pitchman, sees the ends (winning the argument) justifying the means (refusing to grant any assumptions, using ambiguous language, and so forth). Socrates, on the other hand, believes that no good end can come from questionable means.

As you can probably tell, our own sympathies are with Socrates and his view of argument as enlightenment and clarification. But Socrates lived in a much simpler world than we do, if by "simple" we mean a world where the True and the Good can be confidently known. For Socrates, there was one True Answer to any important question. Truth resided in the ideal world of forms, and through philosophic rigor humans could transcend the changing, shadow-like world of everyday reality to perceive the world of universals where Truth, Beauty, and Goodness resided. Even though our sympathies are with Socrates, we acknowledge that Callicles had a vision of truth closer to that of our modern world. Callicles forces us to confront the nature of truth itself. Is there only one possible truth at which all arguments will necessarily arrive? Can there be degrees of truth or different kinds of truths for different situations or cultures? How "true" is a truth if you can't get anybody to accept it? Before we can attempt to resolve the debate between Socrates and Callicles, therefore, it will be useful to look more closely at some notions of truth in the modern world.

WHAT IS TRUTH? THE PLACE OF ARGUMENT IN CONTEMPORARY LIFE

Although the debate between Socrates and Callicles appears to end inconclusively, many readers over the centuries conceded the victory to Socrates almost by default. Callicles was seen as cheating. Sophistry, for good reasons, was synonymous with trickery in argument. The moral relativism of the Sophists was so repugnant to most people that they refused to concede that the Sophists' position might have some merits or that their methodology might be turned to other ends. In our century, however, the Sophists have found a more sympathetic readership, one that takes some of the questions they raised quite seriously. Indeed, the fact that the Sophists are no longer dismissed out of hand is evidence of the shift away from a Platonic world where there was a single, knowable Truth attainable by rational means.

One way of tracing this shift in attitude toward truth is by looking at a significant shift in the definition of the verb *to argue* over the centuries. We have already mentioned that one early meaning of *to argue* was "to clarify." Another early meaning was "to prove." Argument was closely associated with demonstrations of the sort you see in math classes when you move from axioms to proofs through formulae. An argument of this sort is virtually irrefutable—unless we play Callicles and reject the axioms.

Today, on the other hand, *to argue* is usually taken to mean something like "to provide grounds for inferring." Instead of demonstrating some preexisting truth, an argument can hope only to make an audience more likely to agree with its conclusions. The better the argument, the better grounds one provides, the more likely the audience will infer what the arguer has inferred. One contemporary philosopher says that argument can hope only to "increase adherence" to ideas, not absolutely convince an audience of the necessary truth of ideas.

In the twentieth century, absolute, demonstrable truth is seen by many thinkers, from physicists to philosophers, as an illusion. Some would argue that truth is merely a product of human beings' talking and arguing with each other. These thinkers say that with regard to questions of interpretation, meaning, or value, one can never tell for certain whether an assertion is true—not by examining the physical universe more closely nor by reasoning one's way toward some Platonic form nor by receiving a mystical revelation. The closest one can come to truth is through the confirmation of one's views from others in a community of peers. "Truth" in any field of knowledge, say these thinkers, is simply an agreement of experts in that field.

As you can see, the world depicted by many twentieth-century thinkers, although it is certainly different from the world depicted by Callicles, has some important similarities to the Sophists' world view. Whatever else we may say about it, it is a world in which we look toward our social groups more than toward the world of objects to test our beliefs and ideas.

To illustrate the relevance of Callicles to contemporary society, suppose for the moment that we wanted to ask whether sexual fidelity is a virtue. A Socratic approach would assume a single, real Truth about the value of sexual fidelity, one that could be discovered through a gradual peeling away of wrong answers. Callicles' approach would assume that the value of sexual fidelity is culturally relative, so Callicles would point out all the societies in which monogamous fidelity for one or both sexes is not the norm. Clearly, our world is more like Callicles'. We are all exposed to multiple cultural perspectives directly and indirectly. Through TV, newspapers, travel, and education we experience ways of thinking and valuing that are different from our own. It is difficult to ignore the fact that our personal values are not universally shared or even respected. Thus, we're all faced with the need to justify our ideas in such a diverse society.

□ FOR CLASS DISCUSSION

On any given day, newspapers provide evidence of the complexity of living in a pluralist culture. Issues that could be readily decided in a completely homogeneous culture raise many questions for us in a society that has few shared assumptions.

What follows are three brief news stories that appeared on Associated Press wires in late fall 1993. Choose one or more of the stories and conduct a "simulation game" in which various class members role-play the points of view of the characters involved in the controversy. If you choose the first case, for example, one class member should role-play the attorney of the woman refusing the Caesarian section, another the "court-appointed representative of the woman's fetus," and another the doctor. If you wish, conduct a court hearing in which other members role-play a judge, cross-examining attorneys, and a jury. No matter which case you choose, your class's goal should be to represent each point of view as fully and sympathetically as possible to help you realize the complexity of the values in conflict.

ILLINOIS COURT WON'T HEAR CASE OF MOM WHO REFUSES SURGERY

CHICAGO—A complex legal battle over a Chicago woman's refusal to   1
undergo a Caesarean section, even though it could save the life of her
unborn child, essentially was settled yesterday when the state's highest
court refused to hear the case.

The court declined to review a lower court's ruling that the woman   2
should not be forced to submit to surgery in a case that pitted the rights
of the woman, referred to in court as "Mother Doe," against those of her
fetus.

The 22-year-old Chicago woman, now in the 37th week of her preg-   3
nancy, refused her doctors' advice to have the surgery because she
believes God intended her to deliver the child naturally.

The woman's attorneys argued that the operation would violate her   4
constitutional rights to privacy and the free exercise of her religious
beliefs.

Cook County Public Guardian Patrick Murphy, the court-appointed   5
representative of the woman's fetus, said he would file a petition with the
U.S. Supreme Court asking it to hear the case. He has 90 days to file the
petition, but he acknowledged future action would probably come too
late.

Doctors say the fetus is not receiving enough oxygen from the pla-   6
centa and will either die or be retarded unless it is delivered by Caesarean
section. Despite that diagnosis, the mother has stressed her faith in
God's healing powers and refused doctors' advice to submit to the operation.

MARYLAND COURT STRIKES DOWN STATE'S CROSS-BURNING LAW

ANNAPOLIS, Md.—Maryland's cross-burning law was struck down as   1
unconstitutional yesterday by the state's highest court, whose judges said
it interfered with free speech.

U.S. Supreme Court rulings make clear that burning a cross or other   2
religious symbol qualifies as speech under the First Amendment, the
Maryland Court of Appeals said in a unanimous ruling.

"The open and deliberate burning of religious symbols is, needless to   3
say, odious to thoughtful members of our society," wrote Chief Judge
Robert Murphy in an opinion joined by six other judges.

"But the Constitution does not allow the unnecessary trammeling of   4
free expression even for the noblest of purposes."

The decision affirmed a circuit-court ruling dismissing charges in two   5
Prince George's County cases. In one case, a cross was burned on the
property of an African-American family; in the other case, on public property.

The Maryland law, which was adopted in 1966, made it illegal to burn   6
a cross on private property without getting permission of the landowner
and notifying the local fire department.

HOMELESS HIT THE STREETS TO PROTEST PROPOSED BAN

SEATTLE—The homeless stood up for themselves by sitting down in a peaceful but vocal protest yesterday in Seattle's University District.   1

About 50 people met at noon to criticize a proposed set of city ordinances that would ban panhandlers from sitting on sidewalks, put them in jail for repeatedly urinating in public, and crack down on "intimidating" street behavior.   2

"Sitting is not a crime," read poster boards that feature mug shots of Seattle City Attorney Mark Sidran, who is pushing for the new laws. . . . "This is city property; the police want to tell us we can't sit here," yelled one man named R.C. as he sat cross-legged outside a pizza establishment.   3

Marsha Shaiman stood outside the University Book Store holding a poster and waving it at passing cars. She is not homeless, but was one of many activists in the crowd. "I qualify as a privileged white yuppie," she said. "I'm offended that the privileged people in this country are pointing at the poor, and people of color, and say they're causing problems. They're being used as scapegoats."   4

Many local merchants support the ban saying that panhandlers hurt business by intimidating shoppers and fouling the area with the odor of urine, vomited wine, and sometimes even feces.   5

A SUCCESSFUL PROCESS OF ARGUMENTATION: THE WELL-FUNCTIONING COMMITTEE

For many people, committee deliberations are the very antithesis of good argumentation. Committee deliberations seldom display the verbal thrusts and parries of congressional debates or courtroom proceedings; and other than peevishness, they seldom arouse the sort of passion that one can find every morning in the "Letters to the Editor" section of the paper. For many of us, committee experiences are too often muddled, tedious, and downright boring. Our collective suspicion of the committee process is manifest in the many jokes we make about it. (For example, do you know the definition of the word *committee?* It's a place where people keep minutes and waste hours. Or, what is a zebra? A horse designed by a committee.)

Why then, if we are all so uncomfortable with committees, do we continue to rely so heavily on them in nearly every corner of society? Probably for the same reason that Winston Churchill cited for the hardiness of democracy: However imperfect it may be, the alternatives to it are worse.

A single individual making decisions may be quirky, idiosyncratic, and insensitive to the effects of a decision on different groups of people; worse yet, he or she may pursue self-interests to the detriment of an entire group. On the other hand, it's not usually feasible to involve everyone affected by a decision in the decision-making process. Hence, we've generally found it useful to delegate many decision- and policy-making tasks to a smaller, representative group—a committee.

We use the word *committee* in its broadest sense to indicate all sorts of important work that grows out of group conversation and debate. The Declaration of Independence is essentially a committee document with Thomas Jefferson as the chair. Similarly, the U.S. Supreme Court is in effect a committee of nine judges who rely heavily, as numerous books and articles have demonstrated over the years, on group decision-making processes to reach their judgments and formulate their legal briefs. The processes used by the judges are those used in any effective instance of group decision-making. Such processes put a premium on gathering and interpreting information, listening to multiple points of view, and synthesizing and moderating different viewpoints in response to each individual's deepened understanding of the issue's complexity. The process works best when the participants listen well, treat each other with respect, and refrain from pursuing self-interest by manipulating procedures or bullying opponents.

By way of exemplifying our committee model for argument, let's briefly consider the workings of a university committee on which coauthor John Ramage served from 1992 through 1994, the University Standards Committee. The Arizona State University (ASU) Standards Committee plays a role in university life analogous to that of the Supreme Court in civic life. It's the final court of appeal for ASU students seeking exceptions to various rules that govern their academic lives. If they wish to register under a catalog different from the one they are assigned, to be exempted from a General Studies requirement, to be allowed to retake a course for a third time, or to pursue any other sort of irregular course of action, they will, after unsuccessful appeal to their advisors, their home departments, and their colleges, come to the University Standards Committee.

It is a large committee, comprising nearly two dozen members, representing the whole spectrum of departments and offices across campus. Every two weeks, the committee meets for two or more hours to consider between twenty and forty appeals. Several days before each meeting committee members receive a hefty packet of materials relevant to the cases (i.e., originals of the students' appeals, including the responses of those who've heard the appeal earlier, complete transcripts of each student's grades, and any supporting material or new information the student might wish to provide). Students may, if they choose, appear before the committee personally to make their cases.

Like all human institutions, the committee functions imperfectly. For example, there are no extensive records of its deliberations, so it often finds itself returning uncertainly to previously discussed issues whose resolutions have faded from memory. Each time an issue is revisited raises the possibility that the committee will act inconsistently. Committee members in the minority often remind those in the majority of such inconsistencies; but these reminders seldom carry the day.

For the most part, however, the committee functions remarkably well, especially considering the number of people involved. Moreover, the issues that regularly come before the committee comprise almost all the types of arguments and argumentative strategies discussed in detail throughout this text. Hence a brief summary of some of these cases is a good introduction to what is coming later in this book.

In cases that receive an extensive hearing, the committee regularly encounters the three dimensions of argument that we discuss later under the headings of *pathos, logos,* and *ethos.* (Very roughly, these terms mean, respectively, appeals to the audience's emotion, to logic, and to the arguer's personal character). Thus, under the heading of *pathos,* the committee considers the extenuating circumstances that cause appellants to seek relief from some regulation. For example, a young man whose case on paper was weak persuaded the committee to allow him to retake a course after he told them he'd missed a great deal of school while extracting his younger brother from a disastrous home situation and bringing him to live with him at school.

It should be noted, however, that while this student's emotional appeal was cited by many committee members as crucial to the decision, he probably would not have prevailed if he hadn't also established his good character (appeal to *ethos*). For the members of the committee, the young man's *ethos* was established in large part by his school record, which revealed solid grades in very difficult courses. As several of them noted, he was a deserving person who would likely do well in the course he was asking to retake. He was both capable and trustworthy in the committee's eyes.

In most cases reviewed by the committee, the *logos* of the appellant's argument is the primary concern. Thus, for example, students who ask to be exempted from the required math course because of a learning disability must present solid evidence that they have such a disability. Students who claim that their work schedules caused them to fail a course should be prepared to explain why their work schedules didn't appear to harm their performance in any other classes.

In turn, all of the argument types discussed in Part III of this text regularly surface during committee deliberations. The committee deals with definition issues ("What constitutes math anxiety and how bad does it have to be to justify exempting a student from the math requirement?"); cause/consequence issues ("What were the causes of this student's sudden poor performance during spring semester?" "What will be the consequences of approving this appeal?" "What harm might be caused by denying the appeal?"); resemblance issues ("How is this case similar to an earlier case that we considered?"); evaluation issues ("Which criteria should take precedence in assessing this sort of appeal?"); and proposal issues ("Should we make it a policy to allow course X to substitute for course Y in the General Studies requirements?").

Perhaps most of all, the committee's deliberations showed how dialogue can lead to clarification of thinking. On many occasions, committee members' initial views shifted as they listened to opposing arguments. In one case, for example, a student petitioned to change the catalog under which she was supposed to graduate because the somewhat different requirements would allow her to graduate a half year sooner. Initially, most committee members opposed the petition. They reminded the committee that in several earlier cases it had denied such petitions primarily because the requested catalog preceded the implementation of a General Studies curriculum. Petitioners were seen as trying to evade these more rigorous academic standards. Moreover, the committee was reminded that fairness to other students who had to meet the more rigorous graduation standards required the denial of this student's petition.

However, after emphatic negative arguments had been presented, a few committee members began to voice support for the student's case. While acknowledging the truth of what other committee members had said, they pointed out reasons to support the petition. The young woman in question had taken most of the required General Studies courses; it was mostly changes in the requirements for her major that delayed her graduation. Moreover, she had performed quite well in what everyone acknowledged to be a demanding course of study. Although the committee had indeed turned down previous petitions of this nature, in none of those cases had the consequences of denial been so dire for the student.

In the end, the student's defenders prevailed. Although the committee was reluctant to set a bad precedent (those who resisted the petition foresaw the committee being deluged with similar petitions from less worthy candidates), it recognized unique circumstances that legitimately made this petitioner's case different. Moreover, the rigor of the student's curriculum, the primary concern of her detractors, was shown to be greater than the rigor of many who graduated under the newer catalog.

As the previous illustration suggests, what allowed the committee to function as well as it did was the fundamental civility of its members and their collective concern that their decisions be just. Unlike some committees, this committee made many decisions, the consequences of which were not trivial for the people involved. Because of the significance of these outcomes, committee members were more willing than they otherwise might have been to concede a point to another member in the name of reaching a better decision.

To give you first-hand experience at using argument as a process of clarification, we conclude this chapter with an actual case that came before the University Standards Committee during its deliberations in the spring of 1993. We invite you to read the following letter, pretending that you are a member of the University Standards Committee; then proceed to the exercises that follow.

Petition to waive University mathematics requirement

Standards Committee Members,

I am a 43-year-old member of the Pawnee Tribe of Oklahoma and a 1
very non-traditional student currently pursuing Justice Studies at the Arizona State University (ASU) College of Public Programs. I entered college
as the first step toward completion of my goal—becoming legal counsel
for my tribe, and statesman.

I come before this committee in good faith to request that ASU sus- 2
pend, in my special case, its mathematics requirement for undergraduate degree completion so I may enter the ASU college of Law during Fall
1993. The point I wish to make to this committee is this: I do not need
algebraic skills; I will never use algebra in my intended profession; and, if
forced to comply with ASU's algebra requirement, I will be needlessly
prevented from graduating in time to enter law school next fall and face
an idle academic year before my next opportunity in 1994. I will address
each of these points in turn, but a few words concerning my academic
credentials are in order first.

Two years ago, I made a vow of moral commitment to seek out and 3
confront injustice. In September of 1990, I enrolled in college. Although I
had only the benefit of a ninth grade education, I took the General Equiv-
alency Diploma (GED) examination and placed in the top ten percent of
those, nationwide, who took the test. On the basis of this score I was
accepted into Scottsdale Community College (SCC). This step made me
the first in my entire family, and practically in my tribe, to enter college.
During my first year at SCC I maintained a 4.0 GPA, I was placed on the
President's list twice, was active in the Honors Program, received the
Honors Award of Merit in English Humanities, and was conferred an
Honors Scholarship (see attached) for the Academic year of 1991–1992
which I declined, opting to enroll in ASU instead.

At the beginning of the 1991 summer semester, I transferred to ASU. I 4
chose to graduate from ASU because of the courses offered in American
Indian studies, an important field ignored by most other Universities but
necessary to my commitment. At ASU I currently maintain a 3.6 GPA,
although my cumulative GPA is closer to 3.9, I am a member of the Honors and Justice Colleges, was appointed to the Dean's List, and awarded
ASU's prestigious Maroon and Gold Scholarship twice. My academic
standing is impeccable. I will enter the ASU College of Law to study
Indian and criminal law during the Fall of 1993—if this petition is
approved. Upon successful completion of my juris doctorate I will return
to Oklahoma to become active in the administration of Pawnee tribal
affairs as tribal attorney and advisor, and vigorously prosecute our right
to sovereignty before the Congress of the United States.

When I began my "college experience," I set a rigid time schedule for   5
the completion of my goal. By the terms of that self-imposed schedule,
founded in my belief that I have already wasted many productive years, I
allowed myself thirty-five months in which to achieve my Bachelor of Science degree in Justice Studies, for indeed justice is my concern, and
another thirty-six months in which to earn my juris doctorate—summa
cum laude. Consistent with my approach to all endeavors, I fell upon this
task with zeal. I have willingly assumed the burden of carrying substantial
academic loads during fall, spring and summer semesters. My problem
now lies in the fact that in order to satisfy the University's math requirement to graduate I must still take MAT-106 and MAT-117. I submit that
these mathematics courses are irrelevant to my goals, and present a barrier to my fall matriculation into law school.

Upon consideration of my dilemma, the questions emerged: Why do I   6
need college algebra (MAT-117)? Is college algebra necessary for studying American Indian law? Will I use college algebra in my chosen field?
What will the University gain or lose, from my taking college algebra—or
not? I decided I should resolve these questions.

I began my inquiry with the question: "Why do I need college algebra   7
(MAT-117)?" I consulted Mr. Jim _____ of the Justice College and presented this question to him. He referred to the current ASU catalog and
delineated the following answer: I need college algebra (1) for a minimum level of math competency in my chosen field, and (2) to satisfy the
university math requirement in order to graduate. My reply to the first
answer is this: I already possess ample math skills, both practical and
academic; and, I have no need for algebra in my chosen field. How do I
know this? During the spring 1992 semester at ASU I successfully completed introductory algebra (MAT-077), scoring the highest class grade
on one test (see attached transcript and test). More noteworthy is the fact
that I was a machine and welding contractor for fifteen years. I used
geometry and algebra commonly in the design of many welded structures. I am proficient in the use of Computer Assisted Design (CAD) programs, designing and drawing all my own blueprints for jobs. My blueprints and designs are always approved by city planning departments.
For example, my most recent job consisted of the manufacture, transportation and installation of one linear mile of anodized, aluminum
handrailing at a luxury resort condo on Maui, Hawaii. I applied extensive
use of math to calculate the amount of raw materials to order, the logistics of mass production and transportation for both men and materials
from Mesa to Maui, the job site installation itself, and cash flow. I have
successfully completed many jobs of this nature—all without a mathematical hitch. As to the application of math competency in my chosen
field, I can guarantee this committee that there will not be a time in my
practice of Indian law that I will need algebra. If an occasion ever occurs
that I need algebra, I will hire a mathematician, just as I would an engineer if I need engineering, or a surgeon if I need an operation.

I then contacted Dr. _____ of the ASU Mathematics Department 8
and presented him with the same question: "Why do I need college algebra?" He replied: (1) for a well rounded education; (2) to develop creative
thinking; and (3) to satisfy the university math requirement in order to
graduate. Responding to the first answer, I have a "well rounded education." My need is for a specific education in justice and American Indian
law. In fact, I do not really need the degree to practice Indian law as representative of my tribe, just the knowledge. Regarding the second, I do
not need to develop my creative thinking. It has been honed to a keen
edge for many years. For example, as a steel contractor, I commonly create huge, beautiful and intricate structures from raw materials. Contract-
ing is not my only experience in creative thinking. For twenty-five years I
have also enjoyed the status of being one of this country's foremost
designers and builders of racebikes. Machines I have designed and
brought into existence from my imagination have topped some of Japan
and Europe's best engineering efforts. To illustrate this point, in 1984 I
rode a bike of my own design to an international victory over Honda,
Suzuki, Laverda, BMW and Yamaha. I have excelled at creative thinking
my entire life—I called it survival.

Expanding on the question of why I need college algebra, I contacted 9
a few friends who are practicing attorneys. All responded to my question
in similar manner. One, Mr. Billy _____, Esq., whose law firm is in
Tempe, answered my two questions as follows: "When you attended law
school, were there any courses you took which required algebra?" His
response was "no." "Have you ever needed algebra during the many
years of your practice?" Again, his response was "no." All agreed there
was not a single occasion when they had need for algebra in their professional careers.

Just to make sure of my position, I contacted the ASU College of Law, 10
and among others, spoke to Ms. Sierra _____. I submitted the question "What law school courses will I encounter in which I will need algebra?" The unanimous reply was, they knew of none.

I am not proposing that the number of credit hours I need for gradua- 11
tion be lowered. In fact, I am more than willing to substitute another
course or two in its place. I am not trying to get out of anything hard or
distasteful, for that is certainly not my style. I am seeking only to dispose
of an unnecessary item in my studies, one which will prevent me from
entering law school this fall—breaking my stride. So little holds up so
much.

I agree that a young adult directly out of high school may not know 12
that he needs algebraic skills. Understandably, he does not know what
his future holds—but I am not that young adult. I claim the advantage. I
know precisely what my future holds and that future holds no possibility
of my needing college algebra.

Physically confronting injustice is my end. On reservations where gov- 13
ernment apathy allows rapacious pedophiles to pose as teachers; in a

country where a million and a half American Indians are held hostage as second rate human beings whose despair results in a suicide, alcohol and drug abuse rate second to no other people; in prisons where helpless inmates are beaten like dogs by sadistic guards who should be the inmates—this is the realm of my chosen field—the disenfranchised. In this netherworld, algebra and justice exist independently of one another.

In summary, I am convinced that I do not need college algebra for a   14
minimum level of math competency in my chosen field. I do not need college algebra for a well rounded education, nor to develop my creative thinking. I do not need algebra to take the LSAT. I do not need algebra for any courses in law school, nor will I for any purpose in the practice of American Indian law. It remains only that I need college algebra in order to graduate.

I promise this committee that ASU's integrity will not be compromised   15
in any way by approving this waiver. Moreover, I assure this committee that despite not having a formal accreditation in algebra, I will prove to be nothing less than an asset to this University and its Indian community, both to which I belong, and I will continue to set a standard for integrity, excellence and perseverance for all who follow. Therefore, I ask this committee, for all the reasons described above, to approve and initiate the waiver of my University mathematics requirement.

[Signed: Gordon Adams]

☐ For Class Discussion

1. Before class discussion, decide how you would vote on this issue. Should this student be exempted from the math requirement? Write out the reasons for your decision.

2. Working in small groups or as a whole class, pretend that you are the University Standards Committee and arrive at a group decision on whether to exempt this student from the math requirement.

3. After the discussion, write for five to ten minutes in a journal or notebook describing how your thinking evolved during the discussion. Did any of your classmate's views cause you to rethink your own? Class members should share with each other their descriptions of how the process of argument led to clarification of their own thinking.

We designed this exercise to help you experience argument as a clarifying process. But we had another purpose. We also designed the exercise to stimulate thinking about a problem we introduced at the beginning of this chapter: the difference between argument as clarification and argument as persuasion. Is a good argument necessarily a persuasive argument? In our opinion, this student's letter to the committee is a good argument. The student writes well, takes a clear stand, offers good reasons for his position, and supports his reasons with effective evidence. To what extent, however, is the letter a *persuasive* argument? Did it win its case? You know how you and your classmates stand on this issue. But what do you think the University Standards Committee at ASU actually decided during its deliberations in spring 1993?

We will return to this case later in the text when we discuss in more detail the differences between argument with a truth-seeking or referential aim and argument with a persuasive aim.

CONCLUSION: WHAT HAPPENS WHEN THE ARGUING PROCESS FAILS

So far we have been examining successful arguing processes. Let's conclude this chapter by looking at what happens when the arguing process fails. We'll choose an extreme example—something at the opposite end of the spectrum from the rational deliberation of the University Standards Committee or the carefully argued request for exemption from the ASU algebra requirement. We'll call it "The Case of the Crank Letter."

The "Letters to the Editor" section of almost any newspaper will contain occasional examples of breakdowns in argumentation. The worst of these we label as "crank" letters, identifiable by their moral fervor, obscure allusions, and missing logical links. Here is one example, certainly not the worst of the lot, taken from a Montana newspaper.

> I do believe Wiesner overstepped the line a bit Sept. 1 in criticizing the recent letters on creationism and evolution. (He hit a nerve is what he did.) We discuss these things because they are significant and to acquire better knowledge and understanding. Whether it can be proven or not, it can lead to dispellation of ignorance and fallacy. Things don't get accomplished by "having faith" that perhaps God will see to it. Someone has to get out and do it and a certain amount of knowledge and understanding is necessary for proper direction.
>
> In regard to Dr. Freiburger's presentations, I'm reminded of a religious discussion on TV some years ago, what about I don't remember. One so-called clergyman could quote most anything from anywhere to stand on but actual thoughts of his own I couldn't discuss. Quoting studied sources is no doubt valuable but like quoting the Bible, if you can't put it in your own words, you haven't really shown an understanding of it. (I've probably hit some nerves now, myself.)
>
> On a trip to Billings Labor Day, I noticed that the left side parking strip of eastbound I-94 is 10 feet wide only in some places. It's rather misleading to be driving along expecting it to be wide enough to park on and then it isn't. Then it is, then it isn't. Not something for an unconcerned motorist to have to find out at the last minute. That strip should be wide enough so a person at least doesn't have to step out in the grass and weeds on top of a rattlesnake.

Often a crank letter will begin in the middle with insufficient background or summary of the issues ("I do believe Wiesner overstepped the line a bit . . . " "In regard to Dr. Freiburger's presentations . . ."). Who's Wiesner? Who's Dr. Freiburger? What did they say? The writer has assumed, somehow, that all newspaper readers have been following the debate with the same passion as he has.

In addition to starting in the middle, crank letters are often characterized by unclear pronoun references and vague nouns. In the opening paragraph of the above letter, it is difficult to tell what "these things," "they," and the four occurrences of "it" stand for. Such confusion is not simply a matter of being clear to readers. We suggest that the letter writer would be hard pressed to explain their precise meaning to himself.

Showing little concern for the clarity of his own thinking, the crank letter writer typically shows little respect for opposing views ("one so-called clergyman"). Because he doesn't take opposing views seriously or treat them with any thoroughness, the crank writer seldom sees the need to defend his own views reasonably. The result is a tendency to insult the opposition and to ignore the limitations of people and ideas friendly to the writer's own position. The ratio of assertions to evidence in a crank letter is roughly equal to the ratio of salt to pepper in the Dead Sea. And, finally, the logical leap from biblical argument to parking strip widths on I-94 is symptomatic of a writer so caught up in his own world that he can't imagine a need for transitions.

The chief difference between the crank's argument and arguments in the University Standards Committee is that the Committee used argument for clarification, whereas the crank uses it to express personal feelings toward people and ideas. Although individual committee members argued forcefully for their own position, they were willing to let their positions evolve in light of differing arguments. The writer of the crank letter, however, already knows the Truth and treats those who haven't seen the light as ignoramuses.

What is our advice for you, then, at the close of this introductory chapter? Briefly, to see argument first as a process of truth-seeking and clarification and then later, when you are firmly committed to a position, as an occasion for persuasion. We suggest that throughout the process of argumentation you seek out a wide range of views, that you especially welcome views different from your own, that you treat these views respectfully, and that you see them as intelligent and rationally defensible. (Hence you must look carefully at the reasons and evidence upon which they are based).

Our goal in this text is to help you learn skills of argumentation. If you choose, you can use these skills, like Callicles, to argue any side of any issue. And yet we hope you won't. We hope that, like Socrates, you will use argument for clarification and that you will consequently find yourselves, on at least some occasions, changing your position on an issue while writing a rough draft (a sure sign that the process of arguing has been a process of clarification). We believe that the skills of reason and inquiry developed through the writing of arguments can help you get a clearer sense of who you are. If our culture sets you adrift in pluralism, argument can help you take a stand, to say "These things I believe." In this text we will not pretend to tell you what position to take on any given issue. But as responsible beings, you will often need to take a stand, to define yourself, to say "Here are the reasons that choice A is better than choice B, not just for me but for you also." If this text helps you base your commitments on reasonable grounds, then it will be successful.

Reading Arguments

☐

WHY READING ARGUMENTS IS IMPORTANT FOR WRITERS OF ARGUMENT

In the previous chapter we explained how argument is a social phenomenon. It grows out of people's search for the best answers to questions, the best choices among alternative courses of actions. Part of the social nature of argumentation is the requirement to read arguments as well as write them.

Although this chapter focuses on reading, much of its advice applies also to listening. In fact, it is often helpful to think of reading as a conversation. We like to tell students that a college library is not so much a repository of information as a discussion frozen in time until you as reader bring it to life. Those books and articles, stacked neatly on library shelves, are arguing with each other, carrying on a great extended conversation. As you read, you bring those conversations to life. And when you write, you enter those conversations.

So writing and speaking are only half of the arguing process. The other half is careful reading and listening.

SUGGESTIONS FOR IMPROVING YOUR READING PROCESS

Before we offer specific strategies for reading arguments, let's examine some general strategies that can improve your ability to read any kind of college-level material, from complex textbooks to primary sources in a history or philosophy course.

1. Slow down: Advertisements for speedreading mislead us into believing that expert readers read rapidly. In fact, experts read difficult texts slowly, often rereading them two or three times, treating their first readings like first drafts. They hold confusing passages in mental suspension, hoping that later parts of the essay will clarify earlier parts. They "nutshell" or summarize passages in the margins. They interact with the text by asking questions, expressing disagreements, linking the text with other readings or with personal experience.

2. Get the dictionary habit: When you can't tell a word's meaning from context, get in the habit of looking it up. One strategy is to make small tic marks next to words you're unsure of; then look them up after you're done so as not to break your concentration.

3. Lose your highlighter/find your pen: Relying on those yellow highlighters makes you too passive. Next time you get the urge to highlight a passage, write in the margin why you think it's important. Is it a major new point in the argument? A significant piece of support? A summary of the opposition? A particularly strong or particularly weak point? Use the margins to summarize the text, protest vehemently, ask questions, give assent—but don't just color the pages.

4. Reconstruct the rhetorical context: Train yourself to ask questions such as these: Who is this author? What audience is he or she writing for? What occasion prompted this writing? What is the author's purpose? Any piece of writing makes more sense if you think of its author as a real person writing for some real purpose out of real historical context.

5. Join the text's conversation by exploring your views on the issues before reading: To determine the text's issues before reading it through, note the title, read the first few paragraphs carefully and skim the opening sentences of paragraphs. You can then explore your own views on the issue. This sort of personal exploration at the pre-reading stage both increases your readiness to understand the text and enhances your ability to enjoy it.

6. Continue the conversation after your reading: After you've read a text, try completing the following statements in a journal: "The most significant question this essay raises is. . . ." "The most important thing I learned from this essay is. . . ." "I agree with the author about. . . ." "However, I disagree about. . . ." These questions help you remember the reading and urge you to respond actively to it.

7. Try "translating" difficult passages: When you stumble over a difficult passage, try "translating" it into your own words. Converting the passage into your own language forces you to focus on the precise meanings of words. Although your translation may not be exactly what the author intended, you see more clearly where the sources of confusion lie and what the likely range of meanings might be.

STRATEGIES FOR READING ARGUMENTS: AN OVERVIEW

Whereas the above suggestions can be applied to all sorts of reading tasks, the rest of this chapter focuses on reading strategies specific to arguments. Because argument begins in disagreements within a social community, we recommend that you examine any argument as if it were only one voice in a larger conversation. We therefore recommend the following strategies in sequence:

1. Read as a believer.
2. Read as a doubter.
3. Seek out alternative views and analyze sources of disagreement to clarify why participants in the conversation are disagreeing with each other.
4. Evaluate the various positions.

Let's now explore each of these strategies in turn.

STRATEGY 1:   READING AS A BELIEVER

When you read as a believer, you are practicing what psychologist Carl Rogers calls "empathic listening," in which you mentally walk in the author's shoes, trying to join the author's culture and to see the world through the author's eyes. Reading as a believer helps you guard against coloring the author's ideas with your own biases and beliefs.

Because empathic listening is such a vital skill, we ask you now to try it on an influential and controversial article by conservative political writer Charles Murray. The article, published in the October 29, 1993 *Wall Street Journal,* concerns Murray's approach to the growing problem of American babies born outside of wedlock. According to syndicated political columnist John Leo (also a conservative), Murray's article "may turn out to be the most potent op-ed article in about 10 years. . . . [It] has had an explosive impact in policy discussions [at the presidential level]."* Before reading the article, reflect briefly on your own attitudes toward single parenthood. Do you think it is a problem that 30 percent of American babies are now born to unmarried mothers? Can a single parent raise a child as effectively as a married couple? What are the causes for the rise in single parenthood in our culture? If you think the 30 percent illegitimacy rate is a problem, what can be done about it?

---

* John Leo, "New Cultural Conscience Shifts the Welfare Debate," *Seattle Times* 14 Dec. 1993: B4.

THE COMING WHITE UNDERCLASS

Charles Murray

Every once in a while the sky really is falling, and this seems to be the case with the latest national figures on illegitimacy. The unadorned statistic is that, in 1991, 1.2 million children were born to unmarried mothers, within a hair of 30 percent of all live births. How high is 30 percent? About four percentage points higher than the black illegitimacy rate in the early 1960s that motivated Daniel Patrick Moynihan to write his famous memorandum on the breakdown of the black family.[1]   1

The 1991 story for blacks is that illegitimacy has now reached 68 percent of births to black women. In inner cities, the figure is typically in excess of 80 percent. Many of us have heard these numbers so often that we are inured. It is time to think about them as if we were back in the mid-1960s with the young Moynihan and asked to predict what would happen if the black illegitimacy rate were 68 percent.   2

Impossible we would have said. But if the proportion of fatherless boys in a given community were to reach such levels, surely the culture must be "Lord of the Flies" writ large,[2] the values of unsocialized male adolescents made norms—physical violence, immediate gratification and predatory sex. That is the culture now taking over the black inner city.   3

But the black story, however dismaying, is old news. The new trend that threatens the U.S. is white illegitimacy. Matters have not yet quite gotten out of hand, but they are on the brink. If we want to act, now is the time.   4

In 1991, 707,502 babies were born to single white women, representing 22 percent of white births. The elite wisdom holds that this phenomenon cuts across social classes, as if the increase in Murphy Browns[3] were pushing the trendline. Thus, a few months ago, a Census Bureau study of fertility among all American women got headlines for a few days because it showed that births to single women with college degrees doubled in the last decade to 6 percent from 3 percent. This is an interesting trend, but of minor social importance. The real news of that study is that the proportion of single mothers with less than a high school education who gave birth jumped to 48 percent from 35 percent in a single decade.   5

---

[1]   A reference to a controversial Department of Labor study, *The Negro Family: The Case for National Action* (Office of Planning and Research, March 1965).

[2]   A reference to William Golding's novel *Lord of the Flies*, in which a group of adolescent males become stranded on an island and create their own society with no adult supervision. As soon as adult "norms" begin to fade, the boys' culture gradually descends into savagery and violence.

[3]   Murphy Brown, the star of a TV sitcom by the same name, became a single mother on a TV episode made famous in 1992 by then Vice President Quayle, who used her as a symbol of the breakdown of the traditional family.

These numbers are dominated by whites. Breaking down the numbers   6
by race (using data not available in the published version), women with
college degrees contribute only 4 percent of white illegitimate babies,
while women with a high school education or less contribute 82 percent.
Women with family incomes of $75,000 or more contribute 1 percent of
white illegitimate babies, while women with family incomes under
$20,000 contribute 69 percent.

The National Longitudinal Study of Youth, a Labor Department study   7
that has tracked more than 10,000 youths since 1979, shows an even
more dramatic picture. For white women below the poverty line in the
year prior to giving birth, 44 percent of births have been illegitimate,
compared with only six percent for women above the poverty line. White
illegitimacy is overwhelmingly a lower-class phenomenon.

This brings us to the emergence of a white underclass. In raw num-   8
bers, European-American whites are the ethnic group with the most people in poverty, most illegitimate children, most women on welfare, most
unemployed men, and most arrests for serious crimes. And yet whites
have not had an "underclass" as such, because the whites who might
qualify have been scattered among the working class. Instead, whites
have had "white trash" concentrated in a few streets on the outskirts of
town, sometimes a Skid Row of unattached white men in the large cities.
But these scatterings have seldom been large enough to make up a
neighborhood. An underclass needs a critical mass, and white America
has not had one.

But now the overall white illegitimacy rate is 22 percent. The figure in   9
low-income, working-class communities may be twice that. How much
illegitimacy can a community tolerate? Nobody knows, but the historical
fact is that the trendlines on black crime, dropout from the labor force,
and illegitimacy all shifted sharply upward as the overall black illegitimacy
rate passed 25 percent.

The causal connection is murky—I blame the revolution in social pol-   10
icy during that period, while others blame the sexual revolution, broad
shifts in cultural norms, or structural changes in the economy. But the
white illegitimacy rate is approaching that same problematic 25 percent
region at a time when social policy is more comprehensively wrong-
headed than it was in the mid-1960s, and the cultural and sexual norms
are still more degraded.

The white underclass will begin to show its face in isolated ways. Look   11
for certain schools in white neighborhoods to get a reputation as being
unteachable, with large numbers of disruptive students and indifferent
parents. Talk to the police; listen for stories about white neighborhoods
where the incidence of domestic disputes and casual violence has been
shooting up. Look for white neighborhoods with high concentrations of
drug activity and large numbers of men who have dropped out of the
labor force. Some readers will recall reading the occasional news story
about such places already.

As the spatial concentration of illegitimacy reaches critical mass, we   12
should expect the deterioration to be as fast among low-income whites in
the 1990s as it was among low-income blacks in the 1960s. My proposition is that illegitimacy is the single most important social problem of our
time—more important than crime, drugs, poverty, illiteracy, welfare or
homelessness because it drives everything else. Doing something about
it is not just one more item on the American policy agenda, but should
be at the top. Here is what to do.

In the calculus of illegitimacy, the constants are that boys like to sleep   13
with girls and that girls think babies are endearing. Human societies have
historically channeled these elemental forces of human behavior via thick
walls of rewards and penalties that constrained the overwhelming majority of births to take place within marriage. The past 30 years have seen
those walls cave in. It is time to rebuild them.

The ethical underpinning for the policies I am about to describe is   14
this: Bringing a child into the world is the most important thing that most
human beings ever do. Bringing a child into the world when one is not
emotionally or financially prepared to be a parent is wrong. The child
deserves society's support. The parent does not.

The social justification is this: A society with broad legal freedoms   15
depends crucially on strong nongovernmental institutions to temper and
restrain behavior. Of these, marriage is paramount. Either we reverse the
current trends in illegitimacy—especially white illegitimacy—or America
must, willy-nilly, become an unrecognizably authoritarian, socially segregated, centralized state.

To restore the rewards and penalties of marriage does not require   16
social engineering. Rather, it requires that the state stop interfering with
the natural forces that have done the job quite effectively for millennia.
Some of the changes I will describe can occur at the federal level; others
would involve state laws. For now, the important thing is to agree on what
should be done.

I begin with the penalties, of which the most obvious are economic.   17
Throughout human history, a single woman with a small child has not
been a viable economic unit. Not being a viable economic unit, neither
have the single woman and child been a legitimate social unit. In small
numbers they must be a net drain on the community's resources. In
large numbers, they must destroy the community's capacity to sustain
itself. *Mirabile dictu,* communities everywhere have augmented the economic penalties of single parenthood with severe social stigma.

Restoring economic penalties translates into the first and central pol-   18
icy prescription: to end all economic support for single mothers. The
AFDC (Aid to Families with Dependent Children) payment goes to zero.
Single mothers are not eligible for subsidized housing or for food
stamps. An assortment of other subsidies and in-kind benefits disappear.
Since universal medical coverage appears to be an idea whose time has
come, I will stipulate that all children have medical coverage. But with

that exception, the signal is loud and unmistakable. From society's per-spective, to have a baby that you cannot care for yourself is profoundly irresponsible, and the government will no longer subsidize it.

How does a poor young mother survive without government support? 19 The same way she has since time immemorial. If she wants to keep a child, she must enlist support from her parents, boyfriend, siblings, neighbors, church or philanthropies. She must get support from some-where, anywhere, other than the government. The objectives are three-fold.

First, enlisting the support of others raises the probability that other 20 mature adults are going to be involved with the upbringing of the child, and this is a great good in itself.

Second, the need to find support forces a self-selection process. One 21 of the most short-sighted excuses made for current behavior is that an adolescent who is utterly unprepared to be a mother "needs someone to love." Childish yearning isn't a good enough selection device. We need to raise the probability that a young single woman who keeps her child is doing so volitionally and thoughtfully. Forcing her to find a way of sup-porting the child does this. It will lead many young women who shouldn't be mothers to place their babies for adoption. This is good. It will lead others, watching what happens to their sisters, to take steps not to get pregnant. This is also good. Many others will get abortions. Whether this is good depends on what one thinks of abortion.

Third, stigma will regenerate. The pressure on relatives and communi- 22 ties to pay for the folly of their children will make an illegitimate birth the socially horrific act it used to be, and getting a girl pregnant something boys do at the risk of facing a shotgun. Stigma and shotgun marriages may or may not be good for those on the receiving end, but their deter-rent effect on others is wonderful—and indispensable.

What about women who can find no support but keep the baby any- 23 way? There are laws already on the books about the right of the state to take a child from a neglectful parent. We have some 360,000 children in foster care because of them. Those laws would still apply. Society's main response, however, should be to make it as easy as possible for those mothers to place their children for adoption at infancy. To that end, state governments must strip adoption of the nonsense that has encumbered it in recent decades.

The first step is to make adoption easy for any married couple who 24 can show reasonable evidence of having the resources and stability to raise a child. Lift all restrictions on interracial adoption. Ease age limita-tions for adoptive parents.

The second step is to restore the traditional legal principle that placing 25 a child for adoption means irrevocably relinquishing all legal rights to the child. The adoptive parents are parents without qualification. Records are sealed until the child reaches adulthood, at which time they may be unsealed only with the consent of biological child and parent.

Given these straightforward changes—going back to the old way, which worked—there is reason to believe that some extremely large proportion of infants given up by their mothers will be adopted into good homes. This is true not just for flawless blue-eyed blond infants but for babies of all colors and conditions. The demand for infants to adopt is huge.

26

Some small proportion of infants and larger proportion of older children will not be adopted. For them, the government should spend lavishly on orphanages. I am not recommending Dickensian barracks. In 1993, we know a lot about how to provide a warm, nurturing environment for children, and getting rid of the welfare system frees up lots of money to do it. Those who find the "orphanages" objectionable may think of them as 24-hour-a-day preschools. Those who prattle about the importance of keeping children with their biological mothers may wish to spend some time in a patrol car or with a social worker seeing what the reality of life with welfare-dependent biological mothers can be like.

27

Finally, there is the matter of restoring the rewards of marriage. Here, I am pessimistic about how much government can do and optimistic about how little it needs to do. The rewards of raising children within marriage are real and deep. The main task is to shepherd children through adolescence so that they can reach adulthood—when they are likely to recognize the value of those rewards—free to take on marriage and family. The main purpose of the penalties for single parenthood is to make that task easier.

28

One of the few concrete things that the government can do to increase the rewards of marriage is make the tax code favor marriage and children. Those of us who are nervous about using the tax code for social purposes can advocate making the tax code at least neutral.

29

A more abstract but ultimately crucial step in raising the rewards of marriage is to make marriage once again the sole legal institution through which parental rights and responsibilities are defined and exercised.

30

Little boys should grow up knowing from their earliest memories that if they want to have any rights whatsoever regarding a child that they sire—more vividly, if they want to grow up to be a daddy—they must marry. Little girls should grow up knowing from their earliest memories that if they want to have any legal claims whatsoever on the father of their children, they must marry. A marriage certificate should establish that a man and a woman have entered into a unique legal relationship. The changes in recent years that have blurred the distinctiveness of marriage are subtly but importantly destructive.

31

Together, these measures add up to a set of signals, some with immediate and tangible consequences, others with long-term consequences, still others symbolic. They should be supplemented by others based on a re-examination of divorce law and its consequences.

32

That these policy changes seem drastic and unrealistic is a peculiarity of our age, not of the policies themselves. With embellishments, I have

33

endorsed the policies that were the uncontroversial law of the land as recently as John Kennedy's presidency. Then, America's elites accepted as a matter of course that a free society such as America's can sustain itself only through virtue and temperance in the people, that virtue and temperance depend centrally on the socialization of each new generation, and that the socialization of each generation depends on the matrix of care and resources fostered by marriage.

Three decades after that consensus disappeared, we face an emerg- 34
ing crisis. The long, steep climb in black illegitimacy has been calamitous in black communities and painful for the nation. The reforms I have described will work for blacks as for whites, and have been needed for years. But the brutal truth is that American society as a whole could survive when illegitimacy became epidemic within a comparably small ethnic minority. It cannot survive the same epidemic among whites.

Now that you have finished the article, ask yourself how well you "listened" to it. The best way to demonstrate such listening is through your ability to restate the author's argument fairly and accurately in your own words—that is, to summarize it.

Summary Writing as a Way of Reading to Believe

A summary (also called an abstract or a precis) condenses the original by eliminating supporting data and leaving only the major points. Summaries can vary in length from one sentence to several pages (if, say, you are summarizing a book). Summaries of articles typically range from a single paragraph (containing, say, 100–250 words) to several paragraphs that reduce the original to about one-third its original length.

If you practice the following steps, you should eventually find yourself writing summaries with relative ease.

1. The first time through, read the essay for general meaning. Follow the flow of the argument without judgment or criticism, trying to see the world as the author sees it.

2. Reread the essay carefully, writing brief statements in the margins that sum up what each paragraph (or group of closely related paragraphs) says and does. A "what it says" statement summarizes a paragraph's content. A "what it does" statement identifies a paragraph's function, such as "summarizes opposition," "develops second supporting reason," "offers illustrative anecdote," "provides statistical data to support a point," and so on. Figure 2–1 shows a page from Murray's article with "says" and "does" statements intermixed in the margin.

The first few times you summarize an article, you might find it helpful to write "says" and "does" statements on a separate page to help you under-

Figure 2–1. Reading-to-believe annotations on Murray text

> But now the overall white illegitimacy rate is 22 percent. The figure in low-income, working-class communities may be twice that. How much illegitimacy can a community tolerate? Nobody knows, but the historical fact is that the trendlines on black crime, dropout from the labor force, and illegitimacy all shifted sharply upward as the overall black illegitimacy rate passed 25 percent.   [9]

White illegitimacy rate approaching danger point of 25%.

> The causal connection is murky—I blame the revolution in social policy during that period, while others blame the sexual revolution, broad shifts in cultural norms, or structural changes in the economy. But the white illegitimacy rate is approaching that same problematic 25 percent region at a time when social policy is more comprehensively wrong-headed than it was in the mid-1960s, and the cultural and sexual norms are still more degraded.   [10]

What is the cause?

| Murray blames social policy | Others blame sexual revolution, shifts in culture, economy |

> The white underclass will begin to show its face in isolated ways. Look for certain schools in white neighborhoods to get a reputation as being unteachable, with large numbers of disruptive students and indifferent parents. Talk to the police; listen for stories about white neighborhoods where the incidence of domestic disputes and casual violence has been shooting up. Look for white neighborhoods with high concentrations of drug activity and large numbers of men who have dropped out of the labor force. Some readers will recall reading the occasional news story about such places already.   [11]

danger signs

> As the spatial concentration of illegitimacy reaches critical mass, we should expect the deterioration to be as fast among low-income whites in the 1990s as it was among low-income blacks in the 1960s. My proposition is that illegitimacy is the single most important social problem of our time—more important than crime, drugs, poverty, illiteracy, welfare, or homelessness because it drives everything else. Doing something about it is not just one more item on the American policy agenda, but should be at the top. Here is what to do.   [12]

Illegitimacy single most important problem.

> In the calculus of illegitimacy, the constants are that boys like to sleep with girls and that girls think babies are endearing. Human societies have historically channeled these elemental forces of human behavior via thick walls of rewards and penalties that constrained the overwhelming majority of births to take place within marriage. The past 30 years have seen those walls cave in. It is time to rebuild them.   [13]

Turning point: Here is what to do.

(1) We must rebuild walls that used to constrain births within marriage.

> The ethical underpinning for the policies I am about to describe is this: Bringing a child into the world is the most important thing that most human beings ever do. Bringing a child into the world when one is not emotionally or financially prepared to be a parent is wrong. The child deserves society's support. The parent does not.   [14]

It is wrong to have a baby unless parents are emotionally and financially prepared.

> The social justification is this: A society with broad legal freedoms depends crucially on strong nongovernmental institutions to temper and restrain behavior. Of these, marriage is paramount. Either we reverse the recent trends in illegitimacy—especially white illegitimacy—or America must, willy-nilly, become an unrecognizably authoritarian, socially segregated, centralized state.   [15]

> To restore the rewards and penalties of marriage does not require social engineering. Rather, it requires that the state stop interfering with the natural forces that have done the job quite effectively for millennia.

Either we restore cultural norms against illegitimacy or we will degenerate into an authoritarian state.

stand the structure and argument of the essay. To illustrate this powerful strategy, we provide paragraph-by-paragraph "says" and "does" statements for approximately two-thirds of Murray's essay (numbers in boldface refer to original paragraph numbers).

DOES/SAYS ANALYSIS OF MURRAY

Paragraphs 1–2: *Does:* Introduces problem and uses comparison of present illegitimacy birth rates with earlier rates to underscore significance of problem.

Says: Illegitimate birthrates have soared in recent years, far exceeding the 25 percent danger level that prompted Daniel Moynihan in the 1960s to prophesy the breakdown of the black family.

Paragraph 3:   *Does:*   Lends presence to his claim by drawing an analogy between communities full of fatherless adolescents and a novel about adolescent boys marooned on an island. *Says:*   Like the boys in *Lord of the Flies,* contemporary illegitimate children will create a savage society.

Paragraph 4:   *Does:*   Provides a transition from discussion of black illegitimacy rates to white illegitimacy rates. *Says:*   The white illegitimacy problem is growing but there's still time to get it under control.

Paragraphs 5–7:   *Does:*   Supports and limits the claim that white illegitimacy rate is growing. *Says:*   Although 22 percent of white births are illegitimate, the proportions are much larger among working class whites.

Paragraph 8:   *Does:*   Defines the illegitimacy problem as a part of the larger problem of an "emergent white underclass." *Says:*   The white underclass is now large enough to constitute a "critical mass."

Paragraphs 9 and 11:   *Does:*   Compares white illegitimacy rate to historical black rates and predicts bad consequences. *Says:*   As white illegitimacy rates approach 25 percent, we can expect to see crime and unemployment figures rise dramatically as they did when black rates achieved a similar level.

Paragraph 10:   *Does:*   Claims a causal connection between illegitimacy rates and social problems. *Says:*   While admitting the connection is "murky," Murray identifies "social policy"—not changes in sexual mores or cultural economic shifts—as the key to illegitimacy rates.

Paragraph 12:   *Does:*   Sums up and restates problem. *Says:*   Illegitimacy is the "single most important social issue of our time" because it drives other social problems.

....

Paragraphs 23–25:   *Does:*   Anticipates objection that not all mothers will find aid or place children for adoption voluntarily. *Says:*   When mothers don't act responsibly, we have the legal means to remove them and place them in sound families, if we ease adoption restrictions.

Paragraphs 26–27:   *Does:*   Predicts large numbers of children will be given up for adoption and offers an alternative for those who are not placed. *Says:*   For those illegitimate children not adopted, we need to provide "24-hour-a-day preschools" (orphanages).

Paragraphs 28–32:   *Does:*   Offers second prong of proposal, rewarding marriage. *Says:*   In addition to penalizing illegitimacy, we need to reward marriage by favoring it in the tax code and in civil laws defining parental rights and responsibilities.

Paragraph 33:   *Does:*   Cites a precedent for the current proposal. *Says:*   Most aspects of the current proposal were law of the land in the Kennedy era.

Paragraph 34:   *Does:*   Underscores significance by returning to earlier precedents. *Says:*   If we don't act, we can look for the same sorts of problems in the white underclass that we've already seen in the black underclass.

☐ FOR CLASS DISCUSSION

Working individually or in groups, make "what it does" and "what it says" statements for the middle paragraphs (paragraphs 13–22) of Murray's article.

3. After you've analyzed the essay paragraph by paragraph, try locating the main divisions or parts of the argument. At the largest level, Murray's article divides into two major parts: the first part (paragraphs 1–12) describes the problem, while the second part (paragraphs 13–35) explains Murray's proposed solution. Subdividing the essay further, we identified the following main sections (different readers might subdivide the sections in a slightly different way):

- an introductory section describing the problem of illegitimacy among inner-city blacks and showing that the illegitimacy rate is also rising among lower-class whites (paragraphs 1–7)
- a section showing how the increase in the illegitimacy rate among lower-class whites is reaching a critical mass that will lead to the emergence of a white underclass and a dramatic increase in crime, unemployment, drug use (paragraphs 8–12)
- an overview paragraph saying that we must rebuild the "walls" that restrict childbirth to married couples (paragraph 13)
- a section giving the ethical and social justification for his proposal (paragraphs 14–16)
- a section showing the three "good" results of ending all economic aid to single mothers (paragraphs 17–27). This section also includes a subsection on improving the process of adoption (paragraphs 23–27)
- a section showing that we must re-establish the rewards for marriage (paragraphs 28–32)
- a conclusion showing the importance of the proposal and claiming that this proposal is not radical.

Instead of listing the sections as we did above, many readers might prefer to make an outline, flowchart, or diagram of the article showing its main parts and subparts. (See our diagram of Murray's article in Figure 2–2.)

4. Turn your list, outline, flowchart, or diagram into a prose summary. Typically, writers do this in one of two ways. Some start with a lengthy paragraph-by-paragraph summary and then prune it in successive drafts. Others start with a one-sentence summary of the argument's thesis and major supporting reasons and then gradually flesh it out with more supporting ideas.

5. Continue writing drafts until your summary is the desired length and is sufficiently clear, complete, and concise that someone who hasn't read the original could read your summary and explain the original to a third party.

As illustrations, consider the following three summaries of Murray's article.

ONE-SENTENCE SUMMARY

To solve the problem of illegitimacy, which has long been at crisis levels for black culture and now is reaching crisis proportions among lower-class whites, the United States should end all economic support for single mothers, thereby reawakening social stigmas against single parenthood. (45 words)

Figure 2–2. Branch diagram of Murray's argument

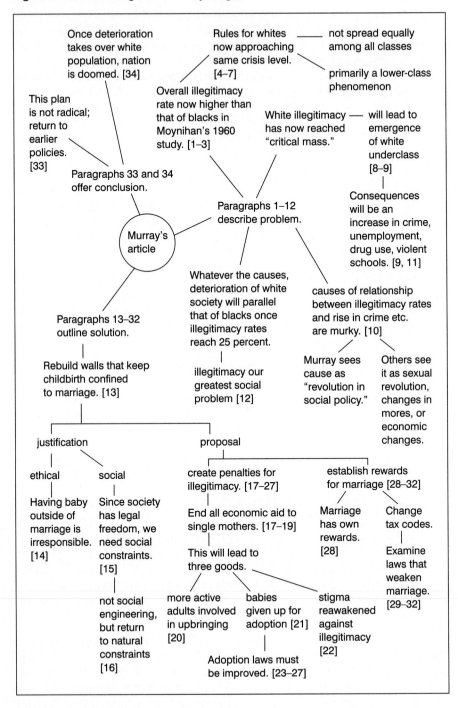

100-WORD SUMMARY

The illegitimacy rate in America, now 30 percent of all live births, has increased most dramatically among lower class whites, where we can now predict the same kind of social breakdown that characterized black inner-city culture when illegitimacy rates soared above 25 percent. The solution is to revitalize cultural constraints against illegitimacy by ending all economic support for single mothers. Three good results will follow: (1) More family and friends will be involved in raising the child; (2) more infants will be given for adoption; and (3) social stigmas against illegitimacy will be reawakened. This approach, although seemingly drastic, returns our nation to earlier policies. (101 words)

250-WORD SUMMARY

The illegitimacy rate in America has reached 30 percent of all live births, thus exceeding the 25 percent black illegitimacy rate in the 1960s that sparked Moynihan's prophetic warnings about the breakdown of the black family. Illegitimate births among lower-class whites have risen so dramatically that a new white underclass is beginning to emerge. We can thus predict the same kind of social breakdown among working-class whites (increase in crime, drug abuse, unemployment, unmanageable schools) that has characterized the black inner city. The solution, which can be justified on both ethical and social grounds, is to revitalize cultural constraints against illegitimacy. We should begin by ending all economic support for single mothers, forcing them to seek assistance from family, boyfriends, or charities. Three good results will follow: (1) more adults will be involved in raising the child; (2) many single mothers will decide against keeping infants and offer them for adoption; and (3) angry families will reawaken the social stigma against illegitimacy. To make the solution workable, we must ease adoption laws and be prepared to spend lavishly on orphanages. Finally, we must increase the rewards of marriage through restructured tax codes and reexamination of divorce laws and other regulations that undermine the social importance of marriage. Although this approach seems drastic, it merely returns our nation to the policies that prevailed up through John Kennedy's presidency. Unless we return to the values of virtue and temperance, the social catastrophe that has undermined black culture will sweep through white culture also, thus destroying our nation. (253 words)

We don't want to pretend that these summaries were easy to write. They weren't. Murray's argument is quite difficult to summarize because he doesn't always make the links between parts explicit. Moreover, some readers might fault our summaries for overemphasizing some aspects of the essay while neglecting others. Such differences are to be expected in the absence of prominently stated transitions and other structural markers.

Incorporating Summaries into Your Writing

Suppose you were writing your own argument on welfare reform and wanted to incorporate a summary of Murray's views into your own essay. Any of the above summaries could be woven into your own essay through the use of *attributive tags,* which are phrases such as "Murray says," "according to Murray," and so forth. These tags, together with a bibliographic citation to Murray's article, indicate that you are reporting someone else's views rather than your own. If you were to copy any phrases directly from Murray's article, you would also need quotation marks around the part you copied. The following example uses the Modern Language Association (MLA) citation system.*

SUMMARY OF MURRAY INCORPORATED INTO YOUR OWN ESSAY

The conservative social critic Charles Murray, writing in the October 29, 1993, *Wall Street Journal,* has argued that America's skyrocketing illegitimacy rate is "the single most important social problem of our time" (29). Citing extensive statistical evidence, Murray argues that the illegitimacy rate in America has reached 30 percent of all live births, thus exceeding the 25 percent black illegitimacy rate in the 1960s that sparked Daniel Patrick Moynihan's prophetic warnings about the breakdown of the black family. According to Murray, illegitimate births among lower-class whites have risen so dramatically that a new white underclass is beginning to emerge. Murray thus predicts the same kind of social breakdown among working-class whites (increase in crime, drug abuse, unemployment, unmanageable schools) that has characterized the black inner city. Murray's proposed solution, for which he gives both ethical and social justification, is to revitalize cultural constraints against illegitimacy. We should begin, he claims, by ending all economic support for single mothers, forcing them to seek assistance from family, boyfriends, or charities. He wants to send adolescents a "loud and unmistakable" (30) message. "From society's perspective, to have a baby that you cannot care for yourself is profoundly irresponsible, and the government will no longer subsidize it" (30). Murray claims that three good results will follow from the withdrawing of economic support: (1) more adults will be involved in raising the child; (2) many single mothers will decide against keeping infants and offer them for adoption; and (3) angry families will reawaken the social stigma against illegitimacy. To make the solution workable, Murray argues that we must ease adoption laws and be prepared to spend lavishly on orphanages. Finally, Murray wants to increase the rewards of marriage through restructured tax codes and reexamination of divorce laws and other regulations that undermine the social importance of marriage. Although this approach seems drastic, Murray argues that it merely returns our nation to the policies that prevailed up through John Kennedy's presidency. Unless we return to the values of virtue and temperance, claims Murray, the social catastrophe that has undermined black culture will sweep through white culture also, thus destroying our nation.

WORKS CITED

Murray, Charles. "The Coming White Underclass." *Wall Street Journal* 29 Oct. 1993: A13. Rpt. in *Writing Arguments: A Rhetoric with Readings.* John D. Ramage and John C. Bean. 3rd ed. Needham, MA: Allyn and Bacon, 1995. 27–32.

---

*   In this example, numbers in parentheses indicate page numbers in this text where the quotations can be found. A listing of complete bibliographic information would be included on a separate page at the end of the essay under the heading "Works Cited." See Chapter 17, "Using and Documenting Sources," for further discussion of documentation systems.

STRATEGY 2: READING AS A DOUBTER

But reading as a believer isn't enough. You must also read as a doubter by raising objections, asking questions, expressing skepticism, and withholding assent. In the margins you add a new layer of notations demanding more proof, doubting evidence, challenging the author's assumptions and values, and so forth. Figure 2–3 shows one reader's doubting commentary as she made marginal notations on a page from Murray's article. (For purposes of illustration, this reader's believing commentary—efforts to understand and summarize the argument—aren't shown. Marginal notations of a text usually intermingle both believing and doubting commentary.)

☐ FOR CLASS DISCUSSION

Before we inform you of some of the doubts and queries raised by our own students, we ask you to return now to the Murray article and read it skeptically yourself. Raise questions, offer objections, express all your doubts. Then, working as a whole class or in small groups, make a list of problems you find with Murray's argument.

We hope that you have now done your own doubting of Murray's article. What follows is a selective list of doubts and queries raised by students in our classes:

- Murray seems to have no compassion for the individuals who would suffer from his proposal. He treats people like abstract numbers.
- Murray glosses over the question of cause, calling it "murky" (paragraph 9). He believes that the "revolution in social policy" is the primary cause, and thus he thinks that changing the social policy will reverse the trend. But what if the other factors are more important—sexual revolution, shift in cultural norms, or changes in the economy?
- Will changing welfare rules really change attitudes of sexually active teenagers or young adults? Murray seems to assume that desire for welfare money is a primary motivation for getting pregnant. Perhaps the desire of poor women to have a baby is the result of alienation and hopelessness in living a life of poverty.
- Is illegitimacy really the root cause that drives all the other social problems such as crime, drug use, unemployment, and so forth? Perhaps poverty is the root cause. What good will it do to force the boyfriend to marry the girl (shotgun wedding) if the boyfriend has no job?
- What would happen to single mothers and their children if welfare payments suddenly stopped and they were unable to get help from family and friends? How many babies would starve or be abandoned? Would these "lavish" orphanages really work?
- Our group felt the article was racist. Murray seemed to think we could tolerate illegitimacy among blacks but not among whites. He seems to have completely given up on Black America.

Figure 2–3. Reading-to-doubt annotations on Murray text

But now the overall white illegitimacy rate is 22 percent. The figure in low-income, working-class communities may be twice that. How much illegitimacy can a community tolerate? Nobody knows, but the historical fact is that the trendlines on black crime, dropout from the labor force, and illegitimacy all shifted sharply upward as the overall black illegitimacy rate passed 25 percent.   [9]

The causal connection is murky—I blame the revolution in social policy during that period, while others blame the sexual revolution, broad shifts in cultural norms, or structural changes in the economy. But the white illegitimacy rate is approaching that same problematic 25 percent region at a time when social policy is more comprehensively wrongheaded than it was in the mid-1960s, and the cultural and sexual norms are still more degraded.   [10]

> How much does Murray's "sol-ution" depend on his analysis of the cause here? What if the primary causes are economic, or changes in sexual or cultural norms?

The white underclass will begin to show its face in isolated ways. Look for certain schools in white neighborhoods to get a reputation as being unteachable, with large numbers of disruptive students and indifferent parents. Talk to the police; listen for stories about white neighborhoods where the incidence of domestic disputes and casual violence has been shooting up. Look for white neighborhoods with high concentrations of drug activity and large numbers of men who have dropped out of the labor force. Some readers will recall reading the occasional news story about such places already.   [11]

As the spatial concentration of illegitimacy reaches critical mass, we should expect the deterioration to be as fast among low-income whites in the 1990s as it was among low-income blacks in the 1960s. My proposition is that illegitimacy is the single most important social problem of our time—more important than crime, drugs, poverty, illiteracy, welfare, or homelessness because it drives everything else. Doing something about it is not just one more item on the American policy agenda, but should be at the top. Here is what to do.   [12]

> Murray claims that illegitimacy drives all other social problems. But maybe he has causality reversed. Maybe there would be less illegitimacy if poor people had better jobs—they would have greater sense of self-worth and more sexual responsibility. Seems to claim that most single mothers wanted to get pregnant. What if lack of sex education has a lot to do with this problem?

In the calculus of illegitimacy, the constants are that boys like to sleep with girls and that girls think babies are endearing. Human societies have historically channeled these elemental forces of human behavior via thick walls of rewards and penalties that constrained the overwhelming majority of births to take place within marriage. The past 30 years have seen those walls cave in. It is time to rebuild them.   [13]

The ethical underpinning for the policies I am about to describe is this: Bringing a child into the world is the most important thing that most human beings ever do. Bringing a child into the world when one is not emotionally or financially prepared to be a parent is wrong. The child deserves society's support. The parent does not.   [14]

The social justification is this: A society with broad legal freedoms depends crucially on strong nongovernmental institutions to temper and restrain behavior. Of these, marriage is paramount. Either we reverse the recent trends in illegitimacy—especially white illegitimacy—or America must, willy-nilly, become an unrecognizably authoritarian, socially segregated, centralized state.   [15]

> But he wants to reverse this trend by punishing single mothers. Not providing economic help seems authoritarian to me.
>
> He seems to think that the middle-class, two-parent family is the "natural" way. What about other cultures where polygamy or communal child raising is the norm?

To restore the rewards and penalties of marriage does not require social engineering. Rather, it requires that the state stop interfering with the natural forces that have done the job quite effectively for

- Murray seems to have a sentimental attachment to the past. He assumes that all earlier cultures were modeled on 1950s two-parent nuclear families. What worked in the 50s he believes has worked "for millennia." Were the 50s really all that great?

- Murray is a sexist when it comes to sex. He assumes that boys like sex and that girls want babies. He thus puts no emphasis on birth control or safe sex. But girls like sex too and need to be taught how to have sex without getting pregnant. Perhaps we need better sex education and family planning programs rather than changes in welfare rules.

These are only some of the objections that might be raised against Murray's article. Perhaps you and your classmates have other objections that are equally important. Our point is that you should practice "doubting" an argument as well as "believing" it. Both skills are essential. Whereas believing helps you expand your view of the world or modify your arguments and beliefs in response to others, doubting helps protect you from becoming overpowered by others' arguments and teaches you to stand back, consider, and weigh carefully.

STRATEGY 3:   ANALYZING WHY DISPUTANTS DISAGREE

As we have shown, argument is a social phenomenon in which reasonable people disagree about a question at issue. When you analyze an argument, therefore, you shouldn't isolate it from the general conversation of differing views that form its context. If you were an arbitrator, you wouldn't think of settling a dispute between A and B on the basis of A's testimony only. You would also insist on hearing B's side of the story. It is therefore important that you actively seek out opposing or differing views so that you see an issue in its fullest context.

Once you have heard differing views on an issue, it is profitable to ask why the disputants disagree. We suggest that you examine four primary sources of disagreement: (1) disagreement about the facts of the case or about the kind of "truth" that the facts show; (2) disagreement about definitions; (3) disagreement about appropriate analogies; and (4) disagreement about beliefs, basic assumptions, and values. Let's look at each in turn.

Disagreement about Facts or Truth

Theoretically, a fact is a piece of empirical data on which everyone agrees. Often, however, what one person takes as fact another takes as a misconception or mere opinion. Thus person A might say that B was breaking the speed limit because the police officer's radar gun clocked him at 85 mph. B might respond, "I was going 60 mph. The officer must have misused the radar gun or perhaps clocked a different car. Cars were zooming past me all the time." This is a basic disagreement about the facts. A different kind of factual disagreement occurs when facts that are important and relevant to one person are insignificant and irrelevant to another. Writer A supports her claim using one set of facts. Writer B supports an opposing claim using a different set of facts. As a reader, you won't know whom to believe without further research. At a still more complex level, writers might agree on a certain set of facts or statistics but interpret them in different ways so that the "truth of the matter" is still disputable. For example, scientists might agree that the amount of carbon dioxide in the earth's atmosphere has increased but disagree about both the causes and the effects of this phenomenon. There is agreement at the level of basic data but disagreement about how the data are to be interpreted or explained. Here we might say the dispute is about truth rather than facts. Examples of disagreements about facts or truth include the following:

- In arguing whether silver/mercury amalgam tooth fillings should be banned, dental researchers disagree on the amount of mercury vapor released by older fillings; they also disagree on how much mercury vapor has to be present before it is harmful.
- In arguing about the legalization of drugs, writers disagree about the degree to which Prohibition reduced alcohol consumption; they also disagree on whether crack cocaine is "crimogenic" (has chemical properties that induce violent behavior).
- In arguing what to do about the problem of illegitimacy, disputants agree that the illegitimacy rate is rising but disagree about causes.

Disagreement about Definitions

Sometimes disagreements between people are really disputes about definitions. For example, A and B may disagree about whether *Playboy* exploits women. But this disagreement may stem primarily from different definitions of *exploit*. Or to take another example, when arguing whether a therapy based on behavioral modification leads to improvement in a client's mental health, persons A and B might disagree on what is meant by *improvement*.

Disagreement about Appropriate Analogies

Other disagreements arise from the use of analogies, or comparisons. As we will see throughout this text, a powerful arguing strategy is to compare one thing to another. For example, in supporting a Texas law forbidding flag burning, Chief Justice William Rehnquist argued that desecration of a flag in the name of free speech is similar to desecrating the Washington Monument by posting leaflets all over it. Just as we would forbid desecration of a national monument, so should we forbid desecration of the flag. Opposing justices did not think the analogy was valid.

Here is another example. Person A and Person B disagree on whether it is ethically acceptable to have Down's syndrome children undergo plastic surgery to correct some of the facial abnormalities associated with this genetic condition. Person A supports the surgery, arguing it is similar to any other cosmetic surgeries done to improve appearance. Person B argues against such surgery, comparing it to the racial self-hatred of some minority persons who have tried to change their ethnic appearance and become lily-white. (The latter analogy argues that Down's syndrome is nothing to be ashamed of and that persons should take pride in their difference.)

Disagreement about Values, Beliefs, or Assumptions

A fourth source of disagreement concerns differences in values, beliefs, or assumptions. These are often the chief causes of disagreement and the least likely to be changed through argumentation. It is very helpful, however, to identify the conflicting values in order to clarify the debate and help you develop your own beliefs and values. Here are some examples:

- Persons A and B might agree that a huge tax on gasoline would cut down on the consumption of petroleum. They might agree further that the world's supply of petroleum will eventually run out. Thus A and B agree at the level of facts. But they might disagree about whether the United States should enact a huge gas tax. Person A might support the law in order to conserve oil while B might oppose it, perhaps because B believes that scientists will find alternative energy sources before the petroleum runs out or because B believes the short-term harm of such a tax outweighs distant benefits.

- Person A and Person B might agree that capital punishment deters potential murderers (an agreement on facts). Person A supports capital punishment for this reason, but person B opposes it, believing that the taking of a human life is always wrong in principle even if the state does it legally (a disagreement about basic beliefs).

□ FOR CLASS DISCUSSION

As discussed in Chapter 1, we live in a pluralistic world wherein many differing systems of values and beliefs compete for our allegiance. It follows that one of the most frequent sources of disagreement among participants in a conversation is disagreement about values, beliefs, or basic underlying assumptions. What follows are three different responses to Charles Murray's proposal to cut off welfare support for single mothers. The first two are letters to the editor that appeared in the *Wall Street Journal* on November 15, 1993. The third is part of a newspaper editorial by conservative columnist John Leo. Read the three pieces carefully. Then, working as a whole class or in small groups, answer the following questions.

1. What does each piece reveal about the underlying beliefs, assumptions, and values of its writer?

2. In what way do these writers' underlying beliefs, assumptions, and values cause them to agree or disagree with Charles Murray and with each other?

◼

PIECE 1: LETTER TO THE EDITOR
IN RESPONSE TO CHARLES MURRAY

Charles Murray's Oct. 29 editorial page piece "The Coming White Underclass" raises a profound moral paradox that he himself appears not to fully appreciate.   1

With considerable thoughtfulness and conservative passion over the mounting tragedy of illegitimate births in this country, Mr. Murray calls essentially for a return to the social values and policies of "as recently as John Kennedy's presidency": i.e., holding up marriage as the only socially acceptable venue for bearing and raising children and removing all government support for single women who bear and raise the children, however well or poorly, by themselves.   2

His respect for the institution of marriage is laudable. He's right to say that the optimum human environment from within which a child can become a productive, responsible, compassionate member of society is the marriage commitment. But in prescribing his bitter pills of social stigmatization and sink-or-swim governmental policy, he almost ignores the patient's most convenient remedy for this social illness—abortion.   3

At the staggering rate of 1.6 million times a year, American women and teenage girls, married and unmarried, are aborting their unborn children. The unmarried are doing it for many reasons, one of which is that an illegitimate birth is still a "socially horrific act" throughout much of society. But an increasingly more compelling reason for this profoundly destructive act is that "the old way" on the subject of abortion has also been dramatically altered since John Kennedy's presidency. It has been legal to elect abortion for any reason in this country since 1973. Even more alarmingly, it has become a "reproductive right" that virtually defines a woman's bodily and emotional integrity while it defines away the other human life involved.   4

Mr. Murray's reasoning seems either astoundingly sloppy or astoundingly "pro-choice" in this regard. In order to argue against the irresponsibility of pre-marital sex and single motherhood, he uses language like "bringing a child into the world" and "having a baby." But after the pre-marital sex and before the single motherhood, there's another human life involved with a right to be born. Mr. Murray acknowledges that many women may have abortions when AFDC and other pub-   5 lic supports are withdrawn as he recommends. He then casually concludes that "whether this is good depends on what one thinks of abortion."

Among socially horrific acts, abortion has to rank far above even illegitimacy.

Patricia Bucalo, Burlingame, Calif.

PIECE 2: LETTER TO THE EDITOR
IN RESPONSE TO CHARLES MURRAY

There is no question that virtually every social problem facing our nation—in his words, "crime, drugs, poverty, illiteracy, welfare, [and] homelessness"—is vastly exacerbated by the epidemic of unintended and unwanted births. But Mr. Murray's assessment of the roots of the problem and his proposed solutions are dangerously off course. 1

Mr. Murray begins with the patronizing and treacherous premise that out-of-wedlock births happen because "boys like to sleep with girls and . . . girls think babies are endearing." He ends with a call to restore "economic penalties [and] severe social stigma" on single parents. Along the way, he makes clear that by "single parents," he really means single mothers—suggesting that women spontaneously generate not only babies, but poverty itself. 2

In sum, Mr. Murray wants to pull the plug on our nation's most vulnerable women and children. Every tub on its own bottom, he says: Able mothers will eke out a subsistence without government help; and as for the others, well, let's just cart their children off to "lavishly [funded] orphanages." This is a grotesque vision. First, it maligns the many single mothers who are doing all they can to achieve independence. Worse, it's a prescription for disaster. Already, 360,000 children languish in a child welfare system plagued by funding shortages, inadequate facilities and staffing crises. Mr. Murray's plan would crush this overburdened system, leaving more and more babies to be abandoned in alleys, Dumpsters, and public restrooms. 3

Here are some real solutions to the epidemic of teen pregnancy and its attendant cycle of hopelessness: America must provide universal access to comprehensive sexuality education and confidential, affordable contraception. We must make safe, legal abortion available to all women, with federal and state funding for those who need it. We must raise our expectations of young men, making them equal partners in preventing unintended pregnancy and in caring for the children they father; as U.S. Surgeon General Joycelyn Elders has said, "There is more to being a father than providing the sperm." 4

Above all, we must equip our young people with self-esteem and   5
hope—through decent education, better job opportunities, and meaningful life options. In short, we must give them a future worth protecting.

Pamela J. Maraldo, Ph.D., R.N.
President, Planned Parenthood Federation of America

PIECE 3: EXCERPT FROM "NEW CULTURAL CONSCIENCE SHIFTS WELFARE DEBATE"

John Leo

. . . Reflecting the current state of the argument, President Clinton seems   1
to say things like this, over and over: "Would we be a better-off society if
babies were born to married couples? You bet we would." He told ministers in Memphis, Tenn., that if the Rev. Martin Luther King Jr. were to
reappear today, he would say, among other things, "I did not live and die
to see the American family destroyed." We are a long way here from last
year's general babble about "family diversity" and "new family forms."

It says a lot about the current cultural moment that a Democratic   2
president is starting to echo conservative scholar Charles Murray. . . .
Murray wants America to go cold-turkey on welfare—eliminating it
completely. On Oct. 29, *The Wall Street Journal* published a piece by
Murray that may turn out to be the most potent op-ed article in about
10 years. . . .

Murray's piece has had an explosive impact in policy discussions. He   3
says it's like striking a spike into the earth and feeling "enormous pressure in the ground ready to explode." He feels there's a chance now for
"real radical reform." That's the new cultural moment. Like it or not,
President Clinton seems to feel it, too. He said in an interview with Tom
Brokaw that Murray's op-ed piece is "essentially right," though he questions the prescription of eliminating welfare entirely.

The debate on welfare will now take place on Murray's terms, not Clin-   4
ton's, a rather amazing phenomenon that nobody could have predicted a
few weeks ago. Murray's analysis removes race from the welfare debate,
since he sees whites and blacks going through the same process. And it
calls into question all the sex programs and condom distribution
schemes that sustain the highly sexualized youth culture driving the illegitimacy rate. Welcome to a new moment and a very different debate.

The preceding short responses to Murray's essay reveal disagreements
occurring primarily at the level of values, assumptions, and beliefs. But

Murray's article provoked longer responses also—responses that show disagreements in all four of the categories we have outlined: disagreements about facts or interpretation of facts; disagreements about definitions; disagreements about appropriate analogies; and disagreements about values, assumptions, and beliefs. As you read the following opinion-editorial by columnist Dorothy Gilliam (it appeared in the *Washington Post* in mid-December 1993) ask yourself what the primary sources of disagreement are between herself and Murray.

■

WRONG WAY TO REFORM WELFARE

Dorothy Gilliam

With an eye toward reducing the rate of teenage pregnancy, the White House task force on welfare reform wants to curtail additional benefits to unmarried mothers who have more children while on welfare.   1

Taking this drive to discourage out-of-wedlock births among young welfare recipients a step further, Charles Murray, a fellow at the conservative American Enterprise Institute, wants to cut off all economic support to single mothers who have additional children while on welfare—no monetary assistance, no food stamps, no subsidized housing.   2

I agree with the underlying analysis that the problem of children born to poor, single mothers is a crucial issue in welfare reform because it helps drive so many other social problems: crime, drugs, violence, poverty and illiteracy.   3

But the task force proposal and Murray's draconian "solutions" are not the answer.   4

Not only is there a lack of substantiated evidence linking welfare benefits to increases in illegitimate births, but the task force's approach also is really a punitive, morally questionable attempt at social engineering on the backs of poor people.   5

President Clinton has not received the task force's final report on welfare reform, which includes the aforementioned proposal and several others meant to discourage additional births among single, young mothers. But, thank God, he already has had the good sense to question whether that alternative would be "morally right."   6

Meanwhile, many children and family advocacy groups are working hard to turn the tide against the idea.   7

"Frankly, I'm sick and tired of social engineering on the backs of poor women," said David S. Liederman, executive director of the Child Welfare League of America.   8

Citing New Jersey's current experiment with "child exclusion" provi-   9
sions for mothers on public assistance, Liederman said trying to stop
women from having additional children is "nonsense."

"There is no history that says these kinds of behavior-modification   10
schemes have any effect on whether or not women have children," Liederman said in an interview. "It assumes women have children for
money, and that is not true. The children suffer, and the baby who needs
support doesn't get it."

Murray, writing recently in the *Wall Street Journal* that the United   11
States is quickly developing a white underclass that is larger and potentially more devastating than the black underclass, goes on to propose a
myriad of solutions to reduce the rising number of births among poor,
single white women.

But the fallacy of Murray's argument is his belief that punitive action   12
would change behavior. It's an argument that does not take into account
why such behavior exists. Pamela J. Maraldo, president of Planned Parenthood Federation of America, believes too much attention is being
paid to the issue of marital status, and too little to the more crucial issue
of mutual commitment of parents to each other and their children.

"The issue is not whether a child is illegitimate, but whether that child   13
is wanted or unwanted," Maraldo said.

Though a great deal of attention has been focused on the huge cost   14
of welfare, Liederman notes that the budget for Aid to Families with
Dependent Children equals 1 percent of the federal budget.

"To hear some folks rail about welfare, you'd think it's the terrible   15
monster that is causing all of the evils," he said. "But to care for almost
10 million children with 1 percent of the budget is miraculous."

If Clinton is serious about "ending welfare as we know it," as he   16
pledged in his campaign, his planners must take seriously what most
advocates have long said: Most women do not want to be on welfare and
would prefer jobs that position them to get off the rolls permanently.

Though welfare certainly includes a fringe of recipients who abuse the   17
system, the focus should be on the majority of poor mothers and children who earnestly want better lives.

It's a quick-fix mentality that presumes that welfare can be reformed in   18
isolation of all the root social problems that feed into it: poor housing,
drug-related violence, joblessness, lack of opportunity. It's a cowardly
mentality that targets the poor because they lack clout.

Why not, instead, exploit the current momentum for welfare reform by   19
offering more continuing education and job-training opportunities for
people who want meaningful work? That way reform would help them
and their children, not punish them because they had the bad luck to be
born disadvantaged and poor.

It would be a sad day if this country chooses the proposed alternative: 20
to throw poor women and their children overboard.

☐ For Class Discussion

Now that you have read the Dorothy Gilliam editorial, compare its argument with that of Charles Murray. Working as a whole class or in small groups, analyze why the authors disagree, answering each of these questions:

1. Do the two sides disagree about facts and/or interpretations of facts?
2. Do the two sides disagree about definitions of key terms?
3. Do the two sides use different analogies or comparisons that suggest sources of disagreement?
4. Do the two sides differ in values, beliefs, or basic assumptions about the world?

Writing an Analysis of a Pro/Con Controversy

The above For Class Discussion exercise is an oral version of a common writing assignment in argumentation courses: a formal paper analyzing the sources of disagreement in a dispute. To illustrate how our four questions can help you write such an analysis, we've constructed the following model: our own brief analysis of the sources of disagreement between Murray and Gilliam written as a short, formal essay.

AN ANALYSIS OF THE SOURCES OF DISAGREEMENT BETWEEN MURRAY AND GILLIAM

In their response to the problem of illegitimacy, Charles Murray and   1
Dorothy Gilliam have one major area of agreement. Both agree that illegitimacy *is* a major social problem that drives many other social problems. A bulk of their disagreement is over how to solve the problem, a disagreement involving dissension about both truth and values.

Murray and Gilliam agree on the relevant statistics. Both agree that   2
the current illegitimacy rate among lower-class whites is rising and that high illegitimacy rates drive other social problems such as crime, drugs, violence, poverty, and illiteracy. But they disagree in their analysis of causes. Whereas Murray asserts a causal relationship between welfare benefits and illegitimacy, Gilliam rejects this causal connection. She states her case first in her own words: There is "a lack of substantiated evidence linking welfare benefits to increases in illegitimate births" (47). Then she cites the authority of David Liederman, executive director of the Child Welfare League of America, who said in an interview, "'There is no history that says these kinds of behavior-modification schemes have any effect on whether or not women have children. . . . It assumes women

have children for money, and that is not true'" (48). Although Gilliam denies Murray's claim, she herself provides no evidence against a causal link between welfare benefits and illegitimacy rates other than Lieder-man's testimony. For her own part, Gilliam attributes the rising illegitimacy rate to the more basic problems of "poor housing, drug-related violence, joblessness, [and] lack of opportunity" [48]. Neither writer, however, offers empirical evidence to support his or her position on this causal issue.

As can be expected, Gilliam's disagreement with Murray about the causes of rising illegitimacy rates leads her toward dramatically different solutions as well. She argues that by providing job training and meaningful work to low-income people, we could avoid Murray's more "draconian" solution. The difference between Murray's and Gilliam's solutions indicates a substantial difference in values. For Gilliam, Murray's solution is not only unworkable, it's morally repugnant as well. She sees his solution as "punitive" (47) and part of a "cowardly mentality that targets the poor because they lack clout" (48). To Gilliam, Murray chooses to "throw poor women and their children overboard" (48) in lieu of offering them means to solve their own problems. While she doesn't directly cite Murray's "ethical underpinning" ("The child deserves society's support. The parent does not" [Murray, 29]), she clearly thinks it's not possible to separate the moral interests of the child from those of the parent. All in all, Murray reveals values that we typically think of as conservative—belief that the old ways are better than the present, that we should make individuals responsible for their actions by restoring penalties and bad consequences for wrong choices, and that we should place the good of the social order above the individual happiness of each member. Gilliam, on the other hand, espouses values that we typically associate with liberalism—attributing problems to their social or economic causes rather than to individual mistakes, believing the state should help the "victims" of a bad economy or social environment, and believing that education, job training, and fuller employment will solve many social problems.

These values differences also give rise to some interesting disputes involving definitions or analogies. For example, is Murray's plan a form of "social engineering"? Murray takes pains to deny that his plan involves social engineering. "To restore the rewards and penalties of marriage," he says, "does not require social engineering. Rather, it requires that the state stop interfering with the natural forces that have done the job quite effectively for millennia" (29). He thus sees his proposal as a way of returning to the "natural" (and hence better) way of doing things. Gilliam, on the other hand, believes that helping poor mothers and their children is the "natural" thing to do. She therefore pointedly calls Murray's proposal an instance of "social engineering" (47) as well as a "'behavior modification scheme'" (48).

Their value differences are also reflected in the meanings they attach to "illegitimacy." Gilliam wants to shift attention away from mere marital status to consider the broader issue of "'mutual commitment of parents to each other and their children'" (48). According to Gilliam, an "illegitimate" child is not by definition an "unwanted" or neglected one. Gilliam wants us to see that many illegitimate children may in fact be well loved and well nurtured while many "legitimate" children may be unwanted and abused. Thus for Gilliam, legitimacy is not a necessary condition for a functional family unit or for happy, well-adjusted children. In contrast, Murray uses illegitimacy as a statistical gauge of social health. In his abstract use of numbers, any out-of-wedlock child (no matter how loved) counts in the negative column while any in-wedlock child (no matter how neglected or abused) counts in the positive column.

To conclude, the disagreement between Murray and Gilliam hinges on   6
disagreements over the causes of the rise in illegitimacy rates and the basic values that each writer brings to the debate. To accept Murray, one would have to believe that eliminating welfare benefits would lead to a dramatic drop in illegitimate births, that this reduction in illegitimacy would lead to greater family stability and a corresponding drop in crime, and that the long-range good to society would outweigh the hardships it would impose on current welfare mothers and children. To accept Gilliam, one would have to believe that eliminating welfare benefits would have little effect on reducing illegitimacy rates, that the suffering imposed on welfare recipients would outweigh whatever long-range social good might come from Murray's proposal, and that better sex education programs, job training, and employment opportunities would be more effective than Murray's proposal in solving the problems of illegitimacy.

WORKS CITED*

Gilliam, Dorothy. "Wrong Way to Reform Welfare." *The Washington Post* 11 Dec. 1993: B01. Rpt. in *Writing Arguments: A Rhetoric with Readings.* John D. Ramage and John C. Bean. 3rd ed. Needham, MA: Allyn and Bacon, 1995. 27–32.

Murray, Charles. "The Coming White Underclass." *Wall Street Journal* 29 Oct. 1993: A13. Rpt. in *Writing Arguments: A Rhetoric with Readings.* John D. Ramage and John C. Bean. 3rd ed. Needham, MA: Allyn and Bacon, 1995. 47–48.

STRATEGY 4:   EVALUATING THE CONFLICTING POSITIONS

When we ask you to evaluate an argument or a set of arguments, we aren't asking you to choose a winner. Rather, we are asking you to take stock as you make your own journey toward clarity. Which lines of reasoning seem strong to you? Which seem weak? Before you could make up your mind on

---

*   When you type your own documented essays, the "Works Cited" list begins on a separate page.

the issue, what additional research would you want to pursue? What value questions do you still need to resolve? As we have seen in the dispute between Murray and Gilliam, writers don't always address neatly the questions you would like them to address. For example, neither Murray nor Gilliam satisfactorily analyzes the causes of rising illegitimacy rates. The one blames welfare benefits, the other blames hopelessness and poverty, but neither provides supporting data. Therefore, before we formulated our own position on illegitimacy and welfare reform, we would want to do more research. Specifically, we would like to address issues such as the following:

- What did Daniel Moynihan say in his 1960s study of the black family, the study that is so crucial to Murray's analogy argument?
- How does the present welfare system actually work? Who gets AFDC money and how? What percentage of single parents receive welfare payments?
- What evidence is there that the opportunity to receive welfare money actually motivates a girl to have a baby out of wedlock? What evidence is there that a change in welfare policy will affect social attitudes toward illegitimate pregnancy?
- Is it true that children are better off in two-parent families than in a single-parent family? What about unhappy two-parent families forced together "by shotgun"? What percentage of single parents are doing a good job raising their children?
- What other kinds of welfare reform or family policies are being considered at the federal or state level?

Our point, then, is that evaluation of opposing arguments doesn't mean picking sides. Rather, it means examining the conversation carefully to determine the lines of debate, the essential questions at issue, and the research remaining to be done. It also forces us to examine our own values because ultimately the position we take will grow out of our own beliefs, values, and underlying assumptions.

JOINING AN ARGUMENT: A BRIEF CASE STUDY

In addition to analyzing arguments, you also need to learn how to write your own. In many cases, your own desire to write an argument grows out of issues that emerge from your reading. The argument you write, in other words, joins an ongoing conversation.

We close this chapter recounting how one of our students, Sandra Nelson, joined a conversation based on readings she did in an argument course. Her involvement began when her class was given the following case:

Situation: A middle-aged couple despair because their seventeen-year-old daughter is dying of leukemia. Doctors can't find a compatible bone marrow donor for a transplant, her only hope. The couple decides to conceive a child, hoping that the baby's bone marrow would match the daughter's. The transplant operation would not be life-threatening to the baby. *Your problem:* Is it morally permissible to conceive a child in order to provide bone marrow for a dying sibling?

□ FOR CLASS DISCUSSION

As a class or in small groups, try to reach consensus on whether this couple's decision to conceive a baby is morally justified. Articulate reasons for your consensus position. If consensus is impossible, articulate majority and minority views.

If your class is like ours, you'll find people equally divided on this issue. Students supportive of the couple focused on the dying daughter's plight, arguing that her life could be saved with very little risk to the baby. Those opposed to the couple's decision focused on the ethics of imposing even a small risk on an infant too young to give consent. They also wondered if the couple would love the baby for its own sake.

This dilemma is based on a real case. After the above discussion, the instructor passed out the following article, complete with pictures of the family, from a February 1990 *People* magazine.

■

TO SAVE THEIR DAUGHTER FROM LEUKEMIA, ABE AND MARY AYALA CONCEIVED A PLAN—AND A BABY

Anissa Ayala had always hated hypodermic needles; even the thought of going to the doctor made her nervous. So when mysterious lumps appeared around her ankles two years ago and she began experiencing cramplike stomach pains, the athletic teenager from Walnut, Calif., decided not to tell her parents. "I was scared to go to a doctor," Anissa recalls. "My main fear was that I would have to get a blood test."   1

Soon afterward, Ayala discovered that having blood drawn would be the least of her worries. On Easter Sunday 1988, just a few days after she celebrated her 16th birthday, her agony reached the point where she realized she needed medical care. Hospital tests were performed, and the doctors came back with a grim diagnosis: Anissa was suffering from chronic myelogenous leukemia—a disease that would kill her in three to five years unless a donor could be found for a bone marrow transplant.   2

Testing of Anissa's extended family, including her mother, Mary, 43, her father, Abe, 45, and brother Airon, 19, failed to locate a suitable donor. A search by the National Bone Marrow Donor Registry for an unrelated transplant candidate—the odds against a successful match are 20,000 to 1—also failed. So, in desperation, Mary and Abe Ayala, who own a speedometer-repair business, seized upon a final alternative. Told that the chances of a sibling marrow match were one in four, they   3 decided to try to conceive another child. Little did they know that their gamble to save Anissa would catapult them into a heated medical-ethics controversy and raise troublesome questions about the rightful reason for having a baby.

Not that bringing another Ayala into the world would be easy. Aside   4
from the couple's relatively advanced age, Abe first had to undergo surgery to reverse a vasectomy performed 16 years earlier. But he had the operation, and just six months later Mary became pregnant. Then came more good news: The Ayalas learned from amniocentesis and tissue-typing tests that bone marrow cells of the baby—a girl to be born in April—will almost certainly be compatible with Anissa's.

"This is our miracle baby," a jubilant Abe Ayala told reporters last   5
week.

"We are all very, very blessed," sobbed his wife.   6

Those who knew only that the Ayalas had conceived for the purpose   7
of finding a marrow match, however, were troubled by the implications of the pregnancy. "What they're doing is ethically very troubling," said Alexander M. Capron, a professor of law and medicine at USC. "The major objection," says Dr. Arthur Caplan, Director of Biomedical Ethics at the University of Minnesota in Minneapolis, "[is that]it's wrong to have a child just to have a donor."

For their part, the Ayalas insist that their baby was conceived in a spirit   8
of love. "She's my baby sister, and we're going to love her for who she is, not what she can give to me," says Anissa. Mary Ayala believes the baby has already proved her healing powers, regardless of the success of the transplant. "She has given Anissa more of a reason to live," she says. The special circumstances of her conception are underscored by the name the family has chosen for her: Marissa, a combination of Mary and Anissa.

From the outset, Anissa's illness has been a burden shared by her   9
family. Though Anissa herself remained remarkably calm—"I wanted to know everything," she says—her parents were panic-stricken. "The first thing you think is, 'She's going to die,'" says Abe Ayala. "I started getting flashbacks to when she was a little girl. I remember going into her room at home when she was in the hospital and thinking that maybe she'd never come back. It's really hard on the heart."

Luckily, Anissa responded well to initial chemotherapy treatments and   10
was able to leave the hospital after only nine days. Compared with many leukemia patients, Anissa has been fortunate so far. She has not had to undergo radiation treatments or massive chemotherapy. Still, the possibility of premature death has cast a shadow on her and her family. "At the beginning, the stress was really bad," says Mary. "I was trying to stay up for her, and she was trying to stay up for me. She would look at me, and I would start crying." Inevitably, there are moments of fear. When Anissa is plagued by nightmares, she sleeps with her parents in their king-size bed. "I'll sing to her," says Mary, "or read the Bible to her."

That kind of support was especially necessary after a heartbreaking 11 episode last October, when the UCLA Medical Center contacted the Ayalas to tell them a perfect marrow match had been found for Anissa. But the donor backed out at the last moment. Apparently, he had been willing to give blood but not to go through the more complex and time-consuming procedure of donating bone marrow. "Anissa was devastated," says Mary. "She took it personally, and it was a good two weeks before she got over the trauma of it."

Fortunately, eight months earlier, Mary and Abe had considered having 12 another child—at an age when most of their friends were having grandchildren. "I had a dream," says Mary. "God told me everything was going to be okay. I woke up and told Abe, 'God told me to go ahead and have a baby.'"

Although the prognosis for Anissa is favorable now, she is hardly out 13 of jeopardy. Anissa's doctors hope to obtain stem cells from the baby's umbilical cord at the time of birth, a painless procedure for the infant. When Marissa is 6 months old, those stem cells will be combined with additional bone marrow cells that have been taken from the child. They will then be injected into Anissa's body, where the transplant has a 70 percent chance of success. Should the transplant fail, or if Anissa's condition deteriorates seriously between now and next fall, she will need to find another donor.

Meanwhile, Anissa has found another source of hope in the Life- 14 Savers Foundation of America (900-990-1414), a group that raises money and recruits donors for those in need of bone marrow transplants. "Anissa is a really effective spokesperson," says Mary. "She's not afraid to go up to people and say, 'I'm dying, and I need your help.'" Though she continues to project remarkable optimism, Anissa has been robbed of some of the simple pleasures of being a teenager. She broke up with her boyfriend recently and despairs of finding another. "I want a boyfriend, but I can't stand how immature a lot of the guys I meet can be," she says. "I have a totally different outlook on life now."

After graduating from Walnut High this spring, Anissa hopes to attend 15 Azusa Pacific University and study to become a psychologist or a social worker specializing in treating cancer patients. But even if a transplant from her new baby sister cures her leukemia, she is resigned to surrendering one childhood dream. "I've always wanted to get married early and have a baby," she says wistfully. "But now I figure this baby is enough. I mean, she could be like my own."

This article by itself, in its favorable treatment of the Ayalas, convinced a number of students that the couple made the right decision. That judgment was strengthened by the following editorial written by nationally syndicated columnist Ellen Goodman.

WE HAVE CHILDREN FOR ALL SORTS OF REASONS, AND NOW ONE IS MADE TO SAVE HER SIBLING

Ellen Goodman

BOSTON—When the Prince and Princess of Wales did their royal duty, and begat two children, a British colleague of mine referred to their little boys in a poetic fashion. He called them "The Heir and The Spare."   1

It was a phrase that rang wildly off-key in the American ears of this second child. A spare? In the unroyal Western world, we don't have children for the sake of the crown. We don't set out to conceive a little regal understudy.   2

What then are we to think about the couple in California who conceived a child in hopes of providing their older daughter with a bone-marrow donor? Is this a new family designation: "The Heir and The Spare Part"?   3

Abe and Mary Ayala didn't plan to have a second child until their 17-year-old daughter Anissa came down with leukemia, a cancer of the blood cells that can sometimes be cured by transplanting bone-marrow cells from a compatible donor. After a futile search for such a donor, the Ayalas decided to create a child, taking a one-in-four chance that it would be compatible.   4

Abe had his vasectomy reversed, Mary was impregnated and seven months later their gamble may be paying off. Testing has suggested that the female fetus is compatible with the sister. At birth, they may be able to use the cells from her umbilical cord. At six months, they may be able to use her bone marrow.   5

This is a birthday tale that raises all sorts of ethical hackles. Is it right to conceive one person to serve the needs of another? Can parents distribute one child's bodily parts to save another child? Are there moral and immoral motives for creating life?   6

Not long ago, when fetal tissue was first used in treating Parkinson's disease, a woman considered deliberately conceiving and aborting a fetus to donate the tissue to her father. The ethicists' response was unanimous horror.   7

Last year, a medical journal reported the case of a couple prepared to conceive and abort any fetuses that were incompatible, until they got what they wanted: a marrow donor for their first child. The creation of human life as a means to an end rather than an end in itself also was regarded as horrific.   8

The Ayala case isn't that simple. No, it is true, this couple wouldn't have decided on a second child if Anissa hadn't needed a donor. But they also determined to raise and love this child for itself whether it was compatible or not. As the mother said, "If it's not a match we'll love our baby just the same."   9

If we accept the parents' intentions, then, there are a variety of good   10
intentions in this act. The desire to save their older daughter. The decision to lovingly raise another child. The hope that one can help the other.

Calculated carefully, these goods don't add up to a bad. The Ayalas   11
have skated across the thin ethical ice to safety. But the ice is indeed very
thin. I don't know how many other couples could negotiate the passage.

Bone-marrow transplants are relatively risk-free and pretty successful.   12
The decision might look quite different if this baby were created to be a
kidney or liver donor. Parents don't have an unfettered right to sacrifice
one child for another, or to give a piece of a child to another.

Even in this case, if Anissa goes into some medical crisis that could   13
rush the need for a transplant, there should be safeguards to make sure
that the baby's health is a matter of equal concern. I will leave it to the
parents to ensure the baby's mental health. How do you explain to a
child that she was created for her sister? What if that sister dies anyway?

The entire story raises a long-dormant set of questions about motives   14
for having children. Throughout human history, people had children for
all sorts of reasons. And mostly for no reason at all. We had children to
be our farm workers and children to take care of us in old age. We had
one child as a sibling for another or even, like the royals, as an insurance
policy.

It's only since children began to survive longer, and since birth control,   15
and since the family as an economic unit was replaced by its role as an
emotional unit, that we have devised a list of right and wrong reasons to
have children. Today, the one reason we admit to in public is an altruistic
desire to raise and nourish and love human beings for themselves.

Now the new world of medical choices has offered us another entry   16
onto the wrong side of the ledger. It is wrong to create a child only for its
spare parts. Wrong to regard a person exclusively as something to be
used.

But the Ayalas present us with a case of mixed motives, and mixed   17
motives are more common than we allow. It is possible to decide to have
a child for one reason and love it for other reasons. If this family is very,
very, very lucky, they will have reason to be grateful for two children.

Goodman asks "Is it right to conceive one person to serve the needs of
another?" Her implicit answer: "Not usually, but in the Ayalas' case, yes—
just barely." Goodman's very tentative conclusion reflects her complex
moral view, a view she justifies on the basis of three reasons.

REASON 1:   The Ayalas seem committed to raising and loving the baby
for its own sake. In contrast, Goodman wouldn't tolerate
aborting a fetus simply to use its tissues, or aborting and
reconceiving until a correct match was found.

tures of formal writing. Often several drafts are needed at the revision stage.

Fifth Stage—Editing: Writers now polish their drafts, worrying about the clarity of each sentence and the links between sentences. Often writers are still trying to clarify their meanings at the level of individual sentences and paragraphs. Thus, they try to make each sentence more precise—reworking structure to keep each sentence focused on intended meaning. They are also concerned about surface features such as spelling, punctuation, and grammar. Before they submit a finished product, writers proofread carefully and worry about the appearance and form of the final typed manuscript.

STRATEGIES FOR IMPROVING YOUR WRITING PROCESSES

The stages of the writing process described above are based on observations of skilled writers actually composing. Unskilled writers, however, generally go through a quite different process, one that takes less time and is less rigorous in its demand for clarity. Many student writers, for example, compose rough drafts without sufficient exploration and rehearsal beforehand and revise without sufficient concern for the needs of readers. A good, long-range way for most college students to improve their writing, then, is to try to enrich their processes of composing. Here are some strategies you might try.

Talking about ideas in small groups: This is especially helpful in the very early stages of writing when you may have an issue in mind but not yet a claim to make or a sense of how to develop your argument. The greatest power of groups is their ability to generate ideas and present us with multiple perspectives. Listen to objections your classmates make to your arguments, trying to get a sense of what kinds of reasons and evidence succeed or fail. Appendix 3 in the back of this text suggests ways to make group work as successful as possible.

Using expressive writing for discovery and exploration: Expressive writing is writing you do for yourself rather than for others; it is like talking to yourself on paper. Its purpose is to help you think through ideas and get them recorded for later recall. At the end of this chapter we provide some expressive writing tasks that will help you discover and explore ideas for your argument essays.

Talking your draft: After you have written a draft, it's often helpful to talk through your argument with another person (classmate, roommate, tutor, instructor). Without reading from your draft or even looking at it, explain your argument orally to your listener. Be prepared for interruptions when your listener looks confused or unpersuaded. The act of talking through your argument forces you to formulate your ideas in new language. Often you will immediately see ways to improve your draft.

Inventing with research: *Invention* is a term used by the rhetoricians of ancient Greece and Rome. It is the art of finding "the best available means of persuasion"—that is, the art of generating ideas and finding arguments. One good way to do so is through reading in the library, where you can gather evidence related to your issue and examine the argumentative strategies used by others. Although most students know how to use a card catalog, few are experienced in using indexes to find articles appearing in magazines, journals, and newspapers. Yet these are often the best sources for arguers. If you don't know how to use a library or how to incorporate sources into your arguments, read Part IV in this text, which deals with research writing.

Inventing with heuristic strategies: Another strategy for generating ideas for an argument is to use one or more structured processes called "heuristics" (derived from the Greek word *heuresis* meaning "to discover"). In the next section we will explain several heuristic strategies in more detail. You may find them helpful as ways to think of ideas for your arguments.

Using visual techniques for brainstorming and shaping: Cognitive psychologists have conducted extensive research on the way human beings think. One of their discoveries is that verbal modes of thinking can often be enhanced when supplemented with visual modes. In our own teaching, we have had good results emphasizing visual techniques such as idea-maps and tree diagrams as ways of helping writers imagine the content and shape of their emerging arguments. Later in this chapter we will explain idea-maps and tree diagrams in more detail.

Seeking out opposing views: Although you will often address your arguments to a neutral audience who will be weighing arguments on all sides of the issue, you can get excellent help by discussing your ideas directly with someone skeptical of your position or downright opposed to it. Unlike friendly audiences, who will usually tell you that your argument is excellent, skeptical audiences will challenge your thinking. Skeptics may find holes in your reasoning, argue from different values, surprise you by conceding points you thought had to be developed at length, and dismay you by demanding development of points you thought could be conceded. In short, opponents will urge you to "re-see" your draft.

Extensive revision: Don't manicure your drafts, rebuild them. Make sure you leave lots of white space between lines and in the margins for rewriting. And be sure to apply some of the systematic strategies described later in this text for testing the logic and evidence of an argument. Apply these tests to your own drafts as well as to opposing arguments as a means of being more objective about the substance of your argument.

Exchanging drafts: Get other people's reactions to your work in exchange for your reactions to theirs. Exchanging drafts is a different process from conversing with an opponent. Conversation with an opponent is aimed at invention and clarification of ideas; it focuses on content. An exchange of drafts, however, is aimed at the creation of well-written arguments. In addition to content, partners in a draft exchange focus on organization, development, and style. Their concern is on the quality of the draft as product.

Saving "correctness" for last: Save your concern for sentence correctness, spelling, and punctuation for last. Focusing on it at the early stages of writing can shut down your creative processes.

USING EXPRESSIVE WRITING FOR DISCOVERY AND EXPLORATION

We have already suggested the usefulness of expressive writing as a way to talk to yourself on paper. We recommend that you keep all your expressive writings for this course in a notebook, portfolio, or journal where you will have them as a permanent record of your exploratory thinking.

What follows is a compendium of strategies to help you discover and explore ideas. Some of these strategies may not work very well for you, but many of them might work and all of them are worth trying. Each of them takes practice before you become good at it, so don't give up too soon if the strategy doesn't seem to work for you when you first try it.

Freewriting

Freewriting is a brainstorming activity useful at almost any stage of the writing process. When you freewrite, you put pen to paper and write rapidly *nonstop,* usually ten to fifteen minutes at a stretch. Don't worry about grammar, spelling, organization, transitions, or other features of edited writing. The object is to think of as many ideas as possible. Some freewriters achieve almost a stream-of-consciousness style: Their ideas flow directly onto the paper, stutters and stammers and all, without editing or rearrangement. Other freewriters record their thinking in more organized and focused chunks, but nevertheless they keep pushing ahead without worrying whether or not the chunks connect clearly to each other or whether they fully make sense to a strange reader. Many freewriters, perhaps most, find that their initial reservoir of ideas runs out in three to five minutes. When this happens, force yourself to keep your pen moving. If you can't think of anything to say, write "relax" over and over (or "this is stupid," or "I'm stuck," or whatever) until new ideas emerge.

Here is an example of a freewrite from Steve, a student writer, at the start of a research project on homelessness. (Steve eventually wrote the proposal argument on pp. 339–50 of this text). This freewrite explores his thinking on the question, "What can be done about the homeless?"

> Lets take a minute and talk about the homeless. Homeless homeless. Today on my way to work I passed a homeless guy who smiled at me and I smiled back though he smelled bad. What are the reasons he was out on the street? Perhaps an extraordinary string of bad luck. Perhaps he was pushed out onto the street. Not a background of work ethic, no place to go, no way to get someplace to live that could be afforded, alcoholism. To what extent do government assistance, social spending, etc, keep people off the street? What benefits could a person get that stops "the cycle"? How does welfare affect homelessness, drug abuse programs, family planning? To what extent does the individual have control over

homelessness? This question of course goes to the depth of the question of how community affects the individual. Relax, relax. What about the signs that I see on the way to work posted on the windows of businesses that read, "please don't give to panhandlers it only promotes drug abuse etc" a cheap way of getting homeless out of the way of business? Are homeless the natural end of unrestricted capitalism? What about the homeless people who are mentally ill? How can you maintain a living when haunted by paranoia? How do you decide if someone is mentally ill or just laughs at society? If one can't function obviously. How many mentally ill are out on the street? If you are mentally ill and have lost the connections to others who might take care of you I can see how you might end up on the street. What would it take to get treatment? To what extent can mentally ill be treated? When I see a homeless person I want to ask, How do you feel about the rest of society? When you see "us" walk by how do you think of us? Do you possibly care how we avoid you.

☐ FOR CLASS DISCUSSION

Individual task: Choose one of the following controversial claims (or another chosen by your instructor) and freewrite your response to it for ten to fifteen minutes. **Group task:** Working in pairs, in small groups, or as a whole class, share your freewrite with classmates. Don't feel embarrassed if your freewrite is fragmentary or disjointed. Freewrites are not supposed to be finished products; their sole purpose is to generate a flow of thought. The more you practice the technique, the better you will become.

1. A student should report a fellow student who is cheating on an exam or plagiarizing an essay.
2. States should legalize marriages between homosexuals.
3. For the most part, after-school jobs have a long-range harmful effect on high school students.
4. Spanking children should be considered child abuse.
5. State and federal governments should legalize hard drugs.
6. For grades 1–12, the school year should be extended to eleven months.
7. Certain advertisements such as the "Joe Camel" cigarette campaign are so immoral they should be made illegal.
8. Violent video games such as Mortal Kombat should be made illegal.
9. Rich people are morally obligated to give part of their wealth to the poor.
10. Women should be assigned to combat duty equally with men.

Idea-mapping

Another good technique for exploring ideas is idea-mapping, which is more visual than freewriting and causes you to generate ideas in a different way. When you make an idea-map, you draw a circle in the center of the page and write some trigger idea (usually a broad topic area, a question, or your working thesis statement) in the center of the circle. Then you record your ideas on branches and subbranches that extend from the center circle. As long as you pursue one train of thought, you keep recording your ideas on subbranches off the main branch. But as soon as that chain of ideas runs dry, you go back and start a new branch. Often your thoughts jump back and forth between one branch and another. That's a major advantage of "picturing" your thoughts. You can see them as part of an emerging design rather than as strings of unrelated ideas.

An idea-map usually records more ideas than a freewrite, but these ideas are not so fully developed. Writers who practice both techniques report that they think of ideas in quite different ways, depending on which strategy they are using. Figure 3–1 is an idea-map created by Steve, the student who wrote the previous freewrite on homelessness. When Steve made this idea-map, he had completed approximately ten hours of research on the issue, "What should society do about the mentally ill homeless?" He used the idea-map to try to find some order in his evolving and as yet unclarified thinking on this topic.

□ FOR CLASS DISCUSSION

Choose a current national, local, or campus issue that is interesting to the class and about which members of the class are divided. The instructor will lead a class discussion on this issue, recording ideas on an idea-map as they emerge. Your goal is to appreciate the fluidity of idea-maps as a visual form of idea generation halfway between an outline and a list.

Playing the Believing and Doubting Game

To argue effectively, you must appreciate that positions different from your own can be reasonably defended. An excellent way to imagine opposing views is to play the "believing and doubting" game.*

When you play the believing side of this game, you try to become sympathetic to an idea or point of view; you listen carefully to it, opening yourself up to the possibility of its being true. You try to appreciate why the idea has force for so many people; you try to accept the idea by discovering as many reasons as you can for believing it. It is easy to play the believing game with ideas you already believe in, but the game becomes more difficult, sometimes even frightening and dangerous, when you try believing ideas that seem untrue or disturbing to you.

The doubting game is the opposite of the believing game. It calls for you to be judgmental and critical, to find faults with an idea rather than to accept it. When you doubt a new idea, you try your best to falsify it, to find counterexamples that disprove it, to find flaws in its logic. Again, it is easy to play the doubting game with ideas you don't like, but it too can be threatening when you try to doubt ideas that are dear to your heart or central to your own world view.

---

*   A term coined by Peter Elbow, *Writing without Teachers* (Oxford University Press, 1973), pp. 147–90.

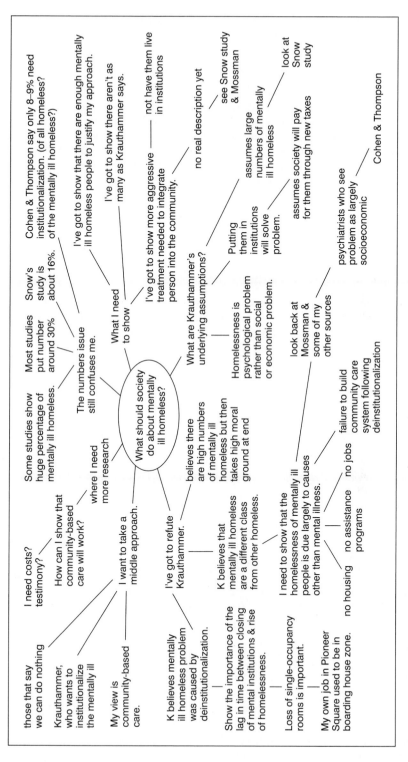

Figure 3–1 Steve's initial idea-map on issue of "What should society do about the mentally ill homeless?"

Here is how one student played the believing and doubting game with the assertion "Pornography serves a useful function in society."

DOUBT

Pornography is smutty, indecent, outlandish usage of the human body. People who look at that have to be indecent nonmoralistic sexists with nothing better to do. Pornography uses the human body to gain pleasure when the human body is supposed to be like a temple that you take care of. I feel very strongly against pornography especially when they use it with young children and pets, etc. I just don't understand how people can get such a big kick out of it. It really surprised me how Dr. Jones [a guest speaker in this student's psychology course] admitted that he had bought pornographic materials, etc. I would think that it would be something that someone wouldn't readily admit to. It seems socially unacceptable to me.

BELIEVE

Pornography is something that people look at when they are feeling sexually frustrated or lonely. It is a form of escape that everyone needs at one time or another. There is always a time where one is unhappy with their sexual relationships and looking at pornography helps. Pornography is an art form. The human body is a beautiful thing and these pictures are for everyone to see the beauty of it all. People should not be afraid to be open about sex and their bodies. Everyone feels the same things. Why not share the experience with others? There is nothing dirty or smutty about being open. It is so individualistic, another way of getting out of the rut of conformity. Sex is beautiful and pornography helps share it with others that aren't quite so lucky to share these moments. (I feel this doubting game with this topic for me opens no new ideas because my mind is so set against pornography but I guess it is good to open up the new avenues of thinking.)

It is easy to see from this entry how the believing game threatens this student's moral views. Yet she does a good job of starting to get inside the head of someone who believes that pornography serves a useful purpose. Although she denies at the end of her entry that playing this game opened up new ideas, the game certainly helped her to see what the issue is and to appreciate that not all people share her values.

When you play the believing and doubting game with an assertion, simply write two different chunks, one chunk arguing for the assertion (the believing game) and one chunk opposing it (the doubting game). Freewrite both chunks, letting your ideas flow without censoring. Or, alternatively, make an idea-map with believing and doubting branches.

☐ FOR CLASS DISCUSSION

Return to the ten controversial claims in the For Class Discussion exercise following the section on freewriting (p. 65). **Individual task:** Choose one of the claims and play the believing and doubting game with it by freewriting for five minutes trying to believe the claim and then for five minutes trying to doubt the claim. Or, if you prefer, make an idea-map by creating a believing spoke and a doubting spoke off the main hub. Instead of freewriting, enter ideas onto your idea-map, moving back and forth between believing and doubting. **Group task:**   Share what you produced with members of your group or with the class as a whole.

Repeat the exercise with another claim.

Brainstorming for Pro and Con "Because Clauses"

This activity is similar to the believing and doubting game in that it asks you to brainstorm ideas for and against a controversial assertion. In the believing and doubting game, however, you simply freewrite or make an idea-map on both sides of the issue. In this activity, you try to state your reasons for and against the proposition as "because clauses." The value of doing so is discussed in depth in Chapter 4, which shows how a claim with because clauses can form the core of an argument.

Here is an example of how you might create because clauses for and against the claim, "Pornography serves a useful function in society."

PRO

Pornography serves a useful function in society

- because it provides a sexual outlet for lonely men.
- because what some people call pornography might really be an art form.
- because it helps society overcome Victorian repression.
- because many people obviously enjoy it.
- because it may relieve the sexual frustration of a person who would otherwise turn to rape or child molestation.

CON

Pornography is harmful to society

- because it is degrading and oppressive to women.
- because it depersonalizes and dehumanizes sexuality.
- because it gives teenagers many wrong concepts about loving sexuality.
- because it is linked with racketeering and crime and destroys neighborhoods.
- because it often exploits children.
- because it might incite some people to commit rape and violence (serial murderer Ted Bundy's claim).

☐ FOR CLASS DISCUSSION

Generating because clauses like these is an especially productive discussion activity for groups. Once again return to the ten controversial claims in the For Class Discussion exercise in the freewriting section (p. 65). Select one or more of these claims (or others provided by your instructor) and, working in small groups, generate pro and con because clauses supporting and attacking the claim. Share your group's because clauses with those of other groups.

The preceding strategies for exploring ideas should help you develop, expand, and complicate your thinking on an issue. Later in this text several additional strategies for exploring and developing arguments are introduced. They include the Toulmin system for analyzing the structure of an argument (in Chapter 5), the "principles/consequences/analogies" strategy for finding persuasive reasons (in Chapter 9), and the "stock issues" strategy for developing proposal arguments (in Chapter 14).

SHAPING YOUR ARGUMENT: THE POWER OF TREE DIAGRAMS

We turn now from discovery strategies to strategies for organizing and shaping your argument. When you begin writing the first draft of an argument, you probably need some sort of plan, but how elaborate or detailed that plan is varies considerably from writer to writer. Some writers need to plan extensively before they can write; others need to write extensively before they can plan. But somewhere along the way, whether at the first draft stage or much later in the process, you need to concentrate on the shape of your argument. At that point, we believe that tree diagrams are often more powerful than traditional outlines.

A tree diagram differs from an outline in that headings and subheadings are indicated through spatial locations rather than through a system of letters and numerals. An example of a simple tree diagram is shown in Figure 3–2. It reveals the plan for a three-reason argument opposing the installation of university-purchased carpets in dorm rooms. The writer's introduction is represented by the inverted triangle at the top of the tree above her claim. Her three main reasons appear as because clauses beneath the claim, and the supporting evidence and argumentation for each reason are displayed vertically underneath each reason.

This same argument displayed in outline form would look like this:

THESIS: The university should not provide carpets for the dorms.

I. Many students want the freedom to decorate their rooms in their own way.
   A. University carpets would be ugly.
   B. Many students have their own carpets and their own decorating style.
   C. Many students don't want the responsibility of carpets.
II. Carpeting the dorms would be too expensive.
   A. Initial cost would be high.
   B. Cost of upkeep would be high.

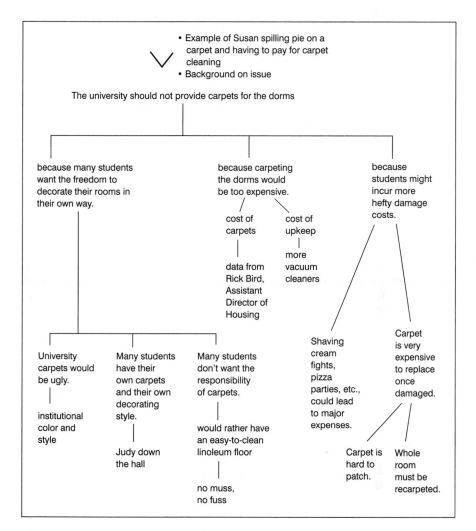

Figure 3–2 Tree diagram of argument on carpets

III. Students might incur hefty damage costs.
   A. Shaving cream fights, pizza parties, etc., could lead to major expenses.
   B. Carpet is very expensive to replace once it is damaged.
      1. Carpet is hard to patch.
      2. Whole room must be recarpeted.

   Although the traditional outline may be the more familiar way to plan an argument, tree diagrams have distinct advantages. First, they are visual. The main points of an argument are laid out horizontally, while the evidence and details supporting each point are displayed vertically. In planning the argument, a writer can move back and forth between both dimensions, working horizontally to develop the main reasons of the argument and then working vertically to find supporting data and evidence. Our own teaching experience suggests that this visual/spatial nature of tree diagrams leads writers to produce fuller, more detailed, and more logical arguments than does traditional outlining.

A related advantage of tree diagrams is their flexibility in representing different mental operations. Traditional outlines represent the division of a whole into parts and of parts into subparts. Consequently, a rule of outlining is that you can't divide a whole into just one part (that is, if you divide something, you must have at least two pieces). Thus every A must have a B, every 1 must have a 2, and so forth. Tree diagrams can easily represent this mental operation by showing two or more lines branching off a single point.

But tree diagrams can also show a single line descending vertically from a higher-level point. Such a line might represent a sequence of step-by-step ideas as in a flowchart (in Figure 3–2, see the branch ending "no muss, no fuss"). Such a line might also represent a movement from a generalization to a specific, as when you choose to support a point with a single example. Thus you could logically have the following structure on a tree diagram:

If you tried to put that same structure on an outline, however, it would look like this:

A. Generalization
    1. example

and some stuffy traditionalist might tell you you were being illogical. Note the amount of information on the tree diagram that could not easily be represented on the traditional outline and was hence omitted (for example, the entries "Judy down the hall," "more vacuum cleaners," and so forth).

Finally, tree diagrams can be powerful aids to invention because you can put question marks anywhere on a tree to hold a space open for ideas that you haven't thought of yet. Consider the value of tree diagraming for student writer Steve as he began drafting his argument on the mentally ill homeless. His first tree diagram is shown in the dark continuous lines of Figure 3–3. As he wrote his first draft, he returned to his idea-map (Figure 3–1) for more ideas, which he added to the tree (shown in the dotted lines on Figure 3–3). Note his use of question marks at places where he needs to add more ideas. His final tree diagram, produced after another draft, is shown in Figure 3–4.* The fluid, evolving nature of tree diagrams, in which

---

* If you would like to read Steve's final essay, it is reproduced in its entirety on pages 339–50.

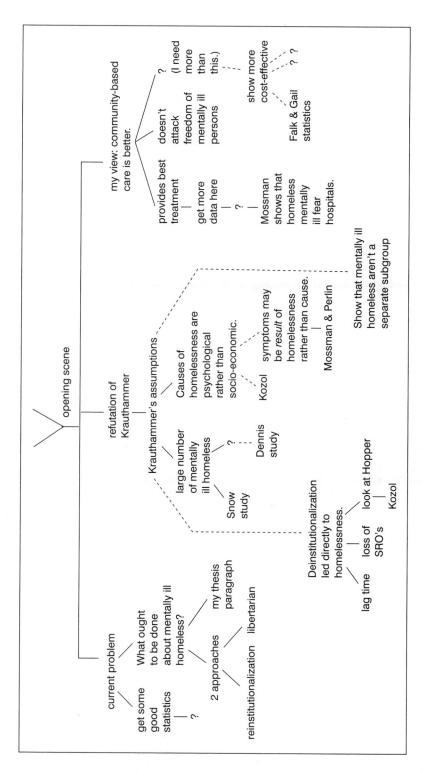

Figure 3–3 Steve's initial tree diagram with later additions and notations (solid lines = original tree diagram; broken lines = later additions)

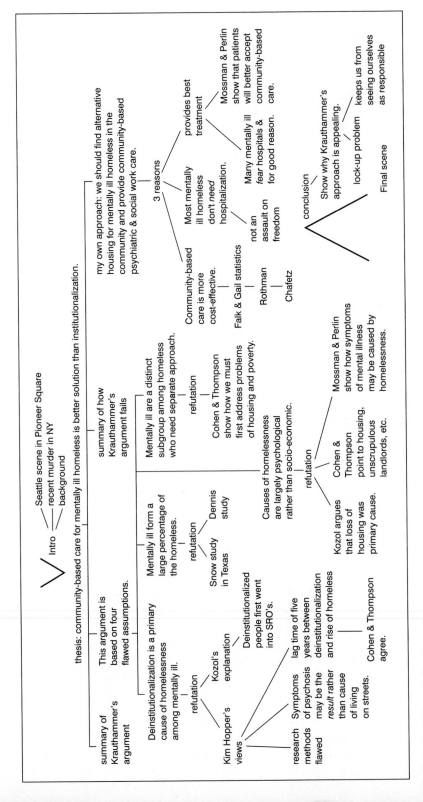

Figure 3–4 Steve's final tree diagram

branches can be added or moved around, makes them particularly valuable planning tools for writers.

A CASE STUDY: SANDRA'S ARGUMENT

To conclude this chapter, let's return briefly to our case study of Sandra, whom we left in Chapter 2 contemplating an argument that Abe and Mary Ayala were not justified morally in conceiving a child to provide bone mar-row for their sixteen-year-old daughter dying of leukemia. Something about the Ayalas' decision troubled Sandra. Early in the course, she explored what was bothering her in the following freewrite.

> OK I read Ellen Goodman and I read the *People* magazine article, but I am not convinced. What sways me in an argument is: when the actions match the words. In other words, when what is being claimed as a future reality is supported by past history or personal performance. This to me makes me believe they will keep their intentions. And it is precisely this that bothers me in the leukemia case: Vasectomy after two children, as opposed to 3 does not say to me that they just wanted another child. Daughter's statement. "I've always wanted a baby sister. Whatever happens she will be loved." On the surface it would seem that this statement clearly supports the notion that the child will be loved. But underneath the surface, why haven't the parents given her a baby sister before. Therefore, I have to ask "Loved by who, the parents or the daughter?"

Sandra's argument went through several drafts before it reached the stage printed next. Although we will not ask you to observe the changes that she made from draft to draft, you can sense how much her ideas evolved by comparing her final version with the initial freewrite.

■

WAS IT MORALLY WRONG FOR THE AYALAS TO CONCEIVE A CHILD TO ACT AS A BONE-MARROW DONOR FOR THEIR OLDER DAUGHTER?

Sandra Nelson (student)

How far should the love for a child take parents? A California couple, Abe and Mary Ayala, believed that their love for their sixteen-year-old daugh-ter, Anissa, who was dying of leukemia, warranted the conception of another child to act as a bone-marrow donor. Was this morally wrong? Some believe it wasn't, that the parents' love obligated them to any means open. Columnist Ellen Goodman pointed out that the medical procedure would cause no harm to the child and that, should the older daughter die anyway, the parents would have the new baby to love.

The decision to have another child is one that grieving parents often make, but usually after the death of the other child. In the February 1990 issue of *People Weekly,* the Ayalas gave a family interview and, if one is not reading carefully, it would appear that they offer a secure, well-adjusted, and loving home. However, several statements made by the family members themselves convinced me that the Ayalas did indeed decide to have this child to save their daughter rather than to have another child to love. It is for this reason that I believe that their decision to give birth was morally wrong.

Both those in favor of the birth and those opposed to it agree that the unconditional love of the parents for the child is prerequisite to a child's developing a strong sense of self-worth and identity. It is the lack of evidence of this vital component of parenting that first raises my concern. It is the daughter, not the parents, who makes this statement:

> I've always wanted a baby sister. . . . Whatever happens she will be loved. . . . She's my baby sister and we're going to love her for who she is, not what she can give to me.

While there is obviously a pledge to unconditional love, the only references to it come from the daughter and not the parents. Mary Ayala relates her fear and concern for her older daughter and calls the baby a "miracle that has given Anissa more of a reason to live." Abe Ayala, too, speaks only of his grief and fear that he will lose Anissa.

The second vital component of parenting is the commitment to meet all the psychological and emotional needs of a child for fifteen to twenty years. To remain consistent in this regard requires purposeful intent on the part of the parents. Having had a son and a daughter, the Ayalas apparently assessed their parenting desires sixteen years ago and chose to prevent further conception through a vasectomy. I see no evidence of a reassessment, change of heart, or reversal of their decision until the daughter's illness threatened to take her life. Therefore, I must ask, who is prepared to raise this child? The only clear pledge that is made toward this responsibility, once again, comes from the daughter, who says, "I've always wanted to get married early and have a baby . . . but now, I figure this baby is enough. I mean, she could be like my own."

My third concern centers on the many family attitudes voiced by the family that could conceivably prevent the child from perceiving herself to be loved in her own right. Abe Ayala is clearly focused on this baby's usefulness to his older daughter as he speaks about his belief that Anissa is going to die, his panic, and his desire to stop the wear and tear on his heart. Mary Ayala states that she conceived to save her daughter at divine direction and that proof of the child's healing powers is already evident in her older daughter's enthusiasm. Anissa herself is unabashedly elated that, should she live, the disease will not have robbed her of the opportunity to be a parent. Most symbolic of the many expectations this child will have to fill before she will be viewed and valued simply because she has arrived is the name chosen for the baby by the mother and daughter. When the new Ayala arrives, she will be christened Marissa—a combination of their own two names.

To my way of thinking, these underlying motivations and overlying agendas cannot help but create confusion for the child and all but obscure the sacred trust of personhood through birth. Although the Ayalas are well intended, the decision to conceive does not reflect the same level of responsible commitment that they have made toward their other two children. It was, therefore, morally incorrect.

USING EXPRESSIVE WRITING TO DISCOVER AND EXPLORE IDEAS: TWO SETS OF EXPLORATORY TASKS

The tasks that follow are intended to help you use expressive writing to generate ideas. The first set of tasks, which we call "Starting Points," helps you build a storehouse of ideas early in a writing project, either by helping you think of issues to write about (if your course gives free choice of topics) or by helping you deepen and complicate your response to readings. The second set of tasks, designed as an aid to drafting almost any kind of argument, helps you think systematically through your ideas before composing a first draft.

Set 1:   Starting Points

These tasks help you take an inventory of issues that already interest you and about which you may have had personal experiences. They also give you ideas for responding to readings.

Task 1:   Making an Inventory of Issues That Interest You

If your course gives you free choice of topics for some assignments, this task and the next will help you take an inventory of possible topics that interest you. Using one or more of the following "trigger questions" as a way to stimulate thinking, make a list of ten to fifteen possible issues or topic areas that you might like to write about. Share your list with classmates, adding to your list ideas from theirs.

- My friends and I disagree about . . .
- I think it is wrong when . . .
- Our campus (this city, my hometown, our state, the country) would be better if . . .
- Person X believes . . . ; however, I believe . . .
- When people discuss X (plug in different possible topic areas), what do they disagree about? (For example, when people discuss money [cars, baseball, guns, cooking], what do they disagree about?)

Task 2:   Choosing Several Areas of Controversy and Exploring Them

For this task, choose two or three possible areas of controversy from your previous list and explore them in your journal through freewriting or idea-mapping. Try responding to the following questions:

a. What is my position on this issue and why?

b. What are opposing or alternative positions on this issue?

c. Why do people disagree about this issue? Use the same exploratory procedures suggested in Chapter 2: Do people disagree about the facts of the
case? About definitions? About analogies and comparisons? About
underlying values, assumptions, and beliefs?

d. If I were to argue my position on this issue, what evidence would I need
to gather and what research might I need to do?

Once again, share your explorations with those of classmates. Your goal is
to find issues that engage you, that are controversial, and that seem
arguable. If your topic areas are good, you should have been able to
freewrite several pages in response to the previous questions.

Task 3: Identifying Issues That Are Problematic for You

A major assignment commonly given in argument courses is to write a
research-based argument that takes a stand on a problem initially puzzling
to you. Steve's proposal argument on the homeless mentally ill (pp. 339–50)
and Lynnea's argument on women police officers (pp. 419–27) are examples
of arguments written for an assignment of this type. Perhaps you don't
know where you stand on an issue because you haven't been able to study
it enough (for example, global warming, legalized gambling, endangered
species controversies). Or perhaps the issue draws you uncomfortably into a
conflict of values (for example, euthanasia, legalization of drugs, noncrimi-
nal incarceration of sexual predators). This course may give you an opportunity to clarify your views on such an issue through systematic research and
exploratory writing and talking. Your goal for this task is to identify several
such issues, preferably issues of public policy or enduring concern. Try
making an inventory of several possible topics in response to this trigger
question:

I am not sure where I stand on the issue of . . .

Task 4: Exploring Your Current Thinking on a
Problematic Issue

For this task, choose one of your issues from Task 3 and explore your current
thinking about it through freewriting or idea-mapping. What is your gut
feeling about the issue? What confuses you about it? Why can't you make
up your mind? What personal experiences, if any, link you to the issue?
What research questions about it do you need to try to answer?

Task 5: Deepening Your Response to Readings

Another common assignment in argument classes asks you to join an argumentative conversation. Typically, the class will read and discuss a collection
of arguments on an issue and then write either analyses of these arguments
or their own position papers on the same issue. Before doing the writing for
this task, read carefully a collection of arguments assigned by your instruc-

tor, annotating the margins with believing and doubting notes as explained in Chapter 2. Then deepen your engagement with these readings through freewriting or idea-mapping by responding to one or more of the following trigger questions:

- What are the sources of disagreement in these readings? Are there disagreements about facts? About definitions? About analogies? About underlying values, beliefs, and assumptions?
- Review the readings and identify "hot spots"—passages that you particularly agree with or disagree with, or that make you angry, confuse you, or otherwise stick in your mind. Copy or summarize several hot spot passages into your journal. Then explore your reaction to these passages.
- Explore the evolution of your thinking as you read the essays and later reviewed them. What new questions have the readings raised for you? What changes have occurred in your own thinking? Where do you currently stand and why?
- If you could talk back to one or more of the authors (imagine meeting them in a tavern or as seatmates on a plane), what would you say to them?

Set 2: Exploration and Rehearsal

The previous set of tasks helps you explore ideas for possible argumentative topics, including deepening your response to readings. The following set of tasks is designed to help you at the exploration and rehearsal stage of writing, after you have chosen a topic for an essay and begun to clarify your thesis. Most students take two or three hours to complete the following tasks; the time pays off, however, because most of the ideas you need for your rough draft will be on paper. We recommend that you freewrite your responses to these tasks each time you are given a formal essay assignment for this course.

Task 1
Write out the issue question you think you would like to focus on in this essay. Then try wording your question in several different ways. Sometimes slight changes in the way you word the question—for example, making it somewhat broader or somewhat narrower—will help you clarify the way your argument will proceed. Finally, write the question in the way that currently seems best. Put a box around it.

Task 2
Look back at the issue question you placed in the box in Task 1. Now write out your own tentative answer to the question. This will be your beginning thesis statement or claim—the position you will try to defend in your essay. Put a box around this answer. Next write out one or more different answers to your question. These will be the possible alternative claims that a neutral

audience will be considering—summaries of the equally plausible opposing positions you will be arguing against. Finally, explore whether or not your issue question seems to be a two-sided issue—one on which people in the conversation will divide neatly into pro and con sides—or whether it is a multisided issue with many different points of view. Your exploration here can make a difference later when you try to achieve a final focus for your argument.

Task 3

For this task, explain why you think people disagree on your issue. In other words, why is this issue controversial? Is there not yet enough evidence to resolve the issue? Is the evidence controversial? Is there disagreement about the definition of key terms? Do different parties in the controversy hold different values, assumptions, or beliefs?

Task 4

What personal interests or personal experiences do you have with this issue? (By "personal experiences" we mean not only firsthand experiences but also memories from things you've read, TV news stories you've seen, lectures you've heard, and so forth.) Exploring these questions should help you clarify your personal interest in this topic, as well as its relationship to concerns and values in your own life.

Task 5

What reasons and evidence can you think of to support your position on this issue? Brainstorm for every possible point you can think of in support of your position. You might want to use an idea-map here instead of freewriting. Get as many ideas as possible on paper. In this task, you will be "rehearsing" the main body of your paper, which will set forth reasons and then support them with evidence or chains of other reasons.

As you generate ideas for reasons and evidence, you are likely to find gaps in your knowledge where you need to do further research either in the library or through interviews. If your claim could be strengthened through the use of statistics, testimony of experts, and so forth, develop a plan for conducting your research.

Task 6

In this task, begin by rereading what you wrote in Task 5 and then reconsider your argument from the perspective of a neutral or opposing audience. What values, beliefs, or assumptions would your audience have to hold in order to accept your argument? Do you think your audience holds these values, assumptions, or beliefs?

Task 7

Continue your exploration of audience by assuming the role of someone who opposes your position. Writing from that person's perspective, try to construct a counterargument that opposes your own views. (In other words, play the doubting game with the argument you created in Task 5.)

Task 8
Why is this an important issue? What are its broader implications and consequences? What other issues does it relate to? Thinking of possible answers to these questions may prove useful when you write your introduction or conclusion.

■ WRITING ASSIGNMENTS FOR PART I

OPTION 1: *A LETTER TO YOUR INSTRUCTOR ABOUT YOURSELF AS A WRITER* Write a letter to your instructor about yourself as a writer. In the first part of your letter, give your instructor a complete picture of how you go about writing. Describe the process you normally go through, using examples from recent writing experiences. Address questions such as the following:

Mechanical procedures: When and where do you like to do your writing? Do you compose your drafts by hand, by typewriter, or by word processor? If by hand, what kind of paper and pens do you use for your first drafts? Subsequent drafts? Do you single-space or double-space your early drafts? One side of the page or two? If you handwrite, do you write large or small? Big margins or little margins? Do you write rapidly or slowly? Do you use the same procedures for second and later drafts? If you use a word processor, do you compose directly at the terminal or do you write out a draft and then type it in? Do you revise at the terminal or make changes on hard copy?

Mental procedures: Do you procrastinate when you need to write? Do you suffer writer's block or anxiety? Do you write a paper the night before it is due or spread your writing time out over several days? Do you normally do exploratory writing such as freewriting and idea-mapping? Do you organize your ideas before drafting or draft first and then organize? How many drafts do you typically make? What kinds of changes do you typically make as you revise? Do you discuss your ideas with friends before you write or between drafts? Do you exchange drafts with friends?

Writing preferences: Do you like to write? What kind of writing do you most like to do? Least like to do? Do you like to choose your own topics or have the teacher choose topics for you? Do you like open-ended assignments or assignments with clear guidelines and constraints? How much time are you willing to put into a paper?

In the second part of your letter, analyze your strengths and weaknesses as a writer. Address questions such as these:

Strengths and weaknesses in final products: What have you been praised for or criticized for in the past as a writer? How consistent are you in coming up with good ideas for your papers? In general, do you have trouble organizing your papers or is organization a strength? Are your sentences usually clear and grammatically correct? Do you have trouble with punctuation? Are you a good speller?

Strengths and weaknesses in writing process: How does your writing process compare with the typical writing processes of experienced writers as described in Chapter 3? If you were to improve your writing process, what would you work on most?

These questions are meant to be representative only. Use them as suggestions for the kinds of information your instructor needs to get to know you as a writer. Your goal is to give your instructor as much helpful information as possible.

OPTION 2:   *AN ARGUMENT SUMMARY*   Write a 250-word summary of an argument selected by your instructor. Then write a one-sentence summary of the same argument. Use as models the summaries of Charles Murray's essay in Chapter 2 (pp. 35–37).

OPTION 3:   *AN ANALYSIS OF THE SOURCES OF DISAGREEMENT IN OPPOSING ARGUMENTS*   Using as a model the analysis in Chapter 2 of the Murray/Gilliam controversy over welfare reform (pp. 49–51), write an analysis and evaluation of any two pro/con articles selected by your instructor.

OPTION 4:   *A DEBATE ESSAY*   Write a debate essay on an issue of your own choosing. Write your essay as a mini-play in which two or more characters argue about an issue. Create any kind of fictional setting that you like: a group of students having beers at a local tavern, two people on a date, a late-night dorm room bull session. Have the characters disagree with each other on the issue, but make your characters reasonable people who are trying to argue logically and intelligently.

The purpose of such an assignment is to free you from strict demands of organization in order to let you explore an issue from all sides. Try to have characters find weaknesses in each other's arguments as well as present their own side of the issue.

Here is a brief example of the format. Imagine that you are looking in on the middle of a debate essay on whether writing courses should be pass/fail:

JOE: Here's another thing. Pass/fail would make students a lot more creative. They wouldn't worry so much about pleasing the teacher.

ANN: Hogwash, Joe. Pass/fail would make them less creative.

JOE: Why?

ANN: They'd put less time into the course. If a course is pass/fail students won't work as hard. They'll put their energy into the courses that will be graded. That's what happened to me when I took an art class pass/fail my freshman year. I started out really interested in it and vowed to spend a lot of time. But by midterms I was getting behind in my other classes, so I neglected art in order to get good grades where they would show up on my transcripts.

JOE: But pass/fail will make you examine your values. Maybe you would quit working just for grades. Besides, in a writing class you would have a different motivation. In a writing class you would have the motivation of knowing that your writing skills will make a big difference in other classes and in your future careers.

ANN: Yes, but students don't worry about long-range benefits. They always take the short-range benefit.

JOE: But maybe you would really get into writing for its own sake. If you don't have to follow a teacher's silly rules, writing can be really creative, like doing art. Remember how much time you spent drawing pictures when you were a little girl? You weren't motivated by grades then. You liked to draw because people are naturally creative. We would still be creative if we weren't afraid. A pass/fail course would take away the fear of failure. How long would you have painted those little kid pictures if some teacher came along and marked up your painting with red ink and said, "Shame, look at all the mistakes you made." You'd quit drawing right away. That is what has happened to writing. Students hate to write because all they get for it is criticism. A pass/fail course would allow us to get praise and to explore writing in new ways.

ANN: You have too much faith, Joe, in the natural creativity of students. You can't overcome twelve years of schooling in one pass/fail course. Look at some other consequences of a pass/fail system. First . . .

OPTION 5:   **PROPOSE A PROBLEM FOR A MAJOR COURSE PROJECT**   An excellent major project for an argument course is to research an issue about which you are initially undecided. Your final essay for the course could be an argument in which you take a stand on this issue. Choose one of the issues you listed in "Starting Points," Task 3, "I am unable to take a stand on the issue of . . ." and make this issue a major research project for the course. During the term keep a log of your research activities and be ready, in class discussion or in writing, to explain what kinds of arguments or evidence turned out to be most persuasive in helping you take a stand.

For this assignment, write a short letter to your instructor identifying the issue you have chosen and explain why you are interested in it and why you can't make up your mind at this time.

4

The Core of an Argument: A Claim with Reasons

THE RHETORICAL TRIANGLE

Before looking at the way arguments are structured, we should recognize that arguments occur within a social context. They are produced by writers or speakers who are addressing an audience—a relationship that can be visualized as a triangle with points labeled "message," "writer/speaker," and "audience" (see Figure 4–1). In composing an effective argument, writers must concern themselves with all three elements of this "rhetorical triangle." As we will see in later chapters, when you alter one point of the triangle (for example, you change the audience for whom you are writing or you re-imagine the role you want to take as a writer—switching, say, from angry protestor to listening friend), then you may also need to restructure the message itself.

The rhetorical triangle's focus on message, speaker/writer, and audience relates also to the three kinds of persuasive appeals identified by classical rhetoricians: *logos, ethos,* and *pathos.*

Logos (Greek for "word") refers to the internal consistency of the message—the clarity of its claim, the logic of its reasons, and the effectiveness of its supporting evidence. The impact of *logos* on an audience is sometimes called the argument's "logical appeal."

Ethos (Greek for "character") refers to the trustworthiness or credibility of the writer or speaker. *Ethos* is often conveyed through the tone and style of the message and through the way the writer or speaker refers to opposing views. It can also be affected by the writer's reputation as it exists independently from the message—his or her expertise in the field, his or her previous record of integrity, and so forth. The impact of *ethos* is often called the argument's "ethical appeal" or the "appeal from credibility."

Our third term, *pathos* (Greek for "emotion"), is perhaps the most difficult to define. It refers to the impact of the message on the audience, the power with which the writer's message moves the audience to decision or action. Although *pathos* refers primarily to the emotional appeal of an argument, it is difficult to disentangle such appeals from the logical structure of an argument. As we show in the following chapters, a successful logical structure is rooted in assumptions, values, or beliefs shared by the audience so that an effective logical appeal necessarily evokes a reader's or listener's emotions. Whereas *logos* engages our rational faculties, *logos* and *pathos* together engage our imaginations. The impact of *pathos* on an audience is often called the "appeal to emotions" or the "motivational appeal."

Using the rhetorical triangle, we can create a checklist of questions that can help a writer plan, draft, and revise an argument (see Figure 4–1). As the checklist suggests, writers should consider ways to make their messages as logically sound and well developed as possible, but they should also take care to link their arguments to the values and beliefs of the audience and to convey an image of themselves as credible and trustworthy.

The chapters in Part II of this text treat all three elements in the rhetorical triangle. Chapters 4–6 are concerned primarily with *logos*, whereas Chapter 7 is concerned with *pathos* and *ethos*. However, all these terms overlap so that it is impossible to make neat separations among them.

Given this background on the rhetorical triangle, we are ready now to turn to *logos*—the logic and structure of arguments.

ISSUE QUESTIONS AS THE ORIGINS OF ARGUMENT

At the heart of any argument is an issue, which we can define as a topic area such as "criminal rights" or "the minimum wage," that gives rise to a dispute or controversy. A writer can usually focus an issue by asking an issue question that invites at least two opposing answers. Within any complex issue—for example, the issue of abortion—there are usually a number of separate issue questions: Should abortions be legal? Should the federal government authorize Medicaid payments for abortions? When does a fetus become a human being (at conception? at three months? at quickening? at birth?)? What are the effects of legalizing abortion? (One person might stress that legalized

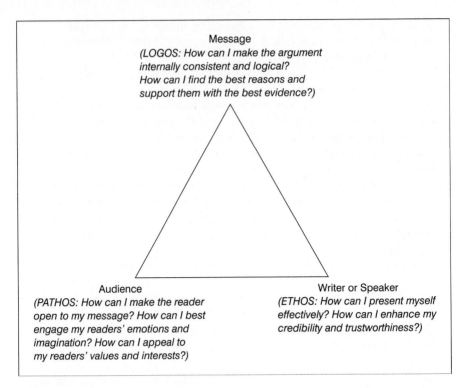

Message
(LOGOS: How can I make the argument
internally consistent and logical?
How can I find the best reasons and
support them with the best evidence?)

Audience
(PATHOS: How can I make the reader
open to my message? How can I best
engage my readers' emotions and
imagination? How can I appeal to
my readers' values and interests?)

Writer or Speaker
(ETHOS: How can I present myself
effectively? How can I enhance my
credibility and trustworthiness?)

FIGURE 4–1 The rhetorical triangle

abortion leads to greater freedom for women; another person might respond that it lessens a society's respect for human life.)

Difference Between an Issue Question and an Information Question

Of course, not all questions are issue questions that can be answered reasonably in two or more opposing ways; thus, not all questions can lead to effective argument essays. Rhetoricians have traditionally distinguished between "explication," which is writing that sets out to inform or explain, and "argumentation," which sets out to change a reader's mind. On the surface, at least, this seems like a useful distinction. If a reader is interested in a writer's question mainly to gain new knowledge about a subject, then the writer's essay could be considered explication rather than argument. According to this view, the following questions about abortion might be called information questions rather than issue questions:

How does the abortion rate in the United States compare with the rate in Sweden?

If the rates are different, why?

Although both questions seem to call for information rather than for argument, we believe the latter one would be an issue question if reasonable people disagreed on the answer. Thus, two writers might agree that abortion rates in the United States and Sweden differ significantly, but they might disagree in their explanations of why. One might say that Sweden has a higher abortion rate because of the absence of a large Catholic or conservative Protestant population in the country. The other might say, "No, the real reasons are linked to the country's economic structure." Thus, underneath the surface of what looks like a simple explication of the "truth" is really a controversy.

You can generally tell whether a question is an issue question or an information question by examining your purpose in relationship to your audience. If your relationship to your audience is that of teacher or learner, so that your audience hopes to gain new information, knowledge, or understanding that you possess, then your question is probably an information question. But if your relationship to your audience is that of advocate to decision maker or jury, so that your audience needs to make up its mind on something and is weighing different points of view, then the question you address is an issue question. Often the same question can be an information question in one context and an issue question in another. Let's look at the following examples:

- How does a diesel engine work? (This is probably an information question since reasonable people who know about diesel engines will probably agree on how they work. This question would be posed by an audience of new learners.)

- Why is a diesel engine more fuel-efficient than a gasoline engine? (This also seems to be an information question since all experts will probably agree on the answer. Once again, the audience seems to be new learners, perhaps students in an automotive class.)

- What is the most cost-effective way to produce diesel fuel from crude oil? (This could be an information question if experts agree and you are addressing new learners. But if you are addressing engineers and one engineer says process X is the most cost-effective and another argues for process Y, then the question is an issue question.)

- Should the present highway tax on diesel fuel be increased? (This is certainly an issue question. One person says yes; another says no; another offers a compromise.)

□ FOR CLASS DISCUSSION

Working as a class or in small groups, try to decide which of the following questions are information questions and which are issue questions. Many of them could be either, depending on the rhetorical context. For such questions, create hypothetical contexts to show your reasoning.

1. What percentage of single-parent families receive welfare support?

2. What is the cause for the recent dramatic increases in the number of out-of-wedlock births in the United States?

3. Should the United States eliminate welfare support for unwed mothers?

4. What percentage of TV shows during prime-time hours depict violence?

5. What is the effect of violent TV shows on children?

6. Are chiropractors legitimate health professionals?

7. How does chiropractic treatment of illness differ from a medical doctor's treatment?

8. Are extended-wear contact lenses safe?

9. Should a woman with a newly detected breast cancer opt for a radical mastectomy (complete removal of the breast and surrounding lymph tissue) or a lumpectomy (removal of the malignant lump without removal of the whole breast)?

10. Is Simone de Beauvoir correct in calling marriage an outdated, oppressive, capitalist institution?

DIFFERENCE BETWEEN A GENUINE ARGUMENT AND A PSEUDO-ARGUMENT

We have said that the heart of an argument is an issue question that invites two or more competing answers. This does not mean, however, that every disagreement between people can lead to a rational argument. Rational arguments depend also on two additional factors: (1) reasonable participants, that is, participants who agree to operate within the conventions of reasonable behavior, and (2) potentially shareable assumptions that can serve as a starting place or foundation for the argument. You should learn to recognize the difference between genuine arguments, which proceed reasonably, and pseudo-arguments, which generate a lot of heat but are as irresolvable as a game of chess in which the players do not agree on how the pieces move.

Pseudo-arguments: Fanatics and Skeptics

As you know, many arguments that at first seem like reasonable disputes are really shouting matches masquerading as arguments. Without really listening to each other, these disputants carry on into the night asserting as facts statements they are unsure of, citing vague authorities, moving illogically into tangential issues, and trying, in general, to rationalize a position based more on feeling and opinion than on careful thought.

Often such disputants belong to one of two classes, Fanatics and Skeptics. Fanatics are people who believe their claims are true because they say so, period. Oh, they may assure us that their claims rest on some authoritative text—the Bible, the *Communist Manifesto*, Benjamin Spock's books on child raising—but in the end it's their narrow and quirky reading of the text, a reading claiming to be fact, that underlies their argument. When you disagree with a Fanatic, therefore, you'll get a desk-thumping rehash of the Fanatic's preconceived convictions.

The Skeptic, on the other hand, dismisses the possibility that anything could be proven right. Because the sun has risen every day in recorded history is inadequate reason for the Skeptic to claim that it will rise tomorrow. Short of absolute proof, which never exists, Skeptics accept no proof. Skeptics, in short, do not understand that an argument cannot be a proof. We can hope that a good argument will increase its readers "adherence" to a claim by making the claim more plausible, more worthy of consideration, but only rarely will it eliminate doubt or overcome the influence of opposing views. In the presence of Fanatics or Skeptics, then, genuine argument becomes impossible.

Another Source of Pseudo-arguments: Lack of Shared Assumptions

A reasonable argument is difficult to conduct unless the participants share common assumptions on which the argument can be grounded. These assumptions are like axioms in geometry or the self-evident truths in the Declaration of Independence—starting points or foundations for the argument. Consider the following conversation in which Randall refuses to accept Rhonda's assumptions.

RHONDA: Smoking is bad because it causes cancer. (Rhonda assumes that Randall will agree with her that cancer is bad. This is the assumption that lets her say that smoking is bad.)

RANDALL: I agree that smoking causes cancer, but what's so bad about that? I like cancer. (Rhonda looks at him in amazement.)

RHONDA: Come on, Randy! Cancer is bad because it causes suffering and death. (Now she hopes Randall will accept her new assumption that suffering and death are bad.)

RANDALL: What's so bad about suffering and death?

RHONDA: Suffering reduces pleasure, while death is a total absence of being. That's awful!

RANDALL: No way. I am a masochist, so I like suffering. And if you don't have any being, you can't feel anything anyway.

RHONDA: O.K., wise guy. Let's assume that instead of absence of being you are dropped head-first into an everlasting lake of boiling oil where you must stay for eternity.

RANDALL: Hey, I said I was a masochist.

As you can see, the conversation becomes ludicrous because Randall refuses to share Rhonda's assumptions. Rhonda's self-evident "truths" (cancer is bad, suffering is bad, an everlasting lake of boiling oil is bad) seem to have no force for Randall. Without assumptions held in common, an argument degenerates into an endless regress of reasons that are based on more reasons that are based on still more reasons, and so forth. Randall's technique here is a bit like Callicles' rebuttals of Socrates—a refusal to accept the starting points of Socrates' argument. Attacking an argument's assumptions is, in fact, a legitimate way of deepening and complicating our understanding of an issue. But taken to an extreme, this technique makes argument impossible.

Perhaps you think the above argument about smoking is a cornball case that would never crop up in real situations. In fact, however, a slight variation of it is extremely common. We encounter the problem every time we argue about purely personal opinions: opera is boring, New York City is too big, pizza tastes better than nachos, baseball is more fun than soccer. The problem with these disputes is that they rest on personal preferences rather than on shared assumptions. In other words, there are no common criteria for "boring" or "too big" or "tastes better" that writer and reader can share.

Of course, reasonable arguments about these disputes become possible once common assumptions are established. For example, a nutritionist could argue that pizza is better than nachos because it provides more balanced nutrients per calorie. Such an argument can succeed if the disputants accept the nutritionist's assumption that "more balanced nutrients per calorie" is a criterion for "better." But if one of the disputants responds, "Nah, nachos are better than pizza because nachos taste better," then he makes a different assumption—"My sense of taste is better than your sense of taste." This is a wholly personal standard, an assumption that others are unable to share.

□ For Class Discussion

The following questions can all be answered in competing ways. However, not all of them will lead to reasonable arguments. Try to decide which questions will lead to reasonable arguments and which will lead only to pseudo-arguments:

1. Is Spike Lee a good film director?
2. Are science fiction films better than westerns?
3. Should our city subsidize the development of a convention center?
4. Is this abstract oil painting by Bozo, the ape from the local zoo, a true work of art?
5. Is Danish Modern furniture attractive?
6. Is football a fun sport to play?
7. Does extrasensory perception (ESP) exist?
8. Which would look more attractive in this particular living room, Early American furniture or Danish Modern furniture?

9. Which are better, argumentation essays or short stories?

10. Which is better, Pete's argumentation essay or Jaynee's?

FRAME OF AN ARGUMENT: A CLAIM SUPPORTED BY REASONS

We have said earlier that an argument originates in an issue question, which by definition is any question that can be answered in two or more competing ways. When you write an argumentation essay, your task is to commit yourself to one of the answers and to support it with reasons and evidence. The claim of your essay is the position you are trying to defend. To put it another way, your position on the issue is your essay's thesis statement, a one-sentence summary answer to your issue question. Your task, then, is to make a claim and defend it with reasons.

What Is a Reason?

A reason (also called a premise) is a claim used to support another claim. In speaking or writing, a reason is usually linked to the claim with such connecting words as *because, since, for, so, thus, consequently,* and *therefore,* indicating that the claim follows logically from the reason.

Let's take an example. Suppose you were interested in the issue question "Are after-school jobs beneficial for teenagers?" Here are frameworks for two possible arguments on this issue:

PRO

Claim: Holding an after-school job can be beneficial for teenagers (aimed, say, at parents who forbid their teenager to get a job).

REASON 1:   An after-school job provides extra spending money.

REASON 2:   It develops responsibility.

REASON 3:   It teaches time management.

REASON 4:   It establishes a record of employment experience useful for later job hunting.

CON

Claim: An after-school job can often be harmful to teenagers (aimed, say, at teenagers seeking an after-school job).

REASON 1:   An after-school job takes time away from schoolwork, thus sacrificing long-range career success for short-range pocket money.

REASON 2:   It reduces opportunities for valuable social and recreational time during high school years.

REASON 3:   Too often it encourages materialism and conspicuous consumption (if extra money is spent on cars, clothes, etc.).

Formulating a list of reasons in this way breaks your argumentative task into a series of smaller parts. It gives you a frame, in other words, on which to build your essay. The preceding "pro" argument could consist of four main parts. In the first part you would support the first reason—an after-school job provides extra spending money. You might give some examples and show how your making extra spending money would help out the family or improve the quality of your life. In each of the other parts you would proceed the same way, trying to convince the reader that each reason is both true and significant—in other words, you would try to show not only that it is true that a job teaches time management but also that learning time management is valuable. If your argument is to be persuasive to your intended audience, each reason should link your claim to an assumption or belief held by the audience.*

To summarize our point in this section, the frame of an argument consists of a claim (the thesis statement of the essay), which is supported by one or more reasons (other claims linked logically to the main claim), which are in turn supported by evidence or chains of further reasons.

Advantages of Expressing Reasons in "Because" Statements

Chances are that when you were a child the word *because* contained magical explanatory powers:

DOROTHY: I want to go home now.

TOMMY: Why?

DOROTHY: Because.

TOMMY: Because why?

DOROTHY: Just because.

Somehow *because* seemed decisive. It persuaded people to accept your view of the world; it changed people's minds. Later, as you got older, you discovered that *because* only introduced your arguments and that it was the reasons following *because* that made the difference. Still, the word *because* introduced you to the powers potentially residing in the adult world of logic.

---

* The values appealed to in the pro argument are these: It is good to have extra spending money, to develop responsibility, to learn time management, and to have greater potential for job success. These values are likely to be granted by parents, who are the intended audience. What values are appealed to in the con argument? Are the intended readers in the con argument—teenagers—likely to share these values?

Of course, there are many additional ways to express the same connection between reasons and claim. Our language is rich in ways of stating "because" relationships:

- An after-school job is valuable for teenagers because it teaches time management.

- An after-school job teaches time management. Therefore, it is valuable for teenagers.

- An after-school job teaches time management, so it is valuable for teenagers.

- One reason after-school jobs are valuable for teenagers is that they teach time management.

- My argument favoring an after-school job for teenagers is based partly on the fact that such jobs teach time management.

Even though logical relationships can be stated in various ways, writing out one or more "because" clauses seems to be the most succinct and manageable way to clarify an argument for oneself. We therefore suggest that sometime in the writing process you create a "working thesis statement" that summarizes your main reasons as because clauses attached to your claim.* Just when you compose your own working thesis statement depends largely on your writing process. Some writers like to plan out their whole argument from the start and often compose their working thesis statements with because clauses before they write their rough drafts. Others discover their arguments as they write. And sometimes it is a combination of both. For these writers an extended working thesis statement is something they might write halfway through the composing process, as a way of ordering their argument when various branches seem to be growing out of control. Or they might compose a working thesis statement at the very end as a way of checking the unity of the final product.

Whenever you write your extended thesis statement, the act of doing so can be simultaneously frustrating and thought-provoking. Composing because clauses can be a powerful discovery tool, causing you to think of many different kinds of arguments to support your claim. But it is often difficult to wrestle your ideas into the because clause shape, which sometimes seems to be overly tidy for the complex network of ideas you are trying to

---

* The working thesis statement for the essay supporting after-school jobs would look like this: "Holding an after-school job can be beneficial for teenagers because it provides extra spending money, because it helps develop responsibility, because it helps teenagers learn time management, and because it helps them establish a record of employment experience useful for later job hunting." You probably wouldn't put such a statement into your essay itself; rather, it is a way of summarizing your argument for yourself so that you can see it whole and clear.

work with. Nevertheless, trying to summarize your argument as a single claim with reasons should help you see more clearly what you have to do.

☐ FOR CLASS DISCUSSION

Try the following group exercise to help you see how writing because clauses can be a discovery procedure.

Divide into small groups. Each group member should contribute an issue that he or she might like to explore. Discussing one person's issue at a time, help each member write a working thesis statement by creating several because clauses in support of the person's claim. Then try to create because clauses in support of an opposing claim for each issue. Recorders should select two or three working thesis statements from the group to present to the class as a whole. Report in twenty-five minutes.

APPLICATION OF THIS CHAPTER'S PRINCIPLES TO YOUR OWN WRITING

In Chapter 2, during our discussion of summary writing, we mentioned that not all arguments are equally easy to summarize. Generally, an argument is easiest to summarize when the writer places her thesis or claim in the essay's introduction and highlights each reason with explicit transitions as the argument progresses. We say that such arguments have a "self-announcing structure," in that the essay announces its thesis (and sometimes its supporting reasons) and forecasts its shape before the body of the argument begins. Such arguments aim at maximum clarity for readers by focusing attention on the content and structure of the writer's ideas.

Arguments with self-announcing structures can be distinguished from those with "unfolding structures." An argument with an unfolding structure often delays its thesis until the end or entwines the argument into a personal narrative, story, or analysis without an explicitly argumentative shape. Often the reader must tease out the writer's thesis and supporting reasons, which remain implied only. Unfolding arguments are often stylistically complex and subtle.

The strategy for generating ideas set forth in this chapter—thinking of parallel because clauses and combining them into a working thesis statement that nutshells your argument—leads naturally to an argument with a self-announcing structure. Each because clause, together with its supporting evidence, becomes a separate building block of your argument. The building blocks, which can vary in length from a single paragraph to a whole series of paragraphs, are linked back to the thesis through appropriate transitions.

In our own classes we ask students early in the course to write arguments with self-announcing structures because such structures force writers to articulate their arguments clearly to themselves and because such structures help students master the art of organizing for readers. Later on in the course we encourage students to experiment with structures that unfold their meanings rather than announce them in the introduction.

In writing self-announcing arguments, students often ask how much of the argument to summarize in the introduction. Consider the following options. Within the introduction you could choose to announce only your claim:

> After-school jobs are beneficial for teenagers.

Or you could also predict a series of parallel reasons:

> After-school jobs are beneficial for teenagers for several reasons.

Or you could forecast the actual number of reasons:

> After-school jobs are beneficial for teenagers for four reasons.

Or you could forecast the whole argument:

> After-school jobs are beneficial for teenagers because they provide extra spending money, because they help develop responsibility, because they help teenagers learn time management, and because they help teenagers establish a record of employment experience useful for later job hunting.

These, of course, are not your only options. If you choose to delay your thesis until the end (a simple kind of unfolding argument), you might place the issue-question in the introduction but not give away your own position:

> Are after-school jobs beneficial for teenagers or not?

There are no hardbound rules to help you decide how much of your argument to forecast in the introduction. In Chapter 7 we discuss the different *ethos* projected when the writer places the claim in the introduction versus withholding it until later in the essay. It is clear at this point, though, that in making this decision a writer trades off clarity for surprise. The more you forecast, the clearer your argument is and the easier it is to read quickly. The less you forecast, the more surprising the argument is because the reader doesn't know what is coming. The only general rule is this: Readers sometimes feel insulted by too much forecasting. In writing a self-announcing argument, announce at the beginning only what is needed for clarity. In a short argument readers usually don't need all the because clauses stated explicitly in the introduction. In longer arguments, however, or in especially complex ones, readers appreciate having the whole argument forecast at the outset.

Of course, stating your reasons in because clauses is only one part of generating, organizing, and developing an argument. In the next chapter we will see how to support a reason by examining its logical structure, uncovering its unstated assumptions, and planning a strategy of development.

5

The Logical Structure of Arguments

In Chapter 4 you learned that the core of an argument is a claim supported by reasons and that these reasons can often be stated as because clauses attached to a claim. In the present chapter we examine the logical structure of arguments in more depth.

OVERVIEW TO *LOGOS:* WHAT DO WE MEAN BY THE "LOGICAL STRUCTURE" OF AN ARGUMENT?

As you will recall from our discussion of the rhetorical triangle, *logos* refers to the strength of an argument's support and its internal consistency. *Logos* is the argument's logical structure. But what do we mean by "logical structure"?

First of all, what we *don't* mean by logical structure is the kind of precise certainty you get in a philosophy class in formal logic. Logic classes deal with symbolic assertions that are universal and unchanging, such as "If all p's are q's and if r is a p, then r is a q." This statement is logically certain so long as p, q, and r are pure abstractions. But in the real world, p, q, and r turn into actual things, and the relationships among them suddenly become fuzzy. For example, p might be a class of actions called "Sexual Harassment," while q could be the class of "Actions That Justify Dismissal from a Job." If r is the class "Telling Off-Color Stories," then the logic of our p–q–r statement suggests that telling off-color stories (*r*) is an instance of sexual harassment (*p*), which in turn is an action justifying dismissal from one's job (*q*).

Now, most of us would agree that sexual harassment is a serious offense that might well justify dismissal from a job. In turn, we might agree that telling off-color stories, if the jokes are sufficiently raunchy and are inflicted on an unwilling audience, constitutes sexual harassment. But few of us would want to say categorically that all people who tell off-color stories are harassing their listeners and ought to be fired. Most of us would want to know the particulars of the case before making a final judgment.

In the real world, then, it is difficult to say that *p*'s are always *q*'s or that every instance of a *q* results in an *r*. That is why we discourage students from using the word *prove* in claims they write for arguments (as in "This paper will prove that euthanasia is wrong"). Real-world arguments seldom *prove* anything. They can only make a good case for something, a case that is more or less strong, more or less probable. Often the best you can hope for is to strengthen the resolve of those who agree with you or weaken the resistance of those who oppose you. If your audience believes *x* and you are arguing for *y*, you cannot expect your audience suddenly, as the result of your argument, to start believing *y*. If your argument causes an audience to experience a flicker of doubt or an instant of open-mindedness, you've done well. So proofs and dramatic shifts in position are not what real-world arguments are about.

A key difference, then, between formal logic and real-world argument is that real-world arguments are not grounded in abstract, universal statements. Rather, as we shall see, they must be grounded in beliefs, assumptions, or values granted by the audience. A second important difference is that in real-world arguments these beliefs, assumptions, or values are often unstated. So long as writer and audience share the same assumptions, then it's fine to leave them unstated. But if these underlying assumptions aren't shared, the writer has a problem.

To illustrate the nature of this problem, consider the following argument.

> After-school jobs are bad for teenagers because they take away study time.

On the face of it, this is a plausible argument. But the argument works only if we agree with the writer's assumption that loss of study time is bad. Suppose that we were skeptical of this assumption and believed that time spent on a job might be more valuable in the long run than time spent studying. Suppose we believed that a high school job teaches kids good work habits, gives them marketable skills, creates contacts and sources for future job references, and so forth. Thus we might believe that developing a good work reputation might lead to greater career success than getting higher grades through more studying. To succeed with the "loss of study time" reason, the writer would then have to create an explicit argument for the value of study time instead of leaving this crucial part of the argument unstated and undeveloped.

The Greek philosopher Aristotle would have called the preceding core argument ("After-school jobs are bad for teenagers because they take away study time") an *enthymeme*. An enthymeme is an incomplete logical structure that depends, for its completeness, on one or more unstated assumptions (values, beliefs, principles) that serve as the starting point of the argument. The successful arguer, said Aristotle, is the person who knows how to formulate and develop enthymemes so that the argument hooks into the audience's values and beliefs.

To clarify the concept of "enthymeme," let's go over this same territory again more slowly, examining what we mean by "incomplete logical structure." The sentence "After-school jobs are bad for teenagers because they take away study time" is an enthymeme. It combines a claim ("After-school jobs are bad for teenagers") with a reason expressed as a because clause ("because they take away study time"). To render this enthymeme logically complete, one must supply an unstated assumption—"loss of study time is bad for teenagers."* If your audience accepts this assumption, then you have a starting place on which to build an effective argument. If your audience doesn't accept this assumption, then you must supply another argument to support it, and so on until you find common ground with your audience.

To sum up:

1. Claims are supported with reasons. You can usually state a reason as a because clause attached to a claim (see Chapter 4).

2. A because clause attached to a claim is an incomplete logical structure called an enthymeme. To create a complete logical structure from an enthymeme, the unstated assumption (or assumptions) must be articulated.

3. To serve as an effective starting point for the argument, this unstated assumption should be a belief, value, or principle that the audience grants.

Let's illustrate this structure by putting the previous example—plus two new ones—into schematic form.

INITIAL ENTHYMEME:	After-school jobs are bad for teenagers because they take away study time.
CLAIM:	After-school jobs are bad for teenagers.
STATED REASON:	because they take away study time

---

* Later in this chapter we use the term *warrant* as the technical name for these often unstated assumptions, values, or beliefs that underlie your argument.

UNSTATED ASSUMPTION: Loss of study time is bad.

INITIAL ENTHYMEME: After-school jobs are good for teenagers because they teach responsibility and time management.

CLAIM: After-school jobs are good for teenagers.

STATED REASON: because they teach responsibility and time management

UNSTATED ASSUMPTION: Activities that teach responsibility and time management are good.

INITIAL ENTHYMEME: Cocaine and heroin should be legalized because legalization would eliminate the black market in drugs.

CLAIM: Cocaine and heroin should be legalized.

STATED REASON: because legalization would eliminate the black market in drugs

UNSTATED ASSUMPTION: An action that eliminates the black market in drugs is good. (Or, to state the assumption more fully, the benefits to society of eliminating the black market in drugs outweigh the negative effects to society of legalizing drugs.)

☐ FOR CLASS DISCUSSION

Working individually or in small groups, identify the claim, stated reason, and unstated assumption that completes each of the following enthymemic arguments.

EXAMPLE

Rabbits make good pets because they are gentle.

CLAIM: Rabbits make good pets.
STATED REASON: because they are gentle
UNSTATED ASSUMPTION: Gentle animals make good pets.

1. Joe is a bad leader because he is too bossy.
2. Buy this stereo system because it has a powerful amplifier.
3. Drugs should not be legalized because legalization would greatly increase the number of drug addicts.
4. Practicing the piano is good for kids because it teaches discipline.
5. Welfare benefits for unwed mothers should be eliminated because doing so will greatly reduce the nation's illegitimacy rate.
6. Welfare benefits for unwed mothers should not be eliminated because these benefits are needed to prevent unbearable poverty among our nation's most helpless citizens.
7. We should strengthen the Endangered Species Act because doing so will preserve genetic diversity on the planet.
8. The Endangered Species Act is too stringent because it severely damages the economy.

9. Bill Jones is a great leader because he is open-minded yet decisive.

10. Abortion should be legal because a woman has the right to control her own body. (This enthymeme has several unstated assumptions behind it; see if you can recreate all the missing premises.)

ADOPTING A LANGUAGE FOR DESCRIBING ARGUMENTS: THE TOULMIN SYSTEM

Understanding a new field usually requires us to learn a new vocabulary. For example, if you were taking biology for the first time, you'd spend days memorizing dozens and dozens of new terms. Luckily, the field of argument requires us to learn a mere handful of new terms. A particularly useful set of argument terms, one we'll be using throughout the rest of this text, comes from philosopher Stephen Toulmin. In the 1950s, Toulmin rejected the prevailing models of argument based on formal logic in favor of a very audience-based courtroom model.

Toulmin's courtroom model differs from formal logic in that it assumes (1) that all assertions and assumptions are contestable by "opposing counsel," and (2) that all final "verdicts" about the persuasiveness of the opposing arguments will be rendered by a neutral third party, a judge or jury. Keeping in mind the "opposing counsel" forces us to anticipate counterarguments and to question our assumptions; keeping in mind the judge and jury reminds us to answer opposing arguments fully, without rancor, and to present positive reasons for supporting our case as well as negative reasons for disbelieving the opposing case. Above all else, Toulmin's model reminds us not to construct an argument that appeals only to those who already agree with us.

The system we use for analyzing arguments combines Toulmin's system with Aristotle's concept of the enthymeme. The purpose of this system is to provide writers with an economical language for articulating the structure of argument and, in the process, to help them anticipate their audience's needs. More particularly, it helps writers see enthymemes—in the form of a claim with because clauses—as the core of their argument, and the other structural elements from Toulmin as strategies for elaborating and supporting that core.

This system builds on the one you have already been practicing. We simply need to add a few more key terms from Toulmin. The first key term is Toulmin's *warrant*, the name we will now use for the unstated assumption that turns an enthymeme into a complete logical structure. For example:

INITIAL ENTHYMEME:	After-school jobs are bad for teenagers because they take away study time.
CLAIM:	After-school jobs are bad for teenagers.
STATED REASON:	because they take away study time
WARRANT:	Loss of study time is bad.
INITIAL ENTHYMEME:	Cocaine and heroin should be legalized because legalization would eliminate the black market in drugs.

CLAIM:	Cocaine and heroin should be legalized.
STATED REASON:	because legalization would eliminate the black market in drugs
WARRANT:	An action that eliminates the black market in drugs is good.

Toulmin derives his term *warrant* from the concept of "warranty" or "guarantee." The warrant is the value, belief, or principle that the audience has to hold if the soundness of the argument is to be guaranteed or warranted. We sometimes make similar use of this word in ordinary language when we say "That is an unwarranted conclusion," meaning one has leapt from information about a situation to a conclusion about that situation without any sort of general principle to justify or "warrant" that move. Thus if we claim that cocaine and heroin ought to be legalized because legalization would end the black market, we must be able to cite a general principle or belief that links our prediction that legalization would end the black market to our claim that legalization ought to occur. In this case the warrant is the statement, "An action that eliminates the black market for drugs is good." It is this underlying belief that warrants or guarantees the argument. Just as automobile manufacturers must provide warranties for their cars if they want skeptical customers to buy them, we must provide warrants linking our reasons to our claims if we expect skeptical audiences to "buy" our arguments.

But arguments need more than claims, reasons, and warrants. These are simply one-sentence statements—the frame of an argument, not a developed argument. To flesh out our arguments and make them convincing we need what Toulmin calls *grounds* and *backing*. Grounds are the supporting evidence—facts, data, statistics, testimony, or examples—that cause you to make a claim in the first place or that you produce to justify a claim in response to audience skepticism. Toulmin suggests that grounds are "what you have to go on" in an argument. In short, they are collectively all the evidence you use to support a reason. It sometimes helps to think of grounds as the answer to a "How do you know that . . . ?" question preceding a reason. (How do you know that after-school jobs take away study time? How do you know that legalizing drugs will end the black market?) Here is how grounds fit into our emerging argument schema.

CLAIM:	After-school jobs are bad for teenagers.
STATED REASON:	because they take away study time
GROUNDS:	data and evidence showing that after-school jobs take away study time (examples of teenagers who work late and don't study, statistics showing that teenagers with jobs study less than those without jobs, testimony from teachers that working teenagers study less than those without jobs, etc.)

CLAIM:	Cocaine and heroin should be legalized.
STATED REASON:	because legalization would eliminate the black market in drugs
GROUNDS:	data and evidence showing how legalizing cocaine and heroin would eliminate the black market (statistics, data, and examples

describing the size and effect of current black market, followed by arguments showing how selling cocaine and heroin legally in state-controlled stores would lower the price and eliminate the need to buy them from drug dealers)

In many cases, successful arguments require just these three components: a claim, a reason, and grounds. If the audience already accepts the unstated assumption behind the reason (the warrant), then the warrant can safely remain in the background unstated and unexamined. But if there is a chance that the audience will question or doubt the warrant, then the writer needs to back it up by providing an argument in its support. *Backing* is the argument that supports the warrant. Backing answers the question, "How do you know that . . . ?" or "Why do you believe that . . . ?" prefixed to the warrant. (Why do you believe that loss of study time is bad? Why do you believe that the benefits of ending the black market outweigh the costs of legalizing cocaine and heroin?) Here is how *backing* is added to our schema.

WARRANT: Loss of study time is bad.

BACKING: argument showing why loss of study time is bad (it leads to poor grades, to inadequate preparation for college, to less enjoyment of school, to lower self-image as a student, etc.)

WARRANT: An action that eliminates the black market in drugs is good.

BACKING: an argument supporting the warrant by showing why eliminating the black market in drugs is good (statistics and examples about the ill effects of the black market, data on crime and profiteering, evidence that huge profits make drug dealing more attractive than ordinary jobs, the high cost of crime created by the black market, the cost to taxpayers of waging the war against drugs, the high cost of prisons to house incarcerated drug dealers, etc.)

Finally, Toulmin's system asks us to imagine how a shrewd adversary would try to refute our argument. Specifically, the adversary might attack our reason and grounds by showing how an after-school job does *not* lead to loss of study time or how legalizing drugs would *not* end the black market. Or the adversary might attack our warrant and backing by showing how loss of study time may not be bad or how the negative consequences of legalizing drugs might outweigh the benefit of ending the black market.

In the case of the after-school job debate, an adversary might offer one or both of the following rebuttals:

CONDITIONS OF REBUTTAL: *Rebutting the reason and grounds:*   evidence of teenagers who combine work with good study habits; argument showing that having a job can teach time management, which leads in turn to an increase in studying.

Rebutting the warrant and backing: argument showing that advantages of holding a job may outweigh disadvantages of reduced study time;

argument showing that job experience and achieving a track record as a good worker may be more highly valued by employers than GPA.

If either of these rebuttals seems valid, the author of an argument critical of after-school jobs must build a response into her argument. To help writers imagine such responses, conditions of rebuttal are often stated as conditionals using the word *unless,* such as "After school jobs take away study time *unless* it turns out that holding a job may teach teenagers to use time more efficiently and to study more effectively." Conditions of rebuttal name the exceptions to the rule, the circumstances under which your reason or warrant might not hold. Stated in this manner, the conditions of rebuttal for the legalization-of-drugs argument might look like this:

CONDITIONS OF REBUTTAL: *Rebutting the reason and grounds:*   Ending the black market is good unless taxes on legal drugs would keep the price high enough that a black market would still exist; unless new kinds of illegai designer drugs would be developed and sold on the black market.

Rebutting the warrant and backing: Ending the black market is good unless the increased numbers of drug users and addicts were unacceptably high; unless harmful changes in social structure due to acceptance of drugs were too severe; unless the health and economic consequences of increased number of drug users were catastrophic; unless social costs to families and communities associated with addiction or erratic behavior during drug-induced "highs" were too great.

Toulmin's final term, used to limit the force of a claim and indicate the degree of its probable truth, is *qualifier.* The qualifier reminds us that real-world arguments almost never prove a claim. We may say things like "very likely," "probably," or "maybe" to indicate the strength of the claim we are willing to draw from our grounds and warrant. Thus if there are exceptions to your warrant or if your grounds are not very strong, you will have to qualify your claim. For example, you might say "Holding an after-school job is a bad idea for many teenagers" or "With full awareness of the potential dangers, I suggest we consider the option of legalizing drugs as a way of ending the ill effects of the black market." Placed in our schema, the qualifier might be stated this way:

CLAIM: After-school jobs are bad for teenagers.

QUALIFIER: in many cases; for many teenagers

CLAIM: Cocaine and heroin should be legalized.

QUALIFIER: perhaps, tentatively

Although the system just described might at first seem complicated, it is actually fairly easy to use after you've had some opportunity to practice. The following chart will help you review the terms.

ORIGINAL ENTHYMEME: your claim with because clause

CLAIM: The point or position you are trying to get your audience to accept

STATED REASON: your because clause;* your reasons are the subordinate claims you make in support of your main claim

GROUNDS: the evidence (data, facts, testimony, statistics, examples) supporting your stated reason

WARRANT: the originally unstated assumption behind your enthymeme, the statement of belief, value, principle, and so on, that, when accepted by an audience, warrants or underwrites your argument

BACKING: evidence or other argumentation supporting the warrant. (If the audience already accepts the warrant, then backing is usually not needed. But if the audience doubts the warrant, then backing is essential.)

QUALIFIER: words or phrases limiting the force of your claim

CONDITIONS OF REBUTTAL: your acknowledgement of the limits of your claim—those conditions under which it does not hold true, in anticipation of an adversary's counterargument, against your reason and grounds or against your warrant and backing

To help you practice using these terms, here are two more examples, displayed this time so that the conditions of rebuttal are set in an opposing column next to the reason/grounds and the warrant/backing.

ORIGINAL ENTHYMEME: The Mustangs will win the football championship because they have the best running backs in the league.

CLAIM: The Mustangs will win the football championship.

STATED REASON: because they have the best running backs in the league

CONDITIONS OF REBUTTAL: *Rebuttal of reason and grounds:* unless the Mustangs don't have the best running backs in the league (evidence that the running backs are not as strong as those of several other teams; data showing weaknesses in the running backs—propensity

---

*   Most arguments have more than one because clause or reason in support of your claim. Each enthymeme thus develops only one line of reasoning, one piece of your whole argument.

GROUNDS: physical description of the excellence of the running backs, statistics on their accomplishments, comparative data showing that no other team in the league has running backs of this quality

WARRANT: The team with the best running backs will win the football championship.

BACKING: argument showing the value of running backs to a winning team; statistics linking strong running backs to wins in this league

QUALIFIER: probably

to fumble, inability to read unexpected defenses, etc.)

Rebuttal of warrant and backing: unless other teams alter their defenses to protect against the run, unless passing teams win more games than running teams, unless the Mustangs have serious weaknesses in defense, etc. (evidence that different defenses are more effective against the run; evidence that passing teams outscore running teams; evidence that the Mustangs have a weak defense and don't have a strong enough passing attack to keep opponents from concentrating on rush defense)

ORIGINAL ENTHYMEME: The exclusionary rule is a bad law because it allows drug dealers to escape prosecution.*

CLAIM: The exclusionary rule is a bad law.

STATED REASON: because it allows drug dealers to escape prosecution

GROUNDS: numerous cases wherein the exclusionary rule prevented police from presenting evidence in court; examples of nitpicking rules and regulations that allowed drug dealers to go free; testimony from prosecutors and police about how the exclusionary rule hampers their effectiveness

WARRANT: It is beneficial to our country to prosecute drug dealers.

BACKING: arguments showing the extent and danger of the drug problem; arguments showing that prosecuting and imprisoning drug dealers will reduce the drug problem

QUALIFIER: perhaps, tentatively

CONDITIONS OF REBUTTAL: *Rebuttal of reason and grounds:* unless the exclusionary rule does not allow many drug dealers to escape prosecution (counterevidence showing numerous times when police and prosecutors followed the exclusionary rule and still obtained convictions; statistical analysis showing that the percentage of cases in which exclusionary rule threw evidence out of court is very low)

Rebuttal of warrant and backing: unless reversing exclusionary rule would have serious costs that outweigh benefits; unless greatly increasing the pursuit and prosecution of drug dealers would have serious costs (arguments showing that the value of protecting individual liberties outweighs the value of prosecuting drug dealers; statistical evidence showing that the expense of building more prisons and incarcerating drug dealers is prohibitive; arguments showing that the high social cost of diverting police attention from other crimes in order to track drug dealers harms society)

---

* The exclusionary rule is a court-mandated set of regulations specifying when evidence can and cannot be introduced into a trial. It excludes all evidence that police obtain through irregular means. In actual practice, it demands that police follow strict procedures. Opponents of the exclusionary rule claim that its "narrow technicalities" handcuff police.

□ FOR CLASS DISCUSSION

Working individually or in small groups, imagine that you have to write arguments developing the ten enthymemes listed in the For Class Discussion exercise on pages 101-102. Use the Toulmin schema to help you determine what you need to consider when developing each enthymeme. As an example, we have applied the Toulmin schema to the first enthymeme.

ORIGINAL ENTHYMEME: Joe is a bad leader because he is too bossy.

CLAIM: Joe is a bad leader.

STATED REASON: because he is too bossy

GROUNDS: various examples of Joe's bossiness; testimony about his bossiness from people who have worked with him

WARRANT: Bossy people make bad leaders.

BACKING: arguments showing that other things being equal, bossy people tend to bring out the worst rather than the best in those around them; bossy people tend not to ask advice, make bad decisions; etc.

QUALIFIER: In most circumstances, he isn't a good leader. Many people think he isn't a good leader.

CONDITIONS OF REBUTTAL: *Rebuttal of reason and grounds:* unless Joe isn't really bossy (counterevidence of Joe's cooperativeness and kindness; testimony that Joe is easy to work with; etc.)

Rebuttal of the warrant and backing: unless bossy people sometimes make good leaders (arguments showing that at times a group needs a bossy person who can make decisions and get things done); unless Joe has other traits of good leadership that outweigh his bossiness (evidence that, despite his bossiness, Joe has many other good leadership traits such as high energy, intelligence, charisma, etc.)

USING TOULMIN'S SCHEMA TO DETERMINE A STRATEGY OF SUPPORT

Having introduced you to Toulmin's terminology for describing the logical structure of arguments, we can turn directly to a discussion of how to use these concepts for developing your own arguments. Let's imagine, for example, that you wanted to defend the following enthymemic argument put forth by the woman president of a major corporation:

Women often make better managers than men because they are more people-conscious. They are better listeners and more aware of other people's feelings. They like to find out where people are coming from.

Figure 5–1 shows how one student used the Toulmin schema to examine this enthymeme. The warrant behind this argument is that persons who are "people-conscious" are better managers than those who aren't. In examining the stated reason and the warrant, the writer can see that the argument must be supported in two parts: The writer will have to show that women are more people-conscious than men (this is the original stated reason, the because clause); the writer will also have to show that being people-conscious is the key to being a good manager (this is the unstated warrant or major premise). For this particular argument, supporting the warrant with backing might be even more crucial than supporting the stated reason.

As Figure 5–1 shows, the writer complicated her sense of the issue by also considering Toulmin's conditions of rebuttal. In considering how her stated reason might be rebutted, the writer discovers that she has to define *people-consciousness* clearly and then find some way to demonstrate that women are more people-conscious than men. The writer decides to qualify the argument by saying "women are *frequently* more people-conscious than men"; this qualification helps defend the argument against the exceptions that a skeptical audience might raise. The writer also sees that she should explain what traits or actions characterize a "people-conscious" manager. Then, in order to support the stated reason that women are frequently more people-conscious than men, the writer can look for research studies that might support the claim, think of persuasive representative examples from personal experience, or develop a causal argument based on women's being

Stated Reason:
Women are more people-conscious than men.

Grounds:
Let's see, how could I support this? Examples of people-conscious women: Mrs. Raxborne at church. Examples from books. I could talk about the way girls are raised differently from boys—emphasis on being listeners; earlier development of verbal skills. Maybe I could find some testimony. I'll brainstorm this with my group.

Warrant:
Other things being equal, being people-conscious makes a person a better manager.

Backing:
People trust you more: They realize you aren't just a number. People-conscious managers will be more supportive if you have a down time. They will recognize your need for family. They will look out for your welfare, not just company profits. Build a better team.

Claim:
Women are often better managers than men.

Conditions of Rebuttal:
How could I doubt the stated reason and grounds? Why not say men are more people-conscious than women? I know quite a few people-conscious men and bitchy women. What does it mean to be people-conscious anyway? How could you ever define that? Are you people-conscious just because you are a good listener?

How could I doubt the warrant? Maybe being too people-conscious means you are a weak manager who can't make hard economic decisions. Maybe in the list of criteria for excellence as a manager, being "people-conscious" is less important than being decisive, fair, creative, knowledgeable about marketing, etc.

Qualifier:
"Other things being equal"

FIGURE 5–1 Toulmin schema of argument about women managers

socialized as nurturers, and so forth. These supporting examples and arguments would become the grounds for the stated reason.

Similarly, considering conditions for rebuttal helps the writer see how to qualify the warrant—what to concede to the opposition and what to support. Rather than make the sweeping generalization that people-consciousness is an essential aspect of good management, the writer might argue more narrowly that people-conscious managers build trust and cooperation in an organization. Once again, the writer may uncover some data about the effectiveness of different management styles or bring in personal examples from job experience. In sum, the purpose of brainstorming for opposing views under "Conditions for rebuttal" is to sharpen your sense of the potential strengths and weaknesses of your argument.

CREATING SUPPORT: USING EVIDENCE/CHAINS OF REASONS FOR GROUNDS AND BACKING

The majority of words in any argument are devoted to grounds and backing—the supporting sections that develop the argument frame, consisting of a claim, reasons, and warrants. Generally these supporting sections take one of two forms: either (1) *evidence* such as facts, examples, case studies, statistics, testimony from experts, and so forth; or (2) a *chain of reasons*—that is, further conceptual argument. Let's look at each kind of support separately.

Evidence as Support

It's often easier for writers to use evidence rather than chains of reasons for support because using evidence entails moving from generalizations to specific details—a basic organizational strategy that most writers practice regularly. Consider the following hypothetical case. A student, Ramona, wants to write a complaint letter to the head of the Philosophy Department about a philosophy professor, Dr. Choplogic, whom Ramona considers incompetent. Ramona plans to develop two different lines of reasoning: first, that Choplogic's courses are disorganized and, second, that Choplogic is unconcerned about students.

Let's look briefly at how she can develop her first main line of reasoning, which is based on the following enthymeme:

Dr. Choplogic is an ineffective teacher because his courses are disorganized.

The grounds for this argument will be all the evidence she can muster showing that Choplogic's courses are disorganized. Figure 5–2 shows Ramona's initial brainstorming notes based on the Toulmin schema. The information Ramona lists under "grounds" is what she sees as the facts of the case—the hard data she will use as evidence to support her reason. Here is how this argument might look when placed into written form:

Claim: Dr. Choplogic is an ineffective teacher.
Stated reason: because his courses are disorganized
Grounds: What evidence is there that his courses are disorganized?
    —no syllabus in either Intro or Ethics
    —never announced how many papers we would have
    —didn't know what would be on tests
    —didn't like the textbook he had chosen; gave us different terms
    —didn't follow any logical sequence in his lectures

FIGURE 5–2   Ramona's initial planning notes

One reason that Dr. Choplogic is ineffective is that his courses are poorly organized. I have had him for two courses—Introduction to Philosophy and Ethics—and both were disorganized. He never gave us a syllabus or explained his grading system. At the beginning of the course he wouldn't tell us how many papers he would require, and he never seemed to know how much of the textbook material he planned to cover. For Intro he told us to read the whole text, but he covered only half of it in class. A week before the final I asked him how much of the text would be on the exam and he said he hadn't decided. The Ethics class was even more disorganized. Dr. Choplogic told us to read the text, which provided one set of terms for ethical arguments, and then he told us he didn't like the text and presented us in lecture with a wholly different set of terms. The result was a whole class of confused, angry students.

Claim and reason

*Grounds
(evidence in
support of reason)*

As you can see, Ramona has plenty of evidence to support her contention that Choplogic is disorganized. But how effective is this argument as it stands? Is this all she needs? The Toulmin schema also encourages Ramona to examine the warrant, backing, and conditions of rebuttal for this argument. Figure 5–3 shows how her planning notes continue.

This section of her planning notes helps her see her argument more fully from the audience's perspective. She believes that no one can challenge her reason and grounds—Choplogic is indeed a disorganized teacher. But she recognizes that some people might challenge her warrant ("Disorganized teachers are ineffective"). An adversary might say that some teachers, even though they are hopelessly disorganized, might nevertheless do an excellent job of stimulating thought and discussion. Moreover, such teachers might possess other valuable traits that outweigh their disorganization. Ramona therefore decides to address these concerns by adding another section to this portion of her argument.

Claim: Dr. Choplogic is an ineffective teacher.

Stated reason: because his courses are disorganized

Grounds: What evidence is there that his courses are disorganized?

—no syllabus in either Intro or Ethics

—never announced how many papers we would have

—didn't know what would be on tests

—didn't like the textbook he had chosen; gave us different terms

—didn't follow any logical sequence in his lectures

Warrant: Disorganized teachers are ineffective.

Backing:

—organization helps you learn

—gets material organized in a logical way

—helps you know what to study

—helps you take notes and relate one part of course to another

—when teacher is disorganized you think he hasn't prepared for class; makes you lose confidence

Conditions of rebuttal: Would anybody doubt my reasons and grounds?

—No. Every student I have ever talked to agrees that these are the facts about Choplogic's courses. Everyone agrees that he is disorganized. Of course, the department chair might not know this, so I will have to provide evidence.

Would anybody doubt my warrant and backing? Maybe they would.

—Is it possible that in some cases disorganized teachers are good teachers? Have I ever had a disorganized teacher who was good? My freshman sociology teacher was disorganized, but she really made you think. You never knew where the course was going but we had some great discussions. Choplogic isn't like that. He isn't using classtime to get us involved in philosophic thinking or discussions.

—Is it possible that Choplogic has other good traits that outweigh his disorganization? I don't think he does, but I will have to make a case for this.

FIGURE 5–3 Ramona's planning notes continued

Dr. Choplogic's lack of organization makes it difficult for students to take notes, to know what to study, or to relate one part of the course to another. Moreover, students lose confidence in the teacher because he doesn't seem to care enough to prepare for class.

Backing for warrant (shows why disorganization is bad)

In Dr. Choplogic's defense, it might be thought that his primary concern is involving students in class discussions or other activities to teach us thinking skills or get us involved in philosophical discussions. But this isn't the case. Students rarely get a chance to speak in class. We just sit there listening to rambling, disorganized lectures.

Response to conditions of rebuttal

As the marginal notations show, this section of her argument backs the warrant that disorganized teachers are ineffective and anticipates some of the conditions for rebuttal that an audience might raise to defend Dr. Choplogic. Throughout her draft, Ramona has supported her argument with effective use of evidence. The Toulmin schema has shown her that she needed evidence primarily to support her stated reason ("Choplogic is disorganized"). But she also needed some evidence to support her warrant ("Disorganization is bad") and to respond to possible conditions of rebuttal ("Perhaps Choplogic is teaching thinking skills").

In general, the evidence you use for support can come either from your own personal experiences and observations or from reading and research. Although many arguments depend on your skill at research, many can be supported wholly or in part from your own personal experiences, so don't neglect the wealth of evidence from your own life when searching for data. Chapter 6 is devoted to a more detailed discussion of evidence in arguments.

When evidence is incorporated into your essays, it can take several different forms. In the previous example of Ramona's complaint against Dr. Choplogic, it took the form of a series of relevant facts. Other common forms of evidence include examples, statistics, and testimony. Let's look at each in turn.

Examples

A great number of arguments can be supported by examples. If you want to argue that Joe is a bad leader because he is bossy, you could use some examples of his bossiness as grounds for your argument. Similarly, you might use the example of your grandparents to argue that welfare reforms have caused new hardships to the elderly in your community. The following quotation illustrates how one writer used examples to support his claim that the city of Seattle needs a stronger antidiscrimination law. His main argument is that current laws are not preventing discrimination, an argument he supports by piling up eight different examples (we quote only his first two examples as illustration of the strategy):

> If you don't think such an ordinance is necessary, possibly the following incidents will convince you:
>
> —Christmas Eve 1983—Sewage began to back up at the residence of Steve Reiswig and Ray Woods. Because they couldn't find their landlord, they dialed 911 to contact the Seattle Fire Department for assistance. They say a member of the department answered and replied to their request, "You guys have hepatitis and AIDS," and refused assistance.
>
> —January 1984—The owner of a downtown tavern placed a large hand-lettered sign in the window that said, "Cubans Keep Out." [Six more examples follow.]*

---

* From Steven L. Kendall, "Why We Need New Anti-Discrimination Law," *Seattle Times* 12 Sept. 1987: A11.

Statistics

Another common form of evidence is statistics. Since statistical data pose tricky problems in arguments—some people claim you can prove almost anything with statistics—we have devoted a special section of this text to arguing with numbers (Appendix 2). Here is how the writer of a *Newsweek* article used statistical data to argue that the use of fluorocarbons is harming the earth's ozone layer:

> The ozone layer also blocks out harmful ultraviolet light, which causes skin cancer and other damage. The U.S. Environmental Protection Agency claims that a loss of 2.5 percent of the ozone layer would lead to 15,000 additional victims of the deadliest forms of skin cancer per year. Additionally, UV light kills plankton, a major food source for much of the ocean's fish, as well as the larva of some kinds of fish. A 20 percent increase in UV light, for example, could destroy 5 percent of the ocean's anchovie larvae, which is a major source of animal feed worldwide.*

Testimony

Finally, much evidence comes in the form of testimony, whereby you cite an expert to help bolster your case. Testimony is often blended with other kinds of evidence, as in the above example where the U.S. Environmental Protection Agency is cited as the source of the skin cancer statistics. Citing authorities is particularly common in those arguments where lay persons cannot be expected to be experts—the technical feasibility of cold fusion, the effects of alcohol on fetal tissue development, and so forth. Often, a noteworthy quotation from an expert will have considerable persuasive power. The author of the *Newsweek* article from which we drew our previous example used such a quotation as the thesis statement of her essay:

> But the world may no longer have the luxury of further study. As Senator John Chafee put it last week, at a hearing of his Subcommittee on Environmental Pollution, "There is a very real possibility that man—through ignorance or indifference or both—is irreversibly altering the ability of our atmosphere to [support] life."

Later in the article, more authorities are cited:

> This greenhouse effect, according to a parade of witnesses at last week's hearings, is no longer a matter of scientific debate, but a frightening reality. "Global warming is inevitable—it's only a question of magnitude and time," concluded Robert Watson of the National Aeronautics and Space Administration, the agency whose satellites monitor the upper atmosphere.

Chain of Reasons as Support

So far we have been discussing how to support reasons with evidence. Many reasons, however, cannot be supported this way; rather, they must be

---

* The information on fluorocarbons in this and the following examples is based on Sharon Begley, "Silent Summer: Ozone Loss and Global Warming," *Newsweek* 23 June 1986: 64–66.

supported with a chain of other reasons. Such passages are often more diffi-cult to write. Let's take as an example a student who wants to argue that the state should require the wearing of seatbelts. His claim, along with his main supporting reason, is as follows:

> The state should require the wearing of seatbelts in moving vehicles because seat-belts save lives.

In planning out the argument, the writer determines the unstated war-rant, which in this case is that the state should enact any law that would save lives. The writer's argument thus looks like this:

> CLAIM: The state should enact a mandatory seatbelt law.
>
> STATED REASON: Such a law will save lives.
>
> WARRANT: Laws that save lives should be enacted by the state.

The writer's next step is to consider the conditions for rebuttal for these premises. He realizes that he will have no trouble supporting the stated rea-son ("Seatbelts save lives") since he can use evidence in the form of exam-ples, statistics, and testimony. But the warrant of the argument ("Laws that save lives should be enacted by the state") cannot be defended by an appeal to such data. Although this statement operates as a warrant in the original seatbelt argument, it is actually a new claim that must itself be supported by additional reasons. As this example illustrates, a statement serving as a rea-son in one argument can become a claim in another, setting off a potentially infinite regress of reasons.

Examining the conditions for rebuttal reveals to the writer how vulnera-ble the warrant is. If the state is supposed to enact any law that saves lives, should it then pass laws requiring you to take your vitamins, get your blood pressure checked, or put safety strips in your bathtub? How could the writer argue that the state has the right to require seatbelts without opening the way for dozens of other do-gooder laws? Unable to use evidence, the writer proceeded to think of chains of reasons that might add up to a con-vincing case.

> The seatbelt law differs from other do-gooder laws:
>
> - Because it mandates behavior only on public property.
> - Because it concerns highway safety, and the state is clearly responsible for public highways.
> - Because the connection between wearing seatbelts and safety is immediately clear.
> - Because it is similar to already established laws requiring the wearing of motorcycle helmets.
> - Because the law is easy to follow, is minimally disruptive, and costs relatively little so that the benefits outweigh the disadvantages.

Each of these arguments distinguishes seatbelt legislation from other, less acceptable laws government might enact in the name of citizen safety, and they thus become ways of qualifying the warrant that the state should enact *all* laws that save lives. Together they constitute some reasons for supporting seatbelt legislation and for arguing that such legislation is not an unreasonable infringement of citizens' rights.

Having worked out these differences between seatbelt laws and other do-gooder laws, the writer is ready to draft the argument in essay form. Here is a portion of the writer's essay, picking up his argument after he has shown that seatbelts do indeed save lives:

> But just because seatbelts save lives does not necessarily mean that the state has the right to make us wear them. Certainly we don't want the state to make us put non-slip safety strips in our bathtubs, to require annual blood-pressure checks, or to outlaw cigarettes, alcohol, and sugar. But seatbelt regulation governs our behavior on public roadways, not in the privacy of our homes, and the government is obviously responsible for making the highways as safe as possible. After all, we can sue the government for negligence if it disregards safety in highway construction. Forcing motor vehicle passengers to wear seatbelts can thus be seen as part of their general program to make the highways safe. Moreover, the use of seatbelts constitutes a minimal restriction of personal freedom. Seatbelts are already standard equipment in cars, it costs us nothing to wear them, and they are now designed for maximum comfort.
>
> There are also a number of precedents for seatbelt legislation. Indeed, there are already government regulations requiring the installation of seatbelts in cars. To require their installation but not their use is silly. It is to require people to be potentially, but not actually, safe. In addition, a number of states, following the same sort of rationale as the one I've followed above, require motorcyclists to wear helmets. Such helmets are often costly and uncomfortable and, according to some cyclists, hurt the biker's image. But because they protect lives and save millions of dollars in insurance and hospital costs, such objections have been overridden.

As you can tell, this section is considerably more complex than one that simply cites data as evidence in support of a reason. Here the writer must use an interlocking chain of other reasons, showing all the ways that a seatbelt law is different from a safety-strip-in-the-bathtub law. Certainly it's not a definitive argument, but it is considerably more compelling than saying that the state should pass any law that protects lives. Although chains of reasons are harder to construct than bodies of evidence, many arguments will require them.

CONCLUSION

Chapters 4 and 5 have provided an anatomy of argument. They have shown that the core of an argument is a claim with reasons that usually can be summarized in one or more because clauses attached to the claim. Often, it is as important to support the unstated premises in your argument as it is to support the stated ones. In order to plan out an argument strategy, arguers can use the Toulmin schema, which helps writers discover grounds, warrants, and backings for their arguments and to test them through conditions for rebuttal. Finally, we saw how stated reasons and warrants are supported through the use of evidence or chains of other reasons. In the next chapter we will look more closely at the uses of evidence in argumentation.

□ FOR CLASS DISCUSSION

1. Working individually or in small groups, consider ways you could use evidence from personal experience to support the stated reason in each of the following partial arguments:

   a. Another reason to oppose a state sales tax is that it is so annoying.

   b. Professor X should be rated down on his (her) teaching because he (she) doesn't design homework effectively to promote real learning.

   c. Professor X is an outstanding teacher because he (she) generously spends so much time outside of class counseling students with personal problems.

2. Now try to create a chain-of-reasons argument to support the warrants in each of the above partial arguments. The warrants for each of the arguments are stated below.

   a. Support this warrant: We should oppose taxes that are annoying.

   b. Support this warrant: The effective design of homework to promote real learning is an important criterion for rating teachers.

   c. Support this warrant: Time spent counseling students with personal problems is an important criterion for rating teachers.

3. Using Toulmin's conditions of rebuttal, work out a strategy for refuting either the stated reasons or the warrants or both in each of the above arguments.

Evidence in Argument

In the previous chapter, we examined the two basic ways that writers support their arguments: through reasons supported by evidence and through reasons supported by chains of other reasons. In this chapter we return to a discussion of evidence. Our purpose in this chapter is to help you develop strategies for finding, using, and evaluating evidence. We focus first on the various ways you can use your own personal experiences to support an argument, including research data gathered from interviews, surveys, and questionnaires. Next we discuss evidence from library research and examine the knotty problem of what to do when the experts disagree. Finally, we discuss how you can evaluate evidence in order to use it fairly, responsibly, and persuasively.

USING EVIDENCE FROM PERSONAL EXPERIENCE

Your own life can be the source of supporting evidence in many arguments. Often a story from your own life can support an important point or show your readers the human significance of your issue. Whenever you include specific, vivid evidence from personal experience, you will be reaching out to your readers, who generally empathize with the personal experiences of others. A writer's credibility is often enhanced if the reader senses the writer's personal connection to an issue.

Using Personal Experience Data

Many issues can make extensive, even exclusive, use of personal experience data. Here is how a student from a small Montana town used a personal experience to support her claim that "small rural schools provide a quality education for children."

> Another advantage of small rural schools is the way they create in students a sense of identity with their communities and a sense of community pride. When children see the active support of the community toward the school, they want to return this support with their best efforts. I remember our Fergus Grade School Christmas programs. Sure, every grade school in Montana has a Christmas program, but ours seemed to be small productions. We started work on our play and songs immediately after Thanksgiving. The Fergus Community Women's Club decorated the hall a few days before the program. When the big night arrived, the whole community turned out, even Mr. and Mrs. Schoenberger, an elderly couple. I and the eleven other students were properly nervous as we performed our play, "A Charlie Brown Christmas." As a finale, the whole community sang carols and exchanged gifts. One of the fathers even dressed up as Santa Claus. Everyone involved had a warm feeling down inside when they went home.

The community bonding described in this paragraph—the father playing Santa Claus, the attendance of the elderly couple, the communal singing of Christmas carols—supports the writer's stated reason that small rural schools help students feel an identity with their communities.

Using Personal Observations

For some arguments you can gather evidence through personal observations. For example, suppose you want to argue that your city should install a traffic light at a particularly dangerous pedestrian crossing. You could draw on your past experience by relating an accident you almost had at that crossing. But even more persuasive might be some facts and statistics you could gather by observing the crossing for an hour or so on several different days. You could count numbers of vehicles, observe pedestrian behavior, take note of dangerous situations, time how long it takes to cross the street, and so forth. These could then become persuasive data for an argument.

EXAMPLE ARGUMENT USING PERSONAL OBSERVATION DATA

> The intersection at 5th and Montgomery is particularly dangerous. Traffic volume on Montgomery is so heavy that pedestrians almost never find a comfortable break in the flow of cars. On April 29, I watched fifty-seven pedestrians cross this intersection. Not once did cars stop in both directions

before the pedestrian stepped off the sidewalk onto the street. Typically, the pedestrian had to move into the street, start tentatively to cross, and wait until a car finally stopped. On fifteen occasions, pedestrians had to stop halfway across the street, with cars speeding by in both directions, waiting for cars in the far lanes to stop before they could complete their crossing.

USING EVIDENCE FROM INTERVIEWS, SURVEYS, AND QUESTIONNAIRES

In addition to direct observations, you can gather evidence by conducting interviews, taking surveys, or passing out questionnaires.

Conducting Interviews

Of these methods, interviews are especially powerful sources of evidence, not only for gathering expert testimony and important data, but also for learning about opposing or alternative views. To conduct an effective interview, you need to have a clear purpose for the interview and to be professional, courteous, efficient, and prepared. Probably most interviews go wrong because the interviewer doesn't have a specific plan of questioning. Before the interview, write out the questions you intend to ask based on your purpose. (Of course, be ready to move in unexpected directions if the interview opens up new territory.) Find out as much as possible about the interviewee prior to the interview. Your knowledge of his or her background will help establish your credibility and build a bridge between you and your source. Be punctual, and remember that the interviewee is probably busy and hasn't time for small talk. Finally, in most cases it is best to present yourself as a listener seeking clarity on an issue, rather than as an advocate of a particular position. Except in rare cases, it is a mistake to enter into argument with your interviewee, or to indicate through body language or tone of voice an antagonism toward his or her position. During the interview, play the believing role. Save the doubting role for later, when you are looking over your notes.

While conducting the interview, plan either to tape it (in which case you must ask the interviewee's permission) or to take good notes. Immediately after the interview, while your memory is fresh, rewrite your notes more fully and completely.

When you use interview data in your own writing, put quotation marks around any direct quotations. Except when unusual circumstances might require anonymity, identify your source by name and indicate his or her title or credentials—whatever will convince the reader that this person's remarks are to be taken seriously. Here is how one student used interview data to support an argument against carpeting dorm rooms.

> Finally, university-provided carpets will be too expensive. According to Robert Bothell, Assistant Director of Housing Services, the cost will be $300 per room for the carpet and installation. The university would also have to purchase more vac-

uum cleaners for the students to use. Altogether, Bothell estimated the cost of carpets to be close to $100,000 for the whole campus. [Here the student writer uses
interview data from Robert Bothell as evidence that university-provided carpets
will be too expensive. As Assistant Director of Housing Services, Bothell has the
credentials to be an authoritative source on these costs.]

Using Surveys or Questionnaires

Still another form of field research data can come from surveys or questionnaires. Sometimes an informal poll of your classmates can supply evidence
persuasive to a reader. One of our students, in an argument supporting
public transportation, asked every rider on her bus one morning the following two questions:

Do you enjoy riding the bus more than commuting by car? If so, why?

She was able to use her data in the following paragraph:

Last week I polled forty-eight people riding the bus between Bellevue and
Seattle. Eighty percent said they enjoyed riding the bus more than commuting by
car, while 20 percent preferred the car. Those who enjoyed the bus cited the following reasons in this order of preference: It saved them the hassle of driving in
traffic; it gave them time to relax and unwind; it was cheaper than paying for gas
and parking; it saved them time.

More formal research can be done through developing and distributing
questionnaires. Developing a good questionnaire is a complex task, so much
so that social science or education majors often have to take special courses
devoted to the topic. In general, problems with questionnaires arise when
the questions are confusing or when response categories don't allow the
respondent enough flexibility of choices. If you are writing an argument
that depends on an elaborate questionnaire, consider checking out a book
from your library on questionnaire design. Simple questionnaires, however,
can be designed without formal training. If you use a questionnaire, type it
neatly so that it looks clean, uncluttered, and easy to complete. At the head
of the questionnaire you should explain its purpose. Your tone should be
courteous and, if possible, you should include some motivational pitch to
urge the reader to complete the questionnaire.

INEFFECTIVE EXPLANATION FOR QUESTIONNAIRE:

The following questionnaire is very important for my research. I need it back by
Tuesday, January 19, so please fill it out as soon as you get it. Thanks.
[doesn't explain purpose; reasons for questionnaire stated in terms of writer's
needs, not audience's need]

MORE EFFECTIVE EXPLANATION

This questionnaire is aimed at improving the quality of Dickenson Library for
both students and staff. It should take no more than three or four minutes of your

time and gives you an opportunity to say what you like and don't like about the present library. Of course, your responses will be kept anonymous. To enable a timely report to the library staff, please return the questionnaire by Tuesday, January 19. Thank you very much.
[purpose is clear; respondents see how filling out questionnaire may benefit them]

When distributing questionnaires, you should seek a random distribution so that any person in your target population has an equal chance of being selected. Surveys lose their persuasiveness if the respondents are biased or represent just one segment of the total population you intended to survey. For example, if you pass out your library questionnaire only to persons living in dorms, then you won't know how commuting students feel about the library.

USING EVIDENCE FROM READING: THE ART OF LIBRARY RESEARCH

Whereas you can sometimes make excellent arguments using only personal experience data, many arguments require data gathered from library research, including books, magazines, journals, newspapers, government documents, computerized data banks, specialized encyclopedias and almanacs, corporate bulletins, and so forth. How to find such data, how to incorporate it into your own writing through summary, paraphrase, and quotation, and how to cite it and document it are treated in detail in Part IV of this text (Chapters 16 and 17). Our purpose in this chapter is to examine some of the theoretical and rhetorical issues involved in selecting and using research evidence.

Seeking Clarity: Library Research as an Analysis of a Conversation

As a researcher, do you enter the library solely to support your own position on an issue (Callicles' goal of victory from Chapter 1)? Or are you seeking the fullest possible understanding of the issue (Socrates' goal of clarification)? The most responsible goal is clarification, but the process of reaching this goal often leads you into a confusing morass of conflicting evidence and testimony. Before continuing with a practical discussion of how to use research evidence, let's pause momentarily to examine this knotty problem.

Suppose you are writing an argument claiming that the United States should take immediate measures to combat global warming. Early in your search for evidence, you come across the following editorial, which appeared in *USA Today* in June 1986.

Imagine a world like this:
Omaha, Neb., sweats through the worst drought in its history. In July 2030, the mercury hits 100 on 20 days. Crops are wiped out; the Midwest is a dust bowl.

New Orleans is under water. The French Quarter has shut down; the Superdome holds a small lake. The governor says property damage will be in the billions.

Washington, D.C., suffers through its hottest summer—87 days above 90 degrees. Water is rationed; brownouts are routine because utilities can't meet demand for electricity. Federal employees, working half-days in unbearable heat, report an alarming rise in skin cancer across the USA.

Abroad, floods have inundated Bangladesh and Indonesia. The seas are four feet above 1986 levels. The United Nations reports millions will die in famines; shocking climate changes have ruined agriculture.

That sounds far-fetched, but if some scientists' worst fears come true, that could be what our children inherit.

Since the beginning of this century, man has been spewing pollutants into the atmosphere at an ever-increasing rate. Carbon dioxide and chlorofluorocarbons—CFC's—are fouling the air, our life support system. Everything that burns releases carbon dioxide. CFC's are used to make refrigerants, Styrofoam, computer chips, and other products.

In the past century, carbon dioxide in the atmosphere has risen 25 percent. The problem is that carbon dioxide holds in heat, just as the roof of a greenhouse does. That's why the Earth's warming is called the greenhouse effect.

CFC's retain heat, too, and break down the atmosphere's protective layer of ozone. If it is damaged, more of the sun's ultraviolet rays will reach Earth, causing skin cancer and damaging sea life.

Combined with the loss of forests that absorb carbon dioxide, the effects of this pollution could be disastrous. By 2030, Earth's temperature could rise 8 degrees, polar ice caps would melt, weather would change, crops would wilt.

There is growing evidence that these pollutants are reaching ominous levels. At the South Pole, the ozone layer has a "hole" in it—it's been depleted by 40 percent. NASA scientist Robert Watson says: "Global warming is inevitable—it's only a question of magnitude and time."

Some say don't panic, probably nothing will happen. The trouble with that is that we know these pollutants are building, and by the time we are sure of the worst effects, it may be too late. Action is needed, now. The USA must:

—Recognize that global warming may worsen and begin planning responses; more research is needed, too.

—Renew the search for safe, clean alternatives to fossil fuels, nuclear fission, and chlorofluorocarbons.

—Report on the extent of the problem to the world and press for international controls on air pollution.

The possible dimensions of this disaster are too big to just "wait and see." If a runaway train heads for a cliff and the engineer does nothing, the passengers are bound to get hurt. Let's check the brakes before it's too late.

When the students in one of our classes first read this editorial, they found it both persuasive and frightening. The opening scenario of potential disasters—New Orleans under water, unbearable heat, water rationing, floods, ruined agriculture, "alarming rise in skin cancer"—scared the dickens out of many readers. The powerful effect of the opening scenario was increased by the editorial's subsequent use of scientific data: carbon dioxide has increased 25 percent, the ozone layer has been depleted by 40 percent, a

NASA scientist says that "[g]lobal warming is inevitable . . . ," and so forth. Additionally, a plausible cause-and-effect chain explains the approaching disaster: the spewing of pollutants and the cutting down of forests lead to increased CO_2, which traps heat; use of CFC's breaks down the ozone layer, allowing more ultraviolet radiation to reach earth's surface, thereby causing cancer.

Inexperienced students writing a researched argument might be tempted to quote data from this article, which they would then cite as coming from *USA Today*. Unwittingly, they might even distort the article slightly by writing something like this:

> According to *USA Today*, our civilization is on a train ride to disaster unless we put on the brakes. If global warming continues on its present course, by the year 2030, New Orleans will be under water, crops will be wiped out by droughts, . . . [and so forth].

But a second reading of this editorial begins to raise questions and doubts. First of all, the article is couched in "could's" and "might's." If we read carefully, we see that the opening scenario isn't represented as factual, inevitable, or even likely. Rather, it is represented as the "worst fears" of "some scientists." Near the end of the editorial we learn that "[s]ome say don't panic" but we aren't told whether these "some" are respectable scientists, carefree politicians, crackpots, or what. But the most puzzling aspect of this editorial is the gap between the alarming worst-case scenario at the beginning of the editorial and the tepid recommendations at the end. The final "call for action" calls for no real action at all. Recommendations 1 and 3 call for more research and for "international controls on air pollution"— nicely vague terms that create little reader discomfort. The second recommendation—renew the search for safe alternatives—reveals the writer's comfortable American optimism that scientists will find a way out of the dilemma without causing Americans any real distress. (A curious item in Recommendation 2 is the sandwiching of "nuclear fission" between "fossil fuels" and "chlorofluorocarbons." Nuclear fission is *not* a cause of the greenhouse effect and may be a plausible alternative energy source in our effort to combat global warming. But since nuclear power poses other environmental dangers, the writer tosses it in as one of the enemies.) If the "possible dimensions of this disaster" are as great as the opening scenario leads us to believe, then perhaps wrenching changes in our economy are needed to cut down our dependence on fossil fuels.

But what is the actual truth here? How serious is the greenhouse effect and what should the United States do about it? A search for the truth involves us in the sequence of reading strategies suggested in Chapter 2, "Reading Arguments": (1) reading as a believer; (2) reading as a doubter; (3) seeking out alternative views and asking why the various sides disagree with each other; and (4) evaluating the various positions. When our students applied this strategy to the greenhouse effect, they discovered an unsettling uncertainty among scientists about the facts of the case combined with complex disagreements over values. In your search for clarity, what do you do when the experts disagree?

Coping with Uncertainty: When the Experts Disagree

Coping with disagreement among experts is a skill experienced arguers must develop. If there were no disagreements, of course, there would be no need for argument. It is important to realize that experts can look at the same data, can analyze the same arguments, can listen to the same authorities, and still reach different conclusions. Seldom will one expert's argument triumph over another's in a field of dissenting claims. More often, one expert's argument will modify another's and in turn will be modified by yet another. Your own expertise is not a function of your ability to choose the "right" argument, but of your ability to listen to alternative viewpoints, to understand why people disagree, and to synthesize your own argument from those disagreements.

Here briefly is our analysis of some of the disagreements about the greenhouse effect.

QUESTIONS OF FACT   At the heart of the controversy is the question "How serious is the greenhouse effect?" On the basis of our own research, we discovered that scientists agree on one fact: The amount of carbon dioxide in the earth's atmosphere has increased 7 percent since accurate measurements were first taken during the International Geophysical Year 1957/58. Additionally, scientists seem agreed that the percentage of carbon dioxide has increased steadily since the start of the Industrial Revolution in the 1860s. The statement in the *USA Today* editorial that carbon dioxide has increased by 25 percent is generally accepted by scientists as an accurate estimate of the total increase since 1860.

Where scientists disagree is on the projected effect of this increase. Predictions of global warming are derived from computer models, none of which seems able to encompass all the factors that contribute to global climate, particularly ocean currents and the movements of air masses above the oceans. Because of the enormous complexity of these factors, projections about the future differ considerably from scientist to scientist. *USA Today* took one of the worst-case projections.

QUESTIONS OF VALUE   There is also widespread disagreement on what actions the United States or other countries should take in response to the potential warming of the earth. In general, these disputes stem from disagreements about value. In particular, participants in the conversation give different answers to the following questions:

1. In the face of uncertain threat, do we react as if the threat were definite or do we wait and see? If we wait and see, will we be inviting disaster?

2. How much faith can we place in science and technology? Some people, arguing that necessity is the mother of invention, assume that scientists will get us out of this mess. Others believe that technofixes are no longer possible.

3. How much change in our way of life can we tolerate? What, for example, would be the consequences to our economy and to our standard of living if we waged an all-out war on global warming by making drastic reductions, say, in our use of carbon fuels? To what extent are we willing to give up the benefits of industrialization?

4. How much economic disruption can we expect other nations to tolerate? What worldwide economic forces, for example, are making it profitable to cut down and burn tropical rain forests? What would happen to the economies of tropical countries if international controls suddenly prevented further destruction of rain forests? What changes in our own economy would have to take place?

Our whole point here is that the problem of global warming is interwoven into a gigantic web of other problems and issues. One of the benefits you gain from researching a complex technical and value-laden issue such as global warming is learning how to cope with ambiguity.

What advice can we give, therefore, when the experts disagree? Here is the strategy we tend to use. First, we try to ferret out the facts that all sides agree on. These facts give us a starting place on which to build an analysis. In the greenhouse controversy, the fact that all sides agree that the amount of CO_2 in the atmosphere has increased by 25 percent and that this amount increases the percentage of infrared radiation absorbed in the atmosphere suggests that there is scientific cause for concern.

Second, we try to determine if there is a majority position among experts. Sometimes dissenting voices stem from a small but prolific group of persons on the fringe. Our instincts are to trust the majority opinions of experts, even though we realize that revolutions in scientific thought almost always start with minority groups. In the case of the greenhouse effect, our own research suggests that the majority of scientists are cautiously concerned but not predicting doomsday. There seems to be a general consensus that increased greenhouse gases will contribute to global warming but how much and how soon, they won't say.

Third, we try as much as possible to focus, not on the testimony of experts, but on the data the experts use in their testimony. In other words, we try to learn as much as possible about the scientific or technical problem and immerse ourselves in the raw data. Doing so in the case of the greenhouse effect helped us appreciate the problems of creating computer models of global climate and especially of gathering data about oceanic impact on climate.

Finally, we try to determine our own position on the values issues at stake because, inescapably, these values influence the position we ultimately take. For example, the authors of this text tend to be pessimistic about tech-nofixes for most environmental problems. We doubt that scientists will solve the problem of greenhouse gases either through finding alternatives to petrocarbon fuels or by discovering ways to eliminate or counteract green-house gases. We also tend not to be risk-takers on environmental matters. Thus we prefer to take vigorous action now to slow the increase of green-house gases rather than take a wait-and-see attitude. The conclusion of our own research, then, is that the *USA Today* editorial is irresponsible in two ways: It uses unfair scare tactics in the opening scenario by overstating the fears of most scientists, yet in its conclusion it doesn't call for enough dis-ruption of our present way of life.

What we have attempted to do in the previous section is show you how we try to reach a responsible position in the face of uncertainty. We cannot claim that our position is the right one. We can only claim that it is a reason-able one and a responsible one—responsible to our own understanding of the facts and to our own declaration of values.

WRITING YOUR OWN ARGUMENT: USING EVIDENCE PERSUASIVELY

Once you have arrived at a position on an issue, often after having written a draft that enables you to explore and clarify your own views, you need to select the best evidence possible and to use it persuasively. Whether your evidence comes from research or from personal experience, the following guidelines may be helpful.

When Possible, Select Your Data from Sources Your Reader Trusts

Other things being equal, choose data from sources you think your reader will trust. After immersing yourself in an issue, you will get a sense of who the participants in a conversation are and what their reputations tend to be. One needs to know the political biases of sources and the extent to which a source has a financial or personal investment in the outcome of a contro-versy. In the greenhouse controversy, for example, well-known writers Carl Sagan and Dixie Lee Ray both hold Ph.D. degrees in science, and both have national reputations for speaking out in the popular press on technical and scientific issues. Carl Sagan, however, is an environmentalist while Dixie Lee Ray tends to support business and industry. To some audiences, neither of these writers will be as persuasive as more cautious and less visible scien-tists who publish primarily in scientific journals. Similarly, citing a conserv-ative magazine such as *Reader's Digest* is apt to be ineffective to liberal audi-ences, just as citing a Sierra Club publication would be ineffective to conservatives.

Increase Persuasiveness of Factual Data by Ensuring Recency, Representativeness, and Sufficiency

Other things being equal, choose data that are recent, representative, and sufficient. The more your data meet these criteria, the more persuasive they are.

Recency: Although some timeless issues don't depend on recent evidence, most issues, especially those related to science and technology or to current political and economic issues, depend on up-to-date information. Make sure your supporting evidence is the most recent you can find.

Representativeness: Supporting examples are more persuasive when the audience believes they are typical examples instead of extreme cases or rare occurrences. Many arguments against pornography, for example, use violent pornography or child pornography as evidence, even though these are extreme cases quite different from the erotica associated, say, with *Playboy.* These nonrepresentative examples are ineffective if one's purpose is to include such publications as *Playboy* in the category of pornography. Assuring representativeness is an especially important concern of statisticians, who seek random samples to avoid bias toward one point of view. Seeking representative examples helps you guard against selective use of data—starting with a claim and then choosing only those data that support it, instead of letting the claim grow out of a careful consideration of all the data.

Sufficiency: One of the most common reasoning fallacies, called "hasty generalization" (see Appendix 1), occurs when a person leaps to a sweeping generalization based on only one or two instances. The criterion of sufficiency (which means having enough examples to justify your point) helps you guard against hasty generalization. The key here isn't to cite every possible example, but to convince your audience that the examples you have cited don't exhaust your whole supply. In our experience, lack of sufficiency occurs frequently in personal experience arguments. The student praised earlier for her personal experience data in an argument about rural schools suffers from this problem in the following paragraph:

> My primary reason for supporting the small, rural grade schools over the larger urban schools is the amount of learning that occurs. I am my own proof. I was the only member of my grade from the third to the eighth grade at Fergus Grade School. I relished the privilege of being able to work on two chapters of math, instead of one, especially if I enjoyed the subject. Upon graduation from the eighth grade, I attended a large high school and discovered that I had a better background than students from larger grade schools. I got straight A's.

The problem here is that the writer's one example—herself—isn't sufficient for supporting the claim that rural schools provide quality learning. To support that claim, she would need either more examples or statistical data about the later achievements of students who attended rural grade schools.

In Citing Evidence, Distinguish Fact from Inference or Opinion

In citing research data, you should be careful to distinguish facts from inferences or opinions. A *fact* is a noncontroversial piece of data that is verifiable through observation or through appeal to communally accepted authorities. Although the distinction between a fact and an inference is a fuzzy one philosophically, at a pragmatic level all of the following can loosely be classified as facts.

The Declaration of Independence was signed in 1776.

An earthquake took place in San Francisco on the opening day of the World Series in 1989.

The amount of carbon dioxide in the atmosphere has increased by 7 percent since 1955.

An *inference,* on the other hand, is an interpretation or explanation of the facts that may be reasonably doubted. This distinction is important because, when reading as a doubter, you often call into question a writer's inferences. If you treat these inferences as facts, you are apt to cite them as facts in your own arguments, thereby opening yourself up to easy rebuttal. For the most part, inferences should be handled as testimony rather than as fact.

WEAK: Flohn informs us that the warming of the atmosphere will lead to damaging droughts by the year 2035. [treats Flohn's inference as a fact about global warming]

BETTER: Flohn interprets the data pessimistically. He believes that the warming of the atmosphere will lead to damaging droughts by the year 2035. [makes it clear that Flohn's view is an inference, not a fact]

To Use Evidence Persuasively, Position It Effectively

Whenever possible, place evidence favorable to your point in rhetorically strong positions in your essay; tuck opposing evidence into rhetorically inconspicuous places. Consider the case of Professor Nutt, who was asked to write a letter of recommendation for Elliot Weasel for a management trainee position at a bank. Professor Nutt remembered Weasel with mixed emotions. On the one hand, Weasel was the most brilliant student Nutt had ever had in class—an excellent mathematical mind, creative imagination, strong writing skills. On the other hand, Weasel was slovenly, rude, irresponsible, and moody. In the first case below, Nutt decides to give Weasel a positive recommendation.

POSITIVE RECOMMENDATION FOR WEASEL

Although Elliot Weasel was somewhat temperamental in my class and occasionally lacked people skills, these problems were the result of brilliance. I am convinced that Weasel is one of the most highly intelligent students I have ever encountered. In fact, in one of my business management classes, he wrote the best term paper I have ever received in five years of teaching management. I gave him an A+ and even learned some new insights from his paper. If he could learn to interact more effectively with others, he would become a superb manager. In sum, I give him a quite high recommendation.

In the next case, Nutt's recommendation is negative.

NEGATIVE RECOMMENDATION FOR WEASEL

Although Elliott Weasel is one of the most intelligent students I have ever encountered, he was somewhat temperamental in my class and occasionally lacked people skills. He would come to class dressed sloppily with unkempt hair and dirty-looking clothes. He also seemed like a loner, was frequently moody, and once refused to participate in a group project. Thus my recommendation of him is mixed. He's highly intelligent and an excellent writer, but I found him rude and hard to like.

Let's analyze the difference between these versions. In the first version, Nutt places the anti-Weasel data in subordinate clauses and phrases and places the pro-Weasel data in main slots, particularly the main clause of the first sentence. The effect is to highlight Weasel's strong points. Because the opening sentence ends with an emphasis on Weasel's brilliance, Nutt brings in additional data to back up the assertion that Weasel is brilliant.

In the second version, Nutt reverses this procedure by putting pro-Weasel data in subordinate positions and highlighting the anti-Weasel data in main clauses. Because the opening sentence ends with an emphasis on Weasel's moodiness and lack of people skills, Nutt brings in additional data to back up these points. Thus through selection of data (deciding which facts to put in and which ones to leave out) and through loading of data into main or subordinate slots in the paragraph, Nutt creates a positive impression in the first version and a negative impression in the second. Although neither version could be regarded as untruthful, neither version tells the "whole truth" either, because the necessity to interpret the data means commitment toward some sort of claim, which necessarily shapes the selection and placement of evidence.

□ FOR CLASS DISCUSSION

Suppose that you developed a questionnaire to ascertain students' satisfaction with your college library as a place to study. Suppose further that you got the following responses to one of your questions (numbers in brackets indicate percentage of total respondents who checked each response):

The library provides a quiet place to study.

Strongly agree (10%)
Agree (40%)
Undecided (5%)
Disagree (35%)
Strongly disagree (10%)

Without telling any lies of fact, you can report these data so that they place the current library atmosphere in either favorable or unfavorable light. Working individually or in small groups, use the above data to complete the following sentences:

> There seemed to be considerable satisfaction with the library as a quiet place to study. In response to our questionnaire ... [complete this sentence by selecting data from the above responses].

> Students seem dissatisfied with the noise level of the library. In response to our questionnaire ... [complete this sentence by selecting data from the above responses].

CONCLUSION

Supporting your reasons with evidence or chains of other reasons is essential if you hope to make your arguments persuasive. As we have seen, evidence includes facts, examples, statistics, testimony, and other forms of data, and it can come from personal experience as well as from reading and research. For many issues, your search for evidence leads you into an ambiguous arena of conflicting views. Adapting to a world where experts disagree requires strategies for sorting out the causes of disagreement and establishing reasonable grounds to justify the claims you finally wish to assert. Learning how to evaluate evidence in your sources and how to use evidence responsibly and persuasively is an important skill that develops gradually. We hope this chapter gives you some helpful groundwork on which to build.

In the next chapters we will consider further strategies for making your arguments as persuasive as possible by turning our attention increasingly toward audience.

■ WRITING ASSIGNMENTS FOR CHAPTERS 4–6

The first four writing options below are short, skill-building exercises that we call "microthemes." They can be done as overnight out-of-class assignments or as in-class writing or group discussion exercises. These one- or two-paragraph assignments are most successful if approached like games. They are designed to help you learn argumentative "moves" that you can apply later to longer, more formal essays.

The last option is a formal writing assignment that asks you to construct a logical, well-developed argument, putting into practice the principles of structure discussed in Chapters 4–6.

OPTION 1:   *A MICROTHEME THAT SUPPORTS A REASON WITH PERSONAL EXPERI-ENCE DATA*   Write a one- or two-paragraph argument in which you support one of the following enthymemes using evidence from personal experience. Most of your microtheme should be devoted to use of personal experience to support the stated reason. However, also include a brief passage supporting the implied warrant for your chosen enthymeme. The opening sentence of your microtheme should be the enthymeme itself, which serves as the thesis statement for your argument.

1. Children should have hobbies because, among other things, hobbies fill up leisure time with enjoyable activity. (Support the stated reason with examples of how hobbies in your life have helped you fill up leisure time with enjoyable activities. Support the warrant by arguing that enjoyable use of leisure time is a good thing for children.)

2. After-school jobs are generally not a good idea for teenagers because they take up too much valuable study time.

3. After-school jobs are beneficial for teenagers because they teach time management.

4. Another reason to oppose a state sales tax is that it is so annoying.

5. X (a teacher/professor of your choosing) is an ineffective teacher because, among other things, he (she) doesn't design homework effectively to promote real learning.

6. X (a teacher/professor of your choosing) is an outstanding teacher because he (she) generously spends so much time outside of class counseling students with personal problems.

7. Any enthymeme (a claim with a because clause) of your choice that can be supported through personal experience. Clear your enthymeme with your instructor before drafting your microtheme.

OPTION 2:   *A MICROTHEME THAT USES EVIDENCE FROM RESEARCH*   The purpose of this microtheme is to help you learn how to support reasons with evidence gathered from research. The following presentation of data attempts to simulate the kinds of research evidence one might typically gather on note cards during a research project. (See Chapters 16 and 17 for further advice on incorporating research data into your own writing. For this assignment, assume you are writing for a popular magazine so that you do not need to use academic citations.)

The situation: By means of startling "before and after" photographs of formerly obese people, the commercial diet industry heavily advertises rapid weight loss diets that use liquids and powders or special low-calorie frozen dinners. **Your task:** Drawing on the following data, write a short argument warning people of the hazards of these diets.

Source: Representative Ron Wyden (D—Oregon), chairman of a congressional subcommittee investigating the diet industry:

- Wyden fears that diet programs now include many shoddy companies that use misleading advertisements and provide inadequate medical supervision of their clients.
- "This industry has been built almost overnight on a very shaky foundation."
- "All the evidence says that losing large amounts of weight very fast does more harm than good."
- Wyden believes that the diet industry may need to be federally regulated.

Source: Theodore B. VanItallie, M.D., a founder of the Obesity Research Center at St. Luke's Roosevelt Hospital Center in New York:

- Rapid weight loss systems (such as liquid diets) were originally designed for morbidly obese individuals.
- For people who are only slightly overweight, rapid weight loss can be hazardous.
- When weight loss is too rapid, the body begins using lean muscle mass for fuel instead of excess fat. The result is a serious protein deficiency that can bring on heart irregularities.
- "If more than 25 percent of lost weight is lean body mass, the stage is set not only for early regain of lost weight but for a higher incidence of fatigue, hair loss, skill changes, depression and other undesirable side effects."

Source: Bonnie Blodgett, freelance writer on medical/health issues:

- Rapid weight loss may accelerate formation of gallstones. 179 people are currently suing a major diet company because of gallstone complications while pursuing the company's diet. The company denies responsibility.
- For every five people who start a commercial weight-loss program, only one stays with it long enough to lose a significant amount of weight.
- Up to 90 percent of dieters who lose more than 25 pounds gain it all back within two years.
- Only one in fifty maintains the weight loss for seven years.
- The best way to lose weight is through increased exercise, moderate reduction of calories, and a lifelong change in eating habits.
- Unless one is grossly obese and dieting under a physician's supervision, one should strive to lose no more than 1 or 2 pounds per week.

Source: Philip Kern, M.D., in a study appearing in *The New England Journal of Medicine*:

- Rapid weight loss programs result in the "yo-yo" syndrome—a pattern of compulsive fasting followed by compulsive bingeing.
- This pattern may upset the body's metabolism by producing an enzyme called lipoprotein lipase.
- This protein helps restore fat cells shrunken by dieting.
- It apparently causes formerly fat people to crave fatty foods, thereby promoting regain of lost weight.*

OPTION 3:   *A MICROTHEME THAT DRAWS ON A NEWSPAPER STORY FOR DATA*   Using the following newspaper article, "Deaths Spur New Call for Child-Labor Crackdown," as a source, write a microtheme that could be part of an argument calling for increased enforcement of child-labor laws. Begin your microtheme with the following sentence: "Recent evidence suggests that the child-labor problem is more severe than most people realize." Then select data from the story that focus on the extent and severity of the problem.

DEATHS SPUR NEW CALL FOR CHILD-LABOR CRACKDOWN

Two children were killed and 4,000 injured on the job in Washington state last year, Department of Labor and Industries officials said yesterday in proposing legislation to protect youngsters in the workplace.

The department investigated 395 of the 4,000 cases and found nearly 44 percent of the employers were violating child-labor laws at the time of a minor's injury.

"Society places a high value on the well-being of children," said Joe Dear, director of the agency. "That should extend to children in the workplace. They're more vulnerable. They're more susceptible to intimidation by employers, and they're less knowledgeable about their rights."

It is the third year in a row that the Labor and Industries Department has drafted a bill to strengthen its enforcement capabilities in regulating child-labor laws.

In the past two sessions, the legislation passed the Democrat-controlled House and died in the Republican-dominated Senate.

Attention was focused on child-labor issues in October 1989 when a 14-year-old boy died after being struck by two cars while selling candy door-to-door in the Graham area south of Tacoma.

The state is seeking an injunction to stop the operation of his employer, Teens for Action Against Drugs. The state contends the boy was not supervised properly.

The Pierce County prosecutor's office also has filed criminal misdemeanor charges against owners Christopher and Nikita Spice, accusing them of failure to register the company with the state, failure to secure work permits for employees and variances for children under 16, and false advertising.

---

*   Source of the above data is Bonnie Blodgett, "The Diet Biz," *Glamour* January 1991: 136ff.

The other death involved a 12-year-old Oregon boy struck by a car in the Federal Way area. Officials could not provide further information about his case.

In other incidents, a 16-year-old Spanaway boy cut off three fingers while using a table saw, a 15-year-old girl was burned by a motorized iron in Mount Vernon, and a 17-year-old boy was burned on the face while pouring molten aluminum in a Spokane foundry.

Dear said all were performing duties prohibited by child-labor laws. In its year-long study, the department found injured children in every industry, but particularly in fast-food and retail businesses.

Another study conducted by the University of Washington, Harborview Medical Center and the Labor and Industries Department found 17,000 children under 18 were hurt on the job from 1986 to 1989.

The proposed legislation would allow the department to impose civil penalties on employers who violate the law and to seek felony prosecution for serious violations. That could mean five years in prison and a fine of $10,000, Dear said.

For less serious violations, the department could issue citations, and employers could avoid penalty by complying with the regulations.

The maximum charge an employer now faces is a misdemeanor, with a fine of up to $1,000.

OPTION 4:   *A MICROTHEME THAT USES STATISTICAL DATA TO SUPPORT A POINT*
Defend one of the following theses:

Thesis A—"Women (blacks) made only negligible progress toward job equality between 1972 and 1981."

Thesis B—"Women (blacks) made significant progress toward job equality between 1972 and 1981."

Support your thesis with evidence drawn from the table on pages 136–37. You can write your microtheme about the job progress of either women or blacks.

OPTION 5:   *A FORMAL ARGUMENT USING AT LEAST TWO REASONS IN SUPPORT OF YOUR CLAIM*   Write a multiparagraph essay in which you develop two or more reasons in support of your thesis or claim. Each of your reasons should be summarizable in a because clause attached to your claim. If you have more than two reasons, develop your most important reason last. Give your essay a self-announcing structure in which you highlight your claim at the end of your introduction and begin your body paragraphs with clearly stated reasons. Open your essay with an attention-grabbing lead that attracts your readers' interest; your introduction should also explain the issue being addressed as well as provide whatever background is needed.

Note that this assignment does not ask you to refute opposing views. Nevertheless, it is a good idea to summarize an opposing view briefly to help the reader see the issue more clearly. Because you will not be refuting this view, the best place to summarize it is in your introduction prior to presenting your own claim. (If you place an opposing view in the body of your essay, its prominence obligates you to refute it or concede to it—issues addressed in Chapter 8 of this text. If you briefly summarize an opposing

TABLE for Option 4.
Employed persons, by sex, race, and occupation, 1972 and 1981 (selected occupations)

Occupation	1972			1981		
	Total Employed (1,000)	Percentage		Total Employed (1,000)	Percentage	
		Female	Black and Other		Female	Black and Other
Professional, Technical	11,538	39.3	7.2	16,420	44.6	9.9
Accountants	720	21.7	4.3	1,126	38.5	9.9
Dentists	108	1.9	5.6	130	4.6	6.2
Engineers	1,111	0.8	3.4	1,537	4.4	7.3
Lawyers	322	3.8	1.9	581	14.1	4.6
Librarians	158	81.6	7.0	192	82.8	5.7
Physicians	332	10.1	8.2	454	13.7	14.5
Registered nurses	807	97.6	8.2	1,654	96.8	12.3
College teachers	464	28.0	9.2	585	35.2	9.2
Managers, Administrators	8,081	17.6	4.0	11,540	27.5	5.8
Bank officers	430	19.0	2.6	696	37.5	5.5
Office managers	317	41.9	1.0	504	70.6	4.0
Sales managers	574	15.7	1.6	720	26.5	4.6

Clerical Workers	14,329	75.6	8.7	18,564	80.5	11.6
Bank tellers	290	87.5	4.9	569	93.5	7.6
File clerks	274	84.9	18.0	315	83.8	22.9
Secretaries	2,964	99.1	5.2	3,917	99.1	7.2
Skilled Crafts	10,867	3.6	6.9	12,662	6.3	8.5
Carpenters	1,052	0.5	5.9	1,122	1.9	5.8
Construction	2,261	0.6	9.0	2,593	1.9	10.2
Mechanics	1,040	0.5	8.5	1,249	0.6	8.7
Transportation	3,233	4.2	14.8	3,476	8.9	15.5
Bus drivers	253	34.1	17.1	360	47.2	21.1
Truck drivers	1,449	0.6	14.4	1,878	2.7	13.9
Unskilled Labor	4,242	6.0	20.2	4,583	11.5	16.5
Service Workers	9,584	57.0	18.5	12,391	59.2	18.4
Food service	3,286	69.8	13.9	4,682	66.2	14.0
Nurses' aides	1,513	87.0	24.6	1,995	89.2	24.3
Domestic cleaners	715	97.2	64.2	468	95.1	51.5

view in the introduction, however, you use it merely to clarify the issue and hence do not need to treat it at length.)

The following essay illustrates this assignment. It was written by a freshman student whose first language is Vietnamese rather than English. Additional essays written to the same assignment include Sandra Nelson's essay in Chapter 3 (pp. 75–77) and the set of essays (some strong, some weak) in the "norming exercise" in Appendix 3 (see pp. 460–67). This exercise is aimed at helping you internalize criteria for a strong performance on this assignment.

■

CHOOSE LIFE!

Dao Do (student)

Should euthanasia be legalized? My classmate Paula and her family think it should be. Paula's grandmother was blind from diabetes. For three years she was constantly in and out of the hospital, but then her kidneys shut down and she became a victim of life supports. After three months of suffering, she finally gave up. Paula believes the three-month period was unnecessary, for her grandmother didn't have to go through all of that suffering. If euthanasia were legalized, her family would have put her to sleep the minute her condition worsened. Then, she wouldn't have had to feel pain, and she would have died in peace and with dignity. Despite Paula's strong argument for legalizing euthanasia, I find it is wrong.

First, euthanasia is wrong because no one has the right to take the life of another person. Just as our society discourages suicide, it should discourage euthanasia because in both the person is running away from life and its responsibilities. Some people say that euthanasia or suicide will end suffering and pain. But what proofs do they have for such a claim? Death is still mysterious to us; therefore, we do not know whether death will end suffering and pain or not. What seems to be the real claim is that death to those with illnesses will end *our* pain. Such pain involves worrying over them, paying their medical bills, and giving up so much of our time. Their deaths end our pain rather than theirs. And for that reason, euthanasia is a selfish act, for the outcome of euthanasia benefits us, the nonsufferers, more. Once the sufferers pass away, we can go back to our normal lives.

My second opposition to euthanasia is its unfavorable consequences. Today, euthanasia is performed on those who we think are suffering from incurable diseases or brain death. But what about tomorrow? People might use euthanasia to send old parents to death just to get rid of them faster, so they can get to the money, the possessions, and the real estate.

Just think of all the murder cases on TV where children killed their parents so they can get to the fortune. Legalizing euthanasia will increase the number of these murder cases. The right of euthanasia not only encourages corruption, it encourages discrimination. People who suffer pain would be put into categories according to which should live longer and which shouldn't. Perhaps poor people or people of color will be more apt to be euthanized than rich people, or perhaps people with AIDS will be euthanized sooner so that society won't have to spend money on this very expensive disease.

My third objection to euthanasia is that it fails to see the value in suffering. Suffering is a part of life. We only see the value of suffering if we look deeply within our suffering. For example, I never thought my crippled uncle from Vietnam was a blessing to my grandmother until I talked to her. My mother's little brother was born prematurely. As a result of oxygen and nutrition deficiency, he was born crippled. His tiny arms and legs were twisted around his body, preventing him from any normal movements such as walking, picking up things, and lying down. He could only sit. Therefore, his world was very limited, for it consisted of his own room and the garden viewed through his window. Because of his disabilities, my grandmother had to wash him, feed him, and watch him constantly. It was hard but she managed to care for him for forty-three years. He passed away after the death of my grandfather in 1982. Bringing this situation out of Vietnam and into Western society shows the difference between Vietnamese and West's views. In West, my uncle might have been euthanized as a baby. Supporters of euthanasia would have said he wouldn't have any quality of life and that he would have been a great burden. But he was not a burden on my grandmother. She enjoyed taking care of him, and he was always her company after her other children got married and moved away. Neither one of them saw his defect as a form of suffering because it brought them closer together. My uncle was there for us to be thankful to God for not letting us be born with such disabilities. We should appreciate our lives, for they are not so limited.

In conclusion, let us be reminded that we do not have the right to take life, but we do have the right to live. We are free to live life to its fullest. Why anticipate death when it ends everything? Why choose a path we know nothing of? There's always room for hope. In hoping, we'll see that forced death is never a solution. Until we can understand the world after, we should choose to live and not to die.

7

Moving Your Audience: Audience-based Reasons, *Ethos*, and *Pathos*

In Chapters 5 and 6 we discussed *logos*—the logical structure of reasons and evidence in an argument. When writers focus primarily on *logos*, they often desire to clarify their own thinking as much as to persuade. In this chapter we shift our attention increasingly toward persuasion, in which our goal is to move our audience as much as possible toward our own position on an issue. Specifically, we discuss strategies for developing arguments that are rooted in your audience's values and beliefs (audience-based reasons); that portray you, the writer, as credible and trustworthy (*ethos*); and that appeal effectively to your audience's feelings and emotions (*pathos*).

Although we talk about persuasion in this chapter, we don't intend the Sophists' meaning of *persuasion* that was examined in the debate between Socrates and Callicles. As you recall, Callicles' interest was not in the truth, but simply in winning the debate. For Callicles, truth became whatever the victor proclaimed. Our meaning of persuasion presupposes an arguer whose position is derived from a reasoned investigation of evidence and a commitment to consistent and articulable values and beliefs. Persuasion is the art of making that position as forceful as possible to different audiences.

STARTING FROM YOUR READERS' BELIEFS: THE POWER OF AUDIENCE-BASED REASONS

Persuasive writing begins with an assessment of your audience's values. What is a good reason to you might not be a good reason to others.

As Aristotle showed, real-world arguments are based on enthymemes, which are incomplete logical statements that depend for their completeness on the audience's acceptance of underlying assumptions, values, or beliefs (see pp. 100–101). Finding audience-based reasons means discovering enthymemes that are effectively rooted in your audience's values.

Difference between Writer- and Audience-based Reasons

To illustrate the difference between writer- and audience-based reasons, let's return to Young Person's argument with Parents over her curfew time. As you may recall from Chapter 1, Young Person tried a couple of arguments that didn't work:

> I should be allowed to stay out until 2:00 A.M. (1) because I am sixteen years old and (2) because all my friends' parents let them stay out until 2:00 A.M.

The reason and grounds for both arguments are irrefutable: Young Person has the documents to prove she's sixteen, and she can cite *ad nauseum* all her fortunate friends whose parents let them stay out until the wee hours. Her arguments fail because both of the warrants, which seem perfectly reasonable to Young Person, are unacceptable to Parents.

Warrant for 1:   All sixteen-year-olds should be allowed to stay out until 2:00 A.M.

Warrant for 2:   The rules in this family should be based on the rules in other families.

To put it another way, Young Person's arguments aren't rooted in Parents' values. She uses writer-based rather than audience-based reasons.

Thus Young Person's rhetorical problem is that she has linked her reasons to her own values instead of to values that she and Parents can share. In effect, she needs to identify shared warrants that won't require extensive backing to gain her parents' acceptance. This search for shared warrants can lead to clarification of the issue and hence will influence the content and shape of the argument itself.

Perhaps Young Person could try a reason like this:

> I should be able to set my own curfew because that will give me the freedom to demonstrate my own maturity to you.

Or, if this reason takes wholesomeness further than she wants to take it, she might put her reason this way:

I should be able to set my own curfew because I need enough freedom to learn through my own mistakes.

These reasons probably link to her parents' values—the desire to see their daughter grow in maturity—and make the case that maturity is best demonstrated when a person is free rather than constrained. We can't say whether this argument will win the night for Young Person, but we can say that it is much more persuasive than giving reasons based only on Young Person's values.

Next let's take a more serious example. Suppose you believed that the government should build a new power generation dam on the nearby Rapid River—a project bitterly opposed by environmentalist groups. Which of the following two arguments would be the most persuasive to this audience (people with strong environmentalist leanings)?

1. The federal government should push ahead with its plan to build a new power generation dam on the Rapid River because the only alternative is a coal-fired plant or a nuclear plant, both of which are much greater environmental hazards than clean, water-generated power.
2. The federal government should push ahead with its plan to build a new power generation dam on the Rapid River because this area needs cheap electricity in order to stimulate the growth of heavy industry.

Although intuitively we know that Argument 1 would be more powerful to environmentalists, let's analyze both arguments to see why.

Clearly, the warrant of Argument 1 ("Given alternative means of generating power, we should choose those least hazardous to the environment") is rooted in the values and beliefs of environmentalists, whereas the warrant of Argument 2 ("Growth of industry is good") is apt to make them wince. To environmentalists, industry is not a good: It means more congestion, more smokestacks, and more pollution. On the other hand, Argument 2 might be very persuasive to out-of-work laborers, to whom industry means jobs.

From the perspective of *logos* alone, Arguments 1 and 2 are both sound. Both are internally consistent, and both proceed from reasonable premises. But as pieces of persuasion—arguments that work, that move their intended audiences—they have quite different appeals. Argument 1 proceeds from the values of people committed primarily to protecting the environment; Argument 2 proceeds from the values of people committed primarily to economic growth and jobs.

Of course, it should be understood that neither argument proves that the government should build the dam, for both arguments are open to refutation and counterargument. Facing Argument 1, for example, thoroughgoing environmentalists might counter by arguing that the government shouldn't build any power plant at all. They could argue that energy conservation would obviate the need for a new power plant. Or they might argue that building a dam hurts the environment in ways other than pollution. Our point, then, isn't that Argument 1 will persuade environmentalists. Rather, our point is that Argument 1 will be more persuasive than 2 because it is rooted in beliefs and values that the intended audience shares.

Let's take a third example by returning to the argument we presented in Chapter 1, student Gordon Adams' request for exemption from Arizona State University's (ASU's) numeracy requirement. Gordon's central argument, as you will recall, was that as a lawyer he would have no use for algebra. Placed in Toulmin's terms, Gordon's argument goes like this:

CLAIM:	I should be exempted from the ASU algebra requirement.
STATED REASON:	because in my chosen field of law I will have absolutely no use for algebra
GROUNDS:	testimony from lawyers and others that lawyers never use algebra
WARRANT:	(left largely unstated and undeveloped in Gordon's argument) General education requirements should be based on career utility. (More narrowly: If a course doesn't meet an individual student's particular career need, then it should not be required for that student.)
BACKING:	(not provided) arguments that career utility should be the chief criterion for requiring General Studies courses

In our discussions of this case with students and faculty, students generally vote to waive Gordon's numeracy requirement, whereas faculty generally vote against the request. Disapproval of the request, in fact, was the decision at ASU, where the University Standards Committee denied Gordon's appeal, thus requiring him to take college algebra and delaying his entrance into law school.

Why do faculty generally differ from students on this issue? Mainly because faculty won't accept Gordon's warrant that usefulness for careers should be the chief criterion for determining general education requirements. General education, in the view of most teachers, immerses students in the traditional liberal arts, which provide a base of common learning that links us to the past and that teaches us general principles of analysis and interpretation useful in any field. Algebra is required because it is one of the traditional liberal arts, a means of teaching students a mathematical way of knowing and thinking.

Gordon's argument, instead of being rooted in the audience's value system, directly attacks it. Moreover, his argument further threatens faculty because approving Gordon's appeal would set a dangerous precedent. It would open a floodgate of student requests to waive literature, art, history, or any other general education requirement on the grounds of its uselessness for a chosen career.

How might Gordon have created a more persuasive argument? In our view, Gordon may have been more successful had he adopted the faculty's belief in the value of the numeracy requirement and argued that he had met this requirement through alternative means. His best approach, we believe, would have been to base his argument on an enthymeme like this:

> I should be exempted from the algebra requirement because my unusual background as a machine and welding contractor and inventor has already provided me with an equivalent kind of mathematical knowledge.

Following this audience-based approach, he would remove from his argument all the material about algebra's uselessness for lawyers and use the saved space to document more fully his creative achievements and the mathematical ways of thinking he acquired as a welding contractor and an inventor, designer, and maker of racing bikes. This approach, besides accepting the audience's values, would also reduce faculty and administrative fear of setting precedents, because few students would come to ASU with Gordon's unusual background, and those who did could apply for similar exemption. We can't say such an argument would have swayed the committee. We can say it would have been more persuasive than his direct attack on his audience's value system.

On the other hand, arguments like Gordon's that call fundamental assumptions into doubt are potentially valuable. Although he probably would have greatly improved his chances of getting a waiver by accepting his audience's values and beliefs, his challenge of those beliefs might in the long run contribute to systemic change that he values. By arguing that he's a special case, Gordon would have left the rule unchallenged. His requirement would have been waived, but no other cases would have been affected by that ruling. His is a high-risk/high-gain strategy that, while unsuccessful, may place seeds of doubt and questions that could potentially bring about changes in the requirements and affect thousands of students.

□ FOR CLASS DISCUSSION

Working in groups, decide which of the following pairs of reasons is likely to be more persuasive to the specified audience. Be prepared to explain your reasoning to the class as a whole by writing out the implied warrant for each because clause and deciding whether the specific audience would be likely to grant it.

1. Audience: a prospective employer
   a. I would be a good candidate for a summer job at the Happy Trails Dude Ranch because I have always wanted to spend a summer in the mountains and because I like to ride horses.
   b. I would be a good candidate for a summer job at the Happy Trails Dude Ranch because I am a hard worker, because I have had considerable experience serving others in my volunteer work at Mercy Hospital, and because I know how to make guests feel welcome and relaxed.
2. Audience: a prospective buyer of encyclopedias
   a. You should buy these encyclopedias because they are designed especially for students and are written in a more popular, fun-to-read style than its major competitors' encyclopedias.

b. You should buy these encyclopedias because then I will win my company's sales award and my wife and I will win a free trip to Hawaii.

3. Audience: a group of people who oppose the present grading system on the grounds that it is too competitive

a. We should keep the present grading system because it prepares people for the competitive world of business.

b. We should keep the present grading system because it tells students there are certain standards of excellence that must be met if individuals are to reach their full potential.

4. Audience: young people ages fifteen to twenty-five

a. You should become a vegetarian because an all-vegetable diet is better for your heart than a diet that includes meat.

b. You should become a vegetarian because that will help eliminate the suffering of animals caused by factory farming.

Finding Audience-based Reasons: Asking Questions about Your Audience

As the above exercise makes clear, reasons are most persuasive when linked to the audience's values. This principle seems simple enough, yet it is an easy one to forget. Among the most common complaints employers have about job candidates during interviews is candidates' tendency to emphasize what the company can do for the candidate instead of what the candidate can do for the company. Job search experts agree that the best way to prepare for a job interview is to study everything you can about the company in order to relate your skills to the company's problems and needs. The same advice applies to writers of arguments.

To find out all you can about your audience, we recommend that you ask yourself, early in the writing process, a series of questions that can be grouped into five categories:

1. Who is your audience? Are you writing directly to a decision maker, such as a proposal to a board of directors to start a new research and development project in your company? Or are you writing to a wider, more inclusive audience, such as the general readership of a newspaper or magazine? Most formal arguments in college are written to general audiences, but "case" assignments or arguments written for specific occasions in your life (a letter to the financial aid office arguing for a student loan) can give you practice at writing to specific decision makers.

2. How much does your audience know or care about your issue? Are they currently part of the conversation or do they need quite a bit of background? If you are writing to specific decision makers (for example, the administration at your college about restructuring the intramural program), are they currently aware of the issue and do they care about it? If not, you may need to shock them into seeing the problem.

3. What is your audience's current attitude toward your issue? Is your audience opposed to your position on the issue or are they neutral? If neutral, are they open-minded? What other points of view besides your own will your audience be weighing?

4. What weaknesses will your audience find in your own argument? Why might they oppose your view on this issue? What aspects of your position will they find threatening?

5. Finally, what values, beliefs, or assumptions about the world do you and your audience share? Despite differences of view on this issue, where can you find common links with your audience? How might you use these links to build a bridge to your audience?

Suppose, for example, that you support universal mandatory testing for the HIV virus to help reduce unknowing transmission of AIDS. Although your audience will be general readers ranging from people who already accept your view to those who deeply oppose it, you intend to aim your argument at undecided people, who will also be weighing opposing views. What assumptions could you make about those who oppose your views? You imagine that many gay people might oppose mandatory testing as well as many political liberals such as members of the American Civil Liberties Union. You decide to ask first what each of these groups probably fears about your position. Gay people and others in high-risk categories may fear finding out whether they are infected, and they certainly fear discrimination from being publicly identified as HIV carriers. Moreover, mandatory AIDS testing may be seen as part of a conservative backlash against the gay community, who recently have made important strides toward gaining acceptance in American society. Liberals, besides also fearing a gay backlash, will be concerned about the attack on privacy and other civil liberties that mandatory testing might entail.

You should then consider the values that you share with your opponents because such values provide opportunities to build bridges toward your audience. You might decide, at a minimum, that both you and your opponents want to find a cure for AIDS and that both of you fear the horrors of an epidemic. Moreover, you want to stress that you share with your opponents a respect for the dignity and human value of those who are at high risk for AIDS. Particularly, you do not see yourself as part of a gay backlash.

As you begin to write, you must try to develop an argumentative strategy that reduces your audience's fears and incorporates reasons linked to their values. Your thinking might go something like this:

PROBLEM:	How can I create an argument rooted in shared values?
POSSIBLE SOLUTIONS:	I can try to reduce the audience's fear that mandatory AIDS testing implies a criticism of gay people. I could show my acceptance of gays and my sympathy for victims of AIDS. I could make sure my plan assured confidentiality. I must make it clear that my concern is stopping the spread of the disease and that this concern is shared by the gay community.

PROBLEM: How can I reduce fear that mandatory AIDS testing violates civil liberties?

POSSIBLE SOLUTIONS: I must show that the "enemy" here is the AIDS virus and not victims of the disease. Also, I might cite precedents for how we fight other infectious diseases. For example, many states require marriage license applicants to take a VD test, and on numerous occasions communities have imposed quarantines to halt the spread of epidemics. I could also argue that the rights of the gay community to be free from this disease outweigh individual rights to privacy, especially when confidentiality is assured.

The preceding example shows how a writer's focus on audience can shape the actual invention of the argument.

☐ FOR CLASS DISCUSSION

Working individually or in small groups, plan an audience-based argumentative strategy for one or more of the following cases. Follow the thinking process used by the writer of the mandatory AIDS-testing argument: (1) state several problems that the writer must solve to reach the audience and (2) develop possible solutions to those problems.

1. An argument for the right of software companies to continue making and selling violent video games. Aim the argument at parents who deeply oppose their children's playing these games.

2. An argument limiting the number of terms that can be served by members of Congress: Aim the argument at supporters of an influential incumbent who would no longer be eligible to hold office.

3. An argument supporting a one-dollar-per-gallon increase in gasoline taxes as an energy conservation measure: Aim your argument at business leaders who oppose the tax on the grounds that it will raise the cost of consumer goods.

4. An argument supporting the legalization of cocaine: Aim your argument at readers of *Reader's Digest,* a conservative magazine that supports the current war on drugs.

ETHOS AND *PATHOS* AS PERSUASIVE APPEALS: AN OVERVIEW

The previous section focused on audience-based reasons as a means of moving an audience. In terms of the rhetorical triangle introduced in Chapter 4, searching for audience-based reasons can be seen primarily as a function of *logos*—finding the best structure of reasons and evidence to sway an audience—although, as we shall see, it also affects the other points of the triangle. The next sections turn to the power of *ethos* (the appeal to credibility) and of *pathos* (the appeal to emotions) as further means of enhancing the rhetorical effectiveness of your arguments.

From the outset, you shouldn't think of these three kinds of appeals as, say, separate ingredients in a cake. You wouldn't say something like "This argument has enough *logos;* now I need to add some *ethos* and *pathos*." It may be helpful, however, to think of these terms as a series of lenses through which you filter and transform your ideas. Thus, if you intensify the *pathos* lens (such as by using more concrete language or vivid examples), the resulting image will appeal more strongly to the audience's emotions. If you change the *ethos* lens (perhaps by adopting a different tone toward your audience), the projected image of you as a person will be subtly altered. If you intensify the *logos* lens (by adding, say, more data for evidence), you will draw the reader's attention to the logical appeal of the argument. *Logos, ethos,* and *pathos* work together to create an impact on the reader. The three terms give us a common language to talk about the forces that create that impact.

Consider, for example, the variable effects of the following arguments, all having roughly the same logical appeal:

1. People should adopt a vegetarian diet because only through vegetarianism can we prevent the cruelty to animals that results from factory farming.

2. I hope you enjoyed your fried chicken this evening. You know, of course, how much that chicken suffered just so you could have a tender and juicy meal. Commercial growers cram the chickens so tightly together into cages that they have to have their beaks cut off to keep them from pecking each others' eyes out. The only way to end the torture is to adopt a vegetarian diet.

3. People who eat meat are no better than sadists who torture other sentient creatures in order to enhance their own pleasure. Unless you enjoy sadistic tyranny over others, you have only one choice: Become a vegetarian.

4. People committed to justice might consider the extent to which our love of eating meat requires the agony of animals. A visit to a modern chicken factory—where chickens live their entire lives in tiny darkened coops without room to spread their wings—might raise doubts about our right to inflict such suffering on sentient creatures. Indeed, such a visit might persuade us that vegetarianism is a more just alternative.

Each argument has roughly the same logical core:

CLAIM:	People should adopt a vegetarian diet.
STATED REASON:	Vegetarianism is the only way to end the suffering of animals caused by factory farming.
GROUNDS:	the evidence of suffering in commercial chicken farms, where chickens peck each others' eyes out; other evidence of animal suffering in factory farms; evidence that only widespread adoption of vegetarianism will end factory farming
WARRANT:	If we have an alternative to inflicting suffering on animals, we should adopt it.

But the impact of each argument on audiences varies. The difference between Arguments 1 and 2, most of our students report, is the emotional power of 2. Whereas Argument 1 refers only to the abstraction "cruelty to animals," Argument 2 paints a vivid picture of chickens with their beaks cut off to prevent their pecking each other blind. Argument 2 makes a stronger appeal to *pathos* (not necessarily a stronger argument) by stirring feelings—hitting the heart, as it were, as well as the head.

The difference between Arguments 1 and 3 concerns both *ethos* and *pathos.* Argument 3 appeals to the emotions through such highly charged words as "torture," "sadist," and "tyranny." But Argument 3 also draws attention to its writer, and most of our students report not liking that writer very much. His stance is self-righteous and insulting; he prefers shocking his audience by accusing them of sadism rather than by showing empathy for their values. We are not apt to trust such a writer. In contrast, the writer of Argument 4 establishes a more positive *ethos.* He establishes rapport with his audience by assuming they are committed to justice and by qualifying his argument with conditional terms such as "might" and "perhaps." He also invites sympathy for his problem—an appeal to *pathos*—by offering a specific description of chickens crammed into tiny coops.

Which of these arguments is best? They all have appropriate uses. Arguments 1 and 4 seem aimed at receptive audiences reasonably open to exploration of the issue, while Arguments 2 and 3 seem designed to shock complacent audiences or to rally a group of True Believers. Even Argument 3, which borders on being so abusive that it would be ineffective in most instances, might work as a rallying speech at a convention of animal liberation activists.

Our point thus far is that *logos, ethos,* and *pathos* are different aspects of the same whole, different lenses for mixing and coloring the light you project upon the screen. Every choice you make as a writer affects in some way each of the three appeals. The rest of this chapter examines these choices in more detail.

HOW TO CREATE AN EFFECTIVE *ETHOS:* THE APPEAL TO CREDIBILITY

Long ago the classical rhetoricians of Greece and Rome recognized that an argument would be more persuasive if the audience trusted the speaker. Aristotle argued that such trust is created within the speech itself rather than being brought to the speech by the prior reputation of the speaker. In the speaker's manner and delivery, in his tone and voice, in his choice of words, in his arrangement of reasons, in his fairness and sympathy toward opposing views, and in other subtler ways, a speaker could project the image of being a fair-minded, trustworthy person. Aristotle called the impact of the writer's credibility the appeal from *ethos.*

How does a writer create credibility? We will suggest three ways.

Create Credibility by Being Knowledgeable about Your Issue

The first way to gain credibility is to *be* credible; that is, to argue from a strong base of knowledge, to have at hand the examples, personal experiences, statistics, and other empirical data needed to make a sound case. If you have done your homework (people who "do their homework" are highly respected in business, government, and academia) you will command the attention of most audiences.

Create Credibility by Demonstrating Fairness

Besides being knowledgeable about your issue, you need to demonstrate fairness and courtesy to opposing views. In Chapter 1, the members of the well-functioning committee differed from the writer of the crank letter by showing respect rather than contempt for opposing views. Because true argument can occur only where persons may reasonably disagree, your *ethos* will be strengthened if you demonstrate that you understand and empathize with other points of view. Of course, there are times when it's effective to scorn an opposing view, but these times are rare, and they occur mainly when you are addressing an audience predisposed toward your position. As a general rule, demonstrating empathy to opposing views is the best strategy.

Create Credibility by Building a Bridge to Your Audience

A third means of establishing credibility—building a bridge to your audience—has been treated at length in the first part of this chapter in our discussion of audience-based reasons. By grounding your argument in shared values and assumptions, you demonstrate your good will and enhance your image as a trustworthy person. We mention audience-based reasons here to show how this aspect of *logos*—finding the reasons that are most rooted in the audience's values—also affects your *ethos* as a person respectful of your readers' views.

HOW TO CREATE *PATHOS*: THE APPEAL TO EMOTIONS

At the height of the protest movement against the Vietnam War, a group of protesters "napalmed" a puppy by dousing it with gasoline and setting it on fire. All over the country Americans were outraged by the demonstration. Letters began pouring in to local newspapers protesting the cruel killing of the puppy. The protesters responded as follows: "Why are you outraged by the napalming of a single puppy when you are not outraged by the daily napalming of human babies in Vietnam?"

The protesters' argument depended on *pathos. Logos*-centered arguments, the protesters felt, numbed the mind to human suffering. The napalming of the puppy gave presence to the reality of suffering; it reawakened feeling, creating in Americans a gut-level revulsion that, according to protesters, should have been felt all along for the war.

Of course, the napalmed puppy was a real-life event, part of a street theater argument, not a written essay. But the same strategy is often used in written arguments. Anti-abortion arguers use it whenever they present graphic descriptions of the dismembering of a fetus, tiny limb by limb, during the abortion process; proponents of euthanasia use it when they describe the prolonged suffering of a terminally ill patient hooked hopelessly to machines. And students use it when they argue with a professor that their grade should be raised from a C to a B lest the student lose his scholarship and have to return to poverty, shattering the dreams of his dear old grandmother.

Are such appeals to emotion legitimate? Our answer is yes if the emotional appeals clarify an issue rather than cloud it. Emotional appeals have an important place in argument because we can know with our hearts as well as with our minds. When used effectively, appeals to emotion help us clarify an issue by revealing its fullest human meaning. That is why arguments are often improved through the use of sensory detail that allows us to see the reality of a problem or through stories that make specific cases and instances come alive.

Appeals to emotion become illegitimate, we believe, when they serve to cloud issues rather than to clarify them. The student's argument for a grade of B is, we feel, an illegitimate appeal to emotion. We would argue that a student's grade in a course should be based on his or her performance in the course, not on the student's need. The image of the dear old grandmother may provide a legitimate motive for the student to study harder, but not for the professor to change a grade. On the other hand, the same image would be both appropriate and effective in a letter from the student's parents urging him to study harder.

Although it is difficult to classify all the ways that writers can create emotional appeals, we will focus on four strategies: concrete language; examples and illustrations; word choice, metaphors, and analogies; and appeals to audience values.

Appeal to Emotions by Using Concrete Language

In writing courses, teachers often try to help students develop "voice" or "style." In general, these terms refer to the liveliness, interest level, personality, or beauty of the prose. One of the chief strategies for achieving voice is the effective use of concrete language and specific detail. When used in argument, such language usually heightens *pathos*. Consider the differences between the first and second drafts of the following student argument on the advantages of riding the bus over driving a personal car:

FIRST DRAFT

People who prefer driving a car to taking a bus think that taking the bus will increase the stress of the daily commute. Just the opposite is true. Not being able to find a parking spot when in a hurry to work or school can cause a person stress. Taking the bus gives a person time to read or sleep, etc. It could be used as a mental break.

Although the argument is logically structured, the lack of details makes it emotionally flat, even dull.

SECOND DRAFT

Taking the bus can be more relaxing than driving a car. Having someone else behind the wheel gives people time to chat with friends or cram for an exam. They can balance their checkbooks, do homework, doze off, read the daily newspaper, or get lost in a novel rather than foaming at the mouth looking for a parking space. Taking the bus is break time rather than stress time.

In this revision, specific details make the prose livelier by creating images that trigger positive feelings—who wouldn't want some free time to doze off or get lost in a novel?

Appeal to Emotions by Using Examples and Illustrations

Stories, examples, and illustrations give your argument a powerful presence. Such specifics serve two purposes: As data, they provide evidence that supports your stated reasons; simultaneously, they evoke emotional responses that make your argument more vivid and memorable.

Consider the lack of presence in the following passage written by a student arguing that the core curriculum at his university should include multicultural studies.

EARLY DRAFT

Another advantage of a multicultural education is that it will help us see our own culture in a broader perspective. If all we know is our own heritage, then we might not be inclined to see anything bad about this heritage because we won't know anything else. But if we study other heritages, then we can see the pros and cons of our own heritage.

Now note the increase in emotional as well as logical appeal when the writer adds specific examples.

REVISED DRAFT

Another advantage of multicultural education is that it raises questions about traditional Western values. For example, the idea of private property and of ownership is part of the American dream (buying a house with a picket fence in the country, and so forth). It is also one of the basic rights guaranteed in the Constitution of the United States. However, in studying the beliefs of American Indians, students are confronted with an opposing view of property rights. When the U.S. Government wanted to buy land in the Pacific Northwest from Chief Sealth, he replied:

The president in Washington sends words that he wishes to buy our land. But how can you buy or sell the sky? The land? The idea is strange to us. If we do

> not own the freshness of the air and the sparkle of the water, how can you buy them? . . . We are part of the earth and it is part of us. . . . This we know: the earth does not belong to man, man belongs to the earth.

Our class was shocked when we realized the contrast between Western values and Chief Sealth's values. One of our best class discussions was initiated by the above quotation from Chief Sealth. Had we not been exposed to a view from another culture, we would have never been led to question the "rightness" of Western values.

The revised draft is much more persuasive. The writer begins by evoking a traditional middle-class American dream—a little house in the country, far from the stress of city life, bordered with a picket fence—which is then immediately undercut by the haunting speech of Chief Sealth. Chief Sealth's vision is not of land domesticated and enclosed, but of land as open, endless, and unobtainable as the sky. In this one brief quotation, the student shows us how a study of Chief Sealth can problematize our belief in private property and thus brings to life his previously abstract point about a benefit of multicultural education.

Another place where writers often use examples to evoke emotions is in their introductions. At the beginning of an argument, a vivid example—real or hypothetical—can shape your audience's emotional response to your issue. In using an opening example, the writer must be careful to fit the example to the claim. To illustrate the potential and the pitfalls of introductory scenes, consider the following vignettes from two different arguments dealings with homeless people in a downtown business area. The first argument, pleading for public support for legislation to help the poor, aims at creating sympathy for homeless people. It opens this way:

> It hurts the most when you come home from the theater on a cold January night. As you pull your scarf tighter around your neck and push your gloved hands deeper into the pockets of your wool overcoat, you notice the man huddled over the sewer grate, his feet wrapped in newspapers. He blows on his hands, then tucks them under his armpits and lies down on the sidewalk with his shoulders over the grate, his bed for the night. There are hundreds like him downtown, and their numbers are growing. Who in our legislature knows or cares about these people?

The second argument, supporting an anti-loitering law to keep homeless people out of a posh shopping area, creates sympathy not for the homeless but for the shoppers.

> Panhandlers used to sit on corners with tin cups. Not any more. I'm not talking here about the legitimate poor—homeless mothers or the blind or crippled. These are ratty, middle-aged woe salesmen drinking fortified wine from a sack or hostile young men with tattoos who appear to be saving their handouts to buy Harley hogs or uzis. They scuttle up behind you, breathing their foul breath down your neck, tap your arm or grab your sleeve, and demand your money. If you try to ignore them, they just keep following you. I'm sure all these poor souls have a tale to explain their present state. But the bottom line is they don't have a *right* to my money, and I do have a right to walk down a public thoroughfare unaccosted.

Each of these scenes makes a case for a particular point of view toward the homeless. They help us see a problem through the eyes of the person making the argument. Although each is effective in its own way, both will face resistance in some quarters. The first scene will strike some as sentimental; the second will strike others as flippant and indifferent. The emotional charge set by an introductory scene can sometimes work against you as well as for you. If you have doubts about an opening scene, test it out on other readers before using it in your final draft.

□ FOR CLASS DISCUSSION

Suppose that you want to write arguments on the following topics. Working as individuals or in small groups, think of a description, scene, or brief story that could be used in the introduction of your essay to create an emotional appeal favorable to your argument.

1. a. an argument supporting the use of animals for biomedical research

    b. an argument opposing the use of animals for biomedical research

    (Note that the purpose of the first scene is to create sympathy for the use of animals in biomedical research, perhaps by focusing readers' attention on the happy smile of a child cured by a medical breakthrough made possible through animal research. The purpose of the second scene is to create sympathy for the opposing view, perhaps by focusing on the suffering of an animal during an experiment.)

2. a. an argument for a program to restore a national park to its pristine, natural condition

    b. an argument for creating more camping places and overnight sites for recreational vehicles in a national park

    (The purpose of the first scene is to arouse sympathy for restoring a park's beauty; the purpose of the second scene is to arouse sympathy for more camping spaces.)

3. a. an argument favoring legalization of drugs

    b. an argument opposing legalization of drugs

4. a. an argument favoring TV advertising of condoms

    b. an argument opposing TV advertising of condoms

Appeal to Emotions through Appropriate Word Choice, Metaphors, and Analogies

Another way to create emotional appeals is to select words, metaphors, or analogies that have emotional connotations suitable to your purpose. If you oppose a local official, you might call him "a petty bureaucrat," but if you support him, you might call him a "beleaguered administrator." Likewise, the reader's feelings toward the official would be shaped differently if you called him "assertive" as opposed to "pushy," "decisive" as opposed to "obstinate," or "careful about money" as opposed to "miserly."

Similarly, we can use favorable or unfavorable metaphors, analogies, and other comparisons to shape our audience's emotional response to our arguments. A tax bill might be regarded either as a "poison to the economy" or as "economic medicine"; an insurance salesman might be "like a good neighbor" or "like a voracious shark"; or a new set of audiotapes in the library might be "a valuable new learning tool" or "another cheap educational gadget." In each case, the differing comparisons create differing emotional appeals.

The Problem of Slanted Language
The writer's power in choosing one set of words over another raises the problem of how language can be slanted or biased to distort the truth. One of the tricks of the Sophists (see the discussion of Callicles in Chapter 1) is to choose slanted words that bias an argument by evoking emotional responses favorable to the arguer's aims but distortive of the truth. Suppose that you are a real estate developer wishing to attract house buyers to your new subdivision, Paradise Village. Here is what an advertising blurb on Paradise Village might look like:

> Paradise Village, located on the banks of Clearwater Lake, combines the best of city and country life. Dozens of hiking trails through the Clearwater Woods are only minutes away from your doorstep, while the city itself is virtually at your fingertips. An excellent bus transportation system links Paradise Village with the Metropolis City Center only 15 minutes away.

But consider what a disillusioned homebuyer might say when telling the "truth" about Paradise Village.

> Before buying in Paradise Village, check out carefully the "promises" made in those sales brochures. Clearwater Lake isn't really a lake; it was created by developers by damming up Clearwater Creek, and so far it has been an unattractive pond, full of moss and water bugs but no fish. Clearwater Woods is simply a couple acres of trees between housing developments. Nowhere within the woods are you free from freeway noise. As for the city being at your fingertips, the bus ride is indeed 15 minutes—at 7:00 A.M. Sunday mornings. But during commuting hours the ride often takes an hour each way. Moreover, buses run infrequently at approximately one-hour intervals during the week and two-hour intervals on weekends.

As the examples show, it is possible to use language deceptively by choosing words that manipulate a reader's response.

A More Complex Look at Slanting
But this example raises a more complex philosophical question: To what extent is there really an objective truth that can be portrayed fully in language? We tend to think of slanted language as the opposite of objective language or "true" language.

When a witness takes the stand in a trial, he or she swears "to tell the truth, the whole truth, and nothing but the truth." We like to think that "telling the whole truth" is possible in language. We like to believe that objective language tells the whole truth, whereas slanted language distorts it. But can we *ever* tell the whole truth in language? Probably not. When we choose word A rather than word B, when we decide to put this word in the subject slot of our sentence rather than that word, when we select this detail rather than that detail to put into our paragraph, we create bias.

Let's take an illustration, once again focusing on homeless people. When you walk down a city street and see an unshaven man sitting on the sidewalk with his back up against a doorway, wearing old, slovenly clothes, and drinking from a bottle hidden in a sack, what is the "correct" word for this person?

a person on welfare?	a crazy person?
a beggar?	an indigent?
a wino?	a bum?
a homeless person?	a drunk?
a pauper?	a victim of the system?
a hobo?	a mendicant?
a panhandler?	a tramp?
a transient?	a scumbag leech on society?
a brother in need?	a loafer?
a streetperson?	a person down on his luck?

None of these words is the "correct" term because no such objective or correct term exists. When we choose one of the words, we look at the person through that word's lens. If we call the person a "beggar," for example, we bring up connotations from the historical past, particularly the Bible, where begging provided an opportunity for charity. The word *beggar* is associated with words like *alms,* which one gives to beggars. *Beggar,* then is a more favorable word than *panhandler,* which conjures up the image of an obnoxious person pestering you for money. Calling the person "homeless," on the other hand, takes our attention off the person's actions and places it on the cause of the problem, in this case a faulty economic system. Likewise, the word *wino* focuses on a cause, but now the cause is alcoholism rather than economics.

☐ FOR CLASS DISCUSSION

Divide the class into two groups. The task of the first group is to compose a list of words, analogies, or metaphors that create positive feelings for each of the following classes of people: unemployed people, people who sell used cars, lawyers, college professors, professional wrestlers, hunters, publishers of *Playboy,* and cheerleaders. The task of the second group is to compose a list that creates negative feelings. Then compare the lists from the two groups.

EXAMPLE:	CORPORATE EXECUTIVES
Positive connotations:	industrial leaders, chief executive officers, economic decision-makers, top-level corporation heads
Negative connotations:	fat cats, business tycoons, winners in the corporate rat race, country club elite, business kingpins, business moguls

Appeal to Emotions through Sensitivity to Your Audience's Values

We conclude this section by returning to the persuasive strategy introduced at the beginning of the chapter—finding audience-based reasons. What appeals to a writer's emotions may not necessarily appeal to the emotions of her intended audience.

Suppose that your college or university decided to raise tuition substantially, causing you and many of your classmates to feel truly strapped for funds. Typically, college administrators support tuition increases insofar as they enhance the economic stability of the institution. Students, on the other hand, oppose tuition increases insofar as they impose personal hardships. If you wanted to write a powerful argument against raising tuition, you might choose an emotional appeal based on your own values (sorrowful descriptions of hard-up students). But a better route might be emotional appeals aimed at your audience's values: stories of students who plan to transfer or to drop out of school because of the increased tuition costs. Loss of potential revenues through decreased enrollments probably triggers greater consternation among administrators than your having to borrow another grand from the bank. Likewise, administrators explaining the plan to students should focus on reasons that appeal to students' values; for example, a tuition increase allows hiring and retention of top professors, which leads to a better academic reputation of the college, which leads in turn to higher prestige for students' degrees.

APPLYING THIS CHAPTER'S PRINCIPLES TO YOUR OWN WRITING: WHERE SHOULD YOU REVEAL YOUR THESIS?

To demonstrate the interrelatedness of *logos, ethos,* and *pathos* as you compose your own arguments, we conclude this chapter by turning to a question often asked in our argument classes: "Where should I place my thesis? Should I put it in the introduction so that I tell my readers up front where I stand on an issue, or should I wait until later in the paper to reveal where I stand?" Although this may seem like a small technical matter, the placement of the thesis can profoundly affect an audience's perception of you as author (your *ethos*) as well as their emotional experience while reading your essay (your argument's *pathos*).

The standard way of conducting an argument is to state your own position near the beginning of your essay and then to summarize and refute the opposing views. Rhetorically, however, it is not always advantageous to tell your readers where you stand at the start of your argument or to separate yourself so definitively from your opposition. Sometimes it is to your advantage to keep the issue open, delaying the revelation of your own position until the middle or end of the essay. The effect of an up-front thesis—what we might call the "standard form"—is quite different from that of a delayed thesis. Let's explore this difference in more detail.

Standard Form Arguments

Figure 7–1 shows the format of a typical "standard form" argument—the form that results in what we have called a "self-announcing" structure. Like a tract home or a fast-food restaurant, a standard form argument usually gets the job done, but it does not work well in all environments and for all purposes. Teachers often ask students to write their first arguments in standard form as a way of learning and practicing the basic moves of argumentation. Later, students can experiment with variations on standard form to see the different effects various versions of an argument can have on audiences.

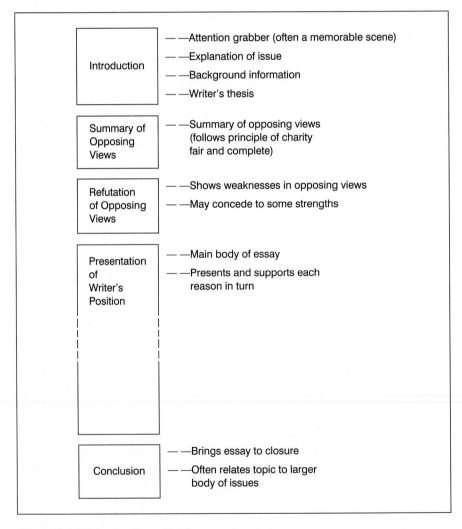

Figure 7–1 Diagram of standard form argument

As Figure 7–1 shows, a standard form argument usually begins with an attention grabber, which may be a startling statistic, a dramatic fact, or a real or hypothetical story or example. The attention grabber is usually followed by an explanation of the issue, which in turn is followed by the writer's thesis statement—often the last sentence of the introduction. Sometimes the writer also needs to provide background information (definitions of key terms, historical information about the origins of the issue, explanations of technical matters, and so forth) before presenting the thesis.

The next major part of a typical standard form argument is a summary and refutation of opposing views. If the opposing argument consists of several parts, the writer has two options for organizing this section: The writer can summarize all of the opposing argument before moving to the refutation, or he or she can summarize and refute one part at a time.

After refuting opposing views, the writer proceeds to present his own position and support it. This is usually the longest part of the argument. Frequently the writer will devote a section, often of several paragraphs or more, to the development of each reason.

Finally, the conclusion of a standard form argument serves to bring the whole argument into focus, thus giving the essay a sense of closure.

The standard form, as we have described it here, has several advantages for newcomers to the writing of arguments. For example, the standard form requires you to summarize opposing views and then to refute them, a challenging conceptual skill well worth practicing. Similarly, there are also conceptual advantages to the standard form's requirement that you put your thesis statement into your introduction. By clearly formulating a thesis statement with because clauses, you can see the whole of your argument in miniature. As your argument becomes increasingly clarified during the drafting process, you can revise your thesis statement to reflect your new intentions.

However, there are many times when the standard form doesn't allow you the subtlety and flexibility necessary to establish an effective and persuasive argument. Let's look now at the differing effect of a delayed thesis argument.

Delayed Thesis Arguments

To illustrate the differences between a standard form and a delayed thesis argument, we have taken a delayed thesis argument by nationally known columnist Ellen Goodman and rewritten it into the standard form. The article appeared shortly after the nation was shocked by a brutal gang rape in New Bedford, Massachusetts, in which a woman was raped on a pool table by patrons of a local bar.* We would like you to read both versions and then answer the class discussion exercises that follow.

---

* The rape occurred in 1985; the event was made into an Academy Award–winning movie, *The Accused,* starring Jodie Foster.

ELLEN GOODMAN'S ORIGINAL VERSION
(DELAYED THESIS)

Just a couple of months before the pool-table gang rape in New Bedford, Mass., *Hustler* magazine printed a photo feature that reads like a blueprint for the actual crime. There were just two differences between *Hustler* and real life. In *Hustler,* the woman enjoyed it. In real life, the woman charged rape.

There is no evidence that the four men charged with this crime had actually read the magazine. Nor is there evidence that the spectators who yelled encouragement for two hours had held previous ringside seats at pornographic events. But there is a growing sense that the violent pornography being peddled in this country helps to create an atmosphere in which such events occur.

As recently as last month, a study done by two University of Wisconsin researchers suggested that even "normal" men, prescreened college students, were changed by their exposure to violent pornography. After just ten hours of viewing, reported researcher Edward Donnerstein, "the men were less likely to convict in a rape trial, less likely to see injury to a victim, more likely to see the victim as responsible." Pornography may not cause rape directly, he said, "but it maintains a lot of very callous attitudes. It justifies aggression. It even says you are doing a favor to the victim."

If we can prove that pornography is harmful, then shouldn't the victims have legal rights? This, in any case, is the theory behind a city ordinance that recently passed the Minneapolis City Council. Vetoed by the mayor last week, it is likely to be back before the Council for an overriding vote, likely to appear in other cities, other towns. What is unique about the Minneapolis approach is that for the first time it attacks pornography, not because of nudity or sexual explicitness, but because it degrades and harms women. It opposes pornography on the basis of sex discrimination.

University of Minnesota Law Professor Catherine MacKinnon, who co-authored the ordinance with feminist writer Andrea Dworkin, says that they chose this tactic because they believe that pornography is central to "creating and maintaining the inequality of the sexes. . . . Just being a woman means you are injured by pornography."

They defined pornography carefully as, "the sexually explicit subordination of women, graphically depicted, whether in pictures or in words." To fit their legal definition it must also include one of nine conditions that show this subordination, like presenting women who "experience sexual pleasure in being raped or . . . mutilated. . . ." Under this law, it would be possible for a pool-table rape victim to sue *Hustler.* It would be possible for a woman to sue if she were forced to act in a pornographic movie.

Indeed, since the law describes pornography as oppressive to all women, it would be possible for any woman to sue those who traffic in the stuff for violating her civil rights.

In many ways, the Minneapolis ordinance is an appealing attack on an appalling problem. The authors have tried to resolve a long and bubbling conflict among those who have both a deep aversion to pornography and a deep loyalty to the value of free speech. "To date," says Professor MacKinnon, "people have identified the pornographer's freedom with everybody's freedom. But we're saying that the freedom of the pornographer is the subordination of women. It means one has to take a side."

But the sides are not quite as clear as Professor MacKinnon describes them. Nor is the ordinance.

Even if we accept the argument that pornography is harmful to women—and I do—then we must also recognize that anti-Semitic literature is harmful to Jews and racist literature is harmful to blacks. For that matter, Marxist literature may be harmful to government policy. It isn't just women versus pornographers. If women win the right to sue publishers and producers, then so could Jews, blacks, and a long list of people who may be able to prove they have been harmed by books, movies, speeches or even records. The Manson murders, you may recall, were reportedly inspired by the Beatles.

We might prefer a library or book store or lecture hall without Mein Kampf or the Grand Whoever of the Ku Klux Klan. But a growing list of harmful expressions would inevitably strangle freedom of speech.

This ordinance was carefully written to avoid problems of banning and prior restraint, but the right of any woman to claim damages from pornography is just too broad. It seems destined to lead to censorship.

What the Minneapolis City Council has before it is a very attractive theory. What MacKinnon and Dworkin have written is a very persuasive and useful definition of pornography. But they haven't yet resolved the conflict between the harm of pornography and the value of free speech. In its present form, this is still a shaky piece of law.

OUR REWRITE OF THE SAME ARGUMENT INTO STANDARD FORM

Just a couple of months before the pool-table gang rape in New Bedford, Mass., *Hustler* magazine printed a photo feature that reads like a blueprint for the actual crime. There were just two differences between *Hustler* and real life. In *Hustler,* the woman enjoyed it. In real life, the woman charged rape. Of course, there is no evidence that the four men charged with this crime had actually read the magazine. Nor is there evidence that the spectators who yelled encouragement for two hours had held previous ringside seats at pornographic events. But there is a growing sense that the violent pornography being peddled in this country helps to create an atmosphere in which such events occur. One city is taking a unique approach to attack this problem. An ordinance recently passed by the Minneapolis City Council outlaws pornography not because it contains nudity or sexually explicit acts, but because it degrades and harms women. Unfortunately, despite the proponents' good intentions, the Minneapolis ordinance is a bad law because it has potentially dangerous consequences.

Let's begin by looking at the opposing view. The proponents of the Minneapolis City Ordinance argue that pornography should be made illegal because it degrades and humiliates women. To show that it degrades women, they cite a recent study done by two University of Wisconsin researchers that suggests that even "normal" men (prescreened college students) are changed by their exposure to violent pornography. After just ten hours of viewing, reported researcher Edward Donnerstein, "the men were less likely to convict in a rape trial, less likely to see injury to a victim, more likely to see the victim as responsible." Pornography may not cause rape directly, he said, "but it maintains a lot of very callous attitudes. It justifies aggression. It even says you are doing a favor to the victim."

The core of their argument runs as follows: "If something degrades and humiliates women, then it discriminates against women. Pornography degrades and humiliates women. Therefore, pornography discriminates against women." Since empirical evidence is mounting that pornography indeed degrades and humiliates women, pornography, their argument goes, is a form of sex discrimination. University of Minnesota Law Professor Catherine MacKinnon, who co-authored the ordinance with feminist writer Andrea Dworkin, says that they chose to focus on pornography as a form of discrimination because they believe that pornography is central to "creating and maintaining the inequality of the sexes. . . . Just being a woman means you are injured by pornography." They defined pornography carefully as "the sexually explicit subordination of women, graphically depicted, whether in pictures or in words." To fit their legal definition it must also include one of nine conditions that show this subordination, like presenting women who "experience sexual pleasure in being raped or . . . mutilated. . . ." Under this law it would be possible for a woman to sue if she were forced to act in a pornographic movie. Indeed, since the law describes pornography as oppressive to all women, it would be possible for any woman to sue those who traffic in the stuff for violating her civil rights.

In many ways, the Minneapolis ordinance is an appealing solution to an appalling problem. The authors have tried to resolve a long and bubbling conflict among those who have both a deep aversion to pornography and a deep loyalty to the value of free speech. "To date," says Professor MacKinnon, "people have identified the pornographer's freedom with everybody's freedom. But we're saying that the freedom of the pornographer is the subordination of women. It means one has to take a side."

One must concede that the argument is attractive. It seems to give liberal thinkers a way of getting around the problem of free speech. But the reasoning behind the ordinance is flawed because its acceptance could lead to the suppression of a wide range of ideas. Even if we accept the argument that pornography is harmful to women—and I do—then we must also recognize that anti-Semitic literature is harmful to Jews and racist literature is harmful to blacks. For that matter, Marxist literature may be harmful to government policy. It isn't just women versus pornographers. If women win the right to sue publishers and producers, then so could Jews, blacks, and a long list of people who may be able to prove they have been harmed by books, movies, speeches, or even records. The Manson murders, you may recall, were reportedly inspired by the Beatles.

We might prefer a library or book store or lecture hall without Mein Kampf or the Grand Whoever of the Ku Klux Klan. But a growing list of harmful expressions would inevitably strangle freedom of speech. The ordinance was carefully written to avoid problems of banning and prior restraint, but the right of any woman to claim damages from pornography is just too broad. It seems destined to lead to censorship. What the Minneapolis City Council has before it is a very attractive theory. What MacKinnon and Dworkin have written is a very persuasive and useful definition of pornography. But they haven't yet resolved the conflict between the harm of pornography and the value of free speech. In its present form, this is still a shaky piece of law.

☐ FOR CLASS DISCUSSION

The following questions are based on Ellen Goodman's pornography essay, which you have just read. Using whichever version of the essay is most helpful, prepare answers to the questions. Work either as individuals or in small groups.

1. In one or two sentences, summarize the argument supporting the Minneapolis ordinance.

2. In one or two sentences, summarize Goodman's own argument.

3. Which version of the essay, 1 or 2, did you find most useful in answering the preceding two questions?

4. Which version of the essay do you think is most effective? Why?

If you are like our own students, two-thirds of you will prefer Goodman's original version over the standard form version. However, a large majority of our students reported that the standard form version was more useful for helping them answer the above questions. By placing the writer's thesis statement at the end of the introduction ("Unfortunately, despite the proponents' good intentions, the Minneapolis ordinance is a bad law because it has potentially dangerous consequences"), the standard form version gives you up front a clear summary of the writer's position (question 2). Similarly, by setting off the Minneapolis ordinance as the opposition and by supplying the syllogistic core of its supporting argument, the standard form version makes it easier to find and summarize the opposing view.

But even though the argument of the standard form version can be grasped more quickly, the majority of readers prefer Goodman's original version. Why is this?

What most people point to is the greater sense of complexity and surprise in the original version, a sense that comes largely from a delay in presenting the writer's own position. Whereas in the standard form version the Minneapolis ordinance is the "opposition," in the original version the ordinance isn't so identified until later, creating more reader sympathy for its argument. Because we aren't told from the start that the author will eventually oppose this ordinance, we are led to examine it more open-mindedly, not knowing for sure what judgment will finally emerge. To the extent that she sympathizes with feminist beliefs, Ellen Goodman does not wish to distance herself from those who see pornography as a violation of women's rights. Thus, in her original version the author's sympathy for the Minneapolis ordinance seems real, so real that we are surprised in the last third of the essay when she finally rejects the ordinance. By not laying out her own position at the beginning—as the standard form requires—Goodman lets us enter her own struggle to think through these issues, and her final rejection of the ordinance is made all the more powerful by her obvious sympathy for what the writers of the ordinance are proposing. Thus Goodman's decision about the arrangement of parts turns out to be a decision about how we as audience will feel about both her and her argument, choices that relate to the sense of self that she wishes to project.

It seems clear, then, that a writer's decision about when to reveal an essay's thesis and when to separate the writer's view from the opposition's has considerable importance. If the thesis is revealed early, the writer comes across as more hard-nosed, more sure of her position, more confident about how to divide the ground into friendly and hostile camps, more in control. If the thesis is delayed, the issues are made to seem more complex, the reader's sympathy for the opposition is often increased, and the writer's struggle for clarity is highlighted. Paradoxically, though, such an essay is sometimes more persuasive to opponents because they feel their own position has been generously listened to. It is obvious that the interplay between *pathos* and *ethos* is complex. By delaying her thesis, Goodman projects an image of herself (*ethos*) as sympathetic to feminism and troubled by her own position. This image of herself increases the reader's sympathy (*pathos*) for her dilemma and thus strengthens her argument.

The Ellen Goodman example reveals the kinds of complex choices writers make when they draft and revise. It is often conceptually easier to write an argument in the standard form, which works well in most rhetorical situations. Variations on this form, however, can sometimes make your argument more persuasive as well as more stylistically subtle.

CONCLUSION

In this chapter, we have explored ways that writers can strengthen the persuasiveness of their arguments by using audience-based reasons and by creating appeals to *ethos* and *pathos*. Arguments are more persuasive if they are rooted in the underlying assumptions, beliefs, and values of the intended audience. Similarly, arguments are more persuasive if readers trust the credibility of the writer and if the argument appeals to readers' hearts and imaginations as well as to their intellects. We have also seen how the placement of a writer's thesis—whether stated explicitly in the beginning or delayed until the end of the essay—can have subtle effects on the way both the argument and the writer are received.

8

Accommodating Your Audience: Treating Opposing Views

☐

In the previous chapter we discussed ways of moving your audience through audience-based reasons and appeals to *pathos* and *ethos*. In this chapter we are concerned with how a writer treats opposing views in a finished product—whether to ignore opposing views, to summarize and refute them, to concede to their strengths, or to seek compromise and conciliation. These choices are determined in part by the stance you wish to take toward your audience and by how you want that audience to perceive you.

OPENING EXERCISE: A CONTROVERSY IN FIRST-YEAR COMPOSITION

As an introduction to these concerns, consider the following case study, which we will refer to occasionally for illustration throughout this chapter.

SHOULD TEAM WRITING BE REQUIRED IN A FIRST-YEAR COMPOSITION COURSE?

A heated controversy recently occurred in the composition program at University X. As an experiment, instructors for several sections of first-year composition asked their students to write a "team" or group proposal argument (written by five-person teams) that offered a solution for a campus problem chosen by each team. Each student's grade for the project was based on the quality of the final team product adjusted upward or downward according to each student's individual contributions to the team effort.

Several teachers in the experiment, enthusiastic about the success of this assignment, proposed to the Composition Committee that a similar team-writing experience be required in all sections of first-year composition. To no one's surprise, this proposal turned out to be controversial with both students and instructors writing letters to the committee supporting or opposing the proposal.

Based on your initial reaction, what position would you take on this controversy?

INITIAL OPINION SURVEY

1. Would you support or oppose a requirement that first-year composition students write one of their formal essays as a group or team?

2. Do you believe that team writing an essay would be a valuable learning experience for you?

3. Explain briefly the primary reasons for your choices.

Now that you know something of the background of this issue and have made your own initial judgment, please read the following two versions of a teacher's letter to the Composition Committee supporting the team-writing proposal. Which of the two versions of the letter do you think is more effective?

VERSION 1

I urge the Composition Committee to approve the proposal that team-writing be required in first-year composition courses. As a teacher in the experimental program, I have required a team-writing assignment for the last three semesters with very positive results. Let me highlight briefly my reasons for supporting this proposal.

First, the team-writing assignment promotes true active learning. I was impressed by my students' ability to identify and analyze a problem on campus, imagine alternative solutions, and then propose and justify their chosen solution to the problem. The group discussions revealed a high level of critical thinking and creativity. Students' views evolved as they did research and gathered data, listened to their teamates' ideas, argued for their own positions, and negotiated differences. No other assignment that I have ever given in composition created such effective group dynamics.

The group work also taught students a lot about writing—especially about revision, editing, and style. Acting alternately as drafters and revisers, the students had to make all the parts of the proposal fit together with unity of structure and consistency in voice and style. When team members are responsible for revising a draft written by another team member, they learn to find and fix problems that they might otherwise overlook in their own drafts. Largely because the process was effective, the final products were excellent. Some of their proposals were so good that I have urged the groups to submit them to appropriate university offices.

Additionally, team writing simulates the kind of writing students will do in professional life. Team writing has long been common in science and engineering, and is increasingly common in the business world, where reports and proposals are typically written by teams. By teaching students to function in a group environment, the team-writing experience imparts an essential career skill.

Finally, from a teacher's perspective, the team-writing assignment gives instructors a breathing space in the semester when they can schedule more student conferences and provide more individual help. Relieved from a heavy paper-grading load during the team-writing unit, I worked with students on revisions of earlier assignments and gave other kinds of individualized help.

For these reasons, I strongly urge you to make a team-writing experience a required part of our first-year composition courses. If you would like to discuss these ideas with me personally or would like to see examples of work produced by my student groups, please contact me at xxxx.

Sincerely,
Professor_____ Jones

VERSION 2

Despite real difficulties associated with team-writing assignments, I urge the composition committee to approve the proposal that team writing be required in first-year composition courses. As a teacher in the program, I have required a team-writing assignment for the last three semesters. Although I have had my share of difficulties in requiring team writing, the positive benefits of the assignment outweigh the costs.

Let me begin, though, by acknowledging the problem areas. Teachers and students who dislike team writing point with justification to such problems as dysfunctional groups, unequal sharing of work, group difficulties in scheduling out-of-class meetings, personality conflicts, willingness of weak writers to let the good writers do the work, and the very knotty problem of assigning grades equitably. I know these problems well. Last semester one of my students became so angry at her group that she stormed out of the classroom, telling me in the hall that she would drop the class before she would return to her group. Students are so used to working individually rather than together that the strain on the teacher of trying to help them function as a team can be overwhelming.

Despite these problems, I still enthusiastically support a required team-writing experience for first-year students. Here are my reasons.

First, the team-writing assignment promotes true active learning. I was impressed by my students' ability to identify and analyze a problem on campus, imagine alternative solutions, and then propose and justify their chosen solution to the problem. With only a few exceptions, the group conversations during this project—even among groups that didn't seem to be working well together—showed a high level of critical thinking and creativity. Students' views evolved as they listened to their team-mates' ideas, did research and gathered data, argued for their own positions, and negotiated differences. No other assignment that I have ever given in composition created such effective group dynamics.

The group work also taught students a lot about writing—especially about revision, editing, and style. Acting alternately as drafters and revisers, the students had to make all the parts of the proposal fit together with unity of structure and consistency in voice and style. When team members are responsible for revising a draft written by another team member, they learn to find and fix problems that they might otherwise overlook in their own drafts. Largely because the process was effective, the final products were excellent. Some of their proposals were so good that I have urged the groups to submit them to appropriate university offices.

Additionally, team writing simulates the kind of writing students will do in professional life. Team writing has long been common in science and engineering, and is increasingly common in the business world, where reports and proposals are typically written by teams. Even the dysfunctional groups benefit from this aspect of team writing. They learn—perhaps the hard way—that professional working groups, unlike friendship groups, require goal orientation, dutiful work habits, and effective cooperation. By teaching students how to work productively in groups, we are imparting an essential career skill.

Finally, from a teacher's perspective, the team-writing assignment gives instructors a breathing space in the semester when they can schedule more student conferences and provide more individual help. Relieved from a heavy paper-grading load, I worked with students on revisions of earlier assignments and gave other kinds of individualized help that would otherwise be impossible.

For these reasons, I strongly urge you to make a team-writing experience a required part of our first-year composition courses. If you would like to discuss these ideas with me personally or would like to see examples of work produced by my student groups, please contact me at xxxx.

Sincerely,

Professor_____ Jones

SECOND OPINION SURVEY

1. Which version do you find most persuasive?
2. Which version do you think the author should submit to the Composition Committee?

☐ FOR CLASS DISCUSSION

1. Working in small groups, describe the main differences between the two versions and compare notes on which version you find most persuasive.
2. Take a class poll on the numbers of persons who prefer each of the versions.
3. What relationship do you find, if any, between a person's initial position on the team-writing issue and that person's preference for Version 1 or Version 2 as most persuasive?

ONE-SIDED VERSUS TWO-SIDED ARGUMENTS

The previous exercise introduces you to the differences between one- and two-sided arguments. Version 1 is a one-sided argument. It presents only a positive view of team writing, without attempting to look at an opposing perspective. Version 2, on the other hand, is a two-sided argument. It still supports team writing, but at various places summarizes the objections that adversaries might raise.

Which version is more effective rhetorically? That is, which is apt to be more persuasive to an audience?

According to some researchers, if people already agree with a writer's thesis, they usually find one-sided arguments more persuasive. A two-sided argument appears wishy-washy and makes the writer seem less decisive. On the other hand, if people initially disagree with a writer's thesis, a two-sided argument often seems more persuasive because it shows that the writer has listened to the other side and thus seems more open-minded and fair.

An especially interesting effect has been documented for neutral audiences. In the short run, one-sided arguments seem more persuasive to neutral audiences, but in the long run two-sided arguments seem to have more staying power. Neutral audiences who've heard only one side of an issue tend to be easily swayed to the other side when they hear opposing arguments. By anticipating and in some cases refuting opposing views, the two-sided argument diminishes the surprise and force of subsequent counter-arguments and also exposes their weaknesses.

Now that you've heard from the researchers, go back and examine the results of your own little experiment. Do they bear out the experts' findings? If not, why not?

BEGINNING A TWO-SIDED ARGUMENT: SUMMARIZING OPPOSING VIEWS

An effective two-sided argument usually begins with a fair summary of an opposing view. (By "two sides" we mean your position versus one or more positions opposing yours. Often you might need to summarize several different opposing views.) When you summarize opposing views, your own credibility is enhanced if you follow the "principle of charity." This principle obliges you to make your opponents' best case, avoiding loaded or biased summaries or "strawman" summaries, which oversimplify opposing arguments, making them easy to knock over.

Consider the differences among the following summaries of the argument supporting team writing. In the following hypothetical cases, the writer, who opposes the team-writing proposal, attempts to summarize the views of our earlier letter writer, whom we have called Professor Jones. The following passages illustrate fair and unfair ways for this writer to summarize Jones' views.

Unfair Summary—Loaded Language

Professor Jones is too caught up in recent educational fads to see the damage she is causing. All her jargon about "active learning," "critical thinking," "group processes," etc. is just a coverup for her failure to stand in front of the class and teach. She pretends to believe that group-writing produces better thinking and prepares students for the world of work. Oh, sure. Her real motivation is obviously to get out of grading papers and to take a week off from preparing classes.

Although this summary shows an opposing view, it doesn't effectively enter into that view. Through sarcasm and ridicule, the writer reveals a bias that prevents him from seeing the issue from a contrary perspective.

UNFAIR SUMMARY—STRAWMAN

Professor Jones supports team-writing primarily because it reduces her paper-grading load. She also claims that a single team-writing experience will lead to sudden improvements in thinking skills and to enhanced career success.

Although less sarcastic than the loaded-language version, this passage both distorts and oversimplifies Jones' position. First, it misrepresents Jones' reason for liking the reduced paper-grading feature of team writing. It also exaggerates and hence oversimplifies Jones' claims about the value of team writing to teach critical thinking and enhance career success. Through distortion and oversimplification, the writer sets up a strawman that is easier to knock down than is Jones' original argument.

FAIR SUMMARY—FOLLOWS THE PRINCIPLE OF CHARITY

Professor Jones presents four main reasons for supporting team writing. First, she argues that team writing promotes active learning and teaches critical thinking; second, it helps students learn revising skills, which in turn leads to better written papers; third, she believes that team writing prepares students for the kind of writing environment that prevails in the world of work; fourth, she argues that the time saved in paper grading can be converted profitably to time helping individuals.

This version role-plays the opposing view, trying to state its argument fairly and accurately.

□ FOR CLASS DISCUSSION

Suppose that you wanted to refute Sandra's argument (pp. 75–77) that the Ayalas were not morally justified in conceiving a baby to save their elder daughter from death by leukemia. Working individually or in groups, prepare three different summaries of Sandra's views as follows:

1. unfair summary using loaded language
2. unfair strawman summary
3. fair summary following the principle of charity.

When you are finished, be prepared to read your summaries aloud to the class as a whole.

Once writers have summarized an opposing view, they can respond to it using one of several strategies: (1) a combative rebuttal strategy; (2) a more moderate concession strategy; or (3) a conciliatory or Rogerian strategy, which eschews combativeness in favor of synthesis and reconciliation.

RESPONSE STRATEGY 1: REBUTTAL OF OPPOSING VIEWS

When rebutting or refuting an argument, you attempt to convince readers that an opposing view is logically flawed, erroneously supported, or in some other way much weaker than the opponent claims.

Using the Toulmin Schema to Find a Strategy for Rebuttal

In planning a rebuttal, the most important principle to keep in mind is that for any given line of reasoning you can attack (1) the writer's stated reason and grounds, or (2) the writer's warrant and backing, or (3) both. Put in common language, you can attack an adversary's reasons and evidence or his underlying assumptions.

Let's illustrate this strategy by continuing with our case study about team writing. Let's assume that you oppose the team-writing requirement and that you want to refute Professor Jones' arguments. For the purposes of this illustration, we focus on Jones' third reason, which can be summarized into a single enthymeme as follows:

PROFESSOR JONES' ENTHYMEME: Team writing should be required in our first-year composition course because this experience prepares students for the team-writing environment of the work world.

Placed in the Toulmin schema, Jones' argument is as follows:

CLAIM:	Team writing should be required in our first-year composition course.
STATED REASON:	because this experience prepares students for the team-writing environment of the work world
GROUNDS:	evidence that team writing is common in the work world (statistical evidence of the frequency of team writing in the work world; examples of team writing; testimony from people in business and industry that team writing is common, etc.); also evidence that the assignment actually teaches students to do this kind of writing (evidence that group interaction in the freshman classroom in some way approximates group interaction in a business setting)
WARRANT:	*Narrowly:* An assignment that prepares students for the team-writing environment of the work world should be one of the requirements of first-year composition. *More broadly:* We should use educational practices that prepare students to function effectively in the work world.
BACKING:	arguments showing the centrality and importance of preparing students for the business world; arguments showing the pedagogical value of career-oriented assignments (increased student motivation, etc.); arguments showing the importance of measuring academic success by work success.

The above list has the major elements of the Toulmin schema, except for the conditions of rebuttal, which we will consider in a moment. Before looking at effective strategies for rebutting the above argument, let's look at a typical example of an ineffective rebuttal, which simply asserts disagreement while bringing in irrelevant arguments and evidence.

INEFFECTIVE REBUTTAL

Professor Jones wrongly claims that writing team essays prepares students for the world of work. The assignment is so stupid it wouldn't prepare anybody to do anything. It just wastes everyone's time. Our group just sat around shooting the bull. I even took a poll of my fellow classmates, and three out of four said that the assignment didn't improve their writing at all.

This rebuttal is ineffective because the writer simply asserts his opinion while failing to say why the assignment is "stupid." The fact that his group "just sat around shooting the bull" would be more effective evidence if we knew how many other groups were similarly disengaged. Finally, the cited poll supports only the point "Many students felt the assignment didn't help their writing." The poll failed to ask whether team writing would help students in the world of work.

To refute this argument more effectively, the writer can return to the Toulmin schema to consider the conditions of rebuttal, which are a series of "unless" statements that identify cases or situations that lessen the force of the reasons and grounds, or warrant and backing. Pretending to be "opposing counsel," the writer might come up with a list like this:

CONDITIONS OF REBUTTAL:
Rebutting the reason and grounds: This reason is a good one unless team writing is not common in the work world; unless the college team-writing situation is so different from the work team-writing situation that the former doesn't prepare you for the latter.

Rebutting the warrant and backing: unless learning to function in a team-writing environment isn't as important as other skills for career success; unless career-oriented assignments shouldn't be stressed in first-year composition.

What follows are examples of how each of these conditions of rebuttal might be expanded into an argument rebutting Professor Jones' original line of reasoning:

REBUTTAL STRATEGY 1:   TEAM WRITING IS NOT COMMON IN THE WORK WORLD

Professor Jones claims that team writing prepares students for careers by simulating work-world writing conditions. Jones' argument depends on our accepting as "fact" this teacher's assertion that team writing is common in the world of work. I don't believe it is. I am majoring in elementary education and decided to take a survey of present elementary teachers. I interviewed a dozen teachers at Irving and Longfellow grade schools, and none of them has ever written a team paper nor even heard of anyone else writing a team paper. Thus, for my profession at least, team writing doesn't seem common at all. Unless supporters of the team-writing requirement could demonstrate that at least half of this class could really expect to do frequent team writing in their careers, this assignment is not worth the time and trouble.

This rebuttal strategy casts doubt on Jones' stated reason and grounds—namely, her claim that team writing is common in the world of work. If team writing is rare in the world of work, then an exercise to give students that skill is irrelevant. The writer doesn't claim that team-writing is not common in the work world in general, only that it is not common in her chosen field of elementary teaching, as based on her survey. This use of evidence, although limited, places the burden of proof back on supporters of the proposal.

REBUTTAL STRATEGY 2:   COLLEGE TEAM-WRITING CONDITIONS DIFFERENT FROM WORK CONDITIONS

Professor Jones says that writing team essays simulates writing conditions in the world of work and therefore prepares students for careers. I agree with her that team writing occurs frequently in the world of work. I also accept her assumption that assignments that prepare us for the world of work are valuable. However, the circumstances under which we do team writing in first-year composition are so different from the circumstances under which scientists or business people do team writing that the one doesn't prepare you for the other. In the business world people have common goals, common interests, and flexible enough time schedules to permit successful team meetings. They have an intrinsic interest in succeeding as a team. In our class, however, the teams are entirely artificial. Some of us care about this class; some of us don't. Some of us want to get A's; some of us will be happy with C's. Nobody in our group has intrinsic interest in our team-writing project. We're motivated only by grades, not by common interests or professional goals. Moreover, our inflexible schedules make scheduling out-of-class team meetings nearly impossible. This situation makes us dislike team writing and leads to bickering and ineffective cooperation. First-year composition courses cannot teach students how to do successful team writing for the world of work unless they can create the kind of environment that occurs in the world of work. That certainly didn't happen in my class.

This strategy accepts Professor Jones' warrant ("An assignment that prepares students for the team-writing environment of the work world is valuable") and also the assumption on which the stated reason is based ("Team writing is common in the world of work"). This writer's approach is to attack the stated reason from another direction by showing that group processes in first-year composition are not comparable to group processes in a real work situation and thus that the team-writing assignment never achieves its goal of teaching valuable work skills.

REBUTTAL STRATEGY 3:   OTHER SKILLS MORE VALUABLE THAN TEAM-WRITING SKILLS

Professor Jones claims that writing team essays is valuable because team essays simulate workplace writing conditions and thus prepare students for careers. I concede that a lot of work-related writing is done in teams and that team practice in first-year composition will probably be of some help in later life. However, I do not accept Jones' assumption that college writing ought to simulate workplace writing or that team essays are the surest preparation for career success. Instead of team essays, first-year composition should teach basic writing skills. When I asked several business people what bothered them most about their employees' writing, not one complained that they didn't know how to write in groups. Rather, they complained about employees who didn't know how to spell or punctuate or write short clear sentences or compose a simple memo. When so many students enter the work force lacking the basics, it's hard to justify spending four class meetings on team writing. Perhaps English teachers could teach team writing in an advanced course in business communication. But in first-year composition they should spend that valuable time on the basics. Our class hasn't spent nearly enough time reviewing punctuation or studying editing skills. Instructors should teach us to walk before we take on some strange kind of dance movement like team writing.

This too is an effective rebuttal, but it takes a much different tack. This writer accepts Jones' reason and grounds, but attacks her warrant ("An assignment that prepares students for the team-writing environment of the work world should be one of the requirements for first-year composition"). Thus, the writer agrees that team writing is common in the world of work and that team writing in college may help students learn to do team writing in the work world. What this writer attacks instead is the value of preparing students for a team-writing environment. The writer argues that team writing is far less important than basic skills to career success.

REBUTTAL STRATEGY 4: CAREER-ORIENTED ASSIGNMENTS SHOULDN'T BE STRESSED IN FIRST-YEAR COMPOSITION

Professor Jones claims that writing team essays is valuable because team essays simulate workplace writing conditions and thus prepare students for careers. I concede that a lot of work-related writing is done in teams and that team practice in first-year composition will probably be of some help in later life. However, I do not accept Jones' assumption that college writing ought to simulate workplace writing or that the function of academics is to prepare students for careers. In recent years, this pervasive focus on practicality and careerism has all but destroyed the liberal arts. Students will have their whole lives to learn how to do workplace writing but only a few precious undergraduate years to immerse themselves in the great traditions of thought which characterize world cultures. Writing assignments for first-year composition ought to be based on academic reading, particularly reading that deepens students' engagement with the liberal arts tradition. Save team-writing for specialized courses later in a student's career.

This approach, which opposes the whole idea of career-oriented undergraduate education, attacks Professor Jones' warrant and backing at its most general level. It questions Jones' underlying assumption that preparing students for careers is an important undergraduate goal, positing instead the value of the traditional liberal arts.

□ FOR CLASS DISCUSSION

Complete each of the following enthymemes by supplying the warrant. Then invent plausible grounds and backing for the argument. Finally, consider conditions for rebuttal by suggesting ways to attack the reason and grounds, or the warrant and backing, or both.

1. Writing courses should be pass/fail because the pass/fail system encourages more creativity.

2. The state should require persons to wear seatbelts because wearing seatbelts saves lives.

3. Majoring in engineering is better than majoring in music because engineers make more money than musicians.
4. Don't elect Sam as committee chair because he is too bossy.
5. The endangered species law is too stringent because it seriously hampers the economy.

Using the Toulmin schema helps you see a variety of strategies for rebutting an argument. Frequently rebuttals occur at the level of grounds or backing, where you attempt to refute an opposing argument's use of evidence. The next section deals specifically with rebutting evidence.

Ways to Rebut Evidence

Among the most common ways to refute an argument is to find weaknesses in the opponent's use of evidence. Here are some strategies that you can use:

Deny the Facticity of the Data

Generally a piece of data can be considered a fact when a variety of observers all agree that the datum corresponds with reality. Often, though, what one writer considers a "fact," another may consider an "interpretation" or simply a case of wrong information. If you have reason to doubt your opponent's facts, then call them into question. Thus, if your opponent claims that elementary teachers don't do team writing, you might point to a jointly written committee report or grant proposal recently completed at a local elementary school.

Cite Counterexamples or Countertestimony

One of the most effective ways to counter an argument based on examples is to cite a counterexample. If your opponent argues that women are more people-conscious than men, several counterexamples of cold, impersonal women or of kindly, warm-hearted men can cast doubt on the whole claim. The effect of counterexamples is to deny the conclusiveness of the original data. Similarly, citing an authority whose testimony counters other expert testimony is a good way to begin refuting an argument based on testimony.

Cast Doubt on the Representativeness or Sufficiency of Examples

Examples are powerful only if the audience feels them to be representative and sufficient. If your opponent argues that pool players are true athletes because they excel at many other sports, not just pool, and then cites as an example a local pool player who is also a varsity track star, you could argue that the mentioned player is not typical of all pool players. You could demand that the opponent provide evidence based on a wide sampling of pool players. To conclude your rebuttal, you might cite examples of one or two pool players who were klutzes at other sports.

Cast Doubt on the Relevance or Recency of the Examples, Statistics, or Testimony

The best evidence is up-to-date. In a rapidly changing universe, data that are even a few years out of date are often ineffective. If your opponent uses demographic data to argue that your community doesn't need a new nursing home, you could raise questions about the recency of the data, arguing that the percentage of elderly has increased since the time the data were collected. Another problem with data is their occasional lack of relevance. For example, in arguing that an adequate ozone layer is necessary for preventing skin cancers, it is not relevant to cite statistics on the alarming rise of lung cancers.

Call Into Question the Credibility of an Authority

One trick of sophistry is to have an authority within one field speak out on issues in a different field. Modern advertising regularly uses this kind of sleight-of-hand whenever movie stars or athletes endorse products about which they have no expertise. The problem of credibility is trickier when an apparent authority has no particular expertise in a specific subfield within the discipline. For example, a psychologist specializing in the appetite mechanisms of monkeys might not be an expert witness on schizophrenic behavior in humans, even though a writer could cite that person as a Ph.D. in psychology. Thus, if you can attack the credibility of the authority, you can sometimes undermine the effectiveness of the testimony. (This procedure is different from the *ad hominem* fallacy discussed in Appendix 1 because it doesn't attack the personal character of the authority but only the authority's expertise on a specific matter.)

Question the Accuracy or Context of Quotations

Frequently evidence based on testimony is distorted by being either misquoted or taken out of context. Often scientists will qualify their findings heavily, but these qualifications will be omitted when their research is reported by the popular media. You can thus attack the use of a quotation by putting it in its original context or by restoring the qualifications accompanying the quotation in its original source.

Question the Way Statistical Data Were Produced or Interpreted

Appendix 2 provides fuller treatment of how to refute statistics. At this point, however, you should appreciate that you can attack your opponent's statistical evidence by calling into account how the data were gathered, treated mathematically, or interpreted. It can make a big difference, for example, whether you cite raw numbers or percentages or whether you choose large or small increments for the axes of graphs.

Anticipating Adversarial Views throughout Your Essay

Although good writers will often devote a specific section of an essay to refutation, they don't ignore adversarial views in the rest of the essay. They will often refer to opposing views even while presenting their own side of the argument. When you draft your essay, try to imagine yourself in a conversation with a reader who has just listened to an opposing view and is weighing its merits against those of your argument. Imagine watching his or her facial expressions as you make your case. At controversial points in your argument, picture your reader recalling an opposing point of view, frowning, giving a shake of the head, and starting to interrupt, "Yes, but. . . ." Your job as a writer is to anticipate those "Yes, but . . ." moments and let your imaginary reader make an opposing case briefly before you go on. The ability to work these opposing views into your arguments gracefully is one hallmark of a skilled writer.

RESPONSE STRATEGY 2: CONCESSION TO OPPOSING VIEWS

Sometimes you encounter portions of an argument that you simply can't refute. For example, if you support the legalization of drugs, adversaries invariably cite alarming statistics enumerating large increases in drug users and addicts that will result from legalization. You might dispute the size of their numbers, but you reluctantly agree that legalization will increase drug use and hence addiction. Your strategy in this case is not to refute the opponent's argument, but to concede to it by admitting that legalization of hard drugs will promote heroin and cocaine addiction. Having made that concession, your task is then to show that the benefits of drug legalization still outweigh the costs you've just conceded.

As this example shows, the strategy of a concession argument is to switch from the field of values employed by your adversaries to a different field of values more favorable to your position. Whereas your opponent opposes legalization because of criterion A (alarming increase in numbers of users and addicts), you support it because of criteria B, C, and D (eliminating the black market in drugs, ending the crime and violence associated with procurement of drugs, thus freeing the police to deal with violent crime, and so forth). To put it another way, in a concession argument you don't try to refute your opponent's stated reason and grounds (by arguing that legalization will *not* lead to increased drug usage and addiction), nor do you directly attack your opponent's warrant (by arguing that increased drug use and addiction are *not* bad). Rather you shift the argument to a new field of values by introducing a new warrant, one that you think your audience can share (eliminating the black market is good). To the extent that opponents of legalization share your desire to stop drug-related crime, shifting to this new field of values is a good strategy. Although it may seem that you weaken your own position by conceding to your opponent's argument, you may actually strengthen it by increasing your credibility and gaining your audience's goodwill. Moreover, conceding to one part of an opponent's argument doesn't mean that you won't refute other parts of that argument.

A good illustration of the concession strategy is Version 2 of the team-writing argument (pp. 168–69). The writer does not try to refute the argument against team writing. She concedes that a team-writing assignment can create a bundle of headaches for teachers, including dysfunctional groups, inequities in grading, and so forth. Rather, her strategy is to shift from the opponents' field of values (teacher comfort, ease of grading, reduction of hassles) to a different field of values (active learning, gaining an important career skill, extra time for teachers to schedule conferences). By conceding to the opponents' argument, the writer achieves a fair-minded *ethos* that may be more persuasive than a combative *ethos*.

RESPONSE STRATEGY 3:   CONCILIATORY OR ROGERIAN APPROACH TO OPPOSING VIEWS

A third way to deal with opposing views is to take a conciliatory approach, often referred to as *Rogerian argument*. Rogerian argument was developed by psychologist Carl Rogers to help people resolve differences.* It emphasizes "empathic listening," which Rogers defined as the ability to see an issue sympathetically from another person's perspective. He trained people to withhold judgment of another person's ideas until after they listened attentively to the other person, understood that person's reasoning, appreciated that person's values, respected that person's humanity—in short, walked in that person's shoes. Before disagreeing with another person, Rogers would tell his clients, you must be able to summarize that person's argument so accurately that he or she will say, "Yes, you understand my position."

What Carl Rogers understood is that traditional methods of argumentation are threatening. When you try to persuade people to change their minds on an issue, Rogers claimed, you are actually demanding a change in their worldviews—to get other people, in a sense, to quit being their kind of person and start being your kind of person. Research psychologists have shown that persons are often not swayed by a logical argument if it somehow threatens their own view of the world. Carl Rogers was therefore interested in finding ways to make arguments less threatening. In Rogerian argument the writer typically waits until the end of the essay to present his position, and that position is often a compromise between the writer's

---

* See Carl Rogers' essay "Communication: Its Blocking and Its Facilitation" in his book *On Becoming a Person* (Boston: Houghton Mifflin, 1961), pp. 329–337. For a fuller discussion of Rogerian argument see Richard Young, Alton Becker, and Kenneth Pike, *Rhetoric: Discovery and Change* (New York: Harcourt Brace, 1972).

original views and those of the opposition. Because Rogerian argument stresses the psychological as well as logical dimensions of argument, and because it emphasizes reducing threat and building bridges rather than winning an argument, it is particularly effective when dealing with emotionally laden issues.

Under Rogerian strategy, the writer reduces the sense of threat to the opposition by showing that *both writer and opponent share many basic values.* Instead of attacking the opponent as wrong-headed, the Rogerian writer respects the opponent's intelligence and demonstrates an understanding of the opponent's position before presenting his or her position. Finally, the Rogerian writer never asks an opponent to capitulate entirely to the writer's side—just to shift somewhat toward the writer's views. By acknowledging that he or she has already shifted toward the opponent's views, the writer makes it easier for an opponent to accept compromise. All of this negotiation ideally leads to a compromise between—or better, a synthesis of—the opposing positions. (A compromise is a middle ground that neither party particularly likes; a synthesis is a new position that both parties like at least as well as their original positions.)

The key to successful Rogerian argument, besides the art of listening, is the ability to point out areas of agreement between the opposing positions. For example, if you support a woman's right to choose abortion and you are arguing with someone completely opposed to abortion, you're unlikely to convert your opponent but you might soften his or her opposition to pro-choice supporters. You begin this process by summarizing your opponent's position sympathetically, stressing your shared values. You might say, for example, that you also value children; that you also are appalled by people who treat abortion as a form of birth control; that you also worry that the easy acceptance of abortion diminishes the value society places on life; and that you also agree that accepting abortion lightly can lead to lack of sexual responsibility. Building bridges like these between you and your opponents makes it more likely that they will meet you halfway when you present arguments that threaten their values.

In its emphasis on establishing common ground, Rogerian argument has much in common with recent feminist theories of argument. Many feminists criticize traditional arguments for being rooted in a male value system and tainted by metaphors of war and combat (such as use of the word "opponent"). Thus, traditional arguments are typically praised for being "powerful," "forceful," or "disarming." The writer "defends" his position and "attacks" his opponent's position using facts and data as "ammunition" and reason as "big guns" to "blow away" his opponent's claim. Throughout this text, our own frequent use of the word "opponent" or "adversary" implicates us in a worldview in which people are divided into opposing camps. According to some feminists, such views can lead to inauthenticity, posturing, and game-playing. The traditional school debate—defined in one of our desk dictionaries as "a formal contest of argumentation in which two opposing teams defend and attack a given proposition"—treats argument as verbal jousting, more concerned to determine a winner than to clarify an issue.

One of our woman students, who excelled as a debater in high school and received straight A's in argument classes, recently explained in an essay her growing alienation from traditional male rhetoric. "Although women students are just as likely to excel in 'male' writing . . . , we are less likely to feel as if we were saying something authentic and true." Later in this same paper the student elaborated on her distrust of "persuasion":

> What many writing teachers have told me is that "the most important writing/ speaking you will ever do will be to persuade someone." My experience as a person who has great difficulty naming and expressing emotions is that the most important communication in my life is far more likely to be simply telling someone how I feel. To say "I love you," or "I'm angry with you," will be far more valuable in most relationship contexts than to say "These are the three reasons why you shouldn't have done what you did. . . ."*

Writers who share this woman's distrust of traditional argumentation often find Rogerian argument appealing because it stresses clarification and accommodation rather than winning, and because it begins with self-examination rather than refutation. Rogerian argument is more in tune with win/win negotiation than with win/lose debate.

To illustrate a conciliatory or Rogerian approach to an issue, let's return to the team-writing controversy. From a Rogerian perspective, the English department's disagreement over team-writing is only a surface manifestation of deeper differences. Using Rogerian listening, supporters of the team-writing proposal would perceive how this issue awakens fears in many of their colleagues and threatens their values. A Rogerian writer listening carefully to her audience might realize that the disagreement over team writing is a symptom of more complex disagreements. Having considered empathically the views of her colleagues who oppose the team-writing proposal, a teacher might use a Rogerian strategy to compose an argument like the following:

An Open Letter to the English Department

The controversy over the team-writing proposal is becoming divisive in the department. I am saddened by this development because people on both sides of the issue are persons of good will with the best interests of their students at heart. As a supporter of the proposal, I think it is time that we recognized the validity and importance of the objections being made against our proposal. There is more at stake here than just the presence or absence of a team-writing unit in first-year composition.

At the very heart of the issue is the perception that we who support the proposal are gradually eroding standards from the writing curriculum. Several years ago many of us urged the department to eliminate the long research paper as

---

* Our thanks to Catherine Brown in an unpublished paper written at Seattle University.

well as the departmental test in editing and grammar. As we have moved more and more to a process approach, the number of papers written by first-year students has declined to accommodate more extensive revision, and many of us have moved from having students read mainstream academic texts to doing analyses of popular culture (cartoons, TV shows, advertisements, etc.). The team-writing proposal seems to many people in our department simply another move away from academic rigor to trendy educational "reform." At every stage of the way, it seems, we have made first-year comp easier rather than harder (analyzing a Gary Larson cartoon rather than a Platonic dialogue) and more fun rather than demanding (watching TV for homework rather than doing library research). The team-writing essay seems to reduce the workload even further; in fact, the lazy student might be able to "hitchhike" his way through the whole project letting the energetic students do all the work. Now if those of us who support the team-writing proposal believe that we do uphold standards and that our courses are characterized by academic rigor and excellence, then we must demonstrate our commitment to these values.

A second perception of our proposal is that it is being used to undermine the traditional role of the teacher. On the surface, at least, use of small groups in the classroom looks lazy, requiring very little preparation and even less classroom skill. Moreover, poorly planned collaborative tasks can often be colossal wastes of time characterized by unfocused and nonproductive talk, fidgeting, and eye-rolling boredom. Once again the burden of proof is on us to show that teaching through collaborative groups requires professional preparation and classroom teaching skill and that our students are at least as likely to learn the knowledge and know-how that all of us expect from them through group work as through traditional means. We know to what extent good lecturing requires professional preparation and skill. We need to show how teaching with small groups requires the same level of professionalism and gets at least as good results.

I therefore suggest that those of us who support the team-writing proposal must demonstrate to the department that we too value the maintenance of high standards for student writing, the centrality and professionalism of the teacher, and commitment to academic excellence and rigor. I recommend therefore that the team-writing proposal be linked to another proposal requiring that the department establish a set of learning outcomes for every class and measure student progress toward those outcomes. If team writing truly is effective, it is up to us to demonstrate that effectiveness by mutually agreeable measures.

The debate over the team-writing proposal gives our department an excellent chance to communicate more fully with each other and to discover that we share a great number of educational values. It is important that all members of the department have their voices heard as we chart out the future of our program. I hope that this compromise proposal gives us a way to move productively forward.

☐ FOR CLASS DISCUSSION

1. In the above letter, what shared values between writer and audience does the writer stress?

2. Compare the argumentative strategy of this letter with those of Versions 1 and 2 on pages 167–69 (all three letters support the team-writing proposal).

a. How do the three essays differ in the way they accommodate their audiences?

b. How do the essays project a different *ethos,* or image of the writer? How do they differ in the kinds of appeals they make to their audience?

c. How would you evaluate the effectiveness of each strategy? Why?

CHAPTER SUMMARY

This chapter has shown you the difference between one- and two-sided arguments and suggested that two-sided arguments are apt to be more persuasive to opposing or neutral audiences. A two-sided argument generally includes a fair summary of the opposing views, followed by either a rebuttal, a concession, or an attempt at Rogerian synthesis or compromise. How much space your essay devotes to opposing views and which strategy you use depend on the rhetorical context in which you find yourself, the audience you are trying to reach, and the ultimate purpose you intend.

APPLICATION OF PRINCIPLES FROM PARTS I AND II TO YOUR OWN WRITING: A GENERAL CHECKLIST FOR EVALUATING DRAFTS

We conclude this chapter by providing a general checklist for evaluating drafts. The checklist serves also as a selective summary of important points and concepts from the first eight chapters of this text. As a writer, you may find such a checklist useful for revising your drafts. But the checklist is most useful, we believe, for readers during an exchange of drafts among peers. When you read a fellow student's draft, your obligation is to provide the most helpful response you can to enable your colleague to revise his or her argument. The following checklist may help you improve the quality of your responses.

General Checklist for Evaluating Drafts

UNDERSTANDING THE WRITER'S INTENTIONS

• What issue is being addressed in this draft?

• What is the writer's thesis (claim, proposition)?

• Where does the writer choose to reveal the thesis? At the beginning? In the middle? At the end? (See discussion of standard form versus delayed thesis, pp. 157–165).

• Can you summarize the writer's main reasons as because clauses?

- Is the draft a one-sided or two-sided argument?
- What audience seems to be addressed? The opposition? Neutral third party? Fellow believers? Other?
- What stance does the writer take toward opposing views? Tough-minded and combative? Conciliatory? Other?

RECONSTRUCTING THE WRITER'S ARGUMENT

- Can you make a tree diagram, flow chart, or outline of the writer's argument? (See pp. 70–75.)
- Summarize the writer's argument in 100–200 words. (If you have trouble summarizing the argument, discuss difficulties with writer. Have him or her talk you through the argument orally and then make recommendations for revision.)

CRITIQUING THE WRITER'S ARGUMENT

- How effective are the writer's supporting reasons? Are there any additional reasons the writer might use?
- Is each reason supported with effective grounds in the form of factual data, evidence, statistics, testimony, or appropriate chains of reasons?
- Do the warrants for any of the reasons need to be explicitly articulated and supported with backing?
- To what extent are the supporting reasons audience-based instead of writer-based? (Do each of the supporting enthymemes rest in values shared by the audience? See pp. 140–47.)
- Does the writer attend adequately to opposing views? As a reviewer of this draft, how would *you* go about refuting the writer's argument?
- If the writer summarizes opposing views, does he or she follow the principle of charity—a fair, accurate, complete summary, making the opponent's "best case" (see pp. 170–71)?
- If the writer rebuts the opposition, is the rebuttal clear and effective? How could it be improved?
- Does the writer project an effective *ethos* (see pp. 149–50)?
- Does the writer make effective use of *pathos?* How could appeals to *pathos* be strengthened through narratives, specific images and details, metaphor and analogy, or word choice (see pp. 150–57)?

CRITIQUING THE ORGANIZATION AND CLARITY OF THE WRITING

- Identify places where the draft is confusing or unclear.
- Do the opening lines engage readers' interest?

- Does the opening introduce the issue and provide enough background?
- If the thesis is presented in the opening, is it clear and is it related effectively to the issue? If the thesis is delayed, is the organization of the draft easy to follow?
- If the essay adopts a self-announcing structure (see pp. 96–97), does the introduction forecast the organizational structure of the essay? Does the essay follow the structure as forecasted? Are transitions between parts clear?
- If the essay adopts an unfolding structure, can you follow the argument? Upon reflection after reading the essay, can you identify the claim and supporting reasons?
- Is the effectiveness of the essay diminished by wordiness, clumsy sentence structure, ineffective passive voice, and other problems of editing, grammar, or style?

SUMMARY OF YOUR RECOMMENDATIONS AS PEER REVIEWER

- What improvements can be made in quality of the writing?
- What improvements can be made in the main reasons supporting the claim?
- What improvements can be made in the use of data and evidence as grounds for the argument?
- What rhetorical changes would you recommend? Adopting a different tone or stance toward audience? Shifting from a one- to two-sided argument? Creating more audience-based reasons? Other?

■ WRITING ASSIGNMENTS FOR CHAPTERS 7 AND 8

The writing options for Chapters 7 and 8 will require you to pay careful attention to the views of your audience. The first option asks you to summarize an opposing view and then to refute it. This assignment calls for a self-announcing structure and asks you to adopt an *ethos* of confident self-assurance about the rightness of your own position.

The second assignment calls for an unfolding, delayed thesis structure in which you arrive at your own position through synthesis with opposing views. In this assignment you adopt a Rogerian *ethos* of conciliator and listener. If in Option 1 you are something of a boxer giving a knockout punch to your opponent, in Option 2 you are an inviter and synthesis-seeker— someone who knits up wounds rather than going for the kill.

OPTION 1:   SUMMARIZING AND REFUTING THE OPPOSITION   Whereas the purpose of most arguments is to develop your own position, the purpose of this assignment is to summarize and refute an opposing view. Before drafting this essay, reread "Response Strategy 1: Rebuttal of Opposing Views" (pp. 171–78).

Write a multiparagraph essay in which you summarize a position opposing yours and then show the weaknesses of that position. Each of the reasons in your opponent's argument should be summarizable in because clauses attached to your opponent's claim.

Your essay should have four main sections. The opening section—your introduction—should introduce your issue, give it presence, and briefly indicate your own position on the issue (but not develop that position). Your second section should summarize an opposing view, following the principle of charity. (Make sure that your transition introducing this section makes clear that this is an *opposing view* that you are summarizing; otherwise your readers will assume it is your view and get confused.) Each of the reasons supporting your opponent's position should be clearly highlighted. The third and longest section of your essay should refute the view you have just summarized by attacking in turn each of the reasons summarized earlier. Finally, your last section should provide a conclusion. The following student essay illustrates this assignment.

■

ABSTRACT VERSUS REPRESENTATIONAL ART

(student essay)

Have you ever come across a painting by Picasso, Mondrian, Pollock, Miro, or any other modern abstract painter of this century and found yourself engulfed in a brightly colored canvas that your senses cannot interpret? Many people, especially out here in the West, would tend to scoff and denounce abstractionism as senseless trash. For instance, these people are disoriented by Miro's bright, fanciful creatures and two-dimensional canvas. They click their tongues and shake their heads at Mondrian's grid works, declaring the poor guy played too many Scrabble games. They guffaw at Pollock's canvases of splashed paint, and silently shake their heads in sympathy for Picasso, whose gruesome, distorted figures must be a reflection of his mental health. Then, standing in front of a Charlie Russell, the famous Western artist, they'll declare it a work of God. People feel more comfortable with something they can relate to and understand immediately without too much thought. This is the case with the work of Charlie Russell. Being able to recognize the elements in his paintings—such as trees, horses, and cowboys—gives people a safety line to their world of "reality." There are some who would disagree when I say abstract art requires more creativity and artistic talent to produce a

1

good piece than does representational art, but there are many weaknesses in their arguments.

People who look down on abstract art have several major arguments to support their beliefs. First, they feel that artists turn abstract because they are not capable of the technical drafting skills that appear in Remington, Russell, and Rockwell pieces. Therefore they created an art form that anyone was capable of and that was less time consuming and then paraded it as artistic progress. Secondly, they feel that the purpose of art is to create something of beauty in an orderly, logical composition. Russell's compositions are balanced and rational; everything sits calmly on the canvas, leaving the viewer satisfied that he has seen all there is to see. The modern abstractionists, on the other hand, seem to compose their pieces irrationally. For example, upon seeing Picasso's *Guernica,* a girlfriend of mine was confused as to the center of focus and turned to ask me, "What's the point?" Finally, many people feel that art should portray the ideal and real. The exactness of detail in Charlie Russell's work is an example of this. He has been called a great historian because his pieces depict the life style, dress, and events of the times. His subject matter is derived from his own experiences on the trail, and reproduced to the smallest detail.

I agree in part with many of these arguments, and at one time even endorsed them. But now, I believe differently. First I object to the opponent's argument that abstract artists are not capable of drafting—representational drawing—and therefore created a new art form that required little technical skill. Many abstract artists, such as Picasso, are excellent draftsmen. As his work matured, Picasso became more abstract in order to increase the expressive quality of his work. *Guernica* was meant as a protest against the bombing of that city by the Germans. To express the terror and suffering of the victims more vividly, he distorted the figures and presented them in a black and white journalistic manner. If he had used representational image and color, much of the emotional content would've been lost and the piece probably would not have caused the demand for justice that it did. Secondly, I disagree that a piece *must* be logical and aesthetically pleasing to be art. More important, I feel, is the message it conveys to its viewers. It should reflect the ideals and issues of its time and be true to itself, not just a flowery, glossy surface. For example, through his work, Mondrian was trying to present a system of simplicity, logic, and rational order. As a result, his pieces did end up looking like a Scrabble board. Miro created powerful, surrealistic images from his dreams and subconscious. Pollock's huge splatter paint canvases surround the viewer with a fantastic linear environment. All of these artists were trying to evoke a response from society through an expressionistic manner, not just create a pretty picture to be admired and passed by. Finally, abstract artists and representational artists maintain different ideas about "reality." To the representational artist, reality is what he sees with his eyes. This is the reality he *reproduces* on canvas.

2

3

To the abstract artist, reality is what he feels about what his eyes see. This is the reality he *interprets* on canvas. This can be illustrated by Mondrian's *Trees* series. You can actually see the progression from the early recognizable, though abstracted, *Trees,* to his final solution, the grid system.

A cycle of abstract and representational art began with the first   4
scratching of prehistoric man. From the abstractions of ancient Egypt to representational, classical Rome, returning to abstractionism in early Christian art and so on up to the present day, the cycle has been proved. But this day and age may witness its death through the camera. With film, there is no need to produce finely detailed, historical records manually; the camera does this for us faster and more efficiently. Perhaps we will soon be heading for a time where representational art is nonexistent and artists and their work will be redefined. With abstractionism as the victor of the first battle, maybe another cycle will be touched off and another cyclical interval. Possibly, some time in the distant future—thousands of years from now—art will be physically nonexistent. I heard it said somewhere that some artists even now believe that once they have planned and constructed a piece in their mind, there is no sense doing it with their hands; it has already been done and could never be duplicated. Echoing the birth, life, and death of man, art too would cycle.

OPTION 2:   CONCILIATORY OR ROGERIAN STRATEGY   Write a multiparagraph essay that refrains from presenting your position until the conclusion. The opening section introduces the issue and provides needed background. The second section summarizes the views of the opposition in a sympathetic manner. The third section creates a bridge between writer and opponent by pointing out major areas of agreement that writer and opponent have in common. After examining this common ground, the third section then points out areas of disagreement but stresses that these are minor compared with the major areas of agreement already discussed. Finally, the last section presents the writer's position, which, if possible, should be a compromise or synthesis indicating that the writer has shifted his original position (or at least his sympathies) toward the opposition's view and is now asking the opposition to make a similar shift toward the writer's new position. Your goal here, through tone, arrangement, and examination of common values, is to reduce the threat of your argument in the eyes of your opponent. Before drafting this essay, reread pages 179–83, where we discuss a conciliatory or Rogerian strategy. The following student essay illustrates this strategy:

LETTER TO BETH DOWNEY

(student essay)

Ms. Beth Downey, Owner/Manager
Downey's Music
Grayfish

Dear Ms. Downey:

I would just like to comment on the success of "Downey's Music" in Grayfish and say that, as owner and manager, you have done a wonderful job. I'm sure that you have the most extensive classical music, music teaching books, piano and acoustic guitar inventory of any store in a 100-square-mile area. After working for you for three years, I have encountered music teachers and classical music lovers coming as far as 70 miles to buy their music from Downey's. All have had nothing but compliments for you and for the store. However, I would once again like to bring up the subject of introducing an inventory of electronic music equipment to the store. Since Grayfish is mainly a tourist town, many times a week I have people from touring bands, visiting Canadians, and also locals coming into the store looking for such things as electronic keyboards, electric guitars, and amplifiers. I know that you have qualms about this idea, but I believe that I have a suggestion that we could both agree on.

First, let me restate your reasons for objecting to such a move. You have already stated that if a change will benefit the store, the initial investment is well worth the expense in the long run (e.g., when pianos were added to the inventory). Therefore, I assume that cost is not a factor at this time. However, you feel that the "kind of people" that electronics may draw could possibly offend our present clientele. You feel, as well as others, that the people who are drawn by electronics are often long haired, dirty, and give a bad impression. This would in effect change the store's image. Also, you are afraid that the noise caused by these instruments could turn classical music lovers away from the store. The sounds of electronic instruments are not always pleasing, and since most of our clientele are older, more refined persons, you feel that these sounds will force some to go to other stores. Mainly, however, you are worried about the result that the change in the store's image could have upon a community the size of Grayfish. Many people in this area, I realize, feel that electronic music means heavy rock music, while this in turn means alcohol and drugs.

Basically, I agree with you that Grayfish needs a "classical" music store and that the culture that your store brings to Grayfish greatly enhances the area. I also love classical music and want to see it growing and alive. I also have some of the same fears about adding electronic music to the inventory. I enjoy the atmosphere of Downey's, and I have always enjoyed working there, so I don't want to see anything adverse happen to it either. On the other hand, I feel that if a large electronic music section were added to the store with sound-proof rooms, a "sit and try it" atmosphere, and a catalog inventory large enough to special order anything that a customer might want that is not in the store, it would help immensely in the success of the store. With the way that Downey's is built, on two levels, it would be very easy to accommodate the needs of both departments. Even now we are only using about half the floor space available, while the rest is empty storage area. By building sound-proof rooms on the lower level, we could easily double the in-use floor area, increase our tourist clientele, have the music business in *all* areas cornered for approximately 60 square miles, and also add practice rooms for our present customers to use when they are choosing music.

I know that you are wrestling with this idea of such a drastic changeover, so I would like to propose a solution that I feel we could both agree on. My solution is to start slowly, on a trial basis, and see how it works. I suggest that we start with a few small electronic keyboards, a few electric guitars, and one or two amps. In this way, we could begin to collect the information and literature on other electronic equipment that may be added later on, see how the community responds to such a move, find out how our present clientele reacts, get a feel for the demand in this field, and yet still be a small home-town music store without a great investment in this electronic area. I still feel that a large addition would be more successful, but I also believe that this little test may help prove to you, or disprove to me, that electronic music instruments in this area are in high demand. I honestly feel that electronics could produce fantastic profits for the people who get in the business first. I would love it if these "people" could be the owners and workers at Downey's Music.

Sincerely,
Mary Doe

OPTION 3:   A FORMAL ARGUMENT IN THE STANDARD FORM   Write a formal argument following the standard form as explained on pages 158–59. In essence, this essay combines the two or more reasons assignment on page 135 (Option 5) with the summary and refutation assignment on pages 185–86 (Option 1). A standard-form argument has a self-announcing structure. Your introduction will present your issue, provide needed background, and announce your thesis. It may also provide a brief forecasting passage to help the reader anticipate the shape of your essay. (See pp. 96–97.) In the body of your essay, you summarize and refute opposing views as well as present your own reasons and evidence in support of your position. It is your choice whether you summarize and refute opposing views before or after you have made your own case. Generally, try to end your essay with your strongest arguments.

Arguments in Depth: Five Categories of Claims

□

9

Using the Categories of Claim to Generate Ideas

In Parts I and II, we discussed the arguing process, the basic structure of arguments, and the relation of arguments to audience. In Part III, our goal is to show you how arguments can be categorized according to the patterns of thought they typically require; that is, each category of argument typically has its own characteristic structure that reflects a characteristic kind of thinking. If you learn these common "moves"—these common patterns of organization and thought—you can use them to help you generate ideas and greatly expand your own argumentative powers. In particular, Part III introduces you to five different categories of arguments: definitional arguments, cause/consequence arguments, analogy/resemblance arguments, evaluation arguments, and proposal arguments. The first three of these categories deal with questions of truth; the last two deal with questions of value.

The benefit of our five-category schema is not that it helps you classify all arguments; in fact, you will come across many arguments that resist and some that defy classification. Rather, the benefit of the five-category schema is that it helps you generate ideas for an argument by teaching you some common patterns that arguments follow. By playing with the categories—by treating an argument you are developing, for example, as if it were a causal or evaluational argument—you open new avenues of support and refutation. Knowing the patterns, then, becomes a powerful tool for invention.

The present chapter introduces you to the five-category schema, gives you an overview of its structure, and explains a simple three-step strategy you can use to generate ideas for arguments. The remaining chapters of Part III deal in turn with each of the category types.

WHAT IS A TRUTH ARGUMENT?

The first three categories in our schema—sometimes called "truth arguments"—involve disputes about the way reality is (or was or will be). Unlike facts, which can be confirmed or disconfirmed by using agreed-on empirical measures, a truth claim involves interpretation of facts, which, like all interpretations, must be supported by reasons.

However, locating the point at which a "fact" turns into a "claim" is a tricky issue. The French mathematician Poincaré said that a fact is something that is "common to several thinking beings and could be common to all." This definition seems simple enough. Water freezes at 32 degrees; Chicago is in Illinois; the state of Illinois did not ratify the Equal Rights Amendment. These are all facts. No problem. But what about the statement "Life is preferable to death." That seems like a statement that could be common to all. But it isn't. The fact that thousands of people voluntarily take their own lives each year establishes that it's not a factual statement. And what makes the number of suicides a fact?—the possibility that we could all go look the information up in a source we all agreed was authoritative and find the same number.

But what about an apparently "factual" statement such as "Joe is literate." Does that mean that Joe can read a newspaper? A traffic sign? A fourth-grade reader? A novel? Or does it mean that he's read a number of books that we've agreed are essential for all educated members of our culture to have read? Anytime an apparent statement of fact requires interpretation (in this case because of a dispute over the definition of *literate*), anytime all who know the thing being referred to don't share a common understanding of that thing, we are in the realm of truth claims, not of facts. Here are some examples of the kinds of truth claims that the next three chapters examine:

Sam is/is not an alcoholic. (X is a Y—definitional argument)

Gun control laws will/will not reduce the violent crime rate in the United States. (X causes Y—causal argument)

Investing in the stock market is/is not like gambling. (X is like Y—resemblance argument)

WHAT IS A VALUES ARGUMENT?

For many people, the only sort of argument we can legitimately have is over claims of truth. Values, after all, are personal, whereas truth can be looked at objectively. But the notion that values are purely personal is a dangerous one. If for no other reason, it's dangerous because every day we encounter value issues that must be resolved. If you think you deserve a promotion and your boss doesn't, your own sense of self-worth won't let you ignore the resulting values dispute. If you think your community needs a new school and a majority of voters is unpersuaded, you need to articulate your views before election day or else your vote may be wasted.

Values may begin as feelings founded on private experience, but a real value must go beyond these beginnings and be capable of being justified. Otherwise, it remains an opinion, which is a feeling limited to personal experiences, your own private collection of likes and dislikes that couldn't be justified even if it were necessary. But values can be justified; they are transpersonal and shareable. We can articulate criteria that others would agree are significant and coherent and then we can apply those criteria to situations, people, and things and come to some agreement.

Here then are some examples of the kinds of values claims that the following chapters will examine:

Dr. Jones is/is not a good teacher. (X is a good Y—evaluation claim)

Congress should/should not pass a balanced-budget amendment. (We should do X—proposal argument)

Dr. Jones is/is not a good person. (special case of evaluation claim—moral argument)

THREE-STEP STRATEGY FOR DISCOVERING AUDIENCE-BASED REASONS

The power of the five-category schema becomes quickly evident when we realize that the supporting reasons for value claims are frequently truth claims. As a quick example, consider the arguments used in the early nineties when conservative politicians objected to the use of taxpayer dollars to fund a controversial exhibition of the Mapplethorpe photographs, which focused on homoerotic themes. The conservative argument, in varying ways, used all three of the different kinds of truth claims to support a value claim:

Taxpayer funding for the Mapplethorpe exhibits ought to be withdrawn [a proposal claim]because the photographs are pornographic [a definitional claim], because they promote community acceptance of homosexuality [a cause/consequence claim], and because the photographs are more like political statements than like art [analogy/resemblance claim].

Whatever you might think of the argument, the example shows how the "because clauses" in support of the proposal claim are truth claims of definition, cause/consequence, and analogy/resemblance. The example suggests how the three truth claims can be used as a strategy to help you think of ways to support value arguments. The rest of this chapter explains this three-step strategy in more detail.

The three-step strategy works by focusing your attention on three different approaches to developing a value argument:

1. An "argument from definition," in which you argue that doing X is right (wrong) according to some value, assumption, principle, or belief that you share with your audience. (This strategy is also called by various other names, such as an "argument from principle" or an "argument from genus or category.")

2. An "argument from consequence," in which you argue that doing X is right (wrong) because doing X will lead to consequences that you and your audience believe are good (bad).

3. An "argument from resemblance," in which you argue that doing X is right (wrong) because doing X is like doing Y, which you and your audience agree is right (wrong).

Let's now illustrate the strategy in more detail. In a recent college course, the instructor asked students whether they would report a classmate for plagiarizing a paper. To the instructor's dismay, the majority of students said they would not. The issue question at stake is this "Should a student report a classmate who plagiarizes an essay?" The teacher wanted to argue "yes," whereas her students argued "no." How could the teacher support her claim?

An Argument From Definition or Principle

One strategy she could use is to argue as follows: "A student should report a classmate for plagiarizing a paper because plagiarism is fraud." We can call this an "argument from principle" because it is based on the assumption that the audience opposes fraud as a kind of unchanging rule or law—in short, that it opposes fraud on principle. Such an argument can also be called an "argument from definition" because it places the term X (plagiarizing a paper) inside the class or category Y (fraud).

ARGUMENT FROM DEFINITION/PRINCIPLE

To think of ideas with this strategy, you conduct the following kind of search:

> We should (should not) do X because X is _____.

Try to fill in the blank with an appropriate adjective or noun (*good, just, ethical, criminal, ugly, violent, peaceful, wrong, inflationary, healing; an act of kindness, terrorism, murder, true art, political suicide,* and so forth). The point is to try to fill in the blank with a noun or adjective that appeals in some way to your audience's values. Your goal is to show that X belongs to the chosen class or category.

In saying that plagiarism is fraud, the teacher assumes that students would report classmates for other kinds of fraud (for example, for counterfeiting a signature on a check, for entering the university's computer system to alter grades, and so forth). In other words, she knows that the term *fraud* has force on the audience because most people will agree that instances of fraud should be reported. Her task is to define *fraud* and show how plagiarism fits that definition. She could show that fraud is an act of deception to obtain a benefit that doesn't rightly belong to a person. She could then argue that plagiarism is such an act in that it uses deception to procure the benefits of a grade that the plagiarizer has not earned. Although the person whose work is plagiarized may not be directly damaged, the reputation and stature of the university is damaged whenever it grants credentials that have been fraudulently earned. The degree earned by a plagiarizer is fraudulent. Although convincing students that plagiarism is fraud won't guarantee that students will report it, it does make such whistle blowing more likely to putting plagiarism inside the class of seriously bad things.

An Argument from Consequence

Besides arguing from principle, the teacher could argue from consequence: "A student should report a classmate for plagiarizing a paper because the consequences of plagiarism are bad for everyone concerned." This is a consequence argument (X produces these consequences) based on the warrant that these consequences are bad; it shows first that X causes Y and then that Y is bad.

ARGUMENT FROM CONSEQUENCE

To think of reasons using this strategy, conduct the following kind of search:

We should (should not) do X because X leads to these consequences: _____, _____, _____, _____.

Then think of consequences that your audience will agree are good or bad, as your argument requires.

Using this strategy, the teacher now focuses on the ill effects that plagiarism can have. She might argue that plagiarism raises the grading curve to the disadvantage of honest students or that it can lead to ill-trained people getting into critical professions. How would you like to undergo brain surgery, she might ask, from someone who cheated her way through medical school? She might argue that acceptance of plagiarism leads to acceptance of moral sloppiness throughout the society—acceptance of tax dodging, of shoddy workmanship, of taking small "loans" from the company till. She might even argue that plagiarism hurts the person who plagiarizes by preventing that person from developing needed skills for later success in life. Finally, she would probably want to argue at some point that reporting plagiarism cases will prevent or limit plagiarism. All these examples would be arguments from consequence.

An Argument from Resemblance

But there is a third strategy the teacher might employ. She could say, "You should report someone for plagiarizing an essay just as you would report someone for submitting someone else's art project in an art class." Although this argument looks similar to saying that "plagiarism is fraud," it actually represents a different kind of reasoning, what we call reasoning from resemblance or analogy.

In using this strategy, the teacher hopes that her audience will see that if someone else's painting is a piece of property, then someone else's essay is a piece of property also. This recognition in turn will help students see plagiarism as theft, because we typically associate theft with property. The teacher will have to show how an essay represents the same kind of artistic craft as a painting and how cheating works the same way in both art and writing.

ARGUMENT FROM RESEMBLANCE

To think of reasons with this strategy, make the following kind of search:

We should (should not) do X because doing X is like _____.

Then think of analogies or precedents that are similar to doing X but that currently have more force on your audience. Your goal is then to transfer to X the audience's attitude toward the precedent or analogy.

Arguing from analogy in this way is among the most persuasive yet tricky of all argumentative strategies. It is the subject of Chapter 12, which treats resemblance arguments in depth.

These three strategies, then—imagining your argument from the perspectives of principle, consequence, and resemblance—can be useful ways to find reasons for your arguments. In creating reasons, of course, you will be guided by your knowledge of your audience, trying to create reasons that appeal to their values and beliefs.

When you use the above strategy for generating ideas, you shouldn't feel you are limited to reasons derived solely from the strategy. You can discover all kinds of excellent reasons for your arguments that don't fit neatly into one of the three claim types. Although a reason can often be reworded so that it more clearly fits a strategy, getting the reasons to match the strategies isn't the purpose. Rather, the purpose is to stimulate your thinking, to give you something to fall back on when your mind gets stuck. With this understanding in mind, you are now ready to try your hand at using the three-step strategy.

□ FOR CLASS DISCUSSION

1. Working individually or in small groups, use the strategies of principle, consequence, and resemblance to think of because clauses to support each of the following claims. Try to have at least one because clause from each of the strategies, but generate as many reasons as possible. Don't worry about whether any individual reason exactly fits the strategy. Again, the purpose is to stimulate thinking, not to fill in slots.

EXAMPLE:

CLAIM: Pit bulls make bad pets

PRINCIPLE: because they are vicious

CONSEQUENCE: because owning a pit bull leads to conflicts with neighbors

RESEMBLANCE: because owning a pit bull is a little like having a shell-shocked friend—the friend is wonderful most of the time, but you never know when some event will turn him violent

   a. The United States should pass a constitutional amendment forbidding abortion

PRINCIPLE: because abortion is _____

CONSEQUENCE: because abortion will have the consequences of _____, _____, _____

RESEMBLANCE: because aborting a fetus is like _____

   b. Marijuana should be legalized.

   c. Despite its high cost, America should continue its space exploration program.

   d. Couples should live together before getting married.

   e. The United States should end its energy dependence on other nations.

   f.–j. Repeat the above exercise, taking a different position on each issue. You might try beginning with the claim. "Pit bulls make good pets."

2. Again working individually or in small groups, use the principle/consequence/resemblance heuristic to explore arguments on both sides of the following issues.

   a. Should spanking be made illegal?

   b. Has affirmative action been good or bad for the nation?

c. Should the United States pass a law mandating universal national service for all American citizens following graduation from high school or college? (*Universal national service* means being drafted into the military or some alternative means of serving the country.)

d. Should high schools pass out free contraceptives?

e. Would it be better to grade college writing classes on the basis of effort rather than performance?

10

Definition Arguments:
X Is/Is Not a Y

□

CASE 1

In 1989 the city of Seattle passed the Family Leave Ordinance, which allowed city employees to use their sick leave to care for a "domestic partner" who is ill. To be eligible for domestic partnership, a couple, whether heterosexual or homosexual, had to file affidavits declaring that they share the same home with their partners, are each other's sole partners, and are responsible for each other's common welfare. For purposes of sick and bereavement leave, domestic partnership was synonymous with marriage. Supporters of this ordinance argued that, in the words of one local columnist, "[i]f sick and bereavement leave is given to married workers, then those in domestic partnerships equivalent to marriage ought to have the same privilege."* Opponents of the ordinance argued that domestic partnerships are not marriages and shouldn't be treated as such.

CASE 2

In a famous Los Angeles criminal case, black motorist Rodney King was stopped for erratic driving after a high-speed chase. According to the arresting officers, King then became verbally abusive, threatened the officers, and violently resisted arrest. The subsequent events were captured on a seventeen-minute video made by an amateur filmmaker. The video showed numerous officers with nightsticks and "stun guns" beating and

---

* Terry Tang, *Seattle Times*, November 1, 1990, p. A10.

stunning King until he was lying on the ground and then continuing the beating for several more minutes. The key point in the trial and subsequent retrial of the officers was whether they had used "reasonable force" in subduing a suspect who was resisting arrest. Clearly the police must protect themselves and use sufficient force to put a suspect under their control, but at what point does reasonable force cross the line and become itself criminal violence?

CASE 3

Economist Isabella Sawhill believes that the current distinctions among "poor," "middle income," and "rich" don't help us understand the real problem of poverty in America. She proposes a new term "underclass." According to her definition, the defining characteristic of the underclass is "dysfunctional behavior," which means failure to follow four major norms of middle-class society: (1) Children are supposed to study hard in school; (2) no one is supposed to become a parent until able to afford a child; (3) adults are supposed to hold regular jobs; and (4) everyone is supposed to obey laws. If we use this definition instead of income level, a rich drug dealer may be a member of the underclass while a poor widow might not be. Sawhill believes society can improve the lives of the underclass by changing these dysfunctional characteristics rather than by relieving poverty directly. A new definition thus aims at changing social policy.*

THE SPECIAL NATURE OF A DEFINITIONAL ISSUE

Many arguments require a definition of key terms. If you are arguing, for example, that after-school jobs are harmful to teenagers because they promote materialism, you will have to define *materialism* somewhere in your argument. Writers regularly define words for their readers either by providing synonyms, by citing a dictionary definition, by stipulating a special definition ("Ordinarily word X means such and so, but in this essay I am using word X to mean this"), or by giving an extended definition in which the writer defines the term and then illustrates the definition with several clarifying examples. This chapter shows you ways to provide such definitions for your readers.

However, this chapter does not focus primarily on writing occasional definitions within arguments. Rather, its purpose is to describe

---

* Spencer Rich, "Economist: Behavior draws lines between the classes," *Seattle Times,* September 13, 1989, p. A4.

how an entire argument can be devoted to a definitional issue. Definitional arguments, according to our usage, occur whenever people disagree about the actual definition of a term or about the "match" or "fit" between an agreed-on definition and a specific object or concept. For example, an argument about whether or not *Penthouse* magazine is pornographic is a definitional argument; as such it will involve two related issues: (1) What do we mean by "pornographic" (the definition issue)? and (2) Does *Penthouse* fit that definition (the match issue)?

Before proceeding with our explanation of definitional arguments, we will present the writing assignment for Chapter 10. This chapter will be more meaningful to you if you read it in the light of a definitional problem that you will need to solve for one of your own essays.

☐ WRITING ASSIGNMENT FOR CHAPTER 10: EXTENDED DEFINITION/BORDERLINE CASE: IS THIS X A Y?

This assignment asks you to solve a definitional problem. In your essay, you must argue whether or not a given X (a borderline case) belongs to concept Y, which you must define.* You will need to write an extended definition of a concept such as "police brutality," "courageous action," "child abuse," "creative act," "cruelty to animals," "free speech," or another, similar concept that is both familiar yet tricky to define precisely. After you have established your definition, you will need to apply it to a "borderline case," arguing whether the borderline case fits or does not fit the definition. For example:

1. Is a daring bank robbery an "act of courage?"

2. Is accounting a "creative profession?"

3. Are highly skilled videogame players "true athletes?"

4. Is a case like the following an instance of "cruelty to animals?"

> A bunch of starlings build nests in the attic of a family's house, gaining access to the attic through a torn vent screen. Soon the eggs hatch, and every morning at sunrise the family is awakened by the sounds of birds squawking and wings beating against rafters as the starlings fly in and out of the house to feed the hatchlings. After losing considerably early morning sleep, the family repairs the screen. Unable to get in and out, the parent birds are unable to feed their young. The birds die within a day.

---

* The writing assignment for this chapter, as well as the collaborative exercises for exploration and development of ideas, is based on the work of George Hillocks and his research associates at the University of Chicago. See George Hillocks, Jr., Elizabeth A. Kahn, and Larry R. Johannessen, "Teaching Defining Strategies as a Mode of Inquiry: Some Effects on Student Writing," *Research in the Teaching of English*, 17 (October 1983), pp. 275–284. See also Larry R. Johannessen, Elizabeth A. Kahn, and Carolyn Calhoun Walter, *Designing and Sequencing Prewriting Activities*, Urbana, Ill.: NCTE, 1982.

One part of your essay should be an extended definition of your Y term (in the above case, cruelty to animals), in which you set forth the criteria for your chosen Y, illustrating each criterion with positive and contrastive examples. Once you have established your definition of Y, you will use it to decide whether your chosen X term (the borderline case—in the preceding case, the repairing of the screen, which leads to the death of the starlings) meets or does not meet the criteria. The rest of this chapter explains this arguing strategy in detail.

THE CRITERIA-MATCH STRUCTURE OF DEFINITIONAL ARGUMENTS

Definitional arguments take the form "X is/is not a Y." This claim can be restated in various ways: "X is/is not a case of Y," X is/is not an instance of Y," "X does/does not belong to the class of Y," and so forth. The Y term can be either a noun phrase ("Writing graffiti on walls is *vandalism*") or an adjective phrase ("Writing graffiti on walls is *politically useless*"—that is, "*belongs to the class of politically useless things*").

To appreciate the structure of a definitional argument, consider the shape of a typical definitional claim when its reasons are stated as because clauses: X is a Y because it possesses feature A, because it possesses feature B, and because it possesses feature C. Placed in the Toulmin schema, the argument looks like this:

ENTHYMEME:	X is a Y because it possesses features A, B, and C.
CLAIM:	X is a Y.
STATED REASON:	because it possesses features A, B, and C
GROUNDS:	evidence that X possesses features A, B, and C
WARRANT:	Features A, B, and C are sufficient criteria for calling something a Y.
BACKING:	chains of reasons and evidence (or citing of statutes, etc.) that show that true Y's have features A, B, and C
CONDITIONS OF REBUTTAL:	*Attacking the grounds:* Unless X doesn't possess features A, B, and C or doesn't possess sufficient quantities of A, B, and C; unless X possesses, in addition to features A, B, and C, a fourth feature Z, which makes it impossible to be a Y.
	Attacking the warrant: unless features A, B, and C are not sufficient criteria for calling something a Y.
QUALIFIER:	Depends on level of certainty of definition or level of certainty that X meets definition.

As shown above, definitional arguments of the type "X is a Y" tend to have a two-part structure: (1) How do we define Y? and (2) Does X fit that definition? We use the term *criteria-match* to describe this structure, which occurs regularly not only in definitional arguments but also, as we shall see in Chapter 13, in values arguments of the type "X is a good/bad Y." The "criteria" part of the structure defines the Y term by setting forth the criteria that must be met to be considered a Y (these criteria are the warrants for the argument). The "match" part examines whether or not the X term meets these criteria (evidence that X meets the criteria is the grounds for the argument). Let's consider several more examples:

Definitional claim: Weaving is a craft, not an art.

>Criteria part: What are the criteria for a craft?

>Match part: Does weaving meet these criteria?

Definitional claim: A Honda assembled in Ohio is/is not an American-made car.

>Criteria part: What criteria have to be met before a car can be called "American-made"?

>Match part: Does a Honda assembled in Ohio meet these criteria?

□ FOR CLASS DISCUSSION

Consider the following definitional claims. Working as individuals or in small groups, identify the criteria issue and the match issue for each of the following claims. (Any of these examples could be potential topics for an "extended definition/borderline case" argument of the kind you are asked to write for this chapter.)

1. Childbirth is/is not a creative act.
2. Writing graffiti on subways is/is not vandalism.
3. The language "spoken" by porpoises is/is not true language.
4. Beauty contests are/are not sexist events.
5. For purposes of state regulation, bungee jumping from a crane is/is not a "carnival amusement ride."
6. Psychology is/is not a true science.
7. Designing advertisements for television is/is not a creative activity.
8. A surrogate mother—one who has had another woman's fertilized egg implanted in her uterus—is/is not the true mother of the child.
9. Cheerleaders are/are not athletes.
10. Poker is/is not a game of luck.

CONCEPTUAL PROBLEMS OF DEFINITION

Before moving on to discuss ways of defining the Y term in a definitional argument, we need to discuss some of the conceptual difficulties of definition. Language, as you quickly discover when you try to analyze it, is a slippery subject. Definitions aren't as easy to make, or as certain, as a handy pocket dictionary might lead you to believe.

Language as a Way of Ordering the World

Language is our primary means of making sense of the world. Through language we convert what psychologist William James called the "buzz and confusion" of the world into a system of classes and relationships that are represented by a network of verbal signs called words. Each naming word in a language depends on our perceiving a set of attributes that any object or concept must have in order to bear that name. Naming words (with the exception of proper names) don't designate particular items but rather attributes of items. Hence, when we want to know what *king* means, we don't need to know every king in history. We simply need to know the characteristics of kings and kingship to understand and use the term. Through naming we are set free from the world of immediate particulars where we can see only this rock or that flower; through naming we are liberated into a shareable world where we possess with other humans the concept "rock" and the concept "flower" along with arbitrary signs—the vocal sounds "rock" and "flower"—that call forth the concepts.

But if naming is the "first act" of language users, it's far from a simple one. Words allow us to share concepts, but they certainly don't assure perfect mutual understanding. Inevitably, as soon as we've named something, someone else will ask "Whaddya mean by that?" Language, for all its wonderful powers, is an arbitrary system that requires agreement among its users before it can work. And it's not always easy to get that agreement. Thus, the second act after naming is defining. And even at the most basic level, defining things can be devilishly complex.

Why Can't We Just Look in the Dictionary?

"What's so hard about defining?" you might ask. Why not just look in a dictionary? To get a sense of the complexity of defining something, consider the word *red*. What does it mean? Although you might agree with us that *red* is difficult to define in words, you could argue that you can escape the problem simply by pointing to something red. Maybe. But consider the following example cited by I. A. Richards and C. K. Ogden in *The Meaning of Meaning*.

An English explorer, investigating an unknown Congolese language, found himself in a hut with five natives standing around a wooden table. The explorer tapped the table and asked "What's this?" Each of the five Congolese gave him a different answer, causing the explorer to congratulate himself for "working among a people who possessed so rich a language that they had five words for one article" (*Meaning*, p. 78).

Only later did he discover that the natives had understood his apparently straightforward gesture in five different ways. One thought he was asking the word for "wood"; another for "table covering"; the third thought he wanted the word for "hardness"; the fourth for "tapping." Only one guessed his actual intention and gave him the Congolese word for "table." Even when we can point to an object in reality, then, there is possibility for confusion. Think how these difficulties multiply as we move on to words standing for things that can't be pointed toward, words like *love* and *freedom* and *cruelty to animals*.

But let's go back to dictionaries and their limitations in resolving definitional disputes. Say you wanted to resolve the debate over whether or not cheerleaders are athletes by turning to your dictionary. An athlete, according to our dictionary, is "one who is trained to compete in exercises, sports, or games requiring physical strength, agility, or skill." So, are cheerleaders athletes? They do train, and the activity itself of leading cheers would appear to require "strength, agility, and skill." But is it a form of "competition"? Do they "compete" against the rival cheerleaders? And is cheerleading "exercise, sport, or game?" Well, you're going to have to keep looking in your dictionary before you can even begin to address these questions. And take it from us, you won't be able to stop once you've defined all the attributes of your first definition.

Dictionaries usually can't resolve real definitional disputes because their function is to tell us the commonly held meanings of words. That is, their purpose is to tell us what words mean in general usage, without getting into the shades and nuances of meaning that are at the heart of most definitional disputes. People arguing over the definition of *athlete* probably already know the approximate dictionary definition of the word. But words aren't facts and an exact meaning common to all is impossible when words are always changing their meaning over time and between contexts. Moreover, dictionary definitions rarely tell us such things as *to what degree* a given condition must be met before it qualifies for class membership. How much do you need to train to qualify as an athlete? *To what extent* must you compete? How strong or agile does an athlete have to be? On all such critical matters, dictionaries are too often silent to settle definitional disputes.

Definitions and the Rule of Justice: At What Point Does X Quit Being a Y?

For some people, all this concern about definition may seem misplaced. How often, after all, have you heard people accuse each other of getting bogged down in "mere semantics"? But how we define a given word can have significant implications for people who must either use the word or have the word used on them. Take, for example, what some philosophers refer to as "the rule of justice." According to this rule, "beings in the same essential category should be treated in the same way." Should an insurance company, for example, treat a woman who needs to miss work following childbirth the same way it treats a woman who needs to miss work following an appendectomy? Should childbirth belong within the category "illness" as far as insurance payments are concerned? Similarly, if a company gives "new baby" leave to a mother, should it also be willing to give "new baby" leave to a father? In other words, is this kind of leave "new mother" leave or is it "new parent" leave? And what if a couple adopts an infant? Should "new mother" or "new parent" leave be available to them also? These questions are all definitional issues involving arguments about what class of beings an individual belongs to and about what actions to take to comply with the "rule of justice," which demands that all members of that class be treated equally.

Let's take a slightly less elevated (and less complex) problem of definitional justice. If your landlord decides to institute a "no pets" rule, then the rule of justice requires that all pets have to go—not just your neighbor's barking dog, but also Mrs. Brown's cat, the kids' hamster downstairs, and your own pet tarantula. In order to keep your friendly spider, though, mightn't you argue that your pet tarantula isn't really a "pet"? Because the rule of justice demands that all pets must be treated equally, the only fair way to save your spider is to get it removed from the class "pets." The rule of justice thus forces the question "How much can any given X vary before it is no longer a Y?"

The rule of justice becomes even harder to apply when we consider X's that grow, evolve, or otherwise change through time. When Young Person back in Chapter 1 argued that she could set her own curfew because she was mature, she raised the question "What are the attributes or criteria of a 'mature' person?" In this case, a categorical distinction between two separate kinds of things ("mature" versus "not mature") evolves into a distinction of degree ("mature enough"). So perhaps we should not ask whether Young Person is mature, but whether she is "mature enough." At what point does a child become an adult? (When does a fetus become a human person? When does a B essay become an A essay? When does a social drinker become an alcoholic?)

Although we may be able arbitrarily to choose a particular point and declare, through stipulation, that "mature" means eighteen years old or that "human person" includes a fetus at conception, or at three months, or at birth, in the everyday world the distinction between child and adult, between egg and person, between social drinking and alcoholism seems an evolution, not a sudden and definitive step. Nevertheless, our language requires an abrupt shift between classes. In short, applying the rule of justice often requires us to adopt a digital approach to reality—switches are either on or off, either a fetus is a human person or it is not—whereas our sense of life is more analogical—there are numberless gradations between on and off, there are countless shades of gray between black and white.

As we can see in the above case, the promise of language to fix the buzz and confusion of the world into an orderly set of categories turns out to be elusive. In most definitional debates, an argument, not a quick trip to the dictionary, is required to settle the matter.

CONDUCTING A CRITERIA-MATCH ARGUMENT

Having raised some philosophical issues about definition, let's now proceed directly to a discussion of how to conduct a criteria-match argument. When you prepare to develop and write a definitional argument, you need first to determine if the criteria or the match or both are primarily at issue.

In some arguments the criteria part—that is, determining the defining characteristics of Y—is the most difficult. The Minneapolis ordinance against pornography, referred to in Chapter 7, is an example of this kind of argument. According to that ordinance, if a magazine or film meets any of nine criteria, it can be considered pornographic. The major difficulty faced by drafters of the ordinance was establishing the nine criteria.

In other arguments the match part will take the majority of your time. If you wanted to argue that your calculus course was badly organized you would probably spend most of your time showing examples of disorganization in the course and little time, if any, defining *disorganized*. In still other arguments—such as the extended definition/borderline case assignment in this chapter—the criteria and match parts might both demand considerable attention. The point is, however, that all definitional arguments have at their core a criteria-match structure even if one part of the structure can be virtually eliminated in specific cases.

DEFINING THE Y TERM (ESTABLISHING CRITERIA FOR Y)

Unless your Y term is easy to define, you will have to present an extended definition in which you gradually bring your reader step by step toward understanding your criteria. In this section we discuss two methods of definition—Aristotelian and operational.

Aristotelian Definition

In Aristotelian definitions, regularly used in dictionaries, one defines a term by placing it within the next larger class or category and then showing the specific attributes that distinguish the term from other terms within the same category. For example, a *pencil* is a "writing implement" (next larger category) that differs from other writing implements in that it makes marks with lead or graphite rather than ink. You could elaborate this definition by saying "usually the lead or graphite is a long, thin column embedded in a slightly thicker column of wood with an eraser on one end and a sharpened point, exposing the graphite, on the other." You could even distinguish a wooden pencil from a mechanical pencil, thereby indicating again that the crucial identifying attribute is the graphite, not the wooden column.

As you can see, an Aristotelian definition of a Y term creates specific criteria that enable you to distinguish it from the next larger class. But whereas our example of a pencil is relatively easy, most criteria arguments are more complex, requiring you not just to state your criteria but to argue for them. For example, when trying to define *true sports car* for the claim "A Dodge Stealth is/is not a true sports car," you might have to defend such criteria as these: "A true sports car is an automobile that has seats for only two people" or "A true sports car is an automobile designed specifically for racing on narrow curving roads." Most of the space in the criteria section of your essay would be spent justifying the criteria you have chosen, usually through examples, contrastive examples, and refutation of opposing criteria.

In constructing Aristotelian definitions it is sometimes helpful to understand and use the concepts of "accidental," necessary," and "sufficient" criteria. An "accidental" criterion is a usual but not essential feature of a concept. For example, "made out of wood" is an accidental feature of a pencil. Most pencils are made out of wood, but something can still be a pencil even if it isn't made out of wood (a mechanical pencil).

Although the distinction between accidental and essential features is relatively clear when discussing things such as pencils, it gets increasingly cloudy as we move into complex definitional debates (for example, what are the accidental, as opposed to essential, characteristics of sexist acts?)

A "necessary" criterion is an attribute that *must* be present for something to be a Y. For example, "is a writing implement" is a necessary criterion for a pencil; "marks with graphite or lead" is also a necessary criterion. However, neither of these criteria by itself is a sufficient criterion for a pencil. Many writing implements aren't pencils (for example, pens); also, many things that mark with lead or graphite aren't pencils (for example, a lead paperweight will make pencil-like marks on paper). To be a pencil both these criteria together must be present. We say, then, that these two criteria together are *sufficient* criteria for the concept "pencil."

You can appreciate how these concepts can help you carry on a definitional argument with more precision. Felix Ungar might argue that a Stealth is not a true sports car because it has rear seats. (To Felix, having seating for only two people is thus a necessary criterion for a true sports car.) Oscar Madison might argue, however, that having two seats is only an accidental feature of sports cars and that a Stealth is indeed a true sports car because it has a racy appearance and because it handles superbly on curves. (For

Oscar, racy appearance and superb handling are together sufficient criteria for a true sports car.)

□ FOR CLASS DISCUSSION

Working individually or in small groups, try to determine whether each of the following is a necessary criterion, a sufficient criterion, an accidental criterion, or no criterion for defining the indicated concept. Be prepared to explain your reasoning.

CRITERION	CONCEPT TO BE DEFINED
presence of gills	fish
having yellow hair (applied to person)	blond
born inside the United States	American citizen
over sixty-five	senior citizen
knows several programming languages for computers	meets foreign language requirement for graduation
line endings form a rhyming pattern	poem
teaches classes at a college	college professor
eats no meat, ever	vegetarian
kills another human being	murderer
good sex life	happy marriage

Effect of Rhetorical Context on Aristotelian Definitions

It is important to appreciate how the context of a given argument can affect your definition of a term. The question "Is a tarantula kept in the house a pet?" may actually have opposing answers, depending on the rhetorical situation. You may argue that your tarantula is or is not a pet, depending on whether you are trying to exclude it from your landlord's "no pet" rule or include it in your local talk show's "weird pet contest." Within one context you will want to argue that what your landlord really means by "pet" is an animal (next larger class) capable of disturbing neighbors or harming the landlord's property (criteria that distinguish it from other members of the class). Thus you could argue that your tarantula isn't a pet in your landlord's sense because it is incapable of harming property or disturbing the peace (assuming you don't let it loose!). In the other context you would argue that a pet is "any living thing" (note that in this context the "next larger class" is much larger) with which a human being forms a caring attachment and which shares its owner's domicile. In this case you might say, "Tommy Tarantula here is one of my dearest friends and if you don't think Tommy is weird enough, wait 'til I show you Vanessa, my pet Venus's-flytrap."

To apply the same principle to a different field of debate, consider whether or not obscene language in a student newspaper should be protected by the First Amendment. The purpose of school officials' suspending editors responsible for such language is to maintain order and decency in the school. The school officials thus hope to narrow the category of acts that are protected under the free speech amendment in order to meet their purposes. On the other hand, the American Civil Liberties Union (which has long defended student newspaper editors) is intent on avoiding any precedent that will restrict freedom of speech any more than is absolutely necessary. The different definitions of *free speech* that are apt to emerge thus reflect the different purposes of the disputants.

The problem of purpose shows why it is so hard to define a word out of context. Some people try to escape this dilemma by returning to the "original intent" of the authors of precedent-setting documents such as the Constitution. But if we try to determine the original intent of the writers of the Constitution on such matters as "free speech," "cruel and unusual punishment," or the "right to bear arms," we must still ask what their original purposes were in framing the constitutional language. If we can show that those original purposes are no longer relevant to present concerns, we have begun to undermine what would otherwise appear to be a static and universal definition to which we could turn.

Operational Definitions

In some rhetorical situations, particularly those arising in the physical and social sciences, writers need precise definitions that can be measured empirically and are not subject to problems of context and disputed criteria. Consider, for example, an argument involving the concept "aggression." "Do violent television programs increase the incidence of aggression in children?" To do research on this issue a scientist needs a precise, measurable definition of *aggression*. Typically, a scientist might measure "aggression" by counting "the number of blows or kicks a child gives to an inflatable bozo doll over a fifteen-minute period when other play options are available." The scientist might then define "aggressive behavior" as six or more blows to the bozo doll. Such definitions are useful in that they are precisely measurable, but they are also limited in that they omit criteria that may be unmeasurable but important. Is it adequate, for example, to define a "superior student" as someone with a 3.2 GPA or higher? Or is it adequate to define an "aggressive child" as one who pummels bozo dolls instead of playing with trucks?

CONDUCTING THE MATCH PART OF A DEFINITIONAL ARGUMENT

As we showed at the beginning of this chapter, a typical enthymeme for a definitional argument is as follows: "X is a Y because it possesses attributes A, B, and C." In the criteria part of the argument you show that A, B, and C are the necessary and sufficient criteria for something to be called a Y. Then in the match part of your argument you show that X possesses the attributes A, B, and C. Generally you do so by using either examples or analysis.

Suppose you wanted to argue that your history teacher was an "authoritarian." Since he is in some ways rather lax—for example, he doesn't count off for late papers and he doesn't require class attendance—some of your classmates say he isn't authoritarian at all. (They are in effect saying that harsh treatment for late papers and absences is a necessary condition for calling a teacher "authoritarian.") Consequently you establish the following criteria for "authoritarian": repression of alternative points of view and strict adherence to certain arbitrary procedures. You now need to show that your history teacher meets these criteria. You write the following enthymeme to serve as the core of your argument:

> My history professor is an authoritarian because he represses questions and alternate points of view in his class and because he demands strict adherence to arbitrary procedures for doing the assignments.

To support this argument, you would give various examples of his meeting these two criteria: To show his repression of alternative points of view, you might cite, among other examples, the time he embarrassed a student for disagreeing with him on the rightness of Harry Truman's decision to drop the atomic bomb on Hiroshima. And to show his adherence to arbitrary procedures, you could, among other things, mention how he reduces the grade on an essay if the margins aren't precisely one and a half inches.

In other kinds of arguments, you may have to analyze the features of your X rather than just cite examples. For instance, if you argue that one *necessary* criterion for "police brutality" is "intention"—that is, the police officer must intend the harm—then you will need to analyze your borderline case to see if the police officer intentionally (as opposed to accidentally) harmed the victim. If the harm was accidental, then you could relieve the officer of the charge "police brutality." Thus through the power of example or analysis you show that X possesses the attributes of Y.

■ WRITING YOUR DEFINITIONAL ARGUMENT

With this background, you are now ready to begin writing your "extended definition/borderline case" argument. The following steps should help you in that process.

Starting Points: Finding a Definitional Controversy

The key to this assignment is finding a good controversy about a definition. A fruitful way to begin is through discussion with others. Perhaps your instructor will use the following discussion exercise in class; if not, start a similar conversation with friends.

☐ FOR CLASS DISCUSSION

1. Suppose you wanted to define the concept "courage." Working in groups, try to decide whether each of the following cases is an example of courage:

   a. A neighbor rushes into a burning house to rescue a child from certain death and emerges, coughing and choking, with the child in his arms. Is the neighbor courageous?

   b. A fireman rushes into a burning house to rescue a child from certain death and emerges with the child in his arms. The fireman is wearing protective clothing and a gas mask. When a newspaper reporter calls him courageous, he says, "Hey, this is my job." Is the fireman courageous?

   c. A teenager rushes into a burning house to recover a memento given to him by his girlfriend, the first love of his life. Is the teenager courageous?

   d. A parent rushes into a burning house to save a trapped child. The fire marshal tells the parent to wait because there is no chance the child can be reached from the first floor. The fire marshal wants to try cutting a hole in the roof to reach the child. The parent rushes into the house anyway and is burned to death. Was the parent courageous?

   e. Are mountain climbers and parachutists courageous in scaling rock precipices or jumping out of airplanes during their leisure hours?

   f. Is a robber courageous in performing a daring bank robbery?

   g. Mutt and Jeff are standing on a cliff high above a lake. Mutt dares Jeff to dive into the water. Jeff refuses, saying it is too dangerous. Mutt double dares Jeff, who still refuses. So Mutt dives into the water and, on surfacing, yells up to Jeff, calling him a coward and taunting him to dive. Jeff starts to dive, but then backs off and takes the trail down to the lake, feeling ashamed and silly. Was Mutt courageous? Was Jeff courageous?

2. As you make your decisions on each of these cases, create and refine the criteria you use.

3. Make up your own series of controversial cases, like those above for "courage," for one or more of the following concepts:

   a. cruelty to animals

b. child abuse

c. true athlete

d. sexual harassment

e. free speech protected by the First Amendment

Once you complete the preceding exercise, choose one of the most controversial cases within a topic area you enjoy and consider using that as the subject of your essay. Or look back through your earlier exploratory writing to see if any of your entries focus on definitional issues. Clear your definitional issue with your instructor.

Exploration Stage I: Developing Criteria for Your Y Term

One effective way to discover criteria is to use a definitional heuristic in which you search for cases that are instances of "Y," "not Y," and "maybe Y." You will find that criteria for Y begin to emerge as your group discusses the characteristics of obvious instances of Y, contrastive instances of not Y, and then borderline instances of maybe Y.

Suppose, for example, you wanted to argue the claim that "accounting is/is not a creative profession." Your first goal is to establish criteria for a creative profession. Using this heuristic, you would begin by thinking of examples of obvious creative behaviors, then of contrastive behaviors that seem similar to the previous behaviors but yet are clearly not creative, and then finally of borderline behaviors that may or may not be creative. Your list might look like this:

EXAMPLES OF CREATIVE BEHAVIORS

Beethoven composes a symphony.

An architect designs a house.

Edison invents the light bulb.

An engineer designs a machine that will make widgets in a new way.

A poet writes a poem (later revised to "A poet writes a poem that poetry experts say is beautiful"—see following discussion).

CONTRASTIVE EXAMPLES OF NONCREATIVE BEHAVIORS

A conductor transposes Beethoven's symphony into a different key.

A carpenter builds a house from the architect's plan.

I change a lightbulb in my house.

A factory worker uses the new machine to stamp out widgets.

A graduate student writes stupid "love/dove" poems for birthday cards.

EXAMPLES OF BORDERLINE CASES

A woman gives birth to a child.

An accountant figures out your income tax.

A musician plays Beethoven's symphony with great skill.

A monkey paints an oil painting by smearing paint on canvas: a group of art critics, not knowing a monkey was the artist, call the painting beautiful.

After you have brainstormed for your various cases, develop your criteria by determining what features the "clearly creative" examples have in common and what features the "clearly noncreative" examples lack. Then refine your criteria by deciding on what grounds you might include or eliminate your borderline cases from the category "creative." For example, you might begin with the following criterion:

DEFINITION: FIRST TRY

For an act to be creative, it must result in an end product that is significantly different from other products.

But then, by looking at some of the examples in your creative and noncreative columns, you decide that just producing a different end product isn't enough. A bad poem might be different from other poems, but you don't want to call a bad poet creative. So you refine your criteria.

DEFINITION: SECOND TRY

For an act to be creative, it must result in an end product that is significantly different from other products and is yet useful or beautiful.

This definition would allow you to include all the acts in your creative column but eliminate the acts in the noncreative column.

Your next step is to refine your criteria by deciding whether to include or reject items in your borderline list. You decide to reject the childbirth case by arguing that creativity must be a mental or intellectual activity, not a natural process. You reject the monkey as painter example on similar grounds, arguing that although the end product may be both original and beautiful, it is not creative because it is not a product of the monkey's intellect. Finally, you reject the example of the musician playing Beethoven's symphony. Like the carpenter who builds the house, the musician possesses great skill but doesn't design a new product; rather, he or she follows the instructions of the designer. (A music major in your group reacts bitterly, arguing that musicians "interpret" music and that such behavior is creative. She notes that the music department is housed in a building called the "Creative Arts Complex." Your group, however, can't figure out a way to reword the definition to include performance rather than production. If you call performing musicians creative, the rest of the group argues, then the rule of justice forces you to call carpenters creative also, because both kinds of craftspeople reproduce the creative intentions of others. Once we call performers creative, they argue, the concept of creativity will get so broad that it will no longer be useful.) Your group's final definition, then, looks like this (with the music major dissenting):

DEFINITION: THIRD TRY

For an act to be creative, it must be produced by intellectual design, and it must result in an end product that is significantly different from other products and is yet useful or beautiful.

Having established these criteria, you are ready for your final borderline case, your original issue of whether or not accounting is a creative profession. Based on your criteria, you might decide that accounting is not generally a creative profession because the final products are not significantly new or different. For the most part, accountants do elaborately complex calculations, but they generally follow established procedures in doing so. However, the profession can sometimes offer creative opportunities when an accountant, for example, develops a new kind of computer program or develops new, improved procedures for handling routine business (Accounting majors may argue that accounting is creative in other ways).

The definitional heuristic thus produces a systematic procedure for developing criteria for a definitional argument. Moreover, it provides an organizational strategy for writing the criteria part of your argument because one good way to conduct a definitional argument is to take your reader step by step through the process of establishing your criteria. In other words, you would use the examples from your list to show your reader first your rough criteria and then your increasingly refined criteria derived from consideration of your borderline cases.

□ FOR CLASS DISCUSSION

1. Working as a group, try the definitional heuristic on the topic "cruelty to animals" (or some other Y chosen by the instructor or your group). Make three lists.

   a. obvious examples of cruelty to animals

   b. contrastive examples, that is, behaviors that are not cruel to animals (Try to vary a few features of each entry under "a" above so that the example switches from cruelty to noncruelty.)

   c. borderline cases (Include the starling example from p. 205)

2. Once you have created your list of cases, create a one-sentence definition of "cruelty to animals" following the pattern described earlier for creativity. Your definition should include each of the criteria you established.

3. In your journal, make a similar three-column list for the Y term you have chosen for your own definitional essay. Then create a working definition for your Y term by deciding on your criteria.

Exploration Stage II: Exploring Your Match Argument

In doing the earlier class discussion exercises, you have practiced arguing whether borderline cases met your definitions for "courage" or "cruelty to animals." Now try this exercise as a form of exploratory writing. List the criteria for your chosen Y term; then freewrite for five or ten minutes exploring whether your borderline case meets each of the criteria. Before writing the first draft of your argument, you might also explore your ideas further by doing the eight freewriting tasks on pages 79–81 in Chapter 3.

Writing the Discovery Draft—A Possible Organizational Structure for Your Essay

You are now ready to write your discovery draft. At this stage it may be helpful to look at a typical organizational structure for an extended definition/borderline case essay. Such an organization is shown in Figure 10–1. The argument typically begins by introducing the reader to the controversy and by showing that the definition of the Y term or the match between the Y definition and the X term is problematic. The body of the essay usually begins with an extended definition of the Y term, followed by an argument showing that the X term does or does not meet the definition. Sometimes a writer will present all the criteria for the Y term before moving to the match argument. At other times, the writer might choose to proceed one criterion at a time by first describing the criterion, arguing that the X term meets it, and then proceeding to the next criterion.

Revision Stage

Once you have written a discovery draft, you will better appreciate the complexity of your issue and see it more clearly. As you revise your draft, your goal will be to make your argument clear and persuasive for readers. You might find it helpful at this time to summarize your argument as a claim with because clauses and to test it with Toulmin's schema. Here is how student writer Kathy Sullivan used Toulmin to analyze a draft of her essay examining the possible obscenity of photographs displayed in a gay bar in Seattle. The final version of this essay is printed on pages 224–26.

ENTHYMEME:	The photographs displayed in the Oncore bar are not obscene because they do not violate the community standards of the patrons of the bar, because they do not appeal to prurient interest, because children are not apt to be exposed to them, and because they promote an important social value, safe sex, in order to prevent AIDS.
CLAIM:	The photographs are not obscene.
STATED REASONS:	(1) They don't violate community standards; (2) they do not appeal to prurient interests; (3) children are not exposed to them; and (4) they promote an important social purpose of preventing AIDS through safe sex.

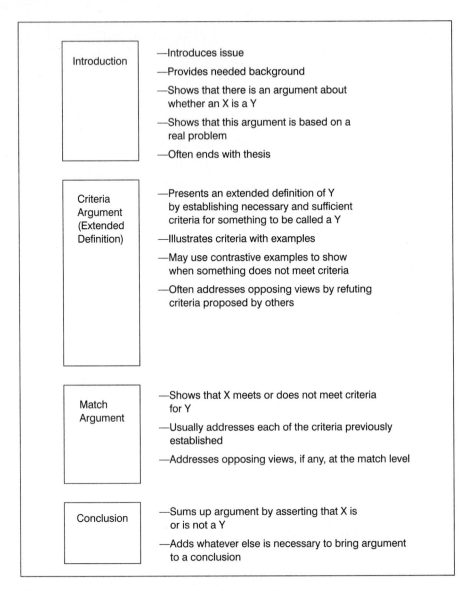

Figure 10–1 Possible organizational pattern for definition argument

GROUNDS: (1) evidence that most Oncore patrons are homosexual and that these photographs don't offend them (no complaints, etc.); (2) purpose of photographs is not prurient sexuality, they don't depict explicit sexual acts, the only thing complained about by the liquor board is visible body parts; (3) because this is a bar, children aren't allowed; (4) evidence that the purpose of these photographs is to promote safe sex, thus they have a redeeming social value

WARRANT:	Things that don't violate community standards, do not appeal to prurient interests, don't come in view of children, and promote an important purpose are not obscene.
BACKING:	These criteria come from the definition of obscenity in *Black's Law Dictionary,* which in turn is based on recent court cases. This is a very credible source. In addition, arguments showing why the community standard here should be that of the homosexual community rather than the community at large; arguments showing that the social importance of safe sex overrides other considerations.
CONDITIONS OF REBUTTAL:	An opponent might say that the community standards should be those of the Seattle community at large, not those of the gay community. An opponent might say that photographs of male genitalia in a gay bar appeal to prurient interest.
QUALIFIER:	Those photographs would be obscene if displayed anywhere but in a gay bar.

As a result of this analysis, Kathy revised her final draft considerably. By imagining where her arguments were weak ("conditions of rebuttal"), she realized that she needed to include more backing by arguing that the community standards to be applied in this case should be those of the homosexual community rather than the community at large. She also added a section arguing that visible genitalia in the photographs didn't make the photos obscene. By imagining how your argument can be rebutted, you will see ways to strengthen your draft. Consequently, we close out this chapter by looking more carefully at the ways a definitional argument can be rebutted.

CONDITIONS FOR REBUTTAL: TESTING A DEFINITIONAL ARGUMENT

In refuting a definitional argument, you need to appreciate its criteria-match structure. Your refutation can attack either the argument's criteria or its match, or both.

Attacking the Criteria

Might an opponent claim that your criteria are not the right ones?   This is the most common way to attack a definitional argument. Opponents might say that A, B, and C are only accidental criteria for Y, not necessary and sufficient criteria. Or they might say that A, B, and C are necessary but not sufficient and that you don't have a real Y until you have a feature D. For example, you might argue that an action is courageous so long as the doer risks something of value, which you might define as "reputation," "family honor," and so forth. But an opponent might say that an action is truly courageous only if a person risks life and limb. The argument will turn, then, on how much is risked.

Might an opponent find counterexamples—things that possess features A, B, and C but may not be a Y?   If you say that cruelty to animals occurs any time a human being intentionally causes an animal to suffer, an opponent might call this criterion into question by bringing up the case of animal research in medicine. Opponents might argue that causing an animal to suffer intentionally is not cruelty to animals so long as the suffering serves a sufficient human good.

Might an opponent cite extraordinary circumstances that weaken your criteria?   An opponent may aso find that the criteria you've developed are perfectly acceptable in ordinary circumstances but are rendered unacceptable by extraordinary circumstances. If you say that starving the starlings (p. 205) is cruelty to animals because the life of the starlings outweighs the inconvenience to the family, an opponent might challenge you by asking, "What if one of the people in the bedroom was ill and needed absolute quiet?" By invoking extraordinary circumstances, an opponent can force us to look at questions of degree—How far are we willing to stretch our criteria?

Might an opponent object to your criteria on the basis of "purpose"?   We have seen how definitional arguments occur in context. If your criteria for "sexual harassment" are based on a male view of the world, with the intention of protecting males from being sued for ogling women, might not your criteria be challenged from a woman's perspective?

Attacking the Match

A match argument usually uses examples to show that X indeed possesses characteristics A, B, and C and thus qualifies as a Y.

Might an opponent claim that your examples are too narrow and unrepresentative?   The most common way to refute a match argument is to show that the examples are too narrow and unrepresentative. In arguing that Dr. Booley, president of State Technical College, is an imaginative leader, you may have cited as examples Booley's creative handling of a labor dispute with the food service and his institution of a new accounting system. But in so doing, have you ignored other, equally important problem areas on campus where Booley has shown no imagination (for example, the clumsy advising system, low faculty morale, outdated curriculum, poor library, etc.)?

Might an opponent claim that your examples are not accurate?   In the previous illustration, an opponent might point out that it was not Dr. Booley's leadership that deserves credit for resolving the labor dispute; rather, it was Vice President Conehead's steady intervention that won the day.

Will your opponent accuse you of using extreme examples?   For example, if you are arguing that pornography is degrading to humans, you may well have turned to extreme instances of child pornography. But might your opponent point out that most pornography is different? Your opponent might simply say: "OK, granted explicit sexual material involving children is degrading to humans. But everything else, so long as it involves consenting adults, is OK."

□ FOR CLASS DISCUSSION

Read the following two definitional arguments. The first is by a student writer in response to the "extended definition/borderline case" assignment in this chapter. The second is by professional commentator Charles Krauthammer. In Krauthammer's argument, definitional issues are embedded in a larger proposal issue. Krauthammer proposes to rebuild a national system of asylums in which homeless mentally ill persons could be involuntarily confined. Krauthammer's definitional issues are these: What are the criteria by which a mentally ill person could be involuntarily institutionalized? How can one tell when eccentric behavior means mental illness?

1. Working as a whole class or in small groups, share your responses to the following questions: (a) How persuaded are you by each writer's argument? (b) If you find the arguments persuasive, which parts of them were particularly influential or effective? (c) If you are not persuaded, which parts of the arguments do you find weak or ineffective? (d) How would you attempt to rebut each argument?*

2. Working individually or in groups, create scenarios of cases that would "test" Krauthammer's criteria for permitting involuntary institutionalization of a homeless mentally ill person: (a) a case of a homeless mentally ill person who could be involuntarily confined under both the present criteria (danger to self or others) and Krauthammer's proposed criteria (degradation or helplessness); (b) a case of a homeless mentally ill person who could remain on the streets according to the danger criterion but could be institutionalized involuntarily under Krauthammer's degradation criterion; (c) a case of a homeless mentally ill person who could stay on the streets according to both criteria.

3. If Krauthammer's definition were to become law, how might his criteria be clarified or restricted so that the state couldn't place any eccentric homeless person in an insane asylum?

---

* For a counterargument that attempts to rebut Krauthammer's plan, see the student essay "What Should Be Done about the Mentally Ill Homeless?" on pp. 339-50.

ONCORE, OBSCENITY, AND
THE LIQUOR CONTROL BOARD

Kathy Sullivan (student)

In early May, Geoff Menasee, a Seattle artist, exhibited a series of pho-   1
tographs with the theme of "safe sex" on the walls of an inner city, predominantly homosexual restaurant and lounge called the Oncore. Before
hanging the photographs, Menasee had to consult with the Washington
State Liquor Control Board because, under the current state law, art work
containing material that may be considered indecent has to be approved
by the board before it can be exhibited. Of the almost thirty photographs,
six were rejected by the board because they partially exposed "private
parts" of the male anatomy. Menasee went ahead and displayed the
entire series of photographs, placing bandaids over the "indecent" areas,
but the customers continually removed the bandaids.

The liquor control board's ruling on this issue has caused controversy   2
in the Seattle community. The *Seattle Times* has provided news coverage, and a "Town Meeting" segment was filmed at the restaurant. The
central question is this: Should an establishment that caters to a
predominantly homosexual clientele be enjoined from displaying
pictures promoting "safe sex" on the grounds that the photographs are
obscene?

Before I can answer this question, I must first determine whether the   3
art work should truly be classified as obscene. To make that determination, I will use the definition of obscenity in *Black's Law Dictionary*:

> Material is "obscene" if to the average person, applying contemporary
> community standards, the dominant theme of material taken as a
> whole appeals to prurient interest, if it is utterly without redeeming
> social importance, if it goes substantially beyond customary limits of
> candor in description or representation, if it is characterized by patent
> offensiveness, and if it is hard core pornography.

An additional criterion is provided by Pember's *Mass Media Laws:* "A
work is obscene if it has a tendency to deprave and corrupt those whose
minds are open to such immoral influences (children for example) and
into whose hands it might happen to fall" (p. 394). The art work in question should not be prohibited from display at predominantly homosexual
establishments like the Oncore because it does not meet the above criteria for obscenity.

First of all, to the average person applying contemporary community   4
standards, the predominant theme of Menasee's photographs is not an
appeal to prurient interests. The first element in this criterion is "average
person." According to Rocky Breckner, manager of the Oncore, 90

percent of the clientele at the Oncore is made up of young white homosexual males. This group therefore constitutes the "average person" viewing the exhibit. "Contemporary community standards" would ordinarily be the standards of the Seattle community. However, this art work is aimed at a particular group of people—the homosexual community. Therefore, the "community standards" involved here are those of the gay community rather than the city at large. Since the Oncore is not an art museum or gallery, which attracts a broad spectrum of people, it is appropriate to restrict the scope of "community standards" to that group who voluntarily patronize the Oncore.

Second, the predominant theme of the photographs is not "prurient   5 interest" nor do the photographs go "substantially beyond public limits of candor." There are no explicit sexual acts found in the photographs; instead, their theme is the prevention of AIDS through the practice of safe sex. Homosexual displays of affection could be viewed as "prurient interest" by the larger community, but same-sex relationships are the norm for the group at whom the exhibit is aimed. If the exhibit were displayed at McDonalds or even the Red Robin it might go "substantially beyond customary limits of candor," but it is unlikely that the clientele of the Oncore would find the art work offensive. The manager stated that he received very few complaints about the exhibit and its contents.

Nor is the material pornographic. The liquor control board prohibited   6 the six photographs based on their visible display of body parts such as pubic hair and naked buttocks, not on the basis of sexual acts or homosexual orientation. The board admitted that the photographs depicted no explicit sexual acts. Hence, it can be concluded that they did not consider the suggestion of same-sex affection to be hard-core pornography. Their sole objection was that body parts were visible. But visible genitalia in art work are not necessarily pornographic. Since other art work, such as Michelangelo's sculptures, explicitly depict both male and female genitalia, it is arguable that pubic hair and buttocks are not patently offensive.

It must be conceded that the art work has the potential of being   7 viewed by children, which would violate Pember's criterion. But once again the incidence of minors frequenting this establishment is very small.

But the most important reason for saying these photographs are not   8 obscene is that they serve an important social purpose. One of Black's criteria is that obscene material is "utterly without redeeming social importance." But these photographs have the explicit purpose of promoting safe sex as a defense against AIDS. Recent statistics reported in the *Seattle Times* show that AIDS is now the leading cause of death of men under forty in the Seattle area. Any methods that can promote the message of safe sex in today's society have strong redeeming social significance.

Those who believe that all art containing "indecent" material should   9
be banned or covered from public view would most likely believe that
Menasee's work is obscene. They would disagree that the environment
and the clientele should be the major determining factor when using criteria to evaluate art. However, in the case of this exhibit I feel that the
audience and the environment of the display are factors of overriding
importance. Therefore, the exhibit should have been allowed to be displayed because it is not obscene.

HOW TO SAVE THE HOMELESS MENTALLY ILL

Charles Krauthammer

Hard cases make bad law. Joyce Brown is a hard case. She was one of   1
the first persons locked up in Bellevue Hospital when New York City
decided to begin sweeping the homeless mentally ill off the streets. And
she was first to challenge in court her forcible hospitalization. She won,
but an appeals court reversed the decision. Now that a court has upheld
her right to refuse treatment, the city will release her any day now. The
case, like Brown herself, is a muddle and making a muddle of the law.
But it dramatically illustrates what is wrong with the current debate about
the homeless mentally ill and with the limits of benevolence that our society permits itself to accord them.

Everything about Brown allows contradictory explanations. Court   2
documents refer not to Joyce Brown but to Billie Boggs, the name of
a local TV personality and one of the several false names Brown adopted.
Is she delusional or did she choose new names the better to hide
from her sisters who in the past had tried to get her hospitalized? She
cut up and publicly urinated on paper money. Is that crazy or, as her
lawyers claim, was she symbolically demonstrating disdain for the
patronizing solicitude of strangers who gave her money? She shouted
obscenities in the street. Is that the result of demented rage or was it her
only effective means of warding off the busybodies of the city's Project
HELP (Homeless Emergency Liaison Project) who might take her away to
a hospital?

In sum, was she living on a grate at 2nd and East 65th because she is   3
mentally ill or because she has chosen the life of a professional (her
word) street person?

"A lucid and rational woman who is down on her luck," Brown's ACLU   4
lawyer calls her. Being down on one's luck can just be that. But it can be

a sign of something graver, namely the downward social mobility that is characteristic of schizophrenia and that is caused by the gradual disintegration of the personality that marks its course. The classic picture is: brilliant physics major drops out, becomes cabbie, becomes unemployed, drifts, becomes homeless. Brown was a secretary, lost her job, did drugs, wandered from sister's house to sister's house, then ended up a bag lady.

She is a puzzle. The first judge thought the ACLU's psychiatrists correct. The appeals court bought the city's diagnosis. Dr. Francine Cournos, the most recent court-appointed (and thus disinterested) psychiatrist, determined that she did suffer from "a serious mental illness," that she "would benefit from medication," but that, since she refused, forcing it upon her would do more harm than good.   5

My guess is that Dr. Cournos is right. Brown most likely is a chronic schizophrenic. But that is a condition more reliably diagnosed by observing a patient's course than by a snapshot observation. The symptoms can remit for a time. When Brown was cleaned up, dressed up, and given attention, she appeared lucid and rational in court. Left on her own, however, her course had been relentlessly downhill. The proof will come if, as is likely, she ends up back at the hospital.   6

But the lawyer's duel was not just over whether Brown is mentally ill. Mental illness is a necessary, but not a sufficient, condition for involuntary commitment. The other condition is dangerousness: a person must also be a danger to himself or to others before he may be forcibly taken care of.   7

Brown's ACLU lawyers argued for the now traditional standard of dangerousness: imminent danger, meaning harm—suicide or extreme neglect leading to serious injury or death—within hours or days. The city was pushing for a broader standard: eventual danger, meaning that Brown's life was such that she inevitably would come to grief, even if it could not now be foreseen exactly when and how. Maureen McLeod, one of the city's lawyers, protested having "to wait until something happens to her. It is our duty to act before it is too late."   8

Is it? Generally speaking, the answer is no. We don't permit preventive detention even for criminals who we "know" are going to commit crimes. We have to wait and catch them. If involuntary commitment requires that dangerousness be shown, then it is not enough to say that something awful will happen eventually. By that standard, heavy smoking ought to be a criterion for commitment.   9

The city, trying desperately to stretch the dangerousness criterion to allow the forced hospitalization of Joyce Brown, had to resort to a very strained logic. After all, Brown had spent a year on the grate without any apparent physical harm from illness, malnutrition, or exposure. As the appeals court dissent pointed out, the city's case came down to a claim that Brown would ultimately be assaulted if she continued living and acting as provocatively as she was. But there is hardly a New Yorker who is   10 not subject to assault merely by passing through the streets of New York. It is odd to blame the pathology of the city on her and lock her up to protect her from it.

The idea of eventual harm as opposed to imminent harm is slippery   11 and arbitrary. Brown had already been exposed to all the things that the city said would do her in—traffic, disease, strangers, the elements—and had survived quite nicely. The city was reduced to arguing that her luck was going to run out. It had to make this claim because it had to prove dangerousness. But why should a civilized society have to prove that a person's mental incapacity will lead to death before it is permitted to save that person? Should not degradation be reason enough?

The standard for the involuntary commitment of the homeless men-   12 tally ill is wrong. It should not be dangerousness but helplessness. We have a whole array of laws (e.g., on drug abuse and prostitution) that prohibit certain actions not primarily because they threaten life but because they degrade the person. In order to override the liberty of the severely mentally ill, one should not be forced to claim—as the city disingenuously claimed in the Brown case—that life is at stake, but that a minimal human dignity is at stake.

Joyce Brown is a tough case because it is at least possible that she is,   13 in fact, not mentally ill at all, only unlucky, eccentric and willful. Fine. But you cannot make that case for thousands of other homeless people. Helen Phillips, for example, picked up in the same New York City round-up as Brown, lives in Pennsylvania Station and is convinced that plutonium is poisoning the water. For the homeless who are clearly mentally ill, why should it be necessary to convince a judge that, left alone, they will die? The vast majority won't. It should be enough to convince a judge that, left alone, they will suffer.

Moreover, the suffering is needless. It can be mitigated by a society   14 that summons the courage to give the homeless mentally ill adequate care, over their objections if need be. In a hospital they will at the very least get adequate clothing and shelter. And for some, medication will relieve the torment of waking dreams.

What prevents us from doing this is the misguided and pernicious   15 civil libertarian impulse that holds liberty too sacred to be overridden for anything other than the preservation of life. For the severely mentally ill, however, liberty is not just an empty word but a cruel hoax. Free to do what? To defecate in one's pants? To wander around Grand Central station begging for sustenance? To freeze to death in Central Park? The week that Joyce Brown won her reprieve from forced medication, three homeless men were found frozen dead in New York. What does freedom mean for a paranoid schizophrenic who is ruled by voices commanded by his persecutors and rattling around in his head?

What to do? The New York City sweep is only the first temporary step. 16
It yields a bath, a check-up, a diagnosis, and the beginning of treatment.
The sicker patients will need long-term custodial care in a psychiatric
hospital. Others might respond to treatment and graduate to the less
restrictive environment of a local clinic or group home. Many of these
people will fall apart and have to be swept up and cycled through the system again.

A sensible approach to the problem begins with the conviction that 17
those helpless, homeless, and sick are the responsibility of the state.
Society must be willing to assert control even if protection and treatment
have to be given involuntarily. These people are owed asylum. Whether
the asylums should be large or small, rural or urban is a matter for
debate. (In my view a mix of asylum size and location would serve the
widest spectrum of patients' needs.) What should by now be beyond
debate is that the state must take responsibility for the homeless mentally ill. And that means asserting control over their lives at least during
their most severe incapacity.

In 1963 President Kennedy helped launch the community mental 18
health revolution that emptied America's state mental hospitals. Kennedy
said in his message to Congress, "Reliance on the cold mercy of custodial isolation will be supplanted by the open warmth of community concern." It wasn't. In the turbulence of urban life even the mentally well
have trouble finding community, let alone deriving from it any warmth.
The mentally ill are even less likely to find it. Everyone is for community
mental health care—until it comes to his community. This may be
deplorable but it is a fact. And it is cruel to allow the mentally ill to suffer
neglect pending rectification of that fact, under the assumption that until
the community is ready to welcome the mentally ill, the street is better
than the asylum. It is not.

In 1955 state psychiatric hospitals had 559,000 patients. Today there 19
are about 130,000, a decline of 75 percent. Now, the incidence of severe
mental illness has not changed. (Schizophrenia, for example, afflicts
about one percent of the population.) Nor have drugs and modern treatment yielded a cure rate of 75 percent. Many of the 75 percent discharged from the state hospitals have simply been abandoned. They
have become an army of grate-dwellers.

Helping them will require, first, rebuilding the mental hospital system. 20
These hospitals do not have to be rural, they do not have to be massive,
and they do not have to be run-down. The entire American medical care
system runs on incentives. Psychiatry, social work, and nursing are not
immune to the inducement that good money would offer to work with
the severely ill.

Second, a new asylum system will require support for a string of less 21
restrictive halfway environments and for the personnel to run them. New
York State has just announced a program to supply another element of

psychiatric care: a new cadre of case workers to supervise intensively the most severely ill. They would follow the mentally ill through all parts of the system, even back onto the streets, and offer supervision, advice, and some services. But facilitators cannot be enough. If there are no beds in a state mental hospital when the patient is severely delusional or self-destructive, if there are no halfway houses during recovery or remission, then the case worker is left helpless. Anybody who has worked with the mentally ill knows that all the goodwill in the world is insufficient if the institutions are not there. Intensive case management can guide a patient through a rebuilt asylum system. Without such a system, however, they can only provide the most superficial succor. The basic facts of the homeless mentally ill, destitution and degradation, will remain unchanged.

Rebuilding an asylum system is one problem we can and should   22 throw money at. It will take a lot. The way to do it is to say to Americans: You are pained and offended by homelessness. We propose to get the most wretched, confused, and disruptive of the homeless off the streets and into clean and humane asylums. We need to pay for them. We propose capping the mortgage interest deduction: less of a tax break on your house so that others can be housed. (A cap at $20,000 would yield $1 billion of revenues annually.) A new asylum system begins with concern for the elementary dignity of the homeless mentally ill. But it does not end there. The rest of us need it too. Not just, as the cynics claim, for reasons of cleanliness, so that the comfortable bourgeois does not have his daily routine disturbed by wretchedness. Getting the homeless mentally ill off the streets is an exercise in morality, not aesthetics.

It is not our aesthetic but our moral sensibilities that are most injured   23 by the spectacle of homelessness. The city, with its army of grate-dwellers, is a school for callousness. One's natural instincts to help are suppressed every day. Moreover, they have to be suppressed if one is to function: there are simply too many homeless. Thirty years ago if you saw a person lying helpless on the street, you ran to help him. Now you step over him. You know that he is not an accident victim. He lives there. Trying to get him out of his cardboard house is not a simple act of mercy of which most people are quite capable. It is a major act of social work that only the professional and the saintly can be expected to undertake. To expect saintliness of the ordinary citizen is bad social policy. Further, to expose him hourly to a wretchedness far beyond his power to remedy is to make moral insensitivity a requirement of daily living. Society must not leave the ordinary citizen with no alternative between ignoring the homeless and playing Mother Teresa. A civilized society ought to offer its people some communal act that lies somewhere in between, such as contributing to the public treasury to build an asylum system to care for these people.

Project HELP, the necessary first stage in such a system, is already   24
under attack. First, because it curtails civil liberties. Second, because it
sets up a revolving door: off the street, into a hospital for 21 days, then to
some lightly supervised home, then back on the streets. In fact, those
picked up in Project HELP have been given a high priority for scarce state
hospital and other psychiatric beds. (Of the 29 New York patients who
have thus far left Bellevue, 21 went to a special 50-bed unit at Creed-
moor Psychiatric Center and eight have been discharged to family or
adult homes.) It is hard to place the rest in state hospitals or in existing
community services because there are few of either: the first as a matter
of conscious policy, the second as a matter of political neglect. The way
to avert the revolving-door problem is not by leaving the homeless mentally ill on the streets, but by building a long-term psychiatric care system
that can accommodate them.

Third, charge the critics, Project HELP deals only with the very tip of   25
the iceberg, so far 70 out of thousands. True. But those 70 are, after all,
real suffering people. Moreover, as proper long-term facilities are built,
there is no reason why Project HELP cannot become their triage service,
assigning the homeless mentally ill to appropriate care.

Still, it will not do to have illusions about what can be achieved. After   26
winning the appeal in the Brown case, Mayor Ed Koch declared himself
eager "to treat her medically. I want this woman to get well, as quickly as
possible." Unfortunately, chronic schizophrenics do not get well quickly.
Some never get well. This is not a question of getting them off the street,
giving them an injection, and letting them go. It is a question of getting
people permanently off the street and into a system of comprehensive
long-term care.

Rebuilding that system is a question of money. But being prepared   27
to pick people up and send them into it—and keep them in it, if
necessary—is a question of political will. It requires relinquishing the
illusions of community and the phony promise of liberty that led to the
dismantling of the system over the last 30 years. It requires a new
consensus that a life of even minimal dignity is preferable to a wretchedness the homeless endure in the name of rights from which, like
the world around them, they have long been alienated. Most of the
homeless mentally ill picked up so far seem to share, as far as they
can, that view. They have not protested the city's efforts. Less than a
fifth of those hospitalized thus far have lodged legal challenges against
their commitment. Two challenges, including Brown's, have met with
some success. Most are grateful for a safe and warm hospital bed. What
they seem to fear is being carted off to one of the wretched emergency
shelters, where they feel—rightly—more endangered than they do on
the street.

A new asylum system will not solve the homeless problem. Obviously   28
the mentally ill are not the only category of homeless people in America.

There are at least two others. Some of the homeless are not helpless but defiantly indigent. This is Joyce Brown, as she depicts herself: a professional street person, a lucid survivor who has chosen a life of drift. "It was my choice to live on the streets," she says. "It was an experience." Such people used to be called hoboes. Then there are the victims of economic calamity, such as family breakup or job loss. Often these are single mothers with children. Unlike the hoboes, they hate the street and want to get off, but lack the money, skills, and social supports. Some nonetheless try very hard: two homeless mothers who testified recently at a House hearing are actually working and putting kids through school.

We can debate for years what to do for these people. Should the   29
hoboes who prefer street life be forced off the street in the name of order? And how best to help the homeless who are simply too poor to buy decent housing in the city? Whatever the answers to these questions, it is both cruel and dishonest to defer addressing the mentally ill homeless—for whom choice is not an issue and for whom poverty is a symptom, not the cause, of their misery—until we have figured out a solution to the rest.

When the mentally ill infiltrate the ranks of another deviant group,   30
criminals, we try to segregate them and treat them differently. We do not await a cure for psychopathy or a solution to criminality before applying different standards of treatment for the criminally insane. There is no reason to defer saving the homeless mentally ill until the solution to the rest of homelessness is found. Moreover, whatever solutions are eventually offered the non-mentally ill homeless, they will have little relevance to those who are mentally ill. Housing vouchers, counseling, and job training won't do much for Helen Phillips until we get the plutonium out of the water. And since we may never succeed, she will need more than housing vouchers, counseling, job training. She will need constant care.

The argument over how many of the homeless are mentally ill is end-   31
less. The estimates, which range from one-quarter to three-quarters, vary with method, definition, and ideology. But so what if even the lowest estimates are right? Even if treating the mentally ill does not end homelessness, how can that possibly justify not treating the tens, perhaps hundreds of thousands who would benefit from a partial solution?

In the end, the Brown case boils down to a problem of category, not a   32
problem of principle. Is she a schizophrenic or a hobo? There is inevitably some blurring of the lines between categories. (Studies of homeless families in New York have shown that many heads of these families exhibit signs of mental illness.) But even the judge who ruled in her favor on the grounds that she was not mentally ill upheld the city's program.

In Brown's case, we will not know which category she really belongs to 33
until her illness, if it is there, plays itself out. We will find out soon enough
if she is a professional street person or a chronic schizophrenic. But
there are others for whom there is no need to wait. The diagnosis is clear,
and treatment, or at least care, is available. In their cases, to wait is a
dereliction of social duty bordering on criminal neglect.

11

Causal Arguments: X Causes/ Does Not Cause Y

CASE 1

In 1970, the Volkswagen company sold 560,000 cars in the United States, the great majority of which were Beetles. In 1993 it sold only 50,000 cars. What accounts for the precipitous decline of Volkswagen's popularity in the United States? According to one analyst, it was VW's decision to drop the Beetle. "While the Beetle was known for ugly styling, cramped quarters and mediocre ride and handling, it became a cult car. Loyalists who swamped VW dealerships to buy one stayed away once a car called the Rabbit hopped in to take its place."* What made the Beetle so popular despite its ugly impracticality? Will Americans buy a "new concept" version of the Beetle ("slightly longer, wider and taller than the legendary Beetle, while still bearing the unmistakable design theme") currently being developed by Volkswagen engineers? These causal issues are at the heart of multimillion dollar manufacturing and marketing decisions for Volkswagen.

CASE 2

Economist James Dunn noted recently that of the 32 economists who won the Nobel Prize in Economics since it was first awarded in 1969, 78 percent were from Great Britain and the United States. At the same time, Dunn goes on to note, those two countries have experienced serious economic declines relative to other countries in the world. Meanwhile, the two countries that have experienced the greatest economic growth over the past several decades—Japan and Germany—have yet to produce a Nobel laureate

---

* "Volkswagen Reinvents the Beetle," *Seattle Times,* January 8, 1994, E1.

economist. This phenomenon raises some intriguing causal questions: Why haven't all these prize-winning economists been able to produce theories or policies that help the economies of their countries? Is it because, as some suspect, their economic theories are little more than "fancy quackery" when put into practice? Or could it possibly be that bright minds are attracted to economics precisely because there are problems in their native economic systems?

CASE 3

A great national debate in the 1990s centers on how to fight the drug war. Some people want to increase penalties for drug pushers and users. Other say that the only way to solve the drug problem is to take the profit out of drugs by legalizing them. At the heart of this controversy is a series of causal issues. What causes people to take drugs? What will be the consequences of different courses of action? For example, opponents of legalization say that open access to drugs will cause an increase, not a decrease, in drug usage and that the greatest losers will be minority communities. Proponents of legalization claim that the glamour of drug pushing is itself a cause of drug demand.

CASE 4

During July and August 1986, the death rate for infants rose an unexplained 235 percent in the state of Washington. A medical school professor at the University of Pittsburgh attributed the increase to radioactive fallout from the Chernobyl nuclear meltdown accident in Ukraine. Using weather reports and empirical evidence gathered in Washington state, he documented the increased radiation received on the northwestern coast of the United States. He used this evidence to bolster his argument that low levels of radiation are more dangerous than the scientific community currently believes. Opponents of the professor's hypothesis urged the public to view his argument with caution. They said that other factors may explain the increase in infant mortality.

THE FREQUENCY OF CAUSAL ARGUMENTS.

We encounter causal issues all the time. What made the VW Beetle a cult car? Will American buyers flock to buy "new concept" Beetles designed for the 1990s? Will legalization of drugs cause an increase or decrease in drug addicts? Will it end drug-related crime? What caused a sudden increase in the infant mortality rate in the Pacific Northwest during the period following the Chernobyl meltdown?

Sometimes an argument will be devoted entirely to a causal issue; just as frequently we encounter causal arguments as part of a "should" argument in which the writer argues that we should do X because X *will lead to specified consequences.* Convincing readers how X will lead to these consequences—a causal argument—thus constitutes much of the "should" argument. (Later in this text we call "should arguments" by the more general term "proposal arguments," which we treat at length in Chapter 14.)

An especially common place to find causal arguments is in debates about moral or legal guilt. For example, before we can assign guilt in a crime, we have to show that those being charged were not driven to act by forces beyond their control. A shrewd attorney might point to her client's life of poverty or to a chemical imbalance such as premenstrual stress syndrome. In one real-life example, a California murderer's sentence was mitigated in part because the defense convinced the jury that the defendant's actions resulted from a diet too heavy in refined sugar. This so-called Twinkie Defense is an extreme case of a causal argument's playing an important role in a judgment about human responsibility.

THE NATURE OF CAUSAL ARGUING

Typically, causal arguments try to show how one event brings about another. Although causation might at first seem like a fairly straightforward phenomenon, it sometimes raises thorny scientific and philosophic issues. Even if we take the classic illustration of causality—one billiard ball striking another on a pool table—and argue that the movement of the second ball was caused by a transfer of energy from the first ball at the moment of contact, there are some philosophers who argue that the human mind has only inferred causality and that all we can know, for sure, is that first one ball moved and then the other. Imagine how complex this issue becomes when we start talking about humans as well as billiard balls.

When human beings are the focus of a causal argument, the first problem that arises is one of definition. When we say that a given factor X "caused" a person to do Y, we might mean that X "forced her to do Y," thereby negating her free will (for example, my taking a certain drug caused me to fall asleep at the wheel); on the other hand, we might simply mean that factor X "motivated" her to do Y, such that doing Y is still an expression of free will (for example, my desire for more freedom caused me to give up my job and join the circus).

A second problem in dealing with human causality is the complexity of describing the causal mechanism. Because we have free will (or at least appear to), we may choose to respond unpredictably, even perversely, to causal forces. A rock dropped from a roof will always fall to the ground at thirty-two feet per second squared; and a rat zapped for making left turns in a maze will always quit making left turns. But can we predict with certainty any human behavior? Numerous psychological and philosophical schools engage in endless debate over their competing explanations of how causal mechanisms affect human beings.

Fortunately, most causal arguments can avoid the worst of these scientific and philosophic quagmires. As human beings we share a number of assumptions about what causes events in the observable world, and we can depend on the goodwill of our audiences to grant us most of these assumptions. Most of us, for example, would be satisfied with the following explanation for why a car went into a skid: "In a panic the driver locked the brakes of his car, causing the car to go into a skid." This sentence asserts a simple causal chain:

panic → slamming brake pedal → locking brakes → skid

We probably do not need to defend this explanation because the audience will grant the causal connections between events A, B, C, and D. The sequence seems reasonable according to our shared assumptions about psychological causality (panic leads to slamming brake pedal) and physical causality (locked brakes lead to skid).

The writer's task is harder, however, when the causal connections between the events either are not clear or go against common assumptions. Suppose that you are an attorney representing Oilcan Floyd, the driver of the car in the above example. Oilcan is suing the Ramjet Goat Automobile Company, claiming that a faulty brake system, not the driver's panic, caused the car to skid. Here is how you might preview your argument for a jury:

> My Dear Jurors,
>
> My client's car went into that disastrous skid not because its driver panicked and slammed the brakes. Oh, no. It skidded because of a flaw in the car's brake system. I propose to demonstrate this to you in the following manner: I propose to show first that the driver, Oilcan Floyd, was a professional race car driver with enormous skill handling cars at racetrack speeds in dangerous situations. I will show further that the driver was not in a panic situation when the accident occurred. Oilcan was maneuvering the car in ordinary traffic conditions and would have had no reasons for a panic stop. Finally, I will provide expert witnesses who will testify that the Ramjet Goat automobile that Oilcan was driving has a design flaw in the brake system that could lead to locked braking of all four wheels upon only a gentle touch of the brake pedal.

As Oilcan's attorney, you will be showing a new causal chain:

normal traffic maneuvering → gentle touch → brake locking → skid

This chain has a key link that violates common sense: How can a gentle touch lead to locking of the brakes? Here you must create an argument to show the workings of an unanticipated causal agent—a faulty brake system:

gentle touch → brake locking
caused by
faulty brakes

Your argument must develop in two stages: First, you must refute the causal chain that your audience would ordinarily assume, namely, that the locked brakes occurred during a panic stop. (You will do this by arguing that Oilcan Floyd is a great driver and that traffic conditions were normal.) Second, you must supply an explanation for the causal connection between a gentle touch on the brake pedal and the locked brakes. (You will do this be explaining the mechanical operation of the faulty brake system—for example, explaining how a leaking seal in the brakes' power assist mechanism caused the wheels to lock.) Our point, then, is that you will need to create an argument for causality, rather than just asserting causality or assuming it, whenever a causal connection seems to violate your audience's normal understanding of cause or whenever the audience is unclear about a cause.

DESCRIBING THE LOGICAL STRUCTURE OF A CAUSAL ARGUMENT: BECAUSE CLAUSES AND THE TOULMIN SCHEMA

Stating a causal argument using because clauses is generally easy ("Oilcan's gentle touch on the brake pedal caused the car to skid because the brakes had a leaking seal in the power assist mechanism"). Typically, causal arguments don't develop every link in the causal chain (or an argument might go on forever). A typical because clause in a causal argument, therefore, summarizes one or two key elements in the causal chain (the leaking seal in the power assist mechanism) rather than describing the entire causal chain.

Like other kinds of arguments, causal argument can often be analyzed using the Toulmin schema, which serves to help arguers see the structure of their arguments and to determine the most effective way to support their claims. Here is how Oilcan's attorney might use Toulmin's schema to prepare his or her court case. (It is easiest to apply Toulmin's schema to causal arguments if you think of the grounds as the observable phenomena at any point in the causal chain and the warrants as the shareable assumptions about causality that join links together.) The attorney's first task is to refute the opposition's argument that Oilcan slammed on the brakes in a panic. The argument could be diagrammed as follows:

ENTHYMEME:	Oilcan did not slam brakes in a panic because traffic conditions were normal and because Oilcan is a professional race car driver.
CLAIM:	Oilcan did not slam brakes in a panic.
STATED REASONS:	(a) because traffic conditions were normal; (b) because Oilcan is a professional race car driver.
GROUNDS:	(a) evidence that traffic conditions were normal (I'll need to call in witnesses); (b) testimony and records showing that Oilcan is a professional race car driver

WARRANT:	(a) People don't panic in normal traffic conditions; (b) Race car drivers are trained not to panic.
BACKING:	I think the jury would accept these warrants. But perhaps I could bring in further testimony from race car drivers about the way they use brakes in order to persuade the jury that race car drivers would never slam on their brakes in dangerous traffic situations, let alone normal conditions.
CONDITIONS OF REBUTTAL:	*Attacking my grounds:* (a) unless there was a momentary cause for panic in otherwise normal conditions (a child ran into the road?); (b) unless Oilcan is a professional race car driver in name only but actually has no real skills (I'll have to be prepared for both these arguments!)
	Attacking my warrants: (a) unless something other than traffic conditions caused Oilcan to panic (stung by a bee? heart attack?); (b) unless Oilcan wasn't his ordinary self (on drugs?)
QUALIFIER:	I will argue for certainty here.

The attorney's second task is to convince the jury that faulty brakes caused the skid. Here is a Toulmin schema for this argument:

ENTHYMEME:	Faulty brakes caused Oilcan Floyd's car to skid because the brake system had a leaky seal.
CLAIM:	Faulty brakes caused Oilcan Floyd's car to skid.
STATED REASON:	because the brake system had a leaky seal
GROUNDS:	expert testimony that brake system had a leaking seal in the power assist mechanism; evidence based on examination of other Ramjet Goat automobiles.
WARRANT:	A leaking seal in the power assist mechanism can cause wheels to lock with a gentle touch of the brake pedal.
BACKING:	Leaking seal causes A, which causes B, which causes C, which causes wheels to lock, which causes skid—I will have to make sure my expert witness can describe each of these links to the jury. We'll have to have charts and diagrams of the brake system.

CONDITIONS OF REBUTTAL: unless Oilcan's car did not have a leaking seal (Can my witness convince jury that *all* Ramjet Goat cars had leaking seals?); unless leaking seals don't always produce skids (Will the opposing attorney argue that wheel locking is rare even with a leaking seal?); unless Oilcan's touch wasn't gentle (Will the jury buy my argument that he didn't panic?)

QUALIFIER: "in all likelihood" (if I argue effectively!)

□ FOR CLASS DISCUSSION

1. Working individually or in small groups, create a causal chain to show how the first mentioned item could help lead to the last one.

   a. invention of the automobile   redesign of cities

   b. invention of the automobile   changes in sexual mores

   c. Elvis Presley brings rock and   rise of the drug culture in the 1960s
   roll to the nation

   d. invention of the telephone   loss of a sense of community
                                         in neighborhoods

   e. development of "the pill"   rise in the divorce rate

   f. development of way to   liberalization of euthanasia laws
   prevent rejections in transplant
   operations

2. For each of your causal chains, compose a claim with an attached because clause summarizing one or two key links in the causal chain. For example, "The invention of the automobile helped cause the redesign of cities because automobiles made it possible for people to live farther away from their places of work."

■ WRITING ASSIGNMENT FOR CHAPTER 11:   AN ARGUMENT INVOLVING "SURPRISING" OR "DISPUTED" CAUSES

By looking back through your previous explorations or by developing new ideas through the exploration tasks at the end of this chapter, choose an issue question about the causes (or consequences) of a trend, event, or other phenomenon. Write a three- to five-page argument that persuades an audience to accept your explanation of the causes (or consequences) of your chosen phenomenon. Within your essay you should examine alternative hypotheses or opposing views and explain your reasons for rejecting them.

You can imagine your issue either as a puzzle or as a disagreement. If a puzzle, your task will be informational as well as argumentative because your role will be that of an analyst explaining causes or consequences of an event to an audience that doesn't have an answer already in mind. If you see your issue as a disagreement, your task will be more directly argumentative since your goal will be to change an opposing audience's views so that they adhere to your position more than their original one.

The rest of this chapter will help you write your essay by giving you more background about causal arguments and by providing suggestions for each stage of the writing process.

THREE METHODS FOR ARGUING THAT ONE EVENT CAUSES ANOTHER

One of the first things you need to do when preparing a causal argument is to note just what sort of causal relationship you're dealing with. Are you concerned with the causes of a specific event or phenomenon such as the increase in homelessness in the 1980s, the collapse of the Soviet Union, the sudden increase in the number of homeruns in the 1993 baseball season, or the breakdown in communication between you and your father? Or are you planning to write about the cause of some recurring phenomenon such as cancer, laughter, math anxiety among females, or teen suicide?

With recurring phenomena, you have the luxury of being able to study multiple cases over long periods of time and establishing correlations between suspected causal factors and effects. In some cases you can even intervene in the process and test for yourself whether diminishing a suspected causal factor results in a lessening of the effect or whether increasing the causal factor results in a corresponding increase in the effect. Additionally, you can spend a good deal of time exploring just how the mechanics of causation might work.

But with a one-time occurrence your focus is on the details of the event and specific causal chains that may have contributed to the event. Sometimes evidence has disappeared or changed its nature. You often end up in the position more of a detective than of a scientific researcher and your conclusion will have to be more tentative as a result.

Having briefly stated these words of caution, let's turn now to the various ways you can argue that one event causes another.

First Method: Explain the Causal Mechanism Directly

The most convincing kind of causal argument occurs when you identify every link in the causal chain, showing how X causes A, which causes B, which in turn causes C, which finally causes Y. In some cases, all you have to do is fill in the missing links; in other cases—when your assumptions about causality may seem questionable to your audience—you have to argue for the causal connection with more vigor. Thus, for example, Oilcan Floyd's attorney will have to argue hard to convince the jury that faulty brakes, not a panicked driver, caused the car to skid.

A careful spelling out of each step in the causal chain is the technique used by astronomer Carl Sagan in "The Warming of the World" (pp. 256–61), in which he explains the greenhouse effect and predicts its consequences. His causal chain looks like this:

STARTING POINT A	STARTING POINT B
Cutting down of forests leads to fewer plants on Earth's land surface.	Burning of fossil fuels produces carbon dioxide.
Fewer plants lead to more carbon dioxide in the atmosphere.	(*Warrant:* because carbon dioxide is a product of combustion)
(*Warrant:* because plants convert carbon dioxide to oxygen)	Production of carbon dioxide leads to more carbon dioxide in the atmosphere.

LINK 2

More carbon dioxide in atmosphere reduces amount of infrared light radiated into space. (*Warrant:*   because carbon dioxide absorbs infrared radiation; Sagan backs this warrant with further explanation)

LINK 3

Earth heats up. (*Warrant:*   because Earth stays cool by reflecting heat back into space through infrared radiation)

LINK 4

Land will become parched; seas will rise. (*Warrant:*   because heat causes changes in precipitation patterns causing land to parch; also because heat causes glacial ice to melt)

LINK 5

Massive global danger (*Warrant:*   because parched farmland and rising seas will cause social and economic upheaval)

Sagan concludes his essay with a proposal based on the above causal argument. Placed into a claim with because clause, Sagan's should argument looks like this:

Nations should initiate worldwide efforts to find alternative energy sources because the continued burning of fossil fuels will lead to global catastrophe.

Thus, in Sagan's essay, a lengthy causal argument in the beginning supports a final should argument.

This causal chain method is also used by student writer Mary Lou Torpey in predicting the consequences of mandatory drug testing (pp. 261–63). Figure 11–1 shows Torpey's planning diagram for her argument "What Drugs I Take Is None of Your Business—The Consequences of Mandatory Drug Testing." Her diagram shows the links of the chain beginning with a mandatory drug-testing program and culminating in prejudice against employees with certain treatable disorders such as narcolepsy.

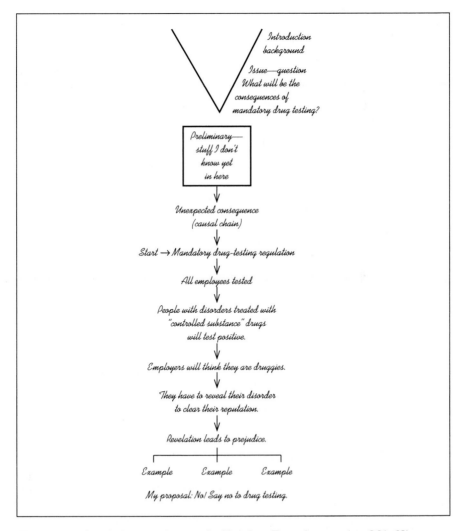

Figure 11–1 Initial planning diagram for Mary Lou Torpey's essay (pp. 261–63)

SECOND METHOD: USE VARIOUS INDUCTIVE METHODS TO ESTABLISH A HIGH PROBABILITY OF A CAUSAL LINK

INFORMAL INDUCTION

Although few of us are scientists, all of us practice the scientific method informally through *induction*. Induction is a form of reasoning by which we make generalizations based on a limited number of specific cases. For example, if on several occasions you got a headache after drinking red wine but not after drinking white wine, you would be apt to conclude inductively that red wine causes you to get headaches. However, because there are almost always exceptions to rules arrived at inductively and because we can't be certain that the future will always be like the past, inductive reasoning gives only probable truths, not certain ones.

When your brain thinks inductively, it sorts through data looking for patterns of similarity and difference. Toddlers are thinking inductively when they learn the connection between flipping a wall switch and watching the ceiling light come on. Like scientists, they are holding all variables constant except the position of the switch. But the inductive process does not explain the causal mechanism itself. Thus, through induction you know that red wine gives you a headache, but you don't know how the wine actually works on your nervous system—the causal chain itself.

Largely because of its power, the process of induction often can lead you to wrong conclusions. You should be aware of two common fallacies of inductive reasoning that can tempt you into erroneous assumptions about causality. (Both fallacies are treated more fully in Appendix 1.)

The *post hoc, ergo propter hoc* fallacy ("after this, therefore because of this") mistakes precedence for cause. Just because event A regularly precedes event B doesn't mean that event A causes event B. The same reasoning that tells us that flipping a switch causes the light to go on can make us believe that the Chernobyl nuclear disaster caused the rise in infant death rates in the state of Washington (see Case 4). The nuclear disaster clearly preceded the rise in death rates. But did it clearly *cause* it? Our point is that precedence alone is no proof of causality and that we are guilty of this fallacy whenever we are swayed to believe that X causes Y primarily because X precedes Y.

The *hasty generalization* fallacy occurs when you make a generalization based on too few cases or too little consideration of alternative explanations: You flip the switch, but the light bulb doesn't go on. You conclude—too hastily—that the power has gone off. (Perhaps the light bulb has burned out or the switch is broken.) How many trials does it take before you can make a justified generalization rather than a hasty generalization? It is difficult to say, for sure. Both the *post hoc* fallacy and the *hasty generalization* fallacy remind us that induction requires a leap from individual cases to a general principle and that it is always possible to leap too soon.

SCIENTIFIC EXPERIMENTATION

One way to avoid inductive fallacies is to examine our causal hypotheses as carefully as possible. When we deal with a recurring phenomenon such as cancer, we can create scientific experiments that give us inductive evidence of causality with a fairly high degree of certainty. If, for example, we were concerned that a particular food source such as spinach might contain cancer-causing chemicals, we could test our hypothesis experimentally. We could take two groups of rats and control their environment carefully so that the only difference between them (in theory anyway) was that one group ate large quantities of spinach and the other group ate none. Spinach eating, then, is the one variable between the two groups that we are testing. After a specified period of time, we would check to see what percentage of rats in each group developed cancer. If twice as many spinach-eating rats contracted cancer, we could probably conclude that our hypothesis had held up.

CORRELATION

Still another method of induction is correlation, which expresses a statistical relationship between X and Y. A correlation between X and Y means that when X occurs, Y is likely to occur also, and vice versa. To put it another way, correlation establishes a possibility that an observed link between an X and a Y is a causal one rather than a mere coincidence. The existence of a correlation, however, does not tell us whether X causes Y, whether Y causes X, or whether both are caused by some third phenomenon. For example, there is a fairly strong correlation between nearsightedness and intelligence. (That is, in a given sample of nearsighted people and people with normal eyesight, a higher percentage of the nearsighted people will be highly intelligent. Similarly, in a sample of high-intelligence people and people with normal intelligence, a higher percentage of the high-intelligence group will be nearsighted.) But the direction of causality isn't clear. It could be that high intelligence causes people to read more, thus ruining their eyes (high intelligence causes nearsightedness). Or it could be that nearsightedness causes people to read more, thus raising their intelligence (nearsightedness causes high intelligence). Or it could be that some unknown phenomenon inside the brain causes both nearsightedness and high intelligence.

In recent years, correlation studies have been made stunningly sophisticated through the power of computerized analyses. For example, we could attempt to do the spinach-cancer study without resorting to a scientific experiment. If we identified a given group that ate lots of spinach (for example, vegetarians) and another group that ate little if any spinach (Eskimos) and then checked to see if their rates of cancer correlated to their rates of spinach consumption, we would have the beginnings of a correlation study. But it would have no scientific validity until we factored out all the other variables between vegetarians and Eskimos that might skew the findings—variables such as life-style, climate, genetic inheritance, differences in diet other than spinach, and so forth. Factoring out such variables is one of the complex feats that modern statistical analyses attempt to accomplish. But the fact remains that the most sophisticated correlation studies still cannot tell us the direction of causality or even for certain that there is causality.

By way of illustrating the uses of correlation arguments, consider Victor Fuchs' article "Why Married Mothers Work" (pp. 263–67). The graph on page 264 shows that the number of married mothers in the workforce has been steadily rising since 1948. Fuchs rejects several common explanations for this phenomenon (growth of feminism, government affirmative action, economic need) on the grounds that the timing is wrong. He proposes another hypothesis: Increased wages and increased job openings in the service sector are for him the best causal candidates because their slow, steady rate of increase correlates with the increase in working married mothers. Moreover, he provides a hypothesis for why women are attracted to service sector jobs (they require less physical strength, offer flexible hours including part-time work, and are located near residential areas).

Note that Fuchs is careful to have two kinds of reasons for his argument. The first is the statistical data that show that the increase of married mothers in the workplace correlates with the increase of wages and the increase of available jobs in the service sector. The second is a hypothesis explaining why increased wages and increased service sector jobs attract married mothers. Whenever you make a causal argument supported by statistical correlations, you should be aware—as is Fuchs—that you must be able to offer some reason for thinking that there is a particular "direction" to the relationship.

CONCLUSION ABOUT INDUCTIVE METHODS

Induction, then, can tell us within varying degrees of certainty whether or not X causes Y. It does not, however, explain the causal mechanism itself. Typically, the because clause structure of an inductive argument would take one of the following three shapes: (1) "Although we cannot explain the causal mechanism directly, we believe that X and Y are very probably causally linked because we have repeatedly observed their conjunction"; (2) "... because we have demonstrated the linkage through controlled scientific experiments"; or (3) "... because we have shown that they are statistically correlated and have provided a plausible hypothesis concerning the causal direction."

□ FOR CLASS DISCUSSION

Working individually or in small groups, develop plausible causal chains that might explain the correlations between the following pairs of phenomena:

a. A person registers low stress level on electrochemical stress meter.

Person does daily meditation.

b. Person regularly consumes frozen dinners.

Person is likely to vote for improved rapid transit.

c. High achiever

First-born child

d. Member of the National Rifle Association

Favors tough treatment of criminals

Third Method: Argue by Analogy or Precedent

Another common method of causal arguing is through analogy or precedent. (See also Chapter 12, "Resemblance Arguments," which deals in more depth with the strengths and weaknesses of this kind of arguing.) When you argue through resemblance, you try to find a case that is similar to the one you are arguing about but is better known and less controversial to the reader. If the reader agrees with your view of causality in the similar case, you then try to transfer this understanding to the case at issue. Causal arguments by analogy and precedent are logically weaker than arguments based on causal chains or on induction and will typically be used in cases where empirical evidence is weak.

Here are some examples of this method in causal arguing:

1. If you wanted to argue that overcrowding in high-density apartment houses causes dangerous stress in humans, you could compare humans to mice, which develop symptoms of high stress when they are crowded together in cages. (This argument depends on the warrant that humans and mice will respond similarly to the condition of crowding.)

2. If you want to argue that doing regular thinking skills exercises will result in improved thinking ability, you could compare the mind to a muscle and the thinking skills exercises to daily weight training. (Because the audience will probably accept the causal chain of weight training leading to improved physical strength, you hope to transfer that acceptance to the field of mental activity. This argument depends on the warrant that the mind is like a muscle.)

3. If you wanted to argue that forced piano lessons won't make a child a musician, you could argue that parents can't mold a child like clay; rather, children are like plants—you can't mold them into something that is not in their nature any more than a gardener can mold a tulip into a rose. (This argument depends on the warrant that children are more like plants than like clay.)

All of these arguments have a persuasive power. However, any two things that are alike in some ways (analogous) are different in others (disanalogous), and these differences are apt to be ignored in arguments from analogy. You should realize, then, that the warrant that says X is like Y can almost always be attacked. Psychologists, for example, have pretty much demonstrated that the mind is not like a muscle, and we can all think of ways that children are not like plants. *All* resemblance arguments, therefore, are in some sense "false analogies." But some analogies are so misleading that logicians have labeled them as fallacious—the fallacy of *false analogy*. The *false analogy* fallacy covers those truly blatant cases where the differences between X and Y are too great for the analogy to hold. An example might be the following: "Putting red marks all over students' papers causes great emotional distress just as putting knife marks over their palms would cause great physical distress." It is impossible to draw a precise line, however, between an analogy that has true clarifying and persuasive power and one that is fallacious.

GLOSSARY OF TERMS ENCOUNTERED IN CAUSAL ARGUMENTS

Because causal arguments are often easier to conduct if writer and reader share a few specialized terms, we offer the following glossary for your convenience.

Fallacy of Oversimplified Cause: One of the greatest temptations when establishing causal relationships is to fall into the habit of looking for *the* cause of something. Most phenomena, especially the ones we argue about, will have multiple causes. For example, few presidents have won elections on the basis of one characteristic or event. Usually elections result from a combination of abilities, stances on key issues, personal characteristics, mistakes on the part of the competition, events in the world, and so forth. Similarly, scientists know that a number of different causes must work together to create a disease such as cancer. But though we know all this, we still long to make the world less complex by attributing a single cause to puzzling effects.

Immediate/Remote Causes: Every causal chain links backward indefinitely into the past. An immediate cause is the closest in time to the event being examined. If a normally passive man goes on a killing rampage, the immediate cause may be a brain tumor or a recent argument with his wife that was the "last straw" in a long chain of events. A number of earlier events may have led up to the present—failure to get medical attention for headaches or failure to get counseling when a marriage began to disintegrate. Such causes going further back into the past are considered remote causes. It's sometimes difficult to determine the relative significance of remote causes insofar as immediate causes are so obviously linked to the event whereas remote causes often have to be dug out or inferred. It's difficult to know, for example, just how seriously to take serial murderer Ted Bundy's defense that he was "traumatized" at age twelve by the discovery that he was illegitimate. How big a role are we willing to grant a causal factor so remote in time and so apparently minor in relation to the murder of thirty-five young women?

Precipitating/Contributing Causes: These terms are similar to *immediate* and *remote* causes but don't designate a temporal linking going into the past. Rather, they refer to a main cause emerging out of a background of subsidiary causes. The contributing causes are a set of conditions that give rise to the precipitating cause, which triggers the effect. If, for example, a husband and wife decide to separate, the precipitating cause may be a stormy fight over money, which itself is a symptom of their inability to communicate with each other any longer. All the factors that contribute to that inability to communicate—preoccupation with their respective careers, anxieties about money, in-law problems—may be considered contributing causes. Note that the contributing causes and precipitating cause all coexist simultaneously in time—none is temporally more remote than another. But the marriage might have continued had the contributing causes not finally resulted in frequent angry fighting, which doomed the marriage.

Constraints: Sometimes an effect occurs, not because X happened, but because another factor—a constraint—was removed. At other times a possible effect will not occur because a given constraint prevents it from happening. A constraint is a kind of negative cause that limits choices and possibilities. As soon as the constraint is removed, a given effect may occur. For example, in the marriage we have been discussing, the presence of children in the home might have been a constraint against divorce; as soon as the children graduate from high school and leave home, the marriage may well dissolve.

Necessary/Sufficient Causes: We speak of necessary causes as those that must be present when a given effect takes place. If a necessary cause is absent, the effect cannot take place. Thus the presence of a spark is a necessary cause for the operation of a gasoline engine. A sufficient cause, on the other hand, is one that guarantees a given effect. An electric spark is thus a *necessary cause* for the operation of a gasoline engine but not a *sufficient cause* since other causes must also be present to make the engine work (fuel, etc.). Few causes are ever both necessary and sufficient to bring about a given effect.

□ FOR CLASS DISCUSSION

The above terms can be used as an effective heuristic for thinking of possible causes of an event. For the following events, try to think of as many causes as possible by making idea-maps with branches labeled *immediate cause, remote cause, precipitating cause, contributing cause,* and *constraint.* (See Figure 11–2).

1. Working individually, make a map identifying causes for one of the following:
   a. your decision to attend your present college
   b. an important event in your life or your family (a divorce, a major move, etc.)
   c. a personal opinion you hold that is not widely shared

2. Working as a group, make a map identifying causes for one of the following:
   a. why many American males began to wear earrings in the mid-1980s
   b. why the majority of teenagers don't listen to classical music
   c. why the number of babies born out of wedlock has increased dramatically in the last thirty years

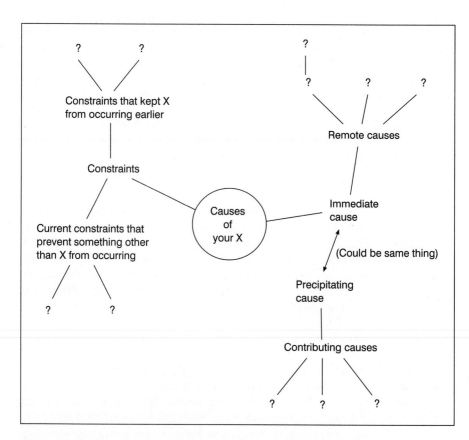

Figure 11–2 Idea-map using kinds of causes for generating ideas

■ WRITING YOUR CAUSAL ARGUMENT

The stages of the writing process that we discussed in Chapter 3 can be fruitfully applied to a causal argument. What follows are some suggestions that may help you find a good causal issue and produce an effective argument.

The Starting Point: Finding a Causal Issue

You already may have discovered some good causal issues and recorded them in your journal. If not, here are some exploration tasks that might help you get started.

Make a List of People's Unusual Likes and Dislikes

One way to become engaged with a causal issue is to make a list of unusual things that anger people, scare them, or inspire their hatred. Alternatively, you can list unusual things that people like, value, or desire. You could then write a causal argument explaining why one of these phenomena produces this emotional response. Try to choose like or dislikes that are fairly common but are puzzling to explain. Typical titles might be: "Why Are People Afraid of Bats?" "Why Do Certain Students Dislike Writing?" or "Why Do So Many People Like Professional Wrestling?"

Make Lists of Trends and Other Puzzling Phenomena

Besides lists of unusual likes and dislikes, try adding your own X's to the following list.

1. trends

    popularity of expensive basketball shoes for street wear

    growth of rap music

    decline of nationwide liquor sales

2. one-time events

    popularity of Ross Perot in 1992 elections

    rash of mysterious illnesses of Gulf War veterans two years after returning to the United States

    riots following acquittal of police officers in Rodney King trial

3. repeatable events

    Why are children attracted to violent video games?

    What are the effects of working swing shifts?

    What are the causes of reading difficulties?

4. other puzzling phenomena

   Why are lotteries popular?

   Why do people watch professional wrestling?

   Why is so much hatred of women reflected in gangsta rap?

Make Some Idea-maps to Explore Causes or Consequences

Another way to find a causal issue is to try out some arguments. Make idea-maps in which you brainstorm possible causes for several of the following phenomena: failure of many sexually active teenagers to use birth control; growth of the home computer industry; decline of interest in home videogames; popularity of rock groups with bisexual identities; increase of popularity of "home birthing" methods; graffiti on subways; the dominance of blacks in college and professional basketball; popularity of Eddie Murphy movies; growth in the pornography industry. Then add at least three phenomena of your own to the list.

Another fruitful area for idea-maps is to explore possible consequences of real or hypothetical events. What might be the consequences, for example, of some of the following: a cure for cancer; worldwide disarmament; the AIDS epidemic; a heavy tax on families having more than two children; replacement of federal income tax with a federal sales tax; a four-day workweek; several topics of your own choice.

Exploration Stage

Once you have decided on a causal issue, we recommend that you explore it by going through the eight guided tasks for exploring an argument (on pp. 79–81). You can also make an idea-map on your causal issue like the ones in the For Class Discussion exercise in the preceding glossary of causal terms.

Writing the Discovery Draft: Typical Ways of Organizing a Causal Argument

Your goal at the discovery draft stage is to get your developing argument onto paper. At this stage it is useful to know some of the standard ways that a causal argument can be organized. Later, you may decide on a quite different organizational pattern, but these standard ways will help you get started.

PLAN 1   When your purpose is to describe and explain all the links in a causal chain:

- Introduce phenomenon to be explained and show why it is problematical.
- Present your thesis in summary form.
- Describe and explain each link in the causal chain.

Carl Sagan's essay on the greenhouse effect (pp. 256–61) follows this format.

PLAN 2   When your purpose is to explore the relative contribution of all causes to a phenomenon or to explore all possible consequences of a phenomenon:

- Introduce the phenomenon to be explained and suggest how or why it is controversial.
- Devote one section to each possible cause/consequence and decide whether it is necessary, sufficient, contributory, remote, and so forth. (Arrange sections so that those causes most familiar to the audience come first and the most surprising ones come last.)

Victor Fuchs' argument "Why Married Mothers Work" (pp. 263–67) follows this format.

PLAN 3   When your purpose is to argue for a cause or consequence that is surprising or unexpected to your audience:

- Introduce a phenomenon to be explained and show why it is controversial.
- One by one, examine and reject the causes or consequences your audience would normally assume or expect.
- Introduce your unexpected or surprising cause or consequence and argue for it.

Plans 2 and 3 are similar in that they examine numerous possible causes or consequences. Plan 2, however, tries to establish the relative importance of each cause or consequence, whereas Plan 3 aims at rejecting the causes or consequences normally assumed by the audience and argues for an unexpected surprising cause or consequence. Plan 3 is the strategy used by Mary Lou Torpey (pp. 261–63) in arguing for an unexpected consequence of drug testing and by Walter S. Minot in proposing an overlooked cause of decline in American education (pp. 267–69).

PLAN 4   When your purpose is to change your audience's mind about a cause or consequence:

- Introduce issue and show why it is controversial.
- Summarize your opponent's causal argument and then refute it.
- Present your own causal argument.

Plan 4 is a standard structure for all kinds of arguments. This is the structure Oilcan Floyd's attorney would use in court to persuade the jury that faulty brakes caused Oilcan's car to skid.

Revision: Seeing Your Argument Afresh

Once you have written a discovery draft, you will have a clearer idea of what you are trying to do in your essay. Through further drafting and discussions with others, your next goal is to clarify your argument for yourself and then finally to make it clear and persuasive for your readers.

If you haven't already done so, now is the time to summarize your argument as a claim with because clauses and to analyze your argument either using the Toulmin schema or making a diagram of your causal chain similar to the one we made for Carl Sagan's essay on the greenhouse effect or that Mary Lou Torpey made for herself (Figure 11–1). To strengthen your argument from the perspective of a skeptical audience, pay particular attention to Toulmin's "conditions for rebuttal." Try to see the weaknesses of your argument from an opposing perspective and use that knowledge to bolster your support. The following section shows you some ways to role play an opposing view in order to discover weaknesses in your own argument.

CONDITIONS FOR REBUTTAL: CRITIQUING CAUSAL ARGUMENTS

Because of the strenuous conditions that must be met before causality can be proven, causal arguments are vulnerable at many points. The following strategies will generally be helpful.

If You Described Each Link in a Causal Chain, Would Skeptics Point out Weaknesses in Any of the Links?

As the diagram of Carl Sagan's article suggests, describing a causal chain can be complex business. A skeptic can raise doubts about an entire argument simply by undercutting one of the links. Your best defense is to make a diagram of the linkages and role play a skeptic trying to refute each link in turn. Whenever you find possible arguments against your position, see how you can strengthen your own argument at that point.

If Your Argument Is Based on a Scientific Experiment, Could Skeptics Question the Validity of the Experiment?

The scientific method attempts to demonstrate causality experimentally. If the experiment isn't well designed, however, the demonstration is less likely to be acceptable to skeptical audiences. Here are ways to critique a scientific argument:

Question the findings.   Skeptics may have reason to believe that the data collected were not accurate or representative. They might provide alternative data or simply point out flaws in the way the data were collected.

Question the interpretation of the data.   Many research studies are divided into a "findings" and a "discussion" section. In the discussion section the researcher analyzes and interprets the data. A skeptic might provide an alternative interpretation of the data or otherwise argue that the data don't support what the original writer claims.

Question the design of the experiment. A detailed explanation of research design is beyond the scope of this text, but we can give a brief example of how a typical experiment did go wrong. A major university recently completed an experiment to test the effect of word processors on students' achievement in Freshman English. They reported that students who used the word processors for revising all their essays did significantly better on a final essay than a control group of students who didn't use word processors.

It turned out, however, that there were at least two major design flaws in the experiment. First, the researchers allowed students to volunteer for the experimental group. Perhaps these students were already better writers than the control group from the start. (Can you think of a causal explanation of why the better students might volunteer to use the computers?) Second, when the teachers graded essays from both the computer group and the control group, the essays were not retyped uniformly. Thus the computer group's essays were typed with "computer perfection" (justified right margins, etc.), whereas the control group's essays were handwritten or typed on ordinary typewriters. Perhaps the readers were affected by the pleasing appearance of the computer-typed essays. More significantly, perhaps the graders were biased in favor of the computer project and unconsciously scored the computer-typed papers higher.

The above example illustrates just a few of the ways a scientific study can be flawed. Our point is that skeptics might not automatically accept your citation of a scientific study as a proof of causality. By considering opposing views in advance, you may be able to strengthen your argument.

If You Have Used Correlation Data, Could Skeptics Argue That the Correlation Is Much Weaker than You Claim or That You Haven't Sufficiently Demonstrated Causality?

As we discussed earlier, correlation data tell us only that two or more phenomena are likely to occur together. They don't tell us that one caused the other. Thus correlation arguments are usually accompanied by hypotheses about causal connections between the phenomena. Correlation arguments can often be refuted as follows:

- Find problems in the statistical methods used to determine the correlation.
- Weaken the correlation by pointing out exceptions.
- Provide an alternative hypothesis about causality.

If You Have Used an Analogy Argument, Could Skeptics Point out Disanalogies?

Although among the most persuasive of argumentative strategies, analogy arguments are also among the easiest to refute. The standard procedure is to counter your argument that X is like Y by pointing out all the ways that X is *not* like Y. Once again, by role playing an opposing view, you may be able to strengthen your own analogy argument.

Could a Skeptic Cast Doubt on Your Argument by Reordering Your Priority of Causes?

Up to this point we've focused on refuting the claim that X causes Y. However, another approach is to concede that X helps cause Y but that X is only one of several contributing causes and not the most significant one at that.

☐ FOR CLASS DISCUSSION

In "Students Who Push Burgers" (pp. 267–69), the author, Walter Minot, blames part-time jobs as a primary cause of the decline of educational performance by American students, a decline that leads in turn (so claims Minot) to a decline in our economy. You, however, want to defend the practice of American teenagers holding part-time jobs. Using procedures outlined in this chapter, how might you attempt to weaken Minot's argument and create greater audience adherence to your own?

1. Do a ten-minute freewrite in which you explore ways to undercut Minot's argument and support your own.
2. In groups, discuss your individual responses.
3. Elect one member of your group to give a brief speech before the class, arguing that Minot's essay either fails to see important benefits in part-time work or diverts attention from other, more important causes of the decline of American education.

■

THE WARMING OF THE WORLD

Carl Sagan

When humans first evolved—in the savannahs of East Africa a few million   1
years ago—our numbers were few and our powers feeble. We knew almost nothing about controlling our environment—even clothing had yet to be invented. We were creatures of the climate, utterly dependent upon it.

A few degrees hotter or colder on average, and our ancestors were in   2
trouble. The toll taken much later by the ice ages, in which average land temperatures dropped some 8° C (centigrade, or Celsius), must have been horrific. And yet, it is exactly such climatic change that pushed our ancestors to develop tools and technology, science and civilization.

Certainly, skills in hunting, skinning, tanning, building shelters and refurbishing caves must owe much to the terrors of the deep ice age.

Today, we live in a balmy epoch, 10,000 years after the last major   3
glaciation. In this climatic spring, our species has flourished; we now cover the entire planet and are altering the very appearance of our world. Lately—within the last century or so—humans have acquired, in more ways than one, the ability to make major changes in that climate upon which we are so dependent. The Nuclear Winter findings are one dramatic indication that we can change the climate—in this case, in the spasm of nuclear war. But I wish here to describe a different kind of climatic danger, this one slower, more subtle and arising from intentions that are wholly benign.

It is warm down here on Earth because the Sun shines. If the Sun   4
were somehow turned off, the Earth would rapidly cool. The oceans would freeze, and eventually the atmosphere itself would condense out and our planet would be covered everywhere by snowbanks of solid oxygen and nitrogen 10 meters (about 30 feet) high. Only the tiny trickle of heat from the Earth's interior and the faint starlight would save our world from a temperature of absolute zero.

We know how bright the Sun is; we know how far from it we are; and   5
we know what fraction of the sunlight reaching the Earth is reflected back to space (about 30 percent). So we can calculate—with a simple mathematical equation—what the average temperature of the Earth should be. But when we do the calculation, we find that the Earth's temperature should be about 20° C below the freezing point of water, in stark contradiction to our everyday experience. What have we done wrong?

As in many such cases in science, what we've done wrong is to forget   6
something—in this case, the atmosphere. Every object in the universe radiates some kind of light to space; the colder the object, the longer the wavelength of radiation it emits. The Earth—much colder than the Sun—radiates to space mainly in the infrared part of the spectrum, not the visible. Were the Sun turned off, the Earth would soon be indetectable in ordinary visible light, though it would be brilliantly illuminated in infrared light.

When sunlight strikes the Earth, part is reflected back into the sky;   7
much of the rest is absorbed by the ground and heats it—the darker the ground, the greater the heating. The ground radiates back upward in the infrared. Thus, for an airless Earth, the temperature would be set solely by a balance between the incoming sunlight absorbed by the surface and the infrared radiation that the surface emits back to space.

When you put air on a planet, the situation changes. The Earth's   8
atmosphere is, generally, still transparent to visible light. That's why we can see each other when we talk, glimpse distant mountains and view the stars.

But in the infrared, all that is different. While the oxygen and nitrogen   9
in the air are transparent in both the infrared and the visible, minor con-

stituents such as water vapor (H_2O) and carbon dioxide (CO_2) tend to be much more opaque in the infrared. It would be useless for us to have eyes that could see at a wavelength, say, of 15 microns in the infrared, because the air is murky black there.

Accordingly, if you add air to a world, you heat it: The surface now has 10 difficulty when it tries to radiate back to space in the infrared. The atmosphere tends to absorb the infrared radiation, keeping heat near the surface and providing an infrared blanket for the world. There is very little CO_2 in the Earth's atmosphere—only 0.03 percent. But that small amount is enough to make the Earth's atmosphere opaque in important regions of the infrared spectrum. CO_2 and H_2O are the reason the global temperature is not well below freezing. We owe our comfort—indeed, our very existence—to the fact that these gases are present and are much more transparent in the visible than in the infrared. Our lives depend on a delicate balance of invisible gases. Too much blanket, or too little, and we're in trouble.

This property of many gases to absorb strongly in the infrared but not 11 in the visible, and thereby to heat their surroundings, is called the "greenhouse effect." A florist's greenhouse keeps its planty inhabitants warm. The phrase "greenhouse effect" is widely used and has an instructive ring to it, reminding us that we live in a planetary-scale greenhouse and recalling the admonition about living in glass houses and throwing stones. But, in fact, florists' greenhouses do not keep warm by the greenhouse effect; they work mainly by inhibiting the movement of air inside, another matter altogether.

We need look only as far as the nearest planet to see an example of an 12 atmospheric greenhouse effect gone wild. Venus has in its atmosphere an enormous quantity of carbon dioxide (roughly as much as is buried as carbonates in all the rocks of the Earth's crust). There is an atmosphere of CO_2 on Venus 90 times thicker than the atmosphere on the Earth and containing some 200,000 times more CO_2 than in our air. With water vapor and other minor atmospheric constituents, this is enough to make a greenhouse effect that keeps the surface of Venus around 470° C (900° F)—enough to melt tin or lead.

When humans burn wood or "fossil fuels" (coal, oil, natural gas, etc.), 13 they put carbon dioxide into the air. One carbon atom (C) combines with a molecule of oxygen (O_2) to produce CO_2. The development of agriculture, the conversion of dense forest to comparatively sparsely vegetated farms, has moved carbon atoms from plants on the ground to carbon dioxide in the air. About half of this new CO_2 is removed by plants or by the layering down of carbonates in the oceans. On human time-scales, these changes are irreversible: Once the CO_2 is in the atmosphere, human technology is helpless to remove it. So the overall amount of CO_2 in the air has been growing—at least since the industrial revolution. If no other factors operate, and if enough CO_2 is put into the atmosphere, eventually the average surface temperature will increase perceptibly.

There are other greenhouse gases that are increasingly abundant in   14
the Earth's atmosphere—halocarbons, such as the freon used in refrigerator cooling systems; or nitrous oxide (N_2O), produced by automobile
exhausts and nitrogenous fertilizers; or methane (CH_4), produced partly
in the intestines of cows and other ruminants.

But let's for the moment concentrate on carbon dioxide: How long, at   15
the present rates of burning wood and fossil fuels, before the global climate becomes significantly warmer? And what would the consequences
be?

It is relatively simple to calculate the immediate warming from a given   16
increase in the CO_2 abundance, and all competent calculations seem to
be in good agreement. More difficult to estimate are (1) the rate at which
carbon dioxide will continue to be put into the atmosphere (it depends
on population growth rates, economic styles, alternative energy sources
and the like) and (2) feedbacks—ways in which a slight warming might
produce other, more drastic, effects.

The recent increase in atmospheric CO_2 is well documented. Over the   17
last century, this CO_2 buildup should have resulted in a few tenths of a
degree of global warming, and there is some evidence that such a warming has occurred.

The National Academy of Sciences estimates that the present atmos-   18
pheric abundance of CO_2 is likely to double by the year 2065, although
experts at the academy predict a one-in-20 chance that it will double
before 2035—when an infant born today becomes 50 years old. Such a
doubling would warm the air near the surface of the Earth by 2° C or
3° C—maybe by as much as 4° C. These are average temperature values;
there would naturally be considerable local variation. High latitudes
would be warmed much more, although a baked Alaska will be some
time coming.

There would be precipitation changes. The annual discharge of rivers   19
would be altered. Some scientists believe that central North America—
including much of the area that is now the breadbasket of the world—
would be parched in summer if the global temperature increases by a
few degrees. There would be some mitigating effects; for example, where
plant growth is not otherwise limited, more CO_2 should aid photosynthe-
sis and make more luxuriant growth (of weeds as well as crops). If the
present CO_2 injection into the atmosphere continued over a few centuries, the warming would be greater than from all other causes over the
last 100,000 years.

As the climate warms, glacial ice melts. Over the last 100 years, the   20
level of the world's oceans has risen by 15 centimeters (6 inches). A
global warming of 3° C or 4° C over the next century is likely to bring a
further rise in the average sea level of about 70 centimeters (28 inches).
An increase of this magnitude could produce major damage to ports all
over the world and induce fundamental change in the patterns of land
development. A serious speculation is that greenhouse temperature

increases of 3° C or 4° C could, in addition, trigger the disintegration of the West Antarctic Ice Sheet, with huge quantities of polar ice falling into the ocean. This would raise sea level by some 6 meters (20 feet) over a period of centuries, with the eventual inundation of all coastal cities on the planet.

There are many other possibilities that are poorly understood, includ-   21
ing the release of other greenhouse gases (for example, methane from peat bogs) accelerated by the warming climate. The circulation of the oceans might be an important aspect of the problem. The scientific community is attempting to make an environmental-impact statement for the entire planet on the consequences of continued burning of fossil fuels. Despite the uncertainties, a kind of consensus is in: Over the next century or more, with projected rates of burning coal, oil and gas, there is trouble ahead.

The problem is difficult for at least three different reasons: 22

(1) We do not yet fully understand how severe the greenhouse conse-   23
quences will be.

(2) Although the effects are not yet strikingly noticeable in everyday   24
life, to deal with the problem, the present generation might have to make sacrifices for the next.

(3) The problem cannot be solved except on an international scale: 25
The atmosphere is ignorant of national boundaries. South African carbon dioxide warms Taiwan, and Soviet coal-burning practices effect productivity in America. The largest coal resources in the world are found in the Soviet Union, the United States and China, in that order. What incentives are there for a nation such as China, with vast coal reserves and a commitment to rapid economic development, to hold back on the burning of fossil fuels because the result might, decades later, be a parched American sunbelt or still more ghastly starvation in sub-Saharan Africa? Would countries that might benefit from a warmer climate be as vigorous in restraining the burning of fossil fuels as nations likely to suffer greatly?

Fortunately, we have a little time. A great deal can be done in decades.   26
Some argue that government subsidies lower the price of fossil fuels, inviting waste; more efficient usage, besides its economic advantage, could greatly ameliorate the CO_2 greenhouse problem. Parts of the solution might involve alternative energy sources, where appropriate: solar power, for example, or safer nuclear fission reactors, which, whatever their other dangers, produce no greenhouse gases of importance. Conceivably, the long-awaited advent of commercial nuclear fusion power might happen before the middle of the next century.

However, any technological solution to the looming greenhouse prob-   27
lem must be worldwide. It would not be sufficient for the United States or the Soviet Union, say, to develop safe and commercially feasible fusion power plants: That technology would have to be diffused worldwide, on terms of cost and reliability that would be more attractive to developing

nations than a reliance on fossil fuel reserves or imports. A serious, very high-level look at patterns of U.S. and world energy development in light of the greenhouse problem seems overdue.

During the last few million years, human technology, spurred in part by climatic change, has made our species a force to be reckoned with on a planetary scale. We now find, to our astonishment, that we pose a danger to ourselves. The present world order is, unfortunately, not designed to deal with global-scale dangers. Nations tend to be concerned about themselves, not about the planet; they tend to have short-term rather than long-term objectives. In problems such as the increasing greenhouse effect, one nation or region might benefit while another suffers. In other global environmental issues, such as nuclear war, all nations lose. The problems are connected: Constructive international efforts to understand and resolve one will benefit the others.   28

Further study and better public understanding are needed, of course. But what is essential is a global consciousness—a view that transcends our exclusive identification with the generational and political groupings into which, by accident, we have been born. The solution to these problems requires a perspective that embraces the planet and the future. We are all in this greenhouse together.   29

■

WHAT DRUGS I TAKE IS NONE OF YOUR BUSINESS— THE CONSEQUENCES OF DRUG TESTING

Mary Lou Torpey (student)

So you have a job interview with a new company tomorrow? Well my advice is to go home, get some rest, and drink plenty of fluids, because chances are you'll have to leave more than just a good impression with your prospective employer. You may have to leave a full specimen bottle to check you out for drug use, too. Imagine having to stand in a line in your business suit with your application in one hand and a steaming cup of urine in the other, waiting to turn each of them in, wondering which one is really more important in the job selection process. Some companies and every branch of the Armed Forces require a witness present during the test so the person being tested doesn't try to switch specimens with someone who is drug or alcohol free. As one can imagine, having to be witnessed during a drug test could give a whole new meaning to the term "stage fright." The embarrassing situation of being drug tested is a real possibility, since mandatory drug testing is becoming more and more prevalent in today's workplaces.   1

Despite the embarrassment, many employers, including western Washington's largest, Boeing, believe the consequences of mandatory   2 drug testing would be beneficial. By trying to ensure safe work environments by cutting down on drug abusers who could create potential hazards for other employees, such companies believe that quality in workmanship will improve. They also believe that their employees will operate at peak performance levels to keep productivity up. However, there is a consequence of mandatory drug testing that is not being considered by the employers who have instituted it, a consequence that will be devastating for hundreds of thousands of people.

Perhaps the most potentially damaging result of mandatory drug testing lies with people who have legitimate uses for controlled substance drugs—people like me. I have narcolepsy, a serious lifelong disorder that causes crippling sleepiness without the help of controlled substance drugs, similar to the way a mobility impaired person would be crippled without crutches, a walker, or a wheelchair. In other words, I, as a narcoleptic, must have a controlled substance drug to maintain any sort of normal lifestyle at all. Without amphetamines, I could not drive a car, go to college, read, or even hold a decent conversation without falling asleep.   3

The damaging consequence of mandatory drug testing here is that if I, or other with a myriad of other chronic disorders requiring the use of controlled substance drugs, such as epilepsy, depression due to chemical imbalance, or a number of other seizure disorders, were seeking employment where a drug test is administered, we would be forced to divulge information about the illness. It should be every person's choice whether or not they will inform their employer, especially if their medications manage their illness adequately.   4

Having to inform a prospective employer about an illness would open the way for prejudice. In all honesty, why would an employer hire a "sick" person when there are so many "normal" ones on the job market? This prejudice is ironic since people like me with narcolepsy or other "silent disabilities" try so hard to compensate that they make exemplary employees. The way I think of it is like that commercial for "Scrubbing Bubbles." That's the commercial where the little bubbles go down the bathtub drain after making it sparkling clean, shouting "we work hard so you don't have to." When it comes to my job, I work hard so my employer doesn't have to think about making special exceptions for me.   5

In the case of a random test for employees already with a company, those individuals would be forced to explain why a controlled substance is coming up on their test results. When this happens to an employee who has not previously told his employer about an illness or medication he must take, that employee runs the strong chance of being terminated or prejudiced against in the promotion process. After all, what would make an employer believe an employee's explanation about a necessary drug if the employer already showed so little trust as to administer a test at all?   6

In addition, the emphasis in drug testing for the abuse of drugs such as Ritalin®and Dexedrine®is making them increasingly difficult to pur-   7 chase in pharmacies. Quotas are now being put on their production, and some states are working on banning them or making them more and more difficult to get. For example, many times I have taken a prescription to be filled into a pharmacy only to find that they had run out of their allotment and would not have any for a few days. A few days is like a lifetime for most narcoleptics without medication, some of whom can be virtually housebound without it. Imagine, in the hysteria over these drugs caused by being targeted in mandatory drug testing, what would happen if a few days turned into weeks or maybe even a month?

There is no denying the need for programs to address drug and alco-   8
hol abuse. The beneficial causes the employers are seeking are reasonable in themselves, but just won't happen through mandatory drug testing. Instead, why can't employers take a positive approach to dealing with substance abuse within the workplace? Employers could set up counseling programs and encourage people with problems to step forward and get help. Employers who show trust and respect for their employees will get trust and respect in return. A positive, caring approach would be better for everyone, considering the far-reaching negative consequences of mandatory drug testing. After all, one should never forget that disorders requiring the use of controlled substance drugs have no prejudice. They can strike anyone at anytime. Believe me, I know.

■

WHY MARRIED MOTHERS WORK

Victor Fuchs

Among single women ages 25–44 four out of five work for pay, and this   1
proportion has not changed since 1950. Divorced and separated women have also traditionally worked, and their participation rates (about 75 percent) have grown only slightly. The truly astonishing changes have taken place in the behavior of married women with children, as shown in Figure 1. . . .

Why has the participation of married mothers grown so *rapidly* and so   2
steadily? Popular discussions frequently attribute this growth to changes in attitudes that were stimulated by the feminist movement, but the time pattern portrayed in Figure 1 does not lend much support to this view. Betty Friedan's *The Feminine Mystique,* which is often credited with sparking the modern feminist movement, was published in 1963, long after the surge of married mothers into the labor force was under way. Moreover, there is no evidence of any sudden acceleration in response to this movement. Similarly, widespread public expressions of feminism *followed* rather than preceded the rise in the age of marriage and the fall in

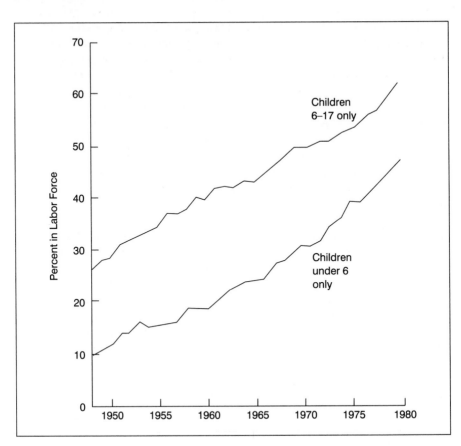

Figure 1 Labor force participation rates of married women with husband present, by presence and age of own children, 1948–1980

(Sources: Employment and Training Administration, *Employment and Training Report of the President, 1980,* table B-4; idem, *Employment and Training Report of the President, 1981,* table B-7.)

the birth rate. Divorce is the one variable whose change coincided with the burgeoning feminist movement, rising rapidly between 1965 and 1975. Thus, the feminist writings and discussion, valid as they may be in their own terms, will probably not be viewed by future historians as a basic cause of social change but primarily as a rationale and a rhetoric for changes that were already occurring for other reasons.

Government affirmative action programs are regarded by many as fos-   3
tering female employment, but the timing again suggests that too much has been claimed for this explanation. These programs, which did not gain force until well into the 1960s, cannot explain the rapid rise in participation of married mothers in the 1950s—a rise that was even more rapid for older women with grown children. The timing of changes in the occupational distribution of employed married women is also contrary to

what one would expect if the feminist movement or government affirmative action had a great deal of effect. The proportion who were in professional and technical occupations rose rapidly between 1948 and 1965, from 7.7 percent to 14.7 percent, but thereafter the rate of increase was more modest, only to 17.7 percent by 1979.

One of the most popular explanations for the two-earner family is that   4
the wife's earnings are "needed to help make ends meet." This answer is the one most frequently given by women to survey researchers, and it receives some support from analytical studies that attempt to explain why, at any particular time, some wives work and some don't. There is a strong consensus among economists that, other things held constant, the higher the husbands income, the less likely it is that the wife will work for pay.

This explanation, however, does not contribute much to an under-   5
standing of changes over time. "Need," in an absolute sense, can hardly be the reason for the rapid rise in labor force participation of married mothers in the 1950s, when the real hourly earnings of their husbands were increasing at an unprecedented pace. Nathan Keyfitz (1980) observed that when women are asked why they work outside the home, they tend to reply that they need the money. "But," he writes, "the answer cannot be correct, since in earlier decades their husbands were earning less, presumably families needed money, and yet wives were content to stay home. Needing money is a universal, a constant, and a first rule of method is that one cannot explain a variable . . . with a constant."

One frequently mentioned but inadequately evaluated explanation for   6
the surge of women into paid employment is the spread of time-saving household innovations such as clothes washers and dryers, frozen foods,and dishwashers. There is little doubt that it is easier to combine paid employment with home responsibilities now than it was fifty years ago, but it is not clear whether these time-saving innovations were the cause of the rise in female labor force participation or whether they were largely a *response* to meet a demand created by working women. Confusion about this point is most evident in comments that suggest that the rapid growth of supermarkets and fast-food outlets is a cause of women going to work. Similar time-saving organizations were tried at least sixty years ago, but with less success because the value of time was much lower then. The absence of supermarkets and fast-food eating places in low-income countries today also shows that their rapid growth in the United States is primarily a *result* of the rising value of time and the growth of women in the work force, not the reverse.

Within the economics profession the explanation that commands the   7
widest consensus is that *higher wages* have attracted more married mothers into the labor force. This explanation is more firmly grounded in economic theory than many of the others and is reasonably consistent with observed behavior, both over time and among families at a given point in time. Ever since the pioneering work of Jacob Mincer (1962),

numerous cross-section analyses—studies that examine differences among individual families or groups of families—uniformly report that the probability of a wife's working is *positively* related to her potential wage rate, holding constant spouse's education. This is the opposite of the previously noted *negative* effect of the husband's wage rate on the wife's labor force participation. . . .

In addition to higher wages, the rapid expansion of jobs in the service   8 sector has contributed to the rise in female labor force participation (Fuchs 1968). The service industries (retail trade, financial service, education, health, personal services, public administration) have traditionally offered much greater employment opportunities for women than have mining, manufacturing, construction, and other branches of the industrial sector. For instance, 73 percent of nonfarm female employment was in the service sector in 1960, whereas the comparable figure for males was only 44 percent.

There are many reasons for this large differential. First, most occupa-   9 tions in the service sector do not place a premium on physical strength. Second, hours of work are frequently more flexible in service industries and there are many more opportunities for part-time work. Other things held constant, mothers of small children are more likely to be working in those metropolitan areas where there is a large variation in the weekly hours of men (King 1978). This variation is a good indicator of the existence of part-time employment opportunities, and women are much more likely than men to seek part-time employment. Third, service sector jobs are more likely to be located in or near residential areas, thus making them more attractive to women who bear large responsibilities for child care and homemaking.

The propensity of women to seek service sector employment is par-   10 ticularly relevant because it is this sector that has provided nearly all of the additional job opportunities in the U.S. economy since the end of World War II. Between 1947 and 1980 U.S. employment expanded by 39 million; the service sector provided 33 million of these additional jobs. To be sure, some of the growth of service employment is the *result* of the increase in female labor force participation rather than the cause (Fuchs 1981a). Families with working mothers are more likely to eat out, to send their children to nursery school, and to purchase a wide range of personal and professional services. This feedback effect, however, accounts for only a part of the growth of service employment. The major explanation is that rapid increases in output per worker in agriculture and industry cut the demand for labor in those sectors and shifted employment to services. A secondary reason is that consumer demand shifted slightly toward services in response to the growth of real income.

I conclude that the growth of real wages and the expansion of the ser-   11 vice sector have been the most important reasons for the growth of female labor force participation. This participation, in turn, has had important effects on marriage, fertility, and divorce, but there is also some feedback from fertility and divorce to labor force participation. Better control of fertility makes a career in the labor market more promising to women, not only because of a reduction in the *number* of children but also because women now have better control over the *timing* of births. The increase in the *probability* of divorce contributes to the rise in female labor force participation because women recognize that complete commitment to home and husband can leave them in a perilous economic position if the marriage should dissolve. Alimony and child support payments are often inadequate, and are not paid at all in a large proportion of cases. An old songs says that "diamonds are a girl's best friend," but today the ability to earn a good wage is likely to prove a more reliable asset.

STUDENTS WHO PUSH BURGERS

Walter S. Minot

A college freshman squirms anxiously on a chair in my office, his eyes   1
avoiding mine, those of his English professor, as he explains that he hasn't finished his paper, which was due two days ago. "I just haven't had the time," he says.

"Are you carrying a heavy course load?"   2
"Fifteen hours," he says—a normal load.   3
"Are you working a lot?"   4
"No, sir, not much. About 30 hours a week."   5
"That's a lot. Do you have to work that much?"   6
"Yeah, I have to pay for my car."   7
"Do you really need a car?"   8
"Yeah, I need it to get to work."   9

This student isn't unusual. Indeed, he probably typifies today's college   10
and high school students. Yet in all the lengthy analyses of what's wrong with American education, I have not heard employment by students being blamed.

I have heard drugs blamed and television—that universal scapegoat. I   11
have heard elaborate theories about the decline of the family, of religion, and of authority, as well as other sociological theories. But nobody blames student employment. The world seems to have accepted the part-time job as a normal feature of adolescence. A parochial school in my town even had a day to honor students who held regular jobs, and parents often endorse this employment by claiming that it teaches kids the value of the dollar.

But such employment is a major cause of educational decline. To   12
argue my case, I will rely on memories of my own high school days and
contrast them with what I see today. Though I do have some statistical
evidence, my argument depends on what anyone over 40 can test
through memory and direct observation.

When I was in high school in the 1950s, students seldom held jobs.   13
Some of us baby-sat, shoveled snow, mowed lawns, and delivered
papers, and some of us got jobs in department stores around Christmas.
But most of us had no regular source of income other than the generosity of our parents.

The only kids who worked regularly were poor. They worked to help   14
their families. If I remember correctly, only about five people in my class
of 170 held jobs. That was in a working-class town in New England. As
for the rest of us, our parents believed that going to school and helping
around the house were our work.

In contrast, in 1986 my daughter was one of the few students among   15
juniors and seniors who didn't work. According to Bureau of Labor statistics, more than 40 percent of high school students were working in
1980, but sociologist Ellen Greenberger and Laurence Steinberg in
"When Teenagers Work" came up with estimates of more than 70 percent working in 1986, though I suspect that the figure may be even
higher now.

My daughter, however, did not work; her parents wouldn't let her. Inter-   16
estingly, some of the students in her class implied that she had an unfair
advantage over them in the classroom. They were probably right, for
while she was home studying they were pushing burgers, waiting on
tables, or selling dresses 20 hours a week. Working students have little
time for homework.

I attended a public high school, while she attended a Roman Catholic   17
preparatory school whose students were mainly middle class. By the
standards of my day, her classmates did not "have to" work. Yet many of
them were working 20 to 30 hours a week. Why?

They worked so that they could spend $60 to $100 a week on   18
designer jeans, rock concerts, stereo and video systems, and, of course,
cars. They were living lives of luxury, buying items on which their parents
refused to throw hard-earned money away. Though the parent would not
buy such tripe for their kids, the parents somehow convinced themselves
that the kids were learning the value of money. Yet, according to Ms.
Greenberger and Mr. Steinberg, only about a quarter of those students
saved money for college or other long-term goals.

How students spend their money is their business, not mine. But as a   19
teacher, I have witnessed the effects of employment. I know that students
who work all evening aren't ready for studying when they get home from
work. Moreover, because they work so hard and have ready cash, they
feel that they deserve to have fun—instead of spending all their free time
studying.

Thus, by the time they get to college, most students look upon stud- 20
ies as a spare-time activity. A survey at Pennsylvania State University
showed that most freshmen believed they could maintain a B average by
studying about 20 hours a week. (I can remember when college guide-
books advised two to three hours of studying for every hour in class—30
to 45 hours a week.)

Clearly individual students will pay the price for lack of adequate time 21
studying, but the problem goes beyond the individual. It extends to
schools and colleges that are finding it difficult to demand quantity or
quality of work from students.

Perhaps the reason American education has declined so markedly is 22
because America has raised a generation of part-time students. And perhaps our economy will continue to decline as full-time students from
Japan and Europe continue to out-perform our part-time students.

12

Resemblance Arguments: X Is/Is Not Like Y

☐

CASE 1

In May 1987, a controversy arose between Israeli and West German historians over the reinterpretation of the Holocaust, the Nazi attempt to destroy
the Jews. According to one West German historian, the Nazi annihilation of
the Jews was comparable to Stalin's massacre of the Russian peasants and
Pol Pot's murder of his opponents in Cambodia. The effect of this comparison, in the eyes of many Israeli historians, was to diminish the horror of the
Holocaust by denying its uniqueness. Israeli historian Shaul Friedlander
responded that while the scale and criminality of the murders might be
compared, "there is no other example to my knowledge of a government
deciding that an entire race of millions of people spread all over a continent
is to be brought together by all means at the disposal of the state and eliminated."*

CASE 2

To further her argument against the notion that motherhood is a predes-
tined role for women, a psychiatrist used the following analogy: "Women
don't need to be mothers any more than they need spaghetti. But if you're
in a world where everyone is eating spaghetti, thinking they need it and
want it, you will think so too."†

---

* From Karen Winkler, "German Scholars Sharply Divided over Place of
Holocaust in History," *Chronicle of Higher Education,* May 27, 1987, pp. 4–5.
† From Betty Rollin, "Motherhood: Who Needs It?"

CASE 3

Lawyer Charles Rembar attacked the American Civil Liberties Union (ACLU) for its opposition to the mandatory reporting of AIDS cases. Rembar claimed that the ACLU position didn't take into account the seriousness of the AIDS problem. According to Rembar, the ACLU "clings to once useful concepts that are inappropriate to current problems. Like the French military, which prepared for World War II by building the Maginot Line, which was nicely adapted to the trench warfare of World War I, the ACLU sometimes hauls up legal arguments effective in old libertarian battles but irrelevant to those at hand. . . ."*

CASE 4

When the voting age was reduced from twenty-one to eighteen, many people argued for the lower voting age by saying, "If you are old enough to fight for your country in a war, you are old enough to vote." But author Richard Weaver claimed that this analogy was true "only if you believe that fighting and voting are the same kind of thing which I, for one, do not. Fighting requires strength, muscular coordination and, in a modern army, instant and automatic response to orders. Voting requires knowledge of men, history, reasoning power; it is essentially a deliberative activity. Army mules and police dogs are used to fight; nobody is interested in giving them the right to vote. This argument rests on a false analogy."†

THE DIFFERENCE BETWEEN RESEMBLANCE ARGUMENTS AND DEFINITION ARGUMENTS

In some cases it may seem that a resemblance argument (X is like Y) is not very different from a definitional argument (X is Y). For example, if you were to say that the Sandinista government of Nicaragua was "like" the Somoza regime that it replaced, you might really be making a definitional argument, claiming that both regimes belong to the same class—say, the class "totalitarian governments" or the class "benevolent dictatorships." Their similarities would be restricted to the traits of whatever class they are being put into. In effect, the "like" statement is a definitional claim in which both X and Y are said to belong to class Z.

But if you were to draw an analogy between the Sandinista regime or the Somoza regime and a third thing different in kind from recent Nicaraguan politics—say, to a skin disease or a sporting event—or if you were to argue that some other situation remote in time—say, American Revolutionary politics or nineteenth-century Balkan poli-

---

*   From the *New York Times*, May 15, 1987.
†   From Richard M. Weaver, "A Responsible Rhetoric," *The Intercollegiate Review,* Winter 1976–1977, pp. 86–87.

tics—should serve as a precedent for Nicaragua, the argument moves over into the realm of resemblance. In either case, there are no preexisting definitional criteria to which the event can be matched. There certainly isn't a "Dictionary of Similar Things" we can use to certify the rightness of our comparison. We have to discover and develop the grounds on which the two terms of our comparison are similar.

When we're developing analogies as opposed to establishing definitions, we must be conscious at all times that the two things being compared are essentially different, not members of the same class. In the end we may well be left with several important points of comparison that don't lead to a neat category or concept that somehow "sums" up all the points of comparison and ties them all together. Analogies, in short, reveal different sides of events or things without forcing us to put the things being compared into the same category.

And although the two (or more) things being compared in a relationship of precedence are going to be closer in identity than the terms of an analogy, a precedent doesn't define a term as strictly as does a definition. In a precedent, we are claiming a relationship of resemblance between two actual events. We're saying that this case and that case have sufficient similarities to warrant our drawing similar conclusions from them; we are not saying that the two cases share an identity. The points of comparison between the two may be numerous, but it would be impossible to establish essential conditions that if met would ensure "class membership."

Obviously, an argument of resemblance has to be considerably more tentative than an argument of definition. Suppose, for example, that you wanted to write an argument favoring a balanced federal budget. In one section of your argument you might develop the following claim of resemblance: "Just as a family will go bankrupt if it continually spends more than it makes, so the federal government will go bankrupt if its expenses exceed its revenues." This claim depends on the resemblance between the fiscal problems of the federal government and the fiscal problems of a private family. For many audiences, this comparison might be persuasive: It uses an area of experience familiar to almost everyone (the problem of balancing the family budget) to help make sense of a more complex area of experience (the problem of balancing the federal budget). At its root is the warrant that what works for the family will work for the Fed.

Such an argument can be powerful, but dangerous, if it ignores important differences ("disanalogies") between the terms of comparison. One can think, for instance, of many differences between the economics of a family and that of the federal government. For example, unlike a private family, the federal government prints its own money and does most of its borrowing from its own members. Perhaps these differences negate the claim that family debt and federal debt are similar in their effects. It is thus essential that an argument based on resemblance acknowledge important disanalogies.

One way of illustrating the necessarily tentative nature of a resemblance claim is to look at it via Toulmin's schema. If we take the above example for our illustration, we might get something like this:

ENTHYMEME:	If the Fed doesn't balance its budget, it will go bankrupt because families that don't balance their budgets go bankrupt.
CLAIM:	If the Fed doesn't balance its debt, it will go bankrupt.
STATED REASON:	because families that don't balance their budgets go bankrupt
GROUNDS:	evidence showing that indeed families overspending their budget do go bankrupt
WARRANT:	The economic laws that apply to families apply also to governments.
BACKING:	evidence that when governments and families behave in economically similar ways, they suffer similar consequences
CONDITIONS OF REBUTTAL:	all cases in which governments and families behaved in similar ways and did not suffer similar consequences; all the ways that families and governments differ
QUALIFIER:	The claim is supported by the analogy only to the extent that family and government economics resemble each other.

As you look at this schema, you can see just how troublesome it would be to support your warrant that economic laws apply equally to families and governments. As noted above, resemblance arguments require you to compare two or more actual cases as opposed to simply applying a concept to an actual case. Whereas the definition of a concept is limited by certain conventions of usage, the comparison between family and government economics is wide open. You have, in sum, undertaken an extraordinary burden of proof since, under the conditions of rebuttal, the possible exceptions to your warrant are in danger of multiplying like exemptions in a tax reform bill (so to speak).

■ ASSIGNMENT OPTIONS FOR CHAPTER 12

OPTION 1:   AN ANALOGY MICROTHEME   Because few arguments are devoted entirely to a resemblance claim and because many arguments from resemblance are used in service of other claims, this assignment asks you simply to write a piece of an argument. Imagine that you are writing a longer argument for or against an X of your choice. As part of your argument you want to influence your reader's emotional or intellectual understanding of X, in either a positive or a negative direction, by comparing it to a more familiar Y. Write the portion of your argument that develops the extended analogy. A good model for this assignment is the argument on pages 275–76. The writer opposes a proficiency exam in writing by comparing it to a proficiency exam in physical fitness. The For Class Discussion exercise on pages 276–77 will give you ideas for topics.

OPTION 2:   A PRECEDENCE MICROTHEME   Imagine that you are writing a proposal argument of the kind "We should/should not do X" and that one of your reasons will develop a precedence argument as follows: "We should/should not do X because doing X will lead to the same good/bad consequences that we experienced when we did Y." Write the portion of your argument that develops this precedence claim.

OPTION 3:   AN ANALYSIS OF A RESEMBLANCE ARGUMENT   Write an analysis of Susan Brownmiller's argument that pornography hurts women (pp. 284–87), which uses an analogy between pornography and Nazi anti-Semitic propaganda, or of some other resemblance argument provided by your instructor.

FIRST TYPE OF RESEMBLANCE ARGUMENT: ARGUMENTS BY ANALOGY

In this section we deal with the first class of resemblance arguments, argument by analogy. Although it's rare to find an entire argument that rests on an analogy, analogies are used extensively in the service of all the other claim types. The ubiquity of analogies in argument is undoubtedly a function of their power to make new relationships clear to reader and writer alike.

The use of analogies can constitute the most imaginative form of argumentation. Consider the case of an outraged prep school student upset about the quality of the high teas at Whitebread-on-Perrier Prep, where he matriculates. Suppose he were to compare his lot to that of a political prisoner in a Russian prison. His resemblance claim would undoubtedly get some attention, particularly from parents paying huge sums of money for their offspring to attend the place.

But getting attention is not enough. In fact, if your argument is particularly weak, getting attention may not be at all desirable. The question now facing our enraged student, the question that faces any author of a resemblance claim, is "How far can I go with this thing?" Analogies can be short and suggestive, used as tools for getting an audience's attention and sympathy, or they can be developed at length and used as tools for guiding their understanding.

Using Undeveloped Analogies

If you put yourself in the shoes of our hypothetical Whitebread-on-Perrier inmate, what would you choose to do? Develop the analogy or let it lie? Our advice would be to get past it as quickly as possible before the disanalogies come back to haunt you. The analogy may serve briefly to suggest certain aspects of the case that you want emphasized—lack of voice in the institution, poor quality of food—but if one goes much past those points of comparison, your suffering is going to pale in comparison to that of the political prisoner. Here, as in many analogies, the differences between the two situations aren't just qualitative but quantitative. And quantitative differences, if extreme, can be fatal to an analogy. In this regard, keep in mind Karl Marx's maxim that "differences in degree, if large enough, become differences in kind."

Using undeveloped analogies to convey feelings and points of view is common in many arguments. The effect is to bring to your argument about topic X (say the importance of discipline to freedom) the full weight, emotion, and understanding your audience already has about Y (the importance of staying on the tracks to the progress of a train). Thus, one writer, arguing against the complexities of recent tax legislation, showed his disgust by drawing an analogy between tax laws and rotting plants or festering wounds.

> It does not take a deep or broadly informed analysis to sense the reek of economic decay and social fester that such irresponsible legislation cultivates.*

Later this writer went on to compare recent tax legislation to an infection by a new virus. Through his use of the analogy, the writer hoped to transfer to the new tax law the audience's already existing revulsion to disease-producing virus.

Using Extended Analogies

Instead of using undeveloped analogies, you may choose to extend your comparison, using your readers' greater understanding of Y to illuminate X. And if your audience is already favorably or unfavorably disposed to Y, then the analogy helps create similar feelings for X. As an example of a claim based on an extended analogy, consider the following excerpt from a professor's argument opposing a proposal to require a writing-proficiency exam for graduation. In the following portion of his argument, the professor compares development of writing skills to the development of physical fitness.

> A writing proficiency exam gives the wrong symbolic messages about writing. It suggests that writing is simply a skill, rather than an active way of thinking and learning. It suggests that once a student demonstrates proficiency then he or she doesn't need to do any more writing.
>
> Imagine two universities concerned with the physical fitness of their students. One university requires a junior-level physical fitness exam in which students must run a mile in less than 10 minutes, a fitness level it considers minimally

---

* From C. Thomas Higgins, *Seattle Times*, September 21, 1986.

competent. Students at this university see the physical fitness exam as a one-time hurdle. As many as 70 percent of them can pass the exam with no practice; another 10–20 percent need a few months' training; and a few hopeless couch potatoes must go through exhaustive remediation. After passing the exam, any student can settle back into a routine of TV and potato chips having been certified as "physically fit."

The second university, however, believing in true physical fitness for its students, is not interested in minimal competency. Consequently, it creates programs in which its students exercise 30 minutes every day for the entire four years of the undergraduate curriculum. There is little doubt which university will have the most physically fit students. At the second university, fitness becomes a way of life with everyone developing his or her full potential.

If you choose to write an extended analogy such as this, you will focus on the points of comparison that serve your purposes. The writer's purpose in the above case is to support the achievement of mastery rather than minimalist standards as the goal of the university's writing program. Whatever other disanalogous elements are involved (for example, writing requires the use of intellect, which may or may not be strengthened by repetition), the comparison reveals vividly that a commitment to mastery involves more than a minimalist test. The analogy serves primarily to underscore this one crucial point. In reviewing the different groups of students as they "prepare" for the fitness exam, the author makes clear just how irrelevant such an exam is to the whole question of mastery. Typically, then, in developing your analogy you are not developing all possible points of comparison so much as you are bringing out those similarities consistent with the point you are trying to make.

☐ FOR CLASS DISCUSSION

The following is a two-part exercise to help you clarify for yourself how analogies function in the context of arguments. Part 1 is to be done outside of class; part 2 is to be done in class. This exercise is an excellent "Starting Point" task for the *Option 1* writing assignment for this chapter.

PART 1   Think of an analogy that accurately expresses your feeling toward each of the following topics. Then write your analogy in the following one-sentence format:

X is like Y: A, B, C . . . (where X is the main topic being discussed; Y is the analogy; and A, B, and C are the points of comparison).

EXAMPLES

Cramming for an exam to get better grades is like pumping iron for ten hours straight to prepare for a weight-lifting contest: exhausting and counterproductive.

A right-to-lifer bombing an abortion clinic is like a vegetarian bombing a cattle barn: futile and contradictory.

a. Spanking a child to teach obedience is like . . .

b. Building low-cost housing for poor people is like . . .

c. The use of steroids by college athletes is like . . .

d. Mandatory AIDS testing for all U.S. residents is like . . .

e. A legislative proposal to eliminate all federally subsidized student loans is like . . .

f. The effect of American fast food on our health is like . . .

g. The personal gain realized by people who have committed questionable or even illegal acts and then made money by selling book and movie rights is like . . .

In each case, begin by asking yourself how you feel about the subject. If you have negative feelings about a topic, then begin by calling up negative pictures that express those feelings (or if you have positive feelings, call up positive comparisons). As they emerge, test each one to see if it will work as an analogy. An effective analogy will convey both the feeling you have toward your topic and your understanding of the topic. For instance, the writer in the "cramming for an exam" example obviously believes that pumping iron for ten hours before a weight-lifting match is stupid. This feeling of stupidity is then transferred to the original topic—cramming for an exam. But the analogy also clarifies understanding. The writer imagines the mind as a muscle (which gets exhausted after too much exercise and which is better developed through some exercise every day rather than a lot all at once) rather than as a large container (into which lots of stuff can be "crammed").

PART 2 Now, bring your analogies to class and compare them to those of your classmates. Select the best analogies for each of the topics and be ready to say why you think they are good. If you choose, you can then use your analogy as the basis for an extended analogy for this chapter's writing assignment.

SECOND TYPE OF RESEMBLANCE ARGUMENT: ARGUMENTS BY PRECEDENT

Precedent arguments are like analogy arguments in that they make comparisons between an X and a Y. In precedent arguments, however, the Y term is always a past event, usually an event where some sort of decision was reached, often a moral, legal, or political decision. An argument by precedent tries to show that a similar decision should or should not be reached for the present issue X because the situation of X is or is not like the situation of Y.

A good example of a precedent argument is the following excerpt from a speech by President Lyndon Johnson in the early years of the Vietnam War:

Nor would surrender in Vietnam bring peace because we learned from Hitler at Munich that success only feeds the appetite of aggression. The battle would be renewed in one country and then another country, bringing with it perhaps even larger and crueler conflict, as we have learned from the lessons of history.*

Here the audience knows what happened at Munich: France and Britain tried to appease Hitler by yielding to his demand for a large part of Czechoslovakia, but Hitler's armies continued their aggression anyway, using Czechoslovakia as a staging area to invade Poland. By arguing that surrender in Vietnam would lead to the same consequences, Johnson brings to his argument about Vietnam the whole weight of his audience's unhappy knowledge of World War II. Administration white papers developed Johnson's precedent argument by pointing toward the similarity of Hitler's promises with those of the Viet Cong: You give us this and we will ask for no more. But Hitler didn't keep his promise. Why should the Viet Cong?

As with analogies, we often turn to precedents in the early stages of planning an argument. Whereas analogies stimulate our thinking about alternative ways of describing a situation or solving a problem, precedents offer us advice from the past. Let's say, for example, that you are arguing for the mandatory use of seatbelts in cars. Here we might turn to the precedent of mandatory motorcycle helmet law in our own state or a mandatory seatbelt law in a neighboring state. We would want to review the whole story of how the seatbelt laws were enacted, how opposition arguments were met, what consequences followed their passage, and so forth, to help us plan our own argument. Once we have explored possible arguments using the precedents as guides, we can also cite those precedents in our arguments, using them as evidence as well as structural models.

In a relatively straightforward legal example such as the seatbelt law example, a precedent argument is particularly persuasive. We can see this more clearly if we apply the Toulmin schema to the argument.

ENTHYMEME:	The state should enact a seatbelt law because seatbelt laws have had good consequences in other states.
CLAIM:	The state should enact a seatbelt law.
STATED REASON:	because seatbelt laws have had good consequences in other states
GROUNDS:	evidence that seatbelt laws in other states have had good consequences (saved lives, relatively high compliance, few enforcement problems)
WARRANT:	Seatbelt laws will be at least as effective in this state as they have been in the other states that have enacted them.

---

* From *Public Papers of the Presidents of the United States,* Vol. 2: *Lyndon B. Johnson,* 1965, p. 794.

BACKING:	evidence that there are no significant differences between this state and other states that might diminish the effectiveness of seatbelt laws in this state
CONDITIONS OF REBUTTAL:	acknowledged differences between states that might well impair the effectiveness of a seatbelt law in this state
QUALIFIERS:	statements to the effect than even if the seatbelt law is less effective here than it has been in other states it will still improve conditions.

As you can see, the key to a precedent argument is showing that the similarities between W and Y outweigh the dissimilarities. In the seatbelt example, it is difficult to imagine how states would differ so that seatbelt laws would be successful in one state but not in another. But if one state is more urban than another (perhaps city drivers are less apt to wear seatbelts because they have to make so many short trips), or if one state regularly elects a Democratic government and the other elects a Republican government (Republicans are generally less tolerant of governmental regulations than Democrats), or if one state has much higher gasoline taxes than another (perhaps people who can afford to drive cars when gasoline is high-priced have a different attitude toward seatbelts than poorer people), then there might be predictable differences in the way citizens would react to a seatbelt law.

☐ For Class Discussion

1. Consider the following claims of precedent and evaluate just how effective you think each precedent might be in establishing the claim:
   a. Don't vote for Governor Frick for president because governors have not proven to be effective presidents.
   b. Gays should be allowed to serve openly in the U.S. military because they are allowed to serve openly in most other Western countries.
   c. The United States should avoid military involvement in the former Yugoslavia because it will end up in another mess like Vietnam.
2. Recently, voters in the state of Montana considered an initiative to abolish property taxes. Supporters of the initiative responded to predictions that it would have disastrous consequences for public service in the state by saying, "Similar dire predictions were made in Massachusetts and California when they passed initiatives to lower property taxes and none of these predictions came to pass, so you can ignore these nay-sayers."

   You have been hired by a lobbying group who opposes the initiative. Your task is to do the background research that your group needs in order to refute the above precedent argument. Working in small groups, make a list of research questions you would want to ask.

WRITING YOUR RESEMBLANCE ARGUMENT

The class discussion exercises in this chapter should help you find a starting point for your analogy or precedent and explore its usefulness. The optional microtheme assignments for this chapter will not require as extensive a process as that required for a full-scale argument. After you have written a rough draft of your microtheme, however, we recommend that you examine your argument using Toulmin's schema. Once again, test your argument by looking carefully at the conditions for rebuttal.

CONDITIONS FOR REBUTTAL: TESTING A RESEMBLANCE ARGUMENT

Once you've written a draft of your resemblance argument, you need to test that argument by attempting to refute it. What follows are some typical questions audiences will raise about arguments of resemblance.

Will My Audience Say I Am Trying to Prove Too Much with My Analogy or Precedent?

The most common mistake people make with resemblance arguments is to ask them to prove more than they're capable of proving. Too often, an analogy is treated as if it were a syllogism or algebraic ratio wherein necessary truths are deduced (*a* is to *b* as *c* is to *d*) rather than as a useful, but basically playful, figure that suggests uncertain but significant insight. The best way to guard against this charge is to qualify your argument and to find other means of persuasion to supplement an analogy or precedent argument.

For a good example of an analogy that tries to do too much, consider former President Reagan's attempt to prevent the United States from imposing economic sanctions on South Africa. Reagan wanted to argue that harming South Africa's economy would do as much damage to blacks as to whites. In making this argument, he compared South Africa to a zebra and concluded that one couldn't hurt the white portions of the zebra without also hurting the black.

Now, the zebra analogy might work quite well to point up the interrelatedness of whites and blacks in South Africa. But it has no force whatsoever in supporting Reagan's assertion that economic sanctions would hurt blacks as well as whites. To refute this analogy, one need only point out the disanalogies between the zebra stripes and racial groups. (There are, for example, no differences in income, education, and employment between black and white stripes on a zebra.)

Will My Audience Point out Disanalogies in My Resemblance Argument?

Although it is easy to show that a country is not like a zebra, finding disanalogies is sometimes quite tricky. Often displaying the argument in Toulmin terms will help. Here is the Toulmin schema for former President Johnson's "Munich analogy" for supporting the war in Vietnam:

ENTHYMEME:	The United States should not withdraw its troops from Vietnam because doing so will have the same disastrous consequences as did giving in to Hitler prior to World War II.
CLAIM:	The United States should not withdraw its troops from Vietnam.
STATED REASON:	because doing so will have the same disastrous consequences as did giving in to Hitler before World War II
GROUNDS:	evidence that withdrawal of military support backfired in Europe in 1939
WARRANT:	The situation in Europe in 1939 closely parallels the situation in Southeast Asia in 1965.
BACKING:	evidence of similarities (for example, in political philosophy, goals, and military strength of the enemy; the nature of the conflict between the disputants; and the American commitment to its allies) between the two situations
CONDITIONS OF REBUTTAL:	acknowledged differences between the two situations that might make the outcome of the present situation different from the outcome of the first situation

Laid out like this, some of the problems with the analogy are quickly evident. One has to make a considerable leap to go from undeniably true, historically verifiable grounds to a highly problematic claim. This means that the warrant will have to be particularly strong to license the movement. And although there are undeniable similarities between the two events (as there will be between any two sufficiently complex events), the differences are overwhelming. Thus, during the Vietnam era, critic Howard Zinn attacked the warrant of Johnson's analogy by claiming three crucial differences between Europe in 1938 and Vietnam in 1967.

First, Zinn argued, the Czechs were being attacked from without by an external aggressor (Germany), whereas Vietnam was being attacked from within by rebels as part of a civil war; second, Czechoslovakia was a prosperous, effective democracy, whereas the official Vietnam government was corrupt and unpopular; finally, Hitler wanted Czechoslovakia as a base for attacking Poland, whereas the Viet Cong and North Vietnamese aimed at reunification of their country as an end in itself.*

The Munich example shows again how arguments of resemblance depend on emphasizing the similarities between X and Y and playing down the dissimilarities. One could try to refute the counterargument made by Zinn by arguing first that the Saigon government was more stable than Zinn thinks and second that the Viet Cong and North Vietnamese were driven by goals larger than reunification of Vietnam, namely, communist domination of Asia. Such an argument would once again highlight the similarities between Vietnam and prewar Europe.

Will My Audience Propose a Counteranalogy

A final way of testing a resemblance claim is to propose an alternative analogy or precedent that counters the original claim. Suppose you wanted to argue for the teaching of creationism along with evolution in the schools and your opponent said that "teaching creationism along with evolution is like teaching the stork theory of where babies come from along with the biological theory." After showing the disanalogies between creationism and the stork theory of reproduction, you could counter with your own analogy: "No, teaching creationism along with evolution is like bilingual education, where you respect the cultural heritage of all peoples." To the extent that your audience values pluralism and the preservation of different beliefs, your analogy may well provide them with a new perspective on the topic, a perspective that allows them to entertain an otherwise alien notion.

□ For Class Discussion

Examine the following resemblance claims and then attempt to refute them by pointing out disanalogies between the phenomena being compared.

1. In the following example, the author is arguing that it is not unconstitutional to require drug testing of federal employees. Within the argument the author draws an analogy between testing for drugs and checking for weapons or bombs at an airport. Using the techniques suggested in this chapter, test the soundness of the argument.

> The Constitution does not prohibit all searches and seizures. It makes the people secure in their persons only from "unreasonable" searches and seizures, and there is nothing unreasonable in Reagan's executive order.
> ... Those who challenge this sensible program [drug testing by urinalysis] ought to get straight on this business of "rights." Like any other employer, the

---

* Based on the summary of Zinn's argument in J. Michael Sproule, *Argument: Language and Its Influence* (New York: McGraw-Hill, 1980), pp. 149–150.

government has a right—within certain well-understood limits—to fix the terms and conditions of employment. The individual's right, if he finds these conditions intolerable, is to seek employment elsewhere. A parallel situation may be observed at every airport in the land. Individuals may have a right to fly, but they have no right to fly without having their persons and baggage inspected for weapons. By the same token, the federal worker who refuses to provide a urine specimen under the president's order can clean out his desk and apply to General Motors or General Electric or Kodak—only to discover that private industry is equally interested in a drug-free work place.*

2. In the following passage, former NAACP administrator Jack Greenberg defends affirmative action on the basis of analogy to other cases in the free market in which certain groups are given preferences not related to merit.

The moral legitimacy of affirmative action and quotas favoring racial minorities must be assessed in a social and historical context, in the light of the many conflicting values that our society holds. . . . [There are many examples of instances in which criteria other than merit result in the selection of persons] other than those best qualified.

A tenured professor will hold his position in spite of competition from younger, better, more vigorous scholars. Tenure is thought, however, to serve the important societal interest in academic freedom by enabling teachers to take controversial positions without fear and by shielding them against petty politics.

Seniority rights advance individual security, worker satisfaction and job loyalty by promoting older workers although younger persons may be objectively more qualified, while, paradoxically, compulsory retirement favors younger persons over older, experienced, and perhaps more competent workers. . . .

[Similarly, preference is given to veterans or union members even though nonveterans or non-union members might be more highly qualified. Both examples serve larger national interests.]

Even the most prestigious schools consider more than marks as criteria for admission—to obtain a geographically and otherwise diverse student body and thereby enhance the educational experience of all. . . .[1]

Analyze Greenberg's argument. Is he right that affirmative action to hire more minorities can be justified by comparison to other instances when criteria other than merit affect hiring decisions: tenure, seniority, union membership, veteran status, geographic diversity?

3. Analyze the strengths and weaknesses of various kinds of resemblance arguments in the following excerpt from Susan Brownmiller's *Against Our Will: Men, Women and Rape.*

---

*   From "A Conservative View" by James J. Kilpatrick. ©Universal Press Syndicate. Reprinted with permission. All rights reserved.
[1]   "Affirmative Action, Quotas, and Merit." *New York Times*, February 7, 1976.

FROM *AGAINST OUR WILL: MEN, WOMEN AND RAPE*

Susan Brownmiller

Pornography has been so thickly glossed over with the patina of chic   1
these days in the name of verbal freedom and sophistication that important distinctions between freedom of political expression (a democratic
necessity), honest sex education for children (a societal good) and ugly
smut (the deliberate devaluation of the role of women through obscene,
distorted depictions) have been hopelessly confused. Part of the problem
is that those who traditionally have been the most vigorous opponents of
porn are often those same people who shudder at the explicit mention of
any sexual subject. Under their watchful, vigilante eyes, frank and free
dissemination of educational materials relating to abortion, contraception, the act of birth, the female biology in general is also dangerous,
subversive and dirty. (I am not unmindful that frank and free discussion
of rape, "the unspeakable crime," might well give these righteous vigi-
lantes further cause to shudder.) Because the battle lines were falsely
drawn a long time ago, before there was a vocal women's movement, the
antipornography forces appear to be, for the most part, religious, Southern, conservative and right-wing, while the pro-porn forces are identified
as Eastern, atheistic and liberal.

But a woman's perspective demands a totally new alignment, or at   2
least a fresh appraisal. The majority report of the President's Commission
on Obscenity and Pornography (1970), a report that argued strongly for
the removal of all legal restrictions on pornography, soft and hard, made
plain that 90 percent of all pornographic material is geared to the male
heterosexual market (the other 10 percent is geared to the male homosexual taste), that buyers of porn are "predominantly white, middle-class,
middle-aged married males" and that the graphic depictions, the meat
and potatoes of porn, are of the naked female body and of the multiplicity of acts done to that body.

Discussing the content of stag films, "a familiar and firmly established   3
part of the American scene," the commission report dutifully, if foggily,
explained, "Because pornography historically has been thought to be primarily a masculine interest, the emphasis in stag films seems to represent the preferences of the middle-class American male. Thus male
homosexuality and bestiality are relatively rare, while lesbianism is rather
common."

The commissioners in this instance had merely verified what purvey-   4
ors of porn have always known: hard-core pornography is not a celebration of sexual freedom; it is a cynical exploitation of female sexual activity
through the device of making all such activity, and consequently all
females, "dirty." Heterosexual male consumers of pornography are

frankly turned on by watching lesbians in action (although never in the final scenes, but always as a curtain raiser); they are turned off with a sudden swiftness of a water faucet by watching naked men act upon each other. One study quoted in the commission report came to the unastounding conclusion that "seeing a stag film in the presence of male peers bolsters masculine esteem." Indeed. The men in groups who watch the films, it is important to note, are *not* naked.

When male response to pornography is compared to female   5
response, a pronounced difference in attitude emerges. According to the commission, "Males report being more highly aroused by depictions of nude females, and show more interest in depictions of nude females than [do] females." Quoting the figures of Alfred Kinsey, the commission noted that a majority of males (77 percent) were "aroused" by visual depictions of explicit sex while a majority of females (68 percent) were not aroused. Further, "females more often than males reported 'disgust' and 'offense.' "

From whence comes this female disgust and offense? Are females   6
sexually backward or more conservative by nature? The gut distaste that a majority of women feel when we look at pornography, a distaste that, incredibly, it is no longer fashionable to admit, comes, I think, from the gut knowledge that we and our bodies are being stripped, exposed and contorted for the purpose of ridicule to bolster that "masculine esteem" which gets its kick and sense of power from viewing females as anony- mous, panting playthings, adult toys, dehumanized objects to be used, abused, broken and discarded.

This, of course, is also the philosophy of rape. It is no accident (for   7
what else could be its purpose?) that females in the pornographic genre are depicted in two cleanly delineated roles: as virgins who are caught and "banged" or as nymphomaniacs who are never sated. The most popular and prevalent pornographic fantasy combines the two: an inno- cent, untutored female is raped and "subjected to unnatural practices" that turn her into a raving, slobbering nymphomaniac, a dependent sex- ual slave who can never get enough of the big, male cock.

There can be no "equality" in porn, no female equivalent, no turning   8
of the tables in the name of bawdy fun. Pornography, like rape, is a male invention, designed to dehumanize women, to reduce the female to an object of sexual access, not to free sensuality from moralistic or parental inhibition. The staple of porn will always be the naked female body, breasts and genitals exposed, because as man devised it, her naked body is the female's "shame," her private parts the private property of man, while his are the ancient, holy, universal, patriarchal instrument of his power, his rule by force over *her.*

Pornography is the undiluted essence of anti-female propaganda. Yet   9
the very same liberals who were so quick to understand the method and purpose behind the mighty propaganda machine of Hitler's Third Reich, the consciously spewed-out anti-Semitic caricatures and obscenities that

gave an ideological base to the Holocaust and the Final Solution, the very same liberals who, enlightened by blacks, searched their own conscience and came to understand that their tolerance of "nigger" jokes and portrayals of shuffling, rolling-eyed servants in movies perpetuated the degrading myths of black inferiority and gave an ideological base to the continuation of black oppression—these very same liberals now fervidly maintain that the hatred and contempt for women that find expression in four-letter words used as expletives and in what are quaintly called "adult" or "erotic" books and movies are a valid extension of freedom of speech that must be preserved as a Constitutional right.

To defend the right of a lone, crazed American Nazi to grind out pro- 10
paganda calling for the extermination of all Jews, as the ACLU has done in the name of free speech, is, after all, a self-righteous and not particularly courageous stand, for American Jewry is not currently threatened by storm troopers, concentration camps and imminent extermination, but I wonder if the ACLU's position might change if, come tomorrow morning, the bookstores and movie theaters lining Forty-second Street in New York City were devoted not to the humiliation of women by rape and torture, as they currently are, but to a systematized commercially successful propaganda machine depicting the sadistic pleasures of gassing Jews or lynching blacks?

Is this analogy extreme? Not if you are a woman who is conscious of 11
the ever-present threat of rape and the proliferation of a cultural ideology that makes it sound like "liberated" fun. The majority report of the President's Commission on Obscenity and Pornography tried to pooh-pooh the opinion of law enforcement agencies around the country that claimed their own concrete experience with offenders who were caught with the stuff led them to conclude that pornographic material is a causative factor in crimes of sexual violence. The commission maintained that it was not possible at this time to scientifically prove or disprove such a connection.

But does one need scientific methodology in order to conclude that 12
the antifemale propaganda that permeates our nation's cultural output promotes a climate in which acts of sexual hostility directed against women are not only tolerated but ideologically encouraged? A similar debate has raged for many years over whether or not the extensive glorification of violence (the gangster as hero; the loving treatment accorded bloody shoot-'em-ups in movies, books and on TV) has a causal effect, a direct relationship to the rising rate of crime, particularly among youth. Interestingly enough, in this area—nonsexual and not specifically related to abuses against women—public opinion seems to be swinging to the position that explicit violence in the entertainment media does have a deleterious effect; it makes violence commonplace, numbingly routine and no longer morally shocking.

More to the point, those who call for a curtailment of scenes of vio- 13
lence in movies and on television in the name of sensitivity, good taste

and what's best for our children are not accused of being pro-censorship or against freedom of speech. Similarly, minority group organizations, black, Hispanic, Japanese, Italian, Jewish, or American Indian, that campaign against ethnic slurs and demeaning portrayals in movies, on television shows and in commercials are perceived as waging a just political fight, for if a minority group claims to be offended by a specific portrayal, be it Little Black Sambo or the Frito Bandido, and relates it to a history of ridicule and oppression, few liberals would dare to trot out a Constitutional argument in theoretical opposition, not if they wish to maintain their liberal credentials. Yet when it comes to the treatment of women, the liberal consciousness remains fiercely obdurate, refusing to be budged, for the sin of appearing square or prissy in the age of the so-called sexual revolution has become the worse offense of all.

13

Evaluation Arguments: X Is/Is Not A Good Y

☐

A young engineer has advanced to the level of a design group leader. She is now being considered for promotion to a management position. Her present supervisor is asked to write a report evaluating her as a prospective manager. He is asked to pay particular attention to the criteria of "creativity," "leadership," "interpersonal skill," "communication skills," and "technical competence."

CASE 2

A medical research group is asked to prepare guidelines for physicians on the best way to manage insulin-dependent diabetes. Some physicians want strict control of blood sugar levels. These physicians expect patients to take readings of their blood sugars every four hours and to take as many as three or four insulin injections per day. Other physicians allow blood sugars to fluctuate through a wider range of readings. They ask patients to monitor their blood sugars less often and to take only one or two injections per day. Which of these management programs is better? The research group has been asked to deal specifically with the following criteria: risk of long-range complications from diabetes; psychological well-being; and quality of life.

CASE 3

When former tennis star Margaret Court argued that Martina Navratilova's admitted homosexuality kept her from being a proper role model for young tennis players, sports writer Steve Kelley disagreed: "Navratilova is, in fact, an excellent role model. . . . She is self-made. She didn't learn the game playing with the privileged classes. She is honest and well-spoken in interviews. She doesn't kiss off questions with stock cliches. . . . Navratilova is a voracious reader, fluent in four languages. She belongs to the Sierra Club, reads several newspapers a day. She is a political junkie who has the courage of her convictions." Additionally, Kelly admires her courage and integrity in openly acknowledging her relationship with her longtime lover Judy Nelson, an admission that "has cost Navratilova millions in endorsements."*

CASE 4

A regional airline company hires a business consulting firm to evaluate the operations of the company's new hub in a large midwestern city. In the first two years of the hub operation, the company has lost money and is now in trouble. They want the consultants to answer two questions: Is this city a good location for a hub? Is the management team in the hub city doing a good job?

In our roles as citizens and professionals we are continually expected to make difficult evaluations, to defend them, and even to persuade others to accept them. Often we will defend our judgments orally—in committees making hiring and promotion decisions, in management groups deciding which of several marketing plans to adopt, or at parent advisory meetings evaluating the success of school policies. Sometimes, too, we will be expected to put our arguments in writing.

Practice in thinking systematically about the process of evaluation, then, is valuable experience. In this chapter we focus on evaluation arguments of the type "X is/is not a good Y" (or "X is a good/bad Y") and the strategy needed for conducting such arguments.† In Chapter 15, we will return to evaluation arguments to examine in more detail some special problems raised by ethical issues.

---

* Steve Kelley, *Seattle Times*, August 26, 1990, C3.

† In addition to the contrasting words *good/bad,* there are a number of other evaluative terms that involve the same kind of thinking: *effective/ineffective, successful/unsuccessful, workable/unworkable,* and so forth. Throughout this chapter, terms such as these can be substituted for *good/bad.*

■ WRITING ASSIGNMENT FOR CHAPTER 13:
EVALUATE A "CONTROVERSIAL" X

Write an argument in which you evaluate something controversial. Possible examples include the following:

- Is a sales tax a good method of taxation? Which method of income tax is preferable, a flat rate or a progressive rate?

- Do Top Forty stations play the best music? Is the classic rock music from the late sixties better than the rock music being produced today? Why is one musician (group) better than another?

- Is *Glory* a great war movie? What is the best horror movie of all time? What is the best Steven Spielberg movie? Does the movie *Taxi Driver* deserve the praise it has received from critics? How good was the Mel Gibson *Hamlet* versus the Laurence Olivier *Hamlet*?

- Is [a controversial teacher at your school] a good teacher? How good is the Canadian health care system? Is Arsenio Hall a good talk show host? Was Pete Rose as great a baseball player as is popularly believed? How effective is homeopathic medicine in treating disease?

- Is *USA Today* a good newspaper? Do network news shows do a good job at giving the news? Are America's prisons effective? How serious a problem is the budget deficit? Have the *Miranda* warnings improved or harmed police enforcement?

The X you choose should be controversial or at least problematic. You would hardly have a surprising essay if you argued that a Mercedes Benz is a good car or that nuclear war is bad. By "controversial" or "problematic," then, we mean that people are apt to disagree with your evaluation of X or that you are somehow opposing the common view of X. By choosing a controversial or problematic X, you will be able to focus on a clear issue. Somewhere in your essay you should summarize opposing views and either refute them or concede to them (see Chapter 8).

Note that this assignment asks you to do something different from a typical movie review, restaurant review, or product review in a consumer magazine. Many reviews are simply informational or analytic, where the writer's purpose is to describe the object or event being reviewed and explain its strengths and weaknesses. In contrast, this assignment calls for an argument, where your purpose is to change someone's mind about the evaluation of X.

The rest of this chapter explains the thinking processes that underlie evaluation arguments and gives you some advice on how to compose an evaluation essay.

CRITERIA-MATCH STRUCTURE OF EVALUATION ARGUMENTS

An "X is/is not a good Y" argument follows the same criteria-match structure that we examined in definitional arguments (Chapter 10). A typical claim for such an argument has the following form:

X is/is not a good Y because it meets/fails to meet criteria A, B, and C.

The main difference between an evaluation argument and a definition argument, in terms of structure, involves the Y term. In a definition argument, one argues whether a particular Y term is the correct class in which to place X. (Is a tarantula a *pet?*) In an evaluation argument, we know the Y term— that is, what class to put X into (Dr. Choplogic is a *teacher*)—but we don't know whether X is a good or bad instance of that class. (Is Dr. Choplogic a *good* teacher?) As in definition arguments, warrants specify the criteria to be used for the evaluation, whereas the stated reasons and grounds assert that X meets these criteria.

Let's look at some examples that, for the sake of illustration, assert just one criterion for "good" or "bad." (Most arguments will, of course, develop several criteria.) For the first example, we examine only the claim, stated reason, and warrant:

ENTHYMEME:	Computer-aided instruction (CAI) is an effective teaching method because it encourages self-paced learning.
CLAIM:	Computer-aided instruction is an effective teaching method.
STATED REASON:	Computer-aided instruction encourages self-paced learning.
WARRANT (CRITERION):	If a teaching method encourages self-paced learning, then it is effective.

To develop this argument, the writer would have to defend both the criterion (warrant) and the match (stated reason). Somewhere in the essay the writer would have to argue that an effective teaching method is one that allows students to work at their own pace; he would also have to argue that CAI instruction actually meets this criterion. (Of course, if self-paced instruction is the only criterion for effectiveness that the writer is proposing, he will have to justify the great weight he is giving to that criterion, which most readers would not believe is a necessary criterion for effectiveness, much less a sufficient one.)

Let's take a second example, and this time display the complete argument according to the Toulmin schema:

ENTHYMEME:	Pete Rose is not a Hall of Fame quality ballplayer because he was strong primarily in batting average and career hits but weak in most other categories.
CLAIM:	Pete Rose does not belong in the Hall of Fame.
STATED REASON:	He wasn't a complete player (he was strong primarily in batting average and career hits but weak in most other categories).
GROUNDS:	A thorough analysis of Pete Rose's career statistics reveals that in many aspects of fielding, hitting, baserunning, and run production his record is below average.

WARRANT:	Well-rounded performance is a necessary criterion for inclusion in the Hall of Fame.
BACKING:	evidence that shows that all present members of the Hall of Fame were well-rounded players; testimony from experts arguing that Hall of Fame players should be well rounded
CONDITIONS OF REBUTTAL:	unless Pete Rose's career records in several areas (e.g., games played, at bats, total career hits, batting average) are so overwhelming that Hall of Fame electors choose to ignore his lack of power, his poor baserunning, his mediocre defense; unless intangibles like competitive zeal are given precedence over the player's record
QUALIFIER:	Given the surprising nature of this claim—most people who oppose Pete Rose's election to the Hall of Fame do so on the basis of his gambling problems and his income tax evasion, not on the basis of his baseball record—one should acknowledge in the qualifier that one faces an uphill battle. Hence, "Pete Rose *may not* belong in the Hall of Fame" is probably as emphatic a claim as one can expect to get away with.

As is often the case with evaluative arguments, the most challenging task is not to establish the match between X and the criteria, but to gain support for the appropriateness of the criteria. Baseball experts probably will agree that Pete Rose was not a well-rounded ball player. What they will disagree about is whether "well-roundedness" is a necessary criterion for election to the Hall of Fame. Similarly, baseball experts will agree that Pete Rose has damaged his reputation through ethical and legal mistakes. But they will disagree whether those problems should be criteria for excluding Rose from the Hall of Fame.

GENERAL STRATEGY FOR EVALUATION ARGUMENTS

The general strategy for evaluation arguments is to establish criteria and then to argue that X meets or does not meet the criteria. In writing your argument, you have to decide whether your audience is apt to accept your criteria or not. If you want to argue, for example, that pit bulls do not make good pets because they are potentially vicious, you can assume that most readers will share your assumption that viciousness is bad. Likewise, if you want to praise the new tax bill because it cuts out tax cheating, you can probably assume readers agree that tax cheating is bad.

Often, however, selecting and defending your criteria are the most difficult parts of a criteria-match argument. For example, people who own pit bulls because they *want* a vicious dog for protection may not agree that viciousness is bad. In this case, you would need to argue that another kind of dog, such as a German shepherd or a doberman, would make a better choice than a pit bull or that the bad consequences of a vicious dog outweigh the benefits. Several kinds of difficulties in establishing criteria are worth discussing in more detail.

The Problem of Standards: What's Normal or What's Ideal?

To get a sense of this problem, consider again Young Person's archetypal argument with The Parents about her curfew (see Chapter 1). She originally argued that staying out until 2:00 A.M. is fair "because all the other kids' parents let their kids stay out late," to which The Parents might respond: "Well, *ideally*, all the other parents should not let their kids stay out that late." Young Person based her criterion for fairness on what is *normal;* her standards arose from common practices of a social group. The Parents, however, argued from what is *ideal*, basing their criteria on some external standard that transcends social groups.

We experience this dilemma in various forms throughout our lives. It is the conflict between absolutes and cultural relativism, between written law and customary practice. There is hardly an area of human experience that escapes the dilemma: Is it fair to get a ticket for going 70 mph on a 65 mph freeway when most of the drivers go 70 mph or higher? Is it better for high schools to pass out free contraceptives to students because the students are having sex anyway (what's *normal*), or is it better not to pass them out in order to support abstinence (what's *ideal*)? When you select criteria for an evaluation argument, you may well have to choose one side or the other of this dilemma, arguing for what is ideal or for what is normal. Neither position should be seen as necessarily better than the other; normal practice may be corrupt just as surely as ideal behavior may be impossible.

The Problem of Mitigating Circumstances

When confronting the dilemma raised by the "normal" versus the "ideal," we sometimes have to take into account circumstances as well as behavior. In particular, we have the notion of "mitigating" circumstances, or circumstances that are extraordinary or unusual enough to cause us to change our standard measure of judgment. Ordinarily it is wrong to be late for work or to miss an exam. But what if your car had a flat tire?

When you argue for mitigating circumstances as a reason for modifying judgment in a particular case, you are arguing against the conditions of both normal behavior and ideal behavior as the proper criterion for judgment. Thus, when you make such an argument, you will likely assume an especially heavy burden of proof. People assume the rightness of usual standards of judgment unless there are compelling arguments for abnormal circumstances.

The Problem of Choosing between Two Goods or Two Bads

Not all arguments of value, of course, clearly deal with bad and good, but with better or worse. Often we are caught between a rock and a hard place. Should we cut pay or cut people? Put our parents in a nursing home or let them stay at home where they have become a danger to themselves? In such cases one has to weigh conflicting criteria, knowing that the choices are too much alike—either both bad or both good.

The Problem of Seductive Empirical Measures

The need to make distinctions among relative goods or relative bads has led many persons to seek quantifiable criteria that can be weighed mathematically. Thus we use grade point averages to select scholarship winners, MCAT scores to decide who gets into medical school, and student evaluation scores to decide which professor gets the University Teaching Award.

In some cases, such empirical measures can be quite acceptable. But they can be dangerous if they don't adequately measure the value of the people or things they purportedly evaluate. (Some people would argue that they *never* adequately measure anything significant.) To illustrate the problem further, consider the problems of relying on grade point average as a criterion for employment. Many employers rely heavily on grades when hiring college graduates. But according to every major study of the relationship between grades and work achievement, grades are about as reliable as palm reading when it comes to predicting life success. Why do employers continue to rely so heavily on grades? Clearly because it is so easy to classify job applicants according to a single empirical measure that appears to rank order everyone along the same scale.

The problem with empirical measures, then, is that they seduce us into believing that complex judgments can be made mathematically, thus rescuing us from the messiness of alternative points of view and conflicting criteria. Empirical measures seem extremely persuasive next to written arguments that try to qualify and hedge and raise questions. We suggest, however, that a fair evaluation of any X might require such hedging.

The Problem of Cost

A final problem that can crop up in evaluations is cost. In comparing an X to others of its kind, we may find that on all the criteria we can develop, X comes out on top. X is the best of all possible Y's. But if X costs too much, we have to rethink our evaluation.*

---

* We can avoid this problem somewhat by placing items into different classes on the basis of cost. For example, a Mercedes may come out far ahead of a Hyundai, but the more relevant evaluative question to ask is, "How does a Mercedes compare to a Cadillac?"

If we're looking to hire a new department head at Median State University, and the greatest scholar in the field, a magnificent teacher, a regular dynamo of diplomacy, says she'll come—for a hundred G's a year—we'll probably have to withdraw our offer. Whether the costs are expressed in dollars or personal discomfort or moral repugnance or some other terms, our final evaluation of X must take cost into account, however elusive that cost might be.

HOW TO DETERMINE CRITERIA FOR YOUR ARGUMENT

Now that we have explored some of the difficulties you may encounter in establishing and defending criteria for your evaluation of X, let's turn to the practical problem of trying to determine criteria themselves. How do you go about finding the criteria you'll need for distinguishing a good teacher from a poor teacher, a good movie from a bad movie, a successful manager from an unsuccessful manager, a healthy diet from an unhealthy diet, and so forth?

Step 1:   Determine the Category in Which the Object Being Evaluated Belongs

In determining the quality or value of any given X, you must first figure out just what your standard of measure is. You can't begin until you determine what class of things you are putting X into. If, for example, you asked one of your professors to write you a letter of recommendation for a summer job, what "class of things" should the professor put you into? Is he or she supposed to evaluate you as a student? a leader? a worker? a party animal? or what? This is an important question because the criteria for excellence in one class (student) may be very different from criteria for excellence in another class (party animal). To write a useful evaluation, your professor will probably need to put you into the general class "summer job holder" and try to give prospective employers an evaluation based on criteria relevant to a summer job.

As a general rule, fairness requires us to judge X according to the smallest applicable class. For example, your professor would do a better job of evaluating you if he or she placed you not in the general class "summer job holder" but in the smaller class "law office intern" or "highway department flagperson" or "golf course groundsperson" and chose criteria accordingly, since excellence in one kind of summer job might differ considerably from excellence in another job.

We thus recommend placing X into the smallest relevant class because of the apples-and-oranges law. That is, to avoid giving a mistaken rating to a perfectly good apple, you need to make sure you are judging an apple under the class "apple" and not under the next larger class "fruit" or a neighboring class "orange." And to be even more precise, you may wish to evaluate your apple in the class "eating apple" as opposed to "pie apple" because the latter class is supposed to be tarter and the former class juicier and sweeter.

Obviously, there are limits to this law. For example, the smallest possible class of apples would contain only one member—the one being evaluated. At that point, your apple is both the best and the worst member of its class. And hence, evaluation of it is meaningless. Also, we sometimes can't avoid apples-and-oranges comparisons because they are thrust upon us by circumstances, tradition, or some other factor. Thus, the Academy Award judges can't distinguish between tragic movies, comic movies, musicals, and satires when choosing the year's "Best Movie."

Step 2:   Determine the Purpose or Function of This Class

Once you have located X in its appropriate class, you should next determine what the purpose or function of this class is. Let's suppose that the summer job you are applying for is tour guide at the city zoo. The function of a tour guide is to make people feel welcome, to give them interesting information about the zoo, to make their visit pleasant, and so forth. Consequently, you wouldn't want your professor's evaluation to praise your term paper on Napoleon Bonaparte or your successful synthesis of some compound in your chemistry lab. Rather, the professor should highlight your dependability, your neat appearance, your good speaking skills, and your ability to work with groups. On the other hand, if you were applying for graduate school, then your term paper on Bonaparte or your chem lab wizardry would be relevant. In other words, the professor has to evaluate you according to the class "tour guide," not "graduate student," and the criteria for each class derive from the purpose or function of the class.

Let's take another example. Suppose that you are the chair of a committee charged with evaluating the job performance of Lillian Jones, director of the admissions office at Clambake College. Ms. Jones has been a controversial manager because several members of her staff have filed complaints about her management style. In making your evaluation, your first step is to place Ms. Jones into an appropriate class, in this case, the general class "manager," and then the more specific class "manager of an admissions office at a small, private college." You then need to identify the purpose or function of these classes. You might say that the function of the general class "managers" is to "oversee actual operations of an organization so that the organization meets its goals as harmoniously and efficiently as possible," whereas the function of the specific class "manager of an admissions office at a small, private college" is "the successful recruitment of the best students possible."

Step 3:   Determine Criteria Based on the Purposes or Function of the Class to Which X Belongs

Once you've worked out the purposes of the class, you are ready to work out the criteria by which you judge all members of the class. Criteria for judgment will be based on those features of Y that help it achieve the purposes of its class. For example, once you determine the purpose and function of the position filled by Lillian Jones, you can develop a list of criteria for managerial success:

1. Criteria related to "efficient operation"
   - articulates priorities and goals for the organization
   - is aggressive in achieving goals
   - motivates fellow employees
   - is well organized, efficient, and punctual
   - is articulate and communicates well
2. Criteria related to "harmonious operation"
   - creates job satisfaction for subordinates
   - is well groomed, sets good example of professionalism
   - is honest, diplomatic in dealing with subordinates
   - is flexible in responding to problems and special concerns of staff members
3. Criteria related to meeting specific goals of a college admissions office
   - creates a comprehensive recruiting program
   - demonstrates that recruiting program works

Step 4:   Give Relative Weightings to the Criteria

Even though you have established criteria, you must still decide which of the criteria are most important. In the case of Lillian Jones, is it more important that she bring in lots of students to Clambake College or that she create a harmonious, happy office? These sorts of questions are at the heart of many evaluative controversies. Thus, a justification for your weighting of criteria may well be an important part of your argument.

DETERMINING WHETHER X MEETS THE CRITERIA

Once you've established your criteria, you've got to figure out how well X meets them. You proceed by gathering evidence and examples. The success of the recruiting program at Clambake College can probably be measured empirically, so you gather statistics about applications to the college, SAT scores of applicants, number of acceptances, academic profiles of entering freshmen, and so forth. You might then compare those statistics to those compiled by Ms. Jones' predecessor or to her competitors at other, comparable institutions.

You can also look at what the recruiting program actually does—the number of recruiters, the number of high school visitations, quality of admissions brochures, and other publications. You can also look at Ms. Jones in action, searching for specific incidents or examples that illustrate her management style. For example, you can't measure a trait such as diplomacy empirically, but you can find specific instances where the presence or absence of this trait was demonstrated. You could turn to examples where Ms. Jones may or may not have prevented a potentially divisive situation from occurring or where she offered or failed to offer encouragement at psychologically the right moment to keep someone from getting demoralized. As with criteria-match arguments in definition, one must provide examples of how the X in question meets each of the criteria that have been set up.

Your final evaluation of Ms. Jones, then, might include an overview of her strengths and weaknesses along the various criteria you have established. You might say that Ms. Jones has done an excellent job with recruitment (an assertion you can support with data on student enrollments over the last five years) but was relatively poor at keeping the office staff happy (as evidenced by employee complaints, high turnover, and your own observations of her rather abrasive management style). Nevertheless, your final recommendation might be to retain Ms. Jones for another three-year contract because you believe that an excellent recruiting record is the most important criterion for her position at Clambake. You might justify this heavy weighting of recruiting on the grounds that the institution's survival depends on its ability to attract adequate numbers of good students.

As a way of testing your argument in preparation for your committee's meeting, you lay out your argument according to Toulmin's schema:

ENTHYMEME:	Despite some weaknesses, Ms. Jones has been a good manager of the admissions office at Clambake College because her office's recruitment record is excellent.
CLAIM:	Ms. Jones has been a good manager of the admissions office at Clambake College.
STATED REASON:	Her office's recruitment record is excellent.
GROUNDS:	statistical data demonstrating the excellence of the recruitment program
WARRANT:	Successful recruitment is the most important criterion for rating job performance of the director of admissions.
BACKING:	Evidence that low recruitment leads to financial problems and even closing of a college; maintaining enrollment through recruitment is the lifeblood of the college. Although her opponents have complained that Ms. Jones has serious problems maintaining harmony among her staff, a happy staff serves no purpose if we don't have enough students to keep the college open.
CONDITIONS OF REBUTTAL:	unless the recruitment record isn't as good as I have said (Note: I'll need to be sure of my standards when I say her record is excellent. Am I arguing about "what's normal" by comparing Clambake's record with other colleges? Or am I arguing about what is ideal? Will one of Jones' critics bring in an argument saying she isn't doing a particularly good job of recruiting? Might they argue that plenty of people in the office could do the same good job of recruitment—after all, Clambake

sells itself—without stirring up any of the personnel problems that Ms. Jones has caused?)

Unless the recruitment record isn't the most important criterion. Ms. Jones is obviously weak in maintaining good relationships with staff. How might an opponent argue that staff problems in Ms. Jones' office are severe enough that we ought to search for a new director? I will have to counter that argument some way.

QUALIFIER: I will need to qualify my general rating of excellent by acknowledging Ms. Jones' weaknesses in some areas. But I want to be definite in saying that recruitment is the most important criterion and that she definitely meets this criterion.

☐ For Class Discussion

The following small-group exercise can be accomplished in one or two class hours. It gives you a good model of the process you will need to go through in order to write your own evaluation essay. Working in small groups, suppose that you are going to evaluate a controversial member of one of the following classes:

    a. a teacher
    b. a political figure
    c. an athlete
    d. a school newspaper
    e. a school policy
    f. a recent Supreme Court decision
    g. a rock singer or group or MTV video
    h. a dorm or living group
    i. a restaurant or college hangout
    j. an X of your choice

1. Choose a controversial member within one of these classes as the specific person, thing, or event you are going to evaluate (Professor Choplogic, the Wild Dog Bar, Madonna, and so forth).
2. Narrow down the general class by determining the smallest relevant class to which your X belongs (from "athlete" to "basketball guard"; from "college hangout" to "college hangout for people who want to hold late-night bull sessions").
3. Make a list of the purposes or functions of that class and then list the criteria that a good member of that class would have to have in order to accomplish the purposes.
4. If necessary, rank order your criteria.
5. Evaluate your X by matching X to each of the criteria.

■ WRITING YOUR EVALUATION ARGUMENT

Starting Point: Finding and Exploring an
Evaluation Issue

If you have not already listed some evaluation issues, try creating idea-maps
with spokes chosen from among the following categories: *people* (athletes,
political leaders, musicians, clergypeople, entertainers, businesspeople); *science and technology* (weapons systems, word-processing programs, spread
sheets, automotive advancements, treatments for diseases); *media* (a newspaper, a magazine or journal, a TV program, a radio station, an advertisement); *government and world affairs* (an economic policy, a Supreme Court
decision, a law or legal practice, a government custom or practice, a foreign
policy); *the arts* (a movie, a book, a building, a painting, a piece of music);
your college or university (a course, a teacher, a textbook, a curriculum, an
administrative policy, the financial aid system); *world of work* (a job, a company operation, a dress policy, a merit pay system, a hiring policy, a supervisor); or any other categories of your choice.

Then brainstorm possibilities for controversial X's that might fit into
the categories on your map. As long as you can imagine disagreement
about how to evaluate X, you have a potentially good topic for this assignment.

Once you have found an issue and have taken a tentative position on it,
explore your ideas by freewriting your responses to the eight guided tasks
in Chapter 3, pages 79–81.

Writing a Discovery Draft: Some Suggestions for
Organizing Your Evaluation Argument

As you write your discovery draft, you might find useful the following typical structure for an evaluation argument. Of course, many evaluation arguments don't follow this shape, but many do, and you can always alter the
shape later if its structure seems too formulaic to you.

- Introduce your issue and show why evaluating X is problematic or con-
troversial.
- Summarize opposing views.
- Refute or concede to opposing views.
- Present your own claim.
     State Criterion 1 and defend it if necessary.
          Show that X meets criterion.
     State Criterion 2 and defend it if necessary.
          Show that X meets criterion.
     Continue with additional criteria and match arguments.
- Sum up your evaluation

Revision

At this stage you should be able to summarize your argument as a claim with because clauses. In order to test the structure of your argument, you may find it useful to analyze it with the Toulmin schema. This method will help you see to what extent you need to defend each of your criteria. As the example on evaluating Lillian Jones shows (pp. 296–99), the main testing of the argument can occur when you consider the conditions of rebuttal. In the final section of this chapter, we turn to some of the questions you might ask yourself when testing your argument.

CONDITIONS FOR REBUTTAL: TESTING YOUR EVALUATION ARGUMENT

After you've gone through a process like the one sketched out above, you should have a thoughtful rough draft ready for more careful scrutiny. Once again, put yourself in the role of the critic.

Will My Audience Accept My Criteria?

Many evaluative arguments are weak because the writers have simply assumed that readers will accept their criteria. Whenever your audience's acceptance of your criteria is in doubt, you will need to make your warrants clear and provide backing in their support.

Are My Criteria Based on the "Smallest Applicable Class" for X?

For example, the James Bond movie *For Your Eyes Only* will certainly be a failure if you evaluate it in the general class "movies," in which it would have to compete with *Citizen Kane* and other great classics. But if you evaluated it as an "escapist movie" or a "James Bond movie" it would have a greater chance for success and hence of yielding an arguable evaluation. All of this isn't to say that you couldn't evaluate "escapist movies" as a class of, say, "popular films" and find the whole class deficient. Evaluations of this type are, however, more difficult to argue because of the numbers of items you must take into account.

Will Readers Accept My General Weighting of Criteria?

Another vulnerable spot in an evaluation argument is the relative weight of the criteria. How much anyone weights a given criterion is usually a function of his or her own interests relative to the X in question. You should always ask whether some particular group affected by the quality of X might not have good reasons for weighting the criteria differently.

Will Readers Question My Standard of Reference?

In questioning the criteria for judging X, we can also focus on the standard of reference used—what's normal versus what's ideal. If you have argued that X is bad because it doesn't live up to what's ideal, you can expect some readers to defend X on the basis of what's normal. Similarly, if you argue that X is good because it is better than its competitors, you can expect some readers to point out how short it falls from what is ideal.

Will Readers Criticize My Use of Empirical Measures?

The tendency to mistake empirical measures for criteria is a common one that any critic of an argument should be aware of. As we have discussed earlier, what's most measurable isn't always significant when it comes to assessing the essential traits needed to fulfill whatever function X is supposed to fulfill. A 95-mph fastball is certainly an impressive empirical measure of a pitcher's ability—but if the pitcher doesn't get batters out, that measure is a misleading gauge of performance.

Will Readers Accept My Criteria but Reject My Match Argument?

The other major way of testing an evaluation argument is to anticipate how readers might object to your stated reasons and grounds. Will readers challenge you by finding sampling errors in your data or otherwise find that you used evidence selectively? For example, if you think your opponents will emphasize Lillian Jones' abrasive management style much more heavily than you did, you may be able to undercut their arguments by finding counterexamples that show Ms. Jones acting diplomatically. Be prepared to counter objections to your grounds.

☐ FOR CLASS DISCUSSION

Read the following examples of evaluation arguments. Then, working as individuals or in a group, answer the following questions:

1. What criteria are used to evaluate the X in question?

2. Does the writer create an argument for the appropriateness of these criteria? If so, how effective is it?

3. How effective is the argument that X matches each of the established criteria?

4. How would you go about refuting each of the arguments?

TARNISHED IMAGE OF ACADEMY AWARDS HASN'T DULLED WORLD'S APPETITE FOR THIS FLAWED FARCE

William Arnold

With a worldwide television audience now in excess of a billion people, the annual Academy Awards ceremony officially has entered the record books as the world's largest spectator event—larger than the World Series, the Super Bowl and the U.S. presidential election, perhaps all put together. 1

Moreover, the Oscars are not only the most popular awards in the history of the planet, they are the most written about, most heatedly debated, most wagered upon, most celebrated in myth and most financially lucrative for the winners—translating into a hard cash value that has been estimated as high as $40 million in increased grosses for a Best Picture win. 2

In short, those little gold statuettes that once again will be handed out tomorrow night are a true phenomenon of 20th-century culture with a credibility that no other award system comes close to matching—not the Tonys, the Grammys, the Emmys, the Pulitzers, the People's Choice, the Medals of Freedom or the Nobel Prizes. 3

And the extraordinary thing is that this phenomenon defies all reason, analysis and common sense. 4

Indeed, it is almost universally accepted—and it certainly has dawned on me during my 10 years of covering the event—that the Oscars are just about the most flawed, tarnished, infuriating and downright perverse awards system ever devised. 5

In fact, when you sit down and examine the case against the Academy Awards, the evidence seems so overwhelming you begin to wonder why the L.A.P.D. bunco squad doesn't move in and padlock the door of the Dorothy Chandler Pavilion some Oscar night. 6

Here, in a nutshell, is everything that is wrong with Oscar, the reasons why you should *not* be glued to your television set tomorrow night: 7

1. The Academy Awards are inherently unfair. The bottom line on the Oscars is that they are not voted upon by any kind of blue-ribbon panel of experts or even a cross section of the movie industry. They are voted upon by the membership of an Academy that is run like a Los Angeles country club. To get in the club one must be nominated by two current members, then voted in by a very picky board of governors. 8

The current membership totals 4,747, which is, of course, only a fraction of the people who actually work in the film industry. 9

This group consists of many older, semiretired people. More than 70 percent of the director's branch of the Academy, for instance, is over age 10

60. Many are from the business and promotion side of filmmaking, including studio executives, who are notorious for knowing nothing about films. And they all are subjected to an unbelievable barrage of influence around Oscar time.

Members are regularly wined and dined by publicists, chauffeured to   11
private screenings in limousines and deluged with free gifts and promotional devices.

Even so, it has been estimated that as few as 60 percent of the total   12
membership actually gets out and votes. And it is likely that even fewer actually see the movies that are being voted upon.

Critic Andrew Sarris once reported the average Academy voter saw as   13
few as 12 films a year, and several illustrious members publicly have admitted voting for or against pictures they hadn't seen.

2.   *The Academy Awards are totally political.*   Although its publi-   14
cists don't much like to admit it, the Motion Picture Academy of Arts and Sciences came into existence in 1927 when Louis B. Mayer, the ruler of MGM, decided the industry needed a company union, a means of stalling the formation of the various guilds that later would get a foothold in the business in the '30s.

Though the Academy slowly has gained its independence from the   15
major studios (who angrily pulled out of financing the Oscar show after a British film, "Hamlet," won Best Picture in 1948), the awards themselves have remained so tied to the big studios that more Oscar outcomes have been decided by studio politics and front-office dictate than any other factor. Even as late as the 1960s, 20th Century-Fox was able to garner Best Picture nominations for big budget flops like "Doctor Doolittle" and "Hello, Dolly" by having its Academy-member employees block vote.

The Oscars also have been influenced by the politics within the mem-   16
bership of the Academy itself. Unofficial Academy historians like Mason Wiley and Damien Bona in their book "Inside Oscar" have had a field day tracing how this power has influenced nominations and winners.

For instance, Walter Brennan's record Best Supporting Actor wins in   17
1936, '38 and '39 can be directly attributed to his popularity with the extras (he was once one of them), who were allowed Academy membership in the '30s and held the balance of power with their numbers.

And, of course, the Academy voting record traditionally has bent with   18
the various outside political breezes, as well: scorning the work of black-listed actors and writers in the redbaiting days, giving Sidney Poitier his Oscar during the height of the civil rights movement in 1964, allowing itself to be swept up in the wave of radical chic of the late 1960s and early '70s to award mavericks like Jane Fonda, George C. Scott and Marlon Brando.

3.   *The Academy Awards are corrupt.*   This is a strong statement   19
but how else to describe a measure of artistic achievement so heavily

influenced by paid advertising? In one year in the early 1980s in which the ad revenue actually was counted, something like $8 million was spent on Oscar advertising, which is roughly $3,000 spent per Academy voter.

And these ad campaigns have an effect. The older voters who deter-   20
mine the elections have proven to be very swayable by these ads. Skillful Oscar campaigns have amassed Best Picture nominations for such totally forgettable movies as "Anne of a Thousand Days," "Oliver!," "Nicholas and Alexandra," "A Touch of Class," "Cleopatra," and "The Alamo."

The last was an infamous 1960 John Wayne-financed campaign in   21
which a barrage of ads depicted cast members kneeling in prayer under copy warning voters that a loss for "The Alamo" would unleash God's wrath on the movie industry.

These campaigns have become a small industry in Los Angeles not   22
only for the trade papers and cable TV stations that get all the ad rev-enue, but for the public relations firms that have sprung up to specialize in Oscar races.

A 1983 California Magazine article chronicling John Lithgow's Best   23
Supporting Actor run for "The World According to Garp" told an amazing story of how the actor put himself in the hands of media specialists who guided his campaign like a race for the presidency—telling him how to dress, what parties to attend, what kind of car to drive and where to live. (In this case, to no avail. He lost.)

4.   *The Academy Awards are a lousy measure of movie immortal-*   24
ity.   To be fair, *all* the movie awards have been poor judges of what ulti-mately would prove to be lasting. With the benefit of hindsight, the selec-tions of the New York Film Critics, the National Board of Review, the Cannes Film Festival and all the others seem amazingly out of touch with posterity.

But the Oscar choices have been the worst.   25

Looking at its list of past winners, one sees an occasional good Best   26
Picture call ("Casablanca" in '42, "Lawrence of Arabia" in '62) but amaz-ingly few accolades to what we now consider the seminal works of Holly-wood art.

No Best Picture honors for "Citizen Kane," "Psycho," "Singin' in the   27
Rain," "2001," "The Searchers," "Dr. Strangelove," "Close Encounters," "Bonnie and Clyde," "Vertigo," "Magnificent Ambersons," "McCabe and Mrs. Miller" or the others that always tend to crop up in the all-time criti-cal 10-best lists.

And a glance at the winning actor lists is even more sobering. The   28
annals of Oscar are clogged with awards for ham performances by the likes of Jose Ferrer, Paul Scofield, George Arliss, Paul Muni and Charles Laughton, but have no place for a Cary Grant.

Oscar voters also have shown themselves to be extraordinarily shallow   29
in other ways, as well.

They're forever rewarding the change-of-pace performance, no matter   30
how dismal (William Hurt as an effeminate homosexual in 1986, Shirley
Jones as a hooker in 1960), constantly letting themselves be influenced
by cheap sentimentality (Liz Taylor's win in 1960 after nearly dying, Ingrid
Bergman's win in 1956 after returning to the Hollywood fold following
years of self-imposed exile), consistently second guessing themselves by
rewarding the previous year's most worthy loser (Bette Davis' win in 1935
for "Dangerous" when she deserved it for "Of Human Bondage" in 1934).

Because of all this shallowness, snobbishness and stupidity, the   31
Oscars simply have failed to acknowledge the work of what often seems
the majority of Hollywood's most important artists.

Alfred Hitchcock, arguably the greatest filmmaker of all time, never   32
took home a Best Director Oscar while the long-forgotten Frank Lloyd
took home two and narrowly missed a third. Edward G. Robinson, my
personal candidate for the greatest film actor of the sound era, was never
nominated in his extraordinary 30-year reign as a top star.

How does one take seriously a movie award that honors Luise Rainer   33
(twice), Ernest Borgnine and Paul Lukas but not Irene Dunne, Carole
Lombard, Marilyn Monroe, Jean Harlow, Myrna Loy, Marlene Dietrich,
Greta Garbo, Robert Mitchum, James Dean, John Garfield, Tyrone
Power, Charles Boyer, Errol Flynn, Charlie Chaplin, Buster Keaton,
William Powell, Kirk Douglas and Fred Astaire?

5.   *The Academy Awards are bad showmanship.*   I suppose all of   34
the above would be forgivable if the Oscar ceremonies themselves were
such a dandy show that made up for these shortcomings in entertainment value. But the truth is that in all the annals of show business, there
probably has been no more tedious, ill-prepared and boring an extrava-
ganza as the annual Oscars consistently have proven themselves to be
since their first television broadcast in 1952.

Whole books have been written ridiculing the unbearably cute repartee   35
between the boy and girl presenters, the ponderous acceptance
speeches, the unimaginative musical numbers, the tasteless attire of the
starlets, the flubbed lines, wrong exits, demonstrations, missed cues and
mispronounced names.

Will anyone who experienced them ever forget Greer Garson's 5 1/2-   36
minute acceptance speech in 1942, or Sally Field's embarrassing out-
burst in 1984 ("You like me—you really like me!"), or Jerry Lewis' excruciating 20-minute ad libbing when the awards inadvertently ended early in
1958, or that tasteless filmed visit in 1976 to the deathbed of a shrunken
little thing that once had been Mary Pickford, America's Sweetheart?

Or that prototypical scene of Hollywood vulgarity played year after   37
year in which the stars unload from their limousines before the bleachers
of screaming fans? How can one look at what Raymond Chandler called
"those awful idiot faces" without feeling, as he did, "a sense of the collapse of human intelligence"?

Indeed, how can anyone in his right mind, in the face of all this well-   38
known evidence of injustice and fraud and epic tackiness, possibly take
the Oscars seriously?

Yet they do. By the thousands. By the millions. With China now added   39
to the Oscarcast, by the billions. By almost everyone I know, including
the snobbiest critics of the most esoteric film journals. And after a
decade of pondering the phenomenon, I think I finally have figured out
why.

Like Christmas and Halloween, Oscar night is a phenomenon that has   40
become completely divorced from its origins. It is an annual ritual, part
Thanksgiving Day parade, part Kentucky Derby, part Everyone's Senior
Prom—a kind of Super Bowl of Celebrity, sanctified by six decades of tradition, united in almost religious communion by the idea that the preservation of human personality on celluloid is a very important thing.

The experience of watching the Academy Awards is a kind of strange   41
cathartic ordeal in which we both voyeuristically witness that great other
world of celebrity we will never make and relieve our sense of inadequacy
by watching these same people one by one make fools of themselves.

As crazy as it sounds, the ritual has a kind of cleansing effect on the   42
psyche, and I'm convinced it has come to serve a valuable function in
our global society. And when it unfolds for the 59th time tomorrow night,
I'll be watching. In fact, I wouldn't miss it for the world.

THE MANDATORY MOTORCYCLE-HELMET LAW IS BAD LAW

Bill C. Healy (student)

For most people, Washington's newly re-instated motorcycle-helmet law,   1
which goes into effect today, is no big deal. The reason: Most people do
not ride motorcycles.

For some people, however, especially motorcyclists and politicians, it   2
is a very big deal. During the last 13 years, especially the last legislative
session, the helmet issue has created heated debate with neither side
willing to compromise. The pro-helmet forces want a mandatory law
because they say it will reduce head injuries, deaths, and cost to taxpayers for medical expenses of unhelmeted riders. Last legislative session,
the pro-helmet people won. But the Legislature made a serious mistake.
When we look at the evidence, it's plain that a mandatory helmet law is a
bad law.

Of course, there are some definite benefits to wearing a helmet. A hel-   3
met will protect the rider from a head injury in some low-speed accidents. Also a helmet with a face shield will protect the wearer from being

pelted with rain and hail, thus making it safer for the rider to operate the motorcycle in foul weather. These benefits mean that responsible motorcyclists will choose to wear a helmet voluntarily when the conditions are appropriate.

However, a helmet won't protect against head injury when traveling at normal traffic speeds. According to the U.S. Department of Transportation, "There is no evidence that any helmet thus far, regardless of cost or design, is capable of rejecting impact stress above 13 mph." The mandatory law is based on the premise that helmet laws reduce injuries and fatalities. But all available evidence shows that they do not. A Washington State Patrol Research Report, No. 039, entitled, "An Evaluation of Washington State's Motorcycle Safety Laws' Effectiveness," reviewed motorcycle fatalities for five years before and five years after the state's previous experiment with a mandatory helmet law. It found virtually no change in cause of death rates with or without a helmet. During 1962–66, when helmet use was voluntary, 47 percent of deaths were due to head injury and 3 percent to neck injury. During 1967–71, when the state mandated wearing of helmets, 45 percent of deaths were attributed to head injury and 6 percent to neck injury. Similar findings were found in other states and by the King County Medical Examiner. It is clear from both state and county records that the mandatory helmet law provided no relief to fatal accident victims. These figures show a mandatory law did not work in the past, and there is no evidence it will work now.

Another reason why the mandatory helmet law is a bad piece of legislation is that wearing a helmet can actually cause accidents. A helmet restricts the wearer's hearing and peripheral vision, two senses a motorcyclist desperately needs for avoiding accidents. Riding a motorcycle while wearing a helmet is like driving an automobile while wearing earplugs and taping paper over your back and side windows and over the right half of your windshield. The Legislature and the police would not allow a person to operate an automobile under these conditions, yet the Legislature passed, and the police will enforce, these same types of sense restrictions for motorcycle riders. A motorcyclist needs to be able to look over his shoulder quickly and efficiently and to be able to hear side traffic, so as to be a safe, alert and defensive rider. It is having the full use of one's senses that helps a motorcyclist avoid accidents. Isn't that what we really want to do?

Finally, the law infringes on my personal freedom. In the motorcycle helmet case, my right to personal freedom clashes with the state's right to save taxpayers' money on medical expenses. But because the state's side of this argument is so weak, my right to personal freedom outweighs the state's right. What non-motorcyclists don't realize is how much the mandatory helmet law reduces the pleasure of motorcycling. Unlike a seatbelt in a car, which is a very minor inconvenience to wear, a motorcycle helmet is a major inconvenience. Not only does the helmet reduce the pleasure of riding—especially in the summer when a helmet is hot and sticky—but it can't be stored on the motorcycle when you reach your destination. Moreover, you can't use your motorcycle to give a pedestrian a lift. But the biggest inconvenience is the increased risk to my safety. Before today, I was a safe and responsible rider when I rode without a helmet because I believed it increased my chances of survival. I still do, and the fact and figures back me. Today and onward I will be a criminal for doing what I have done since I was 16—riding the safest way I know how.

Now my life is in jeopardy because a law was passed for motorcyclists   7
by people who do not ride motorcycles. The mandatory helmet law is a bad law. This is something legislators and the governor will never understand unless they ride a motorcycle.

BEAUTY PAGEANT FALLACIES

Debra Goodwin (student)

"You will be beautiful up there on the stage, Jessica," said the beauty   1
pageant director. "You've spent your whole life preparing for this contest. The judges will examine you and all they will see is a perfect ten. You look gorgeous." There are many in our society who believe beauty pageants are a harmless way to celebrate the beauty of women in our culture. These same individuals boast that the beauty pageants provide many opportunities for the winners of such contests. In some contests women are even awarded scholastic scholarships for their beauty. Advocates of beauty pageants claim that winners of these contests win because of their talent not because of their looks. Despite these claims, I believe that beauty pageants damage our society. First, beauty pageants hurt a woman's self-esteem. Second, beauty contests present women as objects and are thus a kind of pornography. Finally, beauty pageants perpetuate and condone the exploitation of women in our society.

Beauty pageants are harmful because they severely damage a   2
woman's self-esteem by creating an impossible standard of beauty that leads to serious medical and mental problems. My sister Pam pursued her ambition to be a beauty queen. She explained, "I read everything I could find on pageants back to the 1950s to determine if there was a standard of beauty and whether I could seem to fit it. And I could—with the help of heavy makeup to cover my acne scars, enough hair spray to defy gravity for hours, tape for my boobs, and spray adhesive to hold down my swimsuit." Pam felt that being transformed into a beauty queen made absolutely clear how "artificial, dangerous, and self-denying the beauty standard really is." After winning in the local pageants Pam explained, "I was whisked away for a session with two pageant advisors

who dissected my body: 'Okay, you really need to work on your legs; we definitely have to find you a better bra.' No matter how I looked, I was inadequate." Pam's obsession with winning in the beauty pageant circle landed her in the hospital diagnosed as anorexic with a severely low self-esteem. After months of counseling, Pam realized that her identity as a woman was replaced by ideas of what others thought she should act and look like.

Unfortunately, Pam's problem is not an isolated case. She said, "There   3
were women who were always making themselves vomit so that they would not gain any weight. Also, there were women in tears during many of our rehearsals because they didn't look exactly like the pageant orga-nizers wanted." According to Ruby Koppes, a retired beauty pageant organizer whom I interviewed, "Diseases such as anorexia and bulimia are very common problems in the beauty pageant ring. Many girls would have to drop out of the contest because they would become ill from erratic dieting methods." The problems that manifest themselves within the beauty pageant circle indicate the extent to which women have been socialized to pursue the elusive ideal of beauty at any cost.

Another reason why beauty pageants are harmful is that they are a   4
subtle form of pornography which portrays women as objects. Although beauty pageants are not usually thought of as pornographic, they have been a major platform for the reduction of women from full human beings into objects. These competitions are such a way of life that we rarely stop to challenge the concept of a woman walking down a plat-form in a bathing suit, parading in front of a group of male judges who look over her legs, her breasts, and her waist, who compare her bodily measurements with those of other contestants, and who make a choice of the "best" female based primarily on these exterior qualities, just as judges at dog or livestock shows do. Beauty contests create a fantasy world where women are meant to be ogled and men are polite voyeurs. Looking at women as objects helps men to "keep women in their place." When women are totally equated with their physical beauty, they won't be taken seriously in any other respect.

Closely related to the pornographic nature of beauty pageants is the   5
harmful way that they exploit women. There are two major areas of exploitation that I would like to address. First, beauty pageants exploit women by stereotyping their sexuality. For a woman to be successful and to win approval, women must have the unbeatable Madonna-Whore combination—they must be sexy but wholesome. Women who pursue the pageant's approval with more than ordinary determination may get caught by our society's limits on how far women can "properly" go in presenting themselves. The case of Vanessa Williams, chosen Miss America for 1984, is a good example. When a photographer for whom she had posed nude sold her pictures to a magazine for men, she was publicly disgraced and forced to give up her title. Vanessa Williams went "too far." To exhibit one's body scantily clothed and to be seductive con-

forms to our society's standards for womanhood, but over-titillating men with nude photos does not.

Finally, beauty pageants exploit women by perpetuating our society's   6
focus on *young* women. Women are continually reminded that our society does not have any roles for older women. Older women in our society are seen as the antithesis of the beauty pageant queen. The White House Conference on Older Women held in 1981 concluded that "popular images that portray older women as inactive, unhealthy, asexual, unattractive, and ineffectual are prevalent." On television, older women continue to be shown fending off old age with Geritol or aspirin, baking cookies for the grandchildren, or retreating into the world of soap operas. Although the population of older women is expanding and diverse, and older women continue to grow and lead interesting lives, negative stereotypes persist. These prevailing stereotypes will continue as long as beauty pageant contestants are the standard of what our society believes women are and should be.

14

Proposal Arguments: "We Should/ Should Not Do X"

CASE 1

A medical school professor wishes to further her research into the effect of alcohol consumption on fetal development in pregnant women. Focusing on the development of fetal blood vessels, she decides to do a study using laboratory rats. She and her research partner, a professor of anatomy, develop a research design to study how the ingestion of alcohol by pregnant rats affects blood vessel development in fetal eye tissue. She and the anatomist devote three months to the planning and writing of a grant proposal to be submitted to the National Science Foundation.

CASE 2

A student dissatisfied with the noise level in a study lounge in a campus dormitory proposes that a soundproofed wall and door be installed between the study lounge and an adjoining TV/relaxation lounge. In preparing the proposal, which she submits to the university housing office, the student interviews dormitory residents about their study habits and researches the cost of the proposed wall by taking measurements and visiting a local hardware store.

CASE 3

A forestry professor weighs the economic advantages of maintaining a healthy lumber industry versus the environmental advantages of protecting the spotted owl and the grandeur of old growth forests. As a partial solution to the problem of competing needs, he proposes the development of a new industry specializing in thinning and pruning forest lands—making usable products with lumber presently considered scrap and at the same time increasing the quality of forests. [*Seattle Times,* August 27, 1990, A9]

Barry Commoner, director of the Center for the Biology of Natural Systems at Queens College, poses the following dilemma: "To what extent should the choice of production technologies be governed—as it is now—by private, generally short-term, profit-maximizing response to market forces, and to what extent by long-term social concerns like environmental quality?" In examining the problem of atmospheric pollutants, he opts for governmental control based on long-term social concerns. Specifically, he proposes that the government shift from trying to "clean up" pollutants to issuing an outright ban on pollutant-causing technologies.*

THE NATURE OF PROPOSAL ARGUMENTS

Although proposal or "should" arguments are the last type we examine, they are among the most common arguments that you will encounter or be called on to write. Their essence is that they call for action. In reading a proposal, the audience is enjoined to make a decision and then to act upon it—to *do* something. Proposal arguments are sometimes called "should" or "ought" arguments because these helping verbs express the obligation to act: "We *should* do X" or "We *ought* to do X."

For instructional purposes, we will distinguish between two kinds of proposal arguments, even though they are closely related and involve the same basic arguing strategies. The first kind we will call "practical proposals," which propose an action to solve some kind of local or immediate problem. A student's proposal to change the billing procedures for scholarship students would be an example of a practical proposal, as would an engineering firm's proposal for the design of a new bridge being planned by a city government. The second kind we will call "policy proposals," in which the writer offers a broad plan of action to solve major social, economic, or political problems affecting the common good. An argument that the United States should adopt a national health insurance plan or that the terms for senators and representatives should be limited to twelve years would be examples of policy proposals.

The primary difference is the narrowness versus breadth of the concern. Practical proposals are narrow, local, and concrete; they focus on the nuts and bolts of getting something done in the here and now. They are often concerned with the exact size of a piece of steel, the precise duties of a new person to be hired, or a close estimate of the cost of paint or computers to be purchased. Policy proposals, on

---

* "Free Markets Can't Control Pollution," *New York Times,* April 15, 1990.

the other hand, are concerned with the broad outline and shape of a course of action, often on a regional, national, or even international issue. What government should do about overcrowding of prisons would be a problem addressed by policy proposals. How to improve the security alarm system for the county jail would be addressed by a practical proposal.

Learning to write both kinds of proposals is valuable. Researching and writing a policy proposal is an excellent way to practice the responsibilities of citizenship. By researching a complex issue, by attempting to weigh the positive and negative consequences of any policy decision, and then by committing yourself to a course of action, you will be doing the kind of thinking necessary for the survival of a democratic society. On the other hand, writing practical proposals may well be among your most important duties on the job. Writing persuasive practical proposals is the lifeblood of engineering companies and construction firms because through such proposals a company wins bids and creates work. In many companies, employees can initiate improvements in company operations through practical proposals, and it is through grant proposals that innovative people gain funding for research or carry on the work of volunteer and nonprofit organizations throughout our society.

THE GENERAL STRUCTURE AND STRATEGY OF PROPOSAL ARGUMENTS

Proposal arguments, whether practical proposals or policy proposals, generally have a three-part structure: (1) description of a problem, (2) proposed solution, and (3) justification for the proposed solution. Luckily, proposal arguments don't require different sorts of argumentative strategies from the ones you have already been using. In the justification section of your proposal argument, you develop because clauses of the kinds you have practiced all along throughout this text.

SPECIAL REQUIREMENTS OF PROPOSAL ARGUMENTS

Although proposal arguments combine elements from other kinds of claims, they differ from other arguments in that they call for action. Calls to action don't entail any strategies that we haven't already considered, but they do entail a unique set of emphases. Let's look briefly at some of the special requirements of proposal arguments.

Adding "Presence" to Your Argument

It's one thing for a person to assent to a value judgment, but it's another thing to act on that judgment. The personal cost of acting may be high for many people in your audience. That means that you have to engage not only your audience's intellect, but their emotions as well. Thus proposal arguments often require more attention to *pathos* than do other kinds of arguments (see pp. 147–57).

In most cases, convincing people to act means that an argument must have "presence" as well as intellectual force. An argument is said to have presence when the reader senses the immediacy of the writer's words. Not only does the reader recognize the truth and consistency of the argument, but he experiences its very life. An argument with presence is one in which the reader can share the writer's point of view—the writer's emotions, the force of the writer's personal engagement with the issue—as well as assent to the writer's conclusions.

How does one achieve presence in an argument? There are a number of ways. For one, you can appeal directly to the readers' emotions through the effective use of details, brief scenes, and compelling examples that show the reader the seriousness of the problem you are addressing or the consequences of not acting on your proposal. Consider the following example of presence from a policy argument favoring euthanasia:

> There are hundreds of thousands of persons today living in continuing, sustained, baffled misery, pain, and anguish; thousands literally imprisoned in nursing homes and hospitals; thousands isolated, alone, family gone, just prolonging miserable day after miserable day.
>
> Mist clouds my eyes as I remember the last days of my own father, begging the doctors to let him go home and die peacefully in the room he so loved, overlooking the trees and gardens that he had created over the years.
>
> "No," they said, "you must stay here where we can watch you." Maybe brutal is not a strong enough word to describe the situation. And so my father was refused his sacred right to die with integrity, quality and with some dignity left intact in the life of a proud and good man.*

In addition to scenes such as this, writers can use figurative language such as metaphor and analogy to make the problem being addressed more vivid or real to the audience, or they can shift from abstract language to descriptions, dialogues, statistics, and illustrative narratives. Here is how one student used personal experience in the problem section of her proposal calling for redesign of the mathematics department's introductory calculus curriculum.

> My own experience in the Calculus 134 and 135 sequence last year showed me that it was not the learning of calculus that was difficult for me. I was able to catch on to the new concepts. The problem for me was in the fast pace. Just as I was assimilating new concepts and feeling the need to reinforce them, the class was on to a new topic before I had full mastery of the old concept. . . . Part of the reason for the fast pace is that calculus is a feeder course for computer science and engineering. If prospective engineering students can't learn the calculus rapidly, they drop out of the program. The high dropout rate benefits the Engi-

---

* From William Edelen, *The Idaho Statesman.*

neering School because they use the math course to weed out an overabundance of engineering applicants. Thus the pace of the calculus course is geared to the needs of the engineering curriculum, not to the needs of someone like me who wants to be a high school mathematics teacher and who believes that my own difficulties with math—combined with my love for it—might make me an excellent math teacher.

Here the writer creates presence through an effective *ethos:* She is not a complainer or whiner but a serious student genuinely interested in learning calculus. She has given presence to the problem by calling attention to it in a new way.

Overcoming the Natural Conservatism of People

Another difficulty faced by a proposal maker is the innate conservatism of all human beings, whatever their political persuasion. One philosopher refers to this conservatism as the law of inertia, the tendency of all things in the universe, including human beings, to remain at rest if possible. The popular adage "If it ain't broke, don't fix it" is one expression of this tendency. Hence, proposers of change face an extraordinary burden of proof. Specifically, they have to prove that something needs fixing, that it can be fixed, and that the cost of fixing it will be outweighed by the benefits of fixing it.

The difficulty of proving that something needs fixing is compounded by the fact that frequently the status quo appears to be working. So sometimes when writing a proposal, you can't argue that what we have is bad, but only that what we could have is better. Often, then a proposal argument will be based not on present evils but on the evils of lost potential. And getting an audience to accept lost potential may be difficult indeed, given the inherently abstract nature of potentiality.

The Difficulty of Predicting Future Consequences

Further, most proposal makers will be forced to predict consequences of a given act. As we've seen in our earlier discussions of causality, it is difficult enough to argue backward from event Y in order to establish that X caused Y. Think how much harder it is to establish that X will, in the future, cause certain things to occur. We all know enough of history to realize that few major decisions have led neatly to their anticipated results. This knowledge indeed accounts for much of our conservatism. All the things that can go wrong in a causal argument can go wrong in a proposal argument as well; the major difference is that in a proposal argument we typically have less evidence for our conjectures.

The Problem of Evaluating Consequences

A final difficulty faced by all proposal arguments concerns the difficulty of evaluating the consequences of the proposal. In government and industry, managers often turn to a tool known as "cost-benefit" analysis to calculate the potential consequences of a given proposal. As much as possible, a cost-benefit analysis tries to reduce all consequences to a single scale for purposes of comparison. Most often, the scale will be money. Although this scale may work well in some circumstances, it can lead to grotesquely inappropriate conclusions in other situations.

Just how does one balance the money saved by cutting Medicare benefits against the suffering of the people denied benefits? How does one translate the beauty of a wilderness area into a dollar amount? On this score, cost-benefit analyses often run into a problem discussed in the previous chapter: the seductiveness of empirical measures. Because something can't be readily measured doesn't mean it can be safely ignored. And finally, what will be a cost for one group will often be a benefit for others. For example, if social security benefits are cut, those on social security will suffer, but current workers who pay for it with taxes will take home a larger paycheck.

These, then, are some of the general difficulties facing someone who sets out to argue in favor of a proposal. Although not insurmountable, they are at least daunting. Given those difficulties, let's now set forth the writing assignment for this chapter and then turn to the question of how one might put together a proposal argument.

■ WRITING ASSIGNMENT FOR CHAPTER 14: OPTIONS FOR PROPOSAL ARGUMENTS

OPTION 1: A PRACTICAL PROPOSAL ADDRESSING A LOCAL PROBLEM Write a practical proposal offering a solution to a local problem. Your proposal should have three main sections: (1) description of the problem, (2) proposed solution, and (3) justification. You may include additional sections or subsections as needed. Longer proposals often include an "abstract" at the beginning of the proposal to provide a summary overview of the whole argument. (Sometimes called the "executive summary," this abstract may be the only portion of the proposal read by high-level managers.) Sometimes proposals are accompanied by a "letter of transmittal"—a one-page business letter that introduces the proposal to its intended audience and provides some needed background about the writer.

Your proposal can be either an "action" proposal, in which you specify exactly the action that needs to be taken to solve the problem, or a "planning proposal," in which you know what the problem is but don't yet know how to solve it. A planning proposal usually calls for the formation of a committee or task force to address the problem, so that your "solution" doesn't specify an actual solution but rather specifies the mission of the committee you want to establish. To make a planning proposal as effective as possible, you are wise to suggest several ideas for possible solutions, that is, several alternative courses of action that you want the committee to examine in more detail and refine. An example of a practical proposal with a planning focus is included at the end of this chapter ("A Proposal to Restructure the Washington State High School Dance and Drill Team Association Competition" by student writer Karen Kartes).

Document design is important in practical proposals, which are aimed at busy people who have to make many decisions under time constraints. Because the writer of a practical proposal usually produces the finished document (practical proposals are seldom submitted to newspapers or magazines for publication), he or she must pay particular attention to the attractive design of the document. An effective design helps establish the writer's *ethos* as a quality-oriented professional and helps make the reading of the proposal as easy as possible. Document design includes effective use of headings and subheadings, attractive typeface and layout, flawless editing, and other features enhancing the visual appearance of the document.*

OPTION 2:   A POLICY PROPOSAL AS A GUEST EDITORIAL   Write a two- to three-page policy proposal suitable for publication as a feature editorial in a college or city newspaper or in some publication associated with a particular group or activity such as a church newsletter or employee bulletin. By "feature editorial" we mean a well-developed argument as opposed to a short "opinion editorial" that simply sets forth an editorial view without development and support. The voice and style of your argument should be aimed at general readers of your chosen publication. Your editorial should have the following features:

1. the identification of a problem (Persuade your audience that this is a genuine problem that needs solving; give it presence.)
2. a proposal for action that will help alleviate the problem
3. a justification of your solution (the reasons that your audience should accept your proposal and act on it)

OPTION 3:   A RESEARCHED ARGUMENT PROPOSING PUBLIC POLICY   Write an eight- to twelve-page proposal argument as a formal research paper, using research data for support. (See Chapters 16 and 17 for advice on writing a researched argument.) Your argument should include all the features of the

---

* It is usually a mistake, however, to use all the bells and whistles available on recent hardware and software for desktop publishing. Different styles and sizes of fonts, fancy title pages, and extraneous visuals such as pointing fingers, daggers, stars, and so forth, make you look like a computer doodler rather than a serious writer. Tasteful, conservative use of boldface and underlining is usually the best approach. Even if you have available only a typewriter, you can create several levels of attractive headings by using different combinations of indentation, underlining, and capital letters.

shorter argument above (Option 2) and also a summary and refutation of opposing views (in the form of alternative proposals and/or differing cost-benefit analyses of your proposal). An example of a researched policy proposal is student writer Stephen Bean's "What Should Be Done about the Mentally Ill Homeless?" on pages 339–51.

DEVELOPING A PROPOSAL ARGUMENT

Writers of proposal arguments must focus in turn on three main phases or stages of the argument: showing that a problem exists, explaining the proposed solution, and offering a justification.

Convincing Your Readers That a Problem Exists

There is one argumentative strategy generic to all proposal arguments: awakening in the reader a sense of a problem. Typically, the development of a problem occurs in one of two places in a proposal argument—either in the introduction prior to the presentation of the arguer's proposal claim or in the body of the paper as the first main reason justifying the proposal claim. In the second instance the writer's first because clause has the following structure: "We should do X *because a problem exists (and X will solve it)*."

At this stage of your argument, it's important to give your problem presence. You must get people to see how the problem affects people, perhaps through examples of suffering or other loss or through persuasive statistics and so forth. Your goal is to awaken your readers to the existence of a problem, a problem they may well not have recognized before.

Besides giving presence to the problem, a writer must also gain the readers' intellectual assent to the depth, range, and potential seriousness of the problem. Suppose, for illustration, that you wanted to propose a special tax to increase funding for higher education in your state. In trying to convince taxpayers in your state that a problem exists, what obstacles might you face? First of all, many taxpayers never went to college and feel that they get along just fine without it. They tend to worry more about the quality of roads, social services, elementary and secondary schools, police and fire protection, and so forth. They are not too convinced that they need to worry about professors' salaries or better equipped research labs. Thus, it's not enough to talk about the importance of education in general or to cite figures showing how paltry your state's funding of higher education is.

To convince your audience of the need for your proposal, you'll have to describe the consequences of low funding levels in terms they can relate to. You'll have to show them that potential benefits to the state are lost because of inadequate funding. Perhaps you can show the cost in terms of inadequately skilled graduates, disgruntled teachers, high turnover, brain drain to other states, inadequate educational services to farmers and businesspeople, lost productivity, and so forth. Or perhaps you can show your audience examples of benefits realized from better college funding in other states. Such examples give life to the abstract notion of lost potential.

All of this is not to say that you can't or shouldn't argue that higher education is inherently good. But until your reader can see low funding levels as "problematic" rather than "simply the way things are," your proposal stands little chance of being enacted.

Showing the Specifics of Your Proposal

Having decided that there is a problem to be solved, you should lay out your thesis, which is a proposal for solving the problem. Your goal now is to stress the feasibility of your solution, including costs. The art of proposal making is the art of the possible. To be sure, not all proposals require elaborate descriptions of the implementation process. If you are proposing, for example, that a local PTA chapter should buy new tumbling mats for the junior high gym classes, the procedures for buying the mats will probably be irrelevant. But in many arguments the specifics of your proposal—the actual step-by-step methods of implementing it—may be instrumental in winning your audience's support.

You will also need to show how your proposal will solve the problem either partially or wholly. Sometimes you may first need to convince your reader that the problem is solvable, not something intractably rooted in "the way things are," such as earthquakes or jealousy. In other words, expect that some members of your audience will be skeptical about the ability of any proposal to solve the problem you are addressing. You may well need, therefore, to "listen" to this point of view in your refutation section and to argue that your problem is at least partially solvable.

In order to persuade your audience that your proposal can work, you can follow any one of several approaches. A typical approach is to lay out a causal argument showing how one consequence will lead to another until your solution is effected. Another approach is to turn to resemblance arguments, either analogy or precedent. You try to show how similar proposals have been successful elsewhere. Or, if similar things have failed in the past, you try to show how the present situation is different.

The Justification: Convincing Your Reader That Your Proposal Should be Enacted

This phase of a proposal argument will need extensive development in some arguments and minimal development in others, again depending on your particular problem and the rhetorical context of your proposal. If your audience already acknowledges the seriousness of the problem you are addressing and has simply been waiting for the right solution to come along, then your argument will be successful so long as you can convince your audience that your solution will work and that it won't cost too much. Such arguments depend on the clarity of your proposal and the feasibility of its being implemented.

But what if the costs are high? Or what if your audience doesn't think that the problem you are addressing is particularly serious? In such cases you have to develop your main reasons for believing that X should be done. A good strategy is to use the three-step process described in Chapter 9 when you examined arguments from principle, from consequence, and from resemblance. Here are some examples of how the three-step strategy can be used for proposal arguments.

PROPOSAL CLAIM: Our university should abolish fraternities and sororities.

PRINCIPLE: because they are elitist (or "a thing of the past" or "racist" or "sexist" or whatever)

CONSEQUENCE: because eliminating the Greek system will improve our school's academics (or "fill our dormitories," "allow us to experiment with new living arrangements," "replace rush with a better freshman orientation," and so forth)

RESEMBLANCE: because other universities that have eliminated the Greek system have reported good results

PROPOSAL CLAIM: We should eliminate mandatory busing of children to achieve racial equality.

PRINCIPLE: because it is unjust (or "ineffective," "a misuse of judicial authority," "a violation of individual rights," and so forth)

CONSEQUENCE: because it puts too many psychological burdens on kids (or "costs too much," "destroys neighborhood schools," "makes it difficult to have parental involvement in the schools," "splits up siblings," "causes kids to spend too much time on buses," and so forth)

RESEMBLANCE: because busing schoolchildren to solve a social problem such as racism makes about as much sense as sending alcoholics' kids through a detox center to cure their parents

PROPOSAL CLAIM: Our church should start an active ministry to AIDS patients.

PRINCIPLE: because doing so would be an act of love (or "justice" or "an example of Christian courage," and so forth)

CONSEQUENCE: because doing so will help increase community understanding of the disease and also reduce fear

RESEMBLANCE: because Jesus ministered to the lepers and in our society AIDS victims have become the outcasts that lepers were in Jesus' society

Each of these arguments attempts to appeal to the value system of the audience. Each tries to show how the proposed action is within the class of things that the audience already values, will lead to consequences desired by the audience, or is similar to something the audience already values (or will alleviate something the audience disvalues).

Touching the Right Pressure Points

Having defined and weighed the problem, having worked out a feasible solution, and having motivated your audience to act on your proposal, you may well wish to take your argument a step further. You may thus have to determine who has the power to act on your proposal and apply arguments directly to that person's or agency's immediate interests. More than any other form of argument, a proposal argument needs finally to be addressed to those with the power to act on the proposal. You need to know to whom or to what your power source is beholden or responsive and what values your power source holds that can be appealed to. You're looking, in short, for pressure points.

While attempting to get a university to improve wheelchair access to the student union building, one student with multiple sclerosis discovered that the university had recently paid $100,000 to put oak trim in a new faculty office building. She knew officials were a bit embarrassed by that figure, and it became an effective pressure point for her essay. "The university can afford to pay $100,000 for oak trim for faculty, but can't spend one quarter of that amount helping its disabled students get full access to the student union building." This hard-to-justify discrepancy put considerable pressure on the administration to find money for more wheelchair ramps. The moral here is that it makes good sense to tie one's proposal as much as possible to the interests of those in power.

USING THE "STOCK ISSUES" STRATEGY TO DEVELOP A PROPOSAL ARGUMENT

An effective way to generate ideas for a proposal argument is to ask yourself a series of questions based on the "stock issues" strategy. Suppose, for example, you wanted to develop the following argument: "In order to solve the problem of students who won't take risks with their writing, the faculty at Weasel College should adopt a pass/fail method of grading in all writing courses." The stock issues strategy invites the writer to consider "stock" ways (that is, common, usual, frequently repeated ways) that such arguments can be conducted.

Stock issue 1:   *Is there really a problem here that needs to be solved?* Is it really true that a large number of student writers won't take risks in their writing? Is this problem more serious than other writing problems such as undeveloped ideas, lack of organization, poor sentence structure, and so forth? This stock issue invites the writer to convince her audience that a true problem exists. Conversely, an opponent to the proposal might argue that a true problem does not exist.

Stock issue 2: *Will the proposed solution really solve this problem?* Is it true that a pass/fail grading system will cause students to take more risks with their writing? Will more interesting, surprising, and creative essays result from pass/fail grading? Or will students simply put less effort into their writing? This stock issue prompts a supporter to demonstrate that the proposal will solve the problem; in contrast, it prompts the opponent to show that the proposal won't work.

Stock issue 3: *Can the problem be solved more simply without disturbing the status quo?* An opponent of the proposal might agree that a problem exists and that the proposed solution might solve it. However, the opponent might say, "Are there not less radical ways to solve this problem? If we want more creative and risk-taking student essays, can't we just change our grading criteria so that we reward risky papers and penalize conventional ones?" This stock issue prompts supporters to show that *only* the proposed solution will solve the problem and that no minor tinkering with the status quo will be adequate. Conversely, opponents will argue that the problem can be solved without acting on the proposal.

Stock issue 4: *Is the proposed solution really practical? Does it stand a chance of actually being enacted?* Here an opponent to the proposal might agree that the proposal would work but that it involves pie-in-the-sky idealism. Nobody will vote to change the existing system so radically; therefore, it is a waste of our time to debate it. Following this prompt, supporters would have to argue that pass/fail grading is workable and that enough faculty are disposed to it that the proposal is worth debating. Opponents might argue that the faculty at Weasel College are so traditional that pass/fail has utterly no chance of being accepted, despite its merits.

Stock issue 5: *What will be the unforeseen positive and negative consequences of the proposal?* Suppose we do adopt a pass/fail system. What positive or negative consequences might occur that are different from what we at first predicted? Using this prompt, an opponent might argue that pass/fail grading will reduce the effort put forth by students and that the long-range effect will be writing of even lower quality than we have now. Supporters would try to find positive consequences—perhaps a new love of writing for its own sake rather than the sake of a grade.

USING THE TOULMIN SCHEMA TO DEVELOP A PROPOSAL ARGUMENT

The Toulmin schema is also a helpful way to think through a proposal argument. Consider the following proposal argument laid out according to Toulmin's schema and later modified as a result of the Toulmin analysis:

INITIAL ENTHYMEME:	All college students should be required to take an ethics course because most students are not effective ethical thinkers and because an ethics course would help solve this problem.
CLAIM:	All college students should be required to take an ethics course.
STATED REASONS:	a. Students are not effective thinkers about ethical issues; b. An ethics course will help solve this problem.
GROUNDS:	a. evidence that college students lack the ability to think effectively about ethical issues; b. evidence that ethics courses help students think more effectively about ethical issues (e.g., pre- and post-course tests asking students to think coherently about ethical issues; follow-up studies of students who take ethics courses and a control group of students who don't take ethics to see if there are significant differences in ethical behavior)
WARRANT FOR BOTH A AND B:	The ability to think effectively about ethical issues is such an important skill that a proposal to develop that skill should be enacted.
BACKING:	evidence of the benefits of ethical thinking and the costs of ineffective ethical thinking
CONDITIONS OF REBUTTAL:	examples of people who've studied ethics and have been incapable of effective ethical thinking, of effective ethical thinkers who've never had a course in college ethics (perhaps it is the home or the church that teaches ethical thinking, not a college course), or of societies in which effective ethical thinking has not led to the promised benefits
QUALIFIERS:	a statement to the effect that college ethics courses will make it "more likely" that students can think effectively about ethical issues and that more effective ethical thinking will "probably" be beneficial to society

The stated reasons in support of the claim are evaluation and causal claims. The first stated reason—college students are not effective ethical thinkers—is an evaluative claim that requires the writer to create criteria for effective ethical thinking and to show that today's students don't meet the criteria. The second claim—that a course in ethics will help solve this problem—is a causal one and forces the writer to provide evidence that the course will work. The conditions for rebuttal highlight potential weaknesses in the stated reasons and grounds because they point out so many possible exceptions—people who think ethically without taking an ethics course, people who take an ethics course and still don't think ethically, and so forth.

The possibility that one really learns ethics in the home or church seems particularly troubling to the argument.

The main warrant for this proposal—that effective ethical thinking is good and that methods for developing it should therefore be enacted—also presents problems. Although your audience might grant that effective ethical thinking is a good thing, plenty of opponents will not grant that an ethics course should be required. Requiring students to take ethics courses means forcing them to forgo other courses, many of which can lay claim to being inherently good as well. Moreover, students uninterested in ethics and professors who don't teach ethics can't be expected to accept the proposal readily because they are the ones who will bear most of the "costs" of implementing it. So the writer has a considerable burden of proof in getting his readers to accept the warrant.

Seeing the argument displayed this way, the writer decided that more support was needed in two places: First, the writer had to find more evidence that ethics courses really work. Second, the writer had to provide a more convincing argument that the benefits of an ethics course were significant enough to justify a required course for all students. The writer decided to do more research into contemporary problems caused by poor ethical thinking in order to bolster his argument that such a course would bring long-range benefits to society. To strengthen his case further, he decided to argue also that ethics courses would in general make for more thoughtful and questioning students. Finally, he turned to a resemblance argument by citing precedents at many liberal arts colleges around the nation where required courses in ethics have been enacted.

☐ FOR CLASS DISCUSSION

The following collaborative task takes approximately two class days to complete. The exercise takes you through the process of creating a proposal argument.

1. In small groups, identify and list several major problems facing students in your college or university.
2. Decide among yourselves which are the most important of these problems and rank them in order of importance.
3. Take your group's number one problem and explore answers to the following questions. Group recorders should be prepared to present your group's answers to the class as a whole:
   a. Why is the problem a problem?
   b. For whom is the problem a problem?
   c. How will these people suffer if the problem is not solved? (Give specific examples.)
   d. Who has the power to solve the problem?

  e. Why hasn't the problem been solved up to this point?

  f. How can the problem be solved? (That is, create a proposal.)

  g. What are the probable benefits of acting on your proposal?

  h. What costs are associated with your proposal?

  i. Who will bear those costs?

  j. Why should this proposal be enacted?

  k. Why is it better than alternative proposals?

4. As a group, draft an outline for a proposal argument in which you:

  a. describe the problem and its significance,

  b. propose your solution to the problem, and

  c. justify your proposal by showing how the benefits of adopting that proposal outweigh the costs.

5. Recorders for each group should write their group's outline on the board and be prepared to explain it to the class.

■ WRITING THE PROPOSAL ARGUMENT

Starting Points: Finding a Proposal Issue

Since "should" or "ought" issues are among the most common sources of arguments, you may already have good ideas for proposal issues. To think of topics for practical proposals, try making an idea-map of local problems you would like to see solved. For initial spokes, try trigger words such as the following: problems at my university (dorms, parking, registration system, grading system, campus appearance, clubs, curriculum, intramural program, football team); problems in my city or town (dangerous intersections, ugly areas, inadequate lighting, a poorly designed store, a shopping center that needs a specific improvement); problems at my place of work (office design, flow of customer traffic, merchandise display, company policies, customer relations); or problems related to your hobbies, recreational time, life as a consumer, life as a homeowner, and so forth. If you can offer a solution to the problem you identify, consider an action proposal. If you can't solve the problem but believe it is worth serious attention, consider a planning proposal.

To find a topic for policy proposals, stay in touch with the news, which will keep you aware of current debates on regional and national issues. Skimming recent issues of *Time* or *Newsweek*, thumbing through a recent *Wall Street Journal*, or looking at the table of contents in public policy magazines such as *The Atlantic Monthly*, *The New Republic*, *National Review*, and others will also give you excellent leads.

You can also try freewriting in response to trigger questions such as these:

- I would really like to solve the problem of . . .
- I believe that X should . . . [substitute for X words such as *my teachers, the president, the school administration, Congress, my boss,* and so forth]

Exploration Stage

Once you have decided on a proposal issue, we recommend you explore it by trying one or more of the following activities:

Explore ideas by using the "stock issues" strategy. Much of what we say about proposal arguments in this chapter has been influenced by the stock issues questions: (1) Is there really a problem here that has to be solved? (2) Will the proposed solution really solve this problem? (3) Can the problem be solved in a simpler way without disturbing the status quo? (4) Is the proposed solution practical enough that it really stands a chance of being acted upon? (5) What will be the positive and negative consequences of the proposal?

Explore your problem by freewriting answers to the eleven questions (3a.–k.) in the preceding For Class Discussion exercise. These questions cover the same territory as the stock issues strategy, but the arrangement and number of questions might stimulate additional thought.

Explore ideas for the justification section of your proposal by using the three-step strategy introduced in Chapter 9. Briefly, this strategy invites you to justify your proposal to do X by arguing (1) that doing X is the right thing to do in principle, (2) that doing X will lead to various good consequences, and (3) that doing X (or something similar) has been done with good results elsewhere or that doing X is like doing Y, which we agree is good. This strategy is particularly powerful for proposal arguments because it focuses on finding audience-based reasons.

Explore ideas for your argument by completing the eight exploratory tasks in Chapter 3 (pp. 79–81).

Writing the Discovery Draft: Some Ways to Organize a Proposal Argument

When you write your discovery draft, you may find it helpful to have at hand some plans for typical ways of organizing a proposal argument. What follows are two common methods of organization. Option 1 is the plan most typical for practical proposals. Either Option 1 or Option 2 is an effective plan for a policy proposal.

OPTION 1
- presentation of a problem that needs solving:

    description of problem (give problem presence)

background, including previous attempts to solve problem

argumen⸻ e problem is solvable (optional)

- presentatic er's proposal:

    succinct t of the proposed solution serves as thesis statement

    explain f proposed solution.

- summary al of opposing views (In practical proposals, this section is often a summary and rejection of alternative ways of solving the problem.)

- justification persuading reader that proposal should be enacted:

    Reason 1 presented and developed

    Reason 2 presented and developed

    and so forth

- conclusion that exhorts audience to act (Give presence to final sentences.)

OPTION 2

- presentation of issue, including background
- presentation of writer's proposal
- justification

    Reason 1:   Show that proposal addresses a serious problem.

    Reason 2:   Show that proposal will solve problem.

    Reason 3:   Give additional reasons for enacting proposal.

- summary and refutation of opposing views
- conclusion that exhorts audience to act

Revision Stage

Once you have written a discovery draft and have begun to clarify your argument for yourself, you are ready to begin making your argument clear and persuasive for your readers. Once again, exploring your argument using the Toulmin schema should prove useful. Pay particular attention to the ways a skeptical audience might rebut your argument.

CONDITIONS FOR REBUTTAL: TESTING YOUR PROPOSAL ARGUMENT

As we've suggested throughout the foregoing discussion, proposal arguments are vulnerable on many grounds—the innate conservatism of most people, the difficulty of clearly anticipating all the consequences of the proposal, and so forth. What questions, then, can one put specifically to proposal arguments to help us anticipate these vulnerabilities?

Will My Audience Deny That My Problem Is Really a Problem?

The first question to ask of your proposal is "What's so wrong with the status quo that change is necessary?" The second question is "Who loses if the status quo is changed?" Be certain not to overlook this second question. Most proposal makers can demonstrate that some sort of problem exists, but often it is a problem only for certain groups of people. Solving the problem will thus prove a benefit to some people but a cost to others. If your audience examines the problem from the perspective of the potential losers rather than the winners, they can often raise doubts about your proposal.

For example, one state recently held an initiative on a proposed "bottle bill" that would fight litter by permitting the sale of soda and beer only in returnable bottles. Sales outlets would be required to charge a substantial deposit on the bottles in order to encourage people to return them. Proponents of the proposal emphasized citizens as "winners" sharing in the new cleanliness of a landscape no longer littered with cans. In order to refute this argument, opponents showed consumers as "losers" burdened with the high cost of deposits and the hassle of collecting and returning bottles to grocery stores.

Will My Audience Doubt the Effectiveness of My Solution?

Assuming that you've satisfied yourself that a significant problem exists for a significant number of people, a number of questions remain to be asked about the quality of the proposed solution to solve the problem. First, "Does the problem exist for the reasons cited, or might there be alternative explanations?" Here we return to the familiar ground of causal arguments. A proposal supposedly strikes at the cause of a problem. But perhaps striking at that "cause" won't solve the problem. Perhaps you've mistaken a symptom for a cause, or confused two commonly associated but essentially unlinked phenomena for a cause–effect relationship. For example, will paying teachers higher salaries improve the quality of teaching or merely attract greedier rather than brighter people? Maybe more good teachers would be attracted and retained if they were given some other benefit (fewer students? smaller classes? more sabbaticals? more autonomy? more prestige?).

Another way to test your solution is to list all the uncertainties involved. This might be referred to as the "The Devil you know is better than the Devil you don't know" strategy. Remind yourself of all the unanticipated consequences of past changes. Who, for example, would have thought back in the days when aerosol shaving cans were being developed that they might lead to diminished ozone layers, which might lead to more ultraviolet rays getting through the atmosphere from the sun, which would lead to higher incidences of skin cancer? The history of technology is full of such cautionary tales that can be invoked to remind you of the uncertain course that progress can sometimes take.

Will My Audience Think My Proposal Costs Too Much?

The most commonly asked question of any proposal is simply, "Do the benefits of enacting the proposal outweigh the costs?" As we saw above, you can't foresee all the consequences of any proposal. It's easy, before the fact, to exaggerate both the costs and the benefits of a proposal. So, in asking how much your proposal will cost, we urge you to make an honest estimate. Will your audience discover costs you hadn't anticipated—extra financial costs or unexpected psychological or environmental or aesthetic costs? As much as you can, anticipate these objections.

Will My Audience Suggest Counterproposals?

Related to all that's been said so far is the counterproposal. Can you imagine an appealing alternative to both the status quo and the proposal that you're making? The more clearly your proposal shows that a significant problem exists, the more important it is that you be able to identify possible counterproposals. Any potential critic of a proposal to remedy an acknowledged problem will either have to make such a counterproposal or have to argue that the problem is simply in the nature of things. So, given the likelihood that you'll be faced with a counterproposal, it only makes sense to anticipate it and to work out a refutation of it before you have it thrown at you. And who knows, you may end up liking the counterproposal better and changing your mind about what to propose!

□ FOR CLASS DISCUSSION

The following proposal arguments—both by student writers—illustrate the range of proposal writing. The first argument is a practical proposal, the second a policy proposal. Both arguments are reproduced in typewriter format to illustrate conventional typescript form for formal papers. The first argument, as a practical proposal, uses heading and subheadings. When sent to the intended audience, it is accompanied by a single-spaced letter of transmittal following the conventional format of a business letter. The second argument is a formal research paper using the documentation format of the Modern Language Association (MLA). A full explanation of this format occurs in Chapter 17.* Working in groups, identify the argumentation

---

* Stephen Bean's essay attempts to refute a proposal argument by Charles Krauthammer, "How to Save the Homeless Mental Ill," which is reprinted in Chapter 10 (pages 226–33). Bean's method of refutation is to propose a counterproposal. Both Bean's and Krauthammer's arguments are examples of proposals.

strategies used by each writer. Specifically, be able to answer the following questions:

1. Does the writer demonstrate that a problem exists? What strategies does the writer use to demonstrate the problem?

2. Does the writer persuade you that the proposed solution will solve the problem? What strategies does the writer use to try to persuade you that the solution will work?

3. Does the writer attempt to listen to opposing views? How successful is the writer in refuting those views? What strategies does the writer use?

4. Does the writer argue effectively that the solution should be enacted? Does the writer use arguments from principle? from consequence? from resemblance?

5. How would you try to refute each writer's argument?

January 15, 1992

Karen Kartes
12457 Smith Ave.
Seattle, WA 98146

Joanna Benson
WSDDTA President
Evergreen High School
Seattle, WA 98146

Dear Ms. Benson:

Please find enclosed a proposal for improving the annual Washington state dance and drill team competitions. As an active member of the dance and drill community for the past six years—including experience as a team member, team captain, and now co-advisor—I believe that I have the background to appreciate the complex task that WSDDTA undertakes each year in sponsoring the annual competition. My suggestions for improving the structure of the annual competition might help WSDDTA eliminate some persistent problems felt by participants, spectators, and judges.

Basically, I believe that the competition would be more enjoyable if the program were shortened and focused. The enclosed proposal suggests two ways of doing so: through qualifying regional competitions or through separate competitions for the two genres of dance and drill.

The ultimate goal of the WSDDTA's annual competition is to create a rewarding experience for participants and a high level of entertainment for spectators by bringing out the best possible performance from the competing teams. I have found great joy in performing and choreographing, and I hope that through this proposal I can perhaps contribute to enhancing the public image of dance and drill throughout the state. Thank you very much for considering my ideas.

Sincerely,

Karen Kartes
Kennedy Drill Co-Advisor

A PROPOSAL TO RESTRUCTURE THE

WASHINGTON STATE HIGH SCHOOL

DANCE AND DRILL TEAM ASSOCIATION COMPETITION

Submitted to the Washington State
Dance and Drill Team Association

Karen Kartes
Drill Co-Advisor
Kennedy High School

Summary

The present structure of the annual dance and drill team competition sponsored by the Washington State Dance and Drill Team Association (WSDDTA) creates animosity among teams, confusion for viewers, and stress for judges. Additionally, the number of participants makes the competition too lengthy and too taxing for all involved.

The WSDDTA should create a task force to solve the problem of an unwieldy state competition. This proposal suggests two possible solutions to be considered by the task force: (1) regional qualifying competitions preceding the state competition or (2) separate competitions for the two genres of dance and drill.

Background on the WSDDTA Competition

The WSDDTA is a group of elected representatives selected from the advisors of statewide high school dance and drill teams. As a coordinating group, the WSDDTA's primary function is to work with a host high school in Washington state to prepare for the annual state competition, a Friday to Sunday weekend event open to any high school dance or drill team wishing to attend. Each participating team performs for a huge audience of spectators and is critiqued and rated by judges with many years' experience in dance and drill.

Problems with the Current Conference Structure

Several factors in the current structure cause the event to be unfocused, lengthy, tiresome, and demoralizing for weaker teams.

1. The talent level among the 60+ participating teams is too disparate. Some teams have much more skill and experience than others. It does not seem fair for more technically sophisticated teams to perform beside simpler teams at an event which is supposed to be the presentation of the brightest and best work being done in the dance and

1

drill world. A thirty-six member team from a large suburban high school with two faculty advisors and a professional choreographer will put to shame an eight-member team from a tiny rural school that might not even have a full-time advisor. Competing with these "incredible" teams often creates feelings of hopelessness and embarrassment among the weaker teams. Rather than improve from year to year as a result of being intermingled with superior teams (the hope of the WSDDTA), these weaker teams lose motivation.

2. <u>The present competition doesn't distinguish adequately between the genres of dance and drill</u>. Strict military-style drill teams are judged on the same basis as jazzy, dance-oriented novelty squads. Normally, drill teams use sharp movements and employ marching technique, whereas dance squads incorporate complex footwork and flowing, interpretive movements. Although the WSDDTA is proud of this variety, it is as unfair as pitting figure skaters against speed skaters. The WSDDTA judging scale is far too broad if it can be applied to both of these vastly different types of teams. As the judging now stands, teams upset with their final rating blame their scores on judges who "love dance and hate drill" or vice versa. Each year teams don't know whether to focus on drill or on dance in order to improve their ratings at the annual competition. The result is a lessening of overall quality, since teams embark on a neverending crusade to find the perfect style "to please the judges" rather than honing to perfection a style appropriate for their team.

3. <u>The competition is too big an event for one high school to host</u>. Approximately five thousand people pouring into one school is taxing on the organizers and creates an enormous strain on the physical facilities of the school. Organizers report exhaustion from trying to handle the logistics of such a large competition. The spectators, jammed into the seating area of a standard high school gymnasium, complain of

heat, of inadequate drinking fountains and restrooms, of the impossibility of locating a performer for congratulations or a message, and even of claustrophobia.

4. The conference is too long and too emotionally and physically taxing on participants, spectators, and judges. As a spectator, team member, and team advisor, I have witnessed first-hand the stress and fatigue of the conference. Every year complaints flow from spectators and participants about the excessive length of the conference, the hours of sitting, and the tedious waiting—problems compounded by uncomfortable physical conditions in an overcrowded gymnasium. The length is hardest on the performers, who are emotionally and physically drained from months of practicing before the competition begins and who are nervous and anxious throughout the whole weekend.

Proposal

The WSDDTA should select a task force which would decide how to best limit the current scope and length of the competition. What follows are two possible ways in which the competition could be improved. If the scope of the conference is narrowed in either of the following ways, the length of the conference would naturally diminish.

One possible solution: Establishing regional qualifying competitions. Having regional competitions in order to qualify for the state conference would ensure a shorter program involving only top teams. About fifteen teams would attend each regional competition. All teams would perform and be judged, but only three or four would continue on to compete at the state level.

A second possible solution: Hold separate competitions for dance and drill. This alternative would call for two separate state conferences, one for dance squads and one for drill teams. This alternative would require the WSDDTA to separate into two distinct associations. One

3

group would organize a competition for dance squads, the other for drill teams.

Other than separation by genre, the organization of state competitions would be similar to the present structure, except that the size of the competition would be cut in half and the judging system would focus on each particular genre.

Justification

For a number of reasons, limiting the scope of the current state conference would promote quality performances and would increase interest in the sport of dance and drill.

First, with either proposed solution implemented, state judges would be forced to tighten and clarify their criteria for excellence. Their comments would be more respected by teams because criticisms would not be so vague, general, and ambiguous—a problem caused currently by the mixing of genres and by the wide difference in talent levels.

Second, either solution would improve the quality of performances. With regional competitions, teams would strive for higher standards; they would know they had to achieve a certain status to make it to state, just as other sports teams do. At the state level, the head-to-head competition of the best teams would stimulate stronger performances without dilution from weaker teams. With competitions divided by genres, performances would improve because there would no longer be confusion about criteria for excellence.

Third, when teams work harder to achieve a higher standard of excellence, more people will want to stay on the team and more will want to join. Teams' performances at their home schools will boost school spirit and team morale and attract talented new members. Old members will be rewarded with fond memories of success at state and

4

will want to improve further, and new members will yearn to achieve that satisfaction.

Finally, as teams improve and state conferences become more comfortable and enjoyable, more people will take interest in the sport of dance and drill. The great quality and entertainment value of an organized, fair, focused competition will bring about the respect, recognition, and interest that dance and drill activities deserve. Providing the best possible entertainment for audiences is a guaranteed lifeline for the continuation of these activities.

Conclusion

By limiting the scope of the statewide competition, the WSDDTA can simultaneously increase the enjoyment of participants and spectators at competitions while also improving the quality of teams throughout the state and enhancing the public image of dance and drill.

Stephen Bean

Professor Arness

English 110

June 1, 1993

What Should Be Done about the Mentally Ill Homeless?

Winter paints Seattle's streets gray with misting rain that drops lightly but steadily into pools. Walking to work through one of Seattle's oldest districts, Pioneer Square, I see an incongruous mixture of people: both successful business-types and a large population of homeless. Some walk to offices or lunches grasping cups of fresh ground coffee; others slowly push wobbling carts containing their earthly possessions wrapped carefully in black plastic. These scenes of homelessness have become common throughout America's urban centers—so common, perhaps, that despite our feelings of guilt and pity, we accept the presence of the homeless as permanent. The empty-stomach feeling of confronting a ragged panhandler has become an often accepted fact of living in the city. What can we do besides giving a few cents spare change?

Recently, a growing number of commentators have been focusing on the mentally ill homeless. In response to the violent murder of an elderly person by a homeless mentally ill man, New York City recently increased its efforts to locate and hospitalize dangerous homeless mentally ill individuals. New York's plan will include aggressive outreach—actively going out into the streets and shelters to locate mentally ill individuals and then involuntarily hospitalizing those deemed dangerous either to others or themselves (Dugger, "Danger" B1). Although the New York Civil Liberties Union has objected to this action on the grounds that involuntary hospitalization may violate the rights of the mentally ill, many applaud the city's action as a first step in dealing with a problem which the nation has grossly ignored. One highly influential commentator, Charles Krauthammer, has recently called for

Bean 2

widescale involuntary reinstitutionalization of the mentally ill home-less—a seemingly persuasive proposal until one begins to do research on the mentally ill homeless. Adopting Krauthammer's proposal would be a dangerous and wrong-headed policy for America. Rather, research shows that community-based care in which psychiatrists and social workers provide coordinated services in the community itself is a more effective solution to the problems of the mentally ill homeless than widescale institutionalization.

In his article "How to Save the Homeless Mentally Ill," Charles Krauthammer argues that the federal government should assist the states in rebuilding a national system of asylums. He proposes that the criteria for involuntary institutionalization be broadened: The state should be permitted to institutionalize mentally ill persons involuntarily not only if they are deemed dangerous to others or themselves (the current criterion for institutionalization) but also if they are "degraded" or made helpless by their illness. He points to the large number of patients released from state institutions in the 60s and 70s who, finding no support in communities, ended up on the streets. Arguing that the mentally ill need the stability and supervision that only an institution can provide, Krauthammer proposes substantial increases in federal taxes to fund rebuilding of asylums. He argues that the mentally ill need unique solutions because of their unique problems; their homelessness, he claims, stems from mental illness not poverty. Finally, Krauthammer rebuts the argument that involuntary hospitalization violates civil liberties. He argues that "liberty" has no meaning to someone suffering from severe psychosis. To let someone suffer the pains of mental illness and the pains of the street when they could be treated and recover is a cruel right indeed. He points to the project HELP program where less than a fifth of those involuntarily hospitalized protested their commitment; most

Bean 3

are glad, he claims, for a warm bed, nutritious food, and a safe environment.

Krauthammer's argument, while persuasive on first reading, is based on four seriously flawed assumptions. His first assumption is the widely accepted notion that deinstitutionalization of state mental hospitals in the 1960s and 70s is a primary cause of the current homelessness problem in America. Krauthammer talks about the hundreds of thousands released from the hospitals who have become "an army of grate-dwellers" (24). However, recent research has shown that the relationship of deinstitutionalization to homelessness is vastly overstated. Ethnologist Kim Hopper argues that while deinstitutionalization has partly contributed to increased numbers of mentally ill homeless its influence is far smaller than popularly believed. She argues that the data many used to support this claim were methodologically flawed and that researchers who found symptoms of mental illness in homeless people didn't try to ascertain whether these symptoms were the cause or effect of living on the street. Finally, she points out that a lag time of five years existed between the major release of state hospital patients and the rise of mentally ill individuals in shelters. This time lag suggests that other social and economic factors might have come into play to account for the rise of homelessness (Hopper 159-60). Carl Cohen and Kenneth Thompson also point to this time lag as evidence to reject deinstitutionalization as the major cause of mentally ill homelessness (817). Jonathan Kozol argues that patients released from state hospitals in the late sixties and early seventies didn't go directly to the streets but went to single-room occupancy housing, such as cheap hotels or boarding houses. Many of these ex-patients became homeless, he argues, when almost half of single-room occupancy housing was replaced by more expensive housing between 1970 and 1980 (Kozol 18). The effects of this housing shortage might account for the lag time that Hopper and Cohen and Thompson cite.

Krauthammer's focus on mental illness as a cause of much of the homelessness problem leads to another of the implicit assumptions in his argument: that the mentally ill comprise a large percentage of the homeless population. Krauthammer avoids mentioning specific numbers until the end of his article when he writes:

> The argument over how many of the homeless are mentally ill is endless. The estimates, which range from one-quarter to three-quarters, vary with method, definition, and ideology. But so what if even the lowest estimates are right? Even if treating the mentally ill does not end homelessness, how can that possibly justify not treating the tens, perhaps hundreds of thousands who would benefit from a partial solution? (25)

This paragraph is rhetorically shrewd. It downplays the numbers issue and takes the high moral road. But by citing estimates between one-quarter and three-quarters, Krauthammer effectively suggests that a neutral estimate might place the number around fifty percent—a high estimate reinforced by his leap from "tens" to "perhaps hundreds of thousands" in the last sentence.

Close examination of the research, however, reveals that the percentage of mentally ill people on the streets may be even lower than Krauthammer's lowest figure of 25%. In an extensive study conducted by David Snow and colleagues, a team member lived among the homeless for 12 months to collect data on mental illness. Additionally, the researchers tracked the institutional histories of a random sample of homeless. The study found that only 10% of the street sample and 16% of the tracking sample showed mental illness. The researchers pointed to a number of reasons why some previous estimates and studies may have inflated the numbers of mentally ill homeless. They suggest that the visibility of the mentally ill homeless (their odd behaviors make them stand out) combined with the widespread belief that deinstitutionalization poured vast numbers of mentally ill onto the streets caused researchers to bias their data. Thus researchers would often interpret behavior such as socially inappropriate actions, depression, and sleeping disorders as indications of mental illness, when in fact these actions may simply be the natural response to living in the harsh environment of the street. Additionally, the Snow study points to the medicalization of homelessness. This phenomenon means that when doctors and psychiatrists treat the homeless they focus on their medical and psychological problems while ignoring their social and economic ones. Because studies of the mentally ill homeless have been dominated by doctors and psychologists, these studies tend to inflate the numbers of mentally ill on the streets (Snow et al. 419-21).

Another persuasive study showing low percentages of mentally ill homeless—although not as low as Snow's estimates—comes from Deborah Dennis and colleagues who surveyed the past decade of research on mentally ill homeless. The combined findings of all these research studies suggest that the mentally ill comprise between 28% and 37% of the homeless population (Dennis et al. 1130). Thus we see that while the mentally ill make up a significant proportion of the homeless population they do not approach a majority as Krauthammer and others would have us believe.

Krauthammer's third assumption is that the causes of homelessness among the mentally ill are largely psychological rather than socio-economic. By this thinking, the solutions to their problems involve the treatment of their illnesses rather than the alleviation of poverty. Krauthammer writes, "Moreover, whatever solutions are eventually offered the non-mentally ill homeless, they will have little relevance to those who are mentally ill" (25). Closer examination, however, shows that other factors play a greater role in causing homelessness among the mentally ill than mental illness. Jonathan Kozol argues that housing and the economy played the largest role in causing homelessness among the mentally ill. He points to two million jobs lost every year since 1980, an increase in poverty, a massive shortage in low income housing, and a drop from 500,000 subsidized private housing units to 25,000 during the Reagan era (Kozol 17-18). Cohen and Thompson also place primary emphasis on poverty and housing shortages:

> Data suggest that most homeless mentally ill persons lost their rooms in single-room-occupancy hotels or low-priced apartments not because of psychoticism but because they 1) were evicted because of renewal projects and fires, 2) were victimized by unscrupulous landlords or by other residents, or 3) could no longer afford the rent. (Cohen and Thompson 818)

Douglas Mossman and Michael Perlin cite numerous studies which show that mental illness itself is not the primary factor causing homelessness among the mentally ill; additionally, they point out that the severity of mental illness itself is closely linked to poverty. They argue that lack of private health care increases poor health and the frequency of severe mental illness. They conclude, "Homelessness is, if nothing else, a condition of poverty, and poor individuals in general are at increased risk for episodes of psychiatric illness" (Mossman and Perlin 952). Krauthammer's article conveniently ignores the role of poverty, suggesting that much of the homeless problem could be solved by moving the mentally ill back into institutions. But the evidence suggests that symptoms of mental illness are often the <u>results</u> of being homeless and that any efforts to treat the psychological prob-

lems of the mentally ill must also address the socioeconomic problems.

Krauthammer's belief that the causes of mentally ill homelessness
are psychological rather than social and economic leads to a fourth
assumption that the mentally ill homeless are a distinct subgroup who
need different treatment from the other homeless groups. Krauthammer thus divides the homeless into three primary groups: (1) the mentally ill; (2) those who choose to live on the street; and (3) "the victims
of economic calamity, such as family breakup or job loss" (25). By
believing that the mentally ill homeless are not also victims of "economic calamity," Krauthammer greatly oversimplifies their problems.
As Cohen and Thompson show, it is difficult to separate the mentally ill
homeless and the non-mentally ill homeless. "On closer examination,
'not mentally ill' homeless people have many mental health problems;
similarly, the 'mentally ill' homeless have numerous nonpsychiatric
problems that arise from the sociopolitical elements affecting all homeless people" (Cohen and Thompson 817). Because the two groups are
so similar, it is counterproductive to insist on entirely different solutions for both groups.

Krauthammer's proposal thus fails on a number of points. It
won't solve nearly as much of the homelessness problem as he leads
us to believe. It would commit valuable taxpayer dollars to building
asylums rather than attacking the underlying causes of homelessness
in general. And perhaps most importantly, its emphasis on involuntary confinement in asylums is not the best long-range method to treat
the mentally ill homeless. Instead of moving the mentally ill homeless
away from society into asylums, we would meet their needs far more
effectively through monitored community-based care. Instead of building expensive institutions we should focus on finding alternative low
cost housing for the mentally ill homeless and meet their needs

through teams of psychiatrists and social workers who could oversee a number of patients' treatments, monitoring such things as taking medications and receiving appropriate counseling. Involuntary hospitalization may still be needed for the most severely deranged, but the majority of mentally ill homeless people can be better treated in their communities.

From a purely financial perspective, perhaps the most compelling reason to prefer community-based care is that it offers a more efficient use of taxpayer dollars. In a letter to the <u>New York Times</u> on behalf of the Project for Psychiatric Outreach to the Homeless, Drs. Katherine Falk and Gail Albert give us the following statistics:

> It costs $105,000 to keep someone in a state hospital for a year. But it costs only $15,000 to $35,000 (depending on the intensity of services) to operate supported residences in the community with the necessary onsite psychiatrists, case workers, case managers, drug counselors, and other rehabilitation services. (A30)

It can be argued, in fact, that the cost of maintaining state hospitals for the mentally ill actually prevents large numbers of mentally ill from receiving treatment. When large numbers of mentally ill persons were released from state hospitals during the deinstitutionalization movement of the 60s and 70s, the original plan was to convert resources to community-based care. Even though the number of patients in state institutions has dramatically decreased over the past two decades, institutions have continued to maintain large shares of state funding. According to David Rothman of Columbia University, "Historically, the dollars have remained locked in the institutions and did not go into community mental health (Dugger, "Debate" B2). In fact, cutting New York's state hospital budget would provide enough money for over 20,000 units in supported community residences (Falk and Albert A30). Furthermore, Linda Chafetz points out that having the money to pay for such resources as clothes, bathing facilities, meals, and housing is the most urgent concern among caregivers in treating the mentally ill homeless. "The immediate and urgent nature of the resource dilemma can make other issues appear almost frivolous by comparison" (Chafetz 451). With such an obvious shortage of resources, pouring what money we have into the high-cost institutional system would be a grave disservice to the majority of the mentally ill homeless population and to the homeless population as a whole.

A second reason to adopt community-based care over widescale institutionalization is that the vast majority of the homeless mentally ill do not need the tight control of the hospital system. Cohen and Thompson cite a number of studies which show "that only 5%-7% of single adult homeless persons are in need of acute inpatient care" (Cohen and Thompson 820). Involuntarily hospitalizing a large number of homeless who don't demand institutionalized care is not only a waste of resources but also an unnecessary assault on individual freedom for many.

Finally the community-based care system is preferable to institutionalization because it most often gives the best treatment to its patients. Although Krauthammer claims that less than a fifth of involuntarily hospitalized patients have legally challenged their confinement (25), numerous studies indicate there is widespread resistance to institutional care by the homeless mentally ill. Mossman and Perlin cite multiple sources indicating that many mentally ill have legitimate reasons to fear state hospitals. Moreover, they provide evidence that many would rather suffer the streets and their mental illness than suffer the conditions of state hospitals and the side effects of medications. The horrible track record of conditions of state hospitals supports the logic of this thinking. On the other hand, Mossman and Perlin point out many homeless mentally ill will accept treatment from the type of alternative settings community-based care offers (953). Further, Cohen and Thompson tell us that most mentally ill homeless don't see themselves as mentally ill; treatment has often left them feeling humiliated and disempowered (819). Obviously, these feelings of powerlessness would be exacerbated by forced institutionalization. Because the patient plays a large role in the success of his or her treatment, these attitudes make a huge difference. In fact, Mossman and Perlin cite numerous sources that point to the success non-institutional approaches have had in integrating even the chronically mentally ill homeless into the community. For quality of care alone, Mossman and Perlin claim, community-based solutions are the best approach (953).

Given the advantages of community-based care, what is the appeal of Krauthammer's proposal? Involuntary institutionalization appeals to our common impulse to lock our problems out of sight. As crime increases, we want to build more prisons; when we see ragged men and women mumbling in the street, we want to shut them up in institutions. But the simple solutions are not often the most effective ones. Institutionalization is tempting, but alternative methods have shown themselves to be more effective. Community-based care works better because it's based on a better understanding of the problem. Community-based care, by allowing the psychiatrist and social worker to work together, attacks both the mental and social dimensions of the problem: the client not only receives psychological counseling and medication, but also help on how to find affordable housing, how to manage money and shop effectively, and how to live in a community. Without roots in a community, a patient released from a mental asylum will quickly return to the streets. To pour scarce resources into the expensive project of rebuilding asylums—helping

the few while ignoring the many—would be a terrible misuse of taxpayer dollars.

Krauthammer's argument appeals in another way also. By
viewing the homeless as mentally ill, we see them as inherently different from ourselves. We needn't see any connection to those mumbling bag ladies and those ragged men lying on the grates. When we
regard them as mentally ill, we see ourselves as largely unresponsi-
ble for the conditions that led them to the streets. Those professional
men and women carrying their espresso Starbuck's coffees to their
upscale offices in Seattle's Pioneer Square don't have to be reminded
that this historic district used to contain a number of single-occu-
pancy boarding houses. The professionals work where the homeless
used to live. The rich and the poor are thus interconnected, reminding us that homelessness is primarily a social and economic problem, not a mental health problem. And even the most deranged of
the mentally ill homeless are messengers of a nation-wide scourge of
poverty.

Chafetz, Linda. "Withdrawal from the Homeless Mentally Ill."
Community Mental Health Journal 26 (1990): 449-61.

Cohen, Carl I., and Kenneth S. Thompson. "Homeless Mentally Ill
or Mentally Ill Homeless?" American Journal of Psychiatry 149
(1992): 816-23.

Dennis, Deborah L. et al. "A Decade of Research and Services for
Homeless Mentally Ill Persons: Where Do We Stand?" American
Psychologist 46 (1991): 1129-38.

Dugger, Celia W. "A Danger to Themselves and Others." New York
Times 24 Jan. 1993: B1+.

---. "A Debate Unstilled: New Plan for Homeless Mentally Ill Does
Not Address Larger Questions." New York Times 22 Jan. 1993:
B2.

Falk, Katherine, and Gail Albert. Letter. New York Times 11 Feb.
1993: A30.

Hopper, Kim. "More than Passing Strangers: Homelessness and
Mental Illness in New York City." American Ethnologist 15
(1988): 155-57.

Kozol, Jonathan. "Are the Homeless Crazy?" Harper's Magazine
Sept. 1988: 17-19.

Krauthammer, Charles. "How to Save the Homeless Mentally Ill."
New Republic 8 Feb. 1988: 22-25.

Mossman, Douglas, and Michael L. Perlin. "Psychiatry and the
Homeless Mentally Ill: A Reply to Dr. Lamb." American Journal
of Psychiatry 149 (1992): 951-56.

Snow, David A. et al. "The Myth of Pervasive Mental Illness among
the Homeless." Social Problems 33 (1986): 407-23.

15

Ethical Arguments

☐

The line between ethical arguments ("Is X morally good?") and other kinds of values disputes is often pretty thin. Many apparently straight-forward practical values issues can turn out to have an ethical dimen-sion. For example, in deciding what kind of car to buy, most people would base their judgments on criteria such as cost, reliability, safety, comfort, stylishness, and so forth. But some people might feel morally obligated to buy the most fuel-efficient car, or not to buy a car from a manufacturer whose investment or labor policies they found morally repugnant. Depending on how large a role ethical considerations played in the evaluation, we might choose to call this an ethical argu-ment as opposed to a simpler kind of values argument. In any case, we here devote a separate chapter to ethical arguments because we believe they represent special difficulties to the student of argumenta-tion. Let's take a look now at some of those special difficulties.

SPECIAL DIFFICULTIES OF ETHICAL ARGUMENTS

One crucial difficulty with ethical arguments concerns the role of "purpose" in defining criteria for judgment. In Chapter 13, we assumed that every class of beings has a purpose, that the purpose should be defined as narrowly as possible, and that the criteria for judgment derive directly from that purpose. For example, the purpose of a computer repairperson is to analyze the problem with my computer, to fix it, and to do so in a timely and cost-efficient manner. Once I formulate this purpose, it is easy for me to define criteria for a good computer repairperson.

In ethics, however, the place of purpose is much fuzzier. Just what is the purpose of human beings? Before I can begin to determine what ethical duties I have to myself and to others, I'm going to have to address this question; and because the chance of reaching agreement on that question remains remote, many ethical arguments are probably unresolvable. In ethical discussions we don't ask what a "manager" or a "judge" or a "point guard" is supposed to do in situations relevant to the respective classes; we're asking what John Doe is supposed to be or what Jane Doe is supposed to do with her life. Who they are or what their social function is makes no difference to our ethical assessment of their actions or traits of character. A morally bad person may be a good judge and a morally good person may be a bad manager.

As the discussion so far has suggested, disagreements about ethical issues often stem from different systems of belief. We might call this problem the problem of warrants. This is, people disagree because they do not share common assumptions on which to ground their arguments.

If, for example, you say that good manners are necessary for keeping us from reverting to a state of raw nature, your implied warrant is that raw nature is bad. But if you say that good manners are a political tool by which a ruling class tries to suppress the natural vitality of the working class, then your warrant is that liberation of the working classes from the corrupt habits of the ruling class is good. It would be difficult, therefore, for people representing these opposing belief systems to carry on a reasonable discussion of etiquette—their whole assumptions about value, about the role of the natural self, and about political progress are different. This is why ethical arguments are often so acrimonious—they frequently lack shared warrants to serve as starting places for argument.

It is precisely because of the problem of warrants, however, that you should try to confront issues of ethics with rational deliberation. The arguments you produce may not persuade others to your view, but they should lay out more clearly the grounds and warrants of your own beliefs. Such arguments serve the purpose of clarification. By drafting essays on ethical issues, you begin to see more clearly what you believe and why you believe it. Although the arguments demanded by ethical issues require rigorous thought, they force us to articulate our most deeply held beliefs and our richest feelings.

AN OVERVIEW OF MAJOR ETHICAL SYSTEMS

When faced with an ethical issue, such as the issue of whether terrorism can be justified, we must move from arguments of good or bad to arguments of right or wrong. The terms *right* and *wrong* are clearly different from the terms *good* and *bad* when the latter terms mean simply "effective" (meets purposes of class, as in "This is a good stereo system") or "ineffective" (fails to meet purposes of class, as in "This is a bad cookbook"). But "right" and "wrong" often also differ from what seems to be a moral use of the terms *good* and *bad*. We might say, for example, that warm sunshine is good in that it brings pleasure and that cancer is bad in that it brings pain and death, but that is not quite the same thing as saying that sunshine is "right" and cancer is "wrong." It is the problem of "right" and "wrong" that ethical arguments confront.

Thus it is not enough to say that terrorism is "bad"; obviously everyone, including most terrorists, would agree that terrorism is "bad" in that it causes suffering and anguish. If we want to condemn terrorism on ethical grounds, we have to say that it's also "wrong" as well as "bad." In saying that something's wrong, we're saying that all people ought to refrain from doing it. We're also saying that acts that are morally "wrong" are in some way blameworthy and deserve censure, a conclusion that doesn't necessarily follow a negative nonethical judgment, which might lead simply to our not buying something or not hiring someone. From a nonethical standpoint, you may even say that someone like Abu Nidal is a "good" terrorist in that he fully realizes the purposes of the class "terrorist": He causes great damage with a minimum of resources, brings a good deal of attention to his cause, and doesn't (as of this writing) get caught. The ethical question here, however, is not whether or not Nidal is a good member of the class, but whether it is wrong for such a class to exist.

In asking the question "Ought the class 'terrorist' exist?" or, to put it more colloquially, "Are there ever cases where terrorism is justified?" we need to seek some consistent approach or principle. In the phrase used by some philosophers, ethical judgements are typically "universalizable" statements. That is, when we oppose a terrorist act, our ethical argument (assuming it's a coherent one) should be capable of being generalized into an ethical principle that will hold for all similar cases. Ethical disputes usually involve clashes between such principles. For example, a pro-terrorist might say, "My ends justify my means," whereas an antiterrorist might say, "The sanctity of human life is not to be violated for any reason." The differences in principles such as these account for different schools of ethical thought.

There are many different schools of ethical thought—too many to present in this chapter. But to help you think your way through ethical issues, we'll look at some of the most prevalent methods of resolving ethical questions. The first of these methods, "naive egoism," is really less a method than a retreat from method. It doesn't represent a coherent ethical view, but it is a position that many people lapse into on given issues. It represents, in short, the most seductive alternative to rigorous ethical thought.

Naive Egoism

Back in Chapter 1, we touched on the morality of the Sophists and suggested that their underlying maxim was something like "might makes right." That is, in ethical terms, they were essentially egoists who used other people with impunity to realize their own ends. The appeal of this position, however repugnant it may sound when laid out like this, is enormous. It is a rationalization for self-promotion and pleasure seeking. We are all prone to sink into it occasionally. In recent years, people have gotten rich by rationalizing this position into an "enlightened egoism" and by arguing, in numerous best-selling books with words like *Number One* or *Self* in the titles, that if we all follow the bidding of our egos, we'll be happy.

On closer examination, this philosophy proves to be incoherent, incapable of consistent application. Not many philosophers take it seriously, however persistently it returns with new sets of disciples. It should be noted, however, that philosophers don't reject naive egoism simply because they believe "selfishness is bad." Rather, philosophers tend to assess ethical systems according to such factors as their scope (how often will principles derived from a system provide a guide for our moral action?) and their precision (how clearly can we analyze a given situation using the tools of the system?) rather than their intuition about whether the system is right or wrong.

Although naive egoism has great scope (you can always ask "What's in it for me?"), it is far from precise, as we'll try to show. Take the case of young Ollie Unger, who has decided that he wants to quit living irrationally and to join some official school of ethical thought. The most appealing school at the moment—recommended to him by a philosophy major over at the Phi Upsilon Nu house—is the "I'm Number One!" school of scruples. He heads downtown to their opulent headquarters and meets with the school's guru, one Dr. Pheelgood.

"What's involved in becoming a member of your school?" Ollie inquires.

"Ahhh, my apple-cheeked chum, that's the beauty of it. It's so simple. You just give me all your worldly possessions and do whatever I tell you to do."

Ollie's puzzled. He had in mind something a bit more, well, gratifying. He was hoping for something closer to the Playboy philosophy of eat, drink and make merry—all justified through rational thought.

"You seem disappointed," Pheelgood observes. "What's the matter?"

"Well, gee, it just doesn't sound like I'm going to be number one here. I thought that was the idea. To look out for numero uno."

"Of course not, silly boy. This is after all the 'I'm Number One School of Scruples.' And I, *moi*, am the I who's Number One. There can be only one Number One, of course, and since I founded the school, I'm it."

"But I thought the idea of your school was for everyone to have the maximum amount of enjoyment in life."

Peevishness clouds Pheelgood's face. "Look here, Unger, if I arrange things for you to have a good time, my day has to dim. The demand that I curb my own pleasure for the sake of your own, well that's simply subversive, undermines the very foundation of this philosophy. Next you'll be asking me to open soup kitchens and retread the downtrodden. If I'm to look out for Number One, then you've got to act entirely differently from me. I take, you give. Capiche? If you want to be Number One, then you go somewhere else. After paying me to teach you how to do it, of course."

With that, we'll stop the dialogue. As should be obvious by now, it's very difficult to systematize egoism. You have two sets of demands in constant conflict—the demands of your own personal ego and those of everyone else's. It's impossible, hence, to universalize a statement that all members of the school could hold equally without contradicting all other members of the school. Thus, for example, if I write a book saying that it's okay to rip people off to satisfy their own desires, I am authorizing others to steal my book and prevent me from realizing my own desires for profit. In the end, the philosophy is not only contradictory, but also not very efficient at delivering the desired end product—personal gratification.

That's not to say, of course, that people can't or don't act on the principle of me-firstism. It's just to say that it's impossible to systematize it without returning us to what philosopher Thomas Hobbes called the condition of nature, wherein life is "nasty, brutish, and short." The immediate practical problem of any survival-of-the-fittest school of morals is that it benefits a few (the fittest of the fit) at the expense of the many. Some egoists try to get around this problem by conceding that we must limit our self-gratification either by entering into contracts or institutional arrangements with others or by sacrificing short-term interests for long-term ones. We might, for example, give to the poor now in order to avoid a revolution of the masses later. But once they've let the camel's nose of concern for others into the tent, it's tough to hang onto egoistic philosophy. Having considered naive egoism, let's turn to a pair of more workable alternatives.

In shifting to the two most common forms of ethical thought, we shift point of view from "I" to "us." Both groups, those who make ethical judgments according to the consequences of any act and those who make ethical judgments according to the conformity of any act with a principle, are guided by their concern for the whole of humanity rather than simply the self.

Consequences as the Grounds of Ethics

Perhaps the best-known example of evaluating acts according to their ethical consequences is John Stuart Mill's Utilitarianism. The goal of Utilitarianism, according to Mill, is "the greatest good for the greatest number." It is a very down-to-earth philosophy that grew out of nineteenth-century British philosophers' concern to demystify ethics and to make it work in the practical world.

As Mill makes clear, a focus on ethical consequences allows you readily to assess a wide range of acts. You can apply the principle of utility—which says that an action is morally right if it produces a greater net value (benefits minus costs) than any available alternative action—to virtually any situation and it will help you reach a decision. Obviously, however, it's not always easy to make the calculations called for by the principle, since, like any prediction of the future, an estimate of consequences is conjectural. In particular, it's often very hard to assess the long-term consequences of any action. Too often, Utilitarianism seduces us into a short-term analysis of a moral problem simply because long-term consequences are very difficult to predict.

Principles as the Grounds of Ethics

Any ethical system based on principles will ultimately rest on one or two moral tenets that we are duty-bound to uphold, no matter what the consequences. Sometimes the moral tenets come from religious faith—for example, the Ten Commandments. At other times, however, the principles are derived from philosophical reasoning, as in the case of German philosopher Immanual Kant. Kant held that no one should ever use another person as a means to his own ends and that everyone should always act as if his acts were the basis of universal law. In other words, Kant held that we were duty-bound to respect other people's sanctity and to act in the same way that we would want all other people to act. The great advantage of such a system is its clarity and precision. We are never overwhelmed by a multiplicity of contradictory and difficult-to quantify consequences; we simply make sure we are not violating a principle of our ethical system and proceed accordingly.

The Two Systems Compared

In the eyes of many people, a major advantage of a system such as Utilitarianism is that it impels us to seek out the best solution, whereas systems based on principle merely enjoin us not to violate a principle by our action. In turn, applying an ethical principle will not always help us resolve necessarily relativistic moral dilemmas. For instance, what if none of our available choices violates our moral principles? How do we choose among a host of permissible acts? Or what about situations where none of the alternatives is permitted by our principles. How might we choose the least bad alternative?

To further our comparison of the two systems, let's ask what a Mill or a Kant might say about the previously mentioned issue of terrorism. Here the Kantian position is clear: To kill another person to realize your own ends is palpably evil and forbidden.

But a follower of Mill will face a less clear choice. A Utilitarian could not automatically rule out terrorism or any other means so long as it led ultimately to the greatest good for the greatest number. If a nation is being slowly starved by those around it, if its people are dying, its institutions crumbling and its future disappearing, who's to say that the aggrieved nation is not justified in taking a few hundred lives to improve the lot of hundreds of thousands? The Utilitarian's first concern is to determine if terrorism will most effectively bring about that end. So long as the desired end represents the best possible net value and the means are effective at bringing about the end, the Utilitarian can, in theory anyway, justify almost any action.

Given the shared cultural background and values of most of us, not to mention our own vulnerability to terrorism, the Kantian argument is probably very appealing here. Indeed, Kantian ethical arguments have overwhelming appeal for us when the principle being invoked is already widely held within our culture, and when the violation of that principle will have clear and immediate negative consequences for us. But in a culture that doesn't share that principle and for whom the consequences of violation are positive rather than negative, the argument will undoubtedly appear weaker, a piece of fuzzy-headed idealism.

□ FOR CLASS DISCUSSION

Working as individuals or in small groups:

1. Try to formulate a Utilitarian argument to persuade terrorist leaders in a country such a Libya to stop terrorist action.

2. Try to formulate an ethical principle or rule that would permit terrorism.

Some Compromise Positions between Consequences and Principles

In the end, most of us would not be entirely happy with an ethic that forced us to ignore either principles or consequences. We all have certain principles that we simply can't violate no matter what the consequences. Thus, for example, some of us would not have dropped the bomb on Hiroshima even if it did mean saving many lives ultimately. And certainly, too, most of us will compromise our principles in certain situations if we think the consequences justify it. For instance, how many of us would not deceive, harm, or even torture a kidnapper to save the life of a stolen child? Indeed, over the years, compromise positions have developed on both sides to accommodate precisely these concerns.

Some "consequentialists" have acknowledged the usefulness of general rules for creating more human happiness over the long run. To go back to our terrorism example, a consequentialist might oppose terrorist action on the grounds that "Thou shalt not kill another person in the name of greater material happiness for the group." This acknowledgment of an inviolable principle will still be based on a concern for consequences—for instance, a fear that terrorist acts may lead to World War III—but having such a principle allows the consequentialist to get away from a case-by-case analysis of acts and to keep more clearly before himself the long-range consequences of acts.

Among later-day ethics of principle, meanwhile, the distinction between absolute obligation and what philosophers call *prima facie* obligation has been developed to take account of the force of circumstances. An absolute obligation would be an obligation to follow a principle at all times, no matter what. A *prima facie* obligation, on the other hand, is an obligation to do something "other things being equal," that is, in a normal situation. Hence, to use a classic moral example, you would not, other things being equal, cannibalize an acquaintance. But if there are three of you in a lifeboat, one is dying and the other two will surely die if they don't get food, your *prima facie* obligation not to eat another might be waived. (However, the Royal Commission, which heard the original case, took a more Kantian position and condemned the action of the seamen who cannibalized their mate.)

These, then, in greatly condensed form, are the major alternative ways of thinking about ethical arguments. Let's now briefly summarize the ways you can use your knowledge of ethical thought to develop your arguments and refute those of others.

DEVELOPING AN ETHICAL ARGUMENT

To help you see how familiarity with these systems of ethical thought can help you develop an ethical argument, let's take an example case. How, for example, might we go about developing an argument in favor of abolishing the death penalty?

Our first task is to examine the issue from the two points of view just discussed. How might a Utilitarian or a Kantian argue that the death penalty should be abolished? The argument on principle, as is usually the case, would appear to be the simpler of the two. Taking another life is difficult to justify under most ethical principles. For Kant, the sanctity of human life is a central tenet of ethics. Under Judeo-Christian ethics, meanwhile, one is told that "Vengeance is Mine, saith the Lord" and "Thou shalt not kill."

But, unfortunately for our hopes of simplicity, Kant argued in favor of capital punishment:

> There is no sameness of kind between death and remaining alive even under the most miserable conditions, and consequently there is no equality between the crime and the retribution unless the criminal is judicially condemned and put to death.*

Kant is here invoking an important principle of justice—that punishments should be proportionate to the crime. Kant appears to be saying that this principle must take precedence over his notion of the supreme worth of the individual. Some philosophers think he was being inconsistent in taking this position. Certainly, in establishing your own position, you could support a case against capital punishment based on Kant's principles, even if Kant himself did not reach the same conclusion. But you'd have to establish for your reader why you are at odds with Kant in this case. Kant's apparent inconsistency here illustrates how powerfully our intuitive judgments can affect our ethical judgment.

Likewise, with the Judeo-Christian position, passages can be found in the Bible that would support capital punishment, notably, the Old Testament injunction to take "an eye for an eye and a tooth for a tooth." The latter principle is simply a more poetic version of "let the punishment fit the

---

* From Immanuel Kant, *The Metaphysical Elements of Justice.*

crime." Retribution should be of the same kind as the crime. And the commandment "Thou shalt not kill" is often interpreted as "Thou shalt not commit murder," an interpretation that not only permits just wars or killing in self-defense but is also consistent with other places in the Bible that suggest that people have not only the right but the obligation to punish wrongdoers and not leave their fate to God.

So, there appears to be no clearcut argument in support of abolishing capital punishment on the basis of principle. What about an argument based on consequences? How might abolishing capital punishment result in a net good that is at least as great as allowing it?

A number of possibilities suggest themselves. First, in abolishing capital punishment, we rid ourselves of the possibility that someone may be wrongly executed. To buttress this argument, we might want to search for evidence of how many people have been wrongly convicted of or executed for a capital crime. In making arguments based on consequence we must, whenever possible, offer empirical evidence that the consequences we assert exist—and exist to the degree we've suggested.

There are also other possible consequences that a Utilitarian might mention in defending the abolition of capital punishment. These include leaving open the possibility that the person being punished will be reformed, keeping those charged with executing the murderer free from guilt, putting an end to the costly legal and political process of appealing the conviction, and so forth.

But in addition to calculating benefits, you will need also to calculate the costs of abolishing the death penalty and to show that the net result favors abolition. Failure to mention such costs is a serious weakness in many arguments of consequence. Moreover, in the issue at hand, the consequences that favor capital punishment—deterrence of further capital crimes, cost of imprisoning murderers, and so forth—are well known to most members of your audience.

In our discussion of capital punishment, then, we employed two alternative ways of thinking about ethical issues. In pursuing an argument from principle, we looked for an appropriate rule that permitted or at least did not prohibit our position. In pursuing an argument from consequence, we moved from what's permissible to what brings about the most desirable consequences. Most ethical issues, argued thoroughly, should be approached from both perspectives, so long as irreconcilable differences don't present themselves.

Should you choose to adopt one of these perspectives to the exclusion of the other, you will find yourself facing many of the problems mentioned above. This is not to say that you can't ever go to the wall for a principle or focus solely on consequences to the exclusion of principles; it's simply that you will be hard-pressed to convince those of your audience who happen to be of the other persuasion and demand different sorts of proof. For the purpose of developing arguments, we encourage you to consider both the relevant principles and the possible consequences when you evaluate ethical actions.

TESTING ETHICAL ARGUMENTS

Perhaps the first question you should ask in setting out to analyze your draft of an ethical argument is, "To what extent is the argument based on consequences or on ethical principles?" If it's based exclusively on one of these two forms of ethical thought, then it's vulnerable to the sorts of criticism discussed above. A strictly principled argument that takes no account of the consequences of its position is vulnerable to a simple cost analysis. What are the costs in the case of adhering to this principle? There will undoubtedly be some, or else there would be no real argument. If the argument is based strictly on consequentialist grounds, we should ask if the position violates any rules or principles, particularly such commandments as the Golden Rule—"Do unto others as you would have others do unto you"—which most members of our audience adhere to. By failing to mention these alternative ways of thinking about ethical issues, we undercut not only our argument but our credibility as well.

Let's now consider a more developed examination of the two positions, starting with some of the more subtle weaknesses in a position based on principle. In practice people will sometimes take rigidly "principled" positions because they live in fear of "slippery slopes"; that is, they fear setting precedents that might lead to ever more dire consequences. Consider, for example, the slippery slope leading from birth control to euthanasia if you have an absolutist commitment to the sanctity of human life. Once we allow birth control in the form of condoms or pills, the principled absolutist would say, then we will be forced to accept birth control "abortions" in the first hours after conception (IUDs, "morning after" pills), then abortions in the first trimester, then in the second or even the third trimester. And once we have violated the sanctity of human life by allowing abortions, it is only a short step to euthanasia and finally to killing off all undesirables.

One way to refute a slippery-slope argument of this sort is to try to dig a foothold into the side of the hill to show that you don't necessarily have to slide all the way to the bottom. You would thus have to argue that allowing birth control does not mean allowing abortions (by arguing for differences between a fetus after conception and sperm and egg before conception), or that allowing abortions does not mean allowing euthanasia (by arguing for differences between a fetus and a person already living in the world).

Consequentialist arguments have different kinds of difficulties. As discussed before, the crucial difficulty facing anyone making a consequentialist argument is to calculate the consequences in a clear and reliable way. Have you considered all significant consequences? If you project your scenario of consequences further into the future (remember, consequentialist arguments are frequently stronger over the short term than over the long term, where many unforeseen consequences can occur), can you identify possibilities that work against the argument?

As also noted above, consequentialist arguments carry a heavy burden of empirical proof. What evidence can you offer that the predicted consequences will in fact come to pass? Do you offer any evidence that alternative consequences won't occur? And just how do you prove that the consequences of any given action are a net good or evil?

In addition to the problems unique to each of the two positions, ethical arguments are vulnerable to the more general sorts of criticism, including consistency, recency, and relevance of evidence. Obviously, however, consequentialist arguments will be more vulnerable to weaknesses in evidence, whereas arguments based on principle are more open to questions about consistency of application.

□ For Class Discussion

1. Prior to beginning this exercise, read the following short story by Ursula Le Guin. Then, working individually or in small groups, prepare answers to the following questions:

   a. How would someone such as Mill evaluate the actions of those who walk away?

   b. How would someone such as Kant evaluate the same action?

   c. If you are working in groups, try to reach a group consensus on how the action should be evaluated. Recorders for the group should explain how your group's evaluation differs from a Utilitarian or a Kantian approach.

2. Read "The Case for Torture" (pages 395–97) by philosopher Michael Levin. Levin creates an argument that torture not only can be justified but is positively mandated under certain circumstances. Analyze Levin's argument in terms of our distinction between arguments from principle and arguments from consequence.

3. In "The Case for Torture," Levin mentions the possibility of some "murkier" cases in which it is difficult to draw a line demarcating the legitimate use of torture. Try to come up with several examples of these "murkier" cases and explain what makes them murky.

---------------------------------■---------------------------------

THE ONES WHO WALK AWAY FROM OMELAS (VARIATIONS ON A THEME BY WILLIAM JAMES)

Ursula Le Guin

With a clamor of bells that set the swallows soaring, the Festival of Summer came to the city Omelas, bright-towered by the sea. The rigging of the boats in harbor sparkled with flags. In the streets between houses with red roofs and painted walls, between old moss-grown gardens and under avenues of trees, past great parks and public buildings, processions moved. Some were decorous: old people in long stiff robes of   1 mauve and grey, grave master workmen, quiet, merry women carrying their babies, and chatting as they walked. In other streets the music beat faster, a shimmering of gong and tambourine, and the people went dancing, the procession was a dance. Children dodged in and out, their high calls rising like the swallows' crossing flights over the music and the singing. All the processions wound towards the north side of the city, where on the great water-meadow called the Green Fields boys and girls, naked in the bright air, with mud-stained feet and ankles and long,lithe arms, exercised their restive horses before the race. The horses wore no gear at all but a halter without bit. Their manes were braided with streamers of silver, gold, and green. They flared their nostrils and pranced and boasted to one another; they were vastly excited, the horse being the only animal who has adopted our ceremonies as his own. Far off to the north and west the mountains stood up half encircling Omelas on her bay. The air of morning was so clear that the snow still crowning the Eighteen Peaks burned with white-gold fire across the miles of sunlit air, under the dark blue of the sky. There was just enough wind to make the banners that marked the racecourse snap and flutter now and then. In the silence of the broad green meadows one could hear the music winding through the city streets, farther and nearer and ever approaching, a cheerful faint sweetness of the air that from time to time trembled and gathered together and broke out into the great joyous clanging of the bells.

Joyous! How is one to tell about joy? How describe the citizens of Omelas?   2

They were not simple folk, you see, though they were happy. But we   3 do not say the words of cheer much any more. All smiles have become archaic. Given a description such as this one tends to make certain assumptions. Given a description such as this one tends to look next for the King, mounted on a splendid stallion and surrounded by his noble knights, or perhaps in a golden litter borne by great-muscled slaves. But there was no king. They did not use swords, or keep slaves. They were not barbarians. I do not know the rules and laws of their society, but I suspect that they were singularly few. As they did without monarchy and slavery, so they also get on without the stock exchange, the advertisement, the secret police, and the bomb. Yet I repeat that these were not simple folk, not dulcet shepherds, noble savages, bland utopians. They were not less complex than us. The trouble is that we have a bad habit, encouraged by pedants and sophisticates, of considering happiness as something rather stupid. Only pain is intellectual, only evil interesting. This is the treason of the artist: a refusal to admit the banality of evil and the terrible boredom of pain. If you can't lick 'em join 'em. If it hurts, repeat it. But to praise despair is to condemn delight, to embrace violence is to lose hold of everything else. We have almost lost hold; we can no longer describe a happy man, nor make any celebration of joy. How can I tell you about the people of Omelas? They were not naive and happy children—though their children were, in fact, happy. They were mature, intelligent, passionate adults whose lives were not wretched. O miracle! but I wish I could describe it better. I wish I could convince you. Omelas sounds in my words like a city in a fairy tale, long ago and far away, once upon a time. Perhaps it would be best if you imagined it as your own fancy bids, assuming it will rise to the occasion, for certainly I cannot suit you all. For instance, how about technology? I think that there would be no cars or helicopters in and above the streets; this follows from the fact that the people of Omelas are happy people. Happiness is based on a just discrimination of what is necessary, what is neither necessary nor destructive, and what is destructive. In the middle category, however—that of the unnecessary but undestructive, that of comfort, luxury, exuberance, etc.—they could perfectly well have central heating, subway trains, washing machines, and all kinds of marvelous devices not yet invented here, floating light-sources, fuelless power, a cure for the common cold. Or they could have none of that: it doesn't matter. As you like it. I incline to think that people from towns up and down the coast have been coming in to Omelas during the last days before the Festival on very fast little trains and double-decked trams, and that the train station of Omelas is actually the handsomest building in town, though plainer than the magnificent Farmers' Market. But even granted trains, I fear that Omelas so far strikes some of you as goody-goody. Smiles, bells, parades, horses, bleh. If so, please add an orgy. If an orgy would help, don't hesitate. Let us not, however, have temples from which issue beautiful nude priests and priestesses already half in ecstasy and ready to copulate with any man or woman, lover or stranger, who desires union with the deep godhead of the blood, although that was my first idea. But really it would be better not to have any temples in Omelas—at least, not manned temples. Religion yes, clergy no. Surely the beautiful nudes can just wander about, offering themselves like divine souffles to the hunger of the needy and the rapture of the flesh. Let them join the processions. Let tambourines be struck above the copulations, and the glory of desire be proclaimed upon the gongs, and (a not unimportant point) let the offspring of these delightful rituals be beloved and looked after by all. One thing I know there is none of in Omelas is guilt. But what else should there be? I thought at first there were no drugs, but that is puritanical. For those who like it, the faint insistent sweetness of *drooz* may perfume the ways of the city, *drooz* which first brings a great lightness and brilliance to the mind and limbs, and then after some hours a dreamy languor, and wonderful visions at last of the very arcana and inmost secrets of the Universe, as well as exciting the pleasure of sex beyond all belief; and it is not habit-forming. For more modest tastes I think there ought to be beer. What else, what else belongs in the joyous city? The sense of victory, surely, the celebration of courage. But as we did without clergy, let us do without soldiers. The joy built upon successful slaughter is not the right kind of joy; it will not do; it is fearful and it is trivial. A boundless and generous contentment, a magnanimous triumph felt not against some outer enemy but in communion with the finest and fairest in the souls of all men everywhere and the splendor of the world's summer: this is what swells the hearts of the people of Omelas, and the victory they celebrate is that of life. I really don't think many of them need to take *drooz*.

Most of the processions have reached the Green Fields by now. A marvelous smell of cooking goes forth from the red and blue tents of the provisioners. The faces of small children are amiably sticky; in the benign grey beard of a man a couple of crumbs of rich pastry are entangled. The youths and girls have mounted their horses and are beginning to group around the starting line of the course. An old woman, small, fat and laughing, is passing out flowers from a basket, and tall young men wear her flowers in their shining hair. A child of nine or ten sits at the edge of the crowd alone, playing on a wooden flute. People pause to listen, and they smile, but they do not speak to him, for he never ceases playing and never sees them, his dark eyes wholly rapt in the sweet, thin magic of the tune. 4

He finishes, and slowly lowers his hands holding the wooden flute. 5

As if that little private silence were the signal, all at once a trumpet sounds from the pavilion near the starting line: imperious, melancholy, piercing. The horses rear on their slender legs, and some of them neigh in answer. Soberfaced, the young riders stroke the horses' necks and soothe them, whispering, "Quiet, quiet, there my beauty, my hope. . . ." They begin to form in rank along the starting line. The crowds along the racecourse are like a field of grass and flowers in the wind. The Festival of Summer has begun. 6

Do you believe? Do you accept the festival, the city, the joy? No? Then let me describe one more thing. 7

In a basement under one of the beautiful public buildings of Omelas, or perhaps in the cellar of one of its spacious private homes, there is a room. It has one locked door, and no window. A little light seeps in dustily between cracks in the boards, secondhand from a cobwebbed window somewhere across the cellar. In one corner of the little room a couple of mops, with stiff, clotted, foul-smelling heads, stand near a rusty bucket. The floor is dirt, a little damp to the touch, as cellar dirt usually is. The room is about three paces long and two wide: a mere broom closet or disused tool room. In the room a child is sitting. It could be a boy or a girl. It looks about six, but actually is nearly ten. It is feeble-minded. Perhaps it was born defective, or perhaps it has become imbecile through fear, malnutrition, and neglect. It picks its nose and occasionally fumbles vaguely with its toes or genitals, as it sits hunched in the corner farthest from the bucket and the two mops. It is afraid of the mops. It finds them horrible. It shuts its eyes, but it knows the mops are still standing there; and the door is locked; and nobody will come. The door is always locked; and nobody ever comes, except that sometimes— 8 the child has no understanding of time or interval—sometimes the door rattles terribly and opens, and a person, or several people, are there. One of them may come in and kick the child to make it stand up. The others never come close, but peer in at it with frightened, disgusted eyes. The food bowl and the water jug are hastily filled, the door is locked, the eyes disappear. The people at the door never say anything, but the child, who has not always lived in the tool room, and can remember sunlight and its mother's voice, sometimes speaks. "I will be good," it says. "Please let me out. I will be good!" They never answer. The child used to scream for help at night, and cry a good deal, but now it only makes a kind of whining, "eh-haa, eh-haa," and it speaks less and less often. It is so thin there are no calves to its legs; its belly protrudes; it lives on a half-bowl of corn meal and grease a day. It is naked. Its buttocks and thighs a mass of festered sores, as it sits in its own excrement continually.

They all know it is there, all the people of Omelas. Some of them have come to see it, others are content merely to know it is there. They all know that it has to be there. Some of them understand why, and some do not, but they all understand that their happiness, the beauty of their city, the tenderness of their friendships, the health of their children, the wisdom of their scholars, the skill of their makers, even the abundance of their harvest and the kindly weathers of their skies, depends wholly on this child's abominable misery.   9

This is usually explained to children when they are between eight and twelve, whenever they seem capable of understanding; and most of those who come to see the child are young people, though often enough an adult comes, or comes back, to see the child. No matter how well the matter has been explained to them, these young spectators are always shocked and sickened at the sight. They feel disgust, which they had thought themselves superior to. They feel anger, outrage, impotence, despite all the explanations. They would like to do something for the child. But there is nothing they can do. If the child were brought up into the sunlight out of that vile place, it if were cleaned and fed and comforted, that would be a good thing, indeed; but if it were done, in that day and hour all the prosperity and beauty and delight of Omelas would wither and be destroyed. Those are the terms. To exchange all the goodness and grace of every life in Omelas for that single, small improvement: to throw away the happiness of thousands for the chance of the happiness of one: that would be to let guilt within the walls indeed.   10

The terms are strict and absolute; there may not even be a kind word spoken to the child.   11

Often the young people go home in tears, or in a tearless rage, when they have seen the child and faced this terrible paradox. They may brood over it for weeks or years. But as time goes on they begin to realize that even if the child could be released, it would not get much good of its freedom: a little vague pleasure of warmth and food, no doubt, but little more. It is too degraded and imbecile to know any real joy. It has been   12 afraid too long even to be free of fear. Its habits are too uncouth for it to respond to humane treatment. Indeed, after so long it would probably be wretched without walls about it to protect it, and darkness for its eyes, and its own excrement to sit in. Their tears at the bitter injustice dry when they begin to perceive the terrible justice of reality, and to accept it. Yet it is their tears and anger, the trying of their generosity and the acceptance of their helplessness, which are perhaps the true source of the splendor of their lives. Theirs is no vapid, irresponsible happiness. They know that they, like the child, are not free. They know compassion. It is the existence of the child, and their knowledge of its existence, that makes possible the nobility of their architecture, and poignancy of their music, the profundity of their science. It is because of the child that they are so gentle with children. They know that if the wretched one were not there snivelling in the dark, the other one, the flute-player, could make no joyful music as the young riders line up in their beauty for the race in the sunlight of the first morning of summer.

Now do you believe in them? Are they not more credible? But there is one more thing to tell, and this is quite incredible. 13

At times one of the adolescent girls or boys who go to see the child does not go home to weep or rage, does not, in fact, go home at all. Sometimes also a man or woman much older falls silent for a day or two, and then leaves home. These people go out into the street, and walk down the street alone. They keep walking, and walk straight out of the city of Omelas, through the beautiful gates. They keep walking across the farmlands of Omelas. Each one goes alone, youth or girl, man or woman. Night falls; the traveler must pass down village streets, between the houses with yellow-lit windows, and on out into the darkness of the fields. Each alone, they go west or north, towards the mountains. They go on. They leave Omelas, they walk ahead into the darkness, and they do not come back. The place they go towards is a place even less imaginable to most of us than the city of happiness. I cannot describe it at all. It is possible that it does not exist. But they seem to know where they are going, the ones who walk away from Omelas. 14

SPECIALIZED INDEXES: EDUCATION

1. *Education Index.* Indexes by author and subject about 300+ periodicals, proceedings, and yearbooks covering all phases of education. Especially good coverage of topics related to children and child development.

2. *Current Index to Journals in Education.* Detailed author and subject index for articles from more than seven hundred education and education-related journals.

SPECIALIZED INDEXES: HISTORY AND LITERATURE

1. *America: History and Life.* Includes abstracts of scholarly articles on the history of the United States and Canada.

2. *Annual Bibliography of English Language and Literature.* Subject index of scholarly articles in English language and literature. Literature section is arranged chronologically and includes articles on the major writers of each century.

3. *Historical Abstracts.* Includes abstracts of scholarly articles on world history (excluding United States and Canada) from 1775 to 1945.

4. *Humanities Index.* Subject index to various topics in the humanities, including archaeology, classics, folklore, history, language and literature, politics, performing arts, philosophy, and religion. (Before 1974 this was called *Social Sciences and Humanities Index.*)

5. *MLA (Modern Language Association) International Bibliography of Books and Articles in Modern Language and Literature.* Comprehensive index of scholarly articles on the languages and literature of various countries. Arranged by national literatures with subdivisions by literary periods.

SPECIALIZED INDEXES: NURSING AND MEDICAL SCIENCES

1. *Cumulative Index to Nursing and Allied Health Literature.* Major index for topics related to nursing and public health.

2. *Index Medicus.* Monthly index, by subject, of periodical literature on medicine and medical-related topics. Covers publication in all principal languages.

SPECIALIZED INDEXES: PHILOSOPHY AND RELIGION

1. *Philosopher's Index.* Author and subject index to scholarly articles in books and periodicals. Subject section includes abstracts of articles.

2. *Religion Index One: Periodicals.* Subject and author index to scholarly articles on topics in religion. Protestant in viewpoint, but also indexes a number of Catholic and Jewish periodicals.

SPECIALIZED INDEXES: PSYCHOLOGY AND SOCIOLOGY

1. *Psychological Abstracts.* Subject and author index covering books, journals, technical reports, and scientific documents. Each item includes an abstract.

2. *Social Sciences Index.* See under Current Affairs on page 377.

3. *Applied Science and Technology Index.* Subject index to periodical articles in fields of aeronautics and space sciences, automation, earth sciences, engineering, physics, telecommunications, transportation, and related topics.

4. *Biological and Agricultural Index.* Subject index to English-language periodicals in the agricultural and biological sciences.

5. *General Science Index.* See Current Affairs

How to Use Periodical Indexes

Once you locate these indexes in the library, you will quickly get the hang of using them. Most of the indexes listed above (with the exception of the *New York Times Index*) are used in approximately the same way. In general, each volume in an index lists articles that appeared in journals and magazines for a one-year period. The year is stated on the outside cover of the index volume and sometimes at the top of each page. To use the index, you have to be flexible in selecting subject headings. Lynnea, for example, found most of her articles indexed under "policewomen," but one index used the heading "women" and the subheading "and police." It is often difficult to know what headings an index will use, but because most indexes cross-reference listings under a variety of headings, with patience and perseverance you can usually track down what you want.

Because indexes are generally bound by year, you need to look in a different volume for each year you wish to search. Thus, if you wanted to find all the articles written on women in police forces between 1980 and 1990, you would need to look under the subject heading "policewomen" in ten separate volumes. Each entry uses a series of abbreviations (you may have to look in the explanatory codes at the front of the index to decipher some of them) that give you all the information you need to locate the article. Figures 16–2, 16–3, and 16–4 show entries on policewomen from the *Readers' Guide,* the *Social Sciences Index,* and the *Public Affairs Information Service (P.A.I.S.) Bulletin.*

When you find entries that seem relevant to your topic, jot down the title of the article; the name of the magazine or journal; and the volume, year, and page numbers (remember that the year often doesn't appear in the entry; the year is on the cover of the volume).

Once you have a preliminary list of articles, you will need to find out how your library shelves its periodical collection so that you can retrieve the journals or magazines you need. (Small libraries can afford only small-

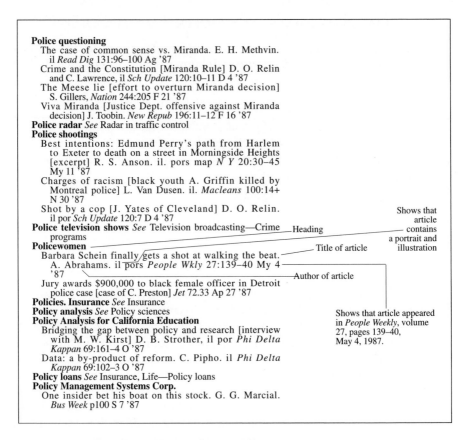

Police questioning
The case of common sense vs. Miranda. E. H. Methvin.
il *Read Dig* 131:96–100 Ag '87
Crime and the Constitution [Miranda Rule] D. O. Relin
and C. Lawrence, il *Sch Update* 120:10–11 D 4 '87
The Meese lie [effort to overturn Miranda decision]
S. Gillers, *Nation* 244:205 F 21 '87
Viva Miranda [Justice Dept. offensive against Miranda
decision] J. Toobin. *New Repub* 196:11–12 F 16 '87
Police radar *See* Radar in traffic control
Police shootings
Best intentions: Edmund Perry's path from Harlem
to Exeter to death on a street in Morningside Heights
[excerpt] R. S. Anson. il. pors map *N Y* 20:30–45
My 11 '87
Charges of racism [black youth A. Griffin killed by
Montreal police] L. Van Dusen. il. *Macleans* 100:14+
N 30 '87
Shot by a cop [J. Yates of Cleveland] D. O. Relin.
il por *Sch Update* 120:7 D 4 '87
Police television shows *See* Television broadcasting—Crime
programs
Policewomen
Barbara Schein finally gets a shot at walking the beat.
A. Abrahams. il pors *People Wkly* 27:139–40 My 4
'87
Jury awards $900,000 to black female officer in Detroit
police case [case of C. Preston] *Jet* 72.33 Ap 27 '87
Policies. Insurance *See* Insurance
Policy analysis *See* Policy sciences
Policy Analysis for California Education
Bridging the gap between policy and research [interview
with M. W. Kirst] D. B. Strother, il por *Phi Delta
Kappan* 69:161–4 O '87
Data: a by-product of reform. C. Pipho. il *Phi Delta
Kappan* 69:102–3 O '87
Policy loans *See* Insurance, Life—Policy loans
Policy Management Systems Corp.
One insider bet his boat on this stock. G. G. Marcial.
Bus Week p100 S 7 '87

Callout labels: Heading; Title of article; Author of article; Shows that article contains a portrait and illustration; Shows that article appeared in *People Weekly*, volume 27, pages 139–40, May 4, 1987.

Figure 16–2   Entry from *Readers' Guide*, 1987

collections of journals, so you may have to cross some of your titles off your list or depend on interlibrary loan.)

Special case: Using the New York Times Index. When you want to find newspaper stories in the *New York Times,* you have to use a slightly different procedure. Each volume of the *New York Times Index* contains a year's worth of condensed news stories arranged chronologically by subject. At the back of the volume, a supplementary index lists all headings with an extensive system of cross-references. By looking under the appropriate headings in this supplementary index, you will find listed, by date, all the year's articles indexed under that heading. For example, the 1988 volume of the *New York Times Index* (Figure 16–5) shows that stories about women in police appeared on March 29 and on December 29. Figure 16–6 shows the mini-summary of the December 29 story from the front of the volume in the section headed "POLICE." A citation to the original story shows that it appeared on December 29, section II, page 1, column 2. To read the full story, you would turn to your library's collection of *New York Times.*

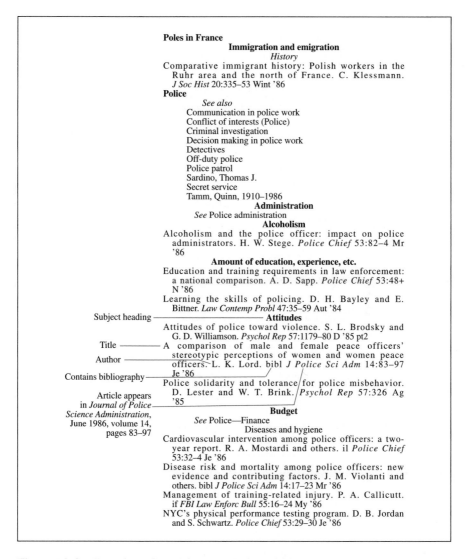

Poles in France
  Immigration and emigration
   History
Comparative immigrant history: Polish workers in the Ruhr area and the north of France. C. Klessmann. *J Soc Hist* 20:335–53 Wint '86
Police
  See also
  Communication in police work
  Conflict of interests (Police)
  Criminal investigation
  Decision making in police work
  Detectives
  Off-duty police
  Police patrol
  Sardino, Thomas J.
  Secret service
  Tamm, Quinn, 1910–1986
     Administration
  See Police administration
     Alcoholism
Alcoholism and the police officer: impact on police administrators. H. W. Stege. *Police Chief* 53:82–4 Mr '86
   Amount of education, experience, etc.
Education and training requirements in law enforcement: a national comparison. A. D. Sapp. *Police Chief* 53:48+ N '86
Learning the skills of policing. D. H. Bayley and E. Bittner. *Law Contemp Probl* 47:35–59 Aut '84

Subject heading —————— **Attitudes**
Attitudes of police toward violence. S. L. Brodsky and G. D. Williamson. *Psychol Rep* 57:1179–80 D '85 pt2

Title ————— A comparison of male and female peace officers'
Author ————— stereotypic perceptions of women and women peace officers. L. K. Lord. bibl *J Police Sci Adm* 14:83–97
Contains bibliography——— Je '86

Article appears — Police solidarity and tolerance for police misbehavior. D. Lester and W. T. Brink. *Psychol Rep* 57:326 Ag
in *Journal of Police* ——— '85
Science Administration,   **Budget**
June 1986, volume 14, *See* Police—Finance
pages 83–97   **Diseases and hygiene**
Cardiovascular intervention among police officers: a two-year report. R. A. Mostardi and others. il *Police Chief* 53:32–4 Je '86
Disease risk and mortality among police officers: new evidence and contributing factors. J. M. Violanti and others. bibl *J Police Sci Adm* 14:17–23 Mr '86
Management of training-related injury. P. A. Callicutt. if *FBI Law Enforc Bull* 55:16–24 My '86
NYC's physical performance testing program. D. B. Jordan and S. Schwartz. *Police Chief* 53:29–30 Je '86

Figure 16–3 Entry from *Social Sciences Index*, 1986

USING COMPUTER SEARCHES

Now that library indexing systems are becoming increasingly computerized, the old-fashioned, one-volume-at-a-time, hands-on searching method described above is becoming obsolete. However, methods of using on-line computer searches vary so much from institution to institution that it is impossible to describe a single, generalized method of conducting a computer search.

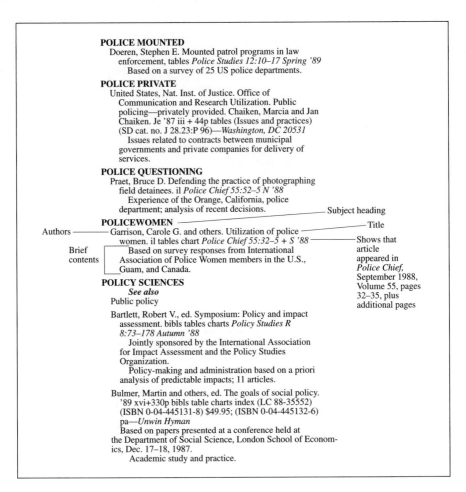

POLICE MOUNTED
Doeren, Stephen E. Mounted patrol programs in law
enforcement, tables *Police Studies 12:10–17 Spring '89*
Based on a survey of 25 US police departments.

POLICE PRIVATE
United States, Nat. Inst. of Justice. Office of
Communication and Research Utilization. Public
policing—privately provided. Chaiken, Marcia and Jan
Chaiken. Je '87 iii + 44p tables (Issues and practices)
(SD cat. no. J 28.23:P 96)—*Washington, DC 20531*
Issues related to contracts between municipal
governments and private companies for delivery of
services.

POLICE QUESTIONING
Praet, Bruce D. Defending the practice of photographing
field detainees. il *Police Chief 55:52–5 N '88*
Experience of the Orange, California, police
department; analysis of recent decisions. ——— Subject heading

Authors ——— **POLICEWOMEN** ———————————— Title
Garrison, Carole G. and others. Utilization of police ———
women. il tables chart *Police Chief 55:32–5 + S '88* ——— Shows that
Brief   Based on survey responses from International   article
contents   Association of Police Women members in the U.S.,   appeared in
               Guam, and Canada.   *Police Chief,*
                                                                       September 1988,
POLICY SCIENCES   Volume 55, pages
See also   32–35, plus
Public policy   additional pages

Bartlett, Robert V., ed. Symposium: Policy and impact
assessment. bibls tables charts *Policy Studies R
8:73–178 Autumn '88*
Jointly sponsored by the International Association
for Impact Assessment and the Policy Studies
Organization.
Policy-making and administration based on a priori
analysis of predictable impacts; 11 articles.

Bulmer, Martin and others, ed. The goals of social policy.
'89 xvi+330p bibls table charts index (LC 88-35552)
(ISBN 0-04-445131-8) $49.95; (ISBN 0-04-445132-6)
pa—*Unwin Hyman*
Based on papers presented at a conference held at
the Department of Social Science, London School of Economics, Dec. 17–18, 1987.
Academic study and practice.

Figure 16–4   Entry from *Public Affairs Information Service (P.A.I.S.) Bulletin,* 1989

Many libraries now have simple, easy-access computer terminals for searching specific databases. One typical system, called INFOTRAC, provides rapid access to a multiyear database of popular journals and magazines. However, the number of entries in the data bank is much smaller than the number in the *Readers' Guide to Periodical Literature* or the *Social Sciences Index* so that INFOTRAC is a good starting place but not an adequate source for an extensive search of periodicals. INFOTRAC is easy to use because of its simple menu options and clear prompts. In general, you type in the subject heading you wish to search and then select from a menu of subheadings. When you have identified the heading and subheading of your choice, you can ask the computer to list its entries in that category. You can either read the entries from the screen or ask for a hard copy printout.

WOLZIEN, VALERIE. See also
Book Reviews—Murder at the PTA Luncheon (Book),
My 22
WOMACK, CECIL. See also
Music, Je 25
WOMACK, JAMES. See also
Sheldahl Inc, F 19, Mr 16
WOMACK, LINDA. See also
Music, Je 25
WOMAN (MAGAZINE)
Magazine will be acquired by Conde Nast Publications
Inc (S). N 16.IV,19:4
WOMAN'S WORKSHOP (NEWSLETTER). See also
Women, O 5
WOMC-FM (RADIO STATION). See also
Radio, Mr 1
WOMEN. See also ————— **Main Heading**
Abortion, Ja 29, F 6,10,29, Mr 6, Jl 29, S 26,27,29
Accounting and Accountants, Jl 12
Acquired Immune Deficiency Syndrome (AIDS), F 20, Mr 6, My
24, Jl 15, Ag 11,14
Advertising, Ja 14, Je 1
Afghanistan, Mr 27, Ap 2, Je 12, D 12
Age, Chronological, S 1
Aged, My 15
Agriculture, Ja 3, F 28
Airlines and Airplanes, F 29, Mr 10, S 13
Airports, My 30
Alcoholism, F 21, Je 19, O 13
Anglican Churches, Jl 20, Ag 2,7,8,14, N 8
Anorexia Nervosa, F 11
Apparel, F 21, Mr 9,11,21,31, Ap 10,12,16,17,19,22, My
1,21,29,30, Je 12, Jl 29, S 25,29, O 11, N 4,8,22, D 13,18,23
Art, Ja 3,15,22, N 20, D 1
Athletics and Sports, Ja 26,31, My 26, Je 8,9,14, Jl 22, S 23,
O 2
Banks and Banking, Mr 9
Baseball, Mr 8,20,21,25, Je 2, Ag 12
Basketball, F 15, Mr 5,18,20,25,27,28, Ap 1,3,4,8,27, N
2,11,12,15, D 20,29
Bathrooms, My 10
Beer, Ap 10
Birth Control and Family Planning, Ja 29, F 6, Jl 28, Ag 4,
S 15
Birth Defects, Ap 27, Je 6, S 28
Blood Pressure, My 15
Boats and Boating, Je 13
Bohemian Club, S 4
Bones, Mr 29
Books and Literature, Mr 20, Ap 21, My 5
Boy Scouts of America, F 14,17, Jl 17, Ag 28
Brooklyn College, My 19
Bulimia, Ag 25
Bush, George (Mrs), D 11
California, University of, Mr 24
Cancer, Ja 7,21, F 2,16, Mr 11,22, My 31, Je 30, S 7,11,21,
29, O 27, N 10,13,16,17,20,28
Cartoons and Cartoonists, N 27
Century Association, N 27
Chemicals, D 15
Child Care, Jl 25
Chilton Club (Boston, Mass), O 30
China, People's Republic of, D 15
Cuba, Ja 5
Curling, F 2
Dartmouth College, S 21, O 19
Data Processing (Computers), Jl 5, 10
Dating (Social), Je 21
Deerfield Academy (Mass), Ja 31
Defense, Department of, My 24
Diamonds, D 18
Drug Addiction and Abuse, Je 23, O 30
Drug Traffic, N 29, D 4
Education and Schools, F 22, O 30, N 30
Electronics, D 15
Emotions, Ag 23
Endometriosis, Mr 8
Engineering and Engineers, Mr 9,30

Ethiopia, My 19, Ag 25
Etiquette, My 11
Executives and Management, Ja 25, My 11, Ag 14, S 25
Exercise, S 5
Families and Family Life, My 22, N 6
Federal Aviation Administration (FAA), Ap 29
Fencing (Sport), Je 25
Fires and Firemen, My 22
Food, Ag 31
Forest Service, US, My 10
Fort Orange Club (Albany, NY), O 8
Friars Club, Jl 19, Ag 27, N 9
Fur, Ap 2
Furniture, Ap 14
Gambling, N 29
Games, Jl 17
Government Employees, Mr 29
Great Britain, Je 3
Guinea-Bissau, Ja 3
Handicapped, Je 18
Harvard University, F 21, My 11,24,26, D 2
Hats and Caps, Mr 25, Ap 24, Je 14
Heart, Ag 3
History, Ja 9
Homeless Persons, Ja 24, D 22
Honda of America Manufacturing Inc, Mr 24
Horse Racing, Mr 6,7,20
Housework, D 8
Housing, Mr 27
Humor and Wit, N 20
Indians, American, O 30
Industrial and Occupational Hazards, Ag 2, O 4,5
Insurance, F 28
International Trade and World Market, Jl 4
Ireland, Northern, My 2
Israel, State of, N 29, D 22
Japan, D 4
Jews, Mr 14,30, My 20, Ag 29, D 2
Jonathan Club (Los Angeles), My 6
Jump Rope, Jl 20
Kissing, D 11
Labor, Ja 18, F 2,12,14, My 30, Je 16,19,30, Jl 31, Ag 14,
O 12,16, N 27
Lacrosse, My 22
Latin America, Jl 27
Lear's (Magazine), F 7
Legal Profession, F 12, Mr 6, Ap 22, Jl 22, Ag 8,11, S 2,30, N 11
Life Insurance, S 5
Lupus Erythematosus, Ap 3
Magazines, My 30
Malaysia, Je 5
Marriages, S 1
Mathematics, Jl 20, N 1
Medicine and Health, Ja 14, Ap 10, Jl 10, O 16, D 9,11,15
Mental Health and Disorders, O 12
Methodist Church, My 4
Murders and Attempted Murders, My 23,24, Je 1
Music, Je 5, O 22, D 25
Names, Personal, Ja 10, F 27, Ap 20
Nashville (Tenn), F 14
Nebraska, O 21
New Hampshire, S 12
New Jersey, Ja 24
New York, City University of (CUNY), My 16, S 30
New York State—Economic Conditions and Trends, Ap 9,19
New York State—Politics and Government, My 20
New York University, Ag 30
Newcomb College, Mr 30
News and News Media, F 4, Ap 14, Jl 14, Ag 3
Plastic Surgery, Ag 28, S 6 ———**Subheading**
Police, Mr 29, D 29
Population, Je 5 —————**Articles in March 29 and**
Pregnancy and Obstetrics —————**December 29 issues of**
Presbyterian Church, F 14 ————— *New York Times*
Presidential Election of 1984, Jl 18
Presidential Election of 1988, My 10,17,19,30, Je 2,17,19,21,27,
Jl 6,18,24,25,28, Ag 14,17,19,29, S 6,11, O 5,27
Presidential Elections (US), Jl 28, Ag 5

Figure 16–5 Index in back of *New York Times Index,* 1988

POLICE (cont.)

Louisa O Dixon, first woman to be Mississippi's Commissioner of Public Safety, wins over most of the doubters in her department, which includes highway patrol, narcotics bureau, crime laboratory, medical examiner's office and law-enforcement training academy; appointment is part of Gov Ray Mabus's continuing effort to bring new ideas to Mississippi government; photo (M), D 22,1,18:5

New Jersey State Trooper Jerome W Johnson is arrested on charges he planned to sell cocaine he confiscated from drug courier who turned out to be an undercover detective (S), D 24,1,30:6

Hemphill, Texas, where black man, Loyal Garner Jr, died in police custody last December, is divided between whites who view incident as tragedy with no villains and blacks embittered by acquittal of three white law-enforcement officers; photos; map (S), D 25,1,18:4

Summary of story ⌐ New York City Police Department, in hopes of attracting more women to careers in police work while helping to ease domestic burdens of employees with pre-school children, begins building on-site day care centers in its Manhattan headquarters building; Judith Dynia, civilian official who is └ in charge of project, comments; photo (S), D 29,11,1:2 ── Story appears in December 29, Section II, page 1, column 2. (S) = short article (M) = medium article (L) = long

Correction of Dec 29 article on plans for day-care center at Police Headquarters in New York City, D 31,1,3:2

POLICE, FRATERNAL ORDER OF. See also
Presidential Election of 1988, O 9

POLICE ATHLETIC LEAGUE (PAL). See also
Children and Youth, Jl 10

Photo of Police Athletic League carnival in Central Park. New York City, Ag 11,11,2:3

POLICE CHIEFS, INTERNATIONAL ASSN OF (LOS ANGELES, CA). See also
Police, My 6

POLICE FOUNDATION. See also
Child Abuse, Mr 15
Koch, Edward I (Mayor), My 24
Police, Ja 31, My 24, N 21

Annual winter benefit dance of New York City Police Foundation at Police Headquarters is held on Feb 11; photo (S), F 12,11,2:3

POLICELLA, ANTHONY. See also
Kinney System Inc, My 4

POLICY AND MANAGEMENT, OFFICE OF (CONN). See also
Prisons and Prisoners, Je 26

POLICY COMMUNICATIONS INC.

William Lilley 3d announces that he is forming his own firm, Policy Communications Inc, to provide policy analysis, lobbying and communications services; photo (S), Mr 2,IV,4:5

POLICY STUDIES, INSTITUTE FOR. See also
United States Politics and Government, Jl 13

Figure 16–6   Story summary from *New York Times Index*

In addition to small, primarily undergraduate systems such as INFO-TRAC, many libraries offer in-house computerized searching of specialized databases such as ERIC (Educational Research Information Center) or NEXIS (for news and public affairs). Most libraries also provide exhaustive, professional on-line searches from a variety of national and international databases. These searches usually require the assistance of a reference librarian and are often quite expensive. The key to these searches is providing the right array of subject headings, called "descriptors," so that you adequately narrow your topic (otherwise you end up paying for hundreds of titles) without getting it so narrow that you miss key titles. Ask your librarian for help.

USING OTHER LIBRARY SOURCES

Besides being a storehouse for books and periodicals, your library has a wealth of material in the reference section that may be useful to you in finding background information, statistics, and other kinds of evidence. Here are some sources that we have found particularly useful in our own research.

1. *Encyclopedias.* For getting quick background information on a topic, you will often find that a good encyclopedia is your best bet. Besides the well-known general-purpose encyclopedias such as the *Encyclopedia Britannica,* there are excellent specialized encyclopedias devoted to in-depth coverage of specific fields. Among the ones you might find most useful are these:

The International Encyclopedia of the Social Sciences

Dictionary of American History

Encyclopedia of World Art

McGraw-Hill Encyclopedia of Science and Technology

2. *Facts on File.* These interesting volumes give you a year-by-year summary of important news stories. If you wish to assemble a chronological summary of a news event such as Hillary Clinton's task force on national health coverage, ethnic wars in the Balkan countries, or the end of apartheid in South Africa, *Facts on File* gives you a summary of the events along with information about exact dates so that you can find the full stories in newspapers. A special feature is a series of excellent maps in the back of each volume, allowing you to find all geographical place names that occur in the year's news stories. The front cover of each volume explains how to use the series.

3. *Statistical Abstracts of the United States.* Don't even consider picking up one of these volumes if you don't have some spare time. You will get hooked on the fascinating graphs, charts, and tables compiled by the Bureau of Statistics. For statistical data about birth rates and abortions, marriages and divorces, trends in health care, trends in employment and unemployment, nutritional habits, and a host of other topics, these yearly volumes are a primary source of quantitative information about life in the United States.

4. *Congressional Abstracts.* For people working on current or historical events related to politics or any controversy related to the public sector, this index can guide you to all debates about the topic in the Senate or the House of Representatives.

5. *Book Review Digest.* For writers of argument, this series can be a god-send because it provides not only a brief summary of a book but also excerpts from a variety of reviews of the book, allowing the writer to size up quickly the conversation surrounding the book's ideas. To use *Book Review Digest,* you need to know the publishing date of the book for which you want to find reviews. Generally, reviews first appear in the same year the book was published and for several years thereafter. If you want to read reviews, for example, of a book appearing in 1992, you would probably find them in the 1992, 1993, and (if the book were very popular or provocative) 1994 volumes of *Book Review Digest.*

□ For Class Discussion

Working in groups, visit your college's library and learn to use the indexes and other sources listed in the preceding pages. Choose an issue of interest to the members of your group (preferably one about current public affairs so that you can find sources from the *New York Times Index* and *Congressional Abstracts*); then locate titles of two or three articles addressing your issue from as many of the indexes and sources as possible. Group members can divide up the work, each person taking several indexes as a special project and then teaching the others how to use them. Your goal is to feel confident that you can use these indexes to unlock most of the resources contained in your library.

BEYOND THE LIBRARY

As you pursue your research project, consider ways you might gather information or ideas through field research as well as library research—interviews, questionnaires, polls, field observations, and so forth. Review Chapter 6 for suggestions on using field research in argumentation.

USING YOUR SOURCES: SITTING DOWN TO READ

Once you have developed a working bibliography of books and articles and have gathered a collection of materials, how do you go about reading and notetaking? There is no easy answer here. At times you need to read articles carefully, fully, and empathically—reading as a believer and as a doubter, as discussed in Chapter 2, trying to understand various points of view on your issue, seeing where the disagreements are located, and so forth. Your goal at this time is to clarify your own understanding of the issue in order to join responsibly the on-going conversation.

At other times you need to read quickly, skimming an article in search of a needed piece of information, an alternative view, or a timely quotation. All these considerations and others—how to get your ideas focused, how to take notes, how to incorporate source material into your own writing, and how to cite and document your sources—are the subjects of the next chapter.

17

Using and
Documenting Sources

☐

The previous chapter helped you pose a good research question and begin unlocking some of the resources of your library. This chapter helps you see what to do with your sources once you have found them—how to use them to clarify your own thinking and how to incorporate them into your writing through effective use of quotations, paraphrases, and summaries along with appropriate conventional formats for citations and documentation.

CLARIFYING YOUR OWN THINKING: THE CASE OF LYNNEA

In the previous chapter, we followed Lynnea's progress as she posed her research question on the effectiveness of policewomen and began her search for sources. Once Lynnea located several articles on policewomen, she found a quiet spot in the library and began to read. She was guided by two related questions: What physical requirements must someone meet in order to be an effective patrol officer? How successful have policewomen been when assigned to patrol duty? After reading some recent articles, Lynnea noticed that writers often referred to significant earlier studies, particularly a 1984 study called *Policewomen on Patrol, Final Report* by P. B. Bloch and D. Anderson. Lynnea tracked down this study as well as several others referred to in the first articles she read.

Both Lynnea's experience and her research strategy are typical. As a researcher becomes familiar with the ongoing conversation on an issue, she will notice that recent writers frequently refer to the same earlier studies or to the same earlier voices in the conversation. In scientific writing, this background reading is so important that the introductions to scientific studies usually include a "review of the literature" section, wherein writers summarize important research done to date on the question under investigation and identify areas of consensus and disagreement.

Therefore, during the first hours of her research project, Lynnea conducted her own "review of the literature" concerning women on patrol. During an early visit to her university's writing center, she reported that she had found three kinds of studies:

1. Studies attempting to identify the attitude of the police establishment (overwhelmingly male) toward women entering the police profession and the attitude of the general public toward women patrol officers. Although the findings weren't entirely consistent, Lynnea reported that male police officers generally distrusted women on patrol and felt that women didn't have the required physical strength or stamina to be patrol officers. The public, however, was more accepting of women patrol officers.

2. Studies attempting to evaluate the success of women on patrol by examining a variety of data such as arrests made, use of force, firing of weapons, interviews with persons involved in incidents, evaluation reports by superiors, and so forth. Lynnea reported that these studies were generally supportive of women police officers and showed that women cops were as successful as men cops.

3. Studies examining the legal and political battles fought by women to gain access to successful careers in police work. Lynnea reported being amazed at how much prejudice against women was evident in the police establishment.

At a writing center conference Lynnea confessed that, as a result of her readings, she was beginning to change her mind: She was now convinced that women could be effective patrol officers. But she wasn't convinced that *all* women could be effective officers any more than *all* men could be. She still felt that minimum size and strength requirements should be necessary. The problem was, she reported, that she couldn't find any information related to size and strength issues. Moreover, the research on women police officers did not mention anything about the size or strength of the women being studied. Were these successful patrol officers "big, husky" women Lynnea asked, or "petite" women? She left the writing center in pursuit of more data.

Lynnea's dilemma is again typical. As we discussed in Chapter 6, the search for clarification often leads to uncertainty. As you immerse yourself in the conversation surrounding an issue, you find that the experts often disagree and that no easy answers emerge. Your goal under these circumstances is to find the best reasons available and to support them with the best evidence you can muster. But the kind of uncertainty Lynnea felt is both healthy and humbling. If your own research leads to similar feelings, we invite you to reread those sections of Chapter 6 where, in our discussion of the greenhouse effect, we suggest our own strategy for coping with ambiguity.

We'll leave Lynnea at this point to take up the technical side of writing research arguments. Besides using research to clarify your own thinking, you also need to have strategies for note taking and for incorporating the results of your reading into your own writing through proper citations and documentation.

DEVELOPING A GOOD SYSTEM OF NOTE TAKING

There is no one right way to take notes. For short research papers, many students keep all their notes in a spiral notebook; others use a system of 3×5 cards (for bibliographic information) and 5×8 cards (for actual notes). A few technological types are even using database software on their personal computers. Whatever system you use, the key is to take notes that are complete enough so that you don't have to keep going back to the library to reread your sources. Some students get around this problem by photocopying all articles they might use in their essays, but this is an expensive habit that may in the long run be less efficient than careful note taking in the first place.

It is much easier to take good notes for a research project if you have your issue question clearly formulated. When you know your issue question, you can anticipate how information from books and articles is apt to get incorporated into your essay. Sometimes you will need to write an accurate summary of a whole article as part of your research notes; at other times you may want to jot down only some facts or figures from an article; at still other times you may want to copy a passage word for word as a potential quotation. There is no way to know what kind of notes you will need to take on each book or article unless you can predict what kind of thesis you will be supporting. We therefore continue our comments on the art of note taking as we discuss ways information can be used in a research essay.

INCORPORATING SOURCES INTO YOUR ARGUMENT: SOME GENERAL PRINCIPLES

To illustrate different ways that you can use a source, we will use the following brief article from the magazine *Science '86.*

READING, WRITING, AND (UGH!) YOU KNOW WHAT

ANN ARBOR, Mich.—Not only are American high school students   1
worse at mathematics than their Japanese and Chinese peers, they start
falling behind in kindergarten.

That's one conclusion of a five-year study done by psychologist   2
Harold Stevenson and graduate student Shin-ying Lee, both of the University of Michigan, and psychologist James Stigler of the University of
Chicago. The study also shows for the first time that parents must share
the blame.

More than 2,000 children in kindergarten and the first and fifth grades   3
were tested and interviewed in Minneapolis, in Sendai, Japan, and in
Taipei, China. The researchers composed the test for each grade from
math problems found in textbooks in all three cities.

All the children in each grade performed equally well on reading and   4
general intelligence tests, but math scores differed from the start. While
average scores for U.S. and Chinese kindergarten students were the
same, Japanese kindergartners scored about 10 percent higher. First
graders in the U.S. were surpassed by their peers in both China and
Japan by an average of 10 percent. Then the gap widened. The top U.S.
fifth-grade class scored below the lowest Japanese class and the second
lowest Chinese class. Of the 100 highest scoring fifth graders, one was
American.

A crucial difference is time: Chinese and Japanese students spend   5
more hours in math class and attend school some 240 days a year,
Americans about 180. But another difference, the researchers found, is
parental influence. Chinese and Japanese parents give their children
more help with math homework than U.S. parents, who tended to believe
that "ability" was the premier reason for academic success, according to
the researchers' interviews. Chinese and Japanese parents, in contrast,
most often said "effort" was most important. And more than 90 percent
of U.S. parents believed the schools did an "excellent" job teaching math
and other subjects; most Japanese and Chinese parents said the schools
did a "fair" job.

"American parents are very involved in teaching reading," says Stigler.   6
"But they seem to think that teaching math is the school's job. It's as if it
gets them off the hook."

Citing Information

Sometimes the complete argument of an article may not be relevant to your
essay. Often you will use only a piece of information from the article. For
example, let's suppose you are writing an argument claiming that American
society, as a whole, values individual creativity more than does Japanese

society. You plan to contrast an open classroom in an American grade school with a more regimented Japanese classroom. At the end of the passage, you might write something like this:

> Not only is education in Japan more regimented than it is in the United States, it continues through a much longer school year. A typical Japanese grade school student attends classes 240 days a year compared with 180 days a year in the United States. (*Science '86* 7). Although such a system might produce more academic achievement, it provides little time for children to be children, to play and daydream—essential ingredients for nurturing creativity.

Here the total argument of the *Science '86* article isn't relevant to the writer's essay. He has borrowed only the small detail about the length of the school year (which, of course, the writer documents by means of a citation in parentheses). In his original notecards, the writer would not have had to summarize the whole *Science '86* article. By knowing his research question, he would have known that only this piece of information was relevant.

Summarizing an Argument: Different Contexts Demand Different Summaries

On other occasions, however, you may need to summarize the entire argument of an essay, or at least a major portion of the argument. How you summarize it depends once again on the context of your own essay because your summary must focus on your own thesis. To illustrate how context influences a summary, we will examine passages by two different writers, Cheryl and Jeff, each of whom uses the *Science '86* article, but in the context of different arguments. Cheryl is writing on the issue of heredity versus environment in the determination of scholastic achievement. She is making the causal claim that environment plays a key role in scholastic high achievement. Jeff, on the other hand, is writing on American mathematics education. He is making the evaluation claim that American mathematics education is in a dangerous shambles. Both writers include a summary of the *Science '86* article,* but their summaries are written in different ways in order to emphasize different aspects of the article.

PASSAGE FROM CHERYL'S ESSAY ON HEREDITY VERSUS ENVIRONMENT

Another argument showing the importance of environment on scholastic achievement comes from a research study done by psychologists at the University of Chicago and the University of Michigan (*Science '86*). These researchers compared the mathematics achievement of 2000 kindergartners, first graders, and fifth graders from the United States, Japan, and China. At the beginning of the study the researchers determined that the comparison groups were equal in terms of reading ability and general intelligence. But the American students were far behind in mathematics achievement. At the first grade level, the researchers reported, American students were 10 percent behind Japanese and Chinese stu-

---

* The citations follow the MLA format described later in this chapter.

dents and considerably further behind by the end of the fifth grade. In fact, only one American student scored in the top 100 of all students.

What is significant about this study is that heredity seems to play no factor in accounting for the differences between American students and their Japanese and Chinese counterparts since the comparison groups were shown to be of equal intelligence at the beginning of the study. The researchers attribute the differences between the groups to the time they spent on math (Japanese students go to class 240 days per year while Americans are in class only 180 days per year) and to parental influence. According to the study, American parents believe that native "ability" is the key factor in math achievement and don't seem to push their children as much. Japanese and Chinese parents, however, believe that "effort" is the key factor and spend considerably more time than American parents helping their children with their math homework (8). Thus, it is the particular environment created by Chinese and Japanese societies, not inherited intelligence, that accounts for the greater math achievement of children in those cultures.

PASSAGE FROM JEFF'S ESSAY ON THE FAILURE OF MATHEMATICS EDUCATION IN THE UNITED STATES

Further evidence of the disgraceful nature of mathematics education in the United States is the dismal performance of American grade school students in mathematics achievement tests as compared to children from other cultures. One study, reported in the magazine *Science '86*, revealed that American kindergarten students scored 10 percent lower on mathematics knowledge than did kindergarteners from Japan. This statistic suggests that American parents don't teach arithmetical skills in the home to preschoolers the way Japanese parents do.

But the most frightening part of the study showed what happens by the fifth grade. The best American class in the study scored below the worst Chinese or Japanese class, and of the top 100 students only one was an American (8). The differences between the American students and their Chinese and Japanese counterparts cannot be attributed to intelligence because the article reports that comparison groups were matched for intelligence at the beginning of the study. The difference can be accounted for only by the quality of education and the effort of students. The researchers who did this study attributed the difference first of all to time. According to the study, Chinese and Japanese students spend 240 days per year in school while Americans spend only 180. The second reason for the difference is parental influence, since Japanese and Chinese parents spend much more time than American parents helping their children with mathematics. The study suggests that if we are to do anything about mathematics education in the United States we need a revolution not only in the schools but in the home.

□ FOR CLASS DISCUSSION

Although both passages above summarize the *Science '86* article, they use the article to support somewhat different claims. Working as individuals or in groups, prepare short answers to the following questions. Be ready to elaborate on your answers in class if called on to defend them.

1. What makes each passage different from a data dump?

2. In what ways are the summaries different? (Compare the summaries to each other and to the original article.)

Death: Suppose a terrorist has hidden an atomic bomb on Manhattan Island which will detonate at noon on July 4 unless . . . (here follow the usual demands for money and release of his friends from jail). Suppose, further, that he is caught at 10 A.M. of the fateful day, but—preferring death to failure—won't disclose where the bomb is. What do we do? If we follow due process—wait for his lawyer, arraign him—millions of people will die. If the only way to save those lives is to subject the terrorist to the most excruciating possible pain, what grounds can there be for not doing so? I suggest there are none. In any case, I ask you to face the question with an open mind.   3

Torturing the terrorist is unconstitutional? Probably. But millions of lives surely outweigh constitutionality. Torture is barbaric? Mass murder is far more barbaric. Indeed, letting millions of innocents die in deference to one who flaunts his guilt is moral cowardice, an unwillingness to dirty one's hands. If *you* caught the terrorist, could you sleep nights knowing that millions died because you couldn't bring yourself to apply the electrodes?   4

Once you concede that torture is justified in extreme cases, you have admitted that the decision to use torture is a matter of balancing innocent lives against the means needed to save them. You must now face more realistic cases involving more modest numbers. Someone plants a bomb on a jumbo jet. He alone can disarm it, and his demands cannot be met (or if they can, we refuse to set a precedent by yielding to his threats). Surely we can, we must, do anything to the extortionist to save the passengers. How can we tell 300, or 100, or 10 people who never asked to be put in danger, "I'm sorry, you'll have to die in agony, we just couldn't bring ourselves to . . ."   5

Here are the results of an informal poll about a third, hypothetical, case. Suppose a terrorist group kidnapped a newborn baby from a hospital. I asked four mothers if they would approve of torturing kidnappers if that were necessary to get their own newborns back. All said yes, the most "liberal" adding that she would like to administer it herself.   6

I am not advocating torture as punishment. Punishment is addressed to deeds irrevocably past. Rather, I am advocating torture as an acceptable measure for preventing future evils. So understood, it is far less objectionable than many extant punishments. Opponents of the death penalty, for example, are forever insisting that executing a murderer will not bring back his victim (as if the purpose of capital punishment were supposed to be resurrection, not deterrence or retribution). But torture, in the cases described, is intended not to bring anyone back but to keep innocents from being dispatched. The most powerful argument against using torture as a punishment or to secure confessions is that such practices disregard the rights of the individual. Well, if the individual is all that important—and he is—it is correspondingly important to protect the rights of individuals threatened by terrorists. If life is so valuable that it   7 must never be taken, the lives of the innocents must be saved even at the price of hurting the one who endangers them.

Better precedents for torture are assassination and pre-emptive 8 attack. No Allied leader would have flinched at assassinating Hitler, had that been possible. (The Allies did assassinate Heydrich.) Americans would be angered to learn that Roosevelt could have had Hitler killed in 1943—thereby shortening the war and saving millions of lives—but refused on moral grounds. Similarly, if nation A learns that nation B is about to launch an unprovoked attack, A has a right to save itself by destroying B's military capability first. In the same way, if the police can by torture save those who would otherwise die at the hands of kidnappers or terrorists, they must.

Idealism: There is an important difference between terrorists and 9 their victims that should mute talk of the terrorists' "rights." The terrorist's victims are at risk unintentionally, not having asked to be endangered. But the terrorist knowingly initiated his actions. Unlike his victims, he volunteered for the risks of his deed. By threatening to kill for profit or idealism, he renounces civilized standards, and he can have no complaint if civilization tries to thwart him by whatever means necessary.

Just as torture is justified only to save lives (not extort confessions or 10 recantations), it is justifiably administered only to those *known* to hold innocent lives in their hands. Ah, but how can the authorities ever be sure they have the right malefactor? Isn't there a danger of error and abuse? Won't We turn into Them?

Questions like these are disingenuous in a world in which terror- 11 ists proclaim themselves and perform for television. The name of their game is public recognition. After all, you can't very well intimidate a government into releasing your freedom fighters unless you announce that it is your group that has seized its embassy. "Clear guilt" is difficult to define, but when 40 million people see a group of masked gunmen seize an airplane on the evening news, there is not much question about who the perpetrators are. There will be hard cases where the situation is murkier. Nonetheless, a line demarcating the legitimate use of torture can be drawn. Torture only the obviously guilty, and only for the sake of saving innocents, and the line between Us and Them will remain clear.

There is little danger that the Western democracies will lose their way if 12 they choose to inflict pain as one way of preserving order. Paralysis in the face of evil is the greater danger. Some day soon a terrorist will threaten tens of thousands of lives, and torture will be the only way to save them. We had better start thinking about this.

For incorporating Levin's ideas into your own writing, you have a number of options.

Summary

When you wish to include a writer's complete argument (or a large sustained portion of it) in your own essay, you will need to summarize it. For a detailed explanation of how to summarize, see Chapter 2. Summaries can be quite long or very short. The following condensation of Levin's essay illustrates a short summary.

> Levin believes that torture can be justifiable if its purpose is to save innocent lives and if it is certain that the person being tortured has the power to save those lives. Torture is not justifiable as punishment. Levin likens the justified use of torture to the justified use of assassination or preemptive strikes in order to preclude or shorten a war.

This short passage summarizes the main points of the Levin argument in a few sentences. As a summary, it condenses the whole down to a small nutshell. For an example of a somewhat longer summary, see Chapter 2, pages 32–39.

Paraphrase

Unlike summary, which is a condensation of an essay, a paraphrase is a "translation" of an essay into the writer's own words. It is approximately the same length as the original, but converts the original into the writer's own voice. Be careful when you paraphrase to avoid both the original writer's words and the original writer's grammatical structure and syntax. If you follow the original sentence structure while replacing occasional words with synonyms, you are cheating: That practice is plagiarism, not paraphrase. Here is a paraphrase of paragraph 4 in Levin's essay:

> Levin asks whether it is unconstitutional to torture a terrorist. He believes that it probably is, but he argues that saving the lives of millions of innocent people is a greater good than obeying the Constitution. Although torture is brutal, so is letting innocent people die. In fact, Levin believes that we are moral cowards if we don't torture a guilty individual in order to save millions of lives.

This paraphrase of paragraph 4 is approximately the same length as the original paragraph. The purpose of a paraphrase is not to condense the original, but to turn the original into one's own language. Even though you are not borrowing any language, you will still need to cite the source to indicate that you are borrowing ideas.

Block Quotation

Occasionally, you will wish to quote an author's words directly. You must be meticulous in copying down the words *exactly* so that you make no changes. You must also be fair to your source by not quoting out of context. When the quoted material takes up more than three lines in your original source, use the following block quotation method:

In his argument supporting torture under certain circumstances, Levin is careful to insist that he doesn't see torture as punishment but solely as a way of preventing loss of innocent lives:

> I am not advocating torture as punishment. Punishment is addressed to deeds irrevocably past. Rather, I am advocating torture as an acceptable measure for preventing future evils. So understood, it is far less objectionable than many extant punishments.

Here the writer wants to quote Levin's words as found in paragraph 7. Because the passage to be quoted is longer than three lines, the writer uses the block quotation method. Note that the quotation is introduced with a colon and that no quotation marks are used. The block format with indentations takes the place of quotation marks.

Inserted Quotation

If the passage you wish to quote is less than three lines, you can insert it directly into your own sentences by using quotation marks instead of the block method:

> In his argument favoring torture, Levin is careful to distinguish between torture and punishment. "I am not advocating torture as punishment," Levin asserts. "Punishment is addressed to deeds irrevocably past. Rather, I am advocating torture as an acceptable measure for preventing future evils."

Here the writer breaks the same quotation into parts so that no part is longer than three lines. Thus the writer uses quotation marks rather than the block quotation method.

If the inserted quotation is a complete sentence in your own essay, then it should begin with a capital letter. The quotation is usually separated from preceding explanatory matter by a colon or comma. However, if the quotation is not a complete sentence in your own essay, then you insert it using quotation marks only and begin the quotation with a small letter.

QUOTATION AS INDEPENDENT SENTENCE

According to Levin, "Punishment is addressed to deeds irrevocably past."

QUOTATION AS CLAUSE OR PHRASE THAT IS NOT AN INDEPENDENT SENTENCE

Levin claims that punishment is concerned with "deeds irrevocably past," while torture is aimed at "preventing future evils."

In the first example, the quotation begins with a capital P because the quotation comprises an independent sentence. Note that it is separated from the preceding phrase by a comma. In the second example the quotations do not comprise independent sentences. They are inserted directly into the writer's sentence, using quotation marks only.

Shortening or Modifying Quotations

Sometimes you wish to quote the exact words from a source, but in order to make the quotation fit gracefully into your own sentence you need to alter it in some way, either by shortening it, by changing it slightly, or by adding explanatory material to it. There are several ways of doing so: through judicious selection of phrases to be quoted or through use of ellipses and brackets.

SHORTEN A PASSAGE BY SELECTING ONLY KEY PHRASES FOR QUOTING

In his argument favoring torture, Levin is careful to distinguish between torture and punishment. "I am not advocating torture as punishment," Levin asserts, but only "as an acceptable measure for preventing future evils."

Here the writer quotes only selected pieces of the longer passage and weaves them into her own sentences.

USE ELLIPSIS TO OMIT MATERIAL FROM A QUOTATION

Levin continues by distinguishing torture from capital punishment:

> Opponents of the death penalty . . . are forever insisting that executing a murderer will not bring back his victim. . . . But torture . . . is intended not to bring anyone back but to keep innocents from being dispatched.

In this block quotation from paragraph 7, the writer uses ellipses in three places. Made with three spaced periods, an ellipsis indicates that words have been omitted. Note that the second ellipsis in the above passage seems to contain four periods. The first period ends the sentence; the last three periods are the ellipsis.

USE BRACKETS TO MAKE SLIGHT CHANGES IN A QUOTATION OR TO ADD EXPLANATORY MATERIAL

According to Levin, "By threatening to kill for profit or idealism, he [the torturer] renounces civilized standards."

The writer puts "the torturer" in brackets to indicate the antecedent of the quoted pronoun "he." This passage is from paragraph 9.

According to Levin, "[T]orture [is] an acceptable measure for preventing future evils."

This passage, from paragraph 7, changes the original slightly: a small *t* has been raised to a capital *T*, and the word *as* has been changed to *is*. These changes are indicated by brackets. You don't usually have to indicate when you change a small letter to a capital or vice versa. But it is important to do so here because the writer is actually changing the grammar of the original by converting a phrase into a sentence.

Using Quotations within Quotations

Sometimes you may wish to quote a passage that already has quotation marks within it. If you use the block quotation method, keep the quotation marks exactly as they are in the original. If you use the inserted quotation method, then use single quotation marks (') instead of double marks (") to indicate the quotation within the quotation.

Levin is quick to dismiss the notion that a terrorist has rights:

> There is an important difference between terrorists and their victims
> that should mute talk of the terrorists' "rights." The terrorist's victims
> are at risk unintentionally, not having asked to be endangered. But
> the terrorist knowingly initiated his actions.

Because the writer uses the block quotation method, the original quotation
marks around *rights* remain. See the original passage in paragraph 9.

> Levin claims that "an important difference between terrorists and their victims . . .
> should mute talk of the terrorists' 'rights.'"

Here the writer uses the inserted quotation method. Therefore the original
double quotation marks (") around *rights* have been changed to single quotation marks ('), which on a typewriter are made with an apostrophe.

An Extended Illustration: Martha's Argument

To help you get a feel for how a writer integrates brief quotations into paraphrases or summaries, consider the following passage written by Martha, a
student who was disturbed by a class discussion of Levin's essay. Several
classmates argued that Levin's justification of torture could also be used to
justify terrorism. Martha did not believe that Levin's argument could be
applied to terrorism. Here is the passage from Martha's argument that summarizes Levin. (Page references in Martha's passage refer to the original
Newsweek source that she used—part of the MLA citation system to be
described shortly.)

> Now it may seem that if terrorism is always wrong then torture should always
> be wrong also since torture, even more so than terrorism, is a barbaric practice
> from a pre-civilized age. But philosopher Michael Levin shows a flaw in this rea-
> soning. Torture is justifiable, says Levin, but only in some cases. First of all, he
> says that torture should be applied only to those "*known* to hold innocent lives in
> their hands" and only if the person being tortured is clearly guilty and clearly can
> prevent a horrible act from occurring (13). Levin uses the example of using tor-
> ture on a captured terrorist to find the location of an atomic bomb set to go off on
> Manhattan Island. The principle here is that you are saving the lives of millions of
> innocent bystanders by applying systematic pain to one person who
> "renounc[ed] civilized standards" (13) when becoming a terrorist. For Levin, sav-
> ing the lives of innocent bystanders is a higher moral imperative than refusing to
> torture the person who can prevent the deaths. In fact, Levin claims, refusal to
> torture the terrorist is "moral cowardice, an unwillingness to dirty one's hands"
> (13). "If life is . . . valuable," Levin argues, then "the lives of the innocents must be
> saved even at the price of hurting the one who endangers them" (13).
>
> We can now return to the problem I posed earlier. If Levin is able to justify tor-
> ture under some conditions, why can't we also justify terrorism under some con-
> ditions? The answer is that . . . [Martha's argument continues].

☐   FOR CLASS DISCUSSION

Working as individuals or as small groups, prepare brief answers for the following questions:

1. How is Martha's passage different from a data dump?

2. Without being able to read her whole essay, can you determine Martha's purpose for summarizing Levin within her own argument on terrorism? If so, what is her purpose?

3. Why did the writer use brackets [ ] within one quotation and ellipses (. . .) within another?

4. What effects did Martha achieve by using only short quotations instead of longer block quotations from Levin's argument?

Signaling Directions: The Use of Attributive Tags

In all of our examples of citing, summarizing, paraphrasing, and quoting, the writers have used attributive tags to signal to readers which ideas are the writer's own and which ideas are being taken from another source. Attributive tags are phrases such as the following: "according to the researchers . . . ," "Levin claims that . . . ," "the author continues . . . ," and so forth. Such phrases signal to the reader that the material immediately following is from the cited source. Parenthetical citations are used only to give readers follow-up information on where the source can be found, not to indicate that the writer is using a source. The source being cited should always be mentioned in the text. Note how confusing a passage becomes if these attributive tags are omitted.

CONFUSING ATTRIBUTION

Now it may seem that if terrorism is always wrong then torture should always be wrong also since torture, even more so than terrorism, is a barbaric practice from a pre-civilized age. But there is a flaw in this reasoning. Torture should be applied only to those *"known* to hold innocent lives in their hands (Levin 13)" and only if the person being tortured is clearly guilty and clearly can prevent a terrorist act from occurring. A good example is using torture on a captured terrorist to find the location of an atomic bomb set to go off on Manhattan Island.

Although this writer cites Levin as the source of the quotation, it is not clear just when the borrowing from Levin begins or ends. For instance, is the example of the captured terrorist on Manhattan Island the writer's own or does it come from Levin? As the following revision shows, the use of attributive tags within the text makes it clear exactly where the writer's ideas leave off and a borrowed source begins or ends.

CLEAR ATTRIBUTION

Now it may seem that if terrorism is always wrong then torture should always be wrong also since torture, even more so than terrorism, is a barbaric practice from a pre-civilized age. But **philosopher Michael Levin shows** a flaw in this reasoning. Torture is justifiable, **says Levin,** but only in some cases. First of all, **he says that** torture should be applied only to those *"known* to hold innocent lives in their hands" and only if the person being tortured is clearly guilty and clearly can prevent a horrible act from occurring (13). **Levin uses** the example of using torture on a captured terrorist to find the location of an atomic bomb set to go off on Manhattan Island.

AVOIDING PLAGIARISM

Plagiarism, a form of academic cheating, is always a serious academic offense. You can plagiarize in one of two ways: (1) by borrowing another person's ideas without indicating the borrowing with attributive tags in the text and a proper citation, or (2) by borrowing another person's language without putting the borrowed language in quotation marks or block indentations. The first kind of plagiarism is usually outright cheating; the writer usually knows he is stealing material and tries to disguise it.

The second kind of plagiarism, however, often begins in a hazy never-never land between paraphrasing and copying. We refer to it in our classes as "lazy cheating" and still consider it a serious offense, like stealing from your neighbor's vegetable garden because you are too lazy to do your own planting, weeding, and harvesting. Anyone who appreciates how hard it is to write and revise even a short passage will appreciate why it is wrong to take someone else's language ready-made. Thus, in our classes, we would fail a paper that included the following passage. (Let's call the writer Lucy.)

> Another argument showing the importance of environment on scholastic achievement comes from a research study done by psychologists at the University of Chicago and the University of Michigan (*Science '86* 7, 8). The study shows that parents must share the blame for the poor math performance of American students. In this study more than 2,000 children in kindergarten and the fifth grade were tested and interviewed in Minneapolis, in Sendai, Japan, and in Taipei, China. The researchers made up a test based on math problems found in textbooks used in all three cities. All the children in each grade performed equally well on reading and general intelligence tests, but their math scores differed from the start. The kindergarteners from Japan scored about 10 percent higher than American kindergarteners. The gap widened by the fifth grade. The top U.S. fifth-grade class scored below the lowest Japanese class and the second lowest Chinese class. Of the 100 highest scoring fifth graders, one was American (*Science '86* 8).

□ For Class Discussion

Do you think it was fair to flunk Lucy's essay? She claimed she wasn't cheating since she gave two different parenthetical citations accurately citing the *Science '86* article as her source. Before answering this question, compare the above passage with the original article on page 391; also compare the above passage with the opening paragraph from Cheryl's summary (pages 392–93) of the *Science '86* article. What justification could a professor use for giving an A to Cheryl's essay while flunking Lucy's essay?

Note Taking to Avoid Plagiarism

When you take notes on books or articles, be extremely careful to put all borrowed language in quotation marks. If you write summaries of arguments, as we strongly recommend you do, take time at the note-taking stage to put the summaries in your own words. If you wish to paraphrase an important passage, make sure you either copy the original into your notes word for word and indicate that you have done so (so that you can paraphrase it later) or paraphrase it entirely in your language when you take the notes. Inadvertent plagiarism can occur if you copy something in your notes word for word and then later assume that what you copied was actually a paraphrase.

DOCUMENTING YOUR SOURCES

To many students, the dreariest aspect of research writing is documenting their sources—that is, getting citations in the proper places and in the correct forms. As we noted at the beginning of the previous chapter, however, documentation of sources is a service to readers who may want to follow up on your research. Documentation in the proper form allows them to find your sources quickly.

There are two questions that you must answer to ensure proper documentation: "When do I cite a source?" and "What format do I use?"

When to Cite Sources

As a general rule, cite everything you borrow. Some students take this rule to unnecessary extremes, arguing that everything they "know" comes from somewhere. They end up citing lectures, conversations with a friend, notes from an old high school class, and so forth. Use common sense. If you successfully avoid writing a data dump essay, then your research will be used to support a thesis, which will reflect your own individual thinking and synthesis of material. You will know when you are using evidence from your own personal experience as source material and when you are using evidence you got from doing library research. Document all the material you got from the library or from another external source.

What Format to Use

Formats for citations and bibliographies vary somewhat from discipline to discipline. At the present time, footnotes have almost entirely disappeared from academic writing as a means of citing sources. Rather, citations for quotations or paraphrased material are now usually made in the text itself by putting brief identifying symbols inside parentheses.

OVERVIEW OF THE MLA AND APA SYSTEMS OF DOCUMENTATION*

The two main systems used today for academic essays aimed at general college audiences are the MLA (Modern Language Association) system, generally favored in the humanities, and the APA (American Psychological Association) system, generally favored in the social sciences. Other general systems are sometimes encountered—for example, the *University of Chicago Manual of Style*—and many specialized disciplines such as biology or chemistry have their own style manuals. But familiarity with the MLA and APA systems should serve you well throughout college. The sample research argument written by Stephen Bean (pp. 339–51) follows the MLA style. The sample research argument written by Lynnea Clark (pp. 421–29) follows the APA style.

Neither the MLA nor the APA system uses footnotes to document sources. In both systems a source is cited by means of a brief parenthetical reference following the quotation or the passage in which the source is used. Complete bibliographic information on each source is then included in an alphabetical list at the end of the text. Let us now turn to a more complete discussion of these two features.

Feature 1: Place a Complete Bibliographic List at the End of the Text

In both the MLA and the APA styles, a list of all the sources you have cited is included at the end of the research paper. In the MLA system, this bibliographic list is called "Works Cited." In the APA system this list is called "References." In both systems, entries are listed alphabetically by author (if no author is given for a particular source, then that source is alphabetized by title).

Let's look at how the two style systems would have you cite the Levin article on torture. The article appears in the June 7, 1982, issue of *Newsweek* on page 13. In the MLA style the complete bibliographic reference would be placed at the end of the paper under "Works Cited," where it would appear as follows:

MLA:

> Levin, Michael. "The Case for Torture." <u>Newsweek</u> 7
> June 1982: 13.

---

* Our description of the MLA style is taken from Joseph Gibaldi and Walter S. Achtert, *MLA Handbook for Writers of Research Papers,* 3rd ed. New York: MLA, 1988. Our description of the APA style is taken from *Publication Manual of the American Psychological Association,* 3rd ed. Washington, D.C.: APA, 1983.

In the APA system, the complete bibliographic reference would be placed at the end of the paper under "References," where it would appear as follows:

APA: Levin, M. (1982, June 7). The case for torture. <u>Newsweek</u>, p. 13.

When you refer to this article in the text—using either system—you place a brief citation in parentheses.

Feature 2:   Cite Sources in the Text by Putting Brief References in Parentheses

Both the MLA and the APA systems cite sources through brief parenthetical references in the text. However, the two systems differ somewhat in the way these citations are structured.

In-text Citation: MLA System

In the MLA system, you place the author's name and the page number of the cited source in parentheses. (If the author's name is mentioned in a preceding attributive tag, then only the page number needs to be placed in parentheses.)

> Torture, claims one philosopher, should only be applied to those "<u>known</u> to hold innocent lives in their hands" and only if the person being tortured is clearly guilty and clearly can prevent a terrorist act from occurring (Levin 13).

or

> Torture, claims Michael Levin, should only be applied to those "<u>known</u> to hold innocent lives in their hands" and only if the person being tortured is clearly guilty and clearly can prevent a terrorist act from occurring (13).

If readers wish to follow up on the source, they will look up the Levin article in the "Works Cited" at the end. If more than one work by Levin has been used as sources in the essay, then you would include in the in-text citation an abbreviated title of the article following Levin's name.

(Levin, "Torture" 13)

Once Levin has been cited the first time and it is clear that you are still quoting from Levin, then you need put in parentheses only the page number and eliminate the author's name.

In-text Citation: APA System

In the APA system, you place the author's name and the date of the cited source in parentheses. If you are quoting a particular passage or citing a particular table, include the page number where the information is found. Use a comma to separate each element of the citation and use the abbreviation *p.* or *pp.* before the page number. (If the author's name is mentioned in a preceding attributive tag, then only the date needs to be placed in parentheses.)

> Torture, claims one philosopher, should only be applied to those
>
> "<u>known</u> to hold innocent lives in their hands" and only if the per-
>
> son being tortured is clearly guilty and clearly can prevent a ter-
>
> rorist act from occurring (Levin, 1982, p. 13).

or

> Torture, claims Michael Levin, should only be applied to those
>
> "<u>known</u> to hold innocent lives in their hands" and only if the per-
>
> son being tortured is clearly guilty and clearly can prevent a ter-
>
> rorist act from occurring (1982, p. 13).

If readers wish to follow up on the source, they will look for the 1982 Levin article in the "References" at the end. If Levin had published more than one article in 1982, the articles would be distinguished by small letters placed alphabetically after the date:

(Levin, 1982a)

or

(Levin, 1982b)

In the APA style, if an article or book has more than one author, the word *and* is used to join them in the text but the ampersand (&) is used to join them in the parenthetical reference:

Smith and Peterson (1983) found that . . .

More recent data (Smith & Peterson, 1983) have shown . . .

Citing a Quotation or Other Data from a Secondary Source

Occasionally, you may wish to use a quotation or other kinds of data from a secondary source. For example, suppose you are writing an argument that the United States should reconsider its trade policies with China. You read an article entitled "China's Gilded Age" by Xiao-huang Yin appearing in the April 1994 issue of *The Atlantic Monthly*. This article contains the following passage appearing on page 42:

Dual ownership has in essence turned this state enterprise into a private business. Asked if such a practice is an example of China's "socialist market economy," a professor of economics at Nanjing University, where I taught in the early 1980's, replied, "Nobody knows what the concept means. It is only rhetoric, and it can mean anything but socialism."

When citing material from a secondary source, it is always best, when possible, to locate the original source and cite your data directly. But in the above case, no other source is likely available. Here is how you would cite it in both the MLA and APA systems.

> **MLA:**   According to an economics professor at Nanjing University, the term "socialist market economy," has become confused under capitalistic influence. "Nobody knows what the concept means. It is only rhetoric, and it can mean anything but socialism" (qtd. in Yin 42).

> **APA:**   According to an economics professor at Nanjing University, the term "socialist market economy," has become confused under capitalistic influence. "Nobody knows what the concept means. It is only rhetoric, and it can mean anything but socialism" (cited in Yin, 1994, p. 42).

In both systems you would place the Yin article in the end-of-text bibliographic list. What follows is a description of the format for the end-of-text bibliographic entries under "Works Cited" in the MLA system and under "References" in the APA system.

FORM FOR ENTRIES IN "WORKS CITED" (MLA) AND "REFERENCES" (APA)

General Format for Books

> MLA: Author. <u>Title</u>. Edition. City of Publication: Publisher, year.
>
> APA: Author. (Year of Publication). Title. City of Publication: Publisher.

ONE AUTHOR

> MLA: Coles, Robert. <u>The Spiritual Life of Children</u>. Boston: Houghton, 1990.
>
> APA: Coles, R. (1990). <u>The spiritual life of children</u>. Boston: Houghton Mifflin.

In the MLA style, author entries include first names and middle initials. In the APA style only the initials of the first and middle names are given, unless full names are needed to distinguish persons with the same initials. In the APA style only the first word and proper names in a title are capitalized. Note also that the year of publication follows immediately after the author's name. In the MLA system, names of publishers have standard abbreviations, listed on pages 214–216 in the *MLA Handbook for Writers of Research Papers,* cited earlier. In the APA system, names of publishers are not usually abbreviated, except for the elimination of unnecessary words such as *Inc., Co.,* and *Publishers.*

TWO LISTINGS FOR ONE AUTHOR

MLA: Doig, Ivan. <u>Dancing at the Rascal Fair</u>. New York:

Atheneum, 1987.

---. <u>English Creek</u>. New York: Atheneum, 1984.

In the MLA style, when two or more works by one author are cited, the works are listed in alphabetical order by title. For the second and all additional entries, type three hyphens and a period in place of the author's name. Then skip two spaces and type the title.

APA: Doig, I. (1984). <u>English Creek</u>. New York: Atheneum.

Doig, I. (1987). <u>Dancing at the rascal fair</u>. New York:

Atheneum.

Selfe, C. L. (1984a). The predrafting processes of four

high- and four low-apprehensive writers. <u>Research in

the teaching of English</u>, 18, 45-64.

Selfe, C. L. (1984b). <u>Reading as writing and revising strat-

egy</u>. ERIC Document Reproduction Service No. ED

244-295.

In APA style, when an author has more than one entry in "References," the author's name is repeated and the entries are listed chronologically (oldest to newest) rather than alphabetically. When two entries by the same author have the same date, they are then listed in alphabetical order. Lower-case letters are added after the year of publication to distinguish them from each other when cited by date in the text.

TWO OR MORE AUTHORS

MLA: Ciochon, Russell, John Olsen, and Jamie James. <u>The

Search for the Giant Ape in Human Prehistory</u>. New

York: Bantam, 1990.

APA: Ciochon, R., Olsen, J., & James, J. (1990). <u>The search for the giant ape in human prehistory</u>. New York: Bantam Books.

Note that the APA style uses the ampersand (&) to join the names of multiple authors.

USING *ET AL.* FOR WORKS WITH SEVERAL AUTHORS

MLA: Maimon, Elaine P. et al. <u>Writing in the Arts and Sciences</u>. Cambridge: Winthrop, 1981.

In the MLA system, if there are four or more authors, you have the option of using *et al.* (meaning "and others") after the name of the first author listed on the title page.

APA: Maimon, E. P., Belcher, G. L., Hearn, G. W., Nodine, B. F., & O'Connor, F. W. (1981). <u>Writing in the arts and sciences</u>. Cambridge: Winthrop.

APA style allows the use of *et al.* only when there are six or more authors for one work.

ANTHOLOGY WITH AN EDITOR

MLA: Rabkin, Norman, Ed. <u>Approaches to Shakespeare</u>. New York: McGraw-Hill, 1964.

APA: Rabkin, N. (Ed.). (1964). <u>Approaches to Shakespeare</u>. New York: McGraw-Hill.

ESSAY IN AN ANTHOLOGY OR OTHER COLLECTION

MLA: Stein, Robert B., Lon Polk, and Barbara Bovee Polk. "Urban Communes." <u>Old Family/New Family</u>. Ed. Nona Glazer-Malbin. New York: Nostrand, 1975. 171-88.

APA: Stein, R. B., Polk, L., & Polk, B. B. (1975). Urban communes. In N. Glazer-Malbin (Ed.), <u>Old family/new family</u> (pp. 171-188). New York: D. Van Nostrand.

BOOK IN A LATER EDITION

MLA: Valette, Rebecca M. <u>Modern Language Testing</u>. 2nd ed. New York: Harcourt, 1977.

Williams, Oscar, Ed. <u>A Little Treasury of Modern Poetry</u>. Rev. ed. New York: Scribner's 1952.

APA: Valette, R. M. (1977). <u>Modern language testing</u> (2nd ed.). New York: Harcourt, Brace, Jovanovich.

Williams, O. (Ed.). (1952). <u>A little treasury of modern poetry</u> (rev. ed.). New York: Scribner's.

MULTIVOLUME WORK

Cite the whole work when you have used more than one volume of the work.

MLA: Churchill, Winston S. <u>A History of the English-Speaking Peoples</u>. 4 vols. New York: Dodd, 1956-58.

APA: Churchill, W. S. (1956-1958). <u>History of the English-speaking peoples</u> (Vols. 1-4). New York: Dodd, Mead.

Include the volume number when you have used only one volume of a multivolume work.

MLA: Churchill, Winston S. <u>The Great Democracies</u>. New York: Dodd, 1957. Vol. 4 of <u>A History of the English-Speaking Peoples</u>. 4 vols. 1956-58.

APA: Churchill, W. S. (1957). <u>A history of the English-speaking peoples: Vol. 4. The great democracies</u>. New York: Dodd, Mead.

REFERENCE WORK WITH FREQUENT EDITIONS

MLA: Pei, Mario. "Language." <u>World Book Encyclopedia</u>. 1976 ed.

In citing familiar reference works under the MLA system, you don't need to include all the normal publication information.

APA: Pei, M. (1976). Language. In <u>World book encyclopedia</u> (Vol. 12, pp. 62-67). Chicago: Field Enterprises.

APA does not give a specific example for use of a reference book. The APA manual directs the writer to follow an example similar to the source and to include more information rather than less.

LESS FAMILIAR REFERENCE WORK WITHOUT FREQUENT EDITIONS

MLA: Ling, Trevor O. "Buddhism in Burma." <u>Dictionary of Comparative Religion</u>. Ed. S. G. F. Brandon. New York: Scribner's, 1970.

APA: Ling, T. O. (1970). Buddhism in Burma. In S. G. F. Brandon (Ed.). <u>Dictionary of comparative religion</u>. New York: Scribner's.

EDITION IN WHICH ORIGINAL AUTHOR'S WORK IS PREPARED BY AN EDITOR

MLA: Brontë, Emily. <u>Wuthering Heights</u>. Ed. V. S. Pritchett. Boston: Houghton, 1956.

APA: Brontë, E. (1956). <u>Wuthering Heights</u> (V. S. Pritchett, Ed.). Boston: Houghton, Mifflin. (Original work published 1847)

TRANSLATION

MLA: Camus, Albert. <u>The Plague</u>. Trans. Stuart Gilbert. New York: Modern Library, 1948.

APA: Camus, A. (1948). <u>The plague</u> (S. Gilbert, Trans.). New York: Modern Library. (Original work published 1947)

In APA style, the date of the translation is placed after the author's name; the date of original publication of the work is placed in parentheses at the end of the reference. In text, this book would be cited

(Camus, 1947/1948)

CORPORATE AUTHOR (A COMMISSION, COMMITTEE, OR OTHER GROUP)

MLA: American Medical Association. <u>The American Medical Association's Handbook of First Aid and Emergency Care</u>. New York: Random, 1980.

APA: American Medical Association. (1980). <u>The American Medical Association's handbook of first aid and emergency care</u>. New York: Random House.

Anonymous Work

MLA: <u>The New Yorker Cartoon Album: 1975–1985</u>. New York: Penguin, 1987.

APA: <u>The New Yorker cartoon album: 1975–1985</u>. (1987). New York: Penguin Books.

Republished Work (For Example, a Newer Paperback Published After the Original Hardbound)

MLA: Sagan, Carl. <u>The Dragons of Eden: Speculations on the Evolution of Human Intelligence</u>. 1977. New York: Ballantine, 1978.

APA: Sagan, C. (1978). <u>The dragons of Eden: Speculations on the evolution of human intelligence</u>. New York: Ballantine. (Originally published in 1977)

General Format for Articles

MLA: Author. "Article Title." <u>Magazine or Journal Title</u> volume number (Date): inclusive pages.

APA: Author. (Date). Article title. <u>Magazine or Journal Title, volume number</u>, inclusive pages.

Scholarly Journal with Continuous Annual Pagination

MLA: Barton, Ellen L. "Evidentials, Argumentation, and Epistemological Stance." <u>College English</u> 55 (1993): 745–69.

APA: Barton, E. L. (1993). Evidentials, argumentation, and epistemological stance. <u>College English 55</u>, 745–769.

Scholarly Journal with Each Issue Paged Separately

MLA: Pollay, Richard W., Jung S. Lee, and David Carter-Whitney. "Separate, but Not Equal: Racial Segmentation in Cigarette Advertising." Journal of Advertising 21.1 (1992): 45–57.

APA: Pollay, R. W., Lee, J. S., & Carter-Whitney, D. (1992). Racial segmentation in cigarette advertising. Journal of Advertising 21 (1), 45–57.

Note that in both systems when each issue is paged separately, both the volume (in this case, 43) and the issue number (in this case, 4) are given.

Magazine Article

MLA: Fallows, James. "Vietnam: Low-Class Conclusions." Atlantic Apr. 1993: 38–44

APA: Fallows, J. (1993, April). Vietnam: Low-class conclusions. Atlantic, pp. 38–44.

Note that the above form is for a magazine published each month. The next entry shows the form for a magazine published each week.

Anonymous Article

MLA: "The Rebellious Archbishop." Newsweek 11 July 1988: 38.

APA: The rebellious archbishop. (1988, July 11). Newsweek, p. 38.

Review

MLA: Bliven, Naomi. "Long, Hot Summer." Rev. of We Are Not Afraid: The Story of Goodman, Schwerner, and Cheney and the Civil Rights Campaign of Mississippi, by Seth Cagin and Philip Dray. New Yorker 11 July 1988: 81+.

This is a review of a book. The *81+* indicates that the review continues later in the magazine. For both movie and book reviews, if the reviewer's name is not given, begin with the title of the reviewed work, preceded by "Rev. of" in the MLA system or "[Review of *title*]" in the APA system. Begin with the title of the review if the review is titled but not signed.

APA: Bliven, N. (1988, July 11). Long, hot summer [Review of
<u>We are not afraid: The story of Goodman, Schwerner,</u>
<u>and Cheney and the civil rights campaign of</u>
<u>Mississippi</u>]. <u>New Yorker</u>, p. 81+

NEWSPAPER ARTICLE

MLA: Healy, Tim. "The Politics of Real Estate." <u>Seattle Times</u> 14
June 1988: 1E.

APA: Healy, T. (1988, June 14). The politics of real estate. <u>The</u>
<u>Seattle Times</u>, p. 1E.

Note that the section is indicated if each section is paged separately.

NEWSPAPER EDITORIAL

MLA: Smith, Charles Z. "Supreme Court Door Opens for a Minority." Editorial. <u>Seattle Times</u> 14 July 1988: 18A.

APA: Smith, C. Z. (1988, July 14). Supreme court door opens for
a minority [Editorial]. <u>The Seattle Times</u>, p. 18A.

LETTER TO THE EDITOR OF A MAGAZINE OR NEWSPAPER

MLA: Fleming, Deb. Letter. <u>Ms</u>. July 1988: 14.

APA: Fleming, D. (1988, July). [Letter to the editor]. <u>Ms.</u>, p. 14.

Include a title if one is given to the letter in the publication.

INFORMATION SERVICE SUCH AS ERIC (EDUCATIONAL RESOURCES INFORMATION
CENTER) OR NTIS (NATIONAL TECHNICAL INFORMATION SERVICE)

MLA: Eddy, P. A. <u>The Effects of Foreign Language Study in High</u>
<u>School on Verbal Ability as Measured by the Scholastic</u>
<u>Aptitude Test-Verbal</u>. Washington: Center for Applied
Linguistics, 1981. ERIC ED 196 312.

APA: Eddy, P. A. (1981). <u>The effects of foreign language study in</u>
<u>high school on verbal ability as measured by the</u>

<u>Scholastic Aptitude Test-Verbal</u>. Washington, D.C.: Center for Applied Linguistics. (ERIC Document Reproduction Service No. ERIC ED 196 312)

Miscellaneous Materials

FILMS, FILMSTRIPS, SLIDE PROGRAMS, AND VIDEOTAPES

MLA: <u>Chagall</u>. Videocassette. Dir. by Kim Evans. Ed. Melvyn Bragg. London Weekend Television, 1985.

APA: Evans, K. (Director), & Bragg, M. (Editor). (1985). <u>Chagall</u> [Videocassette]. London, England: London Weekend Television.

TELEVISION AND RADIO PROGRAMS

MLA: <u>Korea: The Forgotten War</u>. Narr. by Robert Stack. KCPQ, Seattle. 27 June 1988.

APA: Stack, R. (Narrator). (1988, June 27). <u>The forgotten war</u>. KCPQ Seattle.

INTERVIEW

MLA: Deltete, Robert. Personal interview. 27 Feb. 1994.

APA: Deltete, R. (1994, February 27). [Personal interview].

The APA publication manual says to omit nonrecoverable materials—such as personal correspondence, personal interviews, lectures, and so forth—from "References" at the end. However, in college research papers, professors usually like to have such information included.

LECTURE, ADDRESS, OR SPEECH

MLA: North, Oliver. Speech. Washington Policy Council. Seattle, 20 July 1988.

APA: North, O. (1988, July 20). Speech presented to Washington Policy Council, Seattle.

In the MLA system, if the title of the speech is known, give the title in quotation marks in place of the word "Speech." The *Publication Manual of the American Psychological Association* has no provisions for citing lectures, addresses, or speeches because these are nonrecoverable items. However, the manual gives authors leeway to design citations for instances not covered explicitly in the manual. This format is suitable for college research papers.

For more complicated entries, consult the *MLA Handbook for Writers of Research Papers,* third edition, or the *Publication Manual of the American Psychological Association,* third edition. Both books should be available in your library or bookstore.

CONCLUSION

If you see research writing as a variation on the thesis-governed writing you do for all your argument essays, you shouldn't have any particular difficulty writing an argument as a research paper. Keep in mind the issue question, thesis, and purpose of your own essay as a guide to taking notes and incorporating sources into your own work. Avoid data dumping by using borrowed material as a way of supporting your own argument instead of as an end in itself. Take particular care to indicate the beginning and end of borrowed material by putting attributive tags in your text and indicate any borrowed language with quotation marks or block indentations. Simply add the conventions of documentation appropriate to your topic and field, and you will have produced a satisfying research paper.

□ FOR CLASS DISCUSSION

1. Read Stephen's essay, pages 339–51, which is an example of a fully documented argument using the MLA style. Go to your library and locate several of the sources he has cited in his essay. Read one or two of the articles he cites and then prepare a brief report on whether he uses those sources accurately and fairly.*

2. Read Lynnea's essay (following this section), which is an example of a fully documented argument using the APA style. Give this essay the same scrutiny requested for Stephen's essay. Go to your library and locate several of the sources she has cited in her essay. Then prepare a brief report on whether or not she uses those sources accurately and fairly.

3. Pages 418–19, arranged as facing pages for easy comparison, show a "Works Cited" list (MLA) and a "References" list (APA). These lists give you a "quick check" summary of the formats for the most commonly used sources. Review the formats for MLA and APA bibliographic lists, noting similarities and differences. Then respond to the questions on page 420.

---

* The Charles Krauthammer essay cited by Stephen is reprinted on pages 226–33 of this text.

WORKS CITED: MLA STYLE SHEET FOR THE MOST COMMONLY USED SOURCES

Ross 27

Author's last name and page number in upper right corner.

Works Cited

Adler, Freda. <u>Sisters in Crime</u>. New York: McGraw, 1975.

Book entry, one author. Use standard abbreviations for common publishers.

Andersen, Margaret L. <u>Thinking About Women: Sociological Perspectives on Sex and Gender</u>. 3rd ed. New York: Macmillan, 1993.

Book entry in a revised edition.

Bart, Pauline, and Patricia O'Brien. <u>Stopping Rape: Successful Survival Strategies</u>. New York: Pergamon, 1985.

Book with two or three authors. With four or more authors use "et al", as in Jones, Peter, et al.

Durkin, Kevin. "Social Cognition and Social Context in the Construction of Sex Differences." <u>Sex Differences in Human Performances</u>. Ed. Mary Anne Baker. New York: Wiley, 1987. 45-60.

Article in anthology; author heads the entry; editor cited after the title. Inclusive page numbers come two spaces after the period following year.

Fairburn, Christopher G., et al. "Predictors of 12-month Outcome in Bulimia Nervosa and the Influence of Attitudes to Shape and Weight." <u>Journal of Consulting and Clinical Psychology</u> 61 (1993): 696-98.

Article in scholarly journal paginated consecutively throughout year. This article has three or more authors.

Kantrowitz, Barbara. "Sexism in the Schoolhouse." <u>Newsweek</u> 24 Feb. 1992: 62.

Weekly or biweekly popular magazine; abbreviate all months except May, June, and July.

Langewiesche, William. "The World in Its Extreme." <u>Atlantic</u> Nov. 1991: 105-40.

Monthly, bimonthly, or quarterly magazine.

Taylor, Chuck. "After Cobain's Death: Here Come the Media Ready to Buy Stories." <u>Seattle Times</u> 10 Apr. 1994: A1+.

Newspaper article with identified author; if no author, begin with title.

REFERENCES: APA STYLE SHEET FOR THE MOST COMMONLY USED SOURCES

Women, Health, and Crime

27

References

Adler, F. (1975). <u>Sisters in crime</u>. New York: McGraw-Hill.

Andersen, M. L. (1993). <u>Thinking about women: Sociological perspectives on sex and gender</u> (3rd ed.). New York: Macmillan Publishing.

Bart, P., & O'Brien, P. (1985). <u>Stopping rape: Successful survival strategies</u>. New York: Pergamon Press.

Durkin, K. (1987). Social cognition and social context in the construction of sex differences. In M. A. Baker (Ed.), <u>Sex differences in human performances</u> (pp. 45-60). New York: Wiley & Sons.

Fairburn, C. G., Pevaler, R.C., Jones, R., & Hope, R.A. (1993). Predictors of 12-month outcome in bulimia nervosa and the influence of attitudes to shape and weight. <u>Journal of Consulting and Clinical Psychology, 61</u>, 696-98.

Kantrowitz, B. (1992, February 24). Sexism in the schoolhouse. <u>Newsweek</u>, p. 62.

Langewiesche, W. (1991, November). The world in its extreme. <u>Atlantic</u>, pp. 105-40.

Taylor, C. (1993, April 10). After Cobain's death: Here come the media ready to buy stories. <u>Seattle Times</u>, pp. A1+.

Running head with page number doublespaced below.

Book entry, one author. Don't abbreviate publisher but omit unnecessary words.

Book entry in a revised edition.

Book with multiple authors; uses ampersand instead of "and" before last name. Authors' names listed last name first.

Article in anthology; no quotes around article. Name of editor comes before book title.

Article in scholarly journal paginated consecutively throughout year. APA lists all authors rather than using "et al."

Weekly or biweekly popular magazine; abbreviate all months except May, June, and July.

Monthly, bimonthly, or quarterly magazine.

Newspaper article with identified author; if no author, begin with title.

☐ DISCUSSION QUESTIONS

Now that you have reviewed the formats of the most commonly used kinds of sources, consider the differences between the MLA and the APA systems. The MLA system is used most frequently in the humanities, while the APA system is used in the social sciences. Why do you suppose the MLA system gives complete first names of authors as well as middle initials, while the APA system uses only initials for the first and middle names? Why does the APA system emphasize date of publication by putting dates prominently near the front of an entry just after the author's name? On the basis of the MLA and APA formats, could you make some observations about differences in values between the humanities and the social sciences?

Women Police Officers:

Should Size and Strength Be Criteria for Patrol Duty?

Lynnea Clark

English 301

15 November 1990

Running Head: WOMEN POLICE

This research paper follows the APA style for format and documentation.

Women Police Officers:

Should Size and Strength Be Criteria for Patrol Duty?

A marked patrol car turns the corner at 71st and Franklin Avenue and cautiously proceeds into the parking lot of an old shopping center. About a dozen gang members, dressed in their gang colors, stand alert, looking down the alley that runs behind the store. As the car moves toward the gathering, they suddenly scatter in all directions. Within seconds, several shots are fired from the alley. Switching on the overhead emergency lights, the officer bolts from the car when he sees two figures running past him. "Freeze! Police!" the officer yells. The men dart off in opposite directions. Chasing one, the policeman catches up to him, and, observing no gun, tackles him. After a violent struggle, the officer manages to handcuff the man, just as the backup unit comes screeching up.

This policeman is my friend. The next day I am with him as he sits at a cafe with three of his fellow officers, discussing the incident. One of the officers comments, "Well, at least you were stronger than he was. Can you imagine if Connie Jones was on patrol duty last night?" "What a joke," scoffs another officer. "How tall is she anyway?" "About 4'10"and 90 pounds," says the third officer. "She could fit in my backpack." Connie Jones (not her real name) has just completed police academy training and has been assigned to patrol duty in _____. Because she is so small, she has to have a booster seat in her patrol car and has been given a special gun, since she can barely manage to pull the trigger of a standard police-issue .38 revolver. Although she passed the physical requirements at the academy, which involved speed and endurance running, situps, and monkey bar tests, most of the officers in her department doubt her ability to perform competently as a patrol officer. But nevertheless she is on patrol because men and women receive equal assignments in most of today's police forces. But is this a good policy? Can a person who is significantly small and weak make an effective patrol officer?

Because the "small and weak" people in question are almost always women, the issue becomes a woman's issue. Considerable research has been done on women in the police force, and much of it suggests that women, who are on the average smaller and weaker than men, can perform competently in law enforcement, regardless of their size or strength. More specifically, most research concludes that female police workers in general perform just as well as their fellow officers in patrolling situations. A major study by Bloch and Anderson (1984), commissioned by the Urban Institute, revealed that in the handling of violent situations, women performed well. In fact, women and men received equally satisfactory evaluation ratings on their overall performances.

In another more recent study (Grennan, 1987) examining the relationship between outcomes of police-citizen confrontations and the gender of the involved officers, female officers were determined to be just as productive as male officers in the handling of violent situations. In his article on female criminal justice employment, Potts (1982) reviews numerous studies on evaluation ratings of policewomen and acknowledges that "the predominant weight of evidence is that women are equally capable of performing police work as are men" (p. 11). Additionally, female officers score higher on necessary traits for leadership (p. 10), and it has been often found that women are better at dealing with rape and abuse victims. Again, a study performed by Grennan (1987), concentrating on male and female police officers' confrontations with citizens, revealed that the inborn or socialized nurturing ability possessed by female police workers makes them "just as productive as male officers in the handling of a violent confrontation" (p. 84).

This view has been strengthened further by the recent achievement of Katherine P. Heller, who was honored by receiving the nation's top award in law enforcement for 1990 (Proctor, 1990). Heller, a United States park policewoman, risked her life by stepping in the open to shoot dead an assailant while he levelled his gun to shoot at her fellow police officer. Five feet three inches and 107 pounds, Heller is not only the first woman to be awarded with Police Officer of the Year, but she is also the smallest recipient ever. Maybe Heller's decisiveness will help lay to rest doubts about many women's abilities as police workers.

However, despite the evidence provided by the above cited research, I am not convinced. Although these studies show that women make effective police officers, I believe the studies must be viewed with skepticism. My concern is public safety. In light of that concern, the evidence suggests that police departments should set stringent size and strength requirements for patrol officers, even if these criteria exclude many women.

First of all, the research studies documenting the success of women as patrol officers are marred by two major flaws: the amount of evidence gathered is scanty and the way that the data have been gathered doesn't allow us to study factors of size and strength. Because of minimal female participation in patrol work prior to the past decade, limited amounts of research and reports exist on the issue. And of the research performed, many studies have not been based on representative samples. Garrison, Grant, and McCormick (1988) found that

> [l]iterature on women in patrol or nontraditional police roles
> tends to be idiosyncratic. . . . Many of the observations written

> about a relatively small number of women performing success-
> fully in a wider range of police tasks support the assumption that
> they are exceptions rather than the norm. (p. 32)

Similarly, Bloch and Anderson (1984) note that in the course of their
study

> it was not possible to observe enough incidents to be sure that
> men and women are equally capable in all such situations. It
> is clear from the incidents which were described that women
> performed well in the few violent situations which did arise.
> (p. 61)

Another problem with the available research is that little differentiation has been made within the large group of women being considered;
all women officers seem to be grouped and evaluated based on only two
criteria: that they are on the police force and that they are female. But
like men, women come in all shapes and sizes. To say that women as a
class make effective or ineffective police workers is to make too general
a claim. The example of women officers such as Katherine Heller proves
that some women make excellent patrol cops. But, presumably, some
women probably would not make good patrol cops just as some men
would not. The available data do not allow us to determine whether size
and strength are factors. Because no size differentiation has been made
within the groups of women officers under observation in the research
studies, it is impossible to conclude whether or not smaller, weaker
women performed patrol duties as well as larger, stronger women did.
In fact, for Bloch and Anderson's study (which indicates that, from a
performance viewpoint, it is appropriate to hire women for patrol
assignments on the same basis as men) both men and women had to
meet a minimum height requirement of 5'7". Therefore, the performance of smaller, weaker women in handling violent situations

remained unevaluated. Thus the data show that many women are great cops; the data do <u>not</u> show that many small women with minimal strength make great cops.

The case of Katherine Heller might seem to demonstrate that smaller women can perform patrol duties successfully. Heller acknowledged in an interview in <u>Parade</u> magazine that ninety percent of her adversaries will be bigger than herself (Proctor, 1990, p. 5). But she is no fluttering fluffball; rather, she has earned the reputation for being an extremely aggressive cop and has compensated for her size by her bearing. But how many women (or men) of Heller's size or smaller could maintain such "officer presence"? How can we be certain that Heller is in fact representative of small women rather than being an exception?

This question leads to my second reason for supporting stringent size and strength requirements: Many police officers, both male and female, have real doubts about the abilities of small and physically weak patrol workers, most of whom are women. In a study done by Vega and Silverman (1982), almost 75% of male police officers felt that women were not strong enough to handle the demands of patrol duties, and 42% felt women lacked the needed assertiveness to enforce the law vigorously (p. 32). Unfortunately, however, because of frequent media reports of discrimination and sexism among police personnel and because of pressure from the Equal Employment Opportunity Commission (EEOC) on police agencies and other employers (Vega & Silverman, 1982; Lord, 1986), these reservations and attitudes have not been seriously taken into account. The valid concerns and opinions of police workers who feel that some women officers are not strong enough to deal effectively with violent situations have been asphyxiated by the smoldering accusations of civil rights activists and feminists, who see only layers of chauvinism, conservatism, cynicism, and authoritarianism permeating our law enforcement agencies. These activists view the problem as being only a "women" issue rather than a "size" issue. But the fact remains that both male and female officers think that many patrol workers are incapable of handling violent situations because of small stature and lack of physical strength. Another policewoman belonging to the same department as Connie Jones explained, "She [Jones]doesn't have the authoritarian stance needed to compensate for her size. She's not imposing and is too soft spoken. Once she responded to a call and was literally picked up and thrown out the door" (anonymous personal communication, October 6, 1990).

Finally, patrol duties, unlike other areas of police work, constitute one of the few jobs in our society that may legitimately require above average strength. Because the job involves great personal risk and danger, the concern for public safety overrides the concern for equal rights in this instance. Patrolling is a high visibility position in police departments as opposed to jobs such as radio dispatching, academy training, or clerical duties. Patrol workers directly face the challenges presented by the public, and violence is always a threat for officers on patrol (Vega & Silverman, 1982; Grennan, 1987). Due to the nature of patrol work, officers many times must cope with violent situations by using physical force, such as that needed for subduing individuals who resist arrest. However, pressure from liberal groups has prevented special consideration being given to these factors of patrol duty. As long as student officers pass the standard academy Physical Ability Test (in addition to the other academy requirements), then they are eligible for patrol assignments; in fact, everyone out of the academy must go on patrol. But the minimum physical requirements are not challenging. According to Lord (1986), police agencies "struggle to find a nondiscriminatory, empirically valid entry level physical agility test which does not discriminate against women by overemphasizing upper body strength" (Lord, 1986, p. 91). In short, the liberal agenda leading to women on patrol has forced the lowering of strength requirements.

Without establishing minimum size and strength requirements for patrol workers, police departments are not discharging their duties with maximum competency or effectiveness. Police training programs stress that police officers should be able to maintain an authoritarian presence in the face of challenges and possess the ability to diffuse a situation just by making an appearance. But some individuals who are able to pass basic training programs still lack the size needed to maintain an imposing physical stance. And as many citizens obviously do not respect the uniform, police workers must possess the strength to efficiently handle violent encounters. Even if size and strength requirements have a disproportionate impact on women, these physical standards are lawful, so long as they relate to the demands of the job and "constitute valid predictors of an employee's performance on the job" (Steel & Lovrich, 1987, p. 53). Patrol duties demand highly capable and effective workers, and in order to professionalize law-enforcement practices and to maintain the degree of order necessary for a free society, police agencies must maintain a high level of competency in their street-patrol forces.

References

Bloch, P., & Anderson, D. (1974). <u>Police women on patrol: Final report</u>. Washington, D.C.: Police Foundation.

Garrison, C., Grant, N., & McCormick, K. (1988). Utilization of police women. <u>The Police Chief</u>, <u>55</u>(9), 32-73.

Golden, K. (1981). Women as patrol officers: A study of attitudes. <u>Police Studies</u>, <u>4</u>(3), 29-33.

Grennan, S. (1987). Findings on the role of officer gender in violent encounters with citizens. <u>Journal of Police Science and Administration</u>, <u>15</u>(1), 78-84.

Igbinovia, P. (1987). African women in contemporary law enforcement. <u>Police Studies</u>, <u>10</u>(1), 31-34.

Lord, L. (1986). A comparison of male and female peace officers' stereotypic perceptions of women and women peace officers. <u>Journal of Police Science and Administration</u>, <u>14</u>(2), 83-91.

Potts, L. (1981). Equal employment opportunity and female criminal justice employment. <u>Police Studies</u>, <u>4</u>(3), 9-19.

Proctor, P. (1990, September 30). "I didn't have time to taste the fear." <u>Parade Magazine</u>, pp. 4-5.

Steel, B., & Lovrich, N., Jr. (1987). Equality and efficiency trade-offs in affirmative action—real or imagined? The case of women in policing. <u>The Social Science Journal</u>, <u>24</u>(1), 53-67.

Vega, M., & Silverman, I. (1982). Female police officers as viewed by their male counterparts. <u>Police Studies</u>, <u>5</u>(1), 31-39.

APPENDIX 1

Logical Fallacies

In this appendix, we look at ways of testing the legitimacy of an argument. Sometimes, there are fatal logical flaws hiding in the heart of a perfectly respectable looking argument, and if we miss them, we may find ourselves vainly defending the indefensible. Take, for example, the following cases. Do they seem persuasive to you?

Creationism must be a science because hundreds of scientists believe in it.

I am opposed to a multicultural curriculum because it will lead to ethnic separatism similar to what is happening in Eastern Europe.

Smoking must cause cancer because a higher percentage of smokers get cancer than do nonsmokers.

Smoking doesn't cause cancer because my grandfather smoked two packs per day for fifty years and died in his sleep at age ninety.

An abnormal percentage of veterans who were marched to ground zero during atomic tests in Nevada died of leukemia and lung cancer. Surely their deaths were caused by the inhalation of radioactive isotopes.

THE PROBLEM OF CONCLUSIVENESS IN AN ARGUMENT

Although it may distress us to think so, none of the above arguments is conclusive. But that doesn't mean they're false either. So what are they? Well, they are, to various degrees, "persuasive" or "unpersuasive." The problem is that some people will mistake arguments such as those above for "conclusive" or airtight arguments. A person may rest an entire argument on them and then fall right through the holes that observant logicians open in them. Although few people will mistake an airtight case for a fallacious one, lots of people mistake logically unsound arguments for airtight cases. So let's see how to avoid falling into specious reasoning.

Some arguments are flawed because they fail to observe certain formal logical rules. In constructing syllogisms, for example, there are certain formal laws that must be followed if we are to have a valid syllogism. The following argument is beyond doubt invalid and inconclusive:

No Greeks are bald.

No Lithuanians are Greek

Therefore, all Lithuanians are bald.

But to say the argument is invalid isn't to say that its conclusion is necessarily untrue. Perhaps all Lithuanians really are bald. The point is, if the conclusion were true, it would be by coincidence, not design, because the above argument is invalid. All invalid arguments are inconclusive. And, by the same token, a perfectly valid syllogism may be untrue. Just because the premises follow the formal laws of logic doesn't mean that what they say is true. For a syllogistic argument to be absolutely conclusive, its form must be valid and its premises must be true. A perfectly conclusive argument would therefore yield a noncontroversial truth—a statement that no one would dispute.

This is a long way around to reach one point: The reason we argue about issues is that none of the arguments on any side of an issue is absolutely conclusive; there is always room to doubt the argument, to develop a counterargument. We can only create more or less persuasive arguments, never conclusive ones.

We have examined some of these problems already. In Chapter 11 on causal arguments we discussed the problem of correlation versus causation. We know, for example, that smoking and cancer are correlated but that further arguments are needed in order to increase the conclusiveness of the claim that smoking *causes* cancer.

In this appendix we explore the problem of conclusiveness in various kinds of arguments. In particular, we use the "informal" fallacies of logic to explain how inconclusive arguments can fool us into thinking they are conclusive.

AN OVERVIEW OF INFORMAL FALLACIES

The study of informal fallacies remains the murkiest of all logical endeavors. It's murky in the sense that informal fallacies are as unsystematic as formal fallacies are rigid and systematized. Whereas formal fallacies of logic have the force of laws, informal fallacies have little more than explanatory power. Informal fallacies are quirky; they identify classes of less conclusive arguments that recur with some frequency, but they do not contain formal flaws that make their conclusions illegitimate no matter what the terms may say. Informal fallacies require us to look at the meaning of the terms to determine how much we should trust or distrust the conclusion. The most common mistake one can make with informal fallacies is to assume that they have the force of laws like formal fallacies. They don't. In evaluating arguments with informal fallacies, we usually find that arguments are "more or less" fallacious, and determining the degree of fallaciousness is a matter of judgment.

Knowledge of informal fallacies is most useful when we run across arguments that we "know" are wrong, but we can't quite say why. They just don't "sound right." They look reasonable enough, but they remain unacceptable to us. Informal fallacies are a sort of compendium of symptoms for arguments flawed in this way. We must be careful, however, to make sure that the particular case before us "fits" the descriptors for the fallacy that seems to explain its problem. It's much easier, for example, to find informal fallacies in a hostile argument than in a friendly one simply because we are more likely to expand the limits of the fallacy to make the disputed case fit.

Not everyone agrees about what to include under the heading of informal fallacies. In selecting the following set of fallacies, we left out far more candidates than we included. Since Aristotle first developed his list of thirteen elenchi (refutations) down to the present day, there have been literally dozens of different systems of informal fallacy put forward. Although there is a good deal of overlap among these lists, the terms are invariably different, and the definition of fallacy itself shifts from age to age. In selecting the following set of fallacies, we left out a number of other candidates. We chose the following because they seemed to us to be the most commonly encountered.

In arranging the fallacies we have, for convenience, put them into three categories derived from classical rhetoric: *pathos, ethos,* and *logos.* Fallacies of *pathos* rest on a flawed relationship between what is argued and the audience for the argument. Fallacies of *ethos* rest on a flawed relationship between the argument and the character of those involved in the argument. Fallacies of *logos* rest on flaws in the relationship among statements of an argument.

Fallacies of *Pathos*

Argument to the People (Appeal to Stirring Symbols)
This is perhaps the most generic possible example of a *pathos* fallacy. Argument to the people appeals to the fundamental beliefs, biases, and prejudices of the audience in order to sway opinion through a feeling of solidar-

ity among those of the group. For example, when a politician says, "My fellow Americans, I stand here, draped in this flag from head to foot, to indicate my fundamental dedication to the values and principles of these sovereign United States," he's redirecting to his own person our allegiance to nationalistic values by linking himself with the prime symbol of those values, the flag. The linkage is not rational, it's associative. It's also extremely powerful—which is why arguments to the people crop up so frequently.

Appeal to Ignorance (Presenting Evidence the Audience Can't Examine)
Those who commit this fallacy present assumptions, assertions, or evidence that the audience is incapable of judging or examining. If, for example, a critic were to praise the novel *Clarissa* for its dullness on the grounds that this dullness was the intentional effect of the author, we would be unable to respond because we have no idea what was in the author's mind when he created the work.

Appeal to Irrational Premises (Appealing to Reasons That May Have No Basis in Logic)
This particular mode of short-circuiting reason may take one of three forms:

1. Appeal to common practice. (It's all right to do X because everyone else does it.)
2. Appeal to traditional wisdom. (It's all right because we've always done it this way.)
3. Appeal to popularity—the bandwagon appeal. (It's all right because lots of people like it.)

In all three cases, we've moved from saying something is popular, common, or persistent to saying it is right, good or necessary. You have a better chance of rocketing across the Grand Canyon on a motorcycle than you have of going from "is" to "ought" on a because clause. Some examples of this fallacy would include (1) "Of course I borrowed money from the company slush fund. Everyone on this floor has done the same in the last eighteen months"; (2) "We've got to require everyone to read *Hamlet* because we've always required everyone to read it"; and (3) "You should buy a Ford Escort because it's the best-selling car in the world."

Provincialism (Appealing to the Belief That the Known is Always Better than the Unknown)
Here is an example from the 1960s: "You can't sell small cars in America. In American culture, automobiles symbolize prestige and personal freedom. Those cramped little Japanese tin boxes will never win the hearts of American consumers." Although we may inevitably feel more comfortable with familiar things, ideas, and beliefs, we are not necessarily better off for sticking with them.

Red Herring (Shifting the Audience's Attention from a Crucial Issue to an Irrelevant One)

A good example of a red herring showed up in a statement by former Secretary of State James Baker that was reported in the 10 November 1990 *New York Times*. In response to a question about the appropriateness of using American soldiers to defend wealthy, insulated (and by implication, corrupt) Kuwaiti royalty, Baker told an anecdote about an isolated encounter he had with four Kuwaitis who had suffered; he then made a lengthy statement on America's interests in the Gulf. Although no one would argue that America is unaffected by events in the Middle East, the question of why others with even greater interests at stake had not contributed more troops and resources went unanswered.

Fallacies of *Ethos*

Appeal to False Authority (Appealing to the Authority of a Popular Person Rather than a Knowledgeable One)

Appeals to false authority involve relying on testimony given by a person incompetent in the field from which the claims under question emerge. Most commercial advertisements are based on this fallacy. Cultural heroes are paid generously to associate themselves with a product without demonstrating any real expertise in evaluating that product. In at least one case, consumers who fell victim to such a fallacy made a legal case out of it. People bilked out of their life savings by a Michigan mortgage company sued the actors who represented the company on TV. Are people fooled by such appeals to false authority entitled to recover assets lost as a result?

The court answered no. The judge ruled that people gullible enough to believe that George Hamilton's capped-tooth smile and mahogany tan qualify him as a real estate consultant deserve what they get. Their advice to consumers?—"Buyers beware," because even though sellers can't legally lie, they can legally use fallacious arguments—all the more reason to know your fallacies.

Keep in mind, however, that occasionally the distinction between a false authority fallacy and an appeal to legitimate authority can blur. Suppose that Arnold Palmer were to praise a particular company's golf club. Because he is an expert on golf, it is possible that Palmer actually speaks from authority and that the golf club he praises is superior. But it might also be that he is being paid to advertise the golf club and is endorsing a brand that is no better than it competitors'. The only way we could make even a partial determination of Palmer's motives would be if he presented an *ad rem* ("to the thing") argument showing us scientifically why the golf club in question is superior. In short, appeals to authority are legitimate when the authority knows the field and when her motive is to inform others rather than profit herself.

Appeal to the Person/*Ad Hominem* (Attacking the Character of the Arguer Rather than the Argument Itself)

Literally, *ad hominem* means "to the man or person." Any argument that focuses on the character of the person making the argument rather than the quality of the reasoning qualifies as an *ad hominem* argument. Ideally, arguments are supposed to be *ad rem*, or "to the thing." that is, addressed to the specifics of the case itself. Thus an *ad rem* critique of a politician would focus on her voting record, the consistency and cogency of her public statements, her responsiveness to constituents, and so forth. An *ad hominem* argument would shift attention from her record to irrelevant features of her personality or personal life. Perhaps an *ad hominem* argument would suggest that she had a less than stellar undergraduate academic record.

But not all *ad hominem* arguments are *ad hominem* fallacies. It's not always fallacious to address your argument to the arguer. There are indeed times when the credibility of the person making an opposing argument is at issue. Lawyers, for example, when questioning expert witnesses who give damaging testimony, will often make an issue of their credibility, and rightfully so. And certainly it's not that clear, for instance, that an all-male research team of social scientists would observe and interpret data in the same way as a mixed-gender research group. An *ad hominem* attack on an opponent's argument in not fallacious so long as (1) personal authority is what gives the opposing argument much of its weight, and (2) the critique of the person's credibility is fairly presented.

An interesting example of an *ad hominem* argument occurred in the 1980's in context of the Star Wars debate. Many important physicists around the country signed a statement in which they declared their opposition to Star Wars research. Another group of physicists supportive of that research condemned them on the grounds that none of the protesting physicists stood to get any Star Wars research funds anyway.

This attack shifted attention away from the reasons given by the protesting physicists for their convictions and put it instead on the physicists' motives. To some extent, of course, credibility is an issue here, because many of the key issues raised in the debate required some degree of expertise to resolve. Hence, the charges meet the first test for nonfallacious reasoning directed to the arguer.

But we must also ask ourselves if the charges being made are fair. If you'll recall from earlier discussions of fairness, we said that fairness requires similar treatment of similar classes of things. Applying this rule to this situation, we can simply reverse the charge being levied against the anti-Star Wars group and say of its supporters: "Because you stand to gain a good deal of research money from this project, we can't take your support of the Star Wars initiatives seriously." The Star Wars supporters would thus become victims of their own logic. *Ad hominem* attacks are often of this nature: The charges are perfectly reversible. (E.g., "Of course you support abortion; all your friends are feminists." "Of course you oppose abortion; you've been a Catholic all your life.") *Ad hominem* debates resemble nothing so much as mental quick-draw contests. Whoever shoots first wins because the first accuser puts the burden of proof on the opposition.

It's important to see here that an *ad hominem* argument, even if not fallacious, can never be definitive. Like analogies, they are simply suggestive; they raise doubts and focus our attention. Catholic writers can produce reasonable arguments against abortion, and feminists can produce reasonable ones for it. *Ad hominem* attacks don't allow us to discount arguments; but they do alert us to possible biases, possible ways the reasoned arguments themselves are vulnerable.

Several subcategories of the *ad hominem* argument that are almost never persuasive include:

1. name-calling (referring to a disputant by unsavory names)
2. appeal to prejudice (applying ethnic, racial, gender, or religious slurs to an opponent)
3. guilt by association (linking the opposition to extremely unpopular groups or causes)

Name-calling is found far more often in transcripts of oral encounters than in books or essays. In the heat of the moment, speakers are more likely to lapse into verbal abuse than are writers who have time to contemplate their words. The Congressional Record is a rich source for name-calling. Here, for example, one finds a duly elected representative referring to another duly elected representative as "a pimp for the Eastern establishment environmentalists." One of the biggest problems with such a charge is that it's unlikely to beget much in the way of reasoned response. It's far easier to respond in kind than it is to persuade people rationally that one is not a jackass of *that* particular sort.

When name-calling is "elevated" to include slighting reference to the opponent's religion, gender, race, or ethnic background, we have encountered an appeal to prejudice. When it involves lumping an opponent with unsavory, terminally dumb, or extremely unpopular causes and characters, it constitutes guilt by association.

Strawperson (Greatly Oversimplifying an Opponent's Argument to Make it Easier to Refute or Ridicule)

Although typically less inflammatory than the above sorts of *ethos* fallacies, the strawperson fallacy changes the character of the opposition in order to suit the arguer's own needs. In committing a strawperson fallacy, you basically make up the argument you *wish* your opponents had made and attribute it to them because it's so much easier to refute than the argument they actually made. Some political debates consist almost entirely of strawperson exchanges such as: "You may think that levying confiscatory taxes on homeless people's cardboard dwellings is the surest way out of recession, but I don't." Or: "While my opponent would like to empty our prisons of serial killers and coddle kidnappers, I hold to the sacred principles of compensatory justice."

Fallacies of *Logos*

Logos fallacies comprise flaws in the relationships among the statements of an argument. Thus, to borrow momentarily from the language of the Toulmin schema discussed earlier, you can think of *logos* fallacies as breakdowns between argument's warrants and their claims, between their warrants and their backing, or between their claims and their reasons and grounds.

Begging the Question (Supporting a Claim with a Reason That Is Really a Restatement of the Claim in Different Words)

Question begging is probably the most obvious example of a *logos* fallacy in that it involves stating a claim as though it warranted itself. For example, the statement "Abortion is murder because it involves the intentional killing of an unborn human being" is tantamount to saying "Abortion is murder because it's murder." The warrant "If something is the intentional killing of a human life, it is murder" simply repeats the claim; murder is *by definition* the intentional killing of another human being. Logically, the statement is akin to a statement like "That fellow is fat because he's considerably overweight." The crucial issue in the abortion debate is whether or not a fetus is a human being in the legal sense; this crucial issue is avoided in the argument, which begins by assuming that the fetus is a legal human being. Hence the argument goes in an endless circle from claim to warrant and back again.

Or consider the following argument: "How can you say Minnie Minoso belongs in the Hall of Fame? He's been eligible for over a decade and the Selection Committee turned him down every year. If he belonged in the Hall of Fame, the Committee would already have chosen him." Because the point at issue is whether or not the Hall of Fame Selection Committee *should* elect Minnie Minoso (and they should), the use of their vote as proof of the contention that they should not elect him is wholly circular and begs the question.

In distinguishing valid reasoning from fallacious examples of question begging, some philosophers say that the question has been begged when the premises of an argument are at least as uncertain as the claim. In such cases, we are not making any movement from some known general principle toward some new particular conclusion; we are simply asserting an uncertain premise in order to give the appearance of certainty to a shaky claim.

To illustrate the preceding observation, consider the controversy that arose in the late eighties over whether or not to impose economic sanctions against South Africa in order to pressure the South Africans into changing their racial policies. One argument against economic sanctions went like this: "We should not approve economic sanctions against South Africa (claim) because economic sanctions will hurt blacks as much as whites" (premise or stated reason. The claim ("We should not impose economic sanctions") is only as certain as the premise from which it was derived ("because blacks will suffer as much as whites"), but many people argued that that premise was extremely uncertain. They thought that whites would suffer the most under sanctions and that blacks would ultimately benefit. The question would no longer be begged if the person included a documented defense of the premise. But without such a defense, the arguer's claim is grounded on a shaky premise that sounds more certain than it is.

Complex Question (Confronting the Opponent with a Question That Will Put Her in a Bad Light no Matter How She Responds)

A complex question is one that requires, in legal terms, a self-incriminating response. For example, the question "When did you stop abusing alcohol?" requires the admission of alcohol abuse. Hence the claim that a person has abused alcohol is silently turned into an assumption.

False Dilemma/Either–Or (Oversimplifying a Complex Issue So That Only Two Choices Appear Possible)

A good extended analysis of this fallacy is found in sociologist Kai Erickson's analysis of President Truman's decision to drop the A-bomb on Hiroshima. His analysis suggests that the Truman administration prematurely reduced numerous options to just two: Either drop the bomb on a major city or sustain unacceptable losses in a land invasion of Japan. Erickson, however, shows there were other alternatives. Typically, we encounter false dilemma arguments when people are trying to justify a questionable action by creating a false sense of necessity, forcing us to choose between two options, one of which is clearly unacceptable. Hence, when someone orders us to do it "My way or hit the highway," or to "Love it or leave it," it's probably in response to some criticism we made about the "way" we're supposed to do it or the "it" we're suppose to love.

But of course not all dilemmas are false. People who reject all binary oppositions (that is, thinking in terms of pairs of opposites) are themselves guilty of a false dilemma. There are times when we might determine through a rational process of elimination that only two possible choices exist. Deciding whether a dilemma is truly a dilemma or only an evasion of complexity often requires a difficult judgment. Although we should initially suspect any attempt to convert a complex problem into an either/or choice, we may legitimately arrive at such a choice through thoughtful deliberation.

Equivocation (Using to Your Advantage at Least Two Different Definitions of the Same Term in the Same Argument)

For example, if we're told that people can't "flourish" unless they are culturally literate, we must know which of the several possible senses of *flourish* are being used before we can test the persuasiveness of the claim. If by *flourishing* the author means acquiring great wealth, we'll look at a different set of grounds than if *flourishing* is synonymous with moral probity, recognition in a profession, or simple contentment. To the extent that we're not told what it means to flourish, the relationship between the claim and the grounds and between the claim and the warrant remains ambiguous and unassailable.

Confusing Correlation for Cause/*Post Hoc, Ergo Propter Hoc* (after This, Therefore Because of This) (Assuming that Event X Causes Event Y Because Event X Preceded Event Y)

Here are two examples in which this fallacy may be at work:

> Cramming for a test really helps. Last week I crammed for a psychology test and I got an A on it.

> I am allergic to the sound of a lawn mower because every time I mow the lawn I start to sneeze.

We've already discussed this fallacy in our chapter on causal arguments, particularly in our discussion of the difference between correlation and causation. This fallacy occurs when a sequential relationship is mistaken for a causal relationship. To be sure, when two events occur frequently in conjunction with each other in a particular sequence, we've got a good case for a causal relationship. But until we can show how one causes the other, we cannot be certain that a causal relationship is occurring. The conjunction may simply be a matter of chance, or it may be attributable to some as-yet-unrecognized other factor. For example, your A on the psych test may be caused by something other than your cramming. Maybe the exam was easier, or perhaps you were luckier or more mentally alert.

Just when an erroneous causal argument becomes an example of the *post hoc* fallacy, however, is not cut and dried. Many reasonable arguments of causality later turn out to have been mistaken. We are guilty of the *post hoc* fallacy only when our claim of causality seems naively arrived at, without reflection or consideration of alternative hypotheses. Thus in our lawn mower argument, it is probably not the sound that creates the speaker's sneezing, but all the pollen stirred up by the spinning blades.

We arrived at this more likely argument by applying a tool known as Occam's Razor–the principle that "what can be explained on fewer principles is explained needlessly by more," or "between two hypotheses, both of which will account for a given fact, prefer the simpler." If we posit that sound is the cause of our sneezing, all sorts of intermediate causes are going to have to be fetched from afar to make the explanation persuasive. But the blades stirring up the pollen will cause the sneezing more directly. So, until science connects lawn mower noises to human eardrums to sneezing, the simpler explanation is preferred.

Slippery Slope

The slippery slope fallacy is based on the fear that once we take a first step in a direction we don't like we will have to keep going.

> We don't dare send weapons to guerrillas in Central America. If we do so, we will next send in military advisers, then a special forces battalion, and then large numbers of troops. Finally, we will be in all-out war.

> Look, Blotnik, no one feels worse about your need for open-heart surgery than I do. But I still can't let you turn this paper in late. If I were to let you do it, then I'd have to let everyone turn in papers late.

We run into slippery slope arguments all the time, especially when person A opposes person B's proposal. Those opposed to a particular proposal will often foresee an inevitable and catastrophic chain of events that would follow from taking a first, apparently harmless step. In other words, once we put a foot on that slippery slope, we're doomed to slide right out of sight. Often, such arguments are fallacious insofar as what is seen as an inevitable effect is in fact dependent on some intervening cause or chain of causes to bring it about. Will smoking cigarettes lead inevitably to heroin addiction? Overwhelming statistical evidence would suggest that it doesn't. A slippery slope argument would, however, lovingly trace a teenager's inevitable descent from a clandestine puff on the schoolground through the smoking of various controlled substances to a degenerate end in some Needle Park somewhere. The power of the slippery slope argument lies as much as anything in its compelling narrative structure. It pulls us along irresistibly from one plausible event to the next, making us forget that it's a long jump from plausibility to necessity.

One other common place to find slippery slope arguments is in confrontations between individuals and bureaucracies or other systems of rules and laws. Whenever individuals ask to have some sort of exception made for them, they risk the slippery slope reply. "Sorry, Mr. Jones, if we rush your order, then we will have to rush everyone else's order also."

The problem, of course, is that not every slippery slope argument is an instance of the slippery slope fallacy. We all know that some slopes are slippery and that we sometimes have to draw the line, saying "to here, but no farther." And it is true also that making exceptions to rules is dangerous; the exceptions soon get established as regular procedures. The slippery slope becomes a fallacy, however, when we forget that some slopes don't *have* to be slippery unless we let them be slippery. Often we do better to imagine a staircase with stopping places all along the way. The assumption that we have no control over our descent once we take the first step makes us unnecessarily rigid.

Hasty Generalization (Making a Broad Generalization on the Basis of Too Little Evidence)

Typically, a hasty generalization occurs when someone reaches a conclusion on the basis of insufficient evidence. But what constitutes "sufficient" evidence? No generalization arrived at through empirical evidence would meet a logician's strict standard of certainty. And generally acceptable standards of proof in any given field are difficult to determine.

The Food and Drug Administration (FDA), for example, generally proceeds very cautiously before certifying a drug as "safe." However, whenever doubts arise about the safety of an FDA-approved drug, critics accuse the FDA of having made a hasty generalization. At the same time, patients eager to have access to a new drug and manufacturers eager to sell a new product may lobby the FDA to "quit dragging its feet" and get the drug to market. Hence, the point at which a hasty generalization about drug safety passes over into the realm of a prudent generalization is nearly always uncertain and contested.

A couple of variants of hasty generalization that deserve mention are

1. Pars pro toto/*Mistaking the part for the whole (assuming that what is true for a part will be true for the whole).* Pars pro toto arguments often appear in the critiques of the status quo. If, say, someone wanted to get rid of the National Endowment for the Arts, they might focus on several controversial grants they've made over the past few years and use them as justification for wiping out all NEA programs.

2. *Suppressed evidence (withholding contradictory or unsupportive evidence so that only favorable evidence is presented to an audience).* The flip side of *pars pro toto* is suppressed evidence. If the administrator of the NEA were to go before Congress seeking more money and conveniently forgot about those controversial grants, he would be suppressing damaging but relevant evidence.

Faulty Analogy (Claiming that Because X Resembles Y in One Regard, X Will Resemble Y in All Regards)

Faulty analogies occur whenever a relationship of resemblance is turned into a relationship of identity. For example, the psychologist Carl Rogers uses a questionable analogy in his argument that political leaders should make use of discoveries about human communication derived from research in the social sciences. "During the war when a test-tube solution was found to the problem of synthetic rubber, millions of dollars and an army of talent was turned loose on the problem of using that finding. . . . But in the social science realm, if a way is found of facilitating communication and mutual understanding in small groups, there is no guarantee that the finding will be utilized."

Although Rogers is undoubtedly right that we need to listen more carefully to social scientists, his analogy between the movement from scientific discovery to product development and the movement from insights into small group functioning to political change is strained. The laws of cause and effect at work in a test tube are much more reliable and generalizable than the laws of cause and effect observed in small human groups. Whereas lab results can be readily replicated in different times and places, small group dynamics are altered by a whole host of factors, including the cultural background, gender, age of participants, and so forth. The warrant that licenses you to move from grounds to claim in the realm of science runs up against a statute of limitation when it tries to include the realm of social science.

Non Sequitur (Making a Claim That Doesn't Follow Logically from the Premises, or Supporting a Claim with Irrelevant Premises)

The *non sequitur* fallacy (literally, "it does not follow") is a miscellaneous category that includes any claim that doesn't follow logically from its premises or that is supported with irrelevant premises. In effect, any fallacy is a kind of *non sequitur* because what makes all fallacies fallacious is the absence of a logical connection between claim and premises. But in practice the term *non sequitur* tends to be restricted to problems like the following:

A completely illogical leap: "Clambake University has one of the best faculties in the United States because a Nobel Prize winner used to teach there." (How does the fact that a Nobel Prize winner used to teach at Clambake University make its present faculty one of the best in the United States?)

A clear gap in the chain of reasoning: "People who wear nose-rings are disgusting. There ought to be a law against wearing nose-rings in public." (This is a *non sequitur* unless the arguer is willing to state and defend the missing premise: "There ought to be a law against anything that I find disgusting.")

Use of irrelevant reasons to support a claim: "I should not receive a C in this course because I have received B's or A's in all my other courses (here is my transcript for evidence) and because I worked exceptionally hard in this course (here is my log of hours worked)." (Even though the arguer has solid evidence to support each premise, the premises themselves are irrelevant to the claim. Course grades should be based on actual performance in the class, not on performance in other classes or on amount of effort devoted to the material.)

☐ FOR CLASS DISCUSSION

Working individually or in small groups, determine the potential persuasiveness of each argument. If the arguments are nonpersuasive because of one or more of the fallacies discussed in this appendix, identify the fallacies and explain how they render the argument nonpersuasive.

1. a. All wars are not wrong. The people who say so are cowards.
   b. Either we legalize marijuana or we watch a steady increase in the number of our citizens who break the law.
   c. The Bible is true because it is the inspired word of God.
   d. Mandatory registration of handguns will eventually lead to the confiscation of hunting rifles.
   e. All these tornadoes started happening right after they tested the A-bombs. The A-bomb testing has changed our weather.
   f. Most other progressive nations have adopted a program of government-provided health care. Therefore, it is time the United States abandoned its outdated practice of private medicine.
   g. The number of Hollywood movie stars who support liberal policies convinces me that liberalism is the best policy. After all, they are rich and will not benefit from better social services.

h. Society has an obligation to provide housing for the homeless because people without adequate shelter have a right to the resources of the community.

i. I have observed the way the two renters in our neighborhood take care of their rental houses and have compared that to the way homeowners take care of their houses. I have concluded that people who own their own homes take better care of them than those who rent. [This argument goes on to provide detailed evidence about the house-caring practices of the two renters and of the homeowners in the neighborhood.]

j. Since the universe couldn't have been created out of nothing, it must have been created by a divine being.

2. Consider the following statements. Note places where you think the logic is flawed. If you were asked by writers or speakers to respond to their statements, what advice would you give to those who wrote or said them to rescue them from charges of fallaciousness? What would each of these speakers/writers have to show, in addition to what's given, to render the statement cogent and persuasive?

a. "America has had the luxury throughout its history of not having its national existence directly threatened by a foreign enemy. Yet we have gone to war. Why?

"The United States of America is not a piece of dirt stretching mainly from the Atlantic to the Pacific. More than anything else, America is a set of principles, and the historical fact is that those principles have not only served us well, but have also become a magnet for the rest of the world, a large chunk of which decided to change course last year.

"Those principles are not mere aesthetic ideas. Those principles are in fact the distillation of 10,000 years of human social evolution. We have settled on them not because they are pretty; we settled on them because they are the only things that work. If you have trouble believing that, ask a Pole." (novelist Tom Clancy)

b. "What particularly irritated Mr. Young [RepublicanCongressman from Alaska] was the fact that the measure [to prohibit logging in Alaska's Tongass National Forest] was initiated by . . . Robert Mrazek, a Democrat from Long Island. 'Bob Mrazek never saw a tree in his entire life until he went to Alaska' said Mr. Young. . . ." (*New York Times*, 11/10/90)

c. "When Senator Tim Wirth . . . was in Brazil earlier this year on behalf of an effort to save the tropical rain forest of the Amazon basin, the first thing Brazilian President Jose Sarney asked him was, 'What about the Tongass?'" (*New York Times*, 11/10/90)

APPENDIX 2

Statistical Traps In Arguments

According to one thinker, "There are three kinds of lies: lies, damned lies, and statistics." Somehow arguments seem especially persuasive when they are decked out in percentages and ratios, and buttressed with charts, graphs, and tables. But much fallacious reasoning can be masked by statistics. Consequently, we are here devoting some special attention to the use of numbers in arguments.

The heavy reliance on the belief in numbers is unique to modern argumentation. Whereas in ancient times speakers relied primarily on logical proof and the invocation of shared principles to convince an audience to accept their point of view, writers and speakers today rely more on statistics and various other manifestations of numbers to make their points. An opponent of abortion in older times might simply invoke the principle "Thou shalt not kill" and then amplify that principle by citing horrors that occurred in the lives of women who aborted their offspring; however, a latter-day opponent of abortion will have to confront statistical or quantitative issues such as biological data about the day-by-day development of the fetus, the percentage of abortions that result in death for the mother, the comparative death rates for mothers who legally or illegally abort offspring, the economic costs associated with aborting or not aborting an offspring, the increase of decrease in unwanted pregnancy that follows changes in abortion laws, and so on. Although one may argue with the appropriateness of statistical arguments, one cannot argue with the pervasiveness of data in argumentation.

Before moving on to a discussion of arguments based on data, we need to say a word about our infatuation with numbers themselves.

We speak of "hard" data—usually data expressed in numbers—as though they were eternal and unquestionable truths and contrast them sneeringly with the "soft data" that fuzzy thinkers derive from poorly constructed questionnaires. Whereas hard data often seem factual, soft data seem one step removed from opinion.

But how "factual" are hard data? One could, for instance, ask a hundred students to rank professors A and B on "overall effectiveness as a teacher" (on a scale, say, of 1 to 10 with 10 the highest) and find that A scored 8.2 whereas B scored 5.8. What do these "hard" data mean? Do they mean that A is a better teacher than B? Do they necessarily even mean that students think that A is a better teacher than B? Do we have any certainty of what criteria students are using when they evaluate "effectiveness"? Are they all using about the same criteria? What if A teaches consistently through lecture and multiple choice exams and B teaches through small-group discussion interspersed with lots of writing assignments? Do the "hard" data mean that students think A is a better teacher than B or that lecturing is a better teaching method than small-group discussions? What if every student ranked A as either 8 or 9 on the scale, whereas 50 percent of all students ranked B as 10 and the other 50 percent ranked B between 1 and 4?

The point being made is that although some data can be considered more trustworthy than other data, no data are "hard" in quite the way that word suggests. In some sense, all numbers are "soft." You can't pick them up or eat them or build houses out of them. Any number system is "made up" and is meaningful only in relation to other numbers. All that "2" means is twice as many as "1" and half as much as "4." Although numbers can be applied to almost anything in the world, none of them refers directly to anything outside the system of numbers. What all this means is that numbers must be made meaningful by viewing them in the context of other numbers. Hence, a billion is a big number if you're talking about people, but a small number if you're talking about atoms. Numbers alone, then, won't settle arguments, and one of the greatest dangers people fall prey to is to rely too much on numbers and not enough on analysis to make numbers significant.

Numbers, in abundance, can also be extremely boring to the general audience unless you have created a context to make them meaningful— thus the unpersuasiveness of long strings of figures that roll unheeded past the glazed eyes of the reader. Numbers have to be grounded in whatever it is that they describe and the numerical system appropriate to that reality before anyone can know what to make of them.

MAKING NUMBERS MEANINGFUL: CHARTS, TABLES, AND GRAPHS

One of the most common ways of making numbers meaningful is to "picture" them in graphs, charts, or tables. A chart is quite literally a picture of numerical values. A pie chart, for example, gives you an immediate sense of

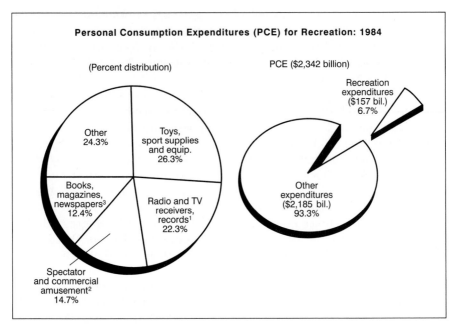

Figure showing:

Personal Consumption Expenditures (PCE) for Recreation: 1984

(Percent distribution)

- Other 24.3%
- Toys, sport supplies and equip. 26.3%
- Books, magazines, newspapers[3] 12.4%
- Radio and TV receivers, records[1] 22.3%
- Spectator and commercial amusement[2] 14.7%

PCE ($2,342 billion)

- Recreation expenditures ($157 bil.) 6.7%
- Other expenditures ($2,185 bil.) 93.3%

[1]Includes musical instruments and radio and TV repair.
[2]Includes admissions to spectator amusements, commercial participant amusement, and parimutuel net receipts.
[3]Includes maps and sheet music.

Source: Chart prepared by U.S Bureau of the Census.

Figure AP2–1   Examples of pie charts

how big a portion of the whole each part claims. Figure AP2–1, for example, shows two pie charts indicating how big a piece of the "personal consumption expenditure" pie Americans spend on recreation and, in turn, how the recreation pie is divided up among various areas. In a table, numerical data can be expressed much more complexly than in a pie chart, but their significance in relation to other numbers is not so visually immediate. A graph, on the other hand, is somewhere between a chart and a table. In a graph, the numbers can be taken from a table and "pictured" either in the form of lines drawn on a grid of squares called "scale units" or in the form of bars drawn out from the vertical or horizontal axis of the graph. "Line" graphs show how one quantity changes as a function of changes in another quantity. Because graphs are the most common—and most commonly misunderstood—form of data presentation, we'll now take a closer look at them.

Interpreting Graphs

In reading a line graph, as in reading a table, we read from the "outside in." We look for a title to the graph which tells us what two values are being related. We then look to see which value is represented on the vertical axis and which is represented on the horizontal axis. We check to see what quantity each scale unit represents for each of the two values. Then we look at the line to see what it tells us about the relationship between the two values.

When the graph line goes in one direction, we know the relationship between the two values is continuous. This means either that every increase in one value is reflected by an increase in the other value, or that every increase in one value is reflected in a decrease in the other value. Squiggly lines that go up and down indicate a variable relationship between the two values.

But graphs can be deceiving. Let's take a look at a graph more closely to see how they are made and what sorts of things one should be careful of in interpreting them. Arranged in tabular form, Table AP2–1 shows some data on the profitability of Bicker Pen Company, manufacturers of cheap ball-point pens.

One can, by looking at the table, get a general sense of Bicker's profit pattern, but it takes a while and the impact is thus diminished. Now let's take a look at a graphic display of the information as compiled by Bernie Bicker, president of the firm (see Figure AP2–2).

Looking at this graph, one might well conclude that Bicker Pen is headed for the stars. Just look at that line, taking off like an Airwolf. But before you grab your checkbook and ring up your broker, let's analyze the graph a bit more closely. One of the trickiest features of graphs is that they often suggest more about relationships than we have any cause to infer. It would appear from looking at this graph that as time passes on the horizontal axis, profitability increases on the vertical axis. Our tendency is to say that the passage of time "results in" an increase in profit. In fact, all we can say is that during the time period depicted in the graph, profits did increase. We cannot legitimately infer that profits will continue to increase over time. No permanent or necessary relationship between the two values has been established, though the picture presented by the graph tends to "fix" that relationship and make it appear permanent.

The graph presents "a" picture of Bicker's profitability, but not "the" picture. The graph is a snapshot of a moving object. To fully understand this graph, we need to have a sense of the larger picture, of other numbers and

Table AP2–1

Monthly Net Profits for Bicker Pen Company, 1987—First Three Quarters

Month	Net Profits (in thousands of $)
Jan.	1.0
Feb.	2.0
Mar.	3.0
Apr.	4.0
May	4.0
June	5.0
July	6.0
Aug.	8.0
Sept.	12.0

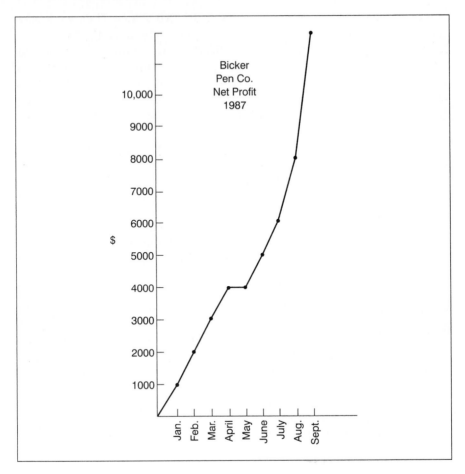

Figure AP2–2   Graph of net profits, Bicker Pen Company, 1987 (Example 1)

other graphs. The assumption we made above was that this particular picture of Bicker's profits was "typical" or "representative" of the larger picture.
But the smaller the particular picture we look at in a graph, the more risky it
is to make inferences about the bigger picture. If, for example, we looked at
a graph that represented Bicker's profits over the life of the company, our
steeply rising line might turn out to be a mere blip upward in an inexorably
descending line. If we looked at profits for the last quarter of 1986 we might
see a precipitous drop. If we looked at the same graphs for 1984 and 1985,
we might see the same pattern, which would indicate that the apparent
steady ascent is merely part of a cyclic pattern of rises and falls, with every
January being a low-sale month (after shoppers have bought their Christmas stocking stuffers) and every September being a high-sale month (when
students return to school).

Another important consideration to keep in mind when interpreting
graphs is the quantity assigned to each square. However truthful one must
be in picturing the correct quantities graphically, the proportion represented

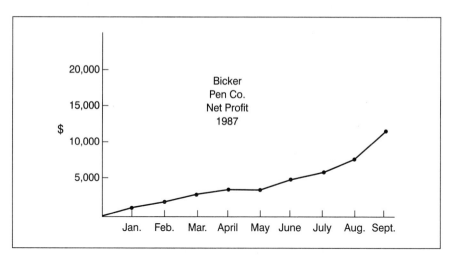

Figure AP2–3 Graph of net profits, Bicker Pen Company, 1987 (Example 2)

by each square is usually a matter of choice and can profoundly influence a reader's perception of the relationship being pictured in the graph. If Bicker, for example, had chosen, instead of $1000, a larger increment for each square on the vertical axis, his company's rise in profitability might not look quite so astonishing. If each of the squares instead represented $5,000, it would appear to be a less remarkable change, barely creeping up to the second square (see Figure AP2–3). Hence one can easily distort or overstate a rate of change on a graph by consciously selecting the quantities one assigns to each scale unit on either the horizontal or the vertical axis. The only guideline we have is the standard practice for graphing phenomena of the type frequently depicted. Thus, Bicker Pen should use the same sort of graph used by other companies of its type and size to depict profitability, thus allowing us to compare the graphs.

Bar graphs are an especially effective way of representing differing quantities. For example, Figure AP2–4 dramatically illustrates both the growth of the cable TV industry over a fifteen-year period, as measured by numbers of subscribers and revenues, and the relatively small increase in cost to the consumer. Because they are generally easier to understand than line graphs, bar graphs are a more effective way of communicating with technically unsophisticated audiences.

NUMBER TRAPS TO AVOID

In addition to these basic sorts of questions about tables, charts, and graphs, one should always be on the lookout for common number traps. For example, beware of "hidden factors," things that influence the picture you're seeing but that aren't mentioned explicitly when a series of numbers is displayed. The discovery of hidden factors requires that you know something about the phenomenon being shown in a chart, table, or graph. First, you

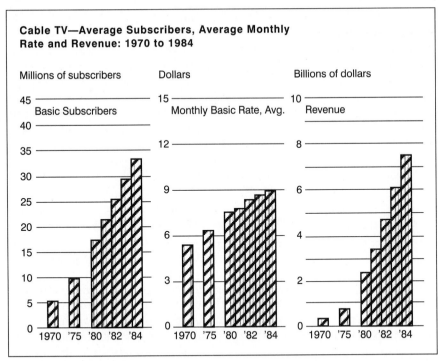

Cable TV—Average Subscribers, Average Monthly Rate and Revenue: 1970 to 1984

Source: Chart prepared by U.S Bureau of the Census.

Figure AP2–4   Example of a bar graph

need to know how the values being related on a graph were derived. In the case of Bicker, for instance, you might want to question why the graph depicts only the first three quarters and ends in September, a month that's bound to be a fat one for a cheap-pen company. You might also want to know how net profit was computed, since there are various bookkeeping procedures that allow companies to hide losses or understate gains. (For example, you need to know whether or not net profit includes sale of land or equipment, or a tax write-off.) Or what about inflation, a major hidden factor in many economic pictures of the mid-1970s through the early 1980s? If inflation was running at a high rate during 1986, so that Bicker felt justified in doubling the price of his pens in July, then Bicker's profit picture might have to be reevaluated.

Also, you need to be especially careful in interpreting data that might be reported either as raw numbers or as percentages. Bicker's profit picture becomes a good deal more meaningful, for example, if we could see it expressed as a percentage of the company's assets. We would then know how good a return on the investment Bicker was providing to its shareholders—which is the point of profit. Turning to the political scene, politicians who enthusiastically report that more Americans are working than ever before may be conveniently forgetting to mention that the percentage of unemployment may be relatively high. In other words, we may have more employed persons because the population has grown, not because the economy is better. Similarly, the increase in the size of the Medicare budget can be made to sound huge if raw numbers are displayed, but much more moderate if the Medicare budget is displayed as a percentage of the gross national product. Thus, in order to comprehend the significance of absolute numbers, you often need to see them both in relation to other absolute numbers and in relation to percentages. For example, "40 percent of the American population would survive nuclear war," doesn't have quite the same ring as "130 million Americans would die in a nuclear war." You need to see the numbers both ways to get a comprehensible picture.

In sum, arguments relying on data, and visual displays of data, demand a knowledge of the sources of those numbers and the context within which those numbers are meaningful. You can always choose to express the same data in a number of ways, and how you say it with numbers is as important as what you say. Whenever you are given numerical evidence of any kind, ask yourself the following questions: "Where did the numbers come from?" "What phenomena do they describe?" "How were they gathered?" "By whom?" and "In relation to what other numbers are these numbers significant?"

☐ FOR CLASS DISCUSSION

Look at Table AP2–2 presented in evidence during a discrimination suit brought by a black teacher. The teacher charged that her salary was artificially low. Looking over the data for her school district, could you infer that a pattern of discrimination against black teachers is indeed apparent? What other information would you require to conclude with certainty that black teachers were being discriminated against?

Table AP2–2

Salary comparison of black and white teachers

Salary Categories	Black Teachers		White Teachers	
	Number	Percentage	Number	Percentage
$4,001–4,500	10	77	3	15
$4,501–5,000	2	15	1	5
$5,001–5,500	1	8	2	10
$5,501–6,000	0	0	9	45
$6,001–6,500	0	0	3	15
$6,501–7,000	0	0	1	5
$7,001–7,500	0	0	0	0
$7,500 and above	0	0	1	5
Total	13	100	20	100

APPENDIX 3

The Writing Community: Working in Groups

In Chapter 1 we stressed that today truth is typically seen as a product of discussion and persuasion by members of a given community. Instead of seeing "truth" as grounded in some absolute and timeless realm such as Plato's forms or the unchanging laws of logic, many modern thinkers assert that truth is the product of a consensus among a group of knowledgeable peers. Our own belief in the special importance of argumentation in contemporary life follows from our assumption that truth arises out of discussion and debate rather than dogma or pure reason.

In this appendix, we extend that assumption to the classroom itself. We introduce you to a mode of learning often called collaborative learning. It involves a combination of learning from an instructor, learning independently, and learning from peers. Mostly it involves a certain spirit—the same sort of inquiring attitude that's required of a good arguer.

FROM CONFLICT TO CONSENSUS: HOW TO GET THE MOST OUT OF THE WRITING COMMUNITY

Behind the notion of the writing community lies the notion that thinking and writing are social acts. At first, this notion may contradict certain widely accepted stereotypes of writers and thinkers as solitary souls who retreat to cork-lined studies where they conjure great thoughts and works. But although we agree that every writer at some point in the process requires solitude, we would point out that most writers and thinkers also require periods of talk and social interchange before they retreat to solitude. Poets, novelists, scientists, philosophers, and technological innovators tend to belong to communities of peers with whom they share their ideas, theories, and work. In this section, we try to provide you with some practical advice on how to get the most out of these sorts of communities in developing your writing skills.

Avoiding Bad Habits of Group Behavior

Over the years, most of us have developed certain bad habits that get in the way of efficient group work. Although we use groups all the time to study and accomplish demanding tasks, we tend to do so spontaneously and unreflectively without asking why some groups work and others don't. Many of us, for example, have worked on committees that just didn't get the job done and wasted our time, or else got the job done because one or two tyrannical people dominated the group. Just a couple of bad committee experiences can give us a healthy skepticism about the utility of groups in general. "A committee," according to some people, "is a sort of centipede. It has too many legs, no brain, and moves very slowly."

At their worst, this is indeed how groups function. In particular, they have a tendency to fail in two opposite directions, failures that can be avoided only by conscious effort. Groups can lapse into "clonethink" and produce a safe, superficial consensus whereby everyone agrees with the first opinion expressed in order to avoid conflict or to get on to something more interesting. At the other extreme is a phenomenon we'll call "egothink." In egothink, all members of the group go their own way and produce a collection of minority views that have nothing to do with each other and would be impossible to act on. Clonethinkers view their task as conformity to a norm; egothinkers see their task as safeguarding the autonomy of individual group members. Both fail to take other people and other ideas seriously.

Successful groups avoid both extremes and achieve unity out of diversity. This means that any successful community of learners must be willing to endure creative conflict. Creative conflict results from an initial agreement to disagree respectfully with each other and to focus that disagreement on ideas, not people. For this reason, we say that the relationship among the members of a learning community is not so much interpersonal or impersonal as transpersonal or "beyond the personal." Each member is personally committed to the development of ideas and does whatever is necessary to achieve that development.

The Value of Group Work for Writers

Because we are basically social animals, we find it natural, pleasurable even, to deal with problems in groups. Proof of this fact can be found on any given morning in any given student union in the country. Around the room you will find many students working in groups. Math, engineering, and business majors will be solving problems together, comparing solutions and their ways of arriving at solutions. Others will be comparing their class notes and testing their understanding of concepts and terms by explaining them to each other and comparing their explanations. To be sure, their discussions will occasionally drift off the topic to encompass pressing social issues such as what they're going to do next weekend, or why they like or dislike the class they're working on, but much of the work of college students seems to get done in convivial conversation over morning coffee or late-night popcorn. Why not ease into the rigors of writing in a similar fashion?

A second major advantage of working on writing in a group is that it provides a real and immediate audience for people's work. Too often, when students write in a school setting they get caught up in the writing-for-teacher racket, which may distort their notion of audience. Argumentative writing is best aimed either at opponents or at a neutral "jury" who will be weighing both sides of a controversy. A group of peers gives you a better sense of a real-world audience "out there" than does a single teacher.

There's danger, of course, in having several audiences consider your writing. Your peer audience well might respond differently to your writing than your instructor. You may feel misled if you are praised for something by a peer and then criticized for the same thing by your instructor. These things can and will happen, no matter how much time you spend developing universally accepted criteria for writing. Grades are not facts but judgments, and all judgments involve uncertainty. Students who are still learning the criteria for making judgments will sometimes apply those criteria differently than an instructor who has been working with them for years. But you should know too that two or more instructors might give you conflicting advice also, just as two or more doctors might give you different advice on what to do about the torn ligaments in your knee. In our view, the risks of misunderstanding are more than made up for by gains in understanding of the writing process, an understanding that comes from working in writing communities where everyone functions both as a writer and a writing critic.

A third advantage to working in writing communities is closely related to the second advantage. The act of sharing your writing with other people helps you get beyond the bounds of egocentrism that limit all writers. By egocentrism, we don't mean pride or stuck-upness; we mean the failure to consider the needs of your readers. Unless you share your writing with another person, your audience is always a "mythical group," a fiction or a theory that exists only in your head. You must always try to anticipate the problems others will have in reading your work, but until others actually read it and share their reactions to it with you, you can never be fully sure you have understood your audience's point of view. Until another reads your writing critically, you can't be sure you aren't talking to yourself.

FORMING WRITING COMMUNITIES: SKILLS AND ROLES

Given that there are advantages to working in groups, just how do we go about forming writing communities in the classroom? We first have to decide how big to make the groups. From our experience, the best groups consist of either five to seven people or simply two people. Groups of three to four tend to polarize and become divisive, and larger groups tend to be unmanageable. Because working in five- to seven-person groups is quite different from working in pairs, we discuss each of these different-sized groups in turn.

Working in Groups of Five to Seven People

The trick to successful group work is to consider the maximum number of viewpoints and concerns without losing focus. Because these two basic goals frequently conflict, you need some mechanisms for monitoring your progress. In particular, it's important that each group member is assigned to perform those tasks necessary to effective group functioning. (Some teachers assign "roles" to individual students, shifting the roles from day to day; other teachers let the groups themselves determine the roles of individuals.) That is, the group must recognize that it has two objectives at all times: the stated objectives of a given task and the objective of making the group work well. It is very easy to get so involved with the given task that you overlook the second objective, generally known as "group maintenance."

The first role is group leader. We hesitate to call persons who fill this role "leaders" because we tend sometimes to think of leaders as know-it-alls who "take charge" and order people about. In classroom group work, however, being a group leader is a role you play, not a fixed part of your identity. The leader, above all else, keeps the groups focused on agreed-on ends and protects the right of every group member to be heard. It's an important function, and group members should share the responsibility from task to task. Here is a list of things for the leader to do during a group discussion:

1. Ensure that everyone understands and agrees on the objectives of any given task and on what sort of final product is expected of the group (for example, a list of criteria, a brief written statement, oral response to a question, and so forth).

2. Ask that the group set an agenda for completing the task and have some sense of how much time they will spend at each stage. (Your instructor should always make clear what time limits you have to operate within and when he or she expects your task to be completed. If a time limit isn't specified, you should request a reasonable estimate.)

3. Look for signs of getting off the track and ask individual group members to clarify how their statements relate to agreed-on objectives.

4. Actively solicit everyone's contributions and take care that all viewpoints are listened to and that the group does not rush to incomplete judgment.

5. Try to determine when the task has been adequately accomplished.

In performing each of these functions, the leader must be concerned to turn criticisms and observations into questions. Instead of saying to one silent and bored-looking member of the group, "Hey, Gormley, you haven't said didley squat here so far; say something relevant or take a hike," the leader might ask, "Irwin, do you agree with what Beth just said about this paper being disorganized?" Remember, every action in nature is met with an equal and opposite reaction—commands tend to be met with resistance, questions with answers.

A second crucial role for well-functioning groups is that of recorder. The recorder's function is to provide the group with a record of their deliberations so they can measure their progress. It is particularly important that the recorder write down the agenda and the solution to the problem in precise form. Because the recorder must summarize the deliberations fairly precisely, he must ask for clarifications. In doing this, he ensures that group members don't fall into the "ya know?" syndrome (a subset of clonethink) in which people assent to statements that are in fact cloudy to them. (Ya know?) At the completion of the task, the recorder should also ask if there are any significant remaining disagreements or unanswered questions. Finally, the recorder is responsible for reporting the group's solutions to the class as a whole.*

If these two roles are conscientiously filled, the group should be able to identify and solve problems that temporarily keep it from functioning effectively. Maybe you are thinking that this sounds dumb. Whenever you've been in a group everyone has known if there were problems or not without leaders or recorders. Too often, however, a troubled group may sense that there is a problem without being perfectly clear about the nature of the problem or the solution. Let's say you are in a group with Elwood Lunt, Jr., who is very opinionated and dominates the discussions. (For a sample of Elwood's cognitive style, see his essay in Task 2 at the end of this Appendix.) Group members may represent their problem privately to themselves with a statement such as "Lunt's such a jerk nobody can work with him. He talks constantly and none of the rest of us can get a word in." The group may devote all of its energies to punishing Lunt with ridicule or silence rather than trying to solve the problem. Although this may make you feel better for a short time, Lunt is unlikely to get any better and the group is unlikely to get much done.

If Lunt is indeed bogging the group down by airing his opinions at great length, it is the leader's job to limit his dominance without excluding him. Because group members all realize that it is the group leader's role to handle such problems, the leader has a sort of license that allows her or him to

---

* There is a debate among experts who study small group communications whether or not the roles of leader and recorder can be collapsed into one job. Your group may need to experiment until it discovers the structure that works best for bringing out the most productive discussions.

deal directly with Lunt. Moreover, the leader also has the explicit responsibility to do so, so that each member is not forced to sit, silently seething and waiting for someone to do something.

The leader might control Lunt in one of several ways: (1) by keeping to the agenda ("Thanks Elwood, hate to interrupt, but we're a bit behind schedule and we haven't heard from everyone on this point yet. Jack, shall we move on to you?"); (2) by simply asking Lunt to demonstrate how his remarks are relevant to the topic at hand. ("That's real interesting, Elwood, that you got to see Sid Vicious in his last performance, but can you tell us how you see that relating to Melissa's point about ending welfare?"); or (3) by introducing more formal procedures such as asking group members to raise their hands and be called on by the chair. These procedures might not satisfy your blood lust, your secret desire to stuff Lunt into a dumpster; however, they are more likely to let the group get its work done and perhaps, just maybe, to help Lunt become a better listener and participant.

The rest of the group, though they have no formally defined roles, have an equally important obligation to participate fully. To ensure full participation, group members can do several things. They can make sure that they know all the other group members by their first names and speak to them in a friendly manner. They can practice listening procedures wherein they try not to dissent or disagree without first charitably summarizing the view with which they are taking issue. Most importantly, they can bring to the group as much information and as many alternative points of view as they can muster. The primary intellectual strength of group work is the ability to generate a more complex view of a subject. But this more complex view cannot emerge unless all individuals contribute their perspectives.

One collaborative task for writers that requires no elaborate procedures or any role playing is reading your essays aloud within the group. A good rule for this procedure is that no one responds to any one essay until all have been read. This is often an effective last step before handing in any essay. It's a chance to share the fruits of your labor with others and to hear finished essays that you may have seen in the draft stages. Hearing everyone else's final draft can also help you get a clearer perspective on how your own work is progressing. Listening to the essays read can both reassure you that your work is on a par with other people's and challenge you to write up to the level of the best student writing in your group.

Many of you may find this process a bit frightening at first. But the cause of your fright is precisely the source of the activity's value. In reading your work aloud, you are taking responsibility for that work in a special way. Writing specialist Kenneth Bruffee, whose work on collaborative learning introduced us to many of the ideas in this chapter, likens the reading of papers aloud to reciting a vow, of saying "I do" in a marriage ceremony. You are taking public responsibility for your words, and there's no turning back. The word has become deed. If you aren't at least a little nervous about reading an essay aloud, you probably haven't invested much in your words. Knowing that you will take public responsibility for your words is an incentive to make that investment—a more real and immediate incentive than a grade.

Working in Pairs

Working in pairs is another effective form of community learning. In our classes we use pairs at both the early-draft and the late-draft stages of writing. At the early-draft stage, it serves the very practical purpose of clarifying a student's ideas and sense of direction at the beginning of a new writing project. The interaction best takes place in the form of pair interviews. When you first sit down to interview each other, each of you should have done a fair amount of exploratory writing and thinking about what you want to say in your essay and how you're going to say it. Here is a checklist of questions you can use to guide your interview:

1. "What is your issue?" Your goal here is to help the writer focus an issue by formulating a question that clearly has alternative answers.

2. "What is your position on the issue and what are alternative positions?" After you have helped your interviewee formulate the issue question, help her clarify this issue by stating her own position and show how that position differs from opposing ones. Your interviewee might say, for example, that "many of my friends are opposed to building more nuclear power plants, but I think we need to build more of them."

3. "Can you walk me through your argument step by step?" Once you know your interviewee's issue question and intended position, you can best help her by having her walk you through her argument talking out loud. You can ask prompting questions such as "What are you going to say first?" "What next?" and so on. At this stage your interviewee will probably still be struggling to discover the best way to support the point. You can best help by brainstorming along with her, both of you taking notes on your ideas. Often at this stage you can begin making a schematic plan for the essay and formulating supporting reasons as because clauses. Along the way give your interviewee any information or ideas you have on the issue. It is particularly helpful at this stage if you can provide counterarguments and opposing views.

The interview strategy is useful before writers begin their rough drafts. After the first drafts have been written, there are a number of different ways of using pairs to evaluate drafts. One practice that we've found helpful is simply to have writers write a one-paragraph summary of their own drafts and of their partner's. In comparing summaries, writers can often discover which, if any, of their essential ideas are simply not getting across. If a major idea is not in the reader's summary, writer and reader need to decide if it's due to a careless reading or to problems within the draft. The nice thing about this method is that the criticism is given indirectly and hence isn't as threatening to either party. At other times, your instructor might also devise a checklist of features for you to consider, based on the criteria you have established for the assignment.

☐ FOR CLASS DISCUSSION

1. As a group, consider the following quotation and then respond to the questions that follow: "In most college classrooms there is a reluctance to assume leadership. The norm for college students is to defer to someone else, to refuse to accept the position even if it is offered. There is actually a competition in humility and the most humble person usually ends up as the leader."*

   a. Do you think this statement is true?

   b. On what evidence do you base your judgment of its truthfulness?

   c. As a group, prepare an opening sentence for a paragraph that would report your group's reaction to this quotation.

2. Read the following statements about group interaction and decide as a group whether these statements are true or false.

   a. Women are less self-assertive and less competitive in groups than are men.

   b. There is a slight tendency for physically superior individuals to become leaders in a group.

   c. Leaders are usually more intelligent than nonleaders.

   d. Females conform to majority opinion more than males in reaching group decisions.

   e. An unconventional group member inhibits group functioning.

   f. An anxious group member inhibits group functioning.

   g. Group members with more power are usually better liked than low-power group members.

   h. Groups usually produce more and better solutions to problems than do individuals working alone.

With the assistance of the group, the recorder should write a four- to five-sentence description of the process your group used to reach agreement on the true/false statements. Was there discussion? Disagreement? Did you vote? Did every person give an opinion on each question? Were there any difficulties?

A SEVERAL-DAYS' GROUP PROJECT: DEFINING "GOOD ARGUMENTATIVE WRITING"

The problem we want you to address in this sequence of tasks is how to define and identify "good argumentative writing." This is a particularly crucial problem for developing writers insofar as you can't begin to measure

---

* Philips, Gerald, Douglas Pederson, and Julia Wood. *Group Discussion: A Practical Guide to Participant Leadership.* Boston: Houghton Mifflin, 1979.

your growth as a writer until you have some notion of what you're aiming for. To be sure, it's no easy task defining good argumentative writing. In order for even experienced teachers to reach agreement on this subject, some preliminary discussions and no small amount of compromise are necessary. By the end of this task you will most certainly not have reached a universally acceptable description of good argumentative writing. (Such a description doesn't exist.) But you will have begun a dialogue with each other and your instructor on the subject. Moreover, you will have developed a vocabulary for sharing your views on writing with each other.

For this exercise, we give you a sequence of four tasks, some being homework and others being in-class group tasks. Please do the tasks in sequence.

TASK 1 (HOMEWORK):   PREPARING FOR THE GROUP DISCUSSION
Freewrite for five minutes on the question: "What is good argumentation writing?" After finishing your freewrite, read fictional student Lunt's argument below and, based on the principles that Lunt seems to break, develop a tentative list of criteria for good argumentative writing.

EXPLANATION
Before you come together with a group of people to advance your understanding and knowledge collectively, you first need to explore your own thoughts on the matter. Too often, groups collapse not because the members lack goodwill, but because they lack preparation. In order to discharge your responsibility as a good group member, you must therefore begin by doing your homework. By using a freewriting exercise, you focus your thinking on the topic, explore what you already know or feel about it, and begin framing questions and problems.

To help you establish a standard for good argumentative writing, we've produced a model of bad arguing by a fictional student, one Elwood P. Lunt, Jr. If you can figure out what's bad about Lunt's argument, then you can formulate the principles of good argument that he violates. Of course, no student of our acquaintance has ever written anything as bad as Lunt's essay. That's the virtue of this contrived piece. It's an easy target. In going over it critically, you may well find that Lunt violates principles of good writing you hadn't thought of in your freewrite. (We tried to ensure that he violated as many as possible.) Thus, you should be sure to go back and modify your ideas from your freewrite accordingly.

A couple of important points to keep in mind here as you prepare to critique another person's work: (1) Remember the principle of charity. Try to look past the muddied prose to a point or intention that might be lurking in the background. Your critique should speak as much as possible to Lunt's failure to realize this intent. (2) Direct your critique to the prose, not the writer. Don't settle for "He just doesn't make sense" or "He's a dimwit." Ask yourself why he doesn't make sense and point to particular places where he doesn't make sense. In sum, give Lunt the same sort of reading you would like to get: compassionate and specific.

—————————————— ■ ——————————————

GOOD WRITING AND COMPUTERS FOR TODAY'S MODERN AMERICAN YOUTH OF AMERICA

(A partial fulfillment of writing an argument in the course in which I am attending)

In todays modern fast paced world computers make living a piece of   1
cake. You can do a lot with computers which in former times took a lot of
time and doing a lot of work. Learning to fly airplanes, for example. But
there are no such things as a free lunch. People who think computers will
do all the work for you need to go to the Iron Curtain and take a look
around, that's the place for people who think they can be replaced by computers. The precious computer which people think is the dawn of a new
civilization but which is in all reality a pig in a poke makes you into a number but can't even add right! So don't buy computers for two reasons.

The first reason you shouldn't buy a computer is writing. So what   2
makes people think that they won't have to write just because they have a
computer on his desk. "Garbage in and garbage out one philosopher
said." Do you want to sound like garbage? I don't. That's why modern
American fast paced youth must conquer this affair with computers and
writing by ourselves is the answer to our dreams and not just by using a
computer for that aforementioned writing. A computer won't make you
think better and thats the problem because people think a computer will
do your thinking for you. No way, Jose.

Another thing is grammar. My Dad Elwood P. Lunt Sr. hit the nail on   3
the head; when he said bad grammar can make you sound like a jerk.
Right on Dad. He would be so upset to think of all the jerks out there
who wasted their money on a computer so that the computer could write
for them. But do computers know grammar? So get on the bandwagon
and write good and get rich with computers. Which can make you write
right. You think any computer could catch the errors I just made? Oh,
sure you do. Jerk. And according to our handbook on writing writing
takes intelligence which computers don't have. Now I'm not against computers. I am just saying that computers have there place.

In conclusion there are two reasons why you shouldn't buy a com-   4
puter. But if you want to buy one that is all right as long as you understand that it isn't as smart as you think.

TASK 2 (IN-CLASS GROUP WORK):   DEVELOPING A MASTER LIST OF CRITERIA
As a group, reach a consensus on at least six or seven major problems with
Lunt's argumentative essay. Then use that list to prepare a parallel list of crite-
ria for a good written argument. Please have your list ready in thirty minutes.

EXPLANATION
Your goal for this task is to reach consensus about what's wrong with Lunt's
argument. As opposed to a "majority decision," in which more people agree
than disagree, a "consensus" entails a solution that is generally acceptable to

all members of the group. In deciding what is the matter with Lunt's essay, you should be able to reach consensus also on the criteria for a good argument. After each group has completed its list, recorders should report each group's consensus to the class as a whole. Your instructor will facilitate a discussion leading to the class's "master list" of criteria.

TASK 3 (HOMEWORK):   APPLYING CRITERIA TO STUDENT ESSAYS
At home, consider the following five samples of student writing. (This time they're real examples.) Rank the essays "1" through "5," with 1 being the best and 5 the worst. Once you've done this, develop a brief rationale for your ranking. This rationale should force you to decide which criteria you rank highest and which lowest. For example, does "quality of reasons" rank higher than "organization and development"? Does "colorful, descriptive style" rank high or low in your ranking system?

EXPLANATION
The essays reprinted below were all written in response to Option 5, pages 135–38, in "Writing Assignments for Chapters 4–6." Before judging the arguments, read over that assignment so you know what students were asked to do. Judge the essays on the basis of the criteria established in class.

BLOODY ICE

It is March in Alaska. The ocean-side environment is full of life and   1
death. Man and animal share this domain but not in peace. The surrounding iceflows, instead of being cold and white, are steaming from the remains of gutted carcasses and stained red. The men are hunters and the animals are barely six weeks old. A slaughter has just taken place. Thousands of baby Harp seals lay dead on the ice and thousands more of adult mothers lay groaning over the death of their babies. Every year a total limit of 180,000 seals set by the U.S. Seal Protection Act is filled in a terrifying bloodbath. But Alaska with its limit of 30,000 is not alone. Canadians who hunt seals off the coast of Northern Newfoundland and Quebec are allowed 150,000 seals. The Norwegians are allowed 20,000 and native Eskimos of Canada and Greenland are allowed 10,000 seals per year. Although this act appears heartless and cruel, the men who hunt have done this for 200 years as a tradition for survival. They make many good arguments supporting their traditions. They feel the seals are in no immediate danger of extinction. Also seal furs can be used to line boots and gloves or merely traded for money and turned into robes or fur coats. Sometimes the meat is even used for food in the off hunting months when money is scarce. But are these valid justifications for the unmerciful killings? No, the present limit on Harp seal killings should be better regulated because the continued hunting of the seals

will lead to eventual extinction and because the method of slaughter is so cruel and inhumane.

The Harp seal killing should be better regulated first because eventual   2
extinction is inevitable. According to *Oceans* magazine, before the limit of 180,000 seals was established in 1950, the number of seals had dwindled from 3,300,000 to 1,250,000. Without these limitations hundreds of thousands were killed within weeks of birth. Now, even with this allotment, the seals are being killed off at an almost greater rate than they can remultiply. Adult female seals give birth once every year but due to pollution, disease, predation, whelping success and malnutrition they are already slowly dying on their own without being hunted. Eighty percent of the seals slaughtered are pups and the remaining twenty percent are adult seals and even sometimes mothers who try attacking the hunters after seeing their babies killed. The hunters, according to the Seal Protection Act, have this right.

Second, I feel the killing should be better regulated because of the   3
inhumane method used. In order to protect the fur value of the seals, guns are not used. Instead, the sealers use metal clubs to bludgen the seal to death. Almost immediately after being delivered a direct blow, the seals are gutted open and skinned. Although at this stage of life the seal's skull is very fragile, sometimes the seals are not killed by the blows but merely stunned; thus hundreds are skinned alive. Still others are caught in nets and drowned, which according to *America* magazine, the Canadian government continues to deny. But the worst of the methods used is when a hunter gets tired of swinging his club and uses the heel of his boot to kick the seal's skull in. Better regulation is the only way to solve this problem because other attempts seem futile. For example, volunteers who have traveled to hunting sites trying to dye the seals to ruin their fur value have been caught and fined heavily.

The plight of the Harp seals has been long and controversial. With the   4
Canadian hunters feeling they have the right to kill the seals because it has been their industry for over two centuries, and on the other hand with humane organizations fearing extinction and strongly opposing the method of slaughter, a compromise must be met among both sides. As I see it, the solution to the problem is simple. Since the Canadians do occasionally use the whole seal and have been sealing for so long they could be allowed to continue but at a more heavily regulated rate. Instead of filling the limit of 180,000 every year and letting the numbers of seals decrease, Canadians could learn to ranch the seals as Montanans do cattle or sheep. The United States has also offered to help them begin farming their land for a new livelihood. The land is adequate for crops and would provide work all year round instead of only once a month every year. As a result of farming, the number of seals killed would be drastically cut down because Canadians would not be so dependent on the seal industry as before. This would in turn lead back to the ranching aspect of sealing and allow the numbers to grow back and keeping the tradition alive for future generations and one more of nature's creatures to enjoy.

RSS SHOULD NOT PROVIDE DORM ROOM CARPETS

Tricia, a University student, came home exhausted from her work-study job. She took a blueberry pie from the refrigerator to satisfy her hunger and a tall glass of milk to quench her thirst. While trying to get comfortable on her bed, she tipped her snack over onto the floor. She cleaned the mess, but the blueberry and milk stains on her brand new carpet could not be removed. She didn't realize that maintaining a clean carpet would be difficult and costly. Tricia bought her own carpet. Some students living in dorm rooms want carpeted rooms provided for them at the expense of the University. They insist that since they pay to live on campus, the rooms should reflect a comfortable home atmosphere. However, Resident Student Services (RSS) should not be required to furnish the carpet because other students do not want carpets. Furthermore, carpeting all the rooms totals into a very expensive project. And lastly, RSS should not have to provide the carpet because many students show lack of respect and responsibility for school property.

Although RSS considers the carpeting of all rooms a strong possibility, students like Tricia oppose the idea. They feel the students should buy their own carpets. Others claim the permanent carpeting would make dorm life more comfortable. The carpet will act as insulation and as a sound proofing system. These are valid arguments, but they should not be the basis for changing the entire residence hall structure. Those students with "cold feet" can purchase house footwear, which cost less than carpet. Unfortunately carpeting doesn't muffle all the noise; therefore, some students will be disturbed. Reasonable quietness should be a matter of respect for other students' privacy and comfort. Those opposed to the idea reason out the fact that students constantly change rooms or move out. The next person may not want carpet. Also, if RSS carpets the rooms, the students will lose the privilege they have of painting their rooms any color. Paint stains cannot be removed. Some students can't afford to replace the carpet. Still another factor, carpet color may not please everyone. RSS would provide a neutral color like brown or gray. With tile floors, the students can choose and purchase their own carpets to match their taste.

Finally, another reason not to have carpet exists in the fact that the project can be expensive due to material costs, installation cost, and the maintenance cost caused mainly by the irresponsibility of many students. According to Rick Jones, Asst. Director of Housing Services, the cost will be $300 per room for the carpet and installation. RSS would also have to purchase more vacuum cleaners for the students use. RSS will incur more expense in order to maintain the vacuums. Also, he claims that many accidents resulting from shaving cream fights, food fights, beverage parties, and smoking may damage the carpet permanently. With floor tiles, accidents such as food spills can be cleaned up easier than carpet. The student's behavior plays an important role in deciding against carpeting. Many students don't follow the rules of maintaining their rooms. They drill holes into the walls, break mirrors, beds, and closet doors, and leave their food trays all over the floor. How could they be trusted to take care of school carpet when they violate the current rules? Many students feel they have the "right" to do as they please. This irresponsible and disrespectful behavior reflects their future attitude about carpet care.

In conclusion, the university may be able to afford to supply the carpets in each room, but maintaining them would be difficult. If the students want carpets, they should pay and care for the carpets themselves. Hopefully, they will be more cautious and value it more. They should take the initiative to fundraise or find other financial means of providing this "luxury." They should not rely on the school to provide unnecessary room fixtures such as carpets. Also, they must remember that if RSS provides the carpet and they don't pay for the damages, they and future students will endure the consequences. What will happen???? Room rates will skyrocket!!!!! 4

STERLING HALL DORM FOOD

The quality of Sterling Hall dorm food does not meet the standard needed to justify the high prices University students pay. As I watched a tall, medium-built University student pick up his Mexican burrito from the counter it didn't surprise me to see him turn up his nose. Johnny, our typical University student, waited five minutes before he managed to make it through the line. After he received his bill of $4.50 he turned his back to the cash register and walked away displeased with his meal. 1

As our neatly groomed University student placed his ValiDine eating card back into his Giorgio wallet, he thought back to the balance left on his account. Johnny had $24 left on his account and six more weeks left of school. He had been eating the cheapest meals he could and still receive a balanced meal, but the money just seemed to disappear. No student, not even a thrifty boy like Johnny could possibly afford to live healthfully according to the University meal plan system. 2

Johnny then sat down at a dirty table to find his burrito only half way cooked. Thinking back to the long-haired cook who served him the burrito, he bit into the burrito and noticed a long hair dangling from his lips. He realized the cook's lack of preparation when preparing his burrito. 3

Since the food costs so much, yet the quality of the food remains low, University students do not get the quality they deserve. From the information stated I can conclude that using the ValiDine service system University students would be jeopardizing their health and wasting their 4 hard-earned money. University students deserve something more than what they have now.

■

ROTC COURSES SHOULD NOT GET COLLEGE CREDIT

One of the most lucrative scholarships a student can receive is a four-year R.O.T.C. scholarship that pays tuition and books along with a living allowance. It was such a scholarship that allowed me to attend an expensive liberal arts college and to pursue the kind of well rounded education that matters to me. Of course, I am obligated to spend four years on active duty—an obligation that I accept and look forward to. What I am disappointed in, however, is the necessity to enroll in Military Science classes. Strong ROTC advocates argue that Military Science classes are essential because they produce good citizens, teach leadership skills, and provide practical experience for young cadets. Maybe so. But we could get the same benefits without having to take these courses for credit. Colleges should make ROTC training an extracurricular activity, not a series of academic courses taken for academic credit.

First of all, ROTC courses, unlike other college courses, do not stress inquiry and true questioning. The ROTC program has as its objective the preparation of future officers committed to the ideals and structure of the military. The structure of the military is based upon obediently following the orders of military superiors. Whereas all my other teachers stress critical thinking and doing independent analysis, my ROTC instructors avoid political or social questions saying it is the job of civilian leaders to debate policies and the job of the military to carry them out. We don't even debate what role the military should play in our country. My uncle, who was an ROTC cadet during the Vietnam war, remembers that not only did ROTC classes never discuss the ethics of the war but that cadets were not allowed to protest the war outside of their ROTC courses. This same obedience is demanded in my own ROTC courses, where we are not able to question administration policies and examine openly the complexity of the situation in Iraq and Kuwait.

A second reason that Army ROTC courses do not deserve academic credit is that the classes are not academically strenuous, thus giving cadets a higher G.P.A. and an unfair advantage over their peers. Much of what a cadet does for academic credit involves non-academic activities such as physical training for an hour three days a week so that at least some of a cadet's grade is based on physical activity, not mental activity. In conducting an informal survey of 10 upper-classmen, I found out that none of them has ever gotten anything lower than an A in a Military Science class and they do not know of anyone who got anything lower than an A. One third-year cadet stated that "the classes are basic. A monkey coming out of the zoo could get college credit for a Military Science class." He went on to say that most of the information given in his current class is a brush-up to 8th grade U.S. history. In contrast, a typical liberal arts college class requires much thought, questioning, and analysis. The ROTC Military Science class is taught on the basis of "regurgitated knowledge," meaning that once you are given a piece of information you are required to know it and reproduce it at any time without thought or question. A good example is in my class Basic Officership. Our first assignment is to memorize and recite in front of the class the Preamble to the Constitution of the United States. The purpose of doing so doesn't seem to be to understand or analyze the constitution because we never talk about that. In fact, I don't know what the purpose is. I just do it because I am told to. Because the "A" is so easy to get in my ROTC class, I spend all my time studying for my other classes. I am a step ahead of my peers in the competition for a high GPA, even though I am not getting as good an education.

Finally, having to take ROTC classes means that I can't take other lib-   4
eral arts courses which would be more valuable. One of the main purposes for ROTC is to give potential officers a liberal education. Many cadets have the credentials to get into an armed forces academy, but they chose ROTC programs because they could combine military training with a well-rounded curriculum. Unfortunately, by taking Military Science classes each quarter, cadets find that their electives are all but eaten up by the time they are seniors. If ROTC classes were valuable in themselves, I wouldn't complain. But they aren't, and they keep me from taking upper division electives in philosophy, literature, and the humanities.

All of these reasons lead me to believe that Army ROTC cadets are   5
getting short-changed when they enroll for Military Science classes. Because cadets receive a lucrative scholarship, they should have to take the required military science courses. But these courses should be treated as extra-curricular activities, like a work-study job or like athletics. Just as a student on a full-ride athletic scholarship does not receive academic credit for football practices and games, so should a student on a full-ride R.O.T.C. scholarship have to participate in the military education program without getting academic credit. By treating R.O.T.C. courses as a type of extra-curricular activity like athletics, students can take more elective credits that will expand their minds, better enabling them to have the knowledge to make moral decisions and to enjoy their world more fully.

LEGALIZATION OF PROSTITUTION

Prostitution . . . it is the world's oldest profession. It is by definition the   1
act of offering or soliciting sex for payment. It is, to some, evil. Yet, the fact is it exists.

Arguments are not necessary to prove the existence of prostitution.   2
Rather, the argument arises when trying to prove something must be
done to reduce the problems of this profession. The problems which exist
are in the area of crime, of health, and of environment. Crime rates are
soaring, diseases are spreading wildly, and the environment on the streets
is rapidly decaying. Still, it has been generally conceded that these problems cannot be suppressed. However they can be reduced. Prostitution
should be legalized because it would reduce the wave of epidemics,
decrease high crime rates, provide good revenue by treating it like other
businesses, and get girls off the streets where sexual crimes often occur.

Of course, there are those who would oppose the legalization of pros-   3
titution stating that it is one of the main causes for the spread of venereal
diseases. Many argue that it is inter-related with drug-trafficking and
other organized crimes. And probably the most controversial is the moral
aspect of the subject; it is morally wrong, and legalizing it would be
enforcing, or even justifying, such an existence.

These points propose good arguments, but I shall counter each point   4
and explain the benefits and advantages of legalizing prostitution. In the
case of prostitution being the main cause for the spread of epidemics, I
disagree. By legalizing it, houses would be set up which would solve the
problem of girls working on the streets and being victims of sexual
crimes. It would also provide regular health checks, as is successfully
done in Nevada, Germany, and other parts of the U.S. and Europe, which
will therefore cut down on diseases spreading unknowingly.

As for the increase of organized crime if prostitution is legalized, I dis-   5
agree again. Firstly, by treating it like businesses, then that would make
good state revenue. Secondly, like all businesses have regulations, so shall
these houses. That would put closer and better control in policing the profession, which is presently a problem. Obviously, if the business of prostitution is more closely supervised, that would decrease the crime rates.

Now, I come to one of the most arguable aspects of legalizing prosti-   6
tution: the moral issue. Is it morally wrong to legalize prostitution? That is
up to the individual. To determine whether anything is "right or wrong" in
our society is nearly impossible to do since there are various opinions. If
a person were to say that prostitution is the root of all evil, that will not
make it go away. It exists. Society must begin to realize that fear or denial
will not make the "ugliness" disappear. It still exists.

Prostitution can no longer go ignored because of our societal atti-   7
tudes. Legalizing it is beneficial to our society, and I feel in time people
may begin to form an accepting attitude. It would be the beginning of a
more open-minded view of what is reality. Prostitution . . . it is the world's
oldest profession. It exists. It is a reality.

TASK 4 (IN-CLASS GROUP WORK):   REACHING CONSENSUS ON RANKING OF
ESSAYS
Working again in small groups, reach consensus on your ranking of the five
essays. Groups should report both their rankings and their justification for

the rankings based on the criteria established in Task 2 or as currently modified by your group.

Explanation
You are now to reach consensus on how you rank the papers and why you rank them the way you do. Feel free to change the criteria you established earlier if they seem to need modification. Be careful in your discussions to distinguish between evaluation of the writer's written product and your own personal position on the writer's issue. In other words, there is a crucial difference between saying "I don't like Pete's essay because I disagree with his ideas" and "I don't like Pete's essay because he didn't provide adequate support for his ideas." As each group reports back the results of their deliberations to the class as a whole, the instructor will highlight discrepancies among the groups' decisions and collate the criteria as they emerge. If the instructor disagrees with the class consensus or wants to add items to the criteria, he or she might choose to make these things known now. By the end of this stage, everyone should have a list of criteria for good argumentative writing established by the class.

A CLASSROOM DEBATE

In this exercise, you have an opportunity to engage in a variant of a formal debate. Although debates of this nature don't always lead to truth for its own sake, they are excellent forums for the development of analytical and organizational skills. The format for the debate is as follows.

First Hour   Groups will identify and reach consensus on "the most serious impediment to learning at this institution." Participants should have come to class prepared with their own individual lists of at least three problems. Once the class has reached consensus on the single most serious impediment to learning on your campus, your instructor will write it out as a formal statement. This statement constitutes the preliminary topic, which will eventually result in a proposition for your debate.

The instructor will then divide the class into an equal number of Affirmative and Negative teams (three to five members per team). Homework for all the Affirmative team members is to identify proposals for solving the problem identified by the class. Negative team members, meanwhile, will concentrate on reasons that the problem is not particularly serious and/or that the problem is "in the nature of things" and simply not soluble by any sort of proposal.

Second Hour   At the beginning of the period, the instructor will pair up each Affirmative team with a Negative team. The teams will be opponents during the actual debate, and there will be as many debates as there are paired teams. Each Affirmative team will now work on choosing the best proposal for solving the problem, while the Negative team pools its resources and builds its case against the seriousness and solubility of the problem. At the end of the period, each Affirmative team will share its proposal with its corresponding Negative team. The actual topic for each of the debates is now set: "Resolved: Our campus should institute Z (the Affirmative team's proposal) in order to solve problem X (the class's original problem statement)."

Homework for the next class is for each team to conduct research (interviewing students, gathering personal examples, polling students, finding data or expert testimony from the library, and so forth) to support its case. Each Affirmative team's research will be aimed at showing that the problem is serious and that the solution is workable. Each Negative team will try to show that the proposal won't work or that the problem isn't worth solving.

THIRD HOUR   At this point each Affirmative team and each Negative team will select two speakers to represent their sides. During this hour each team will pool its ideas and resources to help the speakers make the best possible cases. Each team should prepare an outline for a speech supporting its side of the debate. Team members should then anticipate the arguments of the opposition and prepare a rebuttal.

FOURTH (AND FIFTH) HOUR(S)   The actual debates. (There will be as many debates as there are paired Affirmative and Negative teams.) Each team will present two speakers. Each speaker is limited to five minutes. The order of speaking is as follows:

First affirmative:	Presents best case for the proposal
First negative:	Presents best case against the proposal
Second negative:	Rebuts argument of First Affirmative
Second affirmative:	Rebuts argument of First Negative

Those team members who do not speak will be designated observers. Their task is to take notes on the debate, paying special attention to the quality of support for each argument and to those parts of the argument that are not rebutted by the opposition. By the next class period (fifth or sixth), they will have prepared a brief, informal analysis titled "Why Our Side Won the Debate."

FIFTH OR SIXTH HOUR   The observers will report to the class on their perceptions of the debates by using their prepared analysis as the basis of the discussion. The instructor will attempt to synthesize the main points of the debates and the most telling arguments for either side. At this point, your instructor may ask each of you to write an argument on the debate topic, allowing you to argue for or against any of the proposals presented.

PART V

An Anthology of Arguments

☐

OVERVIEW OF THE ANTHOLOGY

Up to this point, we've concentrated mostly on how to write arguments. In Part V of this text we present a number of finished arguments for you to study. These aren't intended to be "model" arguments in the sense that simply by imitating them you can be guaranteed a great argument. By now, it should be clear that writing is more complex than that. What typically makes these arguments worthy of our attention is the writers' commitment to and knowledge of their subjects and their ability to find a form appropriate to what they have to say. Often, the least "imitable" aspects of an essay are the keys to the essay's success. But this doesn't mean we can't learn something about how to write better arguments from reading a variety of good arguments. And, provided that we don't treat the essays with too much reverence, provided that we're willing to play with them as well as imitate them, we can certainly adapt specific features of various essays to our own ends.

Here we would underscore the need to make the essays work for you. Every argument has a specific occasion, a set of circumstances that gave rise to the writer's choice of voice, structure, and evidence. In order to "translate" another writer's argument to your own occasion, you'll need to make adjustments. An essay you like very much may deal with its topic in an irreverent and funny way; but when you turn to your own topic, you may find humor inappropriate and distracting. Data that are extremely persuasive in one writer's argument may be almost wholly unpersuasive or even irrelevant in the context of your own argument. But by the same token, you may well find that the same author's adroit use of narrative illustrations will serve your essay well. Our advice is to use the following essays as models only in the sense that they are analogues of, not patterns for, arguments you might want to write. The essays represent a range of choices that other writers have made, and in that sense are intended to expand your own sense of available options.

One good method for dealing with the essays in this section is to approach them in the manner of the bricoleur mentioned by French anthropologist Claude Levi-Strauss. A bricoleur is a sort of jack-of-all-trades who keeps a large supply of diverse materials on hand in order to "make do" with them: "A particular cube of oak could be a wedge to make up for the inadequate length of a plank of pine or it could be a pedestal—which would allow the grain and polish of the old wood to show to advantage. In one case it will serve as an extension, in the other as material." If you examine the essays with the bricoleur's irreverent eye for new possibilities and adapt them for your own use, you do them more honor than if you passively "appreciate" them or mechanically ape them.

In order to help you see these essays in the proper spirit, we've attempted to place some of them in the context of the ongoing conversation that they come from. Instead of standing as the last word on some problematical subject, they are presented as positions on an issue. However eloquent and persuasive they may be, each should be recognized as one voice in a conversation. Indeed, we may well decide that one of the essays is right and another wrong. But even then, the essay of choice will almost always be understood differently by virtue of the fact that we've considered another point of view. After reading divergent points of view on a given subject, the reader is left with the responsibility to synthesize what's given and to create yet another point of view. This process of synthesis and dissent is the very lifeblood of argument.

The anthology addresses eleven important social issues. The first four issues are arranged as pro/con pairs so that you can analyze opposing arguments head to head. In the remaining seven issues, we have added additional voices to each of the conversations, blurring somewhat the neatness of sharply contrasted pro/con perspectives but imitating more closely the complexity of actual conversations. Seldom are there just two positions on an issue. Almost always, disputants express a wide range of views with many overlapping areas of agreement and disagreement. The later sections of this anthology reflect this complexity. The collected arguments include essays for general audiences as well as academic essays with academic format and documentation.

As you read through the arguments in Part V, you might want to keep in mind the question of where each of them fits into a larger context of issues—those recurrent questions and dilemmas that we struggle with in different guises all the time. No matter what the specific issue is, certain recurring patterns of concern keep cropping up such as the conflict between principles and consequences in ethical arguments, or between spiritual and material values, individual rights and public duties, duties to self and duties to others, short-range consequences and long-range consequences, and commitment to tradition and commitment to progress. For example, whether you are considering a proposal for mandatory drug testing or for a new zoning regulation to prevent homeowners from building too high a fence, you are dealing with the conflict between "rights of the individual" and "rights of the society." One advantage of an anthology of arguments is that in reading through them, you can see for yourself how frequently these large issues recur in different guises.

GUIDE QUESTIONS FOR THE ANALYSIS AND EVALUATION OF ARGUMENTS

As you read various arguments from this anthology, we hope that you will internalize habits of analysis and evaluation that we believe are essential for arguers. These habits derive from the principles of argument analysis covered throughout this text so that what follows is simply a summary and review of concepts you have already studied.

Questions for Analyzing and Evaluating a Conversation

Whenever you read a pro/con pair or a wide range of arguments addressing the same issue, we recommend that you follow the principles of reading described in Chapter 2.

1. *What does each argument say?* (Reading as a believer, be able to summarize each argument, stating its main claim and supporting reasons in a single sentence, if possible.)
2. *How can each argument be doubted?* (Reading as a doubter, search for weaknesses in the argument and for important questions that you would like to raise if you could talk to the author.)
3. *Why do the disputants disagree?* (Do they disagree about the "facts of the case"? About key definitions? About appropriate comparisons and analogies? About values, assumptions, and beliefs?)
4. *Which arguments appear to be stronger?* (Which arguments seem most persuasive to you? Before you could take a stand on the issue yourself, what further questions would you need to have answered? Which of your own assumptions, values, and beliefs would you have to examine further and clarify?)

Questions for Analyzing and Evaluating an Individual Argument

The previous questions ask you to examine arguments in the context of the conversations to which they belong. This next set of questions asks you to look closely at a single argument, examining in detail its structure, its argumentative strategies, and its rhetorical force.

1. *How effective is the writer at creating logical appeals?*
   - What is the claim?
   - What reasons support the claim?
   - What are the ground and warrants for each of the reasons?
   - How effective is the argument, particularly its use of evidence (grounds) and its support of its basic assumptions (warrants)?
   - Does the argument exhibit any of the *logos* fallacies explained in Appendix 1?

2. *How effective is the writer at creating ethical appeals?*
   - What *ethos* does the writer project? What is the writer's stance toward the audience?
   - Is the writer's *ethos* effective?
   - Does the writer commit any of the *ethos* fallacies explained in Appendix 1?

3. *How effective is the writer at creating emotional appeals?*
   - How effective is the writer at using audience-based reasons?
   - How effective is the writer's use of concrete language, word choice, powerful examples, and analogies for enhancing the emotional appeal of the argument?

4. *How could the writer's argument be refuted?*
   - Can the writer's grounds be attacked or called into question?
   - Can the writer's warrants be attacked or called into question?

Newcomers to Our Shores: Should the United States Place a Moratorium on Immigration?

■

TIMEOUT: THE UNITED STATES NEEDS A MORATORIUM ON IMMIGRATION

Dan Stein

Dan Stein is executive director of a nonprofit public interest organization whose goal is to end illegal immigration and set "reasonable levels" of legal immigration. Here Stein argues that the recent influx of immigrants into the United States exceeds our ability to assimilate them into mainstream culture and prevents our developing policies to stop illegal immigration.

People often talk reverently about our nation's "immigration tradition." 1
So let's begin by citing a few facts to set the record straight:

Between 1820 and 1965 an average of 297,000 new immigrants set- 2
tled in the United States each year. In 1991, the United States admitted more than 1.8 million legal immigrants, up from about 1.5 million in 1990. In addition, it is estimated that between 250,000 and 500,000 illegal immigrants settle here permanently each year.

Thus, the magnitude of immigration we are witnessing today is any- 3
thing but traditional. Moreover, immigration is no longer doing what public policies are supposed to do—namely, serve the interests of the United States and the American people.

In states such as Florida, California, Texas, and New York, state and 4
local budgets are being stretched to the breaking point to pay for the costs of resettling unprecedented numbers of new immigrants. Schools can no longer educate, public hospitals can no longer care for the indigent, and jobs and affordable housing are at a premium.

WE NEED A RESPITE

After 20 years of untraditional high levels of immigration, the United 5
States needs a respite. Throughout our history we have had periods of relatively high levels of immigration followed by extended periods when immigration was quite low.

These periods of low immigration had allowed American society to 6
absorb and assimilate the immigrants and their children and grandchildren. Most notably, the great wave of immigration at the beginning of the 20th century was followed by a more than 40-year period when immigration was extremely low.

Free from the constant cultural and linguistic reinforcement of new   7
arrivals from their countries of origin, the ethnic ghettos eventually dissipated and the second and third generations became part of the American mainstream. Free from the massive influx of immigrant labor, many
African Americans began to migrate north and west, helping to establish
a black middle class.

An immigration moratorium, which would exempt spouses and minor   8
children of U.S. citizens and legitimate refugees, would afford the country
an opportunity to absorb this latest wave of immigration and begin to
deal with the stress it has placed on many states and urban areas.

It would also allow the nation an opportunity to develop legal-immi-   9
gration policies that are suited to the realities of modern times and to get
the problem of illegal immigration under control.

The primary reason that legal immigration numbers have grown so   10
rapidly in recent years is that some 85 percent to 90 percent of the visas
go to family members of other recent immigrants. The right to bring a
relative to this country is not limited to U.S. citizens, and the relatives
who are eligible go well beyond immediate family members.

Thus, not only have we developed never-ending chains of family-   11
based immigration, but each time we admit a new immigrant, we also
actually increase the demand for still further immigration.

Keeping the nuclear family together is an important objective. Immi-   12
grants, when they come, ought to be allowed to bring a spouse and
unmarried minor children. But beyond that, there should be no special
consideration given for extended families. The United States cannot be
responsible for reuniting extended families that immigrants themselves
separate when they immigrate.

Instead, we need to set a firm ceiling on immigration—at the tradi-   13
tional annual levels of about 300,000 annually. And we must choose our
immigrants based on their potential to make a positive contribution to
this country. Other immigrant-receiving nations, like Canada and Australia, have already adopted a merit-based system for selecting newcomers to those countries.

SHUT DOWN OLD SYSTEM

An immigration moratorium would allow us to shut down the old sys-   14
tem, which the vast majority of Americans (of all races and ethnic
groups) believe is failing to serve the national interest. At the same time it
would give us an opportunity to figure out how to deal with the backlog
of 3.4 million people who have already applied for family-based visas.

An additional benefit of a moratorium is that it would free up man-   15
power and resources to deal with the large and ever-growing problem of
illegal immigration. It is estimated that between 2 million and 3 million
people enter the United States illegally each year (though only a fraction
of that number settle permanently). Uncontrolled illegal immigration has

become not only a very costly problem in places like Florida, California and the other states where illegal immigrants settle, but it has become a threat to our national security.

Several of the principal suspects in the World Trade Center bombing   16
and the shooting outside CIA headquarters last winter were illegal aliens. It must be stressed that only a very tiny fraction of illegal aliens are terrorists, but it takes only a handful to perpetrate a lot of murder and mayhem. The same lax rules that permit millions of people to enter the United States without inspection each year made it appallingly easy for terrorists to get here and then live here with little fear of being detected.

Controlling our borders is not an impossible task. Though we share a   17
2,000-mile border with Mexico, nearly all illegal immigration takes place along only about 200 miles of border in California and Texas. Mountainous terrain and unmerciful desert have taken care of the rest.

The entire Border Patrol has about 3,700 agents, roughly the size of   18
the Capitol Hill police force that protects members of Congress. Twice in the past seven years, Congress has promised to increase the Border Patrol manpower to 6,600, and both times it failed to provide the funds. Under a moratorium, additional resources could be redirected to regain control of the border.

WORK VERIFICATION SYSTEM

The most important step in controlling illegal immigration would be to   19
enact a secure work-verification system in this country. Employer sanctions, the law that prohibits the employment of illegal aliens, is being seriously undermined by rampant document fraud. Bogus Social Security cards can be purchased for as little as $25, and 48 out of the 50 states issue drivers' licenses without even checking whether applicants are legal residents of the United States.

In an age when credit cards and ATM cards are routinely verified elec-   20
tronically millions of times a day, there is no reason why the Social Security card—which everyone who works in this country must already have anyway—can't be similarly protected. A verifiable Social Security card would ensure that only those people who are in the country legally could find employment and gain access to public benefits. Moreover, it would make the government, not individual employers, responsible for determining who is here legally.

Most important, a temporary break from extremely high levels of immi-   21
gration would permit the nation to begin absorbing and assimilating the millions of newcomers who have settled here in recent years. Unless we declare a moratorium on most immigration and get a handle on illegal immigration, we will be faced with a further influx of new immigrants during the 1990s equivalent to the entire population of Florida.

It is time to restore our immigration tradition by restoring immigration   22
to its traditional levels. To achieve that, we need to take a timeout.

IMMIGRANTS HELP MAKE AMERICA STRONG

Frank Sharry

Frank Sharry is executive director of a coalition of organizations devoted to assisting refugees and immigrants. "Immigrants help make American strong," claims Sharry, because of their family values, their love of freedom, and their work ethic.

There's a new gang of "drug pushers" on the national scene, and the "drug" they're pushing is immigrant-bashing. Like any other narcotic, taking it distorts one's sense of reality and lulls one into a false sense of security.   1

Use this drug, the anti-immigration pushers insist, and such national problems as crime, poverty, unemployment, poorly managed public school systems and pollution will magically disappear.   2

These pushers are eager to give you a fix, and if recent opinion polls are any indication, numerous Americans are becoming addicted. The trouble is that, once they wake up from their drug-induced stupor, our nation's problems will still be around.   3

In fact, when people take a close look at the effect of immigration on the United States, they find compelling evidence that the immigrants themselves are the antidote to our nation's ills.   4

Immigrants help make America strong. Immigrants who come to the United States are people who fervently believe in freedom and embrace America's opportunities.   5

They work hard, pay taxes and sacrifice for their children's futures. They infuse our aging society with new energy and new ideas; they strengthen our economy; and they breathe life into dying neighborhoods.   6

MYTHS AND DISTORTIONS

The problem is that most Americans simply don't understand how our immigration policies work. This is because those who do most of the explaining are the peddlers of myths and distortions. When Americans are treated with respect, and informed as to why we accept refugees and immigrants, they come to understand that admitting newcomers is both the smart thing to do and the right thing to do.   7

The three values upon which U.S. immigration policy is based are family, freedom and work.   8

Family values. Did you know that more than 70 percent of the refugees and immigrants who enter the United States annually are admitted so they can join loved ones from whom they have been separated?   9

Day after day, in airports around the country, parents and children, husbands and wives, brothers and sisters—many of whom have waited as long as 10 or 15 years to be reunited—rush into each other's arms. They weep with gratitude that they are together, reunited at last in a   10 country that understands the importance of nuclear families as critical to keeping our nation great.

Finding freedom. Our nation was founded in large part by those who were fleeing various kinds of persecution. Today's newcomers are no different. 11

Around the world, there are people who live in fear of the knock on the door in the middle of the night—the Haitian mother living in terror that she may be imprisoned and tortured because soldiers have found a pamphlet in support of deposed President Jean-Bertrand Aristide in her dress pocket; the Peruvian community leader who has been targeted for assassination by Shining Path guerrillas; a Somali man whose entire family has been killed by the minions of some warlord; a Bosnian girl raped and discarded during a "cleansing" operation. 12

These are the refugees who, because they are unwilling to compromise their religious beliefs, their commitment to freedom of speech, or their determination to bring democracy to their homeland, are faced with two choices: Stay in their country and risk death, torture or imprisonment, or flee for freedom. 13

As the world's champion of human rights, we should welcome these refugees, and we should be proud that we live in a country that is a beacon of hope for those who are threatened simply because of what they stand for and what they believe. 14

Work ethic. Immigrants are crucial to strengthening our national economy. Immigrants are three times as likely to save their earnings and start small businesses, which in turn provide jobs for many native-born Americans. 15

In addition, many immigrants are admitted to our country because they have specific skills that contribute to economic growth. We admit immigrants who are engineers, physicists, scientists and other professionals to fill specific jobs for which no American worker can be found. This ensures that U.S. companies maintain a competitive advantage in the global marketplace, and keeps them from moving overseas and taking U.S. jobs with them. 16

CONTRIBUTE MORE THAN UTILIZE

Moreover, newcomers contribute overall far more than they utilize in services. A year ago, a Business Week cover story with the headline "Immigrants: How They're Helping the Economy" reported that, on an annual basis, immigrants pay $90 billion in taxes and receive only $5 billion in welfare. 17

These values—family, freedom and work—constitute a sound and sensible framework for U.S. immigration policies. 18

Just as important, newcomers are admitted to the United States under tightly regulated and orderly refugee and immigration policies. For 19 example, 8 out of 10 refugees and immigrants who enter the country each year do so legally; less than 1.5 percent of the U.S. population has entered the country illegally.

DIFFERENT PICTURE PAINTED

Opponents of immigration paint a different picture. They cite alarming   20
statistics about world population growth and claim that unless we stop all immigration soon we will be overrun by hordes of people. Don't be alarmed. The simple truth is that most people around the world live their entire lives within a few miles of where they were born. They always have and always will. And according to a recent study by the United Nations Population Fund, the vast majority who migrate from developing countries go to other developing countries.

Of course, this is not to suggest that we should open our borders to   21
any who do try to migrate. As a sovereign nation, it is the right and duty of the United States to regulate who enters the country, and without question, there are ways in which the federal government can improve its ability to do so. Professionalizing the Border Patrol and improving the Immigration Service's capacity to quickly and fairly process those who ask for asylum at our ports of entry are two areas that the new administration should focus on in the near future.

But controlling illegal immigration is a far cry from bringing a com-   22
plete halt to legal immigration. Unfortunately, opponents of immigration think Americans are too stupid to understand the difference. Now you know.

Given the potential consequences, just why are the "pushers" of anti-   23
immigrant sentiment working so hard to close the doors on those who want only to build new lives in freedom? Unfortunately, an important ingredient in the immigrant-bashing drug is bigotry.

The Pat Buchanans of the world prey on the public's fears and mis-   24
conceptions to advance their own dubious causes. They use thinly veiled code words and innuendoes to arouse a backlash against people of color who come here in pursuit of the American dream. They even try to turn public opinion against people who have been here for generations but look or sound "foreign." This is nothing more than scapegoating, and does nothing to solve our real problems.

STAND UP TO PUSHERS OF HATE

It's time for the American people and our leaders to stand up to these   25
pushers of hate and division. It's time to make it clear that the newcomers of today, no matter what their skin color happens to be, bring the same kind of courage, determination and commitment to making a better life for themselves and their children as those of years past.

It's time to state clearly and proudly that no other nation has so suc-   26
cessfully combined people from different backgrounds within a single
society, and that the diversity that results from immigration is a unique
source of strength for us as a nation.

☐ FOR CLASS DISCUSSION

1. Analyze and evaluate the disagreement over immigration by applying
   the first set of guide questions from page 473. How do you account for
   the disagreement between Stein and Sharry?

2. Choose one of the arguments for closer analysis, applying the second set
   of guide questions on page 474.

OPTIONAL WRITING ASSIGNMENT   In commenting on the experience of immigrants earlier in U.S. history, Stein notes that, "[f]ree from the constant cultural and linguistic reinforcement of new arrivals from their countries of origin, the ethnic ghettos eventually dissipated and the second and third
generations became part of the American mainstream." To what extent do
you think that immigrants should strive to maintain their own language
and ethnicity as opposed to adopting American ways and blending into
mainstream culture?

Guns and Public Safety: Should the Federal Government Enact Strict Controls on the Ownership of Handguns?

"TWO HUNDRED MILLION GUNS— LET'S NOT MAKE IT ANY WORSE"

Molly Ivins

*"[W]hen one confronts a large, hairy problem," says syndicated columnist
Molly Ivins, "it is always useful to follow the First Rule of Holes: When you're
in one, quit digging." To keep the mess of street violence from getting worse,
Ivins believes we should "ban the sale of all handguns and assault rifles."*

AUSTIN, Texas—Interesting new tack being taken by the gun nuts. For   1
years, whenever anyone brought up gun control, they screeched like the
littlest pig, all the way home, that we shouldn't, we couldn't, we wouldn't
do anything to control guns.

But now that 90 percent of the American people favor gun control,   2
their new tactic is to say, "Sorry, too late to do anything about it now."

simply be more likely to own guns than people in safer circumstances. Getting rid of the gun might not make the renter any safer than buying out the landlord.

Most significantly, the study made no effort to investigate the 99% of   19
protective uses of guns that do not involve a fatality. The folks who got murdered are, after all, the folks for whom protection did not work. A study that ignores survivors, the hundreds of thousands of people who use guns for protection each year, can't say much about the overall protective effect of gun ownership.

Despite the limitations of the study, almost every news report treated   20
the 2.7 figure unquestionably, as a scientific fact. Many academic criminologists thought the study was worthless, but the only dissent reported was from a researcher for the National Rifle Assn.

Other published factoids purporting to show the dangers of gun own-   21
ership are similarly vacuous. If the media spent one-tenth as much effort looking into the truth behind these claims as they spend investigating the conflicting stories about President Clinton's haircuts, the quality of the gun-control debate would improve considerably.

It's true that in some homes, such as those of alcoholics, the mentally   22
ill or ex-felons, the presence of a gun does substantially increase the risk of a homicide. But here, too, the "facts" can be twisted to the gun lobby's favor: The male felon killed by his girlfriend is counted as the victim of a "tragic domestic homicide," not the perpetrator of vicious abuse. But most households are not violence-prone; rather, most gun owners' concern is about violence directed against them from the outside. They know, intuitively, that the government will not protect them from criminal attack. Arthur Boone and Bessie Jones correctly understood this, and they have the support of the tens of millions of other Americans who own guns for protection.

☐ FOR CLASS DISCUSSION

1. Analyze and evaluate the disagreement over handgun control by applying the first set of guide questions from page 473. How do you account for the disagreement between Ivins and Kopel?

2. Choose one of the arguments for closer analysis, applying the second set of guide questions on page 474.

OPTIONAL WRITING ASSIGNMENT   Although these two short arguments touch just the surface of the complex issues that underlie the gun control debate, many readers find the articles surprisingly persuasive. To study their effectiveness, take a poll of your classmates as follows:

1. Ask the class to identify in either of these two articles one passage that caused them to reconsider—even if very slightly—their own initial views on gun control, by making them slightly more certain of their stand on gun control or slightly less certain.

2. Ask everyone to report the passage they chose, and list the passages on the chalkboard.

3. Identify the passage chosen by the most people.

Then, in a short essay (one or two paragraphs), analyze why that passage was effective.

Mercy Killing and the Right to Die: Can Active Euthanasia Be a Moral Good?

RISING TO THE OCCASION OF OUR DEATH

William F. May

Legalizing active euthanasia to eliminate suffering may blind us to the value of suffering. "The community . . . may need its aged and dependent, its sick and its dying, and the virtue they sometimes evince—the virtues of humility, courage, and patience—just as much as the community needs the virtues of justice and love manifest in the agents of care."

For many parents, a Volkswagen van is associated with putting chil- 1
dren to sleep on a camping trip. Jack Kevorkian, a Detroit pathologist, has now linked the van with the veterinarian's meaning of "putting to sleep." Kevorkian conducted a dinner interview with Janet Elaine Adkins, a 54-year-old Alzheimer's patient, and her husband and then agreed to help her commit suicide in his VW van. Kevorkian pressed beyond the more generally accepted practice of passive euthanasia (allowing a patient to die by withholding or withdrawing treatment) to active euthanasia (killing for mercy).

Kevorkian, moreover, did not comply with the strict regulations that 2
govern active euthanasia in, for example, the Netherlands. Holland requires that death be imminent (Adkins had beaten her son in tennis just a few days earlier); it demands a more professional review of the medical evidence and the patient's resolution than a dinner interview with a physician (who is a stranger and who does not treat patients) permits; and it calls for the final, endorsing signatures of two doctors.

So Kevorkian-bashing is easy. But the question remains: Should we 3
develop a judicious, regulated social policy permitting voluntary euthanasia for the terminally ill? Some moralists argue that the distinction between allowing to die and killing for mercy is petty quibbling over technique. Since the patient in any event dies—whether by acts of omission or commission—the route to death doesn't really matter. The way modern procedures have made dying at the hands of the experts and their

machines such a prolonged and painful business has further fueled the euthanasia movement, which asserts not simply the right to die but the right to be killed.

But other moralists believe that there is an important moral distinction   4
between allowing to die and mercy killing. The euthanasia movement, these critics contend, wants to engineer death rather than face dying. Euthanasia would bypass dying to make one dead as quickly as possible. It aims to relieve suffering by knocking out the interval between life and death. It solves the problem of suffering by eliminating the sufferer.

The impulse behind the euthanasia movement is understandable in an   5
age when dying has become such an inhumanly endless business. But the movement may fail to appreciate our human capacity to rise to the occasion of our death. The best death is not always the sudden death. Those forewarned of death and given time to prepare for it have time to engage in acts of reconciliation. Also, advanced grieving by those about to be bereaved may ease some of their pain. Psychiatrists have observed that those who lose a loved one accidentally have a more difficult time recovering from the loss than those who have suffered through an extended period of illness before the death. Those who have lost a close relative by accident are more likely to experience what Geoffrey Gorer has called limitless grief. The community, moreover, may need its aged and dependent, its sick and its dying, and the virtues which they sometimes evince—the virtues of humility, courage, and patience—just as much as the community needs the virtues of justice and love manifest in the agents of care.

On the whole, our social policy should allow terminal patients to die   6
but it should not regularize killing for mercy. Such a policy would recognize and respect that moment in illness when it no longer makes sense to bend every effort to cure or to prolong life and when one must allow patients to do their own dying. This policy seems most consonant with the obligations of the community to care and of the patient to finish his or her course.

Advocates of active euthanasia appeal to the principle of patient   7
autonomy—as the use of the phrase "voluntary euthanasia" indicates. But emphasis on the patient's right to determine his or her destiny often harbors an extremely naive view of the uncoerced nature of the decision. Patients who plead to be put to death hardly make unforced decisions if the terms and conditions under which they receive care already nudge them in the direction of the exit. If the elderly have stumbled around in their apartments, alone and frightened for years, or if they have spent years warehoused in geriatrics barracks, then the decision to be killed for mercy hardly reflects an uncoerced decision. The alternative may be so wretched as to push patients toward this escape. It is a huge irony and, in some cases, hypocrisy to talk suddenly about a compassionate killing when the aging and dying may have been starved for compassion for many years. To put it bluntly, a country has not earned the moral right to

kill for mercy unless it has already sustained and supported life mercifully. Otherwise we kill for compassion only to reduce the demands on our compassion. This statement does not charge a given doctor or family member with impure motives. I am concerned here not with the individual case but with the cumulative impact of a social policy.

I can, to be sure, imagine rare circumstances in which I hope I would   8
have the courage to kill for mercy—when the patient is utterly beyond human care, terminal, and in excruciating pain. A neurosurgeon once showed a group of physicians and an ethicist the picture of a Vietnam casualty who had lost all four limbs in a landmine explosion. The catastrophe had reduced the soldier to a trunk with his face transfixed in horror. On the battlefield I would hope that I would have the courage to kill the sufferer with mercy.

But hard cases do not always make good laws or wise social policies.   9
Regularized mercy killings would too quickly relieve the community of its obligation to provide good care. Further, we should not always expect the law to provide us with full protection and coverage for what, in rare circumstances, we may morally need to do. Sometimes the moral life calls us out into a no-man's-land where we cannot expect total security and protection under the law. But no one said that the moral life is easy.

■

DEATH BY CHOICE: WHO SHOULD DECIDE?

Daniel C. Maguire

Writing before recent court decisions brought these issues to full national consciousness, Catholic theologian Daniel Maguire asks whether any decision to end life can be a moral good. Using the cases of a hydrocephalic boy and a severely deformed infant girl, Maguire argues that it can. He remains in a quandary, however, about who should decide.

Who would dare arrogate to himself the decision to impose death on   1
a child or unconscious person who is not in a position to assent or dissent to the action? What right does any person have to make decisions about life and death in a way that assumes absolute and ultimate authority over another human being? Could a doctor make such a decision? It would seem that he could not. His medical skills are one thing, the moral decision to end a life is another. How would a family feel who learned that a doctor had reached an independent decision to terminate their father's life?

Could the family make such a decision? It would seem not, for several   2
good reasons. There might be a conflict of interest arising from avarice, spite, or impatience with the illness of the patient. And even if these things were not present, the family might be emotionally traumatized

when their pain of loss is complicated by the recollection of their decision. Also, the family might constitute a split and therefore a hung jury. Then what?

Could a court-appointed committee of impartial persons make the decision? No, it would seem not. They would not only be impartial but also uninformed about the personal realities of the patient. The decision to terminate life requires a full and intimate knowledge of all the reality-constituting circumstances of the case. Strangers would not have this. 3

The conclusion, therefore, would seem inescapable that there is no moral way in which death could be imposed on a person who is incapable of consent because of youth or irreversible loss of consciousness. 4

This objection contains so much truth that my reply to it will contain much agreement as well as disagreement. To begin with, it should be noted that we are discussing not the legality but the morality of terminating life without the consent of the patient. Terminating life by a deliberate act of commission in the kinds of cases here discussed is illegal in this country. By an ongoing fiction of American law it would be classified as murder in the first degree. Terminating by calculated omission is murky at best and perilous at worst under current law. Therefore, it can be presumed that any conclusion we reach here will probably be illegal. This is a morally relevant fact; it is not to be presumed morally decisive, however, since there may be good moral grounds to assume the risk of illegality. As we have stated, morality and legality are not identical. 5

With this said, then, let us face up to the objection. There are two parts to my response. First, holding the question of who should decide in abeyance for the moment, I would suggest that there are cases where, if that difficult question could be satisfactorily answered, it would seem to be a morally good option (among other morally good options) to terminate a life. In other words, there are cases where the termination of a life could be defended as a moral good if the proper authority for making the decision could be located. Of course, if the objections raised against all those who could decide are decisive, then this otherwise morally desirable act would be immoral by reason of improper agency. 6

There are cases where it would appear to be arguably moral to take the necessary action (or to make the necessary omission) to end a life. Dr. Ruth Russell tells this story: 7

> I used to annually take a class of senior students in abnormal psychology to visit the hospital ward in a training school for medical defectives. There was a little boy about 4 years old the first time we visited him in the hospital. He was a hydrocephalic with a head so immensely large that he had never been able to raise it off the pillow and he never would. He had a tiny little body with this huge head and it is very difficult to keep him from developing sores. The students asked, "Why do we keep a child like that alive?"
>
> The next year we went back with another class. This year the child's hands had been padded to keep him from hitting his head. Again the

students asked, "Why do we do this?" The third year we went back and visited the same child. Now the nurses explained that he had been hitting his head so hard that in spite of the padding he was injuring it severely and they had tied his arms down to the sides of his crib.[1]

What are the defensible moral options in this kind of case? One might be to keep the child alive in the way that was being done. This might show a great reverence for life and re-enforce society's commitment to weak and defective human life. It may indeed be the hallmark of advancing civilization that continuing care would be taken of this child. Termination of this child's life by omission or commission might set us on the slippery slope that has led other societies to the mass murder of physically and mentally defective persons.

All of this is possibly true but it is by no means self-evidently true to   9
the point that other alternatives are apodictically excluded. This case is a singularly drastic one. Given its special qualities, action to end life here is not necessarily going to precipitate the killing of persons in distinguishably different circumstances.

Furthermore, keeping this child alive might exemplify the materialistic   10
error interpreting the sanctity of life in merely physical terms. This interpretation, of course, is a stark oversimplification. It is just as wrong as the other side of the simplistic coin, which would say that life has no value until it attains a capacity for distinctively personal acts such as intellectual knowledge, love, and imagination. A fetus, while not yet capable of intellectual and other distinctively personal activity, is on a trajectory toward personhood and already shares in the sanctity of human life. (This does not mean that it may never be terminated when other sacred values outweigh its claim to life in a conflict situation.)

The sanctity of life is a generic notion that does not yield a precisely   11
spelled-out code of ethics. Deciding what the sanctity of life requires in conflict situations such as the case of the hydrocephalic child described by Dr. Russell, may lead persons to contradictory judgments. To say that the sanctity of life requires keeping that child alive regardless of his condition and that all other alternatives impeach the perception of life as sacred, is both arrogant and epistemologically unsound. In this case, maintaining this child in this condition might be incompatible with its sacred human dignity. It might not meet the minimal needs of human physical existence. In different terms, the sanctity of death might here take precedence over a physicalist interpretation of the sanctity of life. There is a time when human death befits human life, when nothing is more germane to the person's current needs. This conclusion appears defensible in the case of the hydrocephalic boy.

[1]   See *Dilemmas of Euthanasia,* a pamphlet containing excerpts, papers and discussions from the Fourth Euthanasia Conference, held in New York on December 4, 1971; this is a publication of the Euthanasia Educational Council, Inc. [now called Concern for Dying], New York, p. 35.

brainstem activity can be kept alive almost indefinitely through tubal nourishing and other supportive measures. Would it not seem a clear good if a decision could be made to withdraw support and allow death to have its final say? The spectacle of living with the breathing but depersonalized remains of a loved one could make death seem a needed blessing. In conclusion, then, there are cases where the imposition of death would seem a good. It was logically indicated to state that conclusion before going to the main thrust of the objection, the question of who could decide when the person in question can give no consent.

☐ For Class Discussion

1. Analyze and evaluate the debate on the right to die by applying the first set of guide questions from page 473. How do you account for the disagreement among the disputants?

2. Choose one of the arguments for closer analysis, applying the second set of guide questions on page 474. Also consider student writer Dao Do's essay on page 138–39.

OPTIONAL WRITING ASSIGNMENT   As a member of the state medical board, you have been asked by a local civic organization to give your thoughts on the recent controversy over "Dr. Death," the Detroit physician who designed and made available a "suicide machine" to ensure that those who are suffering from incurable diseases and who wish to kill themselves have a speedy and painless death. (For more background on the Jack Kevorkian case, see the opening of William May's essay, p. 487).

Do people have the right to avail themselves of such machines? Do doctors have a right (or even an obligation) to help patients die? What's the state's role in deciding this issue? These are some of the questions the group would like you to consider in a brief (no more than four pages) speech at their weekly Wednesday luncheon. Drawing on your reading of the preceding essays, personal experience, and any other research you may have done, write your speech.

The Distribution of Wealth: What Responsibility do the Rich Have for the Poor?

LIFEBOAT ETHICS:
THE CASE AGAINST HELPING THE POOR

Garrett Hardin

Hardin argues that rich nations are like lifeboats and that impoverished people are like swimmers in the sea clamoring to climb aboard the lifeboat. If we allow all the swimmers to come aboard, the lifeboat sinks. "Complete justice; complete catastrophe."

Environmentalists use the metaphor of the earth as a "spaceship" in trying to persuade countries, industries and people to stop wasting and polluting our natural resources. Since we all share life on this planet, they argue, no single person or institution has the right to destroy, waste or use more than a fair share of its resources.   1

But does everyone on earth have an equal right to an equal share of its resources? The spaceship metaphor can be dangerous when used by misguided idealists to justify suicidal policies for sharing our resources through uncontrolled immigration and foreign aid. In their enthusiastic but unrealistic generosity, they confuse the ethics of a spaceship with those of a lifeboat.   2

A true spaceship would have to be under the control of a captain, since no ship could possibly survive if its course were determined by committee. Spaceship Earth certainly has no captain; the United Nations is merely a toothless tiger, with little power to enforce any policy upon its bickering members.   3

If we divide the world crudely into rich nations and poor nations, two thirds of them are desperately poor, and only one third comparatively rich, with the United States the wealthiest of all. Metaphorically each nation can be seen as a lifeboat full of comparatively rich people. In the ocean outside each lifeboat swim the poor of the world, who would like to get in, or at least to share some of the wealth. What should the lifeboat passengers do?   4

First, we must recognize the limited capacity of any lifeboat. For example, a nation's land has a limited capacity to support a population and as the current energy crisis has shown us, in some ways we have already exceeded the carrying capacity of our land.   5

ADRIFT IN A MORAL SEA

So here we sit, say fifty people in our lifeboat. To be generous, let us assume it has room for ten more, making a total capacity of sixty. Suppose the fifty of us in the lifeboat see 100 others swimming in the water outside, begging for admission to our boat or for handouts. We have several options: We may be tempted to try to live by the Christian ideal of being "our brother's keeper," or by the Marxist ideal of "to each according to his needs." Since the needs of all in the water are the same, and since they can all be seen as "our brothers," we could take them all into our boat, making a total of 150 in a boat designed for sixty. The boat swamps, everyone drowns. Complete justice, complete catastrophe.   6

Since the boat has an unused excess capacity of ten more passengers, we could admit just ten more to it. But which ten do we let in? How do we choose? Do we pick the best ten, the neediest ten, "first come, first served"? And what do we say to the ninety we exclude? If we do let an extra ten into our lifeboat, we will have lost our "safety factor," an engi-   7 neering principle of critical importance. For example, if we don't leave room for excess capacity as a safety factor in our country's agriculture, a new plant disease or a bad change in the weather could have disastrous consequences.

Suppose we decide to preserve our small safety factor and admit no more to the lifeboat. Our survival is then possible, although we shall have to be constantly on guard against boarding parties.   8

While this last solution clearly offers the only means of our survival, it is morally abhorrent to many people. Some say they feel guilty about their good luck. My reply is simple: "Get out and yield your place to others." This may solve the problem of the guilt-ridden person's conscience, but it does not change the ethics of the lifeboat. The needy person to whom the guilt-ridden person yields his place will not himself feel guilty about his good luck. If he did, he would not climb aboard. The net result of conscience-stricken people giving up their unjustly held seats is the elimination of that sort of conscience from the lifeboat.   9

This is the basic metaphor within which we must work out our solutions. Let us now enrich the image, step by step, with substantive additions from the real world, a world that must solve real and pressing problems of overpopulation and hunger.   10

The harsh ethics of the lifeboat become even harsher when we consider the reproductive differences between the rich nations and the poor nations. The people inside the lifeboats are doubling in numbers every eighty-seven years; those swimming around outside are doubling, on the average, every thirty-five years, more than twice as fast as the rich. And since the world's resources are dwindling, the difference in prosperity between the rich and the poor can only increase.   11

As of 1973, the U.S. had a population of 210 million people, who were increasing by 0.8 percent per year. Outside our lifeboat, let us imagine another 210 million people (say the combined populations of Colombia, Ecuador, Venezuela, Morocco, Pakistan, Thailand and the Philippines), who are increasing at a rate of 3.3 percent per year. Put differently, the doubling time for this aggregate population is twenty-one years, compared to eighty-seven years for the U.S.   12

MULTIPLYING THE RICH AND THE POOR

Now suppose the U.S. agreed to pool its resources with those seven countries, with everyone receiving an equal share. Initially the ratio of Americans to non-Americans in this model would be one-to-one. But consider what the ratio would be after eighty-seven years, by which time the Americans would have doubled to a population of 420 million. By then, doubling every twenty-one years, the other group would have swollen to 3.54 billion. Each American would have to share the available resource with more than eight people.   13

But, one could argue, this discussion assumes that current population trends will continue, and they may not. Quite so. Most likely the rate of   14 population increase will decline much faster in the U.S. than it will in the other countries, and there does not seem to be much we can do about it. In sharing with "each according to his needs," we must recognize that needs are determined by population size, which is determined by the rate of reproduction, which at present is regarded as a sovereign right of every nation, poor or not. This being so, the philanthropic load created by the sharing ethic of the spaceship can only increase.

THE TRAGEDY OF THE COMMONS

The fundamental error of spaceship ethics, and the sharing it requires, is 15
that it leads to what I call "the tragedy of the commons." Under a system of private property, the men who own property recognize their responsibility to care for it, for if they don't they will eventually suffer. A farmer, for instance, will allow no more cattle in a pasture than its carrying capacity justifies. If he overloads it, erosion sets in, weeds take over, and he loses the use of the pasture.

If a pasture becomes a commons open to all, the right of each to use 16
it may not be matched by a corresponding responsibility to protect it. Asking everyone to use it with discretion will hardly do, for the considerate herdsman who refrains from overloading the commons suffers more than a selfish one who says his needs are greater. If everyone would restrain himself, all would be well; but it takes only one less than everyone to ruin a system of voluntary restraint. In a crowded world of less than perfect human beings, mutual ruin is inevitable if there are no controls. This is the tragedy of the commons.

One of the major tasks of education today should be the creation of 17
such an acute awareness of the dangers of the commons that people will recognize its many varieties. For example, the air and water have become polluted because they are treated as commons. Further growth in the population or per-capita conversion of natural resources into pollutants will only make the problem worse. The same holds true for the fish of the oceans. Fishing fleets have nearly disappeared in many parts of the world, technological improvements in the art of fishing are hastening the day of complete ruin. Only the replacement of the system of the commons with a responsible system of control will save the land, air, water and oceanic fisheries.

THE WORLD FOOD BANK

In recent years there has been a push to create a new commons called a 18
World Food Bank, an international depository of food reserves to which nations would contribute according to their abilities and from which they would draw according to their needs. This humanitarian proposal has received support from many liberal international groups, and from such prominent citizens as Margaret Mead, U.N. Secretary General Kurt Waldheim, and Senators Edward Kennedy and George McGovern.

A world food bank appeals powerfully to our humanitarian impulses.   19
But before we rush ahead with such a plan, let us recognize where the
greatest political push comes from, lest we be disillusioned later. Our
experience with the "Food for Peace program," or Public Law 480, gives
us the answer. This program moved billions of dollars' worth of U.S. surplus grain to food-short, population-long countries during the past two
decades. But when P.L. 480 first became law, a headline in the business
magazine *Forbes* revealed the real power behind it: "Feeding the World's
Hungry Millions: How It Will Mean Billions for U.S. Business."

And indeed it did. In the years 1960 to 1970, U.S. taxpayers spent   20
a total of $7.9 billion on the Food for Peace program. Between 1948
and 1970, they also paid an additional $50 billion for other economic-
aid programs, some of which went for food and food-producing
machinery and technology. Though all U.S. taxpayers were forced to-
contribute to the cost of P.L. 480, certain special interest groups gained
handsomely under the program. Farmers did not have to contribute the
grain; the Government, or rather the taxpayers, bought it from them
at full market prices. The increased demand raised prices of farm products generally. The manufacturers of farm machinery, fertilizers and pesti-
cides benefited by the farmers' extra efforts to grow more food. Grain
elevators profited from storing the surplus until it could be shipped.
Railroads made money hauling it to ports, and shipping lines profited
from carrying it overseas. The implementation of P.L. 480 required
the creation of a vast Government bureaucracy, which then acquired
its own vested interest in continuing the program regardless of its
merits.

EXTRACTING DOLLARS

Those who proposed and defended the Food for Peace program in pub-   21
lic rarely mentioned its importance to any of these special interests. The
public emphasis was always on its humanitarian effects. The combination of silent selfish interests and highly vocal humanitarian apologists
made a powerful and successful lobby for extracting money from taxpayers. We can expect the same lobby to push now for the creation of a
World Food Bank.

However great the potential benefit to selfish interests, it should not be   22
a decisive argument against a truly humanitarian program. We must ask
if such a program would actually do more good than harm, not only
momentarily but also in the long run. Those who propose the food bank
usually refer to a current "emergency" or "crisis" in terms of world food
supply. But what is an emergency? Although they may be infrequent and
sudden, everyone knows that emergencies will occur from time to time.
A well-run family, company, organization or country prepares for the likelihood of accidents and emergencies. It expects them, it budgets for
them, it saves for them.

LEARNING THE HARD WAY

What happens if some organizations or countries budget for accidents 23
and others do not? If each country is solely responsible for its own well-
being, poorly managed ones will suffer. But they can learn from experience. They may mend their ways, and learn to budget for infrequent but
certain emergencies. For example, the weather varies from year to year,
and periodic crop failures are certain. A wise and competent government
saves out of the production of the good years in anticipation of bad years
to come. Joseph taught this policy to Pharaoh in Egypt more than 2,000
years ago. Yet the great majority of the governments in the world today
do not follow such a policy. They lack either the wisdom or the competence, or both. Should those nations that do manage to put something
aside be forced to come to the rescue each time an emergency occurs
among the poor nations?

"But it isn't their fault!" some kindhearted liberals argue. "How can we 24
blame the poor people who are caught in an emergency? Why must they
suffer for the sins of their governments?" The concept of blame is simply
not relevant here. The real question is, what are the operational consequences of establishing a world food bank? If it is open to every country
every time a need develops, slovenly rulers will not be motivated to take
Joseph's advice. Someone will always come to their aid. Some countries
will deposit food in the world food bank, and others will withdraw it.
There will be almost no overlap. As a result of such solutions to food
shortage emergencies, the poor countries will not learn to mend their
ways, and will suffer progressively greater emergencies as their populations grow.

POPULATION CONTROL THE CRUDE WAY

On the average, poor countries undergo a 2.5 percent increase in popu- 25
lation each year; rich countries, about 0.8 percent. Only rich countries
have anything in the way of food reserves set aside, and even they do not
have as much as they should. Poor countries have none. If poor countries received no food from the outside, the rate of their population
growth would be periodically checked by crop failures and famines. But if
they can always draw on a world food bank in time of need, their populations can continue to grow unchecked, and so will their "need" for aid. In
the short run, a world food bank may diminish that need, but in the long
run it actually increases the need without limit.

Without some system of worldwide food sharing, the proportion of 26
people in the rich and poor nations might eventually stabilize. The over-
populated poor countries would decrease in numbers, while the rich
countries that had room for more people would increase. But with a well-
meaning system of sharing, such as a world food bank, the growth differential between the rich and the poor countries will not only persist, it will
increase. Because of the higher rate of population growth in the poor

countries of the world, 88 percent of today's children are born poor, and only 12 percent rich. Year by year the ratio becomes worse, as the fast-reproducing poor outnumber the slow-reproducing rich.

A world food bank is thus a commons in disguise. People will have   27
more motivation to draw from it than to add to any common store. The less provident and less able will multiply at the expense of the abler and more provident, bringing eventual ruin upon all who share in the commons. Besides, any system of "sharing" that amounts to foreign aid from the rich nations to the poor nations will carry the taint of charity, which will contribute little to the world peace so devoutly desired by those who support the idea of a world food bank.

As past U.S. foreign-aid programs have amply and depressingly   28
demonstrated, international charity frequently inspires mistrust and antagonism rather than gratitude on the part of the recipient nation.

CHINESE FISH AND MIRACLE RICE

The modern approach to foreign aid stresses the export of technology   29
and advice, rather than money and food. As an ancient Chinese proverb goes: "Give a man a fish and he will eat for a day; teach him how to fish and he will eat for the rest of his days." Acting on this advice, the Rockefeller and Ford Foundations have financed a number of programs for improving agriculture in the hungry nations. Known as the "Green Revolution," these programs have led to the development of "miracle rice" and "miracle wheat," new strains that offer bigger harvests and greater resistance to crop damage. Norman Borlaug, the Nobel Prize winning agroncmist who, supported by the Rockefeller Foundation, developed "miracle wheat," is one of the most prominent advocates of a world food bank.

Whether or not the Green Revolution can increase food production as   30
much as its champions claim is a debatable but possibly irrelevant point. Those who support this well-intended humanitarian effort should first consider some of the fundamentals of human ecology. Ironically, one man who did was the late Alan Gregg, a vice president of the Rockefeller Foundation. Two decades ago he expressed strong doubts about the wisdom of such attempts to increase food production. He likened the growth and spread of humanity over the surface of the earth to the spread of cancer in the human body, remarking that "cancerous growths demand food; but, as far as I know, they have never been cured by getting it."

OVERLOADING THE ENVIRONMENT

Every human born constitutes a draft on all aspects of the environment: 31
food, air, water, forests, beaches, wildlife, scenery and solitude. Food can, perhaps, be significantly increased to meet a growing demand. But what about clean beaches, unspoiled forests, and solitude? If we satisfy a

growing population's need for food, we necessarily decrease its per-capita supply of the other resources needed by men.

India, for example, now has a population of 600 million, which increases by 15 million each year. This population already puts a huge load on a relatively impoverished environment. The country's forests are now only a small fraction of what they were three centuries ago, and floods and erosion continually destroy the insufficient farmland that remains. Every one of the 15 million new lives added to India's population puts an additional burden on the environment, and increases the economic and social costs of crowding. However humanitarian our intent, every Indian life saved through medical or nutritional assistance from abroad diminishes the quality of life for those who remain, and for subsequent generations. If rich countries make it possible, through foreign aid, for 600 million Indians to swell to 1.2 billion in a mere twenty-eight years, as their current growth rate threatens, will future generations of Indians thank us for hastening the destruction of their environment? Will our good intentions be sufficient excuse for the consequences of our actions? 32

My final example of a commons in action is one for which the public has the least desire for rational discussion—immigration. Anyone who publicly questions the wisdom of current U.S. immigration policy is promptly charged with bigotry, prejudice, ethnocentrism, chauvinism, isolationism or selfishness. Rather than encounter such accusations, one would rather talk about other matters, leaving immigration policy to wallow in the crosscurrents of special interests that take no account of the good of the whole, or the interest of posterity. 33

Perhaps we still feel guilty about things we said in the past. Two generations ago the popular press frequently referred to Dagos, Wops, Polacks, Chinks and Krauts, in articles about how America was being "overrun" by foreigners of supposedly inferior genetic stock. But because the implied inferiority of foreigners was used then as justification for keeping them out, people now assume that restrictive policies could only be based on such misguided notions. There are no other grounds. 34

A NATION OF IMMIGRANTS

Just consider the numbers involved. Our Government acknowledges a net inflow of 400,000 immigrants a year. While we have no hard data on the extent of illegal entries, educated guesses put the figure at about 600,000 a year. Since the natural increase (excess of births over deaths) of the resident population now runs about 1.7 million per year, the yearly gain from immigration amounts to at least 19 percent of the total annual increase, and may be as much as 37 percent if we include the estimate for illegal immigrants. Considering the growing use of birth-control devices, the potential effect of educational campaigns by such organizations a Planned Parenthood Federation of America and Zero Population 35

Growth, and the influence of inflation and the housing shortage, the fertility rate of American women may decline so much that immigration could account for all the yearly increase in population. Should we not at least ask if that is what we want?

For the sake of those who worry about whether the "quality" of the   36
average immigrant compares favorably with the quality of the average resident, let us assume that immigrants and nativeborn citizens are of exactly equal quality, however one defines that term. We will focus here only on quantity; and since our conclusions will depend on nothing else, all charges of bigotry and chauvinism become irrelevant.

IMMIGRATION VS. FOOD SUPPLY

World food banks *move food to the people,* hastening the exhaustion of   37
the environment of the poor countries. Unrestricted immigration, on the other hand, *moves people to the food,* thus speeding up the destruction of the environment of the rich countries. We can easily understand why poor people should want to make this latter transfer, but why should rich hosts encourage it?

As in the case of foreign-aid programs, immigration receives support   38
from selfish interests and humanitarian impulses. The primary selfish interest in unimpeded immigration is the desire of employers for cheap labor, particularly in industries and trades that offer degrading work. In the past, one wave of foreigners after another was brought into the U.S. to work at wretched jobs for wretched wages. In recent years, the Cubans, Puerto Ricans and Mexicans have had this dubious honor. The interests of the employers of cheap labor mesh well with the guilty silence of the country's liberal intelligentsia. White Anglo-Saxon Protestants are particularly reluctant to call for a closing of the doors to immigration for fear of being called bigots.

But not all countries have such reluctant leadership. Most educated   39
Hawaiians, for example, are keenly aware of the limits of their environment, particularly in terms of population growth. There is only so much room on the islands, and the islanders know it. To Hawaiians, immigrants from the other forty-nine states present as great a threat as those from other nations. At a recent meeting of Hawaiian government officials in Honolulu, I had the ironic delight of hearing a speaker, who like most of his audience was of Japanese ancestry, ask how the country might practically and constitutionally close its doors to further immigration. One member of the audience countered: "How can we shut the doors now? We have many friends and relatives in Japan that we'd like to bring here some day so that they can enjoy Hawaii too." The Japanese-American speaker smiled sympathetically and answered: "Yes, but we have children now, and someday we'll have grandchildren too. We can bring more people here from Japan only by giving away some of the land that we hope to pass on to our grandchildren some day. What right do we have to do that?"

At this point, I can hear U.S. liberals asking, "How can you justify 40
slamming the door once you're inside? You say that immigrants should
be kept out. But aren't we all immigrants, or the descendants of immigrants? If we insist on staying, must we not admit all others?" Our crav-
ing for intellectual order leads us to seek and prefer symmetrical rules
and morals: a single rule for me and everybody else; the same rule yesterday, today, and tomorrow. Justice, we feel, should not change with
time and place.

We Americans of non-Indian ancestry can look upon ourselves as the 41
descendants of thieves who are guilty morally, if not legally, of stealing
this land from its Indian owners. Should we then give back the land to
the now living American descendants of those Indians? However morally
or logically sound this proposal may be, I, for one, am unwilling to live by
it and I know no one else who is. Besides, the logical consequence would
be absurd. Suppose that, intoxicated with a sense of pure justice, we
should decide to turn our land over to the Indians. Since all our wealth
has also been derived from the land, wouldn't we be morally obliged to
give that back to the Indians too?

PURE JUSTICE VS. REALITY

Clearly, the concept of pure justice produces an infinite regression to 42
absurdity. Centuries ago, wise men invented statutes of limitations to justify the rejection of such pure justice, in the interest of preventing contin-
ual disorder. The law zealously defends property rights, but only relatively
recent property rights. Drawing a line after an arbitrary time has elapsed
may be unjust, but the alternatives are worse.

We are all descendants of thieves, and the world's resources are 43
inequitably distributed. But we must begin the journey to tomorrow from
the point where we are today. We cannot remake the past. We cannot
safely divide the wealth equitably among all peoples so long as people
reproduce at different rates. To do so would guarantee that our grandchildren, and everyone else's grandchildren, would have only a ruined
world to inhabit.

To be generous with one's own possessions is quite different from 44
being generous with those of posterity. We should call this point to the
attention of those who, from a commendable love of justice and equality, would institute a system of the commons, either in the form of a
world food bank, or of unrestricted immigration. We must convince them
if we wish to save at least some parts of the world from environmental
ruin.

Without a true world government to control reproduction and the use 45
of available resources, the sharing ethic of the spaceship is impossible.
For the foreseeable future, our survival demands that we govern our
actions by the ethics of a lifeboat, harsh though they may be. Posterity
will be satisfied with nothing less.

RICH AND POOR

Peter Singer

We have a moral obligation to help those living in "absolute poverty." "Helping is not, as conventionally thought, a charitable act that is praiseworthy to do, but not wrong to omit; it is something that everyone ought to do."

Consider these facts: by the most cautious estimates, 400 million people lack the calories, protein, vitamins and minerals needed for a normally healthy life. Millions are constantly hungry; others suffer from deficiency diseases and from infections they would be able to resist on a better diet. Children are worst affected. According to one estimate, 15 million children under five die every year from the combined effects of malnutrition and infection. In some areas, half the children born can be expected to die before their fifth birthday.

Nor is lack of food the only hardship of the poor. To give a broader picture, Robert McNamara, President of the World Bank, has suggested the term "absolute poverty." The poverty we are familiar with in industrialized nations is relative poverty—meaning that some citizens are poor, relative to the wealth enjoyed by their neighbors. People living in relative poverty in Australia might be quite comfortably off by comparison with old-age pensioners in Britain, and British old-age pensioners are not poor in comparison with the poverty that exists in Mali or Ethiopia. Absolute poverty, on the other hand, is poverty by any standard. In McNamara's words:

> Poverty at the absolute level . . . is life at the very margin of existence.
>
> The absolute poor are severely deprived human beings struggling to survive in a set of squalid and degraded circumstances almost beyond the power of our sophisticated imaginations and privileged circumstances to conceive.
>
> Compared to those fortunate enough to live in developed countries, individuals in the poorest nations have:
> An infant mortality rate eight times higher
> A life expectancy one-third lower
> An adult literacy rate 60% less
> A nutritional level, for one out of every two in the population, below acceptable standards; and for millions of infants, less protein than is sufficient to permit optimum development of the brain.

Absolute poverty is, as McNamara has said, responsible for the loss of countless lives, especially among infants and young children. When absolute poverty does not cause death it still causes misery of a kind not often seen in the affluent nations. Malnutrition in young children stunts both physical and mental development. It has been estimated that the health, growth and learning capacity of nearly half the young children in developing countries are affected by malnutrition. Millions of people on poor diets suffer from deficiency diseases, like goitre, or blindness caused by a lack of vitamin A. The food value of what the poor eat is further reduced by parasites such as hookworm and ringworm, which are endemic in conditions of poor sanitation and health education.

Death and disease apart, absolute poverty remains a miserable condition of life, with inadequate food, shelter, clothing, sanitation, health services and education. According to World Bank estimates which define absolute poverty in terms of income levels insufficient to provide adequate nutrition, something like 800 million people—almost 40% of the people of developing countries—live in absolute poverty. Absolute poverty is probably the principal cause of human misery today. . . .   4

The problem is not that the world cannot produce enough to feed and shelter its people. People in the poor countries consume, on average, 400 lbs of grain a year, while North Americans average more than 2000 lbs. The difference is caused by the fact that in the rich countries we feed most of our grain to animals, converting it into meat, milk and eggs. Because this is an inefficient process, wasting up to 95% of the food value of the animal feed, people in rich countries are responsible for the consumption of far more food than those in poor countries who eat few animal products. If we stopped feeding animals on grains, soybeans and fishmeal the amount of food saved would—if distributed to those who need it—be more than enough to end hunger throughout the world.   5

These facts about animal food do not mean that we can easily solve the world food problem by cutting down on animal products, but they show that the problem is essentially one of distribution rather than production. The world does produce enough food. Moreover the poorer nations themselves could produce far more if they made more use of improved agricultural techniques.   6

So why are people hungry? Poor people cannot afford to buy grain grown by American farmers. Poor farmers cannot afford to buy improved seeds, or fertilizers, or the machinery needed for drilling wells and pumping water. Only by transferring some of the wealth of the developed nations to the poor of the undeveloped nations can the situation be changed.   7

That this wealth exists is clear. Against the picture of absolute poverty that McNamara has painted, one might pose a picture of "absolute affluence." Those who are absolutely affluent are not necessarily affluent by comparison with their neighbors, but they are affluent by any reasonable definition of human needs. This means that they have more income than they need to provide themselves adequately with all the basic necessities of life. After buying food, shelter, clothing, necessary health services and education, the absolutely affluent are still able to spend money on luxuries. The absolutely affluent choose their food for the pleasures of the palate, not to stop hunger; they buy new clothes to look fashionable, not to keep warm; they move house to be in a better neighbourhood or have   8 a play room for the children, not to keep out the rain; and after all this there is still money to spend on books and records, colour television, and overseas holidays.

At this stage I am making no ethical judgments about absolute afflu-   9
ence, merely pointing out that it exists. Its defining characteristic is a significant amount of income above the level necessary to provide for the basic human needs of oneself and one's dependents. By this standard Western Europe, North America, Japan, Australia, New Zealand and the oil-rich Middle Eastern states are all absolutely affluent, and so are many, if not all, of their citizens. The USSR and Eastern Europe might also be included on this list. To quote McNamara once more:

> The average citizen of a developed country enjoys wealth beyond the wildest dreams of the one billion people in countries with per capita incomes under $200. . . .

These, therefore, are the countries—and individuals—who have wealth which they could, without threatening their own basic welfare, transfer to the absolutely poor.

At present, very little is being transferred. Members of the Organization   10
of Petroleum Exporting Countries lead the way, giving an average of 2.1% of their Gross National Product. Apart from them, only Sweden, The Netherlands and Norway have reached the modest UN target of 0.7% of GNP. Britain gives 0.38% of its GNP in official development assistance and a small amount in unofficial aid from voluntary organizations. The total comes to less than £1 per month per person, and compares with 5.5% of GNP spent on alcohol, and 3% on tobacco. Other, even wealthier nations, give still less: Germany gives 0.27%, the United States 0.22% and Japan 0.21%.

The obligation to assist. The path from the library at my university to   11
the Humanities lecture theatre passes a shallow ornamental pond. Suppose that on my way to give a lecture I notice that a small child has fallen in and is in danger of drowning. Would anyone deny that I ought to wade in and pull the child out? This will mean getting my clothes muddy, and either cancelling my lecture or delaying it until I can find something dry to change into; but compared with the avoidable death of a child this is insignificant.

A plausible principle that would support the judgment that I ought to   12
pull the child out is this: if it is in our power to prevent something very bad happening, without thereby sacrificing anything of comparable moral significance, we ought to do it. This principle seems uncontroversial. It will obviously win the assent of consequentialists; but non-consequentialists should accept it too, because the injunction to prevent what is bad applies only when nothing comparably significant is at stake. Thus the principle cannot lead to the kinds of actions of which non-consequentialists strongly disapprove—serious violations of individual rights,

injustice, broken promises, and so on. If a non-consequentialist regards any of these as comparable in moral significance to the bad thing that is to be prevented, he will automatically regard the principle as not applying in those cases in which the bad thing can only be prevented by violating rights, doing injustice, breaking promises, or whatever else is at stake. Most non-consequentialists hold that we ought to prevent what is bad and promote what is good. Their dispute with consequentialists lies in their insistence that this is not the sole ultimate ethical principle: that it is *an* ethical principle is not denied by any plausible ethical theory.

Nevertheless the uncontroversial appearance of the principle that we ought to prevent what is bad when we can do so without sacrificing anything of comparable moral significance is deceptive. If it were taken seriously and acted upon, our lives and our world would be fundamentally changed. For the principle applies, not just to rare situations in which one can save a child from a pond, but to the everyday situation in which we can assist those living in absolute poverty. In saying this I assume that absolute poverty, with its hunger and malnutrition, lack of shelter, illiteracy, disease, high infant mortality and low life expectancy, is a bad thing. And I assume that it is within the power of the affluent to reduce absolute poverty, without sacrificing anything of comparable moral significance. If these two assumptions and the principle we have been discussing are correct, we have an obligation to help those in absolute poverty which is no less strong than our obligation to rescue a drowning child from a pond. Not to help would be wrong, whether or not it is intrinsically equivalent to killing. Helping is not, as conventionally thought, a charitable act which it is praiseworthy to do, but not wrong to omit; it is something that everyone ought to do. 13

This is the argument for an obligation to assist. Set out more formally, it would look like this: 14

First premise:	If we can prevent something bad without sacrificing anything of comparable significance, we ought to do it.
Second premise:	Absolute poverty is bad.
Third premise:	There is some absolute poverty we can prevent without sacrificing anything of comparable moral significance.
Conclusion:	We ought to prevent some absolute poverty.

The first premise is the substantive moral premise on which the argument rests, and I have tried to show that it can be accepted by people who hold a variety of ethical positions. 15

The second premise is unlikely to be challenged. Absolute poverty is, as McNamara put it, "beneath any reasonable definition of human decency" and it would be hard to find a plausible ethical view which did not regard it as a bad thing. 16

The third premise is more controversial, even though it is cautiously   17
framed. It claims only that some absolute poverty can be prevented without the sacrifice of anything of comparable moral significance. It thus
avoids the objection that any aid I can give is just "drops in the ocean"
for the point is not whether my personal contribution will make any
noticeable impression on world poverty as a whole (of course it won't)
but whether it will prevent some poverty. This is all the argument needs
to sustain its conclusion, since the second premise says that any
absolute poverty is bad, and not merely the total amount of absolute
poverty. If without sacrificing anything of comparable moral significance
we can provide just one family with the means to raise itself out of
absolute poverty, the third premise is vindicated.

I have left the notion of moral significance unexamined in order to   18
show that the argument does not depend on any specific values or ethical principles. I think the third premise is true for most people living in
industrialized nations, on any defensible view of what is morally significant. Our affluence means that we have income we can dispose of without giving up the basic necessities of life, and we can use this income to
reduce absolute poverty. Just how much we will think ourselves obliged
to give up will depend on what we consider to be of comparable moral
significance to the poverty we could prevent: colour television, stylish
clothes, expensive dinners, a sophisticated stereo system, overseas holidays, a (second?) car, a larger house, private schools for our children. . . .
For a utilitarian, none of these is likely to be of comparable significance
to the reduction of absolute poverty; and those who are not utilitarians
surely must, if they subscribe to the principle of universalizability, accept
that at least *some* of these things are of far less moral significance than
the absolute poverty that could be prevented by the money they cost.
So the third premise seems to be true on any plausible ethical view—
although the precise amount of absolute poverty that can be prevented
before anything of moral significance is sacrificed will vary according to
the ethical view one accepts.

Taking care of our own. Anyone who has worked to increase over-   19
seas aid will have come across the argument that we should look after
those near us, our families and then the poor in our own country, before
we think about poverty in distant places.

No doubt we do instinctively prefer to help those who are close to us.   20
Few could stand by and watch a child drown; many can ignore a famine
in Africa. But the question is not what we usually do, but what we ought
to do, and it is difficult to see any sound moral justification for the view
that distance, or community membership, makes a crucial difference to
our obligations.

Consider, for instance, racial affinities. Should whites help poor whites   21
before helping poor blacks? Most of us would reject such a suggestion
out of hand: people's need for food has nothing to do with their race,

and if blacks need food more than whites, it would be a violation of the principle of equal consideration to give preference to whites.

The same point applies to citizenship or nationhood. Every affluent 22 nation has some relatively poor citizens, but absolute poverty is limited largely to the poor nations. Those living on the streets of Calcutta, or in a drought stricken region of the Sahel, are experiencing poverty unknown in the West. Under these circumstances it would be wrong to decide that only those fortunate enough to be citizens of our own community will share our abundance. . . .

The element of truth in the view that we should first take care of our 23 own, lies in the advantage of a recognized system of responsibilities. When families and local communities look after their own poorer members, ties of affection and personal relationships achieve ends that would otherwise require a large, impersonal bureaucracy. Hence it would be absurd to propose that from now on we all regard ourselves as equally responsible for the welfare of everyone in the world; but the argument for an obligation to assist does not propose that. It applies only when some are in absolute poverty, and others can help without sacrificing anything of comparable moral significance. To allow one's own kin to sink into absolute poverty would be to sacrifice something of comparable significance; and before that point had been reached, the breakdown of the system of family and community responsibility would be a factor to weigh the balance in favour of a small degree of preference for family and community. This small degree of preference is, however, decisively outweighed by existing discrepancies in wealth and property.

Property rights. Do people have a right to private property, a right 24 which contradicts the view that they are under an obligation to give some of their wealth away to those in absolute poverty? According to some theories of rights (for instance, Robert Nozick's)[1] provided one has acquired one's property without the use of unjust means like force and fraud, one may be entitled to enormous wealth while others starve. This individualistic conception of rights is in contrast to other views, like the early Christian doctrine to be found in the works of Thomas Aquinas, which holds that since property exists for the satisfaction of human needs, "whatever a man has in superabundance is owed, of natural right, to the poor for their sustenance." A socialist would also, of course, see wealth as belonging to the community rather than the individual, while utilitarians, whether socialist or not, would be prepared to override property rights to prevent great evils.. . .

However, I do not think we should accept such an individualistic the-ory. It leaves too much to chance to be an acceptable ethical view. For 25 instance, those whose forefathers happened to inhabit some sandy wastes around the Persian Gulf are now fabulously wealthy, because oil

---

[1] Robert Nozick, *Anarchy, State and Utopia* (New York, Basic Books, 1974).

lay under those sands; while those whose forefathers settled on better land south of the Sahara live in absolute poverty, because of drought and bad harvests. Can this distribution be acceptable from an impartial point of view? If we imagine ourselves about to begin life as a citizen of either Kuwait or Chad—but we do not know which—would we accept the principle that citizens of Kuwait are under no obligation to assist people living in Chad?

Population and the ethics of triage. Perhaps the most serious objection to the argument that we have an obligation to assist is that since the major cause of absolute poverty is overpopulation, helping those now in poverty will only ensure that yet more people are born to live in poverty in the future.   26

In its most extreme form, this objection is taken to show that we should adopt a policy of "triage." The term comes from medical policies adopted in wartime. With too few doctors to cope with all the casualties, the wounded were divided into three categories: those who would probably survive without medical assistance, those who might survive if they received assistance, but otherwise probably would not, and those who even with medical assistance probably would not survive. Only those in the middle category were given medical assistance. The idea, of course, was to use limited medical resources as effectively as possible. For those in the first category, medical treatment was not strictly necessary; for those in the third category, it was likely to be useless. It has been suggested that we should apply the same policies to countries, according to their prospects of becoming self-sustaining. We would not aid countries which even without our help will soon be able to feed their populations. We would not aid countries which, even with our help, will not be able to limit their population to a level they can feed. We would aid those countries where our help might make the difference between success and failure in bringing food and population into balance.   27

Advocates of this theory are understandably reluctant to give a complete list of the countries they would place into the "hopeless" category; but Bangladesh is often cited as an example. Adopting the policy of triage would, then, mean cutting off assistance to Bangladesh and allowing famine, disease and natural disasters to reduce the population of that country (now around 80 million) to the level at which it can provide adequately for all.   28

In support of this view Garrett Hardin has offered a metaphor: we in the rich nations are like the occupants of a crowded lifeboat adrift in a sea full of drowning people. If we try to save the drowning by bringing them aboard our boat will be overloaded and we shall all drown. Since it is better that some survive than none, we should leave the others to drown. In the world today, according to Hardin, "lifeboat ethics" apply. The rich should leave the poor to starve, for otherwise the poor will drag the rich down with them. . . .   29

The consequences of triage on this scale are so horrible that we are 30 inclined to reject it without further argument. How could we sit by our television sets, watching millions starve while we do nothing? Would not that (far more than the proposals for legalizing euthanasia) be the end of all notions of human equality and respect for human life? Don't people have a right to our assistance, irrespective of the consequences?

Anyone whose initial reaction to triage was not one of repugnance 31 would be an unpleasant sort of person. Yet initial reactions based on strong feelings are not always reliable guides. Advocates of triage are rightly concerned with the long-term consequences of our actions. They say that helping the poor and starving now merely ensures more poor and starving in the future. When our capacity to help is finally unable to cope—as one day it must be—the suffering will be greater than it would be if we stopped helping now. If this is correct, there is nothing we can do to prevent absolute starvation and poverty, in the long run, and so we have no obligation to assist. Nor does it seem reasonable to hold that under these circumstances people have a right to our assistance. If we do accept such a right, irrespective of the consequences, we are saying that, in Hardin's metaphor, we would continue to haul the drowning into our lifeboat until the boat sank and we all drowned.

If triage is to be rejected it must be tackled on its own ground, within 32 the framework of consequentialist ethics. Here it is vulnerable. Any consequentialist ethics must take probability of outcome into account. A course of action that will certainly produce some benefit is to be preferred to an alternative course that may lead to a slightly larger benefit, but is equally likely to result in no benefit at all. Only if the greater magnitude of the uncertain benefit outweighs its uncertainty should we choose it. Better one certain unit of benefit than a 10% chance of 5 units; but better a 50% chance of 3 units than a single certain unit. The same principle applies when we are trying to avoid evils.

The policy of triage involves a certain, very great evil: population con- 33 trol by famine and disease. Tens of millions would die slowly. Hundreds of millions would continue to live in absolute poverty, at the very margin of existence. Against this prospect, advocates of the policy place a possible evil which is greater still: the same process of famine and disease, taking place in, say, fifty years time, when the world's population may be three times its present level, and the number who will die from famine, or struggle on in absolute poverty, will be that much greater. The question is: how probable is this forecast that continued assistance now will lead to greater disasters in the future?

Forecasts of population growth are notoriously fallible, and theories 34 about the factors which affect it remain speculative. One theory, at least as plausible as any other, is that countries pass through a "demographic transition" as their standard of living rises. When people are very poor and have no access to modern medicine their fertility is high, but population is kept in check by high death rates. The introduction of sanitation, modern medical techniques and other improvements reduces the death rate, but initially has little effect on the birth rate. Then population grows rapidly. Most poor countries are now in this phase. If standards of living continue to rise, however, couples begin to realize that to have the same number of children surviving to maturity as in the past, they do not need to give birth to as many children as their parents did. The need for children to provide economic support in old age diminishes. Improved education and the emancipation and employment of women also reduce the birthrate, and so population growth begins to level off. Most rich nations have reached this stage, and their populations are growing only very slowly.

If this theory is right, there is an alternative to the disasters accepted   35
as inevitable by supporters of triage. We can assist poor countries to raise the living standards of the poorest members of their population. We can encourage the governments of these countries to enact land reform measures, improve education, and liberate women from a purely child-bearing role. We can also help other countries to make contraception and sterilization widely available. There is a fair chance that these measures will hasten the onset of the demographic transition and bring population growth down to a manageable level. Success cannot be guaranteed; but the evidence that improved economic security and education reduce population growth is strong enough to make triage ethically unacceptable. We cannot allow millions to die from starvation and disease when there is a reasonable probability that population can be brought under control without such horrors.

☐ For Class Discussion

1. Analyze and evaluate the controversy over the obligation of the rich to help the poor by applying the first set of guide questions from page 473. How do you account for the disagreement between Hardin, on the one hand, and Singer or Carnegie on the other?

2. Choose one of the arguments for closer analysis, applying the second set of guide questions on page 474.

Optional Writing Assignment   At last, you've won the lottery. You'll be receiving $250,000 per year for the next 20 years. Ever since you got the news, your phone's been ringing off the hook. Your older brother, Fast Eddie, has called urging you to buy a big house and a fast car and to consider putting a couple of big ones on the Blue Jays for the American League pennant. Your younger sister, Sensible Sarah, has outlined a comprehensive investment strategy for you that will put you into CD's, zero coupon bonds, and a few blue chippers. Then Aunt Teresa calls. "What are your plans for charitable giving?" she wants to know.

"I'm looking into that," you lie. "I have a plan," you lie further.

"Good," she responds. "Send it to me next week in my birthday card."

Your time is running out. What will you tell Aunt Teresa? Just what are your obligations? Some? None? All? Drawing on ideas from the preceding essays, personal experience, and any other research you may have done, write a letter to her justifying your decision.

Civil Disobedience: Is Refusal to Obey Laws Ever a Positive Good?

"LETTER FROM BIRMINGHAM JAIL" IN RESPONSE TO "PUBLIC STATEMENT BY EIGHT ALABAMA CLERGYMEN"

Martin Luther King, Jr.

On April 12, 1963, eight Alabama clergymen signed the following public statement urging "outsiders" to halt the racial demonstrations they had instigated. Writing from the Birmingham jail, Martin Luther King, Jr., gave a compelling justification for his actions: "I am in Birmingham because injustice is here."

We the undersigned clergymen are among those who, in January, issued "An Appeal for Law and Order and Common Sense," in dealing with racial problems in Alabama. We expressed understanding that honest convictions in racial matters could properly be pursued in the courts, but urged that decisions of those courts should in the meantime be peacefully obeyed.

Since that time there had been some evidence of increased forbearance and a willingness to face facts. Responsible citizens have undertaken to work on various problems which cause racial friction and unrest. In Birmingham, recent public events have given indication that we all have opportunity for a new constructive and realistic approach to racial problems.

However, we are now confronted by a series of demonstrations by some of our Negro citizens, directed and led in part by outsiders. We recognize the natural impatience of people who feel that their hopes are slow in being realized. But we are convinced that these demonstrations are unwise and untimely.

We agree rather with certain local Negro leadership which has called for honest and open negotiation of racial issues in our area. And we believe this kind of facing of issues can best be accomplished by citizens of our own metropolitan area, white and Negro, meeting with their knowledge and experience of the local situation. All of us need to face that responsibility and find proper channels for its accomplishment.

Just as we formerly pointed out that "hatred and violence have no sanction in our religious and political traditions," we also point out that such actions as incite to hatred and violence, however technically peaceful those actions may be, have not contributed to the resolution of our local problems. We do not believe that these days of new hope are days when extreme measures are justified in Birmingham.

We commend the community as a whole, and the local news media and law enforcement officials in particular, on the calm manner in which these demonstrations have been handled. We urge the public to continue to show restraint should the demonstrations continue, and the law enforcement officials to remain calm and continue to protect our city from violence.

We further strongly urge our own Negro community to withdraw support from these demonstrations, and to unite locally in working peacefully for a better Birmingham. When rights are consistently denied, a cause should be pressed in the courts and in negotiations among local leaders, and not in the streets. We appeal to both our white and Negro citizenry to observe the principles of law and order and common sense.

Signed by:

C. C. J. Carpenter, D.D., LL.D., *Bishop of Alabama*

Joseph A. Durick, D.D., *Auxiliary Bishop, Diocese of Mobile, Birmingham*

Rabbi Milton L. Grafman, *Temple Emanu-El, Birmingham, Alabama*

Bishop Paul Hardin, *Bishop of the Alabama-West Florida Conference of the Methodist Church*

Bishop Nolan B. Harmon, *Bishop of the North Alabama Conference of the Methodist Church*

George M. Murray, D.D., LL.D., *Bishop Coadjutor, Episcopal Diocese of Alabama*

Edward V. Ramage, *Moderator, Synod of the Alabama Presbyterian Church in the United States*

Earl Stallings, *Pastor, First Baptist Church, Birmingham, Alabama*

Following is the letter Martin Luther King, Jr., wrote in response to the clergymen's public statement.

April 16, 1963

My Dear Fellow Clergymen:

While confined here in the Birmingham city jail, I came across your   1
recent statement calling my present activities "unwise and untimely." Seldom do I pause to answer criticism of my work and ideas. If I sought to answer all the criticisms that cross my desk, my secretaries would have little time for anything other than such correspondence in the course of the day, and I would have no time for constructive work. But since I feel that you are men of genuine good will and that your criticisms are sincerely set forth, I want to try to answer your statement in what I hope will be patient and reasonable terms.

I think I should indicate why I am here in Birmingham, since you have   2
been influenced by the view which argues against "outsiders coming in."
I have the honor of serving as president of the Southern Christian Leadership Conference, an organization operating in every southern state,
with headquarters in Atlanta, Georgia. We have some eighty-five affiliated
organizations across the South, and one of them is the Alabama Christian Movement for Human Rights. Frequently we share staff, educational
and financial resources with our affiliates. Several months ago the affiliate
here in Birmingham asked us to be on call to engage in a nonviolent
direct-action program if such were deemed necessary. We readily con-
sented, and when the hour came we lived up to our promise. So I, along
with several members of my staff, am here because I was invited here. I
am here because I have organizational ties here.

But more basically, I am in Birmingham because injustice is here. Just   3
as the prophets of the eighth century B.C. left their villages and carried
their "thus saith the Lord" far beyond the boundaries of their home
towns, and just as the Apostle Paul left his village of Tarsus and carried
the gospel of Jesus Christ to the far corners of the Greco-Roman world,
so am I compelled to carry the gospel of freedom beyond my own home
town. Like Paul, I must constantly respond to the Macedonian call for
aid.

Moreover, I am cognizant of the interrelatedness of all communities   4
and states. I cannot sit idly by in Atlanta and not be concerned about
what happens in Birmingham. Injustice anywhere is a threat to justice
everywhere. We are caught in an inescapable network of mutuality, tied in
a single garment of destiny. Whatever affects one directly, affects all indirectly. Never again can we afford to live with the narrow, provincial "outside agitator" idea. Anyone who lives inside the United States can never
be considered an outsider anywhere within its bounds.

You deplore the demonstrations taking place in Birmingham. But your   5
statement, I am sorry to say, fails to express a similar concern for the
conditions that brought about the demonstrations. I am sure that none
of you would want to rest content with the superficial kind of social analysis that deals merely with effects and does not grapple with underlying
causes. It is unfortunate that demonstrations are taking place in Birmingham, but it is even more unfortunate that the city's white power structure
left the Negro community with no alternative.

In any nonviolent campaign there are four basic steps: collection of   6
the facts to determine whether injustices exist; negotiation; self-purification; and direct action. We have gone through all these steps in Birmingham. There can be no gainsaying the fact that racial injustice engulfs this
community. Birmingham is probably the most thoroughly segregated city
in the United States. Its ugly record of brutality is widely known. Negroes
have experienced grossly unjust treatment in the courts. There have been
more unsolved bombings of Negro homes and churches in Birmingham
than in any other city in the nation. These are the hard, brutal facts of the

case. On the basis of these conditions, Negro leaders sought to negotiate with the city fathers. But the latter consistently refused to engage in
good-faith negotiation.

Then, last September, came the opportunity to talk with leaders of   7
Birmingham's economic community. In the course of the negotiations,
certain promises were made by the merchants—for example, to remove
the stores' humiliating racial signs. On the basis of these promises, the
Reverend Fred Shuttlesworth and the leaders of the Alabama Christian
Movement for Human Rights agreed to a moratorium on all demonstrations. As the weeks and months went by, we realized that we were the victims of a broken promise. A few signs, briefly removed, returned; the others remained.

As in so many past experiences, our hopes had been blasted, and the   8
shadow of deep disappointment settled upon us. We had no alternative
except to prepare for direct action, whereby we would present our very
bodies as a means of laying our case before the conscience of the local
and the national community. Mindful of the difficulties involved, we
decided to undertake a process of self-purification. We began a series of
workshops on nonviolence, and we repeatedly asked ourselves: "Are you
able to accept blows without retaliating?" "Are you able to endure the
ordeal of jail?" We decided to schedule our direct-action program for the
Easter season, realizing that except for Christmas, this is the main shopping period of the year. Knowing that a strong economic-withdrawal program would be the by-product of direct action, we felt that this would be
the best time to bring pressure to bear on the merchants for the needed
change.

Then it occurred to us that Birmingham's mayoral election was com-   9
ing up in March, and we speedily decided to postpone action until after
election day. When we discovered that the Commissioner of Public
Safety, Eugene "Bull" Connor, had piled up enough votes to be in the
run-off, we decided again to postpone action until the day after the run-
off so that the demonstrations could not be used to cloud the issues.
Like many others, we waited to see Mr. Connor defeated, and to this end
we endured postponement after postponement. Having aided in this
community need, we felt that our direct-action program could be delayed
no longer.

You may well ask: "Why direct action? Why sit-ins, marches and so   10
forth? Isn't negotiation a better path?" You are quite right in calling for
negotiation. Indeed, this is the very purpose of direct action. Nonviolent
direct action seeks to create such a crisis and foster such a tension that a
community which has constantly refused to negotiate is forced to confront the issue. It seeks so to dramatize the issue that it can no longer be
ignored. My citing the creation of tension as part of the work of the non-
violent-resister may sound rather shocking. But I must confess that I am
not afraid of the word "tension." I have earnestly opposed violent tension,
but there is a type of constructive, nonviolent tension which is necessary

for growth. Just as Socrates felt that it was necessary to create a tension in the mind so that individuals could rise from the bondage of myths and half-truths to the unfettered realm of creative analysis and objective appraisal, so must we see the need for nonviolent gadflies to create the kind of tension in society that will help men rise from the dark depths of prejudice and racism to the majestic heights of understanding and brotherhood.

The purpose of our direct-action program is to create a situation so   11
crisis-packed that it will inevitably open the door to negotiation. I therefore concur with you in your call for negotiation. Too long has our beloved Southland been bogged down in a tragic effort to live in monologue rather than dialogue.

One of the basic points in your statement is that the action that I and   12
my associates have taken in Birmingham is untimely. Some have asked: "Why didn't you give the new city administration time to act?" The only answer that I can give to this query is that the new Birmingham administration must be prodded about as much as the outgoing one, before it will act. We are sadly mistaken if we feel that the election of Albert Boutwell as mayor will bring the millennium to Birmingham. While Mr. Boutwell is a much more gentle person than Mr. Connor, they are both segregationists, dedicated to maintenance of the status quo. I have hope that Mr. Boutwell will be reasonable enough to see the futility of massive resistance to desegregation. But he will not see this without pressure from devotees of civil rights. My friends, I must say to you that we have not made a single gain in civil rights without determined legal and nonviolent pressure. Lamentably, it is an historical fact that privileged groups seldom give up their privileges voluntarily. Individuals may see the moral light and voluntarily give up their unjust posture; but, as Reinhold Niebuhr has reminded us, groups tend to be more immoral than individuals.

We know through painful experience that freedom is never voluntarily   13
given by the oppressor; it must be demanded by the oppressed. Frankly, I have yet to engage in a direct-action campaign that was "well timed" in the view of those who have not suffered unduly from the disease of segregation. For years now I have heard the word "Wait!" It rings in the ear of every Negro with piercing familiarity. This "Wait" has almost always meant "Never." We must come to see, with one of our distinguished jurists, that "justice too long delayed is justice denied."

We have waited for more than 340 years for our constitutional God-   14
given rights. The nations of Asia and Africa are moving with jetlike speed toward gaining political independence, but we still creep at horse-and-buggy pace toward gaining a cup of coffee at a lunch counter. Perhaps it is easy for those who have never felt the stinging darts of segregation to say, "Wait." But when you have seen vicious mobs lynch your mothers and fathers at will and drown your sisters and brothers at whim; when you have seen hate-filled policemen curse, kick, and even kill your black

across the pages of history, we were here. For more than two centuries our forebears labored in this country without wages; they made cotton king; they built the homes of their masters while suffering gross injustice and shameful humiliation—and yet out of a bottomless vitality they continued to thrive and develop. If the inexpressible cruelties of slavery could not stop us, the opposition we now face will surely fail. We will win our freedom because the sacred heritage of our nation and the eternal will of God are embodied in our echoing demands.

Before closing I feel impelled to mention one other point in your state-   45
ment that has troubled me profoundly. You warmly commended the Birmingham police force for keeping "order" and "preventing violence." I doubt that you would have so warmly commended the police force if you had seen its dogs sinking their teeth into unarmed, nonviolent Negroes. I doubt that you would so quickly commend the policemen if you were to observe their ugly and inhumane treatment of Negroes here in the city jail; if you were to watch them push and curse old Negro women and young Negro girls; if you were to see them slap and kick old Negro men and young boys; if you were to observe them, as they did on two occasions, refuse to give us food because we wanted to sing our grace together. I cannot join you in your praise of the Birmingham police department.

It is true that police have exercised a degree of discipline in handling   46
the demonstrators. In this sense they have conducted themselves rather "nonviolently" in public. But for what purpose? To preserve the evil system of segregation. Over the past few years I have consistently preached that nonviolence demands that the means we use must be as pure as the ends we seek. I have tried to make clear that it is wrong to use immoral means to attain moral ends. But now I must affirm that it is just as wrong, or perhaps even more so, to use moral means to preserve immoral ends. Perhaps Mr. Connor and his policemen have been rather nonviolent in public, as was Chief Pritchett in Albany, Georgia, but they have used the moral means of nonviolence to maintain the immoral end of racial injustice. As T. S. Eliot has said: "The last temptation is the greatest treason: To do the right deed for the wrong reason."

I wish you had commended the Negro sit-inners and demonstrators of   47
Birmingham for their sublime courage, their willingness to suffer and their amazing discipline in the midst of great provocation. One day the South will recognize its real heroes. They will be the James Merediths, with the noble sense of purpose that enables them to face jeering and hostile mobs, and with the agonizing loneliness that characterizes the life of the pioneer. They will be old, oppressed, battered Negro women, symbolized in a seventy-two-year-old woman in Montgomery, Alabama, who rose up with a sense of dignity and with her people decided not to ride segregated buses, and who responded with ungrammatical profundity to one who inquired about her weariness: "My feets is tired, but my soul is

at rest." They will be the young high school and college students, the young ministers of the gospel and a host of their elders, courageously and nonviolently sitting in at lunch counters and willingly going to jail for conscience' sake. One day the South will know that when these disinherited children of God sat down at lunch counters, they were in reality standing up for what is best in the American dream and for the most sacred values in our Judaeo-Christian heritage, thereby bringing our nation back to those great wells of democracy which were dug deep by the founding fathers in their formulation of the Constitution and the Declaration of Independence.

48   Never before have I written so long a letter. I'm afraid it is much too long to take your precious time. I can assure you that it would have been much shorter if I had been writing from a comfortable desk, but what else can one do when he is alone in a narrow jail cell, other than write long letters, think long thoughts and pray long prayers?

49   If I have said anything in this letter that overstates the truth and indicates an unreasonable impatience, I beg you to forgive me. If I have said anything that understates the truth and indicates my having a patience that allows me to settle for anything less than brotherhood, I beg God to forgive me.

50   I hope this letter finds you strong in faith. I also hope that circumstances will soon make it possible for me to meet each of you, not as an integrationist or a civil-rights leader but as a fellow clergyman and a Christian brother. Let us all hope that the dark clouds of racial prejudice will soon pass away and the deep fog of misunderstanding will be lifted from our fear-drenched communities, and in some not too distant tomorrow the radiant stars of love and brotherhood will shine over our great nation with all their scintillating beauty.

Yours for the cause of Peace and Brotherhood
MARTIN LUTHER KING, JR.

CIVIL DISOBEDIENCE: DESTROYER OF DEMOCRACY

Lewis H. Van Dusen, Jr.

Attorney Lewis H. Van Dusen, Jr., a Rhodes scholar and graduate of Harvard Law School, distinguishes between "conscientious disobedience"—in which one willingly accepts punishment in order to make a moral protest—and active group disobedience aimed at changing laws. "[C]ivil disobedience [e.g., the kind practiced by Martin Luther King, Jr.], whatever the ethical rationalization, is still an assault on our democratic society, an affront to our legal order and an attack on our constitutional government."

As Charles E. Wyzanski, Chief Judge of the United States District   1
Court in Boston, wrote in the February, 1968, *Atlantic:* "Disobedience is
a long step from dissent. Civil disobedience involves a deliberate and
punishable breach of legal duty." Protesters might prefer a different definition. They would rather say that civil disobedience is the peaceable resistance of conscience.

The philosophy of civil disobedience was not developed in our Ameri-   2
can democracy, but in the very first democracy of Athens. It was
expressed by the poet Sophocles and the philosopher Socrates. In
Sophocles's tragedy, Antigone chose to obey her conscience and violate
the state edict against providing burial for her brother, who had been
decreed a traitor. When the dictator Creon found out that Antigone had
buried her fallen brother, he confronted her and reminded her that there
was a mandatory death penalty for this deliberate disobedience of the
state law. Antigone nobly replied, "Nor did I think your orders were so
strong that you, a mortal man, could overrun the gods' unwritten and
unfailing laws."

Conscience motivated Antigone. She was not testing the validity of   3
the law in the hope that eventually she would be sustained. Appealing to
the judgment of the community, she explained her action to the chorus.
She was not secret and surreptitious—the interment of her brother was
open and public. She was not violent; she did not trespass on another
citizen's rights. And finally, she accepted without resistance the death
sentence—the penalty for violation. By voluntarily accepting the law's
sanctions, she was not a revolutionary denying the authority of the state.
Antigone's behavior exemplifies the classic case of civil disobedience.

Socrates believed that reason could dictate a conscientious disobedi-   4
ence of state law, but he also believed that he had to accept the legal
sanctions of the state. In Plato's *Crito,* Socrates from his hanging basket
accepted the death penalty for his teaching of religion to youths contrary
to state laws.

The sage of Walden, Henry David Thoreau, took this philosophy of   5
nonviolence and developed it into a strategy for solving society's injustices. First enunciating it in protest against the Mexican War, he then
turned it to use against slavery. For refusing to pay taxes that would help
pay the enforcers of the fugitive slave law, he went to prison. In Thoreau's
words, "If the alternative is to keep all just men in prison or to give up
slavery, the state will not hesitate which to choose."

Sixty years later, Gandhi took Thoreau's civil disobedience as his strat-   6
egy to wrest Indian independence from England. The famous salt march
against a British imperial tax is his best-known example of protest.

But the conscientious law breaking of Socrates, Gandhi and Thoreau   7
is to be distinguished from the conscientious law testing of Martin Luther
King, Jr., who was not a civil disobedient. The civil disobedient withholds
taxes or violates state laws knowing he is legally wrong, but believing he
is morally right. While he wrapped himself in the mantle of Gandhi and

Thoreau, Dr. King led his followers in violation of state laws he believed were contrary to the Federal Constitution. But since Supreme Court decisions in the end generally upheld his many actions, he should not be considered a true civil disobedient.

The civil disobedience of Antigone is like that of the pacifist who withholds paying the percentage of his taxes that goes to the Defense Department, or the Quaker who travels against State Department regulations to Hanoi to distribute medical supplies, or the Vietnam war protester who tears up his draft card. This civil disobedient has been nonviolent in his defiance of the law; he has been unfurtive in his violation; he has been submissive to the penalties of the law. He has neither evaded the law nor interfered with another's rights. He has been neither a rioter nor a revolutionary. The thrust of his cause has not been the might of coercion but the martyrdom of conscience.   8

WAS THE BOSTON TEA PARTY CIVIL DISOBEDIENCE?

Those who justify violence and radical action as being in the tradition of our Revolution show a misunderstanding of the philosophy of democracy.   9

James Farmer, former head of the Congress of Racial Equality, in defense of the mass action confrontation method, has told of a famous organized demonstration that took place in opposition to political and economic discrimination. The protesters beat back and scattered the law enforcers and then proceeded to loot and destroy private property. Mr. Farmer then said he was talking about the Boston Tea Party and implied that violence as a method for redress of grievances was an American tradition and a legacy of our revolutionary heritage. While it is true that there is no more sacred document than our Declaration of Independence, Jefferson's "inherent right of rebellion" was predicated on the tyrannical denial of democratic means. If there is no popular assembly to provide an adjustment of ills, and if there is no court system to dispose of injustices, then there is, indeed, a right to rebel.   10

The seventeenth century's John Locke, the philosophical father of the Declaration of Independence, wrote in his *Second Treatise on Civil Government:* "Wherever law ends, tyranny begins . . . and the people are absolved from any further obedience. Governments are dissolved from within when the legislative [chamber] is altered. When the government [becomes]. . . arbitrary disposers of lives, liberties and fortunes of the people, such revolutions happen. . . ."   11

But there are some sophisticated proponents of the revolutionary redress of grievances who say that the test of the need for radical action is not the unavailability of democratic institutions but the ineffectuality of those institutions to remove blatant social inequalities. If social injustice exists, they say, concerted disobedience is required against the constituted government, whether it be totalitarian or democratic in structure.   12

Of course, only the most bigoted chauvinist would claim that America   13
is without some glaring faults. But there has never been a utopian society
on earth and there never will be unless human nature is remade. Since
inequities will mar even the best-framed democracies, the injustice rationale would allow a free right of civil resistance to be available always as a
shortcut alternative to the democratic way of petition, debate and assembly. The lesson of history is that civil insurgency spawns far more injustices than it removes. The Jeffersons, Washingtons and Adamses
resisted tyranny with the aim of promoting the procedures of democracy.
They would never have resisted a democratic government with the risk of
promoting the techniques of tyranny.

LEGITIMATE PRESSURES AND ILLEGITIMATE RESULTS

There are many civil leaders who show impatience with the process of   14
democracy. They rely on the sit-in, boycott or mass picketing to gain
speedier solutions to the problems that face every citizen. But we must
realize that the legitimate pressures that won concessions in the past can
easily escalate into the illegitimate power plays that might extort
demands in the future. The victories of these civil rights leaders must not
shake our confidence in the democratic procedures, as the pressures of
demonstration are desirable only if they take place within the limits
allowed by law. Civil rights gains should continue to be won by the persuasion of Congress and other legislative bodies and by the decision of
courts. Any illegal entreaty for the rights of some can be an injury to the
rights of others, for mass demonstrations often trigger violence.

Those who advocate taking the law into their own hands should reflect   15
that when they are disobeying what they consider to be an immoral law,
they are deciding on a possibly immoral course. Their answer is that the
process for democratic relief is too slow, that only mass confrontation
can bring immediate action, and that any injuries are the inevitable cost
of the pursuit of justice. Their answer is, simply put, that the end justifies
the means. It is this justification of any form of demonstration as a form
of dissent that threatens to destroy a society built on the rule of law.

Our Bill of Rights guarantees wide opportunities to use mass meet-   16
ings, public parades and organized demonstrations to stimulate sentiment, to dramatize issues and to cause change. The Washington freedom march of 1963 was such a call for action. But the rights of free
expression cannot be mere force cloaked in the garb of free speech. As
the courts have decreed in labor cases, free assembly does not mean
mass picketing or sit-down strikes. These rights are subject to limitations
of time and place so as to secure the rights of others. When militant students storm a college president's office to achieve demands, when certain groups plan rush-hour car stalling to protest discrimination in
employment, these are not dissent, but a denial of rights to others. Neither is it the lawful use of mass protest, but rather the unlawful use of
mob power.

Justice Black, one of the foremost advocates and defenders of the   17
right of protest and dissent, has said:

> Experience demonstrates that it is not a far step from what to many
> seems to be the earnest, honest, patriotic, kind-spirited multitude of
> today, to the fanatical, threatening, lawless mob of tomorrow. And the
> crowds that press in the streets for noble goals today can be sup-
> planted tomorrow by street mobs pressuring the courts for precisely
> opposite ends.

Society must censure those demonstrators who would trespass on the   18
public peace, as it must condemn those rioters whose pillage would
destroy the public peace. But more ambivalent is society's posture
toward the civil disobedient. Unlike the rioter, the true civil disobedient
commits no violence. Unlike the mob demonstrator, he commits no trespass on others' rights. The civil disobedient, while deliberately violating a
law, shows an oblique respect for the law by voluntarily submitting to its
sanctions. He neither resists arrest nor evades punishment. Thus, he
breaches the law but not the peace.

But civil disobedience, whatever the ethical rationalization, is still an   19
assault on our democratic society, an affront to our legal order and an
attack on our constitutional government. To indulge civil disobedience is
to invite anarchy, and the permissive arbitrariness of anarchy is hardly
less tolerable than the repressive arbitrariness of tyranny. Too often the
license of liberty is followed by the loss of liberty, because into the desert
of anarchy comes the man on horseback, a Mussolini or a Hitler.

Violations of Law Subvert Democracy. Law violations, even for ends   20
recognized as laudable, are not only assaults on the rule of law, but sub-
versions of the democratic process. The disobedient act of conscience
does not ennoble democracy; it erodes it.

First, it courts violence, and even the most careful and limited use of   21
nonviolent acts of disobedience may help sow the dragon-teeth of civil
riot. Civil disobedience is the progenitor of disorder, and disorder is the
sire of violence.

Second, the concept of civil disobedience does not invite principles of   22
general applicability. If the children of light are morally privileged to resist
particular laws on grounds of conscience, so are the children of darkness. Former Deputy Attorney General Burke Marshall said: "If the decision to break the law really turned on individual conscience, it is hard to
see in law how [the civil rights leader] is better off than former Governor
Ross Barnett of Mississippi who also believed deeply in his cause and was
willing to go to jail."

Third, even the most noble act of civil disobedience assaults the rule   23
of law. Although limited as to method, motive and objective, it has the
effect of inducing others to engage in different forms of law breaking
characterized by methods unsanctioned and condemned by classic theories of law violation. Unfortunately, the most patent lesson of civil disobedience is not so much nonviolence of action as defiance of authority.

Finally, the greatest danger in condoning civil disobedience as a per-   24
missible strategy for hastening change is that it undermines our democratic processes. To adopt the techniques of civil disobedience is to
assume that representative government does not work. To resist the decisions of courts and the laws of elected assemblies is to say that democracy has failed.

There is no man who is above the law, and there is no man who has a   25
right to break the law. Civil disobedience is not above the law, but against
the law. When the civil disobedient disobeys one law, he invariably sub-
verts all law. When the civil disobedient says that he is above the law, he
is saying that democracy is beneath him. His disobedience shows a distrust for the democratic system. He is merely saying that since democracy does not work, why should he help make it work. Thoreau expressed
well the civil disobedient's disdain for democracy:

> As for adopting the ways which the state has provided for remedying
> the evil, I know not of such ways. They take too much time and a
> man's life will be gone. I have other affairs to attend to. I came into this
> world not chiefly to make this a good place to live in, but to live in it, be
> it good or bad.

Thoreau's position is not only morally irresponsible but politically rep-   26
rehensible. When citizens in a democracy are called on to make a profession of faith, the civil disobedients offer only a confession of failure. Tragically, when civil disobedients for lack of faith abstain from democratic
involvement, they help attain their own gloomy prediction. They help create the social and political basis for their own despair. By foreseeing failure, they help forge it. If citizens rely on antidemocratic means of protest,
they will help bring about the undemocratic result of an authoritarian or
anarchic state.

How far demonstrations properly can be employed to produce politi-   27
cal and social change is a pressing question, particularly in view of the
provocations accompanying the National Democratic Convention in
Chicago last August and the reaction of the police to them. A line must
be drawn by the judiciary between the demands of those who seek
absolute order, which can lead only to a dictatorship, and those who seek
absolute freedom, which can lead only to anarchy. The line, wherever it is
drawn by our courts, should be respected on the college campus, on the
streets and elsewhere.

Undue provocation will inevitably result in overreaction, human emo-   28
tions being what they are. Violence will follow. This cycle undermines the
very democracy it is designed to preserve. The lesson of the past is that
democracies will fall if violence, including the intentional provocations
that will lead to violence, replaces democratic procedures, as in Athens,
Rome and the Weimar Republic. This lesson must be constantly
explained by the legal profession.

We should heed the words of William James: 29

Democracy is still upon its trial. The civic genius of our people is its only bulwark and . . . neither battleships nor public libraries nor great newspapers nor booming stocks: neither mechanical invention nor political adroitness, nor churches nor universities nor civil service examinations can save us from degeneration if the inner mystery be lost.

That mystery, at once the secret and the glory of our English-speaking race, consists of nothing but two habits. . . . One of them is habit of trained and disciplined good temper towards the opposite party when it fairly wins its innings. The other is that of fierce and merciless resentment toward every man or set of men who break the public peace. (James, *Pragmatism,* 127–28).

FROM *THE CRITO*

Plato

Socrates, who was himself ill-served by the state, here argues in favor of a citizen's absolute obligation to obey the rules of the state. He has been unjustly sentenced to die, and his friend Crito urges him to escape from prison. Socrates declines on ethical grounds.

SOCRATES: . . . Ought a man to do what he admits to be right, or ought he to betray the right?   1

CRITO: He ought to do what he thinks right.   2

SOCRATES: But if this is true, what is the application? In leaving the prison against the will of the Athenians, do I wrong any? Or rather do I not wrong those whom I ought least to wrong? Do I not desert the principles which are acknowledged by us to be just—what do you say?   3

CRITO: I cannot tell, Socrates; for I do not know.   4

SOCRATES: Then consider the matter in this way:—Imagine that I am about to play truant (you may call the proceeding by any name which you like), and the laws of the government come and interrogate me: "Tell us, Socrates," they say: "what are you about? Are you not going by an act of yours to overturn us—the laws, and the whole state, as far as in you lies? Do you imagine that a state can subsist and not be overthrown, in which the decisions of law have no power, but are set aside and trampled upon by individuals?" What will be our answer, Crito, to these and the like words? Any one, and especially a rhetorician, will have a good deal to say on behalf of the law which requires a sentence to be carried out. He will argue that this law should not be set aside; and shall we reply, "Yes, but the state has injured us and given an unjust sentence." Suppose I say that?   5

CRITO: Very good, Socrates.   6

SOCRATES: "And was that our agreement with you?" the law would   7
answer; "or were you to abide by the sentence of the state?" And if I were
to express my astonishment at their words, the law would probably add:
"Answer, Socrates, instead of opening your eyes—you are in the habit of
asking and answering questions. Tell us,—What complaint have you to
make against us which justifies you in attempting to destroy us and the
state? In the first place did we not bring you into existence? Your father
married your mother by our aid and begat you. Say whether you have
any objection to urge against those of us who regulate marriage?" None,
I should reply. "Or against those of us who after birth regulate the nurture
and education of children, in which you also were trained? Were not the
laws, which have the charge of education, right in commanding your
father to train you in music and gymnastics?" Right, I should reply. "Well
then, since you were brought into the world and nurtured and educated
by us, can you deny in the first place that you are our child and slave, as
your fathers were before you? And if this is true you are not on equal
terms with us; nor can you think that you have a right to do to us what
we are doing to you. Would you have any right to strike or revile or do
any other evil to your father or your master, if you had one, because you
have been struck or reviled by him, or received some other evil at his
hands?—you would not say this? And because we think right to destroy
you, do you think that you have any right to destroy us in return, and
your country as far as in you lies? Will you, O professor of true virtue,
pretend that you are justified in this? Has a philosopher like you failed to
discover that our country is more to be valued and higher and holier far
than mother or father or any ancestor, and more to be regarded in the
eyes of the gods and of men of understanding? Also to be soothed, and
gently and reverently entreated when angry, even more than a father, and
either to be persuaded, or if not persuaded, to be obeyed? And when we
are punished by her, whether with imprisonment or stripes, the punishment is to be endured in silence, and if she leads us to wounds or death
in battle, thither we follow as is right; neither may any one yield or retreat
or leave his rank, but whether in battle or in a court of law, or in any other
place, he must do what his city and his country order him; or he must
change their view of what is just: and if he may do no violence to his
father or mother, much less may he do violence to his country." What
answer shall we make to this, Crito? Do the laws speak truly, or do they
not?

CRITO: I think that they do   8

SOCRATES: Then the laws will say, "Consider, Socrates, if we are speaking   9
truly that in your present attempt you are going to do us an injury. For,
having brought you into the world, and nurtured and educated you, and
given you and every other citizen a share in every good which we had to
give, we further proclaim to any Athenian by the liberty which we allow

him, that if he does not like us when he has become of age and has seen the ways of the city, and made our acquaintance, he may go where he pleases and take his goods with him. None of us laws will forbid him or interfere with him. Any one who does not like us and the city, and who wants to emigrate to a colony or to any other city, may go where he likes, retaining his property. But he who has experience of the manner in which we order justice and administer the state, and still remains, has entered into an implied contract that he will do as we command him. And he who disobeys us is, as we maintain, thrice wrong; first, because in disobeying us he is disobeying his parents; secondly, because we are the authors of his education; thirdly; because he has made an agreement with us that he will duly obey our commands; and he neither obeys them nor convinces us that our commands are unjust; and we do not rudely impose them, but give him the alternative of obeying or convincing us;— that is what we offer, and he does neither.

"These are the sort of accusations to which, as we were saying,   10
you, Socrates, will be exposed if you accomplish your intentions; you, above all other Athenians." Suppose now I ask, why I rather than anybody else? They will justly retort upon me that I above all other men have acknowledged the agreement. "There is clear proof," they will say, "Socrates, that we and the city were not displeasing to you. Of all Athenians you have been the most constant resident in the city, which, as you never leave, you may be supposed to love. For you never went out of the city either to see the games, except once when you went to the Isthmus, or to any other place unless when you were on military service; nor did you travel as other men do. Nor had you any curiosity to know other states or their laws: your affections did not go beyond us and our state; we were your special favourites, and you acquiesced in our government of you; and here in this city you begat your children, which is a proof of your satisfaction. Moreover, you might in the course of the trial, if you had liked, have fixed the penalty at banishment; the state which refuses to let you go now would have let you go then. But you pretended that you preferred death to exile, and that you were not unwilling to die. And now you have forgotten these fine sentiments, and pay no respect to us the laws, of whom you are the destroyer; and are doing what only a miserable slave would do, running away and turning your back upon the compacts and agreements which you made as a citizen. And first of all answer this very question: Are we right in saying that you agreed to be governed according to us in deed, and not in word only? Is that true or not?" How shall we answer, Crito? Must we not assent?

CRITO: We cannot help it, Socrates.   11

SOCRATES: Then will they not say: "You, Socrates, are breaking the   12
covenants and agreements which you made with us at your leisure, not in any haste or under any compulsion or deception, but after you have had seventy years to think of them, during which time you were at liberty

to leave the city, if we were not to your mind, or if our covenants appeared to you to be unfair. You had your choice, and might have gone either to Lacedaemon or Crete, both which states are often praised by you for their good government, or to some other Hellenic or foreign state. Whereas you, above all other Athenians, seemed to be so fond of the state, or, in other words, of us her laws (and who would care about a state which has no laws?), that you never stirred out of her; the halt, the blind, the maimed were not more stationary in her than you were. And now you run away and forsake your agreements. Not so, Socrates, if you will take our advice; do not make yourself ridiculous by escaping out of the city.

"For just consider, if you transgress and err in this sort of way, 13 what good will you do either to yourself or to your friends? That your friends will be driven into exile and deprived of citizenship, or will lose their property, is tolerably certain; and you yourself, if you fly to one of the neighboring cities, as, for example, Thebes or Megara, both of which are well governed, will come to them as an enemy, Socrates, and their government will be against you, and all patriotic citizens will cast an evil eye upon you as a subverter of the laws, and you will confirm in the minds of the judges the justice of their own condemnation of you. For he who is a corrupter of the laws is more than likely to be a corrupter of the young and foolish portion of mankind. Will you then flee from well-ordered citizens and virtuous men? and is existence worth having on these terms? Or will you go to them without shame, and talk to them, Socrates? And what will you say to them? What you say here about virtue and justice and institutions and laws being the best things among men? Would that be decent of you? Surely not. But if you go away from well-governed states to Crito's friends in Thessaly, where there is a great disorder and licence, they will be charmed to hear the tale of your escape from prison, set off with ludicrous particulars of the manner in which you were wrapped in a goatskin or some other disguise, and metamorphosed as the manner is of runaways; but will there be no one to remind you that in your old age you were not ashamed to violate the most sacred laws from a miserable desire of a little more life? Perhaps not, if you keep them in a good temper; but if they are out of temper you will hear many degrading things; you will live, but how?—as the flatterer of all men, and the servant of all men; and doing what?—eating and drinking in Thessaly, having gone abroad in order that you may get a dinner. And where will be your fine sentiments about justice and virtue? Say that you wish to live for the sake of your children—you want to bring them up and educate them— will you take them into Thessaly and deprive them of Athenian citizenship? Is this the benefit which you will confer upon them? Or are you under the impression that they will be better cared for and educated here if you are still alive, although absent from them: for your friends will take care of them? Do you fancy that if you are an inhabitant of Thessaly they will take care of them, and if you are an inhabitant of the other world that they will not take of them? Nay: but if they who call themselves friends are good for anything, they will—to be sure they will.

"Listen, then Socrates, to us who have brought you up. Think   14
not of life and children first, and of justice afterwards, but of justice first, that you may be justified before the princes of the world below. For neither will you nor any that belong to you be happier or holier or juster in this life, or happier in another, if you do as Crito bids. Now you depart in innocence, a sufferer and not a doer of evil; a victim, not of the laws of men. But if you go forth, returning evil for evil, and injury for injury, breaking the covenants and agreements which you have made with us, and wronging those whom you ought least of all to wrong, that is to say, yourself, your friends, your country, and us, we shall be angry with you while you live, and our brethren, the laws in the world below, will receive you as an enemy; for they will know that you have done your best to destroy us. Listen, then, to us and not to Crito."

This, dear Crito, is the voice which I seem to hear murmuring in   15
my ears, like the sound of the flute in the ears of the mystic; that voice, I say, is humming in my ears, and prevents me from hearing any other. And I know that anything more which you may say will be vain. Yet speak, if you have anything to say.

CRITO: I have nothing to say, Socrates.   16

SOCRATES: Leave me then, Crito, to fulfill the will of God, and to follow   17
whither he leads.

☐ FOR CLASS DISCUSSION

1. Analyze and evaluate the disagreement between Martin Luther King, Jr., and Lewis Van Dusen, Jr., over the ethics of civil disobedience by applying the first set of guide questions from page 473. How do you account for their disagreement?

2. To what extent do you think that Van Dusen, Jr., and Socrates agree on their reasons for disapproving civil disobedience?

3. Choose one of the arguments for closer analysis, applying the second set of guide questions on page 474.

OPTIONAL WRITING ASSIGNMENTS

1. You are a successful civil rights attorney. The principal of your child's junior high school has approached you with a concern. It seems that none of the social studies textbooks discusses the concept of civil disobedience. He wants to provide the social studies teachers with a statement on civil disobedience.

Drawing on the preceding essays, personal experience and any other research you may have done, write a brief explanation of the role of civil disobedience in a democracy. Before you start writing, believe/doubt the following statement: "There is no place for civil disobedience in a modern democracy." Whatever you decide about that statement, construct a brief explanation of your view that would be appropriate for use in an eighth grade textbook.

2. The aerial bombardment of Iraq at the start of the 1991 war set off waves of student protests on college campuses reminiscent of the Vietnam antiwar movement. Several students at one college missed a midterm exam to join a protest march at the start of the war. When the students showed up the next day asking to take the midterm, the professor refused. He explained that his syllabus specifically stated that students could make up an exam only in cases of illness or personal emergency. Write a letter to the professor either supporting or opposing his decision that political protests do not constitute grounds for missing an exam.

Political Correctness and Diversity: Freedom of Speech at What Cost?

■

"SPEECH CODES" ON THE CAMPUS

Nat Hentoff

Civil libertarian Nat Hentoff reviews various campus attempts to write speech codes that don't imperil free speech and finds them all wanting.

During three years of reporting on anti–free-speech tendencies in higher education, I've been at more than twenty colleges and universities—from Washington and Lee and Columbia to Mesa State in Colorado and Stanford. 1

On this voyage of initially reverse expectations—with liberals fiercely advocating censorship of "offensive" speech and conservatives merrily taking the moral high ground as champions of free expression—the most dismaying moment of revelation took place at Stanford. 2

In the course of a two-year debate on whether Stanford, like many other universities, should have a speech code punishing language that might wound minorities, women, and gays, a letter appeared in the *Stanford Daily*. Signed by the African-American Law Students Association, the Asian-American Law Students Association, and the Jewish Law Students Association, the letter called for a harsh code. It reflected the letter and the spirit of an earlier declaration by Canetta Ivy, a black leader of 3 student government at Stanford during the period of the grand debate. "We don't put as many restrictions on freedom of speech," she said, "as we should."

Reading the letter by this rare ecumenical body of law students (so pressing was the situation that even Jews were allowed in), I thought of twenty, thirty years from now. From so bright a cadre of graduates, from so prestigious a law school would come some of the law professors, civil leaders, college presidents, and maybe even a Supreme Court Justice of the future. And many of them would have learned—like so many other university students in the land—that censorship is okay provided your motives are okay. 4

The debate at Stanford ended when the president, Donald Kennedy, following the prevailing winds, surrendered his previous position that once you start telling people what they can't say, you will end up telling them what they can't think. Stanford now has a speech code. 5

This is not to say that these gags on speech—every one of them so overboard and vague that a student can violate a code without knowing he or she has done so—are invariably imposed by student demand. At most colleges, it is the administration that sets up the code. Because there have been racist or sexist or homophobic taunts, anonymous notes or graffiti, the administration feels it must *do something.* The cheapest, quickest way to demonstrate that it cares is to appear to suppress racist, sexist, homophobic speech. 6

Usually, the leading opposition among the faculty consists of conservatives—when there is opposition. An exception at Stanford was law professor Gerald Gunther, arguably the nation's leading authority on constitutional law. But Gunther did not have much support among other faculty members, conservative or liberal. 7

At the University of Buffalo Law School, which has a code restricting speech, I could find just one faculty member who was against it. A liberal, he spoke only on condition that I not use his name. He did not want to be categorized as a racist. 8

On another campus, a political science professor for whom I had great respect after meeting and talking with him years ago has been silent—students told me—on what Justice William Brennan once called "the pall of orthodoxy" that has fallen on his campus. 9

When I talked to him, the professor said, "It doesn't happen in my class. There's no 'politically correct' orthodoxy here. It may happen in other places at this university, but I don't know about that." He said no more. 10

One of the myths about the rise of p.c. (political correctness) is that, coming from the left, it is primarily intimidating conservatives on campus. Quite the contrary. At almost every college I've been to, conservative students have their own newspaper, usually quite lively and fired by a muckraking glee at exposing "politically correct" follies on campus. 11

By and large, those most intimidated—not so much by the speech   12
codes themselves but by the Madame Defarge-like spirit behind them—
are liberal students and those who can be called politically moderate.

I've talked to many of them, and they no longer get involved in class   13
discussions where their views would go against the grain of p.c. righ-
teousness. Many, for instance, have questions about certain kinds of
affirmative action. They are not partisans of Jesse Helms or David Duke,
but they wonder whether progeny of middle-class black families should
get scholarship preference. Others have a question about abortion. Most
are not pro-life, but they believe that fathers should have a say in whether
the fetus should be sent off into eternity.

Jeff Shesol, a recent graduate of Brown, and now a Rhodes scholar at   14
Oxford, became nationally known while at Brown because of his comic
strip, "Thatch," which, not too kindly, parodied p.c. students. At a forum
on free speech at Brown before he left, Shesol said he wished he could
tell the new students at Brown to have no fear of speaking freely. But he
couldn't tell them that, he said, advising the new students to stay clear of
talking critically about affirmative action or abortion, among other things,
in public.

At that forum, Shesol told me, he said that those members of the left   15
who regard dissent from their views as racist and sexist should realize
that they are discrediting their goals. "They're honorable goals," said
Shesol, "and I agree with them. I'm against racism and sexism. But these
people's tactics are obscuring the goals. And they've resulted in Brown
no longer being an open-minded place." There were hisses from the
audience.

Students at New York University Law School have also told me that   16
they censor themselves in class. The kind of chilling atmosphere they
describe was exemplified last year as a case assigned for a moot court
competition became subject to denunciation when a sizable number of
law students said it was too "offensive" and would hurt the feelings of gay
and lesbian students. The case concerned a divorced father's attempt to
gain custody of his children on the grounds that their mother had
become a lesbian. It was against p.c. to represent the father.

Although some of the faculty responded by insisting that you learn to   17
be a lawyer by dealing with all kinds of cases, including those you
personally find offensive, other faculty members supported the rebellious
students, praising them for their sensitivity. There was little public opposition from the other students to the attempt to suppress the case.
A leading dissenter was a member of the conservative Federalist
Society.

What is p.c. to white students is not necessarily p.c. to black students.   18
Most of the latter did not get involved in the N.Y.U. protest, but throughout the country many black students do support speech codes. A
vigorous exception was a black Harvard Law School student who spoke
during a debate on whether the law school should start punishing

speech. A white student got up and said that the codes are necessary because, without them, black students would be driven away from colleges and thereby deprived of the equal opportunity to get an education.

The black student rose and said that the white student had a hell of a nerve to assume that he—in the face of racist speech—would pack up his books and go home. He'd been familiar with that kind of speech all his life, and he had never felt the need to run away from it. He'd handled it before and he could again.   19

The black student then looked at his white colleague and said that it was condescending to say that blacks have to be "protected" from racist speech. "It is more racist and insulting," he emphasized, "to say that to me than to call me a nigger."   20

But that would appear to be a minority view among black students. Most are convinced they do need to be protected from wounding language. On the other hand, a good many black student organizations on campus do not feel that Jews have to be protected from wounding language.   21

Though it's not much written about in reports of the language wars on campuses, there is a strong strain of anti-Semitism among some—not all, by any means—black students. They invite such speakers as Louis Farrakhan, the former Stokely Carmichael (now Kwame Touré), and such lesser but still burning bushes as Steve Cokely, the Chicago commentator who has declared that Jewish doctors inject the AIDS virus into black babies. That distinguished leader was invited to speak at the University of Michigan.   22

The black student organization at Columbia University brought to the campus Dr. Khallid Abdul Muhammad. He began his address by saying: "My leader, my teacher, my guide is the honorable Louis Farrakhan. I thought that should be said at Columbia Jewniversity."   23

Many Jewish students have not censored themselves in reacting to this form of political correctness among some blacks. A Columbia student, Rachel Stoll, wrote a letter to the *Columbia Spectator:* "I have an idea. As a white Jewish American, I'll just stand in the middle of a circle comprising . . . Khallid Abdul Muhammad and assorted members of the Black Students Organization and let them all hurl large stones at me. From recent events and statements made on this campus, I gather this will be a good cheap method of making these people feel good."   24

At UCLA, a black student magazine printed an article indicating there is considerable truth to the *Protocols of the Elders of Zion.* For months, the black faculty, when asked their reactions, preferred not to comment. One of them did say that the black students already considered the black faculty to be insufficiently militant, and the professors didn't want to make the gap any wider. Like white liberal faculty members on other campuses, they want to be liked—or at least not too disliked.   25

Along with quiet white liberal faculty members, most black professors 26
have not opposed the speech codes. But unlike the white liberals, many
honestly do believe that minority students have to be insulated from
barbed language. They do not believe—as I have found out in a number
of conversations—that an essential part of an education is to learn to
demystify language, to strip it of its ability to demonize and stigmatize
you. They do not believe that the way to deal with bigoted language is to
answer it with more and better language of your own. This seems very
elementary to me, but not to the defenders, black and white, of the
speech codes.

Consider University of California president David Gardner. He has 27
imposed a speech code on all the campuses in his university system.
Students are to be punished—and this is characteristic of the other
codes around the country—if they use "fighting words"—derogatory references to "race, sex, sexual orientation or disability."

The term "fighting words" comes from a 1942 Supreme Court deci- 28
sion, *Chaplinsky v. New Hampshire,* which ruled that "fighting words"
are not protected by the First Amendment. That decision, however, has
been in disuse at the High Court for many years. But it is thriving on college campuses.

In the California code, a word becomes "fighting" if it is directly 29
addressed to "any ordinary person" (presumably, extraordinary people are
above all this). These are the kinds of words that are "inherently likely to
provoke a violent reaction, *whether or not they actually do.*" (Emphasis
added.)

Moreover, he or she who fires a fighting word at any ordinary person 30
can be reprimanded or dismissed from the university because the perpetrator should "reasonably know" that what he or she has said will interfere with the "victim's ability to pursue effectively his or her education or
otherwise participate fully in university programs and activities."

Asked Gary Murikami, chairman of the Gay and Lesbian Association at 31
the University of California, Berkeley: "What does it mean?"

Among those—faculty, law professors, college administrators—who 32
insist such codes are essential to the university's purpose of making *all*
students feel at home and thereby able to concentrate on their work,
there has been a celebratory resort to the Fourteenth Amendment.

That amendment guarantees "equal protection of the laws" to all, 33
and that means to all students on campus. Accordingly, when the
First Amendment rights of those engaging in offensive speech clash with
the equality rights of their targets under the Fourteenth Amendment, the
First Amendment must give way.

This is the thesis, by the way, of John Powell, legal director of the 34
ACLU (American Civil Liberties Union), even though that organization has
now formally opposed all college speech codes—after a considerable
civil war among and within its affiliates.

The battle of the amendments continues, and when harsher codes are   35
called for at some campuses, you can expect the Fourteenth Amendment—which was not intended to censor *speech*—will rise again.

A precedent has been set at, of all places, colleges and universities,   36
that the principle of free speech is merely situational. As college administrators change, so will the extent of free speech on campus. And invariably, permissible speech will become more and more narrowly defined.
Once speech can be limited in such subjective ways, more and more
expression will be included in what is forbidden.

One of the exceedingly few college presidents who speaks out on the   37
consequences of the anti–free-speech movement is Yale University's
Benno Schmidt:

> Freedom of thought must be Yale's central commitment. It is not
> easy to embrace. It is, indeed, the effort of a lifetime. . . . Much expres-
> sion that is free may deserve our contempt. We may well be moved to
> exercise our own freedom to counter it or to ignore it. But universities
> cannot censor or suppress speech, no matter how obnoxious in con-
> tent, without violating their justification for existence. . . .
>
> On some other campuses in this country, values of civility and com-
> munity have been offered by some as paramount values of the univer-
> sity, even to the extent of superseding freedom of expression.
>
> Such a view is wrong in principle and, if extended, is disastrous to
> freedom of thought. . . . The chilling effects on speech of the vague-
> ness and open-ended nature of many universities' prohibitions . . . are
> compounded by the fact that these codes are typically enforced by fac-
> ulty and students who commonly assert that vague notions of commu-
> nity are more important to the academy than freedom of thought and
> expression. . . .
>
> This is a flabby and uncertain time for freedom in the United States.

On the Public Broadcasting System in June, I was part of a Fred   38
Friendly panel at Stanford University in a debate on speech codes versus
freedom of expression. The three black panelists, including a Stanford
student, strongly supported the codes. So did the one Asian-American
on the panel. But then so did Stanford law professor, Thomas Grey, who
wrote the Stanford code, and Stanford president Donald Kennedy, who
first opposed and then embraced the code. We have a new ecumenicism
of those who would control speech for the greater good. It is hardly a
new idea, but the mix of advocates is rather new.

But there are other voices. In the national board debate at the ACLU   39
on college speech codes, the first speaker—and I think she had a lot to
do with making the final vote against codes unanimous—was Gwen
Thomas. A black community college administrator from Colorado, she is
a fiercely persistent exposer of racial discrimination.

She started by saying, "I have always felt as a minority person that we   40
have to protect the rights of all because if we infringe on the rights of any
persons, we'll be next.

"As for providing a nonintimidating educational environment, our   41
young people have to learn to grow up on college campuses. We have to
teach them how to deal with adversarial situations. They have to learn
how to survive offensive speech they find wounding and hurtful."

Gwen Thomas is an educator—an endangered species in higher edu-   42
cation.

■

THE POLITICS OF FEELINGS

John Leo

*Columnist Leo attacks the notion that we can write codes that protect people
from feeling bad. Feelings are ineffably personal, he argues, and to privilege
feelings inevitably diminishes the force of communal standards.*

The original guidelines for the University of Michigan antidiscrimina-   1
tion code said "students must be free to participate in class discussion
without feeling harassed or intimidated." Penn State is striving to forbid
anything on campus that makes people uncomfortable about sexual
issues. Law professor Catharine MacKinnon says "I call it rape whenever
a woman has sex and feels violated."

Note that in these three examples, we are far from any objective   2
or social standard of offense. Instead, we are in the realm of feelings.
Under the Michigan code (since declared unconstitutional), if a student felt intimidated by a professor's remark, even if no one else in the
class saw anything objectionable, the student's negative feeling created
and defined an offense. Apparently, any sexual discomfort felt anywhere by anyone at Penn State does the same thing. And according
to MacKinnon's standard, and some far vaguer than hers, any con-
sensual act of sex can be labeled rape if negative feelings develop.
Since rape and sexual harassment are increasingly being viewed subjec-
tively, definitions of these acts can expand indefinitely and are indeed
doing so.

The use of feelings as a trump card is becoming pervasive. The codes   3
and laws generated by the campus-based race and gender alliance are
aimed at real problems. But almost all are disastrously rooted in the
demand that negative feelings must not be felt. If they are felt, as is so
often the case when the individual collides with the real world, then
someone must be penalized for it. Jonathan Rauch, a writer concerned

with these matters, says this amounts to yet another freshly minted right, "the right not to be offended."

Defusing the news. More and more, this means the abandonment of communal standards in favor of subjective, personal ones. In effect, the right not to be offended has been widely granted. In the media, many militant groups essentially have a veto power over their own bad press. Even in the best newspapers, coverage of such matters as Afrocentrism, the real ideas of Catharine MacKinnon or guerrilla activities of ACT-UP tends to be omitted or carefully softened up to avoid controversy. Editing such stories is like defusing a land mine.

At college, a whole range of discussions is off-limits. On some campuses, affirmative action and set-asides are simply undiscussable; any doubts are apt to be denounced by minority students as arguments that they should not be on campus at all. Some of these arguments are, in fact, racist. And some aren't. But both are being banned, in effect, by feelings.

The loss of consensus and the rise of the right not to be offended explain why *sensitivity* and *insensitivity* have become the nouns of the '90s. Since there are apparently very few social rules that anyone wants to defend, our constant chore is to guess what will trigger negative emotions (sensitivity) and accuse ourselves ruefully when we accidentally step on another person's emotional land mine and set it off (insensitivity). Even the evasive nonapologies of those caught in scandals have taken on this "feelie" quality. William Aramony, stepping down as head of the United Way amid allegations of financial abuses, apologized for a "lack of sensitivity to perceptions." The board, in turn, accepted his "thoughtful and sensitive offer" to leave immediately.

We are hip deep in a bizarre attempt to use emotions as a social standard, mostly thanks to the therapized ethic produced in the '60s and '70s by the Human Potential movement and other pop therapies. These therapies had very little use for rationality or social commitments; the self was autonomous, virtually independent of culture and properly steered by its own feelings, whatever they happened to be. Carl Rogers wrote: "Doing what 'feels right' proves to be a competent and trustworthy guide to behavior which is truly satisfying." This is the basis of the famous phrase "If it feels good, do it," and its not-so-famous corollary, "If it feels bad, attack or ignore it."

Along the way, a great deal of our educational system has been therapized: self-esteem programs that induce a feeling of success, quite apart from any achievement; history as therapy in the high schools and colleges, featuring feel-good stories about each ethnic and sexual group; an unembarrassed relativism based mostly on feelings—all traditions must be equal lest anyone feel inferior.

The enterprise requires a thorough subjectivity. There are no truths, only different views. An offense is what an individual or tribe says it is.

After an insulting racial comment at the University of Washington, a Hispanic professor said that "the abused community [must]define what is or is not acceptable." The implicit argument is that injured feelings, usually under cover of a "hostile environment" theory, must be translated into penalties, codes and laws. But as William Galston of the University of Maryland says, "We have to resist the tendency to make feelings normative for definition of a crime." Yes, indeed. Feelings are private and mercurial; laws are not.

■

SAY THE RIGHT THING—OR ELSE

Judith Martin and Gunther Stent

Etiquette columnist Judith Martin ("Miss Manners") and scientist Gunther Stent argue that universities are within their rights to restrict free speech—just as every other major American institution, including the Supreme Court does—to maintain their sense of civility.

WASHINGTON—Can the university, with its special trust of protecting free speech, be hampered by the restrictions of civility? What kind of a frill is etiquette, anyway, for those in the noble pursuit of truth? 1

These questions are raised whenever a loose-tongued student turns publicly nasty. When Brown University recently expelled such a student, many argued that all restrictions of free speech are intolerable in the university. Brown's president, Vartan Gregorian, agreed with that premise and neatly reclassified the offensive speech as behavior. 2

But the premise is wrong. 3

The special trust of a university is not to foster unlimited speech. It is to foster unlimited inquiry. And totally free speech inhibits rather than enhances the free exchange of ideas. 4

The law cannot restrict such speech without violating our constitutional rights. But etiquette, the extra-legal regulative system that seeks to avert conflict before it becomes serious enough to call in the law, can and does. You may have a legal right to call your mother an idiot, or somebody else's mother a slut, but you won't if you know what's good for you. 5

Nor could you convince many people that the controversy that such remarks are likely to provoke will lead to advances in knowledge. 6

The university needs to enforce rules banning speech that interferes with the free exchange of ideas. It must protect the discussion of offensive topics but not the use of offensive manners. It must enable people freely to attack ideas but not one another. 7

Education is impossible without the order that prevents intimidation and mayhem. When children first enter school, they must be taught to sit 8 still, refrain from taunting their classmates, show respect for their teacher and wait their turn to talk, or they will never be able to learn.

To those who find it horrifying that the university should allow a lesser 9 degree of free speech than the law permits, it might be pointed out that the law itself restricts free speech in its pursuit of juridical truth. Try saying some of the things in a courtroom that the law will protect your right to say in a barroom.

Jurisprudence uses etiquette in courtroom procedure, not only to 10 restrict speech but to impose standards of dress, comportment and forms of address—matters over which universities have long since abandoned authority.

Legislators and diplomats also know the value of keeping speech 11 within the bounds of civility. The parliamentary etiquette book, "Robert's Rules of Order," proscribes "disorderly words" and forbids speakers "to arraign the motives of a member" during strongly worded debate. "It is not the man, but the measure, that is the subject of debate," decrees its section on "Decorum."

The rougher the conflict, the more manners are needed. Only when 12 insults, harassment, disrespect and obscenity are banned can people engage in truly substantive argument.

Of course it is also a personal insult to call someone a racist or a sex- 13 ist. Incivility is no more acceptable in defense than in attack.

Rebuttal, however, is a staple of open debate. Members of the univer- 14 sity community should always have the opportunity to attack ideas—but not to attack people. The university should be obliged to provide a forum for anyone who wants to argue for or against an idea, provided the argument is made in good faith and a polite manner.

This standard of academic etiquette must be required not only in the 15 classroom and lecture hall but wherever the community of scholars gathers—residence halls, dining commons, recreational facilities. Invective, whether spoken or conveyed through posters or graffiti, in the classroom or in the community, is detrimental to rational debate, to which universities are dedicated.

SOME FACTUAL CORRECTNESS
ABOUT POLITICAL CORRECTNESS

Katherine T. Bartlett

Law professor Bartlett argues that PC critics have misrepresented the nature of the debate. They assume that they represent the "natural" (because customary) view of the issue, whereas their opponents argue for merely "political" ends.

Criticizing campus "radicals" for browbeating the majority into some   1
"politically correct" ideological conformity has become more fashionable
than the practice it condemns. But the PC rap is a bum one. PC critics
mischaracterize the enemy, exaggerate its presence, and fail to debate or
even acknowledge the important substantive issues underlying the controversy. In doing so, they not only obscure, but also help to prove, the
insights they themselves do not appear to understand.

The pejorative label "political correctness" represents an effort by PC   2
critics to seize the moral high ground of the First Amendment. They
claim that those protesting the continuation of racism and sexism on college campuses are moral ideologues, intolerant censors, Vietnam-pro-
testers-turned-fascists. They also claim that these ideologues have taken
over the universities, and that from this place of power they are threatening the quality of academic standards and the integrity of free intellectual
inquiry.

Where is this ideological coercion? Where is this threat to open dia-   3
logue? I see little evidence of it, even at Duke University, which has been
cited in these pages as a hotbed of PC. At Duke, courses on Shakespeare, Milton and other "traditional" liberal arts subjects are not under
siege; courses on such subjects as Marxism, women's studies and Afro-
American literature are. The average female Duke student shuns the
label "feminist." In contrast, no shame appears to attach to association
with conservative causes. Outspoken conservative students have their
own newspaper, the Duke Review, and an active chapter of the National
Association of Scholars speaks freely. At Duke, academic traditionalists
head almost all departments and hold almost all chaired professorships.
Duke has only one female dean; all other top leadership positions are
held by white men.

If Duke is typical, what accounts for the perception that university radi-   4
cals have taken over? "Surplus visibility," answers Daphne Patai of the
University of Massachusetts at Amherst. Certain voices are being heard in
the university more often, more loudly, and more insistently than in the
past. Given what we are accustomed to hearing from these voices—
silence—the noise is deafening. As Ms. Patai observes, when members of
groups we do not expect to hear from begin to speak, their voices appear
too loud, out of place, inappropriate, excessive.

Surplus visibility exemplifies a larger phenomenon PC critics have   5
been unwilling to understand: the privilege of those who have power to
say what needs defending and what does not. In any social organization,
the views of the dominant tend to be taken for granted as objective and
neutral. Challenges to these views—like those we are now hearing in the
universities—appear to seek special favors for the "less qualified," or
some compromising of academic standards.

This phenomenon helps to explain why some demands pressed at   6
universities are viewed as "political" or "special pleadings," while others
are not. Some PC critics dismiss as interest-group politics requests that

authors such as Toni Morrison or Mary Wollestonecraft be included in the curriculum; others malign courses in feminist theory or black studies as a "Balkanization" of the curriculum.

In contrast, assignments of writings by Nathaniel Hawthorne or T. S.   7
Eliot draw no notice and require no defense; neither does the "basic" political philosophy course that begins with Aristotle and ends with John Rawls. The difference is *not* that the standard "Western civilization" courses are apolitical. In fact, it is precisely the alignment of these courses with particular points of view—the dominant ones in our society—that makes them appear neutral. This is not to argue that such courses should be abolished, but nobody should pretend that only feminist and minority-studies courses have political content.

PC critics attack as ideologically coercive, condescending and petty   8
the insistence by some "blacks" and "Indians" that they be called "African-Americans" or "Native Americans." Yet they take for granted their own titles of "Professor," "Doctor" or "Judge" as a matter of simple civility.

Most, perhaps all, titles and labels convey substantive political mes-   9
sages about power and self-definition. But those that conform to existing lines of authority are taken as neutral signs of respect, while those that implicitly encroach upon that authority stand out as shamelessly political and arrogant.

It is clear that some PC critics are using a double standard to judge   10
those who do not respect their authority. These critics invoke important principles of academic freedom to shield themselves from criticism of classroom remarks that some students find racist or sexist. Yet they appear to acknowledge no reciprocal freedom on the part of students to resist classroom humiliation; and it is that resistance that is now labeled a "politically correct" effort at censorship.

Most of us who have been labeled "PC" are not seeking special favors.   11
We are not trying to stifle debate. We are trying to begin one—a difficult one that challenges perspectives that are taken for granted in the university and in society. If our critics were true to the free-speech principles they profess, they would be engaging in that debate. All too often, they have chosen personal denunciation and caricature instead.

There is room, and a great need, for a genuine debate in our universi-   12
ties about academic quality and diversity. PC critics have diverted the debate by the distracting assertion, backed by only a few isolated anecdotes, that traditional voices are being silenced.

The one-sidedness of the PC critique mocks this assertion. It also   13
demonstrates a central paradox of the whole PC problem: The more established the status quo, the less defense it requires, and the more easily challenges to it can be made to appear self-serving and tyrannical. The PC charge is a smoke screen. The fact that it packs rhetorical punch demonstrates that there has been far less change in who controls the university, and in what we take for granted there, than many would have us believe.

TEACH DIVERSITY WITH A SMILE

Barbara Ehrenreich

Writer Ehrenreich chides both sides of the PC debate for their humorless partisanship. Acceptance of multiculturalism, points out Ehrenreich, will be a boon to both critics and defendants of monocultural values.

Something had to replace the threat of communism, and at last a   1
workable substitute is at hand. "Multiculturalism," as the new menace is known, has been denounced in the media recently as the new McCarthyism, the new fundamentalism, even the new totalitarianism—take your choice. According to its critics, who include a flock of tenured conservative scholars, multiculturalism aims to toss out what it sees as the Eurocentric bias in education and replace Plato with Ntozake Shange and traditional math with the Yoruba number system. And that's just the beginning. The Jacobins of the multiculturalist movement, who are described derisively as P.C., or politically correct, are said to have launched a campus reign of terror against those who slip and innocently say "freshman" instead of "freshperson," "Indian" instead of "Native American" or, may the Goddess forgive them, "disabled" instead of "differently abled."

So you can see what is at stake here: freedom of speech, freedom of   2
thought, Western civilization and a great many professorial egos. But before we get carried away by the mounting backlash against multiculturalism, we ought to reflect for a moment on the system that the P.C. people aim to replace. I know all about it; in fact it's just about all I *do* know, since I—along with so many educated white people of my generation—was a victim of monoculturalism.

American history, as it was taught to us, began with Columbus' "dis-   3
covery" of an apparently unnamed, unpeopled America, and moved on to the Pilgrims serving pumpkin pie to a handful of grateful red-skinned folks. College expanded our horizons with courses called Humanities or sometimes Civ, which introduced us to a line of thought that started with Homer, worked its way through Rabelais and reached a poignant climax in the pensées of Matthew Arnold. Graduate students wrote dissertations on what long-dead men had thought of Chaucer's verse or Shakespeare's dramas; foreign languages meant French or German. If there had been high technology in ancient China, kingdoms in black Africa or women anywhere, at any time, doing anything worth noticing, we did not know it, nor did anyone think to tell us.

Our families and neighborhoods reinforced the dogma of monocultur-   4
alism. In our heads, most of us '50s teenagers carried around a social map that was about as useful as the chart that guided Columbus to the "Indies." There were "Negroes," "whites" and "Orientals," the latter meaning Chinese and "Japs." Of religions, only three were known—

Protestant, Catholic and Jewish—and not much was known about the last two types. The only remaining human categories were husbands and wives, and that was all the diversity the monocultural world could handle. Gays, lesbians, Buddhists, Muslims, Malaysians, Mormons, etc. were simply off the map.

So I applaud—with one hand, anyway—the multiculturalist goal of   5
preparing us all for a wider world. The other hand is tapping its fingers impatiently, because the critics are right about one thing: when advocates of multiculturalism adopt the haughty stance of political correctness, they quickly descend to silliness or worse. It's obnoxious, for example, to rely on university administrations to enforce P.C. standards of verbal inoffensiveness. Racist, sexist and homophobic thoughts cannot, alas, be abolished by fiat but only by the time-honored methods of persuasion, education and exposure to the other guy's—or, excuse me, woman's—point of view.

And it's silly to mistake verbal purification for genuine social reform.   6
Even after all women are "Ms." and all people are "he or she," women will still earn only 65¢ for every dollar earned by men. Minorities by any other name, such as "people of color," will still bear a hugely disproportionate burden of poverty and discrimination. Disabilities are not just "different abilities" when there are not enough ramps for wheelchairs, signers for the deaf or special classes for the "specially" endowed. With all due respect for the new politesse, actions still speak louder than fashionable phrases.

But the worst thing about the P.C. people is that they are such poor   7
advocates for the multicultural cause. No one was ever won over to a broader, more inclusive view of life by being bullied or relentlessly "corrected." Tell a 19-year-old white male that he can't say "girl" when he means "teen-age woman," and he will most likely snicker. This may be the reason why, despite the conservative alarms, P.C.-ness remains a relatively tiny trend. Most campuses have more serious and ancient problems: faculties still top-heavy with white males of the monocultural persuasion; fraternities that harass minorities and women; date rape; alcohol abuse; and tuition that excludes all but the upper fringe of the middle class.

So both sides would be well advised to lighten up. The conservatives   8
ought to realize that criticisms of the great books approach to learning do not amount to totalitarianism. And the advocates of multiculturalism need to regain the sense of humor that enabled their predecessors in the struggle to coin the term P.C. years ago—not in arrogance but in self-mockery.

Beyond that, both sides should realize that the beneficiaries of multi-   9
culturalism are not only the "oppressed peoples" on the standard P.C. list (minorities, gays, etc.). The "unenlightened"—the victims of monoculturalism—are oppressed too, or at least deprived. Our educations, whether at Yale or at State U, were narrow and parochial and left us ill-equipped

to navigate a society that truly is multicultural and is becoming more so every day. The culture that we studied was, in fact, *one* culture and, from a world perspective, all too limited and ingrown. Diversity is challenging, but those of us who have seen the alternative know it is also richer, livelier and ultimately more fun.

☐ FOR CLASS DISCUSSION

1. Analyze and evaluate the disagreements among these writers concerning political correctness by applying the first set of guide questions from page 473. How do you account for the differing points of view? (Do the writers disagree about questions of truth? About definitions? About appropriate comparisons or analogies? About values, assumptions, and beliefs?)

2. Choose one of the arguments for closer analysis, applying the second set of guide questions on page 474.

OPTIONAL WRITING ASSIGNMENT   As a result of all the national publicity about the prevalence of PC on college campuses, the local paper has sent a reporter out to cover the situation on your campus. She has phoned you and set up an interview with you for tomorrow. Before you speak to her, you want to be sure in your own mind how you feel about the issue. Is PC an issue on your campus? Why or why not? If so, what manifestations of it do you see? Can PC be justified in your view? If so, how and under what circumstances? If not, why not? Write a position paper in which you outline your thoughts on PC for the reporter.

The Legalization of Drugs:
Would America Be Better Off or
Worse Off If Drugs Were Legalized?

■

THE FEDERAL DRUGSTORE

An Interview with Michael S. Gazzaniga

In this interview, Michael S. Gazzaniga, professor of neuroscience at Dartmouth Medical School, provides a scientific perspective on drug use and abuse. Gazzaniga's own stance is a scientifically cautious belief that the benefits of legalizing drugs outweigh the costs.

Q: Professor Gazzaniga, as you know, there are those who have recom-   1
mended the decriminalization of drugs. Before we take up a concrete

proposal coming in from that quarter, we want to ask you a question or two, the answers to which will shed light on any such proposal. The first question is this:

It is said that the drug crack is substantively different from its parent drug, cocaine, in that it is, to use the term of Professor van den Haag, "crimogenic." In other words a certain (unspecified) percentage of those who take crack are prompted to—well, to go out and commit mayhem of some kind. Is that correct? 2

A: No, not in the way you put it. What you are asking is, Is there something about how crack acts on the brain that makes people who take it likelier to commit crime? 3

Let's begin by making it clear what crack is. It is simply cocaine that has been mixed with baking soda, water, and then boiled. What this procedure does is to permit cocaine to be smoked. Now any drug ingested in that way—i.e., absorbed by the lungs—goes more efficiently to the brain, and the result is a quicker, more intense experience. That is what crack gives the consumer. But its impact on the brain is the same as with plain cocaine and, as a matter of fact, amphetamines. No one has ever maintained that these drugs are "crimogenic." 4

The only study I know about that inquires into the question of crack breeding crime reports that most homicides involving crack were the result not of the use of crack, but of dealer disputes. Crack did not induce users to commit crimes. Do some crack users commit crimes? Of course. After all, involvement in proscribed drug traffic is dangerous. Moreover, people who commit crimes tend to use drugs at a high rate, though which drug they prefer varies from one year to the next. 5

Q: You are telling us that an increase in the use of crack would not mean an increase in crime? 6

A: I am saying that what increase there would be in crime would not be simply the result of the pharmacology of that drug. Look, let's say there are 200,000 users/abusers of crack in New York City—a number that reflects one of the current estimates. If so, and if the drug produced violent tendencies in all crack users, the health-care system would have come to a screeching halt. It hasn't. In fact, in 1988 the hospitals in New York City (the crack capital of the world) averaged only seven crack-related admissions, citywide, a day. The perception of crack-based misbehavior is exaggerated because it is the cases that show up in the emergency rooms that receive public notice, and the whole picture begins to look very bleak. All of this is to say: when considering any aspect of the drug problem, keep in mind the matter of selection of the evidence. 7

It is prudent to recall that, in the past, dangerous and criminal behavior has been said to have been generated by other drugs, for instance marijuana (you remember *Reefer Madness?*). And bear it in mind that since cocaine is available everywhere, so is crack available everywhere, since the means of converting the one into the other are easy, and easily 8 learned. It is important to note that only a small percentage of cocaine users actually convert their stuff to crack. Roughly one in six.

Q: Then would it follow that even if there were an increase in the use of crack, the legalization of it would actually result in a decrease in crime?   9

A: That is correct.   10

Q: Isn't crack a drug whose addictive power exceeds that of many other drugs? If that is the case, one assumes that people who opt to take crack do so because it yields the faster and more exhilarating satisfactions to which you make reference.   11

A: That is certainly the current understanding, but there are no solid data on the question. Current observations are confounded by certain economic variables. Crack is cheap—   12

Q: Why? If cocaine is expensive, how can crack be cheap?   13

A: Cocaine costs $1,000 per ounce if bought in quantity. One ounce can produce one thousand vials of crack, each of which sells for $5. The drug abuser is able to experience more drug episodes. Crack being cheap, the next high can come a lot more quickly and since there is a down to every up, or high, the cycle can become intense.   14

So yes, crack is addictive. So is cocaine. So are amphetamines. The special punch of crack, as the result of going quickly via the lungs to the brain, may prompt some abusers to want more. By the way, it is the public knowledge that crack acts in this way that, as several studies document, causes most regular cocaine users to be cautious about crack. The casual-to-moderate user very clearly wants to stay in that category. So, all you can say is that there is a *perception,* widely shared, that crack is more addictive. Whether it is, isn't really known. One thing we do know is that crack does not begin to approach tobacco as a nationwide health hazard. For every crack-related death, there are three hundred tobacco-related deaths.   15

Q: You are confusing us. You say that because of the especially quick effects that come from taking crack, there is a disposition on the part of the user to want more. Isn't that a way of saying that it is more addictive? If someone, after smoking, say, ten cigarettes, begins to want cigarettes every day, isn't tobacco "addictive," as you say it is? Or are you saying that crack finds most users indifferent to the highs it brings on, and for *that* reason it can't be said to be more addictive than cocaine?   16

A: The current, official definition of an addict is someone who compulsively seeks psychoactive drugs. The definition, you will note, focuses on human behavior, not on pharmacologic action on the brain. In respect of crack, there are factors that might lead to a higher rate of addiction. Some of these factors are certainly social in nature and some may be pharmacologic. The purported higher rate of addiction among crack users could be due to social values, for instance the low cost of crack. We simply don't know as yet.   17

Keep in mind our experience with LSD. When it was fashionable to take it, droves did so. But LSD has unpleasant side-effects, and eventu-   18 ally the use of it greatly diminished. In drugs, as in much else, there is a strong tendency to follow the herd. Sorting out the real threat from the hyperbole takes time.

Another example of hyperbole is the recent claim that there were   19
375,000 "crack babies" born last year; how could that possibly be, when the government (the National Institutes on Drug Abuse) informs us that there were only 500,000 crack *users* last year? Exaggeration and misinformation run rampant on this subject.

Q: Well, if crack were legally available alongside cocaine and, say, mari-   20
juana, what could be the reason for a consumer to take crack?

A: You need to keep your drug classifications straight. If your goal   21
were, pure and simple, to get high, you might try crack or cocaine, or some amphetamine. You wouldn't go for marijuana, which is a mild hallucinogen and tranquilizer. So, if you wanted to be up and you didn't have much time, you might go to crack. But then if it were absolutely established that there was a higher addiction rate with crack, legalization could, paradoxically, diminish its use. This is so because if cocaine were reduced to the same price as crack, the abuser, acknowledging the higher rate of addiction, might forgo the more intensive high of crack, opting for the slower high of cocaine. Crack was introduced years ago as offering an alluring new psychoactive experience. But its special hold on the ghetto is the result of its price. Remember that—on another front—we know that 120-proof alcohol doesn't sell as readily as the 86 proof, not by a long shot, even though the higher the proof, the faster the psychological effect that alcohol users are seeking.

Q: The basic question, we take it, has got to be this: It is everywhere   22
assumed that if drugs were legal, their consumption would increase. That guess is based on empirical observations of a past phenomenon. Mr. Bennett, for instance, has said that when Prohibition ended, the consumption of alcohol increased by 400 per cent. What are your comments on that?

A: Books and even careers have been built around studies of the Eigh-   23
teenth Amendment. Arguments about its meaning continue to rage in the scientific journals. Arguments always continue when available data are inconclusive.

Most experts insist that the rate of alcohol use before Prohibition was   24
the same as after. Some qualify that assertion by pointing out that the pre-Prohibition rate of consumption was not realized again until years after Prohibition was over. From this we are invited to conclude that, in that sense, Prohibition was really successful—i.e., it interrupted many potential drinkers on their way to the saloon. And then some point out that although alcohol was freely available during Prohibition, it was harder to get in some parts of America. Even so overall consumption was rising (some say to pre-Prohibition levels) toward the middle and end of Prohibition.

Frankly, here is what's important: *There is a base rate of drug abuse,*   25
and it is achieved one way or another. This is so even though there are
researchers who point to different rates of abuse in different cultures. The
trouble with that generality is that it is usually made without taking into
account correlative factors, such as national traditions, the extent of education programs available, and so on. In which connection, I think the
Federal Government should establish a study group to collect drug information from different cultures in an effort to get useful leads.

Q: Is there evidence that the current consumption of drugs is   26
restrained by their illegality? We have read that ninety million Americans
have experimented, at one time or another, with illegal drugs. Would
more than ninety million have experimented with them if drugs had been
legal?

A: I think illegality has little if anything to do with drug consumption—   27
and, incidentally, I am certain that far more than ninety million Americans
have at some point or other experimented with an illegal drug.

This gets to the issue of actual availability. Drugs are everywhere, sim-   28
ply everywhere. In terms of availability, drugs might just as well be legal
as illegal. Now it has been argued that legalization will create a different
social climate, a more permissive, more indulgent climate. It is certainly
conceivable, primarily for that reason, that there would be greater initial
use—the result of curiosity. But the central point is that human beings in
all cultures tend to seek out means of altering their mental state, and
that although some will shop around and lose the powers of self-disci-
pline, most will settle down to a base rate of use, and a much smaller
rate of abuse, and those rates are pretty much what we have in the
United States right now.

Q: Then the factor of illegality, in your opinion, does not weigh heavily?   29
But, we come to the critical question, if ninety million (or more) Americans have experimented with the use of drugs, why is drug abuse at such
a (relatively) low level?

A: If you exclude tobacco, in the whole nation less than 10 per cent of   30
the adult population abuses drugs. That is, 9 to 12 million adult Americans abuse drugs. That figure includes alcohol, by the way, and the figure remains fairly constant.

Consider alcohol. In our culture alone, 70 to 80 per cent of us use   31
alcohol, and the abuse rate is now estimated at 5 to 6 per cent. We see
at work here a major feature of the human response to drug availability,
namely, the inclination to moderation. Most people are adjusted and are
intent on living productive lives. While most of us, pursuing that goal,
enjoy the sensations of euphoria, or anxiety reduction, or (at times) social
dis-inhibition or even anaesthesia, we don't let the desire for these sensations dominate our behavior. Alcohol fills these needs for many people
and its use is managed intelligently.

It is worth noting that the largest proportion of this drug is sold to the   32
social drinker, not the drunk, just as most cocaine is sold to the casual

user, not the addict. Now, early exposure to alcohol is common and inevitable, and youthful drinking can be extreme. Yet studies have shown that it is difficult to determine which drunk at the college party will evolve into a serious alcoholic. What is known is that the vast majority of early drinkers stop excessive drinking all by themselves. In fact, drug use of all types drops off radically with age.

Q: Wait a minute. Are you telling us that there is only a 10 per cent 33 chance that any user will become addicted to a drug, having experimented with it?

A: The 10 per cent figure includes all drugs except tobacco. The actual 34 risk for abuse of some drugs is much lower. Consider last year's National Household Survey (NHS), which was carried out by the National Institutes on Drug Abuse. It is estimated that some 21 million people tried cocaine in 1988. But according to the NHS only three million defined themselves as having used the drug at least once during the month preceding their interview. Most of the three million were casual users. Now think about it. *All* the cocaine users make up 2 per cent of the adult population, and the addicts make up less than one-quarter of 1 per cent of the total population. These are the government's own figures. Does that sound like an epidemic to you?

Q: But surely an epidemic has to do with the rate at which an undesir- 35 able occurrence is increasing. How many more cocaine users were there than the year before? Or the year before that?

A: The real question is whether or not more and more Americans are 36 becoming addicted to something. Is the rate of addiction to psychoactive substances going up? The answer to that is a flat no. Are there fads during which one drug becomes more popular than another as the drug of abuse? Sure. But, when one drug goes up in consumption, others go down. Heroin use is down, and so is marijuana use. That is why the opiate and marijuana pushers are trying to improve their purity—so they can grab back some of their market share, which apparently they have done for heroin in New York City.

But, having said that, you should know that the actual use of cocaine 37 and all other illicit drugs is on the decline, according to the NHS. The just-published National High School Survey carried out by the University of Michigan reports that the same is true among high-school students. Crack is used at such a low rate throughout the country that its use can hardly be measured in most areas.

Q: Well, if a low addiction rate is the rule, how do we come to terms 38 with the assertion, which has been made in reputable circles, that over 40 per cent of Americans fighting in Vietnam were using heroin and 80 per cent marijuana?

A: Stressful situations provoke a greater use of drugs. Vietnam was one 39 of them. But what happens when the soldiers come home?

That point was examined in a large study by Dr. Lee Robbins at Wash-   40
ington University. During the Vietnam War, President Nixon ordered a
study on the returning vets who seemed to have a drug problem. (Nixon
didn't know what he was looking for, but he was getting a lot of flak on
the point that the war was producing a generation of addicts.) Dr. Robbins chose to study those soldiers returning to the United States in 1971.
Of the 13,760 Army enlisted men who returned and were included in her
sample, 1,400 had a positive urine test for drugs (narcotics, amphetamines, or barbiturates). She was able to re-test 495 men from this sample a few months later. The results were crystal clear: Only 8 per cent of
the men who had been drug positive in their first urine tests remained so.
In short, over 90 per cent of them, now that they were back home,
walked away from drug use. And all of them knew how to get hold of
drugs, if they had wanted them. Incidentally, Dr. Robbins did a follow-up
study a couple of years later on the same soldiers. She reported there
had not been an increase in drug use.

Q: Aha! You are saying that under special circumstances, the use of   41
drugs increases. Well, granted there was stress in Vietnam. Isn't there
stress also in American ghettos?

A: Floyd Bloom of the Scripps Medical Institute—one of the foremost   42
brain scientists in the country—has posited that most psychoactive drugs
work on the brain's reward systems. There is good neurobiologic
research to support this idea. It is an idea that can easily be understood
and applied to everyday life.

What it tells you is that some people want artificial ways of getting   43
their kicks out of life, but also that some people need those artificial
crutches. If you live in poverty and frustration, and see few rewards available to you, you are likelier than your better-satisfied counterpart to seek
the escape of drugs, although the higher rate of consumption does not
result in a higher rate of addiction. Virtually every study finds this to be
the case with one possibly interesting twist. A recent Department of
Defense study showed that drug use in the military was lower for blacks
than for whites, the reverse of civilian life. (It is generally agreed that the
military is the only institution in our country that is successfully integrated.) In short, environmental factors play an important role in the incidence of drug use.

Q: So you are saying that there are social circumstances that will raise   44
the rate of consumption, but that raising the rate of consumption doesn't
in fact raise the rate of addiction. In other words, if 50 per cent of the
troops in Vietnam had been using crack, this would not have affected the
rate at which, on returning to the United States, they became addicted.
They would have kicked the habit on reaching home?

A: That's the idea. Drug consumption can go up in a particular popula-   45
tion, fueled by stress, but the rate of addiction doesn't go up no matter
what the degree of stress. Most people can walk away from high drug use
if their lives become more normal. Of course, the stress of the ghetto

isn't the only situation that fuels high drug consumption. Plenty of afflu-ent people who for some reason or another do not find their lives reward-ing also escape into drugs.

Q: If it is true, then, that only a small percentage of those who take   46
crack will end up addicted, and that that is no different from the small
percentage who, taking one beer every Saturday night, will become alco-holics, what is the correct way in which to describe the relative intensity
of the addictive element in a particular drug?

A: That is an interesting question and one that can't satisfactorily be   47
answered until much more research is done. There are conundrums.
Again, it is estimated that 21 million people tried cocaine in 1988. Yet, of
those, only 3 million currently use it, and only a small percentage are
addicted. As for crack, it is estimated that 2.5 million have used it, while
only a half million say they still do, and *that* figure includes the addicted
and the casual user. Some reports claim that as many as one half of
crack users are addicted. As I have said, crack is cheap, and for that rea-son may be especially attractive to the poor. That is a non-pharmacologi-cal, non-biological factor, the weight of which we have not come to any
conclusions about. We don't even have reliable data to tell us that crack
creates a greater rate of addiction than, say, cocaine. My own guess is it
doesn't. Remember that the drug acts on the same brain systems that
cocaine and amphetamines do.

What is needed, in order to answer your question, is a science of com-   48
parative pharmacology where the various psychoactive drugs could be
compared against some kind of common physiological/psychological
measure. Doing that would be difficult, which is one of the reasons why
those data don't exist. How do you capture fluctuating moods and moti-vations? There are times when the smallest dose of a drug can have a
sublime effect on someone, while at another time it takes ten times the
dose to have any noticeable effect. These are tough problems to quantify
and study, even in the laboratory.

Q: To what extent is the addictive factor affected by education? Here is   49
what I mean by this: Taking a drug, say heroin or cocaine or crack—or,
for that matter, alcohol—is a form of Russian roulette, using a ten-car-tridge revolver. Now, presumably, an educated person, concerned for his
livelihood, wouldn't take a revolver with nine empty cartridges and one
full cartridge, aim it at his head, and pull the trigger. But granted, deci-sions of that kind are based on ratiocinative skills. And we have to
assume these skills don't exist even among college students. If they did,
there would be no drinking in college, let alone drug taking. Comments?

A: Most people perceive themselves as in control of their destiny. They   50
do not think the initial exposure will ruin their lives, because of their per-ceived self-control, and they are right. Take the most difficult case,
tobacco—the most highly addictive substance around. In a now classic
study, Stanley Schachter of Columbia University formally surveyed his

highly educated colleagues at Columbia. At the same time, he polled the working residents of Amagansett, a community on Long Island where he summered. He first determined who were ongoing smokers, and who had been smokers. He took into account how long they had smoked, what they had smoked, and all other variables he could think of.

It wasn't long before the picture began to crystallize. Inform a normally   51
intelligent group of people about the tangible hazards of using a particular substance and the vast majority of them simply stop. It wasn't easy for
some, but in general they stopped, and they didn't need treatment programs, support programs, and all the rest. Dr. Schachter concluded,
after this study, that it is only the thorny cases that show up at the treatment centers, people who have developed a true addiction. For those
people, psychological prophylactics, including education, are of little or
no value. Yet it is these people that are held up as examples of what happens when one uses drugs. This is misleading. It creates an unworkable
framework for thinking about the problem. Most people can voluntarily
stop using a psychoactive substance, and those people who do continue
to use it can moderate their intake to reduce the possibility of health hazards. This is true, as I say, for most substances, but I repeat, less true for
tobacco because of its distinctively addictive nature. The people who
unwisely continue to use tobacco tend to smoke themselves into major
illness even though they are amply warned that this is likely to happen.

Q: So no matter how widely you spread the message, it is in fact going   52
to be ignored, both by PhDs and by illiterates?

A: If they are real abusers, yes. That is the reason for the high recidi-   53
vism rate among graduates of drug treatment centers. Here we are talking about the true addicts. Education appears not to help the recalcitrant
abusers, who are the ones that keep showing up at health centers.

Yet, manifestly, education contributes to keeping the abuse rate as low   54
as it is. I think the message gets to the ghetto, but where there are other
problems—the need for an artificial reward—drugs are going to be taken
by many people because the excruciating pain of a current condition
overrides long-term reason. In short, the ghetto citizen or the psychologically isolated person might well decide that the probability of living a better life is low, so grab some rewards while you can.

Q: At what level of intelligence is a potential drug user influenced to   55
take a less dangerous, rather than a more dangerous, drug? I mean, if it
were known to all PhDs that crack was more dangerous than marijuana,
that the small percentage who became addicted to crack would suffer
greater biological change from it, up to and including death, in contrast
to comparatively lenient sentences from addiction to marijuana, what
percentage of PhDs would be influenced to stay away from the hard stuff,
compared to illiterate 17-year-old ghetto dwellers?

A: Again, this is difficult to answer because the educational message   56
interacts with innumerable social problems. For example, drug abuse is
three times greater among the unemployed. Someone who is unem-

ployed on Monday might be re-employed on Friday, and this may stop, or reduce, his use of drugs. Gainful employment has a bigger effect in a case like this than education does. But in general, education plays a big role, and this is established. Remember, we are a health-oriented society, and we do care about our bodies and minds, by and large. Marijuana is a mild drug, compared to crack, for a variety of biological and psychological reasons. There are studies showing that casual-to-moderate cocaine users will not go the crack route because of fear of a greater chance of addiction or of an immediate physiological crisis. A recent issue of the *New England Journal of Medicine* reports that cocaine use contributes to heart disease in a rather muted way. However, crack may have a far greater impact and be responsible for a much more serious increase in drug-related heart failures. Does that kind of thing influence a kid in the ghetto? I think the message does get there. It certainly gets to Park Avenue first, however.

Q: In that case, education, even in the popular media, is likely to influ- 57
ence primarily the educated classes. That has to mean that the unedu-
cated class will suffer more addiction than the educated class.

A: Well, again, people in the lowest socio-economic status will con- 58
tinue to consume more drugs, but that doesn't change the addiction
rate. Still, legalization shouldn't change the current figures, since drugs
are literally available everywhere in the ghetto. They are also available on
every college campus. They are available in prisons! I suppose if one
wants to conjure up fresh problems brought on by legalization, they will
center on the folks living on Park Avenue, where drugs are less easily
secured, not the ghetto. Legalization of drugs would reduce crime in the
ghetto, and much that is positive would follow.

Q: If the number of addicts would be increased by decriminalization, is 59
the trade-off worth it? Is it wise to decriminalize, even if by doing so: we
a) abort the $150-billion per-year drug-crime business; b) release $10 billion in federal money now going to the pursuit of drug merchants; c) end
the corruption of government subsidized by drug dealers; and d) come
upon a huge sum of money available to give treatment to addicts? Is this,
in your judgment, a moral recommendation to make, given our knowledge of the psychological problems we are talking about?

A: Are you asking me to commit myself at this point to the question of 60
whether that trade-off is wise?

Q: Well, no, not quite yet. Let me describe a situation, the concrete sit- 61
uation I spoke of a while ago, and ask you to comment on it in the light
of the questions put to you above.

Suppose that drugs were made available. All of them, legally, in a Fed- 62
eral Drugstore. But above each of the common drugs—crack, cocaine,
heroin, hash, marijuana, amphetamines, LSD, etc.—there was a graphic
description of what addiction to that drug would do to you. Suppose a
situation in which, for instance, over the punch bowl at the far left of the
counter that contained crack were written: "This drug will create an

and new tax revenues). Street users would be picked up and taken to hospitals, like drunks, instead of arrested.

Legalization would lead to an immediate decrease in murders, bur-   23
glaries and robberies, paralleling the end of alcohol prohibition in 1933. Cheap drugs would mean that most addicts would not be driven to crime to support their habit, and that drug lords would no longer have a turf to fight over. Legalization would be a blow to South American peasants, who would need support in switching back to less lucrative crops, but that would be less devastating than destruction of their crops altogether by aerial spraying or biological warfare. Legalization would enable coun- tries like Peru to regularize the cocaine sector and absorb its money- making capacity in the taxable, legal, unionized economic world. Legal- ization would be a blow to ghetto dealers, who would be deprived of their ticket to riches. It would remove glamorous, Al Capone–type traffickers who are role models for the young, and it would destroy the "cool" status of drug use. It would cancel the corrupting role of the drug cartels in South American politics, a powerful incentive to corruption at all levels of our own government and a dangerous threat to our civil liberties through mistaken enforcement and property confiscation. It would free law- enforcement agencies to focus on other crimes and reduce the strain on the court and prison systems. It would nip in the bud a multibillion-dollar bureaucracy whose prosperity depends on *not* solving the drug probe. It would remove a major cause of public cynicism about obeying the laws of the land.

Legalization would also free up money wasted on interdiction of sup-   24
plies that are needed desperately for treatment, education and research. Clinics in New York have room for only 48,000 of the state's estimated half-million addicts. Only $700 million has been earmarked by the Bush administration for treatment, out of a total expenditure of $8 billion for the drug war. Yet nationally, approximately 90 percent of the addicts who apply to drug treatment and rehabilitation centers are turned away for lack of space, resources and personnel. For those who do persist, the waiting period is six to 18 months. Even then, one-third to one-half of drug abusers turned away do reapply after waiting the extended time.

The worst prospect of legalization is that it might lead to a short-term   25
increase in the use of drugs, due to availability, lower prices and the sud- den freedom from prosecution. The repeal of Prohibition had that result. Drugs cheap enough to destroy their profitability would also be in the range of any child's allowance, just like beer and cigarettes. Cocaine is easily concealable and its effects less overt than alcohol. The possibility of increased teenage use is admittedly frightening.

On the other hand, ending the drug war would free drug control offi-   26
cers to concentrate on protecting children from exploitation, and here stiff penalties would continue to be in effect. The alarmist prediction that cheap available drugs could lead to an addiction rate of 75 percent of regular users simply ignores the fact that 35 to 40 million Americans are

already using some drugs and that only 3 percent become addicts. Most people have strong reasons *not* to become addicts. A major educational program would need to be in effect well before drug legalization took effect.

Fighting the drug war may appear to hold the high moral ground, but this is only an illusion. And while some have argued that legalization would place the state's moral imprimatur on drugs, we have already legalized the most lethal drugs—and no one argues that this constitutes governmental endorsement. But legalizing would indeed imply that drugs are no longer being satanized like "demon rum." It's time we bit the bullet. Addicts will be healed by care and compassion, not condemnation. Dealers will be cured by a ruined world drug market, not by enforcement that simply escalates the profitability of drugs. Legalization offers a nonviolent, nonreactive, creative alternative that will let the drug menace collapse of its own deadly weight.

27

■

THE ECONOMICS OF LEGALIZING DRUGS

Richard J. Dennis

Conducting a cost/benefit analysis of drug legalization, Dennis concludes that "[t]o the pragmatist, the choice is clear: legalization is the best bet." It seems doubtful that making most drugs legal would significantly increase the number of addicts but certain that it would reduce crime and save society money.

Last year federal agents in southern California broke the six-dollar lock on a warehouse and discovered twenty tons of cocaine. The raid was reported to be the largest seizure of illegal narcotics ever. Politicians and law-enforcement officials heralded it as proof not only of the severity of our drug problem but also of the success of our interdiction efforts, and the need for more of the same. However, in reality the California raid was evidence of nothing but the futility and irrationality of our current approach to illegal drugs. It is questionable whether the raid prevented a single person from buying cocaine. Addicts were not driven to seek treatment. No drug lord or street dealer was put out of business. The event had no perceptible impact on the public's attitude toward drug use. People who wanted cocaine still wanted it—and got it.

1

If the raid had any effect at all, it was perverse. The street price of cocaine in southern California probably rose temporarily, further enriching the criminal network now terrorizing the nation's inner cities. William Bennett, the director of national drug-control policy, and his fellow moral authoritarians were offered another opportunity to alarm an already overwrought public with a fresh gust of rhetoric. New support was given to a Bush Administration plan that is meant to reduce supply but in fact

2

drug was legalized, would plummet. This leaves us with approximately 7.5 million new cocaine users. How many of them could we expect to become cocaine addicts? The estimate that there are now one million cocaine addicts suggests a one-in-thirty chance of addiction through experimentation. Thus from the 7.5 million new users we could expect about 250,000 new addicts, or an increase of 25 percent over the number of cocaine addicts that we now have. We can assume about the same increase in the number of users of other hard drugs.

28   Those who argue that wide availability must mean significantly higher usage overlook the fact that there is no economic incentive for dealers to push dirt-cheap drugs. Legalization might thus lead to less rather than more drug use, particularly by children and teenagers. Also, the public evinces little interest in trying legalized drugs. Last year, at the direction of the author, the polling firm Targeting Systems Inc., in Arlington, Virginia, asked a nationwide sample of 600 adults, "If cocaine were legalized, would you personally consider purchasing it or not?" Only one percent said they would.

29   *The drug war will result in a 25 percent decrease in drug use.* That's the midpoint in William Bennett's ten-year plan to cut drug use by 50 percent by the year 2000. Since this figure is based on Bennett's official prediction, we might expect it to be highly optimistic. But to demonstrate the enormous benefits of legalization, let's accept his rosy scenario.

30   *The drug war will cost government at all levels $30 billion a year.* Keeping drugs illegal costs state and local law-enforcement agencies approximately $10 billion a year—a conservative figure derived from the costs of arresting, prosecuting, and imprisoning several hundred thousand people a year for drug violations. Bennett recently implied before Congress that state governments will need to spend as much as $10 billion in new money when he was asked about what it will cost to keep in prison a higher proportion of the country's 20 million or more users of hard and soft drugs. The drug war will also cost the federal government about $10 billion a year, mostly in law enforcement—about what Congress has agreed to spend in the next fiscal year.

31   If marijuana and cocaine were legalized and crack and all drugs for children remained illegal, about 80 percent of current illegal drug use would become legal. This would permit savings of 80 percent—or $8 billion—of the current costs of state and local law enforcement. By rolling back the war on drugs, we could save up to all $20 billion of projected new federal and state expenditures.

32   *The current dollar volume of the drug trade is approximately $100 billion a year.* If Bennett's prediction is accurate and drug consumption is cut by half over the next ten years, Colombian drug lords will still receive, on average, $3.75 billion a year, assuming that they net five percent of gross receipts—a conservative estimate. The money reaped by drug lords can be used for weapons, planes, and bombs, which could

necessitate U.S. expenditures of at least one dollar to combat every dollar of drug profits if a drug war turned into real fighting.

If legalized, taxed drugs were sold for a seventh or an eighth of their   33
current price—a level low enough for illegal dealing to be financially unattractive—the taxes could bring in at least $10 billion at the current level of usage.

The most important—and most loosely defined—variable is the   34
social cost of drug use. The term "social cost" is used indiscriminately. A narrow definition includes only health costs and taxes lost to the government through loss of income, and a broad definition counts other factors, such as the loss of personal income itself and the value of stolen property associated with drug use. The Alcohol, Drug Abuse, and Mental Health Administration has estimated that drug and alcohol abuse cost the nation as much as $175 billion a year, of which alcohol abuse alone accounts for at least $115 billion. These figures probably include costs not really related to drug use, as a result of the Administration's zeal to dramatize the drug crisis. We will assume that $50 billion a year is a realistic estimate of the share for drug use.

Once these usually qualitative factors have been assigned numbers, it   35
is possible to estimate how much the drug war costs in an average year and how much drug peace might save us. Again, this assumes that 25 percent fewer people in a mid-point year will use drugs owing to a successful drug war and 25 percent more people will use drugs with the establishment of drug peace.

If we choose drug peace as opposed to drug war, we'll save $10 billion   36
a year in federal law enforcement, $10 billion a year in new state and local prosecution, about $8 billion a year in other law-enforcement costs (80 percent of the current $10 billion a year), about $6 billion a year in the value of stolen property associated with drug use (80 percent of the current $7.5 billion), and $3.75 billion a year by eliminating the need to match the Colombians' drug profits dollar for dollar. We'll also benefit from taxes of $12.5 billion. These social gains amount to $50.25 billion.

If use rises 25 percent, instead of declining by that amount, it will   37
result in a social cost of $25 billion (50 percent of $50 billion). Therefore, the net social gain of drug peace is $25.25 billion. If legalization resulted in an immediate and permanent increase in use of more than 25 percent, the benefits of drug peace would narrow. But additional tax revenue would partly make up for the shrinkage. For example, if the increase in use was 50 percent instead of 25 percent, that would add another $12.5 billion in social costs per year but would contribute another $2.5 billion in tax revenue.

At the rate at which those numbers converge, almost a 100 percent   38
increase in the number of addicts would be required before the net benefits of drug peace equaled zero. This would seem to be a worst-case scenario. But to the drug warriors, any uncertainty is an opportunity to fan

the flames of fear. Last year Bennett wrote, in *The Wall Street Journal,* "Of course, no one . . . can say with certainty what would happen in the U.S. if drugs were suddenly to become a readily purchased product. We do know, however, that whenever drugs have been cheaper and more easily obtained, drug use—and addiction—have skyrocketed." Bennett cited two examples to prove his thesis: a fortyfold increase in the number of heroin addicts in Great Britain since the drug began to be legally pre-scribed there, and a 350 percent increase in alcohol consumption in the United States after Prohibition.

In fact experts are far from certain about the outcome of the British   39
experiment. The statistics on the increase in the number of drug abusers are unreliable. All that is known is that a significant rise in the number of addicts seeking treatment took place. Moreover, according to some esti-mates, Britain has approximately sixty-two addicts or regular users of heroin per 100,000 population (for a total of 30,000 to 35,000), while the United States has 209 heroin addicts or users per 100,000 population, for a total of 500,000. And very few British heroin addicts engage in seri-ous crime, unlike heroin addicts in America. Bennett's criticism notwith-standing, the British apparently have broken the link between heroin addiction and violent crime.

As for Prohibition, its effects were hardly as dramatic as Bennett   40
implied. During 1916–1919 per capita consumption of pure alcohol among the U.S. drinking-age population was 1.96 gallons a year; during Prohibition it dropped to 0.90 gallons; after Repeal, during 1936–1941, it went up about 70 percent, to 1.54 gallons.

And how does Bennett explain the experience of the Netherlands,   41
where the decriminalization of drugs has resulted in decreased use? Does he think that what made all the difference in Holland is the fact that it has a smaller underclass than we do? In essence, the Dutch policy involves vigorous enforcement against dealers of hard drugs, official tolerance of soft drugs such as marijuana and hashish, and decriminalization of all users. The number of marijuana users began decreasing shortly after the Dutch government decriminalized marijuana, in 1976. In 1984 about four percent of Dutch young people age ten to eighteen reported having smoked marijuana—roughly a third the rate among minors in the United States. In Amsterdam the number of heroin addicts has declined from 9,000 in 1984 to fewer than 6,000 today. Over that same period the aver-age age of addicts has risen from twenty-six to thirty-one, indicating that few new users have taken up the habit. And there is no evidence that crack has made inroads among Dutch addicts, in contrast to its preva-lence in America.

Amsterdam is a capital city close in size (population 695,000), if not in   42
culture and economic demographics, to Washington, D.C. (population 604,000). Amsterdam had forty-six homicides last year, of which perhaps 30 percent were related to the drug trade. Washington had 438 homi-cides, 60 to 80 percent of which were drug related. The rate of homi-

cides per 100,000 population was 6.6 in Amsterdam, less than a tenth the rate of 72.5 in Washington.

Holland's strategy is one of only two that have been shown to cause a real decline in drug use. The other is Singapore's, which consists of imposing the death penalty on people caught in possession of as little as fifteen grams of heroin. If this is Bennett's fallback position, perhaps he should say so explicitly. 43

SOME OBJECTIONS CONSIDERED

The fear that legalization would lead to increased drug use and addiction is not, of course, the only basis on which legalization is opposed. We should address other frequently heard objections here. 44

Crack is our No. 1 drug problem. Legalizing other drugs while crack remains illegal won't solve the problem. Although crack has captured the lion's share of public attention, marijuana has always commanded the bulk of law-enforcement interest. Despite de facto urban decriminalization, more than a third of all drug arrests occur in connection with marijuana—mostly for mere possession. Three fourths of all violations of drug laws relate to marijuana, and two thirds of all people charged with violation of federal marijuana laws are sentenced to prison (state figures are not available). 45

Crack appears to account for about 10 percent of the total dollar volume of the drug trade, according to National Institute on Drug Abuse estimates of the number of regular crack users. Legalizing other drugs would free up most of the law-enforcement resources currently focused on less dangerous substances and their users. It's true that as long as crack remains illegal, there will be a black market and associated crime. But we would still reap most of the benefits of legalization outlined above. 46

Legalization would result in a huge loss in productivity and in higher health-care costs. In truth, productivity lost to drugs is minor compared with productivity lost to alcohol and cigarettes, which remain legal. Hundreds of variables affect a person's job performance, ranging from the consumption of whiskey and cigarettes to obesity and family problems. On a purely statistical level it can be demonstrated that marital status affects productivity, yet we do not allow employers to dismiss workers on the basis of that factor. 47

If legal drug use resulted in higher social costs, the government could levy a tax on the sale of drugs in some rough proportion to the monetary value of those costs—as it does now for alcohol and cigarettes. This wouldn't provide the government with a financial stake in addiction. Rather, the government would be making sure that users of socially costly items paid those social costs. Funds from the tax on decriminalized drugs could be used for anti-drug advertising, which could be made more effective by a total ban on drug advertising. A government that 48

a matter of economics, the prohibition of drug use imposes costs on society that far exceed the benefits. Others, such as the psychoanalyst Thomas Szasz, made the same argument.

We did not take Friedman's advice. (Government commissions rarely   3
do.) I do not recall that we even discussed legalizing heroin, though we did discuss (but did not take action on) legalizing a drug, cocaine, that many people then argued was benign. Our marching orders were to figure out how to win the war on heroin, not to run up the white flag of surrender.

That was 1972. Today, we have the same number of heroin addicts   4
that we had then—half a million, give or take a few thousand. Having that many heroin addicts is no trivial matter; these people deserve our attention. But not having had an increase in that number for over fifteen years is also something that deserves our attention. What happened to the "heroin epidemic" that many people once thought would overwhelm us?

The facts are clear: a more or less stable pool of heroin addicts has   5
been getting older, with relatively few new recruits. In 1976 the average age of heroin users who appeared in hospital emergency rooms was about twenty-seven; ten years later it was thirty-two. More than two-thirds of all heroin users appearing in emergency rooms are now over the age of thirty. Back in the early 1970's, when heroin got onto the national political agenda, the typical heroin addict was much younger, often a teenager. Household surveys show the same thing—the rate of opiate use (which includes heroin) has been flat for the better part of two decades. More fine-grained studies of inner-city neighborhoods confirm this. John Boyle and Ann Brunswick found that the percentage of young blacks in Harlem who used heroin fell from 8 percent in 1970–71 to about 3 percent in 1975–76.

Why did heroin lose its appeal for young people? When the young   6
blacks in Harlem were asked why they stopped, more than half mentioned "trouble with the law" or "high cost" (and high cost is, of course, directly the result of law enforcement). Two-thirds said that heroin hurt their health; nearly all said they had had a bad experience with it. We need not rely, however, simply on what they said. In New York City in 1973–75, the street price of heroin rose dramatically and its purity sharply declined, probably as a result of the heroin shortage caused by the success of the Turkish government in reducing the supply of opium base and of the French government in closing down heroin-processing laboratories located in and around Marseilles. These were short-lived gains for, just as Friedman predicted, alternative sources of supply—mostly in Mexico—quickly emerged. But the three-year heroin shortage interrupted the easy recruitment of new users.

Health and related problems were no doubt part of the reason for the   7
reduced flow of recruits. Over the preceding years, Harlem youth had watched as more and more heroin users died of overdoses, were poi-

soned by adulterated doses, or acquired hepatitis from dirty needles. The word got around: heroin can kill you. By 1974 new hepatitis cases and drug-overdose deaths had dropped to a fraction of what they had been in 1970.

Alas, treatment did not seem to explain much of the cessation in drug   8
use. Treatment programs can and do help heroin addicts, but treatment did not explain the drop in the number of *new* users (who by definition had never been in treatment) or even much of the reduction in the number of experienced users.

No one knows how much of the decline to attribute to personal obser-   9
vation as opposed to high prices or reduced supply. But other evidence suggests strongly that price and supply played a large role. In 1972 the National Advisory Council was especially worried by the prospect that U.S. servicemen returning to this country from Vietnam would bring their heroin habits with them. Fortunately, a brilliant study by Lee Robins of Washington University in St. Louis put that fear to rest. She measured drug use of Vietnam veterans shortly after they had returned home. Though many had used heroin regularly while in Southeast Asia, most gave up the habit when back in the United States. The reason: here, heroin was less available and sanctions on its use were more pronounced. Of course, if a veteran had been willing to pay enough—which might have meant traveling to another city and would certainly have meant making an illegal contact with a disreputable dealer in a threatening neighborhood in order to acquire a (possibly) dangerous dose—he could have sustained his drug habit. Most veterans were unwilling to pay this price, and so their drug use declined or disappeared.

RELIVING THE PAST

Suppose we had taken Friedman's advice in 1972. What would have   10
happened? We cannot be entirely certain, but at a minimum we would have placed the young heroin addicts (and, above all, the prospective addicts) in a very different position from the one in which they actually found themselves. Heroin would have been legal. Its price would have been reduced by 95 percent (minus whatever we chose to recover in taxes). Now that it could be sold by the same people who make aspirin, its quality would have been assured—no poisons, no adulterants. Sterile hypodermic needles would have been readily available at the neighborhood drugstore, probably at the same counter where the heroin was sold. No need to travel to big cities or unfamiliar neighborhoods—heroin could have been purchased anywhere, perhaps by mail order.

There would no longer have been any financial or medical reason to   11
avoid heroin use. Anybody could have afforded it. We might have tried to prevent children from buying it, but as we have learned from our efforts to prevent minors from buying alcohol and tobacco, young people have a way of penetrating markets theoretically reserved for adults. Returning

hundred people, how well would the American civil service have accomplished the same tasks when dealing with tens of thousands of people?

BACK TO THE FUTURE

Now cocaine, especially in its potent form, crack, is the focus of attention. Now as in 1972 the government is trying to reduce its use. Now as then some people are advocating legalization. Is there any more reason to yield to those arguments today than there was almost two decades ago?[1]   20

I think not. If we had yielded in 1972 we almost certainly would have had today a permanent population of several million, not several hundred thousand, heroin addicts. If we yield now we will have a far more serious problem with cocaine.   21

Crack is worse than heroin by almost any measure. Heroin produces a pleasant drowsiness and, if hygienically administered, has only the physical side effects of constipation and sexual impotence. Regular heroin use incapacitates many users, especially poor ones, for any productive work or social responsibility. They will sit nodding on a street corner, helpless but at least harmless. By contrast, regular cocaine use leaves the user neither helpless nor harmless. When smoked (as with crack) or injected, cocaine produces instant, intense, and short-lived euphoria. The experience generates a powerful desire to repeat it. If the drug is readily available, repeat use will occur. Those people who progress to "bingeing" on cocaine become devoted to the drug and its effects to the exclusion of almost all other considerations—job, family, children, sleep, food, even sex. Dr. Frank Gawin at Yale and Dr. Everett Ellinwood at Duke report that a substantial percentage of all high-dose, binge users become uninhibited, impulsive, hypersexual, compulsive, irritable, and hyperactive. Their moods vacillate dramatically, leading at times to violence and homicide.   22

Women are much more likely to use crack than heroin, and if they are pregnant, the effects on their babies are tragic. Douglas Besharov, who has been following the effects of drugs on infants for twenty years, writes that nothing he learned about heroin prepared him for the devastation of cocaine. Cocaine harms the fetus and can lead to physical deformities or neurological damage. Some crack babies have for all practical purposes suffered a disabling stroke while still in the womb. The long-term consequences of this brain damage are lowered cognitive ability and the onset of mood disorders. Besharov estimates that about 30,000 to 50,000 such babies are born every year, about 7,000 in New York City alone. There may be ways to treat such infants, but from everything we now know the treatment will be long, difficult, and expensive. Worse, the   23

---

[1] I do not here take up the question of marijuana. For a variety of reasons—its widespread use and its lesser tendency to addict—it presents a different problem from cocaine or heroin. For a penetrating analysis, see Mark Kleiman, *Marijuana: Costs of Abuse, Costs of Control* (Greenwood Press, 217 pp., $37.95).

mothers who are most likely to produce crack babies are precisely the ones who, because of poverty or temperament, are least able and willing to obtain such treatment. In fact, anecdotal evidence suggests that crack mothers are likely to abuse their infants.

The notion that abusing drugs such as cocaine is a "victimless crime"   24
is not only absurd but dangerous. Even ignoring the fetal drug syndrome, crack-dependent people are, like heroin addicts, individuals who regularly victimize their children by neglect, their spouses by improvidence, their employers by lethargy, and their coworkers by carelessness. Society is not and could never be a collection of autonomous individuals. We have a stake in ensuring that each of us displays a minimal level of dignity, responsibility, and empathy. We cannot, of course, coerce people into goodness, but we can and should insist that some standards must be met if society itself—on which the very existence of the human personality depends—is to persist. Drawing the line that defines those standards is difficult and contentious, but if crack and heroin use do not fall below it, what does?

The advocates of legalization will respond by suggesting that my pic-   25
ture is overdrawn. Ethan Nadelmann of Princeton argues that the risk of legalization is less than most people suppose. Over 20 million Americans between the ages of eighteen and twenty-five have tried cocaine (according to a government survey), but only a quarter million use it daily. From this Nadelmann concludes that at most 3 percent of all young people who try cocaine develop a problem with it. The implication is clear: make the drug legal and we only have to worry about 3 percent of our youth.

The implication rests on a logical fallacy and a factual error. The fal-   26
lacy is this: the percentage of occasional cocaine users who become binge users *when the drug is illegal* (and thus expensive and hard to find) tells us nothing about the percentage who will become dependent when the drug is legal (and thus cheap and abundant). Drs. Gawin and Ellinwood report, in common with several other researchers, that controlled or occasional use of cocaine changes to compulsive and frequent use "when access to the drug increases" or when the user switches from snorting to smoking. More cocaine more potently administered alters, perhaps sharply, the proportion of "controlled" users who become heavy users.

The factual error is this: the federal survey Nadelmann quotes was   27
done in 1985, *before* crack had become common. Thus the probability of becoming dependent on cocaine was derived from the responses of users who snorted the drug. The speed and potency of cocaine's action increases dramatically when it is smoked. We do not yet know how greatly the advent of crack increases the risk of dependency, but all the clinical evidence suggests that the increase is likely to be large.

It is possible that some people will not become heavy users even when   28
the drug is readily available in its most potent form. So far there are no scientific grounds for predicting who will and who will not become

dependent. Neither socio-economic background nor personality traits differentiate between casual and intensive users. Thus, the only way to settle the question of who is correct about the effect of easy availability on drug use, Nadelmann or Gawin and Ellinwood, is to try it and see. But that social experiment is so risky as to be no experiment at all, for if cocaine is legalized and if the rate of its abusive use increases dramatically, there is no way to put the genie back in the bottle, and it is not a kindly genie.

HAVE WE LOST?

Many people who agree that there are risks in legalizing cocaine or heroin still favor it because, they think, we have lost the war on drugs. "Nothing we have done has worked" and the current federal policy is just "more of the same." Whatever the costs of greater drug use, surely they would be less than the costs of our present, failed efforts.   29

That is exactly what I was told in 1972—and heroin is not quite as bad a drug as cocaine. We did not surrender and we did not lose. We did not win, either. What the nation accomplished then was what most efforts to save people from themselves accomplish: the problem was contained and the number of victims minimized, all at a considerable cost in law enforcement and increased crime. Was the cost worth it? I think so, but others may disagree. What are the lives of would-be addicts worth? I recall some people saying to me then, "Let them kill themselves." I was appalled. Happily, such views did not prevail.   30

Have we lost today? Not at all. High-rate cocaine use is not commonplace. The National Institute of Drug Abuse (NIDA) reports that less than 5 percent of high-school seniors used cocaine within the last thirty days. Of course this survey misses young people who have dropped out of school and miscounts those who lie on the questionnaire, but even if we inflate the NIDA estimate by some plausible percentage, it is still not much above 5 percent. Medical examiners reported in 1987 that about 1,500 died from cocaine use: hospital emergency rooms reported about 30,000 admissions related to cocaine abuse.   31

These are not small numbers, but neither are they evidence of a nationwide plague that threatens to engulf us all. Moreover, cities vary greatly in the proportion of people who are involved with cocaine. To get city-level data we need to turn to drug tests carried out on arrested persons, who obviously are more likely to be drug users than the average citizen. The National Institute of Justice, through its Drug Use Forecasting (DUF) project, collects urinalysis data on arrestees in 22 cities. As we have already seen, opiate (chiefly heroin) use has been flat or declining in most of these cities over the last decade. Cocaine use has gone up sharply, but with great variation among cities. New York, Philadelphia, and Washington, D.C., all report that two-thirds or more of their arrestees tested positive for cocaine, but in Portland, San Antonio, and Indianapolis the percentage was one-third or less.   32

In some neighborhoods, of course, matters have reached crisis pro- 33
portions. Gangs control the streets, shootings terrorize residents, and
drug-dealing occurs in plain view. The police seem barely able to contain
matters. But in these neighborhoods—unlike at Palo Alto cocktail parties—the people are not calling for legalization, they are calling for help.
And often not much help has come. Many cities are willing to do almost
anything about the drug problem except spend more money on it. The
federal government cannot change that; only local voters and politicians
can. It is not clear that they will.

It took about ten years to contain heroin. We have had experience with 34
crack for only about three or four years. Each year we spend perhaps
$11 billion on law enforcement (and some of that goes to deal with mari-
juana) and perhaps $2 billion on treatment. Large sums, but not sums
that should lead anyone to say, "We just can't afford this any more."

The illegality of drugs increases crime, partly because some users turn 35
to crime to pay for their habits, partly because some users are stimulated
by certain drugs (such as crack or PCP) to act more violently or ruthlessly
than they otherwise would, and partly because criminal organizations
seeking to control drug supplies use force to manage their markets.
These also are serious costs, but no one knows how much they would be
reduced if drugs were legalized. Addicts would no longer steal to pay
black-market prices for drugs, a real gain. But some, perhaps a great
deal, of that gain would be offset by the great increase in the number of
addicts. These people, nodding on heroin or living in the delusion-ridden
high of cocaine, would hardly be ideal employees. Many would steal simply to support themselves, since snatch-and-grab, opportunistic crime
can be managed even by people unable to hold a regular job or plan an
elaborate crime. Those British addicts who get their supplies from government clinics are not models of law-abiding decency. Most are in
crime, and though their per-capita rate of criminality may be lower
thanks to the cheapness of their drugs, the total volume of crime they
produce may be quite large. Of course, society could decide to support
all unemployable addicts on welfare, but that would mean that gains
from lowered rates of crime would have to be offset by large increases in
welfare budgets.

Proponents of legalization claim that the costs of having more addicts 36
around would be largely if not entirely offset by having more money available with which to treat and care for them. The money would come from
taxes levied on the sale of heroin and cocaine.

To obtain this fiscal dividend, however, legalization's supporters must 37
first solve an economic dilemma. If they want to raise a lot of money to
pay for welfare and treatment, the tax rate on the drugs will have to be
quite high. Even if they themselves do not want a high rate, the politicians' love of "sin taxes" would probably guarantee that it would be high
anyway. But the higher the tax, the higher the price of the drug, and the
higher the price the greater the likelihood that addicts will turn to crime

to find the money for it and that criminal organizations will be formed to sell tax-free drugs at below-market rates. If we managed to keep taxes (and thus prices) low, we would get that much less money to pay for welfare and treatment and more people could afford to become addicts. There may be an optimal tax rate for drugs that maximizes revenue while minimizing crime, bootlegging, and the recruitment of new addicts, but our experience with alcohol does not suggest that we know how to find it.

THE BENEFITS OF ILLEGALITY

The advocates of legalization find nothing to be said in favor of the current system except, possibly, that it keeps the number of addicts smaller than it would otherwise be. In fact, the benefits are more substantial than that.   38

First, treatment. All the talk about providing "treatment on demand" implies that there is a demand for treatment. That is not quite right. There are some drug-dependent people who genuinely want treatment and will remain in it if offered; they should receive it. But there are far more who want only short-term help after a bad crash: once stabilized and bathed, they are back on the street again, hustling. And even many of the addicts who enroll in a program honestly wanting help drop out after a short while when they discover that help takes time and commitment. Drug-dependent people have very short time horizons and a weak capacity for commitment. These two groups—those looking for a quick fix and those unable to stick with a long-term fix—are not easily helped. Even if we increase the number of treatment slots—as we should—we would have to do something to make treatment more effective.   39

One thing that can often make it more effective is compulsion. Douglas Anglin of UCLA, in common with many other researchers, has found that the longer one stays in a treatment program, the better the chances of a reduction in drug dependency. But he, again like most other researchers, has found that drop-out rates are high. He has also found, however, that patients who enter treatment under legal compulsion stay in the program longer than those not subject to such pressure. His research on the California civil-commitment program, for example, found that heroin users involved with its required drug-testing program had over the long term a lower rate of heroin use than similar addicts who were free of such constraints. If for many addicts compulsion is a useful component of treatment, it is not clear how compulsion could be achieved in a society in which purchasing, possessing, and using the drug were legal. It could be managed, I suppose, but I would not want to have to answer the challenge from the American Civil Liberties Union that it is wrong to compel a person to undergo treatment for consuming a legal commodity.   40

Next, education. We are now investing substantially in drug-education programs in the schools. Though we do not yet know for certain what   41 will work, there are some promising leads. But I wonder how credible such programs would be if they were aimed as dissuading children from doing something perfectly legal. We could, of course, treat drug education like smoking education: inhaling crack and inhaling tobacco are both legal, but you should not do it because it is bad for you. That tobacco is bad for you is easily shown; the Surgeon General has seen to that. But what do we say about crack? It is pleasurable, but devoting yourself to so much pleasure is not a good idea (though perfectly legal)? Unlike tobacco, cocaine will not give you cancer or emphysema, but it will lead you to neglect your duties to family, job, and neighborhood? Everybody is doing cocaine, but you should not?

Again, it might be possible under a legalized regime to have effective   42
drug-prevention programs, but their effectiveness would depend heavily, I think, on first having decided that cocaine use, like tobacco use, is purely a matter of practical consequences; no fundamental moral significance attaches to either. But if we believe—as I do—that dependency on certain mind-altering drugs *is* a moral issue and that their illegality rests in part on their immorality, then legalizing them undercuts, if it does not eliminate altogether, the moral message.

That message is at the root of the distinction we now make between   43
nicotine and cocaine. Both are highly addictive; both have harmful physical effects. But we treat the two drugs differently, not simply because nicotine is so widely used as to be beyond the reach of effective prohibition, but because its use does not destroy the user's essential humanity. Tobacco shortens one's life, cocaine debases it. Nicotine alters one's habits, cocaine alters one's soul. The heavy use of crack, unlike the heavy use of tobacco, corrodes those natural sentiments of sympathy and duty that constitute our human nature and make possible our social life. To say, as does Nadelmann, that distinguishing morally between tobacco and cocaine is "little more than a transient prejudice" is close to saying that morality itself is but a prejudice.

THE ALCOHOL PROBLEM

Now we have arrived where many arguments about legalizing drugs   44
begin: is there any reason to treat heroin and cocaine differently from the way we treat alcohol?

There is no easy answer to that question because, as with so many   45
human problems, one cannot decide simply on the basis either of moral principle or of individual consequences; one has to temper any policy by a common-sense judgment of what is possible. Alcohol, like heroin, cocaine, PCP, and marijuana, is a drug—that is, a mood-altering substance—and consumed to excess it certainly has harmful consequences: auto accidents, barroom fights, bedroom shootings. It is also, for some people, addictive. We cannot confidently compare the addictive powers of these drugs, but the best evidence suggests that crack and heroin are much more addictive than alcohol.

Many people, Nadelmann included, argue that since the health and   46
financial costs of alcohol abuse are so much higher than those of
cocaine or heroin abuse, it is hypocritical folly to devote our efforts to
preventing cocaine or drug use. But as Mark Kleiman of Harvard has
pointed out, this comparison is quite misleading. What Nadelmann is
doing is showing that a *legalized* drug (alcohol) produces greater social
harm than *illegal* ones (cocaine and heroin). But of course. Suppose
that in the 1920's we had made heroin and cocaine legal and alcohol illegal. Can anyone doubt that Nadelmann would not be writing that it is
folly to continue our ban on alcohol because cocaine and heroin are so
much more harmful?

And let there be no doubt about it—widespread heroin and cocaine   47
use are associated with all manner of ills. Thomas Bewley found that the
mortality rate of British heroin addicts in 1968 was 28 times as high as
the death rate of the same age group of non-addicts, even though in
England at the time an addict could obtain free or low-cost heroin and
clean needles from British clinics. Perform the following mental experiment: suppose we legalized heroin and cocaine in this country. In
what proportion of auto fatalities would the state police report that the
driver was nodding off on heroin or recklessly driving on a coke high?
In what proportion of spouse-assault and child-abuse cases would the
local police report that crack was involved? In what proportion of industrial accidents would safety investigators report that the forklift or drill-
press operator was in a drug-induced stupor or frenzy? We do not know
exactly what the proportion would be, but anyone who asserts that it
would not be much higher than it is now would have to believe that these
drugs have little appeal except when they are illegal. And that is nonsense.

An advocate of legalization might concede that social harm—perhaps   48
harm equivalent to that already produced by alcohol—would follow from
making cocaine and heroin generally available. But at least, he might
add, we would have the problem "out in the open" where it could be
treated as a matter of "public health." That is well and good, *if* we knew
how to treat—that is, cure—heroin and cocaine abuse. But we do not
know how to do it for all the people who would need such help. We are
having only limited success in coping with chronic alcoholics. Addictive
behavior is immensely difficult to change, and the best methods for
changing it—living in drug-free therapeutic communities, becoming
faithful members of Alcoholics Anonymous or Narcotics Anonymous—
require great personal commitment, a quality that is, alas, in short supply
among the very persons—young people, disadvantaged people—who
are often most at risk for addiction.

Suppose that today we had, not 15 million alcohol abusers, but half a   49
million. Suppose that we already knew what we have learned from our
long experience with the widespread use of alcohol. Would we make
whiskey legal? I do not know, but I suspect there would be a lively debate.

The Surgeon General would remind us of the risks alcohol poses to pregnant women. The National Highway Traffic Safety Administration would point to the likelihood of more highway fatalities caused by drunk drivers. The Food and Drug Administration might find that there is a non-trivial increase in cancer associated with alcohol consumption. At the same time the police would report great difficulty in keeping illegal whiskey out of our cities, officers being corrupted by bootleggers, and alcohol addicts often resorting to crime to feed their habit. Libertarians, for their part, would argue that every citizen has a right to drink anything he wishes and that drinking is, in any event, a "victimless crime."

However the debate might turn out, the central fact would be that the   50
problem was still, at that point, a small one. The government cannot legislate away the addictive tendencies in all of us, nor can it remove completely even the most dangerous addictive substances. But it can cope with harms when the harms are still manageable.

SCIENCE AND ADDICTION

One advantage of containing a problem while it is still containable is   51
that it buys time for science to learn more about it and perhaps to discover a cure. Almost unnoticed in the current debate over legalizing drugs is that basic science has made rapid strides in identifying the underlying neurological process involved in some forms of addiction. Stimulants such as cocaine and amphetamines alter the way certain brain cells communicate with one another. That alteration is complex and not entirely understood, but in simplified form it involves modifying the way in which a neurotransmitter called dopamine sends signals from one cell to another.

When dopamine crosses the synapse between two cells, it is in effect   52
carrying a message from the first cell to activate the second one. In certain parts of the brain that message is experienced as pleasure. After the message is delivered, the dopamine returns to the first cell. Cocaine apparently blocks this return, or "reuptake," so that the excited cell and others nearby continue to send pleasure messages. When the exaggerated high produced by cocaine-influenced dopamine finally ends, the brain cells may (in ways that are still a matter of dispute) suffer from an extreme lack of dopamine, thereby making the individual unable to experience any pleasure at all. This would explain why cocaine users often feel so depressed after enjoying the drug. Stimulants may also affect the way in which other neurotransmitters, such as serotonin and noradrenaline, operate.

Whatever the exact mechanism may be, once it is identified it   53
becomes possible to use drugs to block either the effect of cocaine or its tendency to produce dependency. There have already been experiments using desipramine, imipramine, bromocriptine, carbamazepine, and other chemicals. There are some promising results.

Tragically, we spend very little on such research, and the agencies   54
funding it have not in the past occupied very influential or visible posts
in the federal bureaucracy. If there is one aspect of the "war on drugs"
metaphor that I dislike, it is its tendency to focus attention almost
exclusively on the troops in the trenches, whether engaged in enforcement or treatment, and away from the research-and-develop-
ment efforts back on the home front where the war may ultimately be
decided.

I believe that the prospects of scientists in controlling addiction will be   55
strongly influenced by the size and character of the problem they face. If
the problem is a few hundred thousand chronic, high-dose users of an
illegal product, the chances of making a difference at a reasonable cost
will be much greater than if the problem is a few million chronic users of
legal substances. Once a drug is legal, not only will its use increase but
many of those who then use it will prefer the drug to the treatment: they
will want the pleasure, whatever the cost to themselves or their families,
and they will resist—probably successfully—any effort to wean them
away from experiencing the high that comes from inhaling a legal substance.

IF I AM WRONG . . .

No one can know what our society would be like if we changed the law   56
to make access to cocaine, heroin, and PCP easier. I believe, for reasons
given, that the result would be a sharp increase in use, a more widespread degradation of the human personality, and a greater rate of accidents and violence.

I may be wrong. If I am, then we will needlessly have incurred heavy   57
costs in law enforcement and some forms of criminality. But if I am
right, and the legalizers prevail anyway, then we will have consigned
millions of people, hundreds of thousands of infants, and hundreds
of neighborhoods to a life of oblivion and disease. To the lives and
families destroyed by alcohol we will have added countless more
destroyed by cocaine, heroin, PCP, and whatever else a basement scientist can invent.

Human character is formed by society; indeed, human character is   58
inconceivable without society, and good character is less likely in a bad
society. Will we, in the name of an abstract doctrine of radical individualism, and with the false comfort of suspect predictions, decide to take the
chance that somehow individual decency can survive amid a more general level of degradation?

I think not. The American people are too wise for that, whatever the   59
academic essayists and cocktail-party pundits may say. But if Americans
today are less wise than I suppose, then Americans at some future time
will look back on us now and wonder, what kind of people were they that
they could have done such a thing?

—————————————————————— ■ ——————————————————————

DRUG USE BY U.S. ARMY ENLISTED MEN IN VIETNAM: A FOLLOW-UP ON THEIR RETURN HOME

Lee N. Robins, Darlene H. Davis, and Donald W. Goodwin

This frequently cited research study has been interpreted in different ways (see the conflicting interpretations by Gazzaniga and Wilson in this section). "The results of this study indicate that, contrary to conventional belief, the occasional use of narcotics without becoming addicted appears possible even for men who have previously been dependent on narcotics."

Abstract

Between May and September 1972, 943 men who had returned to the United States from Vietnam in September 1971 as Army enlisted men were sought for interview and collection of urine specimens. Of these men, 470 represented the general population of Army enlisted men returning at that time; 495 represented those whose urine had been positive for opiates at time of departure from Vietnam. At interview 8–12 months after their return, 83 percent were civilians and 17 percent still in service. Nine hundred were personally interviewed and urine specimens collected for 876. Almost half of the "general" sample tried heroin or opium while in Vietnam and one-fifth developed physical or psychological dependence. In the 8- to 12-month period since their return, about 10 percent had some experience with opiates, but less than 1 percent had shown signs of opiate dependence. In the "drug positive" sample, three-quarters felt they had been addicted to narcotics in Vietnam. After return, one-third had some experience with opiates, but only 7 percent showed signs of dependence. Rather than giving up drugs altogether, many had shifted from heroin to amphetamines or barbiturates. Nevertheless, almost none expressed a desire for treatment. Pre-service use of drugs and extent of use in Vietnam were the strongest predictors of continued use after Vietnam. The results indicate that, contrary to conventional belief, the occasional use of narcotics without becoming addicted appears possible even for men who have previously been dependent on narcotics.

INTRODUCTION

During the summer and fall of 1971, drug use by United States servicemen in Vietnam had, by all estimates, reached epidemic proportions. Starting in June 1971, the military screened urines of servicemen for drugs just before scheduled departure from Vietnam. In September 1971, the Department of Defense estimated that 5 per cent of all urines of Army servicemen tested indicated drug use in the immediately preceding period, despite common knowledge that testing would be done and if positive, would result in a six- or seven-day delay in departure from Vietnam.   1

At this time, troop strength in Vietnam was being reduced rapidly, returning to the United States each month thousands of men, of whom about 40 per cent were due for immediate release from service. The   2

Armed Forces, the Veterans Administration, and civilian drug treatment facilities were concerned that the arrival of these men might tax existing drug treatment programs. There was also concern about how drug use might affect veterans' ability to get and hold jobs and their chances of becoming involved in criminal activities if they continued heroin use in the United States, where the price of heroin was many times its price in Vietnam. If the men designated as "drug positives" at DEROS (Date Eligible for Return from Overseas) were actually heroin addicts and if heroin addiction among these soldiers was as chronic and unresponsive to treatment as it had been found to be in the heroin addicts seen in the Public Health Hospitals of Lexington and Fort Worth (1–3), there was reason for concern.

To evaluate these concerns and to learn how many men would require   3
treatment, the kinds of treatment and social services they might need, and how to identify which men needed services, the White House Special Action Office for Drug Abuse Prevention arranged for and assisted in a follow-up study of Army enlisted men who returned from Vietnam to the United States in September 1971. This study promised not only to answer questions relevant to planning programs for these soldiers, but also to teach us something about the natural history of drug utilization and abuse when drugs were readily available to young men from all over the United States and from all kinds of social backgrounds.

Specifically, the study was designed to answer, among other ques-   4
tions, the following:

1. What proportion of Army enlisted men who departed Vietnam for the United States in September 1971, had used drugs in Vietnam? What drugs did they use and how much? What were the distinguishing characteristics of the drug users in terms of demographic variables, civilian history, and prior military record?

2. What proportion of these men had used narcotics or other illicit drugs (marijuana, amphetamines, barbiturates) since their return eight to 12 months previously? How many had been "dependent" on these drugs after return to the United States?

3. How many of them had been treated for drug use since returning? What was the nature of the treatment? Where was it received, and what was its duration? Was there a desire for drug treatment among these veterans that present facilities were not meeting?

4. Among men detected as using narcotics in Vietnam, what factors predicted continued use upon return to the United States?

METHOD

Study design.   Military programs to counter drug abuse among   5
troops in Vietnam have grown and changed over time. As a result, men leaving Vietnam at different dates were exposed to different programs.

Because different military programs might lead to different post-Vietnam adjustments, and because comparisons of outcomes since Vietnam for men who had been detected as drug positive with outcomes for the general run of soldiers would be valid only if the two groups had had equal periods in which to get jobs, begin drug use, or whatever, we decided to study only a single month's departures and to interview the men selected within as circumscribed a time period as possible.

We chose a month of departures, September 1971, thought to repre-   6
sent the period in which use of heroin by soldiers was at its height. And among the military departing Vietnam during that month, we chose the group with the highest rate of positive urines: male Army enlisted personnel. We studied only those who returned to the United States, including all the continental United States plus Hawaii, Puerto Rico and the Virgin Islands. The population we selected for study, Army enlisted men, not only had a high rate of positive urines at departure from Vietnam but also constituted the largest group of returnees to the United States. Thus we were studying the population that should contribute most to veteran candidates for drug treatment. A "general" sample of approximately 500 was to be drawn from this population.

Within the general population of Army enlisted men returning to the   7
United States in September from Vietnam, there was a subpopulation of men who had been detected as drug positive at the time they left Vietnam. From this subpopulation of drug positives we wanted to take a "drug positive" sample of approximately 500 persons. The "general" sample would serve to provide us with estimates of the proportion of Army enlisted men who used drugs in Vietnam, the proportion detected as drug positive at DEROS, the proportion who used drugs after their return to the United States, and the proportion who wanted treatment. Using the "drug positive" sample, we hoped to distinguish between drug users in Vietnam who were likely to be drug users in the United States after their return and those who would use little or no drugs after returning to the United States.

Each man was to be interviewed and asked to contribute a urine spec-   8
imen. The urine specimens were analyzed for morphine, codeine, methadone, quinine, amphetamines, and barbiturates. Army records were also analyzed to test the validity of the interview data and to provide additional information.

Sample selection.   A full description of how the two samples were   9
selected appears elsewhere (4).

The population from which the general sample was drawn—Army   10
enlisted men who left Vietnam in September 1971 to return to the United States—totaled approximately 13,760, according to Department of Defense statistics. Names of approximately 11,000 of these eligible men were made available to us by the military on a tape derived from the master tape of Enlisted Record Briefs for all men on active duty within 120 days of November 30, 1971. (The missing 2760 probably resulted

largely from failure to correct departure dates for men leaving Vietnam at dates other than originally scheduled.) From this tape we selected a simple random sample of 470.

From approximately 1000 eligible names and/or service numbers provided by the Surgeon General of men who had been identified as "drug positive" at DEROS, we selected a simple random sample of 495. There was an overlap between the "general" and "drug positive" samples of 22 men.   11

For each name chosen, the hard copy of the military record was sought to verify the departure date from Vietnam (and thus confirm eligibility for the sample) and to obtain the address of record and the names and addresses of next of kin. Difficulties in locating the military records prolonged sample selection into the interviewing period, greatly reducing the efficiency of travel schedules.   12

The interview.   The interview (also available in reference 4) was a product of repeated revision during pretests with approximately 50 Vietnam veterans who had returned at dates other than September, some recruited through active drug programs.   13

The interview form provided principally precoded answers, plus verbatim answers to open-ended questions. The results in the current report come only from the precoded sections.   14

Questions about drug use referred to five time periods: 1) before service; 2) in service, before Vietnam; 3) in Vietnam; 4) in service, after Vietnam; and 5) after release from active duty. Questions were also asked about deviance of other kinds during these five time periods, about the nature of the man's experience in Vietnam, his opinion as to how the Army and the Veterans Administration should combat drug abuse, and about his adjustment since his return from Vietnam. At the end of the interview, he was asked to give a urine sample.   15

Interviewing was conducted by the National Opinion Research Center. Interviewers received five days of training, which encompassed not only interviewing techniques but also military terminology, the nature of the Vietnam experience, drug language, facts about drug abuse, and the maintenance of confidentiality. A faculty of social scientists and psychiatrists experienced in drug research, a representative of the Veterans Administration, and members of the Armed Forces with Vietnam experience provided the training, along with the staff of supervisors and field directors from the National Opinion Research Center. During training, each interviewer carried out and observed several interviews with veterans currently in drug programs. There were both black and white interviewers, male and female; most but not all were young. Puerto Rican subjects were interviewed by a Puerto Rican interviewer in Spanish.   16

Interviews were conducted in person and in private. They lasted an average of one hour and 40 minutes, and ranged from 30 minutes to more than three and one-half hours.   17

The first contact with the subject was via a letter, signed by the Veterans Administration, asking the subject's cooperation with the project as   18 a person who better than anyone else knew the concerns of men returning from Vietnam. The letter mentioned that the subject would be paid for his cooperation, and invited him to call the National Opinion Research Center to set up an appointment. If the letter was returned as undeliverable, efforts were made to contact a relative to inquire about the man's current address. Interviewers made every possible attempt to contact each man, because other research had indicated that men hard to find at home are much more likely to show social deviance than men readily found at home (5). The subjects constituted a young population in the process of moving to new jobs or getting married, and, therefore, locating them sometimes took great persistence and ingenuity. Because of difficulties in choosing the sample, interviewers had to return to various locations repeatedly. Despite this, they interviewed 97 per cent of the general sample that survived until the time of interview and 96 per cent of the drug positive sample, a completed total of 900 interviews.

Among the 43 men not interviewed, there were six deaths (two auto   19
accidents, one death in a fire, one electrocution on the job, one shot while burglarizing a home, and one overdose of drugs), three refusals, 15 unlocated with no further leads, and 19 still in process of location or arrangement for interview at time of terminating the field work.

Urinalysis.   Of the 900 men interviewed, only 1 per cent refused to   20
provide a urine sample. An additional two were unable to urinate on request, one man was too ill to be asked, and a few urines were lost by leakage in transit. In all, urinalyses were obtained for 98 per cent of the general sample and 96 per cent of the drug positives interviewed.

Urine specimens were sent airmail in sealed containers to the Addic-   21
tion Research Foundation in Toronto for urinalysis. Barbiturates, morphine, codeine, quinine and methadone were screened initially by thin layer chromatography, and positive morphines were confirmed by gas liquid chromatography. Amphetamines and methamphetamines were screened by gas liquid chromatography. Details are described elsewhere (4).

Confidentiality.   Confidentiality was maintained to prevent bias on   22
the part of interviewers and to protect the men's privacy. To avoid bias the interviewers had to be ignorant about whether a subject had been identified as a drug abuser. To be certain that interviewers had no such information, the names composing the two samples were scrambled by giving each a random number. When the interview was complete, it was mailed to the Addiction Research Foundation, Toronto, Canada, in an envelope showing the random number assigned but with no identifying data on the interview and neither name nor address of the subject on the envelope. Waiting for its arrival in Canada was a list showing that random number associated with a single digit which identified the sample from which the case came ("general," "drug" or both) and, for cases in only one of the two samples, whether or not the case appeared in the population from which the other sample had been selected. The possible cate-

gories were: 1) in both general and drug samples; 2) in general sample only, also on Surgeon General's list of drug positives; 3) in general sample only, not on Surgeon General's list; 4) in drug sample only, also on Army tape of September returnees; 5) in drug sample only, not on Army tape of September returnees.

In Canada, the random number was removed and a new number was   23
selected for the interview, the first digit of which was the digit indicating to which sample the case belonged. The only list linking the random number to this newly assigned number was kept in Canada. Therefore, it was impossible for anyone in the United States to link an interview's contents to any individual. Nor was there danger to confidentiality in Canada since nothing was kept there except a list of paired numbers. This method closely follows the recommendations of Astin and Boruch (6). The same technique was used for maintaining the confidentiality of urinalysis reports and abstracts of military records. Because the same new number was assigned to all data pertaining to the same individual, data from various sources could be connected without endangering confidentiality.

Validity.   Most information in this report comes from interviews. This   24
information is valuable to the extent that the interview is accurate. One way of checking accuracy is to look at the rate of admitted drug use by men known to be drug positive by the Surgeon General. In interviews with the drug positive sample, 97 per cent reported having used narcotics in Vietnam. This level of honesty is particularly impressive when we remember that the interviewer had no idea whether the man was, in fact, a member of the drug positive sample.

Men were also asked whether their urines had been drug positive at   25
DEROS. Among the men in the "drug positive" sample, only 7 per cent denied ever having been detected as drug positive while in Vietnam. Eighty-one per cent said they had been positive at DEROS; 7 per cent said they had turned themselves in as users at DEROS rather than go through the DEROS screen; 5 per cent said they were negative at DEROS but had been in a drug treatment program earlier. It seems improbable that men would try to hide having had a positive urine at DEROS if they were willing to reveal other detection as drug positive in Vietnam. Thus it seems likely that 93 per cent of the men identified by the Surgeon General's office gave honest answers, and that the list of "DEROS-positives" provided by the Surgeon General's office actually included some men who had been identified by procedures other than the DEROS screen.

RESULTS

Drug Use in Vietnam

We will present results for the general sample, keeping in mind that   26
this is a random sample of Army enlisted men leaving Vietnam at the

Table 1

Nature of narcotic use in Vietnam (interviewed general sample of Army enlisted men returning to the USA in September 1971: No. = 451)

	%
Tried any narcotic	**43**
Narcotic tried:	
Heroin	34
Opium	38
Morphine	3
Codeine	2
Methadone	2
Each of the others*	1 or less
No. of different narcotic drugs tried:	
1	15
2	23
3 or more	6
Frequency and duration of use:	
Less than 5 times	10
5+ times, not more than once a week	4
More than weekly:	
For less than 6 months	9
For 6–8 months	10
For 9 months or more	10
Consider themselves to have been addicted	20
Ever injected	8
Usual route of administration for those using	
5 times or more (No. = 149):	
Smoking	67
Sniffing	24
Injection	9

*Demerol, Dilaudid, paregoric, Robitussin A/C.

height of public concern over drug abuse. If we had included women officers, personnel from the other services, and Army enlisted men departing Vietnam at other dates, lower rates of drug use would probably have been found.

Narcotic use. Almost half the Army enlisted men who left Vietnam in September 1971 had tried one or more of the narcotic drugs listed in Table 1 while there. About one-third tried heroin and one-third tried opium, and most who tried either, tried both. Only a few tried forms of narcotics such as morphine, codeine, and Dilaudid.

Because the heroin in Vietnam was very pure, it was effective when used in a number of ways: mixed with tobacco and smoked, sniffed, eaten, injected under the skin or into a muscle, or injected into a vein. However, the "kick" or "flash" associated with injection was more intense and preferred by a few.

Most of the use of narcotics in Vietnam was by smoking. Two-thirds of   27
those who used any narcotics more than a few times said their preferred
method in Vietnam was smoking. The next most common method was
sniffing, preferred by 24 per cent of those who used narcotics. Injection
by needle was tried by 18 per cent of users but was the preferred method
for 9 per cent.

Most of those who used narcotics in Vietnam used them repeatedly   28
and over a considerable period. Almost half the users (20 per cent of the
whole general sample) used narcotics more than weekly for six months
to a year. Only one-fourth of the users (11 per cent of the sample) were
"experimenters," that is, tried a narcotic but used it less than five times.

About half (46 per cent) of those who used narcotics at all in Vietnam   29
felt that they had been addicted or "strung out." Over all, one out of five
(20 per cent) of all Army enlisted men returning in September 1971, said
that they felt that they had been "strung out" on heroin while in Vietnam.
While we cannot be certain that all who said they were addicted actually
were so, all had used narcotics regularly for more than one month, and
83 per cent for more than six months, suggesting that the figure of 20
per cent is realistic.

Amphetamines and barbiturates.   One-fourth said that they had   30
used amphetamines while they were in Vietnam (Table 2). Barbiturates
were used by 23 per cent. A few used these drugs heavily; 7 per cent
used amphetamines at least 25 times and 9 per cent used barbiturates at
least 25 times.

If men used any drug in Vietnam, the most common pattern was to   31
use all three types: narcotics, barbiturates, and amphetamines. Eighteen
per cent followed this pattern. The next most common pattern was to
use only narcotics; 15 per cent followed this pattern. A combination of
narcotics with either amphetamines or barbiturates, but not both, was
used by 11 per cent. Two per cent used only amphetamines and less
than 1 per cent used only barbiturates. No man told us that he had used
both amphetamines and barbiturates but not narcotics.

The Vietnam soldier who restricted his use of dangerous drugs to
heroin was atypical—constituting only 23 per cent of drug users. The
more common pattern (54 per cent of drug users) was to use at least two
types of narcotics plus amphetamines or barbiturates. This multiple drug
use is similar to the use patterns of heroin addicts in the United States
(7). What was unusual about drug use in Vietnam as compared with use
in the United States was the infrequency with which amphetamines and
barbiturates were used without the use of narcotics as well. Thus in Vietnam the terms "dangerous-drug user" and "narcotics user" were virtually
synonymous.

Multiple drug use was especially common among men detected as   32
drug positive at DEROS. Almost all (85 per cent) reported use of
amphetamines and barbiturates as well as narcotics, and more than half
(54 per cent) reported having used all three types of drugs, even though

Table 2

Drugs used in Vietnam

	Interviewed general sample (No. = 451) %	Interviewed drug positive sample (No. = 469) %
Any drug: narcotics, amphetamines, or barbiturates	45	97
Narcotics	43	96
Amphetamines	25	59
Barbiturates	23	77
Combinations of drug types:		
All 3: narcotics, amphetamines, and barbiturates	18	54
Narcotics and amphetamines	6	4
Narcotics and barbiturates	5	23
Narcotics only	15	15
Amphetamines only	2	0
Barbiturates only	*	*

*Less than .5%.

the drug detected at DEROS was almost always a narcotic. Only 18 per cent of the men detected as positive had not used either amphetamines or barbiturates in Vietnam.

Distinguishing characteristics of the drug users. As compared with soldiers who used no drugs or only marijuana, drug users tended to be younger, less well educated, to come from larger cities, to be single, and more often reared in broken homes (Table 3). Race was not significantly related to drug use, although blacks were more likely to be detected as positive at DEROS. The majority of users were Regular Army, while the majority of non-users were draftees. Before entering service, more users had had civilian arrests, and somewhat more had had military disciplinary actions before arrival in Vietnam. The most striking difference between users and non-users was in their drug experience before Vietnam. Two-thirds of users in Vietnam had tried marijuana before Vietnam compared with less than one-fifth of non-users, and almost half had tried amphetamines, compared with less than one out of 10 non-users. While more users of drugs in Vietnam than non-users had previously tried barbiturates and narcotics, only a minority had done so. Most of their narcotic experience had been with mild forms: codeine cough syrups, predominantly. Very few had tried heroin.

While pre-Vietnam histories of drug users and non-users differed, it would be a mistake to think of the Vietnam drug user as a highly deviant

Table 3

How men who used drugs in Vietnam differed from non-users at arrival in Vietnam (interviewed general sample of Army enlisted men returning to the USA in September 1971: No. = 451)*

	Users of narcotics, ampheta-mines, or barbiturates (interviewed: No. = 205) %	No drugs or marijuana only (interviewed: No. = 246) %
Demographic differences:		
Under 20 years of age	25	7
Less than 12 years education	39	23
Core city residence	23	14
Never married	81	57
Broken home	36	23
Prior civilian history:		
Civilian arrest	44	20
Drugs ever used—		
Marijuana	69	18
Amphetamines	42	9
Barbiturates	29	1
Narcotics	22	2
Military status:		
Regular Army	65	44
Prior disciplinary history	30	17

*All differences are statistically significant at $p < .05$ or better.

soldier with prior drug experience who could have been expected to get into trouble. While each type of prior deviance was more common in drug users than in non-users, each except marijuana use occurred in only a minority of the drug users.

Drug Use Since Return from Vietnam

Narcotics. In the general sample, 9.5 per cent reported that they had used some narcotics since their return, 2.5 per cent only while they were still in the service and 7 per cent since they had been veterans.

How many of these prospective narcotics users after Vietnam had the Army identified through the DEROS screen program? Of the 43 men in the general sample who reported having used narcotics since their return from Vietnam, 19 (less than half) had any indication in records or interview of having been detected as drug positive at DEROS. Therefore, even if treatment could have deterred every man detected in DEROS from future use, half the number who would be narcotics users after return from Vietnam would not have been reached.

While 9.5 per cent had used narcotics since their return and 3 per   35
cent had used them heavily (more than once a week for more than a month), only 0.7 per cent (three) said that they had been addicted at any time during the eight to 12 months since their return (Table 4). Among the 91 men in the general sample who said they were addicted to Vietnam, only two (2 per cent) reported continuation of that addiction after their return to the United States. Among 348 men in the drug positive sample who said they were addicted in Vietnam, only 9 per cent reported continuation of their addiction in the United States. These are much lower rates of recidivism than one would have predicted based on readdiction rates among treated civilian addicts.

Interview reports may, of course, be unreliable. But urinalyses con-   36
firmed the low rate of current use. In the general sample, 0.7 per cent of the urines collected at interview were positive for morphine or codeine, and in the drug positive sample, urines were positive for morphine or codeine in 2 per cent. While there may have been some abstention from drug use because of the interview appointment, urinalysis results certainly suggest a relatively low level of current addiction.

To find enough users since return to study patterns of post-Vietnam   37
narcotic usage, we turn to the drug positive sample, a third of whom reported having used narcotics since their return (Table 4). Returnees were now using the heroin they were introduced to in Vietnam, rather than the codeine and milder narcotics some were familiar with before Vietnam. Of those using any narcotic since their return, 84 per cent had used heroin (28 per cent of the total drug positive sample). Methadone use had also entered the picture, but it was still much less common than the use of heroin. One striking change in patterns of narcotic use since Vietnam was the shift to injection as the usual mode of administration. Seventy-seven per cent of the frequent users in the United States usually injected, compared to the 18 per cent of the frequent users among drug positives who usually injected in Vietnam. This, of course, reflects the lower strength and higher price of heroin in this country. Smoking narcotics, the most common mode of administration in Vietnam, was hardly used at all after return to the United States.

Initiation of use in the United States occurred almost immediately on return for about one-fourth of the users, but another one-fourth began more than four months after their return. Because the return to narcotics occurred throughout the post-Vietnam period, we cannot be sure that those who had not used narcotics by the time of interview would not use them later.

Most of the men who reported having taken narcotics since their return to the United States denied having used them regularly (defined as

Table 4

Narcotic use since Vietnam

	General sample (No. = 451) %	Drug positives (No. = 469) %
Any narcotic use since return	9.5	33
Type of narcotic used		
Heroin	7	28
Opium	2	7
Codeine	1	6
Methadone	1	5
Morphine	1	3
Robitussin A/C	*	4
Demerol	*	3
Dilaudid	*	2
Paregoric	0	1
Used narcotics heavily (more than once a week for more than one month)	3	15
Felt addicted	0.7	7.2
Current use		
By interview	2	8
By urinalysis	0.7	2.4
Usual method (for those who used 5 times or more)	(No. = 19)	(No. = 82)
Smoking	11	5
Sniffing	21	13
Injection	63	77
Swallowing	5	5
Interval between return and first use, for users	(No. = 43)	(No. = 157)
Less than one week	12	20
Less than one month	23	43
Less than two months	47	57
Less than four months	65	78

*Less than 0.5%.

more than weekly for at least a month), and only about one-fifth of the users felt they had been addicted since their return.

Marijuana, amphetamines, and barbiturates. Marijuana use was widespread among these veterans after their return, whether or not they had been detected as drug positive at DEROS. Half of the general sample and four-fifths of the drug positive sample reported using marijuana since their return to the United States (Table 5). However, less than a quarter of the users had smoked marijuana heavily (three days or more a week for

Table 5

Use of marijuana, amphetamines and barbiturates since Vietnam

	General sample (No. = 451) %	Drug positives (No. = 469) %
Any use:		
Marijuana	45	81
Amphetamines	19	38
Barbiturates	12	30
Heavy use:		
Marijuana	7	18
Amphetamines	5	8*
Barbiturates	2	6
Tolerance or problems:		
Marijuana	5	9
Amphetamines	3	8
Barbiturates	2	4
Current use (shown by urinalysis):		
Amphetamines	11	11*
Barbiturates	2	6

*Not significantly different from general sample. All other differences are significant, $p < .05$.

more than a month) since their return. A small minority of both the general sample and of the drug positives reported that they have been using marijuana "too much" since their return (5 and 9 per cent, respectively). The drug positive sample was almost twice as likely as the general sample to have used marijuana, to have used it heavily, and to have felt they had problems with it.

The drug positive sample was also twice as likely as the general sample to have used amphetamines. Since their return, use of amphetamines created a problem in terms of tolerance, hallucinations, or paranoia for 8 per cent of the drug positives and 3 per cent of the general sample. The drug positive sample reported as much dependence on or problems with amphetamines as with narcotics since their return, while there have been more amphetamine than narcotic problems among members of the general sample.

Among the drug positive sample, 30 per cent had taken barbiturates since their return, as had 12 per cent of the general sample. Tolerance to barbiturates or withdrawal symptoms since their return were reported by 4 per cent of the drug positives and 2 per cent of the general sample.

The analysis of urines collected at interview showed considerably higher rates of amphetamines and barbiturates than of narcotics. In the general sample, 11 per cent of urines were positive for amphetamines, 2 per cent for barbiturates, and 0.7 per cent for narcotics. In the sample of

Table 6

Dangerous drugs used since Vietnam

	General sample (No. = 451) %	Drug positive sample (No. = 469) %
Any drugs: narcotics, amphetamines, barbiturates	23	49
Narcotics	10	33
Amphetamines	19	38
Barbiturates	12	30
Combinations of drug types		
All 3: narcotics, amphetamines, barbiturates	6	14
Amphetamines and barbiturates	3	6
Narcotics and amphetamines	2	7
Narcotics and barbiturates	1	6
Narcotics only	1	7
Amphetamines only	9	10
Barbiturates only	2	5

men detected as positive for drugs at DEROS, amphetamines were found in the urines collected at interview of 11 per cent, barbiturates in the urines of 6 per cent, and narcotics in 2 per cent. (Surprisingly, the two samples showed equally high rates of urines positive for amphetamines.) These urinalysis results would indicate that use of both amphetamines and barbiturates was more common at time of interview among returnees than was the use of narcotics, even among men who had been narcotic-dependent in Vietnam.

Use of dangerous drugs in the first 10 months after Vietnam was about half as common as in Vietnam (compare Tables 6 and 2). The dropoff in use was greatest for narcotics (78 per cent less common) and least for amphetamines (24 per cent less common).

Whereas in Vietnam the user of only a single drug type was usually a narcotics user, after Vietnam he was usually an amphetamine user. Use of multiple drug types was common in both periods, with half of all users trying more than one type since Vietnam.

While men detected as drug positive at DEROS were especially likely to use each type of drug after Vietnam, the same changes in rate of use and choice of drugs had occurred; the rate of use of one or more of these drugs since Vietnam was half the rate in Vietnam (49 vs. 97 per cent); the decrease in use was greatest with respect to narcotics (a 66 per cent drop) and least for amphetamines (a 36 per cent drop). The drug most commonly used alone had changed from narcotics in Vietnam to amphetamines since Vietnam, and about half the drug positives who used a drug since Vietnam have used more than one type of drug.

Post-Vietnam treatment for drug problems

Five per cent of returnees had some treatment for drug use in the eight to 12 months since they returned to the United States. Almost all of that treatment was while still in service. Among men detected as drug positive in Vietnam, 46 per cent had had some drug treatment since their return to the United States, again almost all while still in service, although 4 per cent got treatment through the Veterans Administration, 3 per cent had been inpatients in other hospitals, 1 per cent attended drug clinics, and 2 per cent entered some nonmedically oriented program. The treatment was usually brief, averaging about two weeks. Entering methadone maintenance programs was rare—only 0.4 per cent of the general sample and 5 per cent of the drug positive sample reported it. **41**

Reporting at time of interview that they were in treatment were: none of the general sample, 3 per cent of all drug positives, 8 per cent of the drug positives still on active duty, and 2.5 per cent of those released from service. Two men reported being currently in a methadone maintenance program, a low rate confirmed by urinalysis: only two men showed methadone in their urines. **42**

Asked whether they were interested in continuing or beginning drug treatment, 0.7 per cent of the general sample and 5.2 per cent of the drug positive sample showed interest. To learn whether those showing interest could be expected to have difficulty finding a treatment facility that would accept them, men were asked whether they had asked for treatment at any place where they failed to get it. Among the general sample 0.4 per cent, and among drug positives 4 per cent had sought treatment and not received it. These few failures to receive treatment resulted as often from the applicant's changing his mind as from rejection by the agency. Thus the low rate of treatment received after leaving service did not seem to reflect a lack of treatment opportunities. **43**

Since civilian treatment facilities typically get histories of addiction of several years' duration from men admitted for the first time, it is possible that a demand for treatment may emerge later among veterans now drug dependent but not yet ready to seek help. **44**

Predictors of Post-Vietnam Drug Use

The man most likely to be detected as drug positive in Vietnam was a young, single, black, low-ranking member of the Regular Army who had little education, came from a broken home, had an arrest history before service, and had used drugs before service. **45**

None of the demographic characteristics which had forecast detection as drug positive at DEROS were of any use in forecasting continuing narcotic use after return to the United States among those detected as positive by the DEROS screen. Blacks and whites had about the same risk of using narcotics once they returned to the United States. Men under 22 **46**

Table 7

Significant predictors of narcotic use after return to the USA for men detected positive at DEROS*

| Predictors of narcotic use after return by drug positives | % using a narcotic after return | | | |
| | Of men with this characteristic | | Of men without this characteristic | |
	No.	%	No.	%
Prior to Vietnam:				
Civilian arrest	168	45	301	27
Did not finish high school	216	40	253	27
Tried marijuana	170	54	299	22
Tried a narcotic	106	63	363	25
Disciplinary action	166	42	255	28
In Vietnam:				
Used any amphetamines	275	43	192	19
25+ times	75	52	394	20
Used any barbiturates	363	38	104	16
25+ times	144	53	325	19
No drinking or less than weekly	351	38	117	21
Narcotic used:				
Opium	331	41	138	15
Codeine	50	50	419	32
Methadone	63	59	406	30
Morphine	63	71	406	28
Used narcotics heavily 6+ months	319	43	150	13
Usually injected narcotics	84	54	385	27
Usually "sniffed" narcotics	210	51	259	19
Felt addicted to narcotics	349	40	118	14

*Date eligible for return from overseas.

had the same risk as older men. Single men and married men had equal risks. It made no difference whether the man had grown up in a large city or a small town. Neither did low military rank nor being in the Regular Army predict use on return.

The only pre-service factors that predicted continuing use were delinquency, high school dropout, and drug experience (Table 7). The strongest of these predictors was pre-service narcotic use. Men with such a history had two and one-half times the risk of continuing narcotic use as did men first introduced to narcotics in Vietnam. The only pre-Vietnam military indicator was disciplinary action.

47

Use of barbiturates or amphetamines in Vietnam, and particularly frequent use of either drug, was associated with use of narcotics after return. About half of those reporting taking amphetamines or barbiturates 25 times or more while in Vietnam continued their narcotic use after returning to the United States.

The heavy use of alcohol in Vietnam was negatively related to narcotic use after return. Among men drug positive at DEROS who drank at least weekly in Vietnam, only 21 per cent used narcotics after return to the United States, as compared with 36 per cent of those who drank less than once a week.

Furthermore, the type of narcotic used in Vietnam was a predictor of continued use. Heroin had been used in Vietnam by almost every man detected as drug positive, and one-third of heroin users used narcotics in the United States after their return. Addition of the less common narcotics to the use of heroin was associated with a greater likelihood of using some narcotic after return. Rates of use after return were especially high for morphine users (71 per cent) and methadone users (59 per cent). Even the addition of codeine, a less addicting narcotic than heroin, was associated with a greater risk of continuing narcotics (50 vs. 35 per cent). [48]

Prolonged narcotic usage in Vietnam increased the chance that a man would continue use after leaving Vietnam. Only 13 per cent of the men who confined their use to less than a six-month period used any narcotic after return, while use for more than six months was followed by use in the United States for 43 per cent. [49]

Asked their usual method of administration of narcotics in Vietnam, one-sixth of the drug positives said the needle was the preferred method, one-quarter preferred sniffing, and half preferred smoking. Those who preferred sniffing or injecting were more likely to use on return. There was little difference in later use between those who sniffed or injected. [50]

Drug positives who said they were addicted or "strung out" in Vietnam were more likely to continue use than those denying addiction (40 vs. 14 per cent), but more than half of the drug positives who considered themselves addicted in Vietnam never tried narcotics after their return from overseas. [51]

In summary, patterns of drug use, both before and in Vietnam, were the best predictors of narcotics use after return to the United States by the drug positives. Social status and military status indicators were not helpful. Pre-service delinquency and failure to complete high school were reasonably good predictors, although less powerful than drug use patterns. [52]

There are many ways in which these correlates of drug use after return to the United States could be combined to serve as a predictive tool. One successful combination we discovered was regular narcotic use in Vietnam for more than a month, plus two of the three following correlates: a) use of narcotics before service, b) frequent use of amphetamines or bar- [53]

biturates in Vietnam, and c) little use of alcohol in Vietnam. This combination identified 67 per cent of the drug positives who did use narcotics on return, while selecting only 28 per cent of the drug positives who did not use narcotics on return. An index similar to this one may prove useful for selecting those men most in need of intervention.

It would be of much greater interest, of course, to predict *heavy or* 54 *addictive* use on return to the United States rather than predicting *any* use of narcotics. We discovered no information that would have been obtainable before their departure from Vietnam that could have predicted which of the men likely to continue narcotic use in the States would be heavy or addictive users here. The degree of use after return, if a man uses at all, either is determined more by the local scene than by his history prior to his return, or it is determined by factors our interview has not tapped.

DISCUSSION

The Vietnam experience has been a natural experiment in the expo- 55 sure of masses of young men to narcotic drugs. In Vietnam, in 1970, almost every enlisted man was approached by someone offering him heroin, usually within the first month of his arrival. This "natural experiment" provides an opportunity to learn what happens when first exposure to heroin occurs in a foreign and for many a frightening setting, without the deterrents of high prices, impure drugs, or the presence of disapproving family.

What happened in this population of young Army enlisted men return- 56 ing from Vietnam in September 1971 was that almost half of them did try heroin or opium or both while in Vietnam and that about one-fifth of them used narcotics there with sufficient regularity to develop some signs of physical or psychological dependence. Men who came to Vietnam with a history of deviant behavior (crime, drug use, or high school dropout) were more likely than others to use drugs in Vietnam.

Surprisingly, in the light of the common belief that dependence on 57 narcotics is easily acquired and virtually impossible to rid oneself of, most of the men who used narcotics heavily in Vietnam stopped when they left Vietnam and had not begun again eight to 12 months later. Demographic variables and military rank did not predict which men would continue use after Vietnam. Pre-service use of drugs and extent of use in Vietnam were powerful predictors of continued use after Vietnam.

Of those who continued narcotic use after their return to the United 58 States, most reported that they had not become addicted or readdicted. Contrary to conventional belief, the occasional use of narcotics without becoming addicted appears to be possible even for men who have previously been dependent on narcotics. The returnees' lack of interest in obtaining treatment for drug use perhaps reflects this experience with successful voluntary abstinence and light use. The small percentage who did become readdicted on return were not detectably different in terms of prior history; none of the indicators of social or military status or even of deviant behavior and drug use before or in Vietnam predicted which men could use narcotics occasionally in the United States without readdiction, and which men would become addicted if they used narcotics after return.

Public concern about drugs in both the Vietnam and post-Vietnam periods has centered on narcotics, and heroin in particular. While heroin was very commonly used in Vietnam, so was opium. Nor was there a lack of use in Vietnam of dangerous nonnarcotic drugs, both stimulants and sedatives. In Vietnam, the latter drugs were used almost exclusively by men also using narcotics. Since Vietnam, stimulants and sedatives are playing a larger role than narcotics in the drug behavior of veterans. In the light of the wider use of barbiturates and amphetamines than of narcotics and the small number of veterans who feel they need treatment for narcotic addiction, there should be little pressure on the capacities of existing narcotic treatment programs from these veterans at the present time. However, those using narcotics occasionally since return have usually injected heroin rather than smoking or sniffing heroin and opium as they did in Vietnam, or drinking codeine cough syrups as a few did before Vietnam. This choice of method and substance may be associated with increasing addiction rates in the next few years. 59

The high completion rates for interviews and urinalyses in these large, carefully selected random samples, plus the willingness of the subjects to talk freely about their drug experiences, gives us some confidence that the results reported accurately describe the experience of the population studied: Army enlisted men who returned to the United States from Vietnam in September 1971 and who had been in the United States for eight to 12 months. To what extent our findings can be extrapolated to the drug experiences of civilians or other servicemen is not known. 60

REFERENCES

1. Hunt GH, Odoroff ME: Follow-up study of narcotic drug addicts after hospitalization. Public Health Rep 77:41–54, 1962
2. O'Donnell JA: Narcotic addicts in Kentucky. PHS Publ No. 1881, Washington DC, US GPO, 1969
3. Vaillant GE: Twelve year follow-up of New York narcotic addicts. Am J Psychiatry 122:727–737, 1966
4. Robins LN: A follow-up of Vietnam drug users. Special Action Office Monograph, Series A:1, April, 1973
5. Robins LN: Deviant Children Grown Up. Baltimore, The Williams & Wilkins Company, 1966
6. Astin AW, Boruch RF: A "link" system for assuring confidentiality of research data in longitudinal studies. Am Educational Research J 7:615–624, 1970
7. Drug use in America: problem in perspective. Second report of the National Commission on Marihuana and Drug Abuse. Washington, DC, US GPO, 1973

☐ FOR CLASS DISCUSSION

1. Analyze and evaluate the dispute on the legalization of drugs by applying the first set of guide question from page 473. How do you account for
   the enormous disagreements between Wilson and those arguing that
   drugs should be legalized?

2. Choose one of the arguments for closer analysis, applying the second set
   of guide questions on page 474.

OPTIONAL WRITING ASSIGNMENT   Your state has an initiative on the ballot to
legalize all drugs. Because you are a well-known writer of book blurbs, celebrated for your ability to summarize seven-hundred-page tomes in a few
paragraphs, you have been asked by both sides to write up their side of the
case for the voters' pamphlet. You can't help yourself. You're broke. You take
on both clients. Now the day of truth has arrived. Your deadline is tomorrow. Drawing on the preceding essays, personal experience, and any other
research you may have done, write two-hundred-fifty-word arguments for
and against drug legalization suitable for use in a voting pamphlet.

Sexual Harassment:
When Is Offensiveness a Civil Offense?

GENDER DILEMMAS IN SEXUAL HARASSMENT POLICIES AND PROCEDURES

Stephanie Riger

*Psychology professor Riger analyzes reasons for the paucity of sexual
harassment complaints. She concludes that a gender bias is built into the
way sexual harassment policies are written.*

Sexual harassment—unwanted sexually oriented behavior in a work   1
context—is the most recent form of victimization of women to be redefined as a social rather than a personal problem, following rape and wife
abuse. A sizeable proportion of women surveyed in a wide variety of work
settings reported being subject to unwanted sexual attention, sexual
comments or jokes, offensive touching, or attempts to coerce compliance with or punish rejection of sexual advances. In 1980 the U.S. Merit
Systems Protection Board (1981) conducted the first comprehensive
national survey of sexual harassment among federal employees: About 4
out of 10 of the 10,648 women surveyed reported having been the target
of sexual harassment during the previous 24 months. A recent update of

this survey found that the frequency of harassment in 1988 was identical to that reported earlier: 42% of all women surveyed in 1988 reported that they had experienced some form of unwanted and uninvited sexual attention compared to exactly the same percentage of women in 1980 (U.S. Merit Systems Protection Board, 1988).

Women ranging from blue-collar workers (LaFontaine & Tredeau, 1986; Maypole & Skaine, 1982) to lawyers (Burleigh & Goldberg, 1989) to airline personnel (Littler-Bishop, Seidler-Feller, & Opaluch, 1982) have reported considerable amounts of sexual harassment in surveys. Among a random sample of private sector workers in the Los Angeles area, more than one half of the women surveyed by telephone reported experiencing at least one incident that they considered sexual harassment during their working lives (Gutek, 1985). Some estimate that up to about one third of women in educational institutions have experienced some form of harassment (Kenig & Ryan, 1986). Indeed, Garvey (1986) stated that "Unwanted sexual attention may be the single most widespread occupational hazard in the workplace today" (p. 75).

It is a hazard faced much more frequently by women than men. About 40% of the women in the original U.S. Merit Systems Protection Board survey reported having experienced sexual harassment, compared with only 15% of the men (U.S. Merit Systems Protection Board, 1981). Among working people surveyed in Los Angeles, women were nine times more likely than men to report having quit a job because of sexual harassment, five times more likely to have transferred, and three times more likely to have lost a job (Konrad & Gutek, 1986). Women with low power and status, whether due to lower age, being single or divorced, or being in a marginal position in the organization, are more likely to be harassed (Fain & Anderton, 1987; LaFontaine & Tredeau, 1986; Robinson & Reid, 1985).

Sex differences in the frequency of harassment also prevail in educational environments (Fitzgerald et al., 1988). A mailed survey of more than 900 women and men at the University of Rhode Island asked about a wide range of behavior, including the frequency of respondents' experience of sexual insult, defined as an "uninvited sexually suggestive, obscene or offensive remark, stare, or gesture" (Lott, Reilly, & Howard, 1982, p. 309). Of the female respondents, 40% reported being sexually insulted occasionally or often while on campus, compared with 17% of the men. Both men and women reported that women are rarely the source of such insults. Similar differences were found in a survey of social workers, with 2 1/2 times as many women as men reporting harassment (Maypole, 1986).

Despite the high rates found in surveys of sexual harassment of women, few complaints are pursued through official grievance procedures. Dzeich and Weiner (1984) concluded, after reviewing survey findings, that 20% to 30% of female college students experience sexual harassment. Yet academic institutions averaged only 4.3 complaints each during the 1982–1983 academic year (Robertson, Dyer, & Campbell, 1988), a period roughly consecutive with the surveys cited by Dzeich and Weiner. In another study conducted at a university in 1984, of 38 women who reported harassment, only 1 reported the behavior to the offender's supervisor and 2 reported the behavior to an adviser, another professor, or employer (Reilly, Lott, & Gallogly, 1986). Similar findings have been reported on other college campuses (Adams, Kottke, & Padgitt, 1983; Benson & Thompson, 1982; Brandenburg, 1982; Cammaert, 1985; Meek & Lynch, 1983; Schneider, 1987).

Low numbers of complaints appear in other work settings as well. In a survey of federal workers, only about 11% of victims reported the harassment to a higher authority, and only 2.5% used formal complaint channels (Livingston, 1982). Similarly, female social workers reacted to harassment by avoiding or delaying the conflict or attempting to defuse the situation rather than by adopting any form of recourse such as filing a grievance (Maypole, 1986). The number of complaints alleging sexual harassment filed with the Equal Employment Opportunity Commission in Washington, DC, has declined since 1984, despite an increase in the number of women in the workforce during that time (Morgenson, 1989), and surveys suggest that the rate of sexual harassment has remained relatively stable (U.S. Merit Systems Protection Board, 1981, 1988).   6

It is the contention of this article that the low rate of utilization of grievance procedures is due to gender bias in sexual harassment policies that discourages their use by women. Policies are written in gender-neutral language and are intended to apply equally to men and women. However, these policies are experienced differently by women than men because of gender differences in perceptions of harassment and orientation toward conflict. Although victims of all forms of discrimination are reluctant to pursue grievances (Bumiller, 1987), women, who are most likely to be the victims of sexual harassment, are especially disinclined to pursue sexual harassment grievances for at least two reasons. First, the interpretation in policies of what constitutes harassment may not reflect women's viewpoints, and their complaints may not be seen as valid. Second, the procedures in some policies that are designed to resolve disputes may be inimical to women because they are not compatible with the way that many women view conflict resolution. Gender bias in policies, rather than an absence of harassment or lack of assertiveness on the part of victims, produces low numbers of complaints.   7

GENDER BIAS IN THE DEFINITION OF SEXUAL HARASSMENT

The first way that gender bias affects sexual harassment policies stems from differences between men and women in the interpretation of the definition of harassment. Those writing sexual harassment policies for organizations typically look to the courts for the distinction between illegal sexual harassment and permissible (although perhaps unwanted)   8 social interaction (see Cohen, 1987, for a discussion of this distinction in legal cases). The definition of harassment in policies typically is that provided by the U.S. Equal Employment Opportunity Commission (1980) guidelines:

> Unwelcome sexual advances, requests for sexual favors, and other verbal or physical conduct of a sexual nature constitute sexual harassment when (1) submission to such conduct is made either explicitly or implicitly a term or condition of an individual's employment, (2) submission to or rejection of such conduct by an individual is used as the basis for employment decisions affecting such individual, or (3) such conduct has the purpose or effect of unreasonably interfering with an individual's work performance or creating an intimidating, hostile, or offensive working environment. (p. 74677)

The first two parts of the definition refer to a quid pro quo relationship involving people in positions of unequal status, as superior status is usually necessary to have control over another's employment. In such cases bribes, threats, or punishments are used. Incidents of this type need happen only once to fall under the definition of sexual harassment. However, courts have required that incidents falling into the third category, "an intimidating, hostile, or offensive working environment," must be repeated in order to establish that such an environment exists (Terpstra & Baker, 1988); these incidents must be both pervasive and so severe that they affect the victim's psychological well-being (Trager, 1988). Harassment of this type can come from peers or even subordinates as well as superiors.

In all three of these categories, harassment is judged on the basis of conduct and its effects on the recipient, not the intentions of the harasser. Thus, two typical defenses given by accused harassers—"I was just being friendly," or "I touch everyone, I'm that kind of person"—do not hold up in court. Yet behavior may have an intimidating or offensive effect on some people but be inoffensive or even welcome to others. In deciding whose standards should be used, the courts employ what is called the *reasonable person rule,* asking whether a reasonable person would be offended by the conduct in question. The dilemma in applying this to sexual harassment is that a reasonable woman and a reasonable man are likely to differ in their judgments of what is offensive.

Definitions of sexual harassment are socially constructed, varying not only with characteristics of perceiver but also those of the situational context and actors involved. Behavior is more likely to be labelled harassment when it is done by someone with greater power than the victim (Gutek, Morasch, & Cohen, 1983; Kenig & Ryan, 1986; Lester et al., 1986; Popovich, Licata, Nokovich, Martelli, & Zoloty, 1987); when it involves physical advances accompanied by threats of punishment for noncompliance (Rossi & Weber-Burdin, 1983); when the response to it is negative (T.S. Jones, Remland, & Brunner, 1987); when the behavior reflects persistent negative intentions toward a woman (Pryor & Day, 1988); the more inappropriate it is for the actor's social role (Pryor, 1985); and the more flagrant and frequent the harasser's actions (Thomann & Wiener, 1987). Among women, professionals are more likely than those in secretarial–clerical positions to report the more subtle behaviors as harassment (McIntyre & Renick, 1982).

The variable that most consistently predicts variation in people's definition of sexual harassment is the sex of the rater. Men label fewer behaviors at work as sexual harassment (Kenig & Ryan, 1986; Konrad & Gutek, 1986; Lester et al., 1986; Powell, 1986; Rossi & Weber-Burdin, 1983). Men tend to find sexual overtures from women at work to be flattering, whereas women find similar approaches from men to be insulting (Gutek, 1985). Both men and women agree that certain blatant behaviors, such as sexual assault or sexual bribery, constitute harassment, but women are more likely to see as harassment more subtle behavior such as sexual teasing or looks or gestures (Adams et al., 1983; Collins & Blodgett, 1981; Kenig & Ryan, 1986; U.S. Merit Systems Protection Board, 1981). Even when they do identify behavior as harassment, men are more likely to think that women will be flattered by it (Kirk, 1988). Men are also more likely than women to blame women for being sexually harassed (Kenig & Ryan, 1986; Jensen & Gutek, 1982). 12

These gender differences make it difficult to apply the reasonable person rule. Linenberger (1983) proposed 10 factors that permit an "objective" assessment of whether behavior constitutes sexual harassment, regardless of the perception of the victim and the intent of the perpetrator. These factors range from the severity of the conduct to the number and frequency of encounters, and the relationship of the parties involved. For example, behavior is less likely to be categorized as harassment if it is seen as a response to provocation from the victim. But is an objective rating of provocation possible? When gender differences are as clear-cut and persistent as they are in the perception of what behavior constitutes sexual harassment, the question is not one of objectivity, but rather of which sex's definition of the situation will prevail. Becker (1967) asserted that there is a "hierarchy of credibility" in organizations, and that credibility and the right to be heard are differentially distributed: "In any system of ranked groups, participants take it as given that members of the highest group have the right to define the way things really are" (p. 241). Because men typically have more power in organizations (Kanter, 1977), Becker's analysis suggests that in most situations the male definition of harassment is likely to predominate. As MacKinnon (1987) put it, "objectivity—the nonsituated, universal standpoint, whether claimed or aspired to—is a denial of the existence or potency of sex inequality that tacitly participates in constructing reality from the dominant point of view," (p. 136). "The law sees and treats women the way men see and treat women" (p. 140). This means that men's judgments about what behavior constitutes harassment, and who is to blame, are likely to prevail. Linenberger's 10 factors thus may not be an objective measure, but rather a 13 codification of the male perspective on harassment. This is likely to discourage women who want to bring complaints about more subtle forms of harassment.

SEX DIFFERENCES IN THE ATTRIBUTION OF HARASSMENT

Attribution theory provides an explanation for the wider range of behaviors that women define as harassment and for men's tendency to find women at fault (Kenig & Ryan, 1986; Pryor, 1985; Pryor & Day, 1988). Attribution theory suggests that people tend to see their own behaviors as situationally determined, whereas they attribute the behaviors of others to personality characteristics or other internal causes (E. E. Jones & Nisbett, 1971). Those who see sexual harassment through the eyes of the actor are likely to be male. As actors are wont to do, they will attribute their behaviors to situational causes, including the "provocations" of the women involved. They will then not perceive their own behaviors as harassment. In fact, those who take the perspective of the victim do see specific behaviors as more harassing than those who take the perspective of the actor (Pryor & Day, 1988). Women are more likely to view harassment through the eyes of the victim; therefore they will label more behaviors as harassment because they attribute them to men's disposition or personality traits. Another possibility is that men, as potential harassers, want to avoid blame in the future, and so shift the blame to women (Jensen & Gutek, 1982) and restrict the range of behaviors that they define as harassment (Kenig & Ryan, 1986). Whatever the cause, a reasonable man and a reasonable woman are likely to differ in their judgments of whether a particular behavior constitutes sexual harassment. 14

Men tend to misinterpret women's friendliness as an indication of sexual interest (Abbey, 1982; Abbey & Melby, 1986; Saal, Johnson, & Weber, 1989; Shotland & Craig, 1988). Acting on this misperception may result in behavior that is harassing to women. Tangri, Burt, and Johnson (1982) stated that "Some sexual harassment may indeed be clumsy or insensitive expressions of attraction, while some is the classic abuse of organizational power" (p. 52). Gender differences in attributional processes help explain the first type of harassment, partially accounting for the overwhelming preponderance of sexual harassment incidents that involve a male offender and a female victim. 15

GENDER BIAS IN GRIEVANCE PROCEDURES

Typically, procedures for resolving disputes about sexual harassment are written in gender-neutral terms so that they may apply to both women and men. However, men and women may react quite differently to the same procedures. 16

Analyzing this problem requires looking at specific policies and procedures. Educational institutions will serve as the context for this discussion 17 for three reasons. First, they are the most frequent site of surveys about the problem, and the pervasive nature of harassment on campuses has been well documented (Dzeich & Weiner, 1984). Second, although sexual harassment is harmful to women in all occupations, it can be particularly devastating to those in educational institutions, in which the goal of the organization is to nurture and promote development. The violation of relationships based on trust, such as those between faculty and students, can leave long-lasting and deep wounds, yet many surveys find that those in positions of authority in educational settings are often the sources of the problem (Benson & Thomson, 1982; Fitzgerald et al., 1988; Glaser & Thorpe, 1986; Kenig & Ryan, 1986; Maihoff & Forrest, 1983; Metha & Nigg, 1983; Robinson & Reid, 1985; K. R. Wilson & Kraus, 1983). Third, educational institutions have been leaders in the development of sexual harassment policies, in part because of concern about litigation. In *Alexander v. Yale University* (1977) the court decided that sexual harassment constitutes a form of sex discrimination that denies equal access to educational opportunities, and falls under Title IX of the Educational Amendments of 1972. The Office of Civil Rights in the U.S. Department of Education now requires institutions that receive Title IX funds to maintain grievance procedures to resolve complaints involving sexual discrimination or harassment (M. Wilson, 1988). Consequently, academic institutions may have had more experience than other work settings in developing procedures to combat this problem. A survey of U.S. institutions of higher learning conducted in 1984 (Robertson et al., 1988) found that 66% of all responding institutions had sexual harassment policies, and 46% had grievance procedures specifically designed to deal with sexual harassment complaints, with large public schools more likely to have them than small private ones. These percentages have unquestionably increased in recent years, given the government funding regulations. Although the discussion here is focused on educational contexts, the problems identified in sexual harassment policies exist in other work settings as well.

Many educational institutions, following guidelines put forward by the   18
American Council on Education (1986) and the American Association of University Professors (1983), have established policies that prohibit sexual harassment and create grievance procedures. Some use a formal board or hearing, and others use informal mechanisms that protect confidentiality and seek to resolve the complaint rather than punish the offender (see, e.g., Brandenburg, 1982; Meek & Lynch, 1983). Still others use both types of procedures. The type of procedure specified by the policy may have a great impact on victims' willingness to report complaints.

Comparison of Informal and Formal Grievance Procedures

Informal attempts to resolve disputes differ from formal procedures in   19
important ways (for a general discussion of dispute resolution systems, see Brett, Goldberg, & Ury, 1990). First, their goal is to solve a problem,

rather than to judge the harasser's guilt or innocence. The assumptions underlying these processes are that both parties in a dispute perceive a problem (although they may define that problem differently); that both share a common interest in solving that problem; and that together they can negotiate an agreement that will be satisfactory to everyone involved. Typically, the goal of informal processes is to end the harassment of the complainant rather than judge (and punish, if appropriate) the offender. The focus is on what will happen in the future between the disputing parties, rather than on what has happened in the past. Often policies do not specify the format of informal problem solving, but accept a wide variety of strategies of reconciliation. For example, a complainant might write a letter to the offender (Rowe, 1981), or someone might talk to the offender on the complainant's behalf. The offender and victim might participate in mediation, in which a third party helps them negotiate an agreement. Many policies accept a wide array of strategies as good-faith attempts to solve the problem informally.

In contrast, formal procedures generally require a written complaint   20 and have a specified procedure for handling cases, usually by bringing the complaint to a group officially designated to hear the case, such as a hearing board. The informal process typically ends when the complainant is satisfied (or decides to drop the complaint); the formal procedure ends when the hearing board decides on the guilt or innocence of the alleged harasser. Thus, control over the outcome usually rests with the complainant in the case of informal mechanisms, and with the official governance body in the case of a hearing. Compliance with a decision is usually voluntary in informal procedures, whereas the decision in a formal procedure is binding unless appealed to a higher authority. Formal procedures are adversarial in nature, with the complainant and defendant competing to see whose position will prevail.

A typical case might proceed as follows: A student with a complaint   21 writes a letter to the harasser (an informal procedure). If not satisfied with the response, she submits a written complaint to the sexual harassment hearing board, which then hears both sides of the case, reviews available evidence, and decides on the guilt or innocence of the accused (a formal procedure). If the accused is found guilty, the appropriate officer of the institution decides on punishment.

Gender Differences in Orientation to Conflict

Women and men may differ in their reactions to dispute resolution   22 procedures for at least two reasons. First, women typically have less power than men in organizations (Kanter, 1977). Using a grievance procedure, such as appearing before a hearing board, may be inimical because of the possibility of retaliation for a complaint. Miller (1976) suggested that differences in status and power affect the way that people handle conflict:

As soon as a group attains dominance it tends inevitably to produce a situation of conflict and . . . it also, simultaneously, seeks to suppress conflict. Moreover, subordinates who accept the dominant's conception of them as passive and malleable do not openly engage in conflict. Conflict . . . is forced underground (p. 127).

This may explain why some women do not report complaints at all. When they do complain, however, their relative lack of power or their values may predispose women to prefer informal rather than formal procedures. Beliefs about the appropriate way to handle disputes vary among social groups (Merry & Silbey, 1984). Gilligan's (1982) distinction between an orientation toward rights and justice compared with an emphasis on responsibilities to others and caring is likely to be reflected in people's preferences for ways of handling disputes (Kolb & Coolidge, 1988). Neither of these orientations is exclusive to one sex, but according to Gilligan, women are more likely to emphasize caring. Women's orientation to caring may be due to their subordinate status (Miller, 1976). Empirical support for Gilligan's theories is inconclusive (see, e.g., Mednick, 1989, for a summary of criticisms). Yet the fact that most victims of sexual harassment state that they simply want an end to the offending behavior rather than punishment of the offender (Robertson et al., 1988) suggests a "caring" rather than "justice" perspective (or possibly, a fear of reprisals).   23

In the context of dispute resolution, an emphasis on responsibilities and caring is compatible with the goals of informal procedures to restore harmony or at least peaceful coexistence among the parties involved, whereas that of justice is compatible with formal procedures that attempt to judge guilt or innocence of the offender. Thus women may prefer to use informal procedures to resolve conflicts, and indeed most cases in educational institutions are handled through informal mechanisms (Robertson et al., 1988). Policies that do not include an informal dispute resolution option are likely to discourage many women from bringing complaints.   24

Problems with Informal Dispute-Resolution Procedures

Although women may prefer informal mechanisms, they are problematic for several reasons (Rifkin, 1984). Because they do not result in punishment, offenders suffer few negative consequences of their actions and may not be deterred from harassing again. In institutions of higher learning, the most common form of punishment reported is a verbal warning by a supervisor, which is given only "sometimes" (Robertson et al., 1988). Dismissal and litigation are almost never used. It seems likely, then, that sexual harassment may be viewed by potential harassers as low-risk behavior, and that victims see few incentives for bringing official complaints.   25

The confidentiality usually required by informal procedures prevents other victims from knowing that a complaint has been lodged against a   26 multiple offender. If a woman knows that another woman is bringing a complaint against a particular man who has harassed both of them, then she might be more willing to complain also. The secrecy surrounding informal complaint processes precludes this information from becoming public and makes it more difficult to identify repeat offenders. Also, complaints settled informally may not be included in reports of the frequency of sexual harassment claims, making these statistics underestimate the scope of the problem. Yet confidentiality is needed to protect the rights of the accused and may be preferred by those bringing complaints.

These problems in informal procedures could discourage male as well 27 as female victims from bringing complaints. Most problematic for women, however, is the assumption in informal procedures that the complainant and accused have equal power in the process of resolving the dispute. This assumption is likely to put women at a disadvantage. Parties involved in sexual harassment disputes may not be equal either in the sense of formal position within the organization (e.g., student versus faculty) or status (e.g., female versus male students), and position and status characteristics that reflect levels of power do not disappear simply because they are irrelevant to the informal process. External status characteristics that indicate macrolevel social stratification (e.g., sex and age) help explain the patterns of distribution of sexual harassment in the workplace (Fain & Anderton, 1987). It seems likely that these external statuses will influence the interpersonal dynamics within a dispute-resolution procedure as well. Because women are typically lower than men in both formal and informal status and power in organizations, they will have less power in the dispute resolution process.

When the accused has more power than the complainant (e.g., a 28 male faculty member accused by a female student), the complainant is more vulnerable to retaliation. Complainants may be reluctant to use grievance procedures because they fear retaliation should the charge be made public. For example, students may fear that a faculty member will punish them for bringing a complaint by lowering their grades or withholding recommendations. The person appointed to act as a guide to the informal resolution process is usually expected to act as a neutral third party rather than advocate for the complainant, and may hold little formal power over faculty: "Relatively few institutions have persons empowered to be (nonlegal) advocates for the complainants; a student bringing a complaint has little assurance of stopping the harassment and avoiding retaliation" (Robertson et al., 1988, p. 801). The victim then is left without an advocate to face an opponent whose formal position, age, and experience with verbal argument is often considerably beyond her own. The more vulnerable a woman's position is in her organization, the more likely it is that she will be harassed (Robinson & Reid, 1985); therefore sexual harassment, like rape, involves dynamics of power and domination as well as sexuality. The lack of an advocate for the complainant who might equalize power between the disputing parties is particularly troubling. However, if an advocate is provided for the complainant in an informal process, fairness and due process require that the defendant have an advocate as well. The dilemma is that this seems likely to transform an informal, problem-solving process into a formal, adversarial one.

OTHER OBSTACLES TO REPORTING COMPLAINTS

Belief That Sexual Harassment of Women is Normative

Because of differences in perception of behavior, men and women   29
involved in a sexual harassment case are likely to have sharply divergent interpretations of that case, particularly when a hostile environment claim is involved. To women, the behavior in question is offensive, and they are likely to see themselves as victims of male actions. The requirement that an attempt be made to mediate the dispute or solve it through informal processes may violate their perception of the situation and of themselves as victims of a crime. By comparison, a victim of a mugging is not required to solve the problem with the mugger through mediation (B. Sandler, personal communication, 1988). To many men, the behavior is not offensive, but normative. In their eyes, no crime has been committed, and there is no problem to be solved.

Some women may also consider sexual harassment to be normative.   30
Women may believe that these sorts of behaviors are simply routine, a commonplace part of everyday life, and thus not something that can be challenged. Younger women—who are more likely to be victims (Fain & Anderton, 1987; LaFontaine & Tredeau, 1986; McIntyre & Renick, 1982)—are more tolerant of harassment than are older women (Lott et al., 1982; Reilly et al., 1986). Indeed, Lott et al. concluded that "younger women in particular have accepted the idea that prowling men are a 'fact of life' " (p. 318). This attitude might prevent women from labelling a negative experience as harassment. Surveys that ask women about sexual harassment and about the frequency of experiencing specific sexually harassing behaviors find discrepancies in responses to these questions (Fitzgerald et al., 1988). Women report higher rates when asked if they have been the target of specific harassing behaviors than when asked a general question about whether they have been harassed. Women are also more willing to report negative reactions to offensive behaviors than they are to label those behaviors as sexual harassment (Brewer, 1982).

Normative beliefs may deter some male victims of harassment from   31
reporting complaints also, because men are expected to welcome sexual advances if those advances are from women.

Negative Outcome for Victims Who Bring Complaints

The outcome of grievance procedures does not appear to provide   32
much satisfaction to victims who bring complaints. In academic settings, despite considerable publicity given to a few isolated cases in which

tenured faculty have been fired, punishments are rarely inflicted on harassers, and the punishments that are given are mild, such as verbal warnings (Robertson et al., 1988). Among federal workers, 33% of those who used formal grievance procedures to protest sexual harassment found that it "made things worse" (Livingston, 1982). More than 65% of the cases of formal charges of sexual harassment filed with the Illinois Department of Human Rights involved job discharge of the complainant (Terpstra & Cook, 1985). Less than one third of those cases resulted in a favorable settlement for the complainant, and those who received financial compensation got an average settlement of $3,234 (Terpstra & Baker, 1988). Similar findings in California were reported by Coles (1986), with the average cash settlement there of $973, representing approximately one month's pay. Although a few legal cases have resulted in large settlements (Garvey, 1986), these studies suggest that typical settlements are low. Formal actions may take years to complete, and in legal suits the victim usually must hire legal counsel at considerable expense (Livingston, 1982). These small settlements seem unlikely to compensate victims for the emotional stress, notoriety, and financial costs involved in filing a public complaint. Given the consistency with which victimization falls more often to women than men, it is ironic that one of the largest settlements awarded to an individual in a sexual harassment case ($196,500 in damages) was made to a man who brought suit against his female supervisor (Brewer & Berk, 1982), perhaps because sexual aggression by a woman is seen as especially egregious.

Emotional Consequences of Harassment

In academic settings, harassment can adversely affect students' learn- 33 ing, and therefore their academic standing. It can deprive them of educational and career opportunities because they wish to avoid threatening situations. Students who have been harassed report that they consequently avoid taking a class from or working with a particular faculty member, change their major, or leave a threatening situation (Adams et al., 1983; Lott et al., 1982). Lowered self-esteem follows the conclusion that rewards, such as a high grade, may have been based on sexual attraction rather than one's abilities (McCormack, 1985). Decreased feelings of competence and confidence and increased feelings of anger, frustration, depression, and anxiety all can result from harassment (Cammaert, 1985; Crull, 1982; Hamilton, Alagna, King & Lloyd, 1987; Livingston, 1982; Schneider, 1987). The psychological stress produced by harassment is compounded when women are fired or quit their jobs in fear or frustration (Coles, 1986).

Meek and Lynch (1983) proposed that victims of harassment typically 34 go through several stages of reaction, at first questioning the offender's true intentions and then blaming themselves for the offender's behavior. Women with traditional sex-role beliefs are more likely to blame themselves for being harassed (Jensen & Gutek, 1982). Victims then worry about being believed by others and about possible retaliation if they take formal steps to protest the behavior. A victim may be too frightened or confused to assert herself or punish the offender. Psychologists who work with victims of harassment would do well to recognize that not only victims' emotional reactions but also the nature of the grievance process as discussed in this article may discourage women from bringing formal complaints.

PREVENTION OF SEXUAL HARASSMENT

Some writers have argued that sexual harassment does not occur   35
with great frequency, or if it once was a problem, it has been eliminated in recent years. Indeed, Morgenson (1989), writing in the business publication *Forbes,* suggested that the whole issue had been drummed up by professional sexual harassment counselors in order to sell their services. Yet the studies cited in this article have documented that sexual harassment is a widespread problem with serious consequences.

Feminists and union activists have succeeded in gaining recognition   36
of sexual harassment as a form of sex discrimination (MacKinnon, 1979). The law now views sexual harassment not as the idiosyncratic actions of a few inconsiderate males but as part of a pattern of behaviors that reflect the imbalance of power between women and men in society. Women in various occupations and educational settings have sought legal redress for actions of supervisors or coworkers, and sexual harassment has become the focus of numerous organizational policies and grievance procedures (Brewer & Berk, 1982).

Well-publicized policies that use an inclusive definition of sexual harass-   37
ment, include an informal dispute resolution option, provide an advocate for the victim (if desired), and permit multiple offenders to be identified seem likely to be the most effective way of addressing claims of sexual harassment. However, even these modifications will not eliminate all of the problems in policies. The severity of the consequences of harassment for the victim, coupled with the problematic nature of grievance procedures and the mildness of punishments for offenders, makes retribution less effective than prevention of sexual harassment. Organizational leaders should not assume that their job is completed when they have established a sexual harassment policy. Extensive efforts at prevention need to be mounted at the individual, situational, and organizational level.

In prevention efforts aimed at the individual, education about harass-   38
ment should be provided (e.g., Beauvais, 1986). In particular, policymakers and others need to learn to "think like a woman" to define which behaviors constitute harassment and recognize that these behaviors are unacceptable. Understanding that many women find offensive more subtle forms of behavior such as sexual jokes or comments may help reduce the kinds of interactions that create a hostile environment. Educating

personnel about the punishments involved for offensive behavior also may have a deterring effect.

However, education alone is not sufficient. Sexual harassment is the product not only of individual attitudes and beliefs, but also of organizational practices. Dzeich and Weiner (1984, pp. 39–58) described aspects of educational institutions that facilitate sexual harassment, including the autonomy afforded the faculty, the diffusion of authority that permits lack of accountability, and the shortage of women in positions of authority. Researchers are beginning to identify the practices in other work settings that facilitate or support sexual harassment, and suggest that sexual harassment may be part of a pattern of unprofessional and disrespectful attitudes and behaviors that characterizes some workplaces (Gutek, 1985). **39**

Perhaps the most important factor in reducing sexual harassment is an organizational culture that promotes equal opportunities for women. There is a strong negative relationship between the level of perceived equal employment opportunity for women in a company and the level of harassment reported (LaFontaine & Tredeau, 1986): Workplaces low in perceived equality are the site of more frequent incidents of harassment. This finding suggests that sexual harassment both reflects and reinforces the underlying sexual inequality that produces a sex-segregated and sex-stratified occupational structure (Hoffman, 1986). The implementation of sexual harassment policies demonstrates the seriousness of those in authority; the language of the policies provides some measure of clarity about the types of behavior that are not acceptable; and grievance procedures may provide relief and legitimacy to those with complaints (Schneider, 1987). But neither policies nor procedures do much to weaken the structural roots of gender inequalities in organizations. **40**

Reforms intended to ameliorate women's position sometimes have unintended negative consequences (see Kirp, Yudof, & Franks, 1986). The presence of sexual harassment policies and the absence of formal complaints might promote the illusion that this problem has been solved. Assessment of whether organizational policies and practices promote or hinder equality for women is required to insure that this belief does not prevail. A long-range strategy for organizational reform in academia would thus attack the chilly climate for women in classrooms and laboratories (Project on the Status and Education of Women, 1982), the inferior quality of athletic programs for women, differential treatment of women applicants, the acceptance of the masculine as normative, and a knowledge base uninfluenced by women's values or experience (Fuehrer & Schilling, 1985). In other work settings, such a long-range approach would attack both sex-segregation of occupations and sex-stratification within authority hierarchies. Sexual harassment grievance procedures alone are not sufficient to insure that sexual harassment will be eliminated. An end to this problem requires gender equity within organizations. **41**

REFERENCES

Abbey, A. (1982). Sex differences in attributions for friendly behavior: Do males misperceive females' friendliness? *Journal of Personality and Social Psychology, 42,* 830–838.

Abbey, A., & Melby, C. (1986). The effects of nonverbal cues on gender differences in perceptions of sexual intent. *Sex Roles, 15,* 283–298.

Adams, J. W., Kottke, J. L., & Padgitt, J. S. (1983). Sexual harassment of university students. *Journal of College Student Personnel, 23,* 484–490.

Alexander et al. v. Yale University, 459 F. Supp. 1 (D. Conn. 1977), affirmed 631 F. 2d 178 (2nd Cir. 1980).

American Association of University Professors. (1983). Sexual harassment: Suggested policy and procedures for handling complaints. *Academe, 69,* 15a–16a.

American Council on Education. (1986). *Sexual harassment on campus: Suggestions for reviewing campus policy and educational programs.* Washington, DC: Author.

Beauvais, K. (1986). Workshops to combat sexual harassment: A case study of changing attitudes. *Signs: Journal of Women in Culture and Society, 12,* 130–145.

Becker, H. S. (1967). Whose side are we on? *Social Problems, 14,* 239–247.

Benson, D. J., & Thomson, G. (1982). Sexual harassment on a university campus: The confluence of authority relations, sexual interest and gender stratification. *Social Problems, 29,* 236–251.

Brandenburg, J. B. (1982). Sexual harassment in the university: Guidelines for establishing a grievance procedure. *Signs: Journal of Women in Culture and Society, 8,* 320–336.

Brett, J. M., Goldberg, S. B., & Ury, W. L. (1990). Designing systems for resolving disputes in organizations. *American Psychologist, 45,* 162–170.

Brewer, M. (1982). Further beyond nine to five: An integration and future directions. *Journal of Social Issues, 38,* 149–157.

Brewer, M. B., & Berk, R. A. (1982). Beyond nine to five: Introduction. *Journal of Social Issues, 38,* 1–4.

Bumiller, K. (1987). Victims in the shadow of the law: A critique of the model of legal protection. *Signs: Journal of Women in Culture and Society, 12,* 421–439.

Burleigh, N., & Goldberg, S. (1989). Breaking the silence: Sexual harassment in law firms. *ABA Journal, 75,* 46–52.

Cammaert, L. P. (1985). How widespread is sexual harassment on campus? *International Journal of Women's Studies, 8,* 388–397.

Cohen, C. F. (1987, November). Legal dilemmas in sexual harassment cases. *Labor Law Journal,* 681–689.

Coles, F. S. (1986). Forced to quit: Sexual harassment complaints and agency response. *Sex Roles, 14,* 81–95.

Collins, E. G. C., & Blodgett, T. B. (1981). Some see it . . . some won't. *Harvard Business Review, 59,* 76–95.

Crull, P. (1982). The stress effects of sexual harassment on the job. *American Journal of Orthopsychiatry, 52,* 539–543.

Dzeich, B., & Weiner, L. (1984). *The lecherous professor.* Boston: Beacon Press.

Fain, T. C., & Anderton, D. L. (1987). Sexual harassment: Organizational context and diffuse status. *Sex Roles, 5/6,* 291–311.

Fitzgerald, L. F., Schullman, S. L., Bailey, N., Richards, M., Swecker, J., Gold, Y., Ormerod, M., & Weitzman, L. (1988). The incidence and dimensions of sexual harassment in academia and the workplace. *Journal of Vocational Behavior, 32,* 152–175.

Fuehrer, A., & Schilling, K. M. (1985). The values of academe: Sexism as a natural consequence. *Journal of Social Issues, 41,* 29–42.

Garvey, M. S. (1986). The high cost of sexual harassment suits. *Labor Relations, 65,* 75–79.

Gilligan, C. (1982). *In a different voice: Psychological theory and women's development.* Cambridge, MA: Harvard University Press.

Glaser, R. D., & Thorpe, J. S. (1986). Unethical intimacy: A survey of sexual contact and advances between psychology educators and female graduate students. *American Psychologist, 41,* 43–51.

Gutek, B. A. (1985). *Sex and the workplace.* San Francisco: Jossey-Bass.

Gutek, B. A., Morasch, B., & Cohen, A. G. (1983). Interpreting social-sexual behavior in a work setting. *Journal of Vocational Behavior, 22,* 30–48.

Hamilton, J. A., Alagna, S. W., King, L. S., & Lloyd, C. (1987). The emotional consequences of gender-based abuse in the workplace: New counseling programs for sex discrimination. *Women and Therapy, 6,* 155–182.

Hoffman, F. L. (1986). Sexual harassment in academia: Feminist theory and institutional practice. *Harvard Educational Review, 56*(2), 107–121.

Jensen, I. W., & Gutek, B. A. (1982). Attributions and assignment of responsibility in sexual harassment. *Journal of Social Issues, 38,* 121–136.

Jones, E. E., & Nisbett, R. E. (1971). *The actor and the observer: Divergent perceptions of the causes of behavior.* Morristown, N.J.: General Learning Press.

Jones, T. S., Remland, M. S., & Brunner, C. C. (1987). Effects of employment relationship, response of recipient and sex of rater on perceptions of sexual harassment. *Perceptual and Motor Skills, 65,* 55–63.

Kanter, R. M. (1977). *Men and women of the corporation.* New York: Basic Books.

Kenig, S., & Ryan, J. (1986). Sex differences in levels of tolerance and attribution of blame for sexual harassment on a university campus. *Sex Roles, 15,* 535–549.

Kirk, D. (1988, August). *Gender differences in the perception of sexual harassment.* Paper presented at the Academy of Management National Meeting, Anaheim, CA.

Kirp, D. L., Yudof, M. G., & Franks, M. S. (1986). *Gender justice.* Chicago: University of Chicago Press.

Kolb, D. M., & Coolidge, G. G. (1988). *Her place at the table: A consideration of gender issues in negotiation* (Working paper series 88-5). Harvard Law School, Program on Negotiation.

Konrad, A. M., & Gutek, B. A. (1986). Impact of work experiences on attitudes toward sexual harassment. *Administrative Science Quarterly, 31,* 422–438.

LaFontaine, E., & Tredeau, L. (1986). The frequency, sources, and correlates of sexual harassment among women in traditional male occupations. *Sex Roles, 15,* 433–442.

Lester, D., Banta, B., Barton, J., Elian, N., Mackiewicz, L., & Winkelried, J. (1986). Judgments about sexual harassment: Effects of the power of the harasser. *Perceptual and Motor Skills, 63,* 990.

Linenberger, P. (1983, April). What behavior constitutes sexual harassment? *Labor Law Journal, 238–247.*

Littler-Bishop, S., Seidler-Feller, D., & Opaluch, R. E. (1982). Sexual harassment in the workplace as a function of initiator's status: The case of airline personnel. *Journal of Social Issues, 38,* 137–148.

Livingston, J. A. (1982). Responses to sexual harassment on the job: Legal, organizational, and individual actions. *Journal of Social Issues, 38*(4), 5–22.

Lott, B., Reilly, M. E., & Howard, D. R. (1982). Sexual assault and harassment: A campus community case study. *Signs: Journal of Women in Culture and Society, 8,* 296–319.

MacKinnon, C. A. (1979). *Sexual harassment of working women: A case of sex discrimination.* New Haven, CT: Yale University Press.

MacKinnon, C. A. (1987). Feminism, Marxism, method and the state: Toward feminist jurisprudence. In S. Harding (Ed.), *Feminism and methodology: Social science issues.* Bloomington: Indiana University Press.

Maihoff, N., & Forrest, L. (1983). Sexual harassment in higher education: An assessment study. *Journal of the National Association for Women Deans, Administrators, and Counselors, 46,* 3–8.

Maypole, D. E. (1986). Sexual harassment of social workers at work: Injustice within? *Social Work, 31,* 29–34.

Maypole, D. E., & Skaine, R. (1982). Sexual harassment of blue-collar workers. *Journal of Sociology and Social Welfare, 9,* 682–695.

McCormack, A. (1985). The sexual harassment of students by teachers: The case of students in science. *Sex Roles, 13,* 21–32.

McIntyre, D. I., & Renick, J. C. (1982). Protecting public employees and employers from sexual harassment. *Public Personnel Management Journal, 11,* 282–292.

Mednick, M. T. (1989). On the politics of psychological constructs: Stop the bandwagon, I want to get off. *American Psychologist, 44,* 1118–1123.

Meek, P. M., & Lynch, A. Q. (1983). Establishing an informal grievance procedure for cases of sexual harassment of students. *Journal of the National Association for Women Deans, Administrators, & Counselors, 46,* 30–33.

Merry, S. E., & Silbey, S. S. (1984). What do plaintiffs want? Reexamining the concept of dispute. *Justice System Journal, 9,* 151–178.

Metha, J., & Nigg, A. (1983). Sexual harassment on campus: An institutional response. *Journal of the National Association for Women Deans, Administrators, & Counselors, 46,* 9–15.

Miller, J. B. (1976). *Toward a new psychology of women.* Boston: Beacon Press.

Morgenson, G. (1989, May). Watch that leer, stifle that joke. *Forbes,* 69–72.

Popovich, P. M., Licata, B. J., Nokovich, D., Martelli, T., & Zoloty, S. (1987). Assessing the incidence and perceptions of sexual harassment behaviors among American undergraduates. *Journal of Psychology, 120,* 387–396.

Powell, G. N. (1986). Effects of sex role identity and sex on definitions of sexual harassment. *Sex Roles, 14,* 9–19.

Project on the Status and Education of Women. (1982). The campus climate: A chilly one for women? Washington, DC: Association of American Colleges.

Pryor, J. B. (1985). The lay person's understanding of sexual harassment. *Sex Roles, 13,* 273–286.

Pryor, J. B., & Day, J. D. (1988). Interpretations of sexual harassment: An attributional analysis. *Sex Roles, 18,* 405–417.

Reilly, M. E., Lott, B., & Gallogly, S. (1986). Sexual harassment of university students. *Sex Roles, 15,* 333–358.

Rifkin, J. (1984). Mediation from a feminist perspective: Promise and problems. *Mediation, 2,* 21–31.

Robertson, C., Dyer, C. E., & Campbell, D. (1988). Campus harassment: Sexual harassment policies and procedures at institutions of higher learning. *Signs: Journal of Women in Culture and Society, 13,* 792–812.

Robinson, W. L., & Reid, P. T. (1985). Sexual intimacy in psychology revisited. *Professional Psychology: Research and Practice, 16,* 512–520.

Rossi, P. H., & Weber-Burdin, E. (1983). Sexual harassment on the campus. *Social Science Research, 12,* 131–158.

Rowe, M. P. (1981, May–June). Dealing with sexual harassment. *Harvard Business Review,* 42–46.

Saal, F. E., Johnson, C. B., & Weber, N. (1989). Friendly or sexy? It may depend on whom you ask. *Psychology of Women Quarterly, 13,* 263–276.

Schneider, B. E. (1987). Graduate women, sexual harassment, and university policy. *Journal of Higher Education, 58,* 46–65.

Shotland, R. L., & Craig, J. M. (1988). Can men and women differentiate between friendly and sexually interested behavior? *Social Psychology Quarterly, 51,* 66–73.

Tangri, S. S., Burt, M. R., & Johnson, L. B. (1982). Sexual harassment at work: Three explanatory models. *Journal of Social Issues, 38,* 33–54.

Terpstra, D. E., & Baker, D. D. (1988). Outcomes of sexual harassment charges. *Academy of Management Journal, 31,* 185–194.

Terpstra, D. E., & Cook, S. E. (1985). Complainant characteristics and reported behaviors and consequences associated with formal sexual harassment charges. *Personnel Psychology, 38,* 559–574.

Thomann, D. A., & Wiener, R. L. (1987). Physical and psychological causality as determinants of culpability in sexual harassment cases. *Sex Roles, 17,* 573–591.

Trager, T. B. (1988). Legal considerations in drafting sexual harassment policies. In J. Van Tol (Ed.), *Sexual harassment on campus: A legal compendium* (pp. 181–190). Washington, DC: National Association of College and University Attorneys.

U.S. Equal Employment Opportunity Commission. (1980, November 10). Final amendment to guidelines on discrimination because of sex under Title VII of the Civil Rights Act of 1964, as amended. 29 CFR Part 1604. *Federal Register, 45,* 74675–74677.

U.S. Merit Systems Protection Board. (1981). *Sexual harassment in the federal workplace: Is it a problem?* Washington, DC: U.S. Government Printing Office.

U.S. Merit Systems Protection Board. (1988). *Sexual harassment in the federal government: An update.* Washington, DC: Government Printing Office.

Wilson, K. R., & Krause, L. A. (1983). Sexual harassment in the university. *Journal of College Student Personnel, 24,* 219–224.

Wilson, M. (1988). Sexual harassment and the law. *The Community Psychologist, 21,* 16–17.

◾

HARASSMENT BLUES

Naomi Munson

Munson questions present definitions of sexual harassment and confusion between harassing remarks and innuendo. The writer blames "feminist rage," for much of the failure to distinguish between harassment and normal insensitivity in the workplace.

When I was graduated from college in the early '70s, I had the good   1
fortune to land a job at a weekly newsmagazine. It was a wonderful place
to work, financially lucrative, intellectually demanding but not overwhelming, and, above all, fun.

There was, actually, a sort of hierarchy of fun at the office. Ranking   2
lowest were the hard-news departments; although (or perhaps because)
they offered the excitement of late-breaking news and fast-developing
stories, both the national- and the foreign-affairs sections were socially
rather staid. Next up the scale came the business section, where the people were lively enough but where the general tone nevertheless reflected
the serious nature of the subject matter. Then there was the culture
department, a barrel of laughs in its own way, though the staff did seem
to spend a certain amount of time at the opera. At the top of the scale
stood the department where I wound up, which included science, sports,
education, religion, and the like. Though there might be the occasional
breaking news, these sections generally called more for long thought and
thorough research, which led to a very laidback atmosphere and a lot of
down time. Drinking at nearby bars, dining at the finest restaurants, and
dancing at local discos occupied a great deal of that time. And sex
played a major role in all of this. (It did throughout the magazine, of
course, but nowhere so openly and unselfconsciously as here.)

The men were a randy lot, dedicated philanderers, and foul-mouthed   3
to boot; the women, having vociferously demanded—and been
granted—absolutely equal status, were considered fair game (though
there were a couple of secretaries whose advancing age and delicate
sensibilities consigned them to the sidelines).

Imagine my surprise, then, when one day a young woman who   4
worked with me flounced into my office, cheeks flushed, eyes flashing, to
announce that she had just been subjected to sexual harassment. (It
was a fairly new concept back then, at the end of the '70's, but being in
the vanguard of social trends, we had heard of it.) When she explained
that the offense had occurred not in our own neck of the woods but
in the national-affairs section, I was truly shocked. When she identified
the offender, however—sexually, one of the least lively types on the
premises—I began to be skeptical. And when she described his crime—
which was having said something to the effect that he longed for the
good old days of miniskirts when a fellow had a real chance to see great
legs like hers—I scoffed. "Oh, come on," I said. "That's not sexual
harassment; that's just D. trying to pay you a compliment." To myself,
after she had calmed down and left, I said, "She's even dimmer than I
thought. She thinks *that's* what they mean by sexual harassment."

If I was convinced that this woman's experience did not constitute sex-   5
ual harassment, I, like the vast majority of people at that time, had rather
vague notions of what did. Whatever it was, however, it already seemed
clear that the charge of sexual harassment would serve as a perfect
instrument of revenge for disgruntled female employees. This was borne
out by the story I came to know, years later, about a man at another
office who had had several formal harassment charges brought against
him by women who worked for him. The man was someone who would,
as his coworkers saw it, "nail" anything that moved. He had, in fact, had
longstanding affairs—which he had ended in order to move on to fresh
conquests—with the women now accusing him of having offered financial inducements in exchange for sexual favors. The women claimed to
have declined the offers and consequently suffered the loss of promotions.

Disgruntlement aside, however, it still seemed obvious to me that in a   6
case of sexual harassment, something *sexual* might be supposed to
have occurred. That quaint notion of mine was finally laid to rest during
the Clarence Thomas-Anita Hill debacle. Professor Hill's performance
convinced me of nothing save that if she told me the sun was shining, I
would head straight for my umbrella and galoshes. The vast outpouring
of feminist outrage that accompanied the event did, however, succeed in
opening my eyes to the sad fact that it was I, way back when, who had
been the dim one; my erstwhile colleague had merely been a bit ahead of
her time. For, it now turns out, what she described is precisely what they
do mean by sexual harassment.

During the course of the hearing, story after story appeared in the   7
media supporting the claim that men out there are abusive to their
female employees. It was declared, over and over, that virtually every
woman in the country had either suffered sexual harassment herself or
knew someone who had (I myself, I realize, figure in that assessment).
The abuse, it appeared, had been going on since time immemorial and

was so painful to some of the women involved that they had repressed it for decades.

It became clear amid all the hand-wringing that we were not talking 8 here about bosses exacting sexual favors in exchange for promotions, raises, or the like. Even Professor Hill never claimed that Judge Thomas promised to promote her if she succumbed to his charms, or that he threatened to fire her if she failed to do so. What she said, as all the world now knows, was that he pestered her for dates; that he boasted of his natural endowments and of his sexual prowess; that he used obscene language in her presence; that he regaled her with the details of porno flicks; and that he discussed the joys of, as Miss Hill so expressively put it, "(gulp) oral sex." The closest anyone at the hearing came to revealing anything like direct action was a Washington woman who was horrified when a member of Congress played footsie with her under the table at an official function, and a friend of Anita Hill who announced that she had been "touched in the workplace."

What we—or, to be more precise, they—were talking about was sexual 9 innuendo, ogling, obscenity, unwelcome importuning, nude pin-ups; about an "unpleasant atmosphere in the workplace"; about male "insensitivity." One columnist offered behavioral guidelines to men who had been reduced to "whining" that they no longer knew what was appropriate—something to the effect that though it is OK to say, "Gee, I bet you make the best blackened redfish in town," it is not OK to say, "Wow, I bet you're really hot between the sheets." Even Judge Thomas himself declared that if he *had* said the things the good professor was accusing him of, it *would* have constituted sexual harassment.

Yet in response to all of this it also emerged very plainly that the Amer- 10 ican public just was not buying it. Single women were heard to worry that putting a lid on sex at the office might hurt their chances of finding a husband; one forthright woman was even quoted by a newspaper as saying that office sex was the spice of life. Rather more definitively, polls showed that most people, black and white, male and female, thought Judge Thomas should be confirmed, *even if the charges against him were true.*

How can it be that the majority of Americans were dismissing the sig- 11 nificance of sexual harassment (as now defined) even as their elected representatives were declaring it just the most hideous, heinous, gosh-awful stuff they had ever heard of? How is it possible that, at the very moment newspapers and TV were proclaiming that American women were mad as hell and weren't going to take it any more, most of these women themselves—and their husbands—were responding with a raised eyebrow and a small shrug of the shoulders?

For one thing, most Americans—unlike the ideologues who brought 12 us sexual harassment in the first place, and who have worked a special magic on pundits and politicos for more than two decades now—have a keen understanding of life's realities. Having had no choice but to work, in order to feed and clothe and doctor and educate their children, they have always known that, while work has its rewards, financial and otherwise, "an unpleasant atmosphere in the workplace" is something they may well have to put up with. That, where women are concerned, the unpleasantness might take on sexual overtones gives it no more weight than the uncertainties, the frustrations, and the humiliations, petty and grand, encountered by men.

Most people, furthermore, have a healthy respect for the ability of women to hold their own in the battle of the sexes. They know that women have always managed to deal perfectly well with male lust: to evade it, to quash it, even to be flattered by it. The bepaunched and puffing boss, chasing his buxom secretary around the desk, is, after all, a figure of fun—because we realize that he will never catch her, and that even if he did, she would know very well how to put him in his place. 13

The women's movement and its fellow travelers, on the other hand, have never had any such understanding or any such respect. On the contrary, rage against life's imperfections, and a consequent revulsion against men, has been the bone and sinew of that movement. 14

The feminists came barreling into the workforce, some twenty years ago, not out of necessity, but with the loud assertion that here was to be found something called fulfillment. Men, they claimed, had denied them access to this fulfillment out of sheer power-hungry selfishness. Women, they insisted, were no different from men in their talents or their dispositions; any apparent differences had simply been manufactured, as a device to deprive mothers, wives, and sisters of the excitement and pleasure to which men had had exclusive title for so long, and which they had come to view as their sole privilege. 15

No sooner had these liberated ladies taken their rightful place alongside men at work, however, than it began to dawn on them that the experience was not quite living up to their expectations. They quickly discovered, for example, what their fathers, husbands, and brothers had always known: that talent is not always appreciated, that promotions are not so easy to come by, that often those most meritorious are inexplicably passed over in favor of others. But rather than recognizing this as a universal experience, they descried a "glass ceiling," especially constructed to keep them in their place, and they called for the hammers. 16

Feminists had insisted that child-bearing held no more allure for them than it did for men. That insistence quickly began to crumble in the face of a passionate desire for babies. But rather than recognizing that life had presented them with a choice, they demanded special treatment. They reserved the right to take leave from their work each time the urge to procreate came upon them. And they insisted that husbands, employers, and even the government take equal responsibility with them for the care and upbringing of the little bundles of joy resulting from that urge. 17

And as for sex in the workplace, well, that was pretty much what it had   18
always been everywhere: an ongoing battle involving, on the one side,
attentions both unwelcome and welcome, propositions both unappealing
and appealing, and compliments both unpleasing and pleasing, and on
the other, evasive action, outright rejection, or happy capitulation. Having
long ago decided that the terms of this age-old battle were unacceptable
to them, the women of the movement might have been expected to try
to eliminate them. With the invention of sexual harassment, they have
met that expectation, and with a vengeance. Laws have been made,
cases have been tried and, in the Clarence Thomas affair, a decent man
was pilloried.

Having, in other words, finally been permitted to play with the big   19
boys, these women have found the game not to their liking. But rather
than retiring from the field, they have called for a continuous and open-
ended reformation of the rules. Indeed, like children in a temper, who
respond to maternal placating with a rise in fury, they have met every
accommodating act of the men in their lives with a further escalation of
demand. The new insistence that traditional male expressions of sexual
interest be declared taboo, besides being the purest revelation of feminist
rage, is the latest arc in that vicious cycle.

FEAR OF FLIRTING

Erica Jong

Author Jong, while deploring the actions of many recently noted sexual
harassers, argues for more tolerance toward a special class of harassers
who can't "bring [their] intellect and [their] emotions into the same century,"
who support women's issues with their heads but can't find it in their hearts
to quit trying to exploit them.

I have never worked on Capital Hill with Sen. Bob Packwood and his   1
many merry colleagues, so maybe I am not to be considered an expert
on sexual harassment. But in 20 years as a professional author, I've had
my share of midnight phone calls from obscure publishers at the Frank-
furt Book Fair and, as a young miniskirted poet, of being groped at the
Algonquin Round Table by old goats who didn't seem to know whether
they wanted my next folio or my next something-else-that-starts-with-"f"-
that-you-can't-write-in-a-family-newspaper.

In my callow youth, there were no grievance committees to combat   2
sexual harassment. The very term had not yet been invented. You simply
ran around the desk, smiled sweetly and told the old goat that though he
was devastatingly attractive, you had: a) a boyfriend, b) your period (that

generation saw this as a deterrent) or c) a communicable disease (pre-AIDS, this was less daunting than it would be today). You assumed you had to flatter him. After all, he had the power and you didn't. It never occurred to you to call in the Rape Crisis Commandoes. There were none to call.

Now I admit this makes me sound like a fossil. My daughter accuses   3
me of being "from the '70s" in a way that makes '70s sound like "old Stone Age." But few of us got raped by old goats (some did, to be sure) and some of us managed to keep our careers and our values. We hated the condescension of being treated like objects, but we also liked having sexual power over men; above all, we assumed that men were men—i.e., less evolved than we were—and that given the topsy-turvy state of the world—i.e., the less evolved had more power—we had to figure out how to survive and thrive.

We also wanted to change the world, but realizing that might not   4
come soon enough for us to benefit as our daughters will, we evolved various strategies to stay alive. We might not find these strategies ideologically pure, but ideological purity was a luxury we could not afford. Survival was. Survival and the best use of our talents. Look, even Gloria Steinem dressed up as a bunny and got a brilliant piece out of it. That's what you did then: turned second sexdom into intelligence, wit, a glittering piece of prose.

Times change. Generations change. Sen. Packwood can't make the   5
connection between the legislation he votes for and the pretty young things he chases around his desk when drunk (or even when sober). Like Woody Allen, he has a moral blind spot the size of Oregon. He may be pro-choice in his votes, pro-woman in his hiring, but he just doesn't understand that the times they are a-changing. Too bad for him. And too bad for the 15 or so women he harassed. But what is the price he should pay? He did vote for women's rights while he perpetrated these wrongs. His public stance was as enlightened as his private stance was benighted. In a party that had thrown itself fiercely to the right, he stayed with women on women's issues. Meanwhile, he played out a kind of parody of *droit de seigneur* in the back office. Like Woody Allen, he couldn't bring his intellect and his emotions into the same century.

What to do about men like that? They are a vanishing breed, but alas,   6
they aren't vanishing fast enough. They don't know the new rules of male-female interaction. They don't understand that what's wrong with sexual harassment is that it's an abuse of power. They don't see the unfairness of the power they have and they don't understand that with power comes weighty responsibility. They are fiduciaries of female trust—Woody as stepfather, Packwood as senator. We expect more of them, not less. As with Clarence Thomas, we expect exemplary behavior. When we get something less—much less—we are very disappointed.

The Packwood ethics probe is a clash of generations. A man of 30   7
would know better than to do what Packwood did. But even men of 30
are confused. "What's the line between flirtation and harassment?" they
often ask. Terrified of rejection by women they fancy, they now have to
face court-martial by the sexual harassment commandoes. It will be surprising if any erection ever survives this scrutiny. One suspects that the
sexual harassment commandoes will be happy with this outcome
because sex is insufficiently P.C. anyway. Puritans that they are, they want
to rule out even the possibility of the messiness of sex. Babies by artificial
insemination are much neater, not to mention ideologically pure.

While I am glad that sexual harassment is now recognized as a phe-   8
nomenon and glad that Sen. Packwood's and Woody Allen's generation
are inevitably being replaced by younger, more empathetic males, the
question remains: How should we treat these old guys—as antiques or
as rapists? It's a tough question because these dirty old men grew up in
another world, a world where standards were different. They must feel
baffled by being judged the way we would judge younger men, and yet
we cannot allow them to act like Louis XIV in the halls of Versailles—or
even in the halls of Congress, not to mention the Astoria Studios. In a
clockwork-orange world they would be reprogrammed: locked in a room
with Andrea Dworkin until they came to understand the many errors of
their ways. Perhaps that *is* the path they *voluntarily* should take. Or else
we should invent a 12-step program designed especially for men who
abuse power over women: "I discovered I was powerless over my abuse
of power and my life had become unmanageable. . . ." But until such
therapy exists, shall we simply call for their ouster?

I, for one, would have loved to see Les AuCoin elected for his support   9
for the National Endowment for the Arts, if nothing else, but I also recognize that Packwood stood up for women in a dark time. We do not
excuse his egregious blindness to women's needs as autonomous individuals, but should there be a grandfather clause for some of these ideologically impure people who helped us along the way? Who is so ideologically pure that she has never done a non-P.C. thing in her life? Not me.

I am for working to change the system, but I am also for mercy and   10
rehabilitation. A just goddess would make Packwood into a pretty young
aide on Capital Hill for a day. Then he'd understand. But failing the reap-
pearance of Juno in Washington, how to retrain him? More to the point,
shall we allow feminism to become a reign of terror? We are all—men
and women both—stumbling human beings. If we can't forgive each
other, how can we ever forgive ourselves? Above all, how can we eradicate sexism without eradicating sex?

In some curious way, I feel more able to deal with old goats chasing   11
me around the desk than with the ideology commandoes who want
to scrutinize my writing to make sure I never say a non-P.C. thing as long

as I live. I can trip the old goat or I can call his wife, but the P.C. brigade will never be satisfied with anything as ambivalent or murky as human nature. Under their stern care, art will turn to agitprop and humor will be banned for having double vision. Love songs will be silenced for abetting sex, wine for dissolving the superego and miniskirts for provoking lasciviousness. Hollywood will close down—for what happens both on the screen and behind the screens. Broadway will go dark. Novels will all have to be rewritten for political correctness and no one will ever dare make a dirty joke. Apparently, Cotton Mather still rules America.

Much as I loathe the Packwoods and Allens of this world, I *fear* the   12
P.C. commandoes. Packwood and Allen are motivated by lust and power, but the sexual harassment squads claim benevolence and feminism as their only motives. Hah! When people prate of their purity, I reach for my gun.

Something about the sexual harassment hysteria is starting to remind   13
me of the adolescent girls in "The Crucible" or the raving nuns in "The Devils of Loudun." Just as men can use sexuality for political power, women can use anti-sexuality for political power. It has happened before in this country: The Women's Christian Temperance Union arose out of the same social forces that produced the first wave of feminism.

If we get rid of Packwood, what message are we sending to other   14
men who voted for women's legislation? Women will get you no matter what you do? I dare to ask the forbidden question because as a feminist I always worry about feminism when it moves from legislating public issues to legislating private ones. America is a Puritan country and feminists can be just as puritanical as male chauvinists. It is the Amercan disease to want to tell people how to behave in bed, but I am one who thinks feminists should be immune to this disease. When we become infected, I fear we are setting up the next backlash. When we become infected, I fear we have fallen into a right-wing trap. Sexual hot-button issues like harassment serve to distract us from focusing, for instance, on the fact that women continue to be underpaid. But take away economic inequity, and I believe that sexual inequity will eventually wither too.

Yes, I do expect greater enlightenment from women than from men.   15
Call me a female chauvinist, but I believe that women are the more spiritually advanced sex. If we take our power and use it as badly as men have used theirs throughout the centuries, we will not have brought about the world of equality we seek.

I want a feminist movement that allows for singing, dancing, humor,   16
sex and free speech. Punish the villains, but punish them fairly. Reprogram the abusers and get them to use their seniority to make the world safe for women. If we demand a feminism so pure that no human being is good enough, we won't be able to join our own movement.

WATCH THAT LEER, STIFLE THAT JOKE

Gretchen Morgenson

Forbes *writer Morgenson argues that "the alleged increase in sexual harass-ment [is]more a product of propaganda from self-interested parties," than from substantive cases.*

It's been almost ten years since the Equal Employment Opportunity Commission wrote its guidelines defining sexual harassment as a form of sex discrimination and, therefore, illegal under Title VII of the Civil Rights Act of 1964.   1

During that time, women have transformed the workplace, taken on untraditional jobs, excelled in male-oriented businesses, started their own firms and garnered new power on corporate boards.   2

Have women been harassed every inch of the way by leering, lascivi-ous male chauvinists? It sometimes sounds that way. Following the Equal Employment Opportunity Commission's lead, an estimated three out of four companies nationwide have instituted strict policies against harass-ment; millions of dollars are dutifully spent each year educating employ-ees in Title VII etiquette.   3

What are the boundaries? Where does good-humored kidding cease and harassment begin? How deeply should the courts concern them-selves with personal behavior and good manners? Requests or demands for sexual favors are clear-cut cases of behavior that lie beyond the pale. Sleep-with-me-and-you'll-get-promoted propositions are clearly illegal. Where the law gets hazy and goes beyond where some reasonable peo-ple think the law should go is in what is known as hostile environment harassment—the hazing, joking, sexually suggestive talk between men and the women who work alongside them.   4

Both types of behavior are increasing? That's the story you get from the media, which loves a salacious issue, and from employee relations consultants who make money telling corporations how to protect them-selves from costly harassment claims. These are the loudest voices in the din. Loud but not persuasive.   5

The peddlers of sex harassment advice have, of course, their own moneymaking agenda. Equally suspect are those extremists who would politicize all of American life and seek to regulate human behavior to suit their private prejudices. These people want to impose stringently moralis-tic standards on private industry that are not met in any other environ-ment. It's all part of the transformation taking place today in employment law in which employers' responsibilities to their workers seem to grow just as workers' responsibilities to the bosses seem to diminish.   6

A growth industry has sprung up to dispense harassment advice to worried companies in the form of seminars, videos and group gropes.   7

The deeper *Forbes* delved, the more we became convinced that the alleged increase in sexual harassment was more a product of propa-   8 ganda from self-interested parties. "At least 35% and as many as 90% of women get harassed," contends Linda Krystal Doran, president of Krystal & Kalan Associates, a sex harassment consultant in Issaquah, Wash. Doran conjures up images of a major portion of the work force wolfishly and lustfully abused by another portion. If her figures are taken seriously, as many as 49 million women are getting pinched, propositioned or annoyed on the job.

But why then is the number of federal cases alleging harassment on   9
the job actually declining? This, in spite of a growing female work force. According to the EEOC, where anyone bringing a federal sex harassment case must first file a complaint, the number of Title VII complaints in which sexual harassment was mentioned peaked at 6,342 five years ago; last year there were 4,984 cases.

Sound like a lot? It's not. It's 0.0091% of the female work force—one   10
in every 11,000. And that's cases filed, not cases proven. Furthermore, these cases may primarily involve other forms of discrimination: race, national origin, color and religion.

Forbes consulted human rights commissions that compile such fig-   11
ures in four populous, regionally diverse states: California, Michigan, New York and Texas. Excepting California, where there has been a modest increase, sex harassment cases in these states are down.

Yet the money to be made these days advising corporations on the   12
issue of harassment is not insubstantial. Susan Webb, president of Pacific Resource Development Group, a Seattle consultant, says she spends 95% of her time advising on sex harassment. Like most of the consultants, Webb acts as an expert witness in harassment cases, conducts investigations for companies or municipalities and teaches seminars. She charges clients $1,495 to buy her 60-minute sex harassment video program and handbooks. Webb, who's worked for 350 companies or municipalities, is one of a dozen such consultants, and her prices are typical. Solving the problem is supposed to be their business, but hyping the problem is very much in their personal interests.

Michael Connolly, former general counsel to the EEOC, and now a   13
partner at Cross Wrock in Detroit, says: "There are a lot of bad consultants taking advantage of the fact that harassment is in vogue." There are even consultants who act as agents for other consultants. Jennifer Coplon of Resource Group-Videolearning in Boston represents some 15 sex harassment video producers, connecting them with corporations, universities and government agencies. "Among all employment issues, sexual harassment is the biggest concern among companies," she reports happily.

Sexual harassment became a serious legal issue in the early 1980s,   14
just after the Equal Employment Opportunity Commission published its first guidelines. But it was Mentor Savings Bank v. Vinson, a harassment case that made it to the Supreme Court in 1986, that really acted as a full employment act for sex harassment consultants. In Vinson, the

Supreme Court conveyed the idea that employers could limit their liability to harassment claims by implementing antiharassment policies and procedures in the workplace. And so the antiharassment industry was born. Even today corporate attorneys are sometimes the best salespeople for the sexual harassment prevention industry. They tell their bosses that the existence of a corporate program should be part of a company's legal defenses.

No surprise then that sexual harassment consultants like to claim the problem is getting worse, not better.   15

What about those bothersome EEOC numbers? The consultants say that there is a more than offsetting increase in private suits. Really? There's simply no proof that huge or increasing numbers of private actions are being filed and litigated. The San Francisco law firm of Orrick, Herrington & Sutcliffe has monitored private sex harassment cases filed in California since 1984. From 1984 to March 1989, the number of sexual harassment cases in California that were litigated through to a verdict totaled 15. That's in a litigation-happy state with 5.8 million working women.   16

Those sex harassment actions that do get to a jury are the ones that really grab headlines. A few scary awards have been granted recently— five plaintiffs were awarded $3.8 million by a jury in a North Carolina case against a Texas S&L, Murray Savings Association—but mammoth awards are often reduced in subsequent court proceedings. In California the median jury verdict for all sex harassment cases litigated since 1984 is $183,000. The top verdict in the state was just under $500,000, the lowest was $45,000. California, known for its sympathetic jurors, probably produces higher awards than most states.   17

Paul Tobias, a partner at the Cincinnati law firm of Tobias & Kraus and executive director of the Plaintiffs Employment Lawyers Association, for the past decade has focused on individual employees' problems, including sex harassment. His experience? "During a year, 10 or 15 people may come in and complain; maybe one of those cases is winnable."   18

Of the dozen or so labor lawyers *Forbes* interviewed—from both plaintiffs' and defendants' bars—most feel that job-related harassment, though not gone, occurs much less frequently now than it did ten years ago.   19

Well, maybe, the sex harassment industry replies, but that's only because women are afraid or ashamed to complain. Bringing a sex harassment case is similar to filing a rape case, consultants and lawyers say; both are nasty proceedings that involve defamation, possible job loss and threats to family harmony. "More people are experiencing harassment, but they may not want to bring a case," says Webb, the Seattle trainer.   20

Maybe so, but there is no evidence of this. After reading cases and talking to the lawyers who litigate them, it becomes clear that women have become much more aggressive in filing sex harassment claims.   21

According to the New York State Division of Human Rights, more than half of the complaint outcomes from 1980 through 1986 were dismissed for lack of probable cause. Actual number: 521, or 52%. Compare this with the cases in which probable cause was found and a conciliation was reached: 39, or 4% of the total.   22

One explanation for the large percentage of dismissed cases is that hostile environment harassment is difficult to define. Asking a subordinate to perform sexual favors in exchange for a raise is clearly illegal. But a dirty joke? Behavior that one woman may consider harassment could be seen by another as a nonthreatening gag. Whose standards should be used?   23

Under tort law, the standard that must be met is called the reasonable person rule. This means that the behavior that has resulted in a case—such as an assault or the intent to cause emotional distress—must be considered objectionable by a "reasonable person." The EEOC follows this lead and in its guidelines defines environmental harassment as that which "unreasonably interferes with an individual's job performance."   24

How to define that? Says Freada Klein of Klein Associates, a Boston consulting firm: "My goal is to create a corporate climate where every employee feels free to object to behavior, where people are clear about their boundaries and can ask that objectionable behavior stop." Objectionable to whom? By what standards?   25

Can rudeness and annoying behavior really be legislated out of existence? Can women really think they have the right to a pristine work environment free of rude behavior? These are permissive times: Mrs. Grundy has been laughed out of most areas of our life. Should she be allowed to flourish in the workplace alone? Says Susan Hartzoge Gray, an employment lawyer at Haworth, Riggs, Kuhn & Haworth in High Point, N.C.: "We condone sexual jokes and innuendo in the media—a movie might get a PG rating—yet an employer can be called on the carpet because the same thing bothers someone in an office."   26

In a curious way, the news stories, the harassment seminars, the showing of videotapes—even if educational—can act to perpetuate the woman-as-victim mentality. There is even a kind of backlash at work. Increasing numbers of wrongful discharge cases are brought by men who believe they were fired because of a false harassment claim.   27

Yet the noise will probably continue for a long time to come. The demand by some women for a perfect work climate is part of a larger trend in society. Many people feel they are entitled not only to jobs but to work conditions that suit their tastes.   28

Some of those higher standards, as far as sex harassment is concerned, are approaching the unreasonable. To combat incidents of hostile environment harassment, management is effectively being told to shoulder two new and onerous responsibilities. First, provide a pristine work environment, and second, police it as well.   29

But if women want a level corporate playing field on which they can   30
compete with men, should they expect to be coddled and protected from
rudeness or boors? Why can't they be expected to take care of themselves.

Women do themselves and their careers no favors by playing victim.   31
Sexual harassment is not about sex, it is about power. If women act powerless at work, they'll almost certainly be taken advantage of. Women are
more powerful than the sex harassment peddlers will have you believe. A
woman's power is not in her ability to bring a harassment claim, it's in
her ability to succeed on her merits. And to be able to say, "Back off,
bub."

As more and more women recognize this, sex harassment will likely   32
become even less of a real problem in the years ahead than it is today.
But don't expect the sex harassment specialists to go out of business.
They'll only stop levying their special tax on U.S. business and consumers when demand for their services dries up.

A WINK HERE, A LEER THERE: IT'S COSTLY

Susan Crawford

*Attorney Susan Crawford offers a pragmatic defense of sexual harassment
laws based on lost employee work time, inefficient use of the work day and
costly lawsuits growing out of sexual harassment issues.*

Did the Anita Hill-Clarence Thomas hearings serve as a cautionary   1
tale? For many employers, yes; for many others, regrettably, no. Sexual
harassment in the workplace continues to be an insidious problem, as
well as a degrading and career-limiting experience for many women.
Research indicates that 50 to 85 percent of all female employees experience some form of harassment during their careers, and 15 percent in
any given year. Similarly, 90 percent of Fortune 500 companies have
received complaints of sexual harassment, more than a third have been
sued and nearly a quarter have been sued repeatedly.

It is unrealistic to think we can eradicate harassment in a single gener-   2
ation. But huge strides can be made if it is viewed as an *economic* problem.

With more women in the workplace, we must realize that their abili-   3
ties—and productivity—are critical to our nation's economic health. It is
imperative that companies grasp an essential fact: sexual harassment
damages the bottom line.

As we evolve from an industrial economy toward one based on infor-   4
mation and services, human resources are becoming the true engine of
added value. Skilled, experienced and committed employees frequently

provide a company its competitive edge. But many companies fail to understand that valuable human capital can be squandered by tolerance of harassment.

A 1988 study of 160 Fortune 500 companies reached a striking con-   5
clusion: harassment costs the average big company, with 23,750 employees, $6.7 million a year. The study calculated losses linked to absenteeism, low productivity and turnover; it did not count the hard-to-measure costs of legal defense, time lost and tarnished public image. Recent research by the author, Freada Klein, a Cambridge, Mass., analyst, confirmed that the data are still valid; anecdotal evidence suggests the costs may be even higher now.

How can a company lose $6.7 million a year?   6

First, sexual harassment results in a costly tax on employee perfor-   7
mance. At the least, the victim is forced to waste time parrying unwanted attention or enduring improper comments. At the same time, the transgressor is devoting work time to activities that are in no way good for business.

Typically, victims retreat into a passive or even sullen acceptance: 12   8
percent of women who face harassment report stress-related health problems, 27 percent report undermined self-confidence and 13 percent see long-term career damage.

Second, harassment breeds resentment and mistrust. Tension can   9
spread to others, breeding widespread cynicism—and limiting productivity.

Third, harassment contributes to costly turnover. Women are nine   10
times as likely as men to quit because of harassment, five times as likely to transfer and three times as likely to lose jobs. Fully 25 percent of women who believe they have been harassed have been dismissed or have quit.

Every woman who leaves because of harassment represents a large   11
loss of investment, which is compounded by employee replacement costs.

To attack the problem, many forward-thinking companies are using   12
awareness-training programs to help employees understand the pain and indignity of harassment. Such programs, if they are comprehensive and used aggressively, can be highly effective. The cost ranges from $5,000 for a small company to $200,000 for a large one.

Thus, for that Fortune 500 company facing a $6.7 million liability, it is   13
34 times as costly to ignore the problem as to take steps to eradicate it. Looked at another way, a sexual-harassment program can be cost-effective if it averts the loss of one key employee—or prevents one lawsuit.

We are failing to exploit the full potential of half the nation's work   14
force. And the cost to business is increasingly burdensome. As competition intensifies, managers and directors cannot afford sexual harassment. Corporations—indeed, all organizations—should take aggressive action to eliminate it. Not just to avoid litigation, not just because it is "politically

correct" or "the right thing to do," but also because such programs can yield a startlingly positive return on investment.

It's an opportunity we can't afford to miss. 15

UNIVERSAL TRUTH AND MULTIPLE PERSPECTIVES: CONTROVERSIES ON SEXUAL HARASSMENT

Martha Chamallas

Law professor Chamallas argues that the burden of proof in sex discrimination cases ought not to be on the putative victim but on the accuser; antidiscrimination laws, she contends, ought to take "the victim's perspective."

The question I wish to pose has to do with whether the Constitution 1 and the Bill of Rights will prove up to the challenge of a postmodern world. The term "postmodern" is an overused but nonetheless useful way of describing contemporary society—a society that is marked by diversity, contradiction, and complicated interrelationships. In such a postmodern world, invocations of shared values and fundamental rights are not likely to go unchallenged—in almost every conversation, someone will first want to know just who shares these values and who considers these interests to be fundamental? In a postmodern world it makes sense to speak in the plural—to talk about truths rather than a single truth and to think in terms of American cultures rather than the American culture.

In a variety of disciplines, feminist and postmodern scholars have 2 changed their fields by their persistence in investigating the relationship between knowledge and power. There is now a rich body of scholarship demonstrating how particular views of the world come to dominate the discourse, how our knowledge is far less diverse than our people. A central feature of these new critical inquiries is their skepticism about claims of "objectivity" and "neutrality" and of statements that purport to have "universal" applicability. The take home message of much of this work is that frequently what passes for the whole truth is instead a representation of events from the perspective of those who possess the power to have their version of reality accepted. The search is on for multiple meanings and multiple perspectives, whether attached to language, texts, or human events.

One area of the law in which the postmodern challenge to objectivity 3 is the most visible is anti-discrimination law and discourse. I am using anti-discrimination law and discourse here broadly to include specific constitutional protections such as the fifth and fourteenth amendment protections of equality; specific statutory provisions, including the various civil rights legislation prohibiting discrimination based on race, ethnicity, sex, religion, disability and age; as well as public debate on matters such as race and gender equality which highlight the legal dimension of the issues.

These days even law professors must of necessity go beyond the cases decided by appellate courts and become conversant in what is sometimes referred to as "cultural politics." It has occurred to me that the most celebrated sexual harassment case of our time—Professor Anita Hill's accusation of sexual harassment by Clarence Thomas—was not a lawsuit at all. However, Hill's statements generated the most thorough and diverse public discussion of the intersection of gender and race and of the harms caused by sexual harassment that I have ever witnessed. What was most striking for me was the variety of viewpoints from which the controversy was viewed. Opinion about the Thomas matter did not break down neatly along gender lines, nor along racial lines. The response to the hearings dramatically demonstrated that women are not a monolithic group who think alike, nor are African-Americans all of the same mindset.

But this acknowledgement of diversity of opinion among women and among African-American men and women does not mean that perspective was not important to one's understanding of the Thomas hearings. Instead I regard the voluminous commentary generated by the Thomas hearing to be an excellent example of multiple realities and multiple perspectives operating in public debate. It was not just a matter of how inclined a person was to believe that either Hill or Thomas was telling the truth. Rather it seemed that for many people what Hill described as her experience readily fit into a coherent and familiar pattern of behavior for them. There was an immediate sense of recognition. Other people had great difficulty making sense of Hill's story. For them, it just did not seem to add up.

Hill's revelations prompted many women to tell about their own encounters with sexually harassing behavior—both in private and in public. The day after the hearings ended I sat at a public hearing in Des Moines as a member of a statewide taskforce investigating racial and gender bias in the Iowa judicial system. One of the witnesses that day was a woman who is now a United States Magistrate. She told about an incident that happened to her many years before when she was a young attorney. A man who then served as bailiff for the local courthouse had known this young woman since she was in grade school—in fact, he had been the bus driver for her elementary school. At the end of one day, the woman attorney asked the bailiff to get her a file. He walked over to her, put his arm around her, said he'd do anything for her, and kissed her on the lips. The woman attorney was stunned and humiliated and rushed out of the courtroom. She never reported the incident, never told her friends or family, and spent considerable emotional energy trying to avoid the bailiff while she worked in that area. As she told her experiences to the taskforce, she expressed her empathy for Anita Hill. In her assessment, Hill's account had no holes in it. Hill was not simply a credible witness (or, as one of the Senators on the Judiciary Committee put it, Hill did not just "present" herself well). Instead, she shared a similar "victim's perspective" with Anita Hill. For this woman, Hill's story possessed an internal logic and expressed a reality about the working lives of women.

In some feminist groups I have participated in, we talk about being "of the experience." This means being part of a group who has experienced a certain type of discrimination first-hand or supporting close friends through such a period of victimization. And I think it is experiences like these that give people a certain perspective on the world. Only some women and some men share a victim's perspective on sexual harassment. 7

When those in a position to judge insist that the victim respond as they imagine they would in such circumstances, the perspective of the victim most often is erased. 8

If anti-discrimination law and discourse is to respond to a postmodern world, we need to find ways to reach out for and to give weight to suppressed perspectives in the decisional rules that structure legal definitions of equality. We seldom find victim's perspectives embraced in the law. For example, the leading equal protection case—Washington v. Davis (1)—requires that plaintiff prove that defendant intended to discriminate. This means that the perspective that determines whether a constitutional violation has occurred is the perspective of the defendant. Although like all legal standards, the intent requirement is highly manipulable, it symbolizes that the viewpoint of the defendant—not the victim—is the one that should control. It is not surprising that critical race scholars such as Charles Lawrence have renewed their criticism of Washington v. Davis and have urged the courts in constitutional cases to go beyond the motivations of lawmakers and judge the race-based nature of an action by its "cultural meaning." (2) For Lawrence, the cultural meaning of an action is more likely to take into account the perspectives of suppressed minorities than would the intent of those elected to Congress or state legislatures. 9

One area of the law in which we can begin to glimpse the victim's perspective being taken into account is in Title VII sexual harassment cases involving claims of a hostile or intimidating work environment—the kind of claim Anita Hill might have brought against EEOC had she filed suit. In these cases the plaintiff must prove that the harassing conduct "had the purpose or effect of unreasonably interfering with an individual's work performance or creating an intimidating, hostile or offensive working environment." (3) This standard is more victim-friendly than the current constitutional standard. Because there is no requirement to prove bad intent on the part of the defendant, the perpetrator's perspective is not necessarily determinative. 10

Recently, courts have recognized that events can look very different from the standpoint of plaintiff or defendant—and a few courts have opted to credit plaintiff's version of reality in an effort to uncover and vali- 11 date a formerly suppressed perspective. An important recent case is Ellison v. Brady (4), decided by a panel of the Ninth Circuit in 1991. Depending on your perspective you could call this case either the "love letters" case or the "delusional romance" case. The plaintiff in the case, Kerry Ellison, received two letters from Sterling Gray, a man in her office with whom she had had only casual contact as a co-employee. They both worked as trainees for the IRS. The letters described Gray's intense feelings for Ellison. In one note, for example, he wrote: "I cried over you last night and I'm totally drained today. I've never been in such constant term oil [sic]." They also contained several statements that seemed to assume that the two had formed a genuine and mutual relationship. In one single-spaced, three-page letter, Gray wrote to Ellison "I know you are worth knowing with or without sex . . . Leaving aside the hassles and disasters of recent weeks. I have enjoyed you so much over these past months. Watching you. Experiencing you from O so far away. Admiring your style and your elan . . . Don't you think it odd that two people who have never even talked together alone are striking off such intense sparks . . . I will write another letter in the near future." (5)

This pursuit frightened Ellison because as far as she was concerned   12
there was no such relationship: she had rejected several of Gray's invitations to lunch and had asked a male colleague to inform Gray that she had no interest in him and to leave her alone. Ellison then complained about Gray's conduct to her supervisor and insisted that something be done to make Gray stop.

Ellison's perspective was that this was a case of "delusional romance."   13
She saw Gray's actions as a nontrivial threat of sexual coercion. From Ellison's perspective, through no action of her own, she had been made the object of a man's fantasies who had ignored her clear requests to stop his aggressive behavior towards her. This victim's perspective differed sharply from the perspective expressed by the district court which dismissed Ellison's claim as stating no cause of action under Title VII. The district court saw Gray's letters as harmless love letters designed to win over Ellison's affections, and stressed that there had been no explicit threats or physically aggressive conduct.

On appeal to the Ninth Circuit, Ellison won. The plurality consisting of   14
Judge Beezer and Judge Kozinsky held that Ellison had stated a cause of action and that the case ought to be judged from the perspective of a "reasonable woman" in the position of plaintiff who had received such letters. I'll save for another day the very interesting discussion of whether it is best to describe the victim perspective in sexual harassment litigation in terms of the "reasonable woman." What I think is most important about Ellison is the adoption of a perspective other than the perspective of either the accused or the administrators who handled the complaint.

I applaud the result in Ellison because it validates my own perspective   15
on such matters. On more than one occasion I have been consulted by women students who have received similar, one-sided "love" notes from

men in their class. In those cases, the men refused to stop their pursuit of these women, despite warnings from administrators. These "delusional romances" interfered with the women's education. They were afraid to go to class, to go to the library, and they worried when the phone rang when they were alone in their apartments. In my view these were not harmless love letters; they were forms of sexual harassment.

Taking the victim's perspective in anti-discrimination law would mean a profound change and I do not expect the courts to go far in this direction until I am way too old to teach employment discrimination. I do believe, however, that suppressed perspectives are now being publicly expressed with greater clarity and with greater frequency. The days of universal truth are numbered. 16

NOTES

I have explored some of the ideas in this essay in greater depth in Martha Chamallas, "Feminist Constructions of Objectivity: Multiple Perspectives in Sexual and Racial Harassment Litigation," 1. *Texas Journal of Women & the Law* 95 (1992).

1. 426 U.S. 229 (1976).
2. Charles Lawrence, "The Id, the Ego and Equal Protection: Reckoning with Unconscious Racism," 39. *Stan. Law Review* 317 (1987).
3. EEOC Guidelines on Discrimination Because of Sex, 29. C.F.R., §1604.11(a)(3) (1982).
4. 924 F.2d 872 (9th Cir. 1991).
5. Id. at 874.

☐ FOR CLASS DISCUSSION

1. Analyze and evaluate the disagreements among these writers concerning sexual harassment by applying the first set of guide questions from page 473. How do you account for the differing points of view? (Do the writers disagree about questions of truth? About definitions? About appropriate comparisons or analogies? About values, assumptions, belief?)

2. Choose one of the arguments for closer analysis, applying the second set of guide questions on page 474.

OPTIONAL WRITING ASSIGNMENT The following story recently appeared in a local newspaper. It was told originally by a former high federal official at a meeting of bankers:

There was a woman, an old maid, who was looking for some adventure in her life and decided to take a cruise. These are her journal entries.

Day 1: Glorious morning. It's great to be alive.

Day 2: Perfect weather. Having a wonderful time.

Day 3: Sat at the captain's table at dinner. Captain propositioned me. Turned him down.

Day 4: Captain insisted I sleep with him and said that if I didn't, he'd run the ship into rocks and drown all the passengers.

Day 5:   Saved 600 lives last night.

A columnist who reprinted the story called two sexual harassment consultants and asked them if telling the story in the workplace would constitute sexual harassment. They gave the columnist markedly different answers. Drawing on your reading of the preceding arguments, write your own response to the question: "Does telling the above story constitute an act of sexual harassment?"

Global Warming:
How Serious Is the Greenhouse Effect?
What Should Be Done About It?

■

GLOBAL WARMING ON TRIAL

Wallace S. Broecker

Atmospheric scientist Wallace Broecker examines the historical development of theories about global warming and attempts to reach a balanced judgment. Imagining a mock trial between advocates and skeptics in the greenhouse debate, Broecker believes that "each side would have difficulty proving its case." Nonetheless, he arrives at a sobering conclusion: The real enemy to our planet is the population explosion.

Jim Hansen, a climatologist at NASA's Goddard Space Institute, is   1
convinced that the earth's temperature is rising and places the blame on the buildup of greenhouse gases in the atmosphere. Unconvinced, John Sununu, former White House chief of staff, doubts that the warming will be great enough to produce a serious threat and fears that measures to reduce the emissions would throw a wrench into the gears that drive the United States' troubled economy. During his three years at the White House, Sununu's view prevailed, and although his role in the debate has diminished, others continue to cast doubt on the reality of global warming. A new lobbying group called the Climate Council has been created to do just this.

The stakes in this debate are extremely high, for it pits society's short-   2
term well-being against the future of all the planet's inhabitants. Our past transgressions have altered major portions of the earth's surface, but the effects have been limited. Now we can foresee the possibility that to satisfy the energy needs of an expanding human population, we will rapidly change the climate of the entire planet, with consequences for even the most remote and unspoiled regions of the globe.

The notion that certain gases could warm the planet is not new. In 1896 Svante Arrhenius, a Swedish chemist, resolved the longstanding question of how the earth's atmosphere could maintain the planet's relatively warm temperature when the oxygen and nitrogen that make up 99 percent of the atmosphere do not absorb any of the heat escaping as infrared radiation from the earth's surface into space. He discovered that even the small amounts of carbon dioxide in the atmosphere could absorb large amounts of heat. Furthermore, he reasoned that the burning of coal, oil, and natural gas could eventually release enough carbon dioxide to warm the earth. 3

Hansen and most other climatologists agree that enough greenhouse gases have accumulated in the atmosphere to make Arrhenius's prediction come true. Burning fossil fuels is not the only problem; a fifth of our emissions of carbon dioxide now come from clearing and burning forests. Scientists are also tracking a host of other greenhouse gases that emanate from a variety of human activities; the warming effect of methane, chlorofluorocarbons, and nitrous oxide combined equals that of carbon dioxide. Although the current warming from these gases may be difficult to detect against the background noise of natural climate variation, most climatologists are certain that as the gases continue to accumulate, increases in the earth's temperature will become evident even to skeptics. 4

The issue under debate has implications for our political and social behavior. It raises the question of whether we should renew efforts to curb population growth and reliance on fossil fuels. In other words, should the age of exponential growth initiated by the Industrial Revolution be brought to a close? 5

The battle lines for this particular skirmish are surprisingly well balanced. Those with concerns about global warming point to the recent report from the United Nation's Intergovernmental Plan on Climate Change, which suggests that with "business as usual," emissions of carbon dioxide by the year 2025 will be 25 percent greater than previously estimated. On the other side, the George C. Marshall Institute, a conservative think tank, published a report warning that without greenhouse gases to warm things up, the world would become cool in the next century. Stephen Schneider, a leading computer modeler of future climate change, accused Sununu of "brandishing the [Marshall] report as if he were holding a crucifix to repel a vampire." 6

If the reality of global warming were put on trial, each side would have trouble making its case. Jim Hansen's side could not prove beyond a reasonable doubt that carbon dioxide and the other greenhouse gases have warmed the planet. But neither could John Sununu's side prove beyond a reasonable doubt that the warming expected from greenhouse gases has not occurred. 7

To see why each side would have difficulty proving its case, let us review the arguments that might be presented at such a hearing. The pri- 8 mary evidence would be the temperature records that have been kept by meteorologists since the 1850s. A number of independent analyses of these measurements have reached the same basic conclusions. Over the last century the planet has warmed about one degree. This warming was especially pronounced during the last decade, which had eight of the warmest years on record, with 1990 being the hottest. While Sununu's group might question the adequacy of the geographic coverage of weather stations during the early part of the record and bicker a bit about whether the local warming produced by the growth of cities has biased some of the records, in the end they would concede that this record provides a reasonably good picture of the trend in the earth's temperature. Sununu's advocate would then counter by asking, "Isn't it strange that between about 1940 and 1975 no warming occurred?" The Hansen group would have to admit that there is no widely accepted explanation for this leveling. Sununu's advocate would continue, "Isn't it true that roughly half the warming occurred before 1940, even though almost all the emissions of carbon dioxide and other greenhouse gases have taken place after this date?" Again the Hansen group would have to admit this to be the case.

At this point, a wise judge might pose the following question to both   9
sides: "What do we know about the temperature fluctuations that occurred prior to the Industrial Revolution?" The aim of this question would be to determine what course the earth's temperature might have taken if the atmosphere had not been polluted with greenhouse gases. The answer by both sides would have to be that instead of remaining the same as it was in 1850, the planet's temperature would have undergone natural fluctuations, which could have been as large as the changes measured over the last one hundred years. Neither side, however, would be able to supply the judge with an acceptable estimate of what would have happened to the earth's temperature without the release of greenhouse gases.

Perhaps a longer record of the earth's climate would shed light on its   10
natural variability. The climate prior to 1850 can be reconstructed from historical records of changing ice cover on mountaintops and on the sea. The earliest evidence of this type dates from the end of the tenth century A.D., when Eric the Red first sailed from Iceland to Greenland. Ship logs written between that time and 1190 indicate that sea ice was rarely seen along the Viking sailing routes. The temperature was warm enough that grain could be grown in Iceland. At the end of the twelfth century, however, conditions deteriorated, and sea ice appeared along the Viking sailing routes during the winters. By the mid-fourteenth century, these routes were forced far to the south because of the ice, and sometime in the late fifteenth century, ships were cut off altogether from Greenland and Iceland because of severe ice conditions. As temperatures dropped, people could no longer grow grain in Iceland. The Medieval Warm had given way to the Little Ice Age.

After 1600, records of sea-ice coverage around Iceland and of the   11
extent of mountain glaciers in the Alps improved, giving us an even better idea of recent climate change. The glaciers attracted the attention of
seventeenth-century tourists, including artists whose drawings and paintings document the position of a number of major Alpine glaciers. Modern measurements show that the leading edges of these glaciers fluctu-
ated with temperature changes over the last century. Assuming that this
correlation held true throughout the Little Ice Age, the historical evidence
shows a long interval of glacier expansion, and thus cold climate, lasting
until 1860. During the late 1800s, a widespread recession of Alpine glaciers heralded the end of the Little Ice Age. Ridges of rock and earth bull-
dozed into position by the advancing ice still mark the point of maximum
glacial progress into the valleys. (The glaciers are still shrinking; less than
half of their 1860 volume remains.) The mild conditions that prevailed
during the Medieval Warm did not return until this century.

The problem with all this evidence is that it represents only one region   12
of the earth and is, in a sense, anecdotal. An informed judge might also
challenge this evidence by pointing out that the northern Atlantic Ocean
and its surrounding lands are warmed by powerful ocean currents, collectively known as the Great Conveyor, that transport heat away from the
equator (see "The Biggest Chill," Natural History, October 1987). A temporary shutdown of this circulation 11,000 years ago brought about an
800-year cold period called the Younger Dryas, during which northern
Europe was chilled by a whopping 12°F. Could the Little Ice Age have
been brought about by a similar weakening of the Great Conveyor? If
heat release from the northern Atlantic was the key factor, the Little Ice
Age would have been restricted to the surrounding region, and the historical evidence from Iceland and the Alps could not be taken as an index
of global temperatures.

Although records of similar duration and quality are not available from   13
other parts of the world, we do have firm evidence that by 1850, mountain glaciers in some regions, such as New Zealand and the Andes,
reached down into valleys as far as they had at any time during the last
8,000 years. Furthermore, by 1870 these glaciers had also begun their
retreat. This suggests that the Little Ice Age was indeed global in extent.

The global warming that caused the demise of the Little Ice Age con-   14
fuses attempts to estimate how much of the last century's warming is
natural and how much has been caused by pumping greenhouse gases
into the atmosphere. The Sununu side would pin as much of the blame
as possible on the natural warming trend that ended the Little Ice Age,
while Hansen's side would emphasize the role of the greenhouse gases.
What is needed to resolve this dispute is a detailed, continuous temperature record that extends back beyond the Medieval Warm to see if cycles
could be identified. By extending these cycles into the present century,
scientists could estimate the course the earth's temperature would have
taken in the absence of the Industrial Revolution.

I made such an attempt in 1975, at a time when the earth's tempera-   15
ture seemed to have remained almost constant since the mid-1940s.
Puzzled scientists were asking, "Where's the expected greenhouse warming?" I looked for the answer in the only detailed long-term record then
available, which came from a deep hole bored into northern Greenland's
icecap at a place called Camp Century. In the 1950s, Willi Dansgaard, a
Danish geochemist, had demonstrated that the ratio of heavy to light
oxygen isotopes (18 neutrons to 16 neutrons per atom, respectively) in
the snow falling in polar regions reflected the air temperature. Dansgaard
made measurements of oxygen isotopes in different layers of the ice
core; each represented the compressed snowfall of an arctic year. His
results served as a proxy for the changes in the mean annual temperature. Dansgaard and his colleagues analyzed the record to see if the temperature fluctuations were cyclic. They found indications of two cycles,
one operating on an 80-year time scale and a weaker one operating on a
180-year time scale. (The Milankovitch cycles, caused by changes in the
earth's orbit around the sun, operate on a much longer time scale. Ranging from 20,000 years upward, these cycles are thought to control the
large swings between glacial and interglacial climates.)

I took Dansgaard's analysis a step further by extending his cyclic pat-   16
tern into the future. When combined with the expected greenhouse
warming, a most interesting result appeared. Temperatures leveled off
during the 1940s and 1950s and dropped somewhat during the 1960s
and 1970s. Then, in the 1980s, they began to rise sharply. If there is a
natural eighty-year cycle and it was acting in conjunction with a greenhouse effect, I would explain the leveling of temperature after 1940 as
follows: Dansgaard's eighty-year cycle would have produced a natural
warming between 1895 and 1935 and a natural cooling form 1935 to
1975. The cooling in the second half the of cycle might have counterbal-
anced the fledgling greenhouse warming. After 1975, when the natural
cycle turned once again, its warming effect would have been augmented
by the ever stronger greenhouse phenomenon, producing a sharp upturn
in temperature in the 1980s.

My exercise showed that the lack of warming between 1940 and 1975   17
could not be used to discount the possibility that the pollution we are
pumping into the atmosphere will ultimately warm the globe. We cannot
rule out this possibility until that time in the future when the predicted
warming is so great that it can no longer be masked by natural temperature fluctuations. My projection suggested that a firm answer will not be
available until the first decade of the next century.

While the Camp Century record seemed to provide a good method of   18
determining how natural variations and increasing greenhouse gases
were working in concert to produce the measured global temperatures,
additional ice core data only created confusion. Oxygen isotope records
from ice cores extracted from the Antarctica icecap and mountain glaciers in China and Peru do not follow the Camp Century ice core pattern.

Even worse, oxygen isotope records from three additional Greenland ice cores differ significantly from one another and from the original Camp Century record. Perhaps the most disconcerting feature of these ice core records is that the Medieval Warm and Little Ice Age do not even stand out as major features. Local temperature variations could account for these discrepancies, but oxygen isotope ratios also depend on the season the snow falls and the source of the moisture. For these reasons, ice cores may provide good records of large changes, but the smaller ones we are looking for over the last several hundred years are obscured.

At this point, the judge would likely lose his patience and call a halt to   19
this line of argument, saying, "While regional climate changes certainly occurred during the centuries preceding the Industrial Revolution, firm evidence for a coherent global pattern in these natural fluctuations is lacking." The judge might then suggest a different approach to settle the question of whether we are causing the earth to warm. What drives the natural changes? If we could pin down the villain, then perhaps we could say more about how temperature would have changed in the absence of the Industrial Revolution. Witnesses would point to three such mechanisms. First, the sun's energy output may have changed. Second, large volcanic eruptions may have injected enough material into the stratosphere to reflect a substantial amount of solar radiation back into space, cooling the planet. Third, the operation of the ocean-atmosphere system may have changed internally, causing the earth's temperature to wander.

For several centuries astronomers have been observing the cycles of   20
the sun and trying to link them with climate patterns on earth. Sunspots, caused by knots in the sun's magnetic field, undergo cyclic change, alternating between a maximum of spots in the Northern Hemisphere and then a maximum in the Southern Hemisphere. Between these peaks, the number of sunspots drops almost to zero. A complete solar cycle takes twenty-two years. With satellites, astronomers have been able to directly monitor the sun's energy output over the last cycles. Although the energy seems to dip slightly when sunspots disappear, the change seems too small to greatly alter the earth's temperature.

An intriguing proposal was recently made in this regard. Two Danish   21
meteorologists, Eigil Friss-Christensen and Knud Lassen, point out that over the last 130 years for which observations are available, the sunspot cycle has lengthened and shortened with a periodicity of about 80 years, and that these changes closely parallel the earth's temperature. The Danes suggest that during intervals when the sunspot cycle is longer than average, the sun's energy output is a bit lower, and that when the cycle is shorter, the energy output is higher. Could it be that Dansgaard was correct in thinking that the earth's temperature changes on an eighty-year time scale and that these changes are driven by the sun? Most scientists remain skeptical because no physical mechanism has been proposed tying solar output to the length of the sunspot cycle. Oth-

ers say that the strong similarity between the length of the sunspot cycle and the earth's temperature could be a coincidence.

In addition to the twenty-two-year solar cycle, however, change on a longer time scale has been documented. Between 1660 and 1720, sunspots disappeared altogether. Auroras, which are created when charged particles driven out from the sunspots enter the earth's upper atmosphere, were also absent from the skies during this period. Further, we know from measurements of carbon 14 in tree rings that this radioactive element, produced by cosmic rays bombarding the atmosphere, increased substantially during this time. Normally, charged particles streaming outward from sunspots create a magnetic shield that deflects cosmic rays away from the earth and the inner planets. From 1660 to 1720, this magnetic shield failed, permitting a larger number of cosmic rays to strike our atmosphere and form an unusually large number of radioactive carbon atoms.   22

From the record of radiocarbon locked up in tree rings, we can identify two even earlier periods of reduced sunspot activity: the Wolf sunspot minimum, from about 1260 to about 1320, and the Spörer sunspot minimum, from about 1400 to 1540. These three periods span a major portion of the Little Ice Age, but the last ended more than a hundred years before the Little Ice Age did—too long a time lag. This mismatch in timing and the small change in the sun's energy output (as measured by satellites over the last solar cycle) make a link between the Little Ice Age and the absence of sunspots unlikely. But the partial match prevents a firm rejection of the sun as a cause of the earth's natural temperature changes.   23

What about volcanic eruptions? Major volcanic eruptions occur roughly once per decade. Most have little effect on the climate, but occasionally an eruption blasts a large volume of sulfur dioxide high into the stratosphere. Within a month or two, the sulfur dioxide is transformed into droplets of sulfuric acid, which remain aloft in the stratosphere for a year or more. These tiny spheres reflect sunlight away from the earth, cooling the planet. Hansen and his colleagues predict that the recent eruption of Mount Pinatubo in the Philippines (which shot more sulfur dioxide into the upper atmosphere than any other eruption this century) will cool the planet about one degree Fahrenheit over the next two years.   24

Could the Little Ice Age have been caused by 500 years of intense volcanism releasing copious amounts of sulfur dioxide? This seems implausible, as the world's 100 or so major volcanoes erupt independently of one another and no mechanism exists that could cause them all to erupt with great frequency. Therefore, the chance is slim that one long interval would be followed by a similar period of lesser activity.   25

Fortunately, a record is available in ice cores to check this assumption. When the droplets of sulfuric acid from a volcanic eruption drift down from the stratosphere, they are quickly incorporated into raindrops and   26 snowflakes and carried to the earth's surface. So, in the years immediately following a major volcanic eruption, snow layers rich in sulfuric acid are deposited on all the world's icecaps. An ice core taken from the Dye 3 site in southern Greenland reveals that at about the time of the transition from the Medieval Warm to the Little Ice Age the acid content in the ice doubled. On the other hand, low acidity from 1750 to 1780 (during a time of cold weather) and the relatively high acidity from 1870 to 1920 (when the climate was warming) do not fit the pattern of climate change. Therefore, no strong correlation exists between the trends in volcanic sulfur dioxide and the trend in the earth's temperature.

The last of the three mechanisms that might account for the natural   27 variations in the earth's temperature is a dramatic shift in the way the planet's ocean and wind currents operate. Of the three mechanisms, this one is the hardest to build a case around because we have only a rudimentary understanding of how the interacting elements of the earth's climate system might cause natural fluctuations in temperature. The only well-documented example of such a mechanism is the El Niño cycle, in which winds and ocean currents cause the temperatures of the surface waters of the eastern equatorial Pacific to alternate between warm and cold. The cycle was first noticed because of the severe drops in fish production along the west coast of South America during the warm episodes. Since the timing between these disruptive events ranges from three to seven years, scientists became interested in predicting their arrival. What emerged from these studies is that El Niño cycles are the product of a complex interaction between winds and ocean currents. The importance of this discovery to the global warming debate is that it raises the possibility that cycles involving larger-scale interactions between the atmosphere and oceans—over longer periods—may play an important role. If the earth's temperature is being pushed up and down by such an internal cycle, our chances of determining what would have happened in the absence of the extra greenhouse gases are indeed slim.

Again the judge would become restive and call a halt to this line of evi-   28 dence as well. At this point he would likely dismiss the case and suggest that the litigants return a decade from now when additional evidence regarding the warming trend has accumulated.

Sununu would deem this decision a victory, for it would provide an   29 excuse to delay actions directed toward reductions in carbon dioxide emissions. On the other hand, Hansen could surely maintain that in the absence of proof that the world is not warming at the rate predicted by computer simulations, we should follow the standard applied to other environmental threats and rule on the side of caution. Instead of placing the burden of proof on the environmentalists, the proponents of "business as usual" should be obliged to prove that the unfettered release of greenhouse cases will *not* significantly warm the planet. And such proof does not exist; the balance of scientific opinion is that business as usual will alter the climate.

The debate over global warming is merely a small skirmish that marks   30
the beginning of a far broader war. Many of the things that we could do
to curb the buildup of greenhouse gases—such as conserving energy,
switching to renewable energy sources, or increasing our use of nuclear
power—will be stopgap measures if the underlying problem of population growth is not addressed. World population is now 5.5 billion and
growing by about 1.8 percent every year. If this rate is not substantially
reduced, world population will double by the year 2030. If by that time
the rate of population growth has not been greatly reduced, we run the
risk that the population will skyrocket to 20 billion or more before it finally
levels off. Each additional person adds to the pressure to increase the
use of fossil fuels, pumping ever larger amounts of carbon dioxide into
the atmosphere. In countries such as the United States and Canada,
where per capita energy consumption is the highest in the world, each
person, on average, adds twenty tons of carbon dioxide a year to the
atmosphere. In developing countries, where most of the population
growth will occur, per capita energy consumption is much smaller, with
less than three tons of carbon dioxide emitted per person. But as these
countries strive to better the lot of their citizens through industrialization,
their energy demands will climb. Most of the increase will be met by
burning fossil fuels, particularly coal, which releases more carbon dioxide
per unit of energy produced than oil or gas. Therefore, annual emissions
of greenhouse gases are likely to increase.

We are rapidly approaching a limit beyond which we cannot maintain   31
our numbers without long-term damage to our planet's environment and
its remaining wildlife and to the quality of life of its human populations.
While Sununu may be particularly shortsighted with regard to the effects
of greenhouse gases on the climate, most of the world's leaders are
shortsighted with regard to the population problem. They seem to ignore
it completely. I hope the concern about global warming will force us to
develop a broader perspective of our planet's future—one that will
include the reality of the population bomb. Only then will we be able to
begin the extraordinarily difficult task of defusing it.

GLOBAL WARMING: THE WORST CASE

Jeremy Leggett

Jeremy Leggett, director of science in Greenpeace International's Atmos-
phere and Energy Campaign, outlines a worst-case scenario in which the
greenhouse effect creates a positive feedback loop resulting in calamitous
global warming. "In evaluating military threats throughout history, policy
response has been predicated on a worst-case analysis. The standard mili-
tary yardstick must also apply to environmental security."

As recently as two years ago, it looked as if world leaders would soon   1
agree on a far-sighted course of action to insure cutbacks in the production of "greenhouse" gases, to make certain that future generations
would not suffer from excessive global warming.

Many of us, in fact, thought the ceremonial signing of a global warm-   2
ing treaty would be the centerpiece of the U.N.-sponsored "Earth Summit," which convenes this month in Rio de Janeiro.

Political and economic issues that lie beyond the scope of this article   3
help explain why the compromise treaty that will be signed fails to commit governments to a limitation of greenhouse gases. But there is also
the matter of scientific uncertainty. Although the world's scientists share
a broad consensus that the human-enhanced "greenhouse effect" will
lead to potentially dangerous global warming, profound uncertainty
remains as to the exact response of the climate system to an atmosphere
overloaded with greenhouse gases, most of them long-lived.

Formulating a policy response to global warming is, at heart, an exer-   4
cise in risk assessment. Perhaps the world's policy-makers have not been
able to agree on a plan of action partly because we scientists have not
fully explained the nature of the threat—particularly the possibility that a
worst-case scenario might develop.

EARLY WARNING

Scientific consensus on global warming was formalized in May 1990 in   5
a scientific assessment by the Intergovernmental Panel on Climate
Change (IPCC). Its authoritative early warning set most of the world's
governments negotiating for a Global Climate Convention in February
1991. Amid rapid advances in scientific research, the IPCC was asked to
prepare an updated report by January 1992.

When climate scientists gathered in Guangzhou, China, to complete   6
the second IPCC report, the political scrutiny was intense. Progressive
governments (like Germany and Austria) looked for confirmation that
their policies of cutting carbon dioxide emissions—the gas is modern civilization's major contributor to global warming—were sound. Foot-
dragging governments (like the United States and Saudi Arabia) sought
evidence for their arguments that uncertainties about global warming
permitted delays in efforts to cut emissions.

The central question the 300-plus scientists who collaborated on the   7
1992 IPCC report had to tackle was whether the "early warning" in the
1990 report could be confirmed. The scientists, from 44 governments,
concluded that it could. However, the subsequent February session of the
climate negotiations in New York City ended in deadlock, primarily
because the United States refused to concede the need for setting targets and deadlines for limiting carbon dioxide emissions.

Foot-dragging governments, by definition, advocate go-slow   8
approaches to global warming issues. They argue that the science is
uncertain, and that global warming is an unproved process. This view is a

travesty of the science behind global warming. Climate models on which future warming estimates are based attempt to simulate a complex interactive system. They are not perfect, but they give us a clear warning that business-as-usual emissions of greenhouse gases means taking an appalling gamble with the environmental security of the generations to come.

THE FEEDBACK FACTOR

Many experts' concerns go beyond the ecologically dangerous rates of warming now forecast by all the world's climate modeling centers. Many scientists ask if the abundance of greenhouse gases might lead to a worst-case scenario with runaway warming in the next century. How close are we to a self-sustaining warming that would be beyond human control? Recently, Greenpeace collected scientists' gut feelings (something that would never find their way into an institutional document).   9

In a poll of 400 climate scientists conducted by Greenpeace International during January and February, almost half (45 percent) said that a runaway greenhouse effect is possible if action is not taken to cut greenhouse gas emissions. And more than one in ten of those polled believe that such a scenario is probable.   10

The poll included all scientists involved in the 1990 study of the Intergovernmental Panel on Climate Change, and others who have published on issues relevant to climate change in *Science* or *Nature* during 1991. A total of 113 scientists had responded to the questionnaire by the time of the February negotiations.   11

The worst-case hypothesis is viewed as a serious consideration by many of the world's best climate scientists, but they have been unable to communicate that to policy-makers. Meanwhile, best-case advocates have become regular fixtures in the global media simply by advocating the minority view–rejected in the IPCC's reports—that natural climatic dampening mechanisms will suppress the heat-trapping abilities of the greenhouse gases.   12

It is vital that policy-makers appreciate the risks associated with global warming. And policy-makers need to understand what we know—and what we don't know—about feedbacks involved in the climate system.   13

A feedback is a natural component of the climate system that is activated by other system components. The extent to which climate models can simulate and predict reality depends on their ability to simulate these feedbacks. In a warming world, negative feedbacks can act to suppress warming. (An example might be the formation, in a warming atmosphere, of cloud types that reflect more solar radiation back into space than other types.) Positive feedbacks amplify the warming—the release of now-trapped greenhouse gases from melting tundra in the far north would be an example.   14

The feedbacks generated by water vapor and clouds are incorporated in all modern global circulation models. Water vapor concentrations are   15 generally projected to increase in a warming atmosphere: a positive feedback. Clouds, according to the IPCC, can provide positive or negative feedbacks, and it is in simulating clouds that most of the current variance in climate models is found. The ice-albedo feedback (the reflection of solar radiation back to the atmosphere) is also included in global circulation models. In most, it is positive: a warmer world will involve shrinking ice cover, lowering albedo, and reflecting less solar radiation. But many feedbacks, especially biological feedbacks . . . are simply omitted from climate models because they are too difficult to quantify, given the extent of our ignorance of the climate system.

As policy-makers assess risks, they need answers to several vital questions. To what extent are the feedbacks accurately simulated in these climate models? What is the best-case analysis of global warming? What is the worst-case analysis? Between extremes, what is the best-estimate analysis? And if the best-estimate analysis is wrong, on balance, is it more likely to be wrong on the worst-case side or on the best-case side?   16

BEST-CASE ADVOCATES

A minority of world-class atmospheric scientists subscribe to the best-case analysis of feedback interactions. Their analysis suggests that the human-enhanced greenhouse effect is a nonproblem. Advocates of this view do not question the buildup of greenhouse gases in the atmosphere, unprecedented since humans first appeared on earth, which is measured and proven. Neither do they question the heat-trapping capacity of the gases, which is based on simple physics. Rather, the best-case advocates ask policy-makers to place faith in the expectation that negative feedbacks will work to cool the planet.   17

According to Richard Lindzen of MIT, for instance, a warming troposphere will not produce more water vapor in the way anticipated by global warming models. Instead, water vapor will be wrung from the lower atmosphere by the increased vigor of atmospheric circulation. Lindzen and other advocates of this view ask policy-makers to commit the environmental security of future generations to a theoretical negative feedback concept, which has been rejected by a majority of their peers.   18

Global warming risk assessment is complex, unlike risk assessment associated with the ozone depletion problem. Ozone depletion is represented by one main variable: chlorine and bromine from halocarbons. The higher these chemical concentrations, the lower the ozone concentrations. It is a proven process, and the thinning ozone layer can be measured. Measurements in recent years, in fact, have shown that atmospheric scientists have consistently underestimated the pace and extent of ozone depletion. What if the scientific community's underestimation of ozone depletion proves to apply to global warming as well? Bad as the broad-consensus, best-estimate IPCC prognosis is, what might the worse-case analysis of global warming be?   19

Levels of carbon dioxide have increased by 25 percent over the past   26
100 years; and all greenhouse gases taken together have increased car-
bon-dioxide-equivalent levels by about 50 percent. In other words, we
have already gone halfway towards the greenhouse gas doubling which is
often taken as the benchmark for model predictions. One would have
expected a warming of at least 0.75 degrees centigrade by now, and
more likely a rise of 1.5 degrees centigrade, according to the predictions
of many models.

The reality is quite different. Since 1880, temperature has increased   27
only 0.5 degrees centigrade, and that primarily before 1940—that is, before appreciable greenhouse gases were added to the atmosphere. The
global climate record during the last 50 years shows no appreciable temperature increase at all. In the United States, the warmest years were in
the 1930s, not in the 1980s, based on the analyses of the U.S. Climate
Center in Asheville, North Carolina, which uses the U.S. observational
network and also corrects for the "urban heat island" effect.

Many climatologists identify the pre-1940 warming with a recovery   28
from an anomalous cooling of the preceding centuries, known as the
"Little Ice Age." Certainly, the observed global cooling that inspired a fear
of a coming ice age in the 1970s is not in accord with greenhouse models. Adding to the problem, a November 1, 1991 *Science* article by Danish meteorologists, E. Friis-Christensen and K. Lassen, shows that average temperature and solar activity are closely correlated, as measured by
the length of the sunspot cycle. If this is correct, then little or no warming
can be ascribed to the greenhouse effect.

The most appropriate data for validating current climate models is the   29
global temperature record from satellite microwave observations, which
began in 1979. This is the only truly global and continuous set of data
available, with heat islands and other surface distortions of temperatures
eliminated. Contrary to an expected 0.3 degree centigrade rise per
decade, based on current theory, the satellite record shows no significant
temperature trend.

TREND OR FLUCTUATION?

Temperature observations generally show large fluctuations from   30
unknown causes. Some of the fluctuations maybe due to natural influences, such as volcanic activity. Other fluctuations are a consequence of
the chaotic behavior of the system itself, involving feedbacks, both positive and negative, on many different time scales. These fluctuations
make it difficult (if not impossible) to identify small long-term trends
caused by human activities. Interannual and longer-term fluctuations of
global temperature exceed those predicted by many greenhouse model
calculations.

Disentangling natural changes from a greenhouse effect enhanced by   31
human activities will require detailed examination and more refined indicators than simply average global temperature. The climatological record
may contain specific "fingerprints" that are unique to specific mecha-

nisms of change. But, as pointed out by Hugh Ellsaesser, neither the observed latitude, altitude, or hemispheric variations of global warming in the past century are in agreement with greenhouse theory.

(Even the 1990 IPCC report on climate change waffles on that issue.   32
The report says that the data are too ambiguous to fully support greenhouse theory. Nevertheless, the data are not inconsistent with the greenhouse effect.)

One result of detailed climate studies was the discovery that U.S. tem-   33
perature records reflect a warming trend mainly for night-time temperatures; that is, there is a decrease in the day-to-night temperature range. Data on the same effects in the former Soviet Union and China have now been published. If greenhouse gas increases were the cause of this increase in night temperatures—and we don't know that—then the obvious benefits to agriculture would make this climate change a plus rather than a minus. This argument is strengthened by the expectation that the present interglacial (warm) period, which started around 11,000 years ago, must soon come to an end. With a renewed ice age "on the horizon," the possibility of greenhouse warming takes on a relatively beneficial interpretation.

WHAT TO DO

We can sum up present understanding of the enhanced greenhouse   34
effect as follows: experts generally agree that the expected doubling of greenhouse gases in the next century will not cause a severe or catastrophic warming. Many scientists and most agricultural experts would argue that a longer growing season and enhanced carbon dioxide levels are, on the whole, beneficial to crops, which require both warmth and carbon dioxide to flourish. It is also agreed that it will take years, maybe a decade or more, before satellite data can establish a definite climate trend and before theoretical understanding of the atmosphere is comprehensive enough to allow accurate predictions.

This uncertainty raises an important but controversial question. How   35
long should governments wait before taking drastic policy actions—if we cannot now identify a long-term climate trend? And if a trend is eventually identified, how can we be sure of its cause—or whether the cause is man-made? Answers to these questions are crucial if the proposed policy actions have a negative impact on other human values—economic welfare, health, and life expectancy. Environmental pressure groups often say that "we cannot afford to play Russian roulette with the planet's future." But this is an appeal to emotion, instead of the careful analysis that is called for.

Delaying action is not an invitation to disaster, as often claimed. Cal-   36
culations by atmospheric scientist Michael Schlesinger of the University of Illinois, a climate modeler, clearly demonstrate that postponing controls on carbon dioxide for even a decade would have no noticeable impact on the next century's temperature trends. Moreover, even the most drastic limits on carbon dioxide emissions by industrialized coun-

tries would delay the doubling of greenhouse gases in the next century by only a few years.

A contributing factor to global warming is thought to be population growth and economic development in Third World nations, which will soon determine the growth rate of greenhouse gases. Carbon dioxide will increase because of fuel burning and forest clearing, and methane emitted from rice paddies and cattle raising will increase. It is well recognized, but seldom said, that controlling these activities and thus condemning billions to continued poverty, starvation and misery—or to draconian restrictions on population growth—would rightly be regarded as immoral and as a form of "eco-imperialism." 37

If greenhouse warming should become a problem, two reports from the U.S. National Academy of Sciences during the past year have suggested that mitigation of the effects of climate change, or adjustment to the change, is quite possible, and not prohibitively costly. A wide range of technological options can be pursued. These include planting trees on a large scale to replace logged or burned forests, and fertilizing the ocean with trace nutrients for plankton growth to sequester and thus reduce atmospheric carbon dioxide. Using satellites to screen out some incoming solar radiation also has been suggested. Such schemes may sound farfetched, but at one time so did many other futuristic projects that have since been realized. 38

Drastic, precipitous, and especially unilateral steps to roll back carbon dioxide emissions simply to delay an unlikely greenhouse warming will imperil living standards—and even political freedoms—in the industrial world. Yale economist William Nordhaus, who has been trying to deal quantitatively with the economics of this issue, has pointed out that "those who argue for strong measures to slow greenhouse warming have reached their conclusion without any discernible analysis of the costs and benefits." 39

At this stage, there are major uncertainties about greenhouse theory, about the effects of a possible warming, and about the economic and political impacts of hasty, ill-considered policies. Does it make sense to waste $100 billion a year on what is still a phantom threat when there are so many pressing—and real—problems in need of resources. 40

SIGNS OF GLOBAL WARMING FOUND IN ICE

R. Monastersky

In this brief article appearing in Science News, *Monastersky presents evidence for global warming based on melting of glacial ice. It is not clear, however, that the warming is caused by greenhouse gases.*

High-mountain glaciers in the tropics and temperate areas of Earth   1
show signs of accelerated climate change in recent decades, a U.S.
glaciologist said last week. In Africa and Peru, glaciers are shrinking at
record rates, while evidence from central Asian ice caps reveals that this
area also has warmed considerably.

"These glaciers are telling us something," says Lonnie G. Thompson   2
of Ohio State University in Columbus, who testified at a hearing before
the Senate Committee on Commerce, Science and Transportation. "If
you look at a global scale and see the same things happening, you have
to wonder what is the common denominator."

Glaciers that exist outside the polar zones are extremely sensitive to   3
changing conditions and may provide an early warning of abnormal climatic warming. Scientists know that the planet's average surface temperature is rising, but they cannot yet determine whether natural factors or
greenhouse-gas pollutants have caused the warming. Because glaciers
contain information about conditions going back hundreds of years or
more, the ice records can help experts distinguish between natural and
human-caused climate change.

Thompson described work at the Quelccaya Ice Cap in Peru that   4
reveals unprecedented changes in the region. When his group took a
deep core from the Quelccaya summit in 1983, they found that the year-
by-year layering of ice had preserved a five-century-long record of
changes in the ice's oxygen isotopes. In glacial research, scientists often
study the ratio of two oxygen isotopes in ice to determine how temperatures have changed through time. But when the group returned last year,
ice at the summit was melting so rapidly that the glacier had failed to
preserve an isotope record for the most recent years. This degree of
melting had not occurred in the previous 500 years, Thompson says.

The Ohio State scientist also described oxygen isotope studies on   5
cores from three ice caps in China and Kirghizia, in the former Soviet
Union. These analyses show enrichment of the heavy oxygen isotope,
indicating a warming in these regions over the last 50 years, Thompson
says. At one site, the recent warming trend exceeds any in the last
12,000 years.

Thompson reports that many tropical glaciers are shrinking dramati-   6
cally. Since 1984, one glacier from the Quelccaya Ice Cap has receded
up the mountain at a rate of 14 meters per year—nearly triple the speed
recorded between 1963 and 1978. Scientists studying glaciers in East
Africa report seeing similar changes in glaciers there. In the Ruwenzori
mountain range of Uganda, the Speke glacier retreated 35 to 45 meters
during the 19 years between 1958 and 1977. But it receded more than
150 meters in the 13-year span between 1977 and 1990, according to
Georg Kaser and Bernd Noggler of the University of Innsbruck, Austria.

In Kenya, glaciers on Mt. Kenya have also receded dramatically. In the   7
Feb. 6 *Nature*, Stefan Hastenrath of the University of Wisconsin-Madison
and Phillip D. Kruss of the World Meterological Organization in Geneva,

Switzerland, report that the ice-covered area on Mt. Kenya shrank by 40 percent between 1963 and 1987. The average thickness of the ice cap decreased by 14.5 meters during that same period. The scientists suggest the glacier loss stems primarily from increasing water vapor in the atmosphere, which could be a by-product of warmer ocean temperatures.

Thompson says his findings in Peru and Asia hint that current global   8
warming is now exceeding the normal range of climatic variation during the last five centuries—an indication that the warming is not just a natural fluctuation that will soon reverse itself. He cautions, however, that many glaciers in the polar regions are not showing the same sorts of changes. "What we're seeing are changes in the glaciers in the tropics and the subtropics that indicate warming. We do not know that the warming is driven by increasing greenhouse gases," Thompson says.

GLOBAL WARMING: A SKEPTIC'S VIEW

Dixy Lee Ray

Dixy Lee Ray, former chair of the Atomic Energy Commission and former governor of the state of Washington, has long been skeptical of global warming theories. Here she points to some homely evidence against global warming—the latest hardiness zone maps used by farmers and gardeners to predict frosts. These maps show that the frost zone in the United States is moving south, not north.

By now it seems that almost everyone believes that this old world is   1
warming up, and that the increased temperature is due to human activities. Moreover, nearly everyone seems also to believe that such warming would be environmentally disastrous. Is this conventional wisdom correct? I think it is not.

Before we analyze the evidence for and against the theory of global   2
warming, let us establish a few basic premises:

- The term "global warming" is a misnomer. There is no such reality as   3
a "global temperature." Even during the ice ages when the Northern Hemisphere got very cold indeed, there was almost no temperature drop in the tropics. And, though some ice did form in the Southern Hemisphere, South America and Africa were relatively free from the great ice sheets that covered so much of North America and Europe. Incidentally, human activity had nothing to do with these vast temperature fluctuations.

- Of course the climate is changing. It changes all the time. Not so long   4
ago the arid Southwest supported a thriving agricultural society of Native American Pueblo Indians. The climate changes occur slowly

over decades or centuries, so they are hardly noticed. The changes occurring now seem normal.

- Weather also changes; there are hot years and cold ones. Episodes of   5
warmer and colder patterns tend to repeat themselves in cycles. No one knows the cause of these variabilities in weather and climate. But this we do know: the cause is probably to be found in cosmic forces that are beyond human ability to control. Certainly that is true of past changes.

But now, some activist environmentalists charge, man has acquired   6
the power to alter the composition of the atmosphere sufficiently to cause worldwide climate change—global warming—from carbon dioxide produced by the burning of fossil fuels.

Now the first thing that a scientist does when faced with so serious an   7
allegation is to ask two questions:

1. What is the evidence? and,
2. Can the data be substantiated?

The *evidence* is quite clear and well supported. Temperature records   8
taken this century in North America and Europe (mainly in the United States) show an apparent, slight warming up to the year 1938, which incidentally is the warmest year on record. Much of this warming took place rather quickly between 1919 and 1921. Then, after 1938 there was a 40-year period of cooling (1938 to 1976) followed by another slight warming.

Note that this actual record shows no relation to the slow but constant   9
increasing in carbon dioxide in the atmosphere. What these measurements do show is that there are variations in the weather; some years are hotter and some colder. Also, some years have hotter summers or colder winters, but overall there is no discernable upward or downward trend. This conclusion is borne out by 10 years (1978 to 1988) of temperature readings taken daily over both land and ocean surfaces of the Earth from the space satellite TIROS II.

It is unequivocal from the temperature evidence, supported also by   10
150 years of sea surface temperatures, that no overall warming trend is underway.

Another important area of evidence comes from the plant world. In   11
February of 1990 the Department of Agriculture's National Arboretum put out the first revised hardiness zone map since 1965. This is the chart, much consulted by farmers and gardeners, that shows the areas where crops may be safely planted—that is, free from winter damage. The zones have moved southward.

Says Marc Cathey, the National Arboretum director, "The trees and the   12
plants have been telling us unambiguously that the U.S. climate has been cooling, not warming."

Additional evidence comes from the southeastern states. In the last 50   13
years the citrus industry has had to move south. Now it is no longer possi-

Whereas the community psychiatrists initially sought to achieve their   24
ends through a legislative reconstruction of the mental-health system,
the civil-libertarian attorneys favored the judicial route. They attacked the
major mechanism for entry into the public mental-health system, the statutes governing involuntary commitment. These laws, they charged, were
unconstitutionally broad in allowing any mentally ill person in need of
treatment to be hospitalized against his will. Surely individual liberty
could not legitimately be abridged in the absence of a substantial threat
to a person's life or to the life of others. In addition, they alleged that the
wording of the statutes, many little changed for one hundred years, was
impermissibly vague; particularly problematic for the civil libertarians
were the definitions of mental illness and the circumstances that rendered one committable.

In an era of judicial activism, many courts, both federal and state,   25
agreed. Involuntary commitment came to be limited to persons exhibiting danger to themselves or others; strict, criminal-law-style procedures came to be required, including judicial hearings with legal representation. As the trend in the courts became apparent, many
legislatures altered their statutes in anticipation of decisions in their own
jurisdictions, or in emulation of California, where civil libertarians won
legislative approval of a tightened statute even without the threat of court
action.

The final common pathway of this complex set of interests led   26
through the state legislatures. Although concerns about better treatment
for chronic patients and the enhancement of individual liberty were not
foreign here, more mundane concerns made themselves felt as well. The
old state mental hospitals took up a significant proportion of most state
budgets, in some jurisdictions the largest single allocation. Advocates of
closing the old facilities were not reticent in claiming enormous cost
savings if patients were transferred to community-based care. And even if
real costs remained constant, the availability of new federal entitlement
programs such as Supplemental Security Income and Medicaid, to which
outpatients but not inpatients would have access, promised a shift in
the cost of supporting these people from the states to the federal
government.

In many states, this was the final straw. The possibility that patients   27
could be cared for in the community at less expense, perhaps with better
results, and certainly with greater liberty, was an irresistible attraction.
Deinstitutionalization was too valuable a tool of social policy to remain a
discretionary option of state-hospital psychiatrists. It now became an
avowed goal of the states. Quotas were set for reductions in state-
hospital populations; timetables were drawn up for the closure of facilities. Individual discretion in the release of patients was overridden by legislative and administrative fiat. Patients were to be released at all costs.
New admissions were to be discouraged, in some cases prohibited. In
the words of Joseph Morrissey, if the first phase of deinstitutionalization

reflected an opening of the back wards, the second phase was marked by a closing of the front door.[1]

Thus did deinstitutionalization assume the form in which we know it today.   28

IV

If a decrease in patient population is the sole measure for gauging the outcome of deinstitutionalization, the success of the policy is unquestionable. From 1965 to 1975, inpatient populations in state hospitals fell from 475,000 to 193,000. By 1980, the figure was 137,000, and today all indications are that the number is even smaller. Relatively few of the state hospitals closed. The majority shrank from bustling colonies with thousands of patients to enclaves of a few hundred patients, clustered in a few buildings in largely abandoned campuses.   29

Yet by the mid-1970's professionals in the field and policy analysts had begun to ask whether the underlying goals espoused by the advocates of deinstitutionalization were really being met. Are the majority of the mentally ill, by whatever measure one chooses to apply, better off now than before the depopulation of the state hospitals? The inescapable answer is that they are not.   30

A large part of the reason for the movement's failure stems from its overly optimistic belief in the ability of many mentally ill persons to function on their own, without the much-maligned structure of state-hospital care. Rather than liberating patients from the constraints of institutional life, the movement to reduce the role of state hospitals merely shifted the locus of their regimented existences. Indeed, *trans*institutionalization may be a better term to describe the process that occurred. It is estimated that 750,000 chronic mentally ill persons now live in nursing homes, a figure nearly 50 percent higher than the state-hospital population at its 1955 apogee. Additional hundreds of thousands live in board-and-care homes or other group residences. Many of these facilities, particularly the nursing homes, have locked wards nearly indistinguishable from the old state hospitals. They are, in psychiatrist H. Richard Lamb's evocative phrase, the asylums in the community.   31

Many of the mentally ill, of course, have drifted away entirely from any form of care. Given the freedom to choose, they have chosen to live on the streets; according to various estimates they comprise between 40 and 60 percent of homeless persons. They filter into overcrowded shelters—as Juan Gonzalez did before becoming the agent of his fantasies on the Staten Island ferry—where they may experience fleeting contact   32

---

[1] A good comprehensive history of deinstitutionalization has yet to be written. The best of the existing, essay-length works is Joseph Morrissey's "Deinstitutionalizing the Mentally Ill: Process, Outcomes, and New Directions," in W.R. Gove, ed., *Deviance and Mental Illness* (Sage Publications, 1982). Morrissey focuses in particular on the experiences in Massachusetts, New York, and California.

with mental-health personnel. The lack of external structure is reflected in their internal disorganization. Whatever chance they had to wire together their shattered egos has been lost.

What of the hopes of the community psychiatrists that liberating   33
patients from state hospitals would prevent the development of the chronic dependency which stigmatizes the mentally ill and inhibits their reintegration into the community? They learned a sad lesson suspected by many of their colleagues all along. The withdrawal, apathy, bizarre thinking, and oddities of behavior which Goffman and his students attributed to "institutionalism" appear even in populations maintained outside of institutions. They are the effects of the underlying psychiatric illnesses, usually schizophrenia, not of the efforts to treat those conditions. And contrary to the claims of the labeling theorists, it is the peculiar behavior of severely psychotic persons, not the fact that they were once hospitalized and "labeled" ill, that stigmatizes and isolates them in the community. Studies of discharged patients demonstrate that those who continue to display the signs of their illnesses and disrupt the lives of others are the ones who suffer social discrimination.

To some extent, the community psychiatrists never had a chance to   34
test their theories. The community mental-health centers in which they envisioned care taking place were, for the most part, never built. Fewer than half of the projected 2,000 centers reached operation. Of those that did, many turned from the severely ill to more desirable patients, less disturbed, easier to treat, more gratifying, and above all, as federal subsidies were phased out, able to pay for their own care. A few model programs, working with a selected group of cooperative patients, are all the community psychiatrists have to show for their dreams. But the evidence suggests that even optimal levels of community care cannot enable many mentally ill persons to live on their own.

The goals of the civil libertarians, except in the narrowest sense, have   35
fared little better. If one conceives that liberty is enhanced merely by the release of patients from the hospitals to the streets, then perhaps one might glean some satisfaction from the course of deinstitutionalization to date. But if individual autonomy implies the ability to make reasoned choices in the context of a coherent plan for one's life, then one must conclude that few of the deinstitutionalized have achieved autonomy. One study found fewer than half the residents of a large board-and-care home with a desire to change anything at all about their lives, no matter how unrealistic their objectives might be. If the façade of autonomy has been expanded, the reality has suffered.

Finally, and with fitting irony, not even the hope that deinstitutionaliza-   36
tion would save money has been realized. It was originally anticipated that the closing of state hospitals would allow the transfer of their budgetary allocations to community facilities. But state hospitals proved difficult to close. As many hospitals existed in 1980 as in 1955, despite a fourfold reduction in patients. Even with current, broad definitions of who

can survive in the community, tens of thousands of patients nationwide continue to require institutional care, often long-term. They are so regressed, self-destructive, violent, or otherwise disruptive that no community can tolerate them in its midst. Moreover, the communities that derive jobs from the facilities have fought hard to preserve them. As censuses have fallen, per-capita costs of care have increased, pushed up even further by pressure to improve the level of care for those who remain. Many costs for the treatment of outpatients have been redistributed, with the federal and local governments bearing heavier burdens; but no one has ever demonstrated overall savings. Even as the quality of life for many mentally ill persons has fallen, state mental-health budgets have continued to expand.

V

Both the failure of deinstitutionalization and our seeming paralysis in   37
correcting it stem from the same source: the transformation of deinstitutionalization from a pragmatic enterprise to an ideological crusade. The goal of the first phase of the process—to treat in the community all mentally ill persons who did not require full-time supervision and might do equally well or better in alternate settings—was hardly objectionable. Had state-hospital populations been reduced in a deliberate manner, with patients released no faster than treatment, housing, and rehabilitative facilities became available in the community, the visions of psychiatry's Young Turks of the 1950's might well have been realized.

Once the release of state-hospital patients became a matter of faith,   38
however, this individualized approach was thrown to the winds. In the Manichean view that soon predominated, confinement in state hospitals came to be seen as invariably bad. Freedom was always to be preferred, both for its own sake and because it had a desirable, albeit mysterious therapeutic value. Further, we came to doubt our own benevolent impulses, yielding to those who claimed that any effort to act for the welfare of others was illegitimate and doomed to end with their oppression. Thus, although we may now recognize the failure of deinstitutionalization, we as a society have been unable to reverse course; these same ideologies continue to dominate our policies not by the power of logic but by the force of habit.

It is time to rethink these presuppositions. That freedom *per se* will   39
not cure mental illness is evident from the abject condition of so many of the deinstitutionalized. More difficult to deal with is the belief that, even if the lives of hundreds of thousands of mentally ill persons have been made objectively more miserable by the emptying of our state hospitals, we have no right to deprive people of liberty, even for their own benefit. In the currently fashionable jargon of bioethics, the value of autonomy always trumps the value of beneficence.

Interestingly, this position is now being challenged by a number of our   40
leading public philosophers, who have called attention to its neglected

costs. Robert Burt of the Yale Law School and Daniel Callahan of the Hastings Center, for example, have taken aim at the belief that the freedom to do as we please should be our primary societal value. This emphasis on individual autonomy, they point out, has come to mean that in making our choices, as long as we do not actively infringe on the prerogatives of others, we face no obligation to consider them and their needs. The result has been the creation of an atomistic community in which, relieved of the duty to care for others, we pursue our goals in disregard of the suffering that surrounds us. This lack of an obligation to care for others has been transmuted in some cases into an actual duty to ignore their suffering, lest we act in such a way as to limit their autonomy.

Although Burt and Callahan have not addressed themselves to mental-health policy *per se,* there is no better illustration of their thesis. The right to liberty has become an excuse for failing to address, even failing to recognize, the needs of the thousands of abandoned men and women we sweep by in our streets, in our parks, and in the train and bus stations where they gather for warmth. We have persuaded ourselves that it is better to ignore them—that we have an obligation to ignore them—because their autonomy would be endangered by our concern.   41

But the impulse to act for the benefit of others is the adhesive substance that binds human communities together. A value system that looses those bonds by glorifying individual autonomy threatens the cohesion of the polity. Nobody wants to live in a society characterized by unrestrained intervention (even with benevolent intent), but that does not mean we must reject altogether the notion that doing good for others, despite their reluctance, is morally appropriate under some conditions.   42

Meaningful autonomy does not consist merely in the ability to make choices for oneself. Witness the psychotic ex-patients on the streets, who withdraw into rarely used doorways, rigidly still for hours at a time, hoping, like chameleons on the forest floor, that immobility will help them fade into the grimy urban background, bringing safety and temporary peace from a world which they envision as a terrifying series of threats. Can the choices they make, limited as they are to the selection of a doorway for the day, be called a significant embodiment of human autonomy? Or is their behavior rather to be understood on the level of a simple reflex—autonomous only in a strictly formal sense?   43

Far from impinging on their autonomy, treatment of such psychotics, even coercive treatment, would not only hold out some hope of mitigating their condition but might simultaneously increase their capacity for more sophisticated autonomous choices. To adopt the typological scheme of the philosopher Bruce Miller, patients might thereby be enabled to move from mere freedom of action to choices that reflect congruence with personal values, effective rational deliberation, and moral reflection. Our intervention, though depriving them of the right to autonomy in the short term, may enhance that quality in the long run. In   44

such circumstances, benevolence and autonomy are no longer antagonistic principles.

VI

Deinstitutionalization is a remnant of a different era in our political life,   45
one in which we sought broadly-framed solutions to human problems
that have defied man's creativity for millennia. In the 1960's and 70's we
declared war on poverty, and we determined to wipe out injustice and
bigotry; government, we believed, had the tools and resources to accomplish these ends; all that was needed was the will.

This set of beliefs, applied to the mentally ill, allowed us to ignore the   46
failure of a century-and-a-half of mental-health reform in this country, in
the conviction that this time we had the answer. The problem, as it was
defined, was the system of large state hospitals. Like a cancer, it could be
easily excised. And the will was there.

Unfortunately, the analysis was wrong. The problems of severe mental   47
illness have proved resistant to unitary solutions. For some patients, discharge from the state hospitals was a blessing. For all too many others, it
was the ultimate curse. Far from a panacea, the policy created as many
problems as it solved, perhaps more. To be sure, it is never easy to admit
that massive social initiatives have been misconceived. The time has
come, however, to lay deinstitutionalization to rest.

It would not be difficult to outline a reasonable program to restore   48
some sense to the care of the mentally ill: moderate expansion of beds in
state facilities, especially for the most severely ill patients; good community-based services for those patients—and their number is not small—
who could prosper outside of an institution with proper supports; and
greater authority for the state to detain and treat the severely mentally ill
for their own benefit, even if they pose no immediate threat to their lives
or those of others.

Deinstitutionalization has been a tragedy, but it need not be an irre-   49
versible one.

■

ARE THE HOMELESS CRAZY?

Jonathan Kozol

Writer Jonathan Kozol, author of Rachel and Her Children, *offers a social
and economic explanation of homelessness among the mentally ill. "The
notion that the homeless are largely psychotics who belong in institutions,
rather than victims of displacement at the hands of enterprising realtors,
spares us from the need to offer realistic solutions to the deep and widening
extremes of wealth and poverty in the United States."*

It is commonly believed by many journalists and politicians that the   1
homeless of America are, in large part, former patients of large mental
hospitals who were deinstitutionalized in the 1970s—the consequence, it
is sometimes said, of misguided liberal opinion that favored the treatment of such persons in community-based centers. It is argued that this
policy, and the subsequent failure of society to build such centers or to
provide them in sufficient number, is the primary cause of homelessness
in the United States.

Those who work among the homeless do not find that explanation   2
satisfactory. While conceding that a certain number of the homeless are
or have been mentally unwell, they believe that, in the case of most
unsheltered people, the primary reason is economic rather than clinical.
The cause of homelessness, they say with disarming logic, is the lack of
homes and of income with which to rent or acquire them.

They point to the loss of traditional jobs in industry (2 million every   3
year since 1980) and to the fact that half of those who are laid off end up
in work that pays a poverty-level wage. They point out that since 1968
the number of children living in poverty has grown by 3 million, while
welfare benefits to families with children have declined by 35 percent.

And they note, too, that these developments have occurred during a   4
time in which the shortage of low-income housing has intensified as the
gentrification of our major cities has accelerated. Half a million units of
low-income housing are lost each year to condominium conversion as
well as to arson, demolition, or abandonment. Between 1978 and 1980,
median rents climbed 30 percent for people in the lowest income sector,
driving many of these families into the streets. Since 1980, rents have
risen at even faster rates.

Hard numbers, in this instance, would appear to be of greater help   5
than psychiatric labels in telling us why so many people become homeless. Eight million American families now use half or more of their
income to pay their rent or mortgage. At the same time, federal support
for low-income housing dropped from $30 billion (1980) to $7.5 billion
(1988). Under Presidents Ford and Carter, 500,000 subsidized private
housing units were constructed. By President Reagan's second term, the
number had dropped to 25,000.

In our rush to explain the homeless as a psychiatric problem even the   6
words of medical practitioners who care for homeless people have been
curiously ignored. A study published by the Massachusetts Medical Society, for instance, has noted that, with the exceptions of alcohol and drug
use, the most frequent illnesses among a sample of the homeless population were trauma (31 percent), upper-respiratory disorders (28 percent),
limb disorders (19 percent), mental illness (16 percent), skin diseases (15
percent), hypertension (14 percent), and neurological illnesses (12 percent). Why, we may ask, of all these calamities, does mental illness command so much political and press attention? The answer may be that the
label of mental illness places the destitute outside the sphere of ordinary

life. It personalizes an anguish that is public in its genesis; it individualizes a misery that is both general in cause and general in application.

There is another reason to assign labels to the destitute and single out   7
mental illness from among their many afflictions. All these other problems—tuberculosis, asthma, scabies, diarrhea, bleeding gums, impacted
teeth, etc.—bear no stigma, and mental illness does. It conveys a stigma
in the United States. It conveys a stigma in the Soviet Union as well. In
both nations the label is used, whether as a matter of deliberate policy or
not, to isolate and treat as special cases those who, by deed or word or
by sheer presence, represent a threat to national complacence. The two
situations are obviously not identical, but they are enough alike to give
Americans reason for concern.

The notion that the homeless are largely psychotics who belong in   8
institutions, rather than victims of displacement at the hands of enterprising realtors, spares us from the need to offer realistic solutions to the
deep and widening extremes of wealth and poverty in the United States.
It also enables us to tell ourselves that the despair of homeless people
bears no intimate connection to the privileged existence we enjoy—
when, for example, we rent or purchase one of those restored town
houses that once provided shelter for people now huddled in the street.

What is to be made, then, of the supposition that the homeless are   9
primarily the former residents of mental hospitals, persons who were
carelessly released during the 1970s? Many of them are, to be sure.
Among the older men and women in the streets and shelters, as many as
one-third (some believe as many as one-half) may be chronically disturbed, and a number of these people were deinstitutionalized during the
1970s. But to operate on that assumption in a city such as New York—
where nearly half the homeless are small children whose average age is
six—makes no sense. Their parents, with an average age of twenty-
seven, are not likely to have been hospitalized in the 1970s, either.

A frequently cited set of figures tells us that in 1955 the average daily   10
census of non-federal psychiatric institutions was 677,000, and that by
1984 the number had dropped to 151,000. But these people didn't go
directly from a hospital room to the street. The bulk of those who had
been psychiatric patients and were released from hospitals during the
1960s and early 1970s had been living in low-income housing, many in
skid-row hotels or boardinghouses. Such housing—commonly known as
SRO (single-room occupancy) units—was drastically diminished by the
gentrification of our cities that began in the early '70s. Almost 50 percent
of SRO housing was replaced by luxury apartments or office buildings
between 1970 and 1980, and the remaining units have been disappearing even more rapidly.

Even for those persons who are ill and were deinstitutionalized during   11
the decades before 1980, the precipitating cause of homelessness in
1987 is not illness but loss of housing. SRO housing offered low-cost

sanctuaries for the homeless, providing a degree of safety and mutual support for those who lived within them. They were a demeaning version of the community health centers that society had promised; they were the de facto "halfway houses" of the 1970s. For these people too—at most half of the homeless single persons in America—the cause of homelessness is lack of housing.

Even in those cases where mental instability is apparent, homelessness itself is often the precipitating factor. For example, many pregnant women without homes are denied prenatal care because they constantly travel from one shelter to another. Many are anemic. Many are denied essential dietary supplements by recent federal cuts. As a consequence, some of their children do not live to see their second year of life. Do these mothers sometimes show signs of stress? Do they appear disorganized, depressed, disordered? Frequently. They are immobilized by pain, traumatized by fear. So it is no surprise that when researchers enter the scene to ask them how they "feel," the resulting reports tell us that the homeless are emotionally unwell. The reports do not tell us that we have *made* these people ill. They do not tell us that illness is a natural response to intolerable conditions. Nor do they tell us of the strength and the resilience that so many of these people retain despite the miseries they must endure.   12

A writer in the *New York Times* describes a homeless woman standing on a traffic island in Manhattan. "She was evicted from her small room in the hotel just across the street," and she is determined to get revenge. Until she does, "nothing will move her from that spot. . . . Her argumentativeness and her angry fixation on revenge, along with the apparent absence of hallucinations, mark her as a paranoid." Most physicians, I imagine, would be more reserved in passing judgment with so little evidence, but this reporter makes his diagnosis without hesitation. "The paranoids of the street," he says, "are among the most difficult to help."   13

Perhaps so. But does it depend on who is offering the help? Is anyone offering to help this woman get back her home? Is it crazy to seek vengeance for being thrown into the street? The absence of anger, some psychiatrists believe, might indicate much greater illness.   14

"No one will be turned away," says the mayor of New York City, as hundreds of young mothers with their infants are turned from the doors of shelters season after season. That may sound to some like a denial of reality. "Now you're hearing all kinds of horror stories," says the President of the United States as he denies that anyone is cold or hungry or unhoused. On another occasion he says that the unsheltered "are homeless, you might say, by choice." That sounds every bit as self-deceiving.   15

The woman standing on the traffic island screaming for revenge until her room has been restored to her sounds relatively healthy by comparison. If 3 million homeless people did the same, and all at the same time, we might finally be forced to listen.   16

—————————————————— ■ ——————————————————

THE HOMELESS MENTALLY ILL

Steven Vanderstaay

Freelance writer Steven Vanderstaay spent many months living among the homeless and recording their stories. In his book Street Lives: An Oral History of Homeless Americans, *Vanderstaay interweaves homeless persons' own stories with his own interpretive commentary based on research in the literature on homelessness. The following reading is extracted from the chapter on mentally ill homeless in Vanderstaay's book.*

More of the mentally ill now live on our streets than in our public health hospitals.[1] This number—which does not include alcoholics or drug addicts—appears to be increasing, as is the fear of such people, and the number of voices raised to demand to "do" something about them.

This is not to say that most homeless people are mentally ill. They are not. Nor did the much debated deinstitutionalization of mentally ill patients create homelessness—though homelessness would be much easier to understand if it had.

Rather, and like all segments of the homeless population, the homeless mentally ill are a diverse group, more varied than alike. Understanding their situation is a delicate matter of avoiding these and other generalizations, and of accepting multiple truths: truths that may at best yield a pastiche—rather than a single tidy portrait—of the problem and its causes.

The argument that deinstitutionalization created homelessness goes like this:[2] psychiatric institutions released more than half a million patients between 1955 and 1984. The Community Mental Health Centers (CMHCs), originally designed to provide outpatient care for such people, failed to do so.[3] Adrift from their institutional moorings, and unable or unwilling to take the medications they need, hundreds of thousands of these people now live in our streets.

But the crisis in homelessness did not immediately follow deinstitutionalization. State hospitals released most of their patients before 1978, the greatest percentage of patients having been released in the 1960s. Homelessness did not begin to be recognized as a national crisis until the early 1980s, when families and the working poor—as well as the seriously mentally ill—began to overrun shelters and social services heretofore dominated by street alcoholics and transients. As Jonathan Kozol has remarked, if a significant number of the homeless were institutionalized "before they reappeared in subway stations and in public shelters," one might wonder "where they were and what they were doing from 1972 to 1980."[4]

Furthermore, formerly deinstitutionalized patients constitute but a small portion of the present population of homeless people. In fact, while deinstitutionalization did remove more than half a million patients from state hospitals, the bulk of these people ended up in nursing homes— not the street.[5] This is documented in numerous studies, all of which show a direct correlation between deinstitutionalization and nursing home admissions.[6] Reporting on data from across the country, for example, the U.S. General Accounting Office (GAO) announced in 1977 that deinstitutionalization would be more accurately described as "reinstitutionalization," because the nursing home had replaced the state hospital as the "largest single place of care for the mentally ill."[7]

Finally, up to one-fourth of the homeless people in our nation may be children,[8] and the median age for homeless adults is 36—still too young to have been released from state hospitals in the 1960s and 1970s.[9]   7

Certainly, some deinstitutionalized patients were discharged to homeless shelters and did end up homeless. Others may have become homeless after being pushed out of low-income housing, or tenuous situations where they lived with and were cared for by a relative, during the more significant current of homelessness that struck in the early 1980s. But while deinstitutionalization and the subsequent failure of the CMHCs contributed to homelessness, these factors can hardly be considered the precipitating cause of such a widespread, national crisis.

Nevertheless, it is true that rates of mental illness among homeless people are extremely high, many times that of the general population.[10] A portion of that figure can be attributed to the deinstitutionalization of ex-patients,[11] and another can be ascribed to the fact that some of the homeless mentally ill would have been hospitalized under the previous system. This would account for the many homeless schizophrenics who can be shown to have been genetically predisposed to mental illness. But even these considerations do not account for the roughly 30 percent of homeless people who appear mentally ill—especially those who demonstrate no sign of mental illness until after they become homeless.[12] Hence, if the so-called myth of deinstitutionalization is dismissed, one is left with the question of where so many homeless, mentally ill people come from.   8

One approach to this question is to examine the role homelessness may play in mental illness. This is the approach that most homeless people themselves take when considering the issue. Simply put, they think homelessness can drive you insane. In contrast, the great bulk of the psychiatric literature on homelessness assumes only the converse: that insanity can drive you to homelessness.   9

This occurs because the present psychiatric view considers most serious mental illness as the result of biological rather than environmental factors. According to this view, schizophrenia and manic-depressive psychoses, among others, are genetic illnesses—more like diabetes than emotional stress or the residual effects of traumatic childhood experiences. The underlying theory is that serious mental illness is located in the individual, rather than in the social context of the individual's experi-   10 ence. Accordingly, mental illness is seen as preceding (and thereby caus-ing) homelessness for the mentally ill of our streets and shelters.

Homeless people tend to disagree. While acknowledging that many   11
mentally ill people do become homeless, they stress the debilitating
effects of their situations as a chief cause of mental illness among them.
"When you're homeless your mind kind of wags," says Tanya, a homeless, college-educated woman who was hospitalized for depression and
schizophrenia after losing her children to the state. Cyrell, a homeless
man working to create a cooperative survival center in Philadelphia,
explains it this way:

> People become self-absorbed in their own minds when they're home-
> less. People say they're insane or psychotic, but a lot of people are nei-
> ther. What happens is they become absorbed in theirselves and their
> problems. I call it "mental inwardness," because nothing on the out-
> side matters to them.
>
> If you don't have decent clothing, or you're dirty and have no money,
> you're looked down upon. People turn their heads, say "Get away from
> me, scum!" So you don't fit in. Society rejects you, doesn't care for
> you, and you begin to lose hope. When that happens you just sit alone,
> thinking about your problems. Dejected. And with no human contact
> you just totally block everything out. The outer world gets canceled
> out. You get up off the grate, look this way and that. Self-absorbed.

This rather commonsense point of view is frequently corroborated by   12
mental health clinicians like Dr. Anne Braden Johnson, a clinical social
worker who oversees mental health services for women in New York
City's Rikers Island Jail. As she notes in her widely respected book, *Out
of Bedlam: The Truth about Deinstitutionalization:*

> Something that has not been studied to any appreciable degree, sur-
> prisingly, is the relationship between life without a home and mental
> status. Living on the street or in a shelter, as many homeless people
> do, cannot possibly have a positive effect on one's self-esteem or pro-
> vide much in the way of gratifying experience; and homelessness itself
> is a state of such unremitting crisis that one would expect it to provoke
> some kind of emotional or mental disorder, in and of itself. For the
> most part, though, the detachment prized by science has allowed
> researchers to look at specimen homeless people so objectively that
> the possibility of their having been driven mad by worry, fear, grief,
> guilt, or shame has not seriously entered the observers' minds.[13]

The lack of research on this question is particularly egregious because   13
documentation to support it has existed for years. Examining whether
mental illness might be best understood as a "response to conditions in
the social environment," Johns Hopkins sociologist and epidemiologist
M. Harvey Brenner studied the relationship between economic conditions
and admissions to mental hospitals in New York State. He found that
"instabilities in the national economy have been the single most impor-

tant source of fluctuation in mental-hospital admission rates" for the last 127 years. This effect of economic conditions on rates of mental illness, Brenner notes, has been particularly strong "in the last two decades."[14]

Not surprisingly, rates of homicides, suicides, and deaths from alco-   14
hol-related illnesses also correlate with some periods of economic decline.[15] Similarly, unemployment among men has been associated with a myriad of emotional difficulties and psychiatric symptoms, while women in unemployed families have been shown to be inordinately depressed, anxious, and phobic.[16] Homeless people have also been shown to be significantly more "demoralized" than the general population.[17]

This research does not deny that factors predisposing certain people   15
to mental illness exist. Rather, it demonstrates that economic stress correlates with the appearance of mental illness. Thus while mental illness in a dormant or mild form may precede homelessness, the stresses of poverty and homelessness activate or accelerate the disease. As Brenner puts it, "the appearance of mental illness is seen as *the* maladaptive response to the precipitating stress situation."[18]

The ramifications of these findings are startling. First, rates of mental   16
illness would naturally be expected to be higher among those for whom the stress of economic change has been greatest. This would certainly include people who have lost their jobs, homes, friends, and families. Second, the stress of homelessness explains why many of the homeless mentally ill demonstrate no sign of mental illness until after the onset of their homelessness. Third, to the extent that this view is accurate, such rates of mental illness among homeless people must be understood in societal terms, for it is in response to conditions in the larger society that homelessness has occurred. Finally, it follows that any treatment of the mentally ill must address the socioeconomic sources of the stress responsible for the rise in mental illness among those affected. For homeless people such "sources" would include the unavailability of low-income housing, cuts in disability and assistance benefits, unemployment, low wages, and their acute isolation.

Homeless people also question whether the conditions of homeless-   17
ness could generate responses that may be mistaken as symptoms of mental illness. That is, while the conditions of homelessness might elicit or exacerbate mental illnesses, is it not also likely that any "normal" response to such experiences would be apt to include depression, phobias, rage, and other behaviors symptomatic of mental illness?

People who work with homeless people find this a rather obvious   18
assertion. In fact, one counselor has commented that she has learned to treat the displaced rural homeless she sees just as she treats East Asian refugees suffering from cultural displacement and post-traumatic stress syndrome. "Their conditions are surprisingly similar," she remarked.[19]

Common sense deems that one should be cautious in designating a   19
Cambodian refugee as mentally ill for behavior that seems out of place

or odd. Adjustment and behavioral difficulties would be expected in such a situation. Similarly, one should be cautious when interpreting the behavior of homeless people. In point of fact, however, the exigencies of homeless life are rarely considered in examinations of mental illness among homeless people. In this way, psychiatrists and other researchers can misinterpret symptoms and misdiagnose the disease.

Alcoholism, drug abuse, and other medical problems also confuse psychiatric profiles. Homeless diabetics, for example, often lose their insulin, have syringes stolen, or fail to find the proper balance of food they need. Unable to control their disease, such diabetics can appear drunk and severely mentally ill.[20] The same is true of lesser maladies. Soiling oneself may indicate mental illness, or it may indicate a lack of toilets. It may even indicate an attempt to fend off rapists. Sleep deprivation, another common effect of homelessness, also manifests itself in symptoms identical to those of mental illness.

But even if it were accepted that the treatment most needed by homeless people—the mentally ill included—is an income, a community, and stable housing, the question of what to do with those who do need greater psychiatric care would remain unresolved.

Lithium and antipsychotic medications, for instance, control many of the symptoms of mental illness. Regular treatment with such medication could enable some of the homeless mentally ill to hold down jobs and gain greater control of their minds and bodies.[21] But a large proportion of the people who could benefit from medication will not take it. Typically, they are either not aware of their illness (people who are paranoid, for example, do not believe their fears to be delusions), or they fear the medication itself, some of which causes drowsiness, confusion, and tardive dyskinesia, a condition marked by tics and facial contortions.[22]

[The case of] Joshua . . . is a good example. Joshua's problems may be endemic to the trauma of his experience in Vietnam, or he may have acquired them through physical injury or inherited family traits. Regardless of cause, the debilitating conditions of homelessness and unemployment, and the rejection he has suffered as a poor, black veteran exacerbate his frustration and anger. Brenner's research would suggest that the stress of these factors triggered or activated the symptoms of his illness. Homeless people might say the stress caused them. In any case, Joshua is demonstrably violent, having been convicted of murder, and says that he is apt to "hurt somebody" again. For Joshua's good, as well as that of society at large, some kind of assistance is urgently needed.

Fortunately, Joshua is eligible for health care through the Veterans Administration. But he will not accept the treatment (read "medication") they offer. Whether such medication would help him is beside the point—too many of the other "treated" veterans "walk around like zombies" and he refuses to.

The question of whether Joshua should be forced to accept medication occupies much of the debate surrounding the homeless mentally ill.

The major reason for the failure of public psychiatric services has been   9
a fiscal one. It is not, however, a question of *how much* is being spent,
as is commonly supposed; the approximately $20 billion in public funds
currently being spent each year is probably sufficient to buy first-class
services if it were utilized properly. Rather, the problem is *how these
services are funded.* Until the early 1960s, approximately 96 per cent of
public psychiatric services were funded by the states, with the other 4
percent split between federal and local sources. As deinstitutionalization got under way, the released patients were made eligible for federal
Supplemental Security Income (SSI), Social Security Disability Income
(SSDI), Medicaid, Medicare, food stamps, and other federal subsidies.
By 1985 it was estimated that the states' share of the cost for the mentally ill had fallen to 53 per cent of the total, while the federal share had
risen to 38 per cent (it is undoubtedly several percentage points higher
by now).

The shift of the fiscal burden from the states to the Federal Govern-   10
ment was not, by itself, a disaster. The problems arose out of how the
various fiscal supports were related to each other. For example, the
patients in Metropolitan State Hospital and Columbus State Hospital
mentioned above were primarily the fiscal responsibilities of the states of
Massachusetts and Ohio as long as they were in the hospitals. Once discharged, they became primarily the responsibility of the Federal Government. If such patients relapse and need rehospitalization, as most of
them do, they typically are sent to the psychiatric ward of a general hospital, where Medicaid pays most of the bill. Elderly psychiatric patients
were similarly transferred from state hospitals to nursing homes not
because the care was necessarily better (often it was worse) but rather
because such a transfer made them eligible for Medicare and Medicaid.
Even with the states coming up with Medicaid matching funds, it was
extremely cost-effective, from the point of view of state government, to
shift the fiscal burden to the Federal Government.

The fiscal organization of public psychiatric services in the United   11
States is more thought-disordered than most of their patients. The incentives all lead to discharging psychiatric patients from state facilities as
quickly as possible; there is no incentive to worry about where they go,
whether they get aftercare, or whether they become homeless. Indeed, if
you tried to set up a system for funding public psychiatric services in a
way which would guarantee its failure, you would set up just such a system as we have created.

The solution is to meld federal and state funding streams into a single   12
stream with responsibility placed at the state level, unless states wish to
delegate to the county level (as do California, Minnesota, and Wisconsin).
All incentives to shift the fiscal burden to the Federal Government must
be removed. States would rapidly learn that it is cost-effective to provide
good psychiatric aftercare, because the costs of repeated rehospitaliza-
tions are very high. Continuity of care between inpatient and outpatient
programs would become the rule rather than the exception. Existing

model programs for the homeless mentally ill such as Seattle's El Rey Residential Treatment Facility or the widely praised Weingart Center in Los Angeles, which combine treatment, housing, and rehabilitation, would spread quickly. State laws making it difficult to hospitalize obviously impaired individuals would be amended as it became apparent that good psychiatric care does not cost more in the long run than not-so-benign neglect. And the homeless mentally ill, including the emblematic bag ladies, would become a thing of the past.

NOW FOR THE HARDER ONES

The problem of the homeless mentally ill is easy to solve compared with the problems of the other groups. Alcoholics have always made up a significant percentage of the homeless population, from the days of the early American almshouses to the hobos who rode the rails in the years before World War II. When one is addicted to alcohol or drugs the highest priority is to save as much money as possible to feed that addiction. Present homeless policies, which in some cities have guaranteed free beds and food for everyone who asks, have probably exacerbated rather than relieved the problem of homeless substance abusers. 13

Although there is no policy which can force a person to help himself, it stands to reason that public programs should not make alcohol and drug problems worse. All substance abusers who have any income should be required to pay a certain proportion of it for shelter and food and should also be required to attend regular meetings of Alcoholics Anonymous or Narcotics Anonymous. Rehabilitation programs including vocational training should be readily available, but abstinence should be a requirement for participation. For those who refuse to meet minimal requirements for such publicly funded programs, there is a network of private and church-run shelters (such as the Salvation Army's) which have provided exemplary care for alcoholics and drug abusers for many years. 14

Solutions to the down-on-my-luck homeless are both easy and difficult at the same time. Many of them are victims of reduced stocks of low-income housing. It does not take a PhD to realize that when single-room-occupancy (SRO) hotel units were reduced from 127,000 to 14,000, as happened in New York City between 1970 and 1983, or from 1,680 to 15, as happened in Nashville between 1970 and 1990, some people would be left with nowhere to live. 15

But housing is the easy half of solving the down-on-my luck problem. Many of these people have a poor education and marginal job skills. As the workplace demands increasing technological skills for even entry-level positions, this group is likely to continue to grow. Solutions require the whole panoply of often discussed but rarely available services from remedial education to vocational training, job coaching, transitional employment, supported employment, and counseling. This is certainly the most difficult and most expensive segment of the homeless population to rehabilitate, but not rehabilitating them is also expensive. 16

As long as programs for the mentally ill, substance abusers, and con-   17
sumers of low-income housing are part of the ongoing political tug-of-
war between federal and state governments, solutions to the problems of
the homeless will be elusive. The homeless are, in one sense, daily
reminders of the lack of resolution of this issue.

In the area of public psychiatric and substance-abuse services, the   18
Federal Government has a miserable record of achievement. Exhibit A is
the federally funded Community Mental Health Centers program, which
wasted over $3 billion setting up 769 centers, most of which never did
what they were intended to do. It seems likely that service programs conceived by federal officials, who are too far removed from the real world,
will almost inevitably fail.

What, then, should be the Federal Government's role? The setting of   19
minimal standards and enforcement of such standards through fiscal
incentives and disincentives is necessary, e.g., expecting states to reduce
the mentally ill homeless to a specified level and reducing federal subsidies if they fail. The enforcement function should probably be vested in
the Office of Inspector General in departments such as Health and
Human Services (HHS) or Housing and Urban Development (HUD).
Model programs such as those under the McKinney Act, the HHS-HUD
collaborative program to improve housing and services for the homeless
mentally ill, or Senator Pete Domenici's recently introduced "Projects to
Aid the Transition from Homelessness" bill, should be encouraged. The
problem is that from most states' point of view, such programs are not
regarded merely as models, but rather as an ongoing federal commitment to replace the efforts of the states themselves.

The homeless, then, will be with us until we are able to resolve the   20
issue of federal versus state responsibility for social programs. Hallucinat-
ing quietly next to vacant buildings, lying under bushes in the park, or
aggressively accosting strangers on the street, the homeless represent
not only a failure of social programs, but more broadly a failure of government at all levels.

☐ FOR CLASS DISCUSSION

1. Analyze and evaluate the debate on the mentally ill homeless by applying the first set of guide questions from page 473. How do you account for the disagreements among the disputants? This is a particularly good controversy for examining disagreements based on disputes about facts as well as values. Also, many of these arguments turn on knotty definitional questions: When is a person mentally ill? When is a person homeless? At what point does a person lose his or her rights as a free, autonomous individual?

2. Choose one of the arguments for closer analysis, applying the second set of guide questions on page 474.

OPTIONAL WRITING ASSIGNMENT   You are a newly hired research assistant to Senator Sarah Goodperson. For the past several weeks Senator Goodperson has been lobbied extensively by the National Coalition for the Homeless. The lobbyists are urging Senator Goodperson to support new legislation calling for the construction of 2.5 million low-cost, subsidized housing units in major cities across the United States. However, she has been lobbied with almost equal force by organizations devoted to reducing federal taxes and trimming what they see as a huge welfare bureaucracy. To add to her confusion, a coalition of big-city mayors, in partnership with an association of psychiatrists, has been calling for the rebuilding of state mental hospitals to provide treatment for the mentally ill homeless. These persons have sent Senator Goodperson copies of Charles Krauthammer's "How to Save the Homeless Mentally Ill" (pp. 226–33 in this text) and are urging her to support Krauthammer's proposal.

Sarah Goodperson throws up her hands in confusion. "What is the truth about homelessness?" she asks herself. "What ought we to do?" That night she sits at her word processor and writes you the following memo:

To: [Your name goes here]
From: Sarah Goodperson
Re: A national policy on the homeless

I'm being lobbied every which way but loose on the homeless issue, and frankly I'm confused about it. I've spent so much of my time recently focusing on national health care and reduction of the deficit that I haven't devoted much attention to what our country should be doing about the homeless. I want to start again from ground zero and rethink my entire position on the homeless. I want to develop a consistent position for myself, something that I believe in ethically and that I can support with appropriate reasons and data. My long-range goal is to help forge a coalition of legislators to create a long-range national policy on the homeless. But before I can do that I need time to think—and also I need to surround myself with a team of well-informed research assistants to bat around ideas with me.

This is where you come in. I would like you to examine the problem of the mentally ill homeless in light of the attached article by Charles Krauthammer [pp. 226–33 in this text], which is being avidly supported by a group of psychiatrists and big-city mayors. Read what the current literature is saying about the mentally ill homeless and get back to me with your analysis and advice. Should I support Krauthammer's proposal? What alternative approaches are suggested by the literature? Based on your first pass through the literature, which approach do you most recommend and why?

Because I will be using your document for my preliminary planning, all I need at this time is a basic overview of the literature on the mentally ill. I want to know what the alternatives are to Krauthammer's approach and get your recommendation of which approach is best and why. A reasonably short document ought to do the trick—say four or five double-spaced pages.

Your task: Write the document called for by Senator Goodperson.

Illegitimacy, Single Parenthood, and Welfare Reform: Should the Government Enact Policies to Strengthen the Traditional Family? If So, How?*

■

RESTORING BASIC VALUES: STRENGTHENING THE FAMILY

Dan Quayle

Former Vice President Dan Quayle, in a speech given during his last year in office, offers a wide-ranging analysis of American social ills that led up to the LA riots of 1992. In particular, Quayle is concerned with a "poverty of values" and the dissolution of the two-parent family. His criticism of sitcom heroine Murphy Brown's decision to have a child out of wedlock and raise it herself captured the national imagination and sparked a major debate.

As you may know, I've just returned from a week-long trip to Japan.   1
I was there to commemorate the 20th anniversary of the reversion of Okinawa to Japan by the United States, an act that has made a lasting impression on the Japanese.

While I was there, Japan announced its commitment to join with the   2
United States in assisting Eastern and Central Europe with a 400 million dollar aid package. We also announced a manufacturing technology ini-

* Other essays related to this issue are Charles Murray's "The Coming White Underclass" and Dorothy Gilliam's "Wrong Way to Reform Welfare" on pages 26–32 and 47–48 in this text.

tiative that will allow American engineers to gain experience working in Japanese businesses.

Japan and the United States are allies and partners. Though we have   3
our differences, especially in the area of trade, our two countries—with
40 percent of the world's GNP—are committed to a global partnership in
behalf of peace and economic growth.

But in the midst of all of these discussions of international affairs, I   4
was asked many times in Japan about the recent events in Los Angeles.
From the perspective of many Japanese, the ethnic diversity of our
culture is a weakness compared to their homogenous society. I begged
to differ with my hosts. I explained that our diversity is our strength. And
I explained that the immigrants who come to our shores have made,
and continue to make, vast contributions to our culture and our economy.

It is wrong to imply that the Los Angeles riots were an inevitable out-   5
come of our diversified society. But the question that I tried to answer in
Japan is one that needs answering here: What happened? Why? And
how do we prevent it in the future?

One response has been predictable: Instead of denouncing wrongdo-   6
ing, some have shown tolerance for rioters; some have enjoyed saying "I
told you so"; and some have simply made excuses for what happened.
All of this has been accompanied by pleas for more money.

I'll readily accept that we need to understand what happened. But I   7
reject the idea we should tolerate or excuse it.

When I have been asked during these last weeks who caused the riots   8
and the killing in L.A., my answer has been direct and simple: Who is to
blame for the riots? The rioters are to blame. Who is to blame for the
killings? The killers are to blame. Yes, I can understand how people were
shocked and outraged by the verdict in the Rodney King trial. But there
is simply no excuse for the mayhem that followed. To apologize or in any
way to excuse what happened is wrong. It is a betrayal of all those people
equally outraged and equally disadvantaged who did not loot and did not
riot—and who were in many cases victims of the rioters. No matter how
much you may disagree with the verdict, the riots were wrong. And if we
as a society don't condemn what is wrong, how can we teach our children what is right?

But after condemning the riots, we do need to try to understand the   9
underlying situation.

In a nutshell: I believe the lawless social anarchy which we saw is   10
directly related to the breakdown of family structure, personal responsibility and social order in too many areas of our society. For the poor the
situation is compounded by a welfare ethos that impedes individual
efforts to move ahead in society, and hampers their ability to take advantage of the opportunities America offers.

If we don't succeed in addressing these fundamental problems, and in   11
restoring basic values, any attempt to fix what's broken will fail. But one

reason I believe we won't fail is that we have come so far in the last 25 years.

There is no question that this country has had a terrible problem with   12
race and racism. The evil of slavery has left a long legacy. But we have
faced racism squarely, and we have made progress in the past quarter
century. The landmark civil rights bills of the 1960's removed legal barri-
ers to allow full participation by blacks in the economic, social and political life of the nation. By any measure the America of 1992 is more egalitarian, more integrated, and offers more opportunities to black
Americans—and all other minority group members—than the America of
1964. There is more to be done. But I think that all of us can be proud of
our progress.

And let's be specific about one aspect of this progress: This country   13
now has a black middle class that barely existed a quarter century ago.
Since 1967 the median income of black two parent families has risen by
60 percent in real terms. The number of black college graduates has skyrocketed. Black men and women have achieved real political power—
black mayors head 48 of our largest cities, including Los Angeles. These
are achievements.

But as we all know, there is another side to that bright landscape. Dur-   14
ing this period of progress, we have also developed a culture of poverty—
some call it an underclass—that is far more violent and harder to escape
than it was a generation ago.

The poor you always have with you. Scripture tells us. And in America   15
we have always had poor people. But in this dynamic, prosperous nation,
poverty has traditionally been a stage through which people pass on their
way to joining the great middle class. And if one generation didn't get
very far up the ladder—their ambitious, better-educated children would.

But the underclass seems to be a new phenomenon. It is a group   16
whose members are dependent on welfare for very long stretches, and
whose men are often drawn into lives of crime. There is far too little
upward mobility, because the underclass is disconnected from the rules
of American society. And these problems have, unfortunately, been particularly acute for black Americans.

Let me share with you a few statistics on the difference between black   17
poverty in particular in the 1960's and now.

—In 1967 68 percent of black families were headed by married couples. In 1991, only 48 percent of black families were headed by both a
husband and wife.

—In 1965 the illegitimacy rate among black families was 28 percent.
In 1989, 65 percent—two thirds—of all black children were born to
never-married mothers.

—In 1951 9.2 percent of black youth between 16–19 were unemployed. In 1965, it was 23 percent. In 1980 it was 35 percent. By 1989,
the number had declined slightly, but was still 32 percent.

—The leading cause of death of young black males today is homicide.

It would be overly simplistic to blame this social breakdown on the 18 programs of the Great Society alone. It would be absolutely wrong to blame it on the growth and success most Americans enjoyed during the 1980's. Rather, we are in large measure reaping the whirlwind of decades of changes in social mores.

I was born in 1947, so I'm considered one of those "Baby Boomers" 19 we keep reading about. But let's look at one, unfortunate legacy of the "Boomer" generation. When we were young, it was fashionable to declare war against traditional values. Indulgence and self-gratification seemed to have no consequences. Many of our generation glamorized casual sex and drug use, evaded responsibility and trashed authority. Today the "Boomers" are middle-aged and middle class. The responsibility of having families has helped many recover traditional values. And, of course, the great majority of those in the middle class survived the turbulent legacy of the 60's and 70's. But many of the poor, with less to fall back on, did not.

The intergenerational poverty that troubles us so much today is pre- 20 dominantly a poverty of values. Our inner cities are filled with children having children; with people who have not been able to take advantage of educational opportunities; with people who are dependent on drugs or the narcotic of welfare. To be sure, many people in the ghettos struggle very hard against these tides—and sometimes win. But too many feel they have no hope and nothing to lose. This poverty is, again, fundamentally a poverty of values.

Unless we change the basic rules of society in our inner cities, we can- 21 not expect anything else to change. We will simply get more of what we saw three weeks ago. New thinking, new ideas, new strategies are needed.

For the government, transforming underclass culture means that our 22 policies and programs must create a different incentive system. Our policies must be premised on, and must reinforce, values such as: family, hard work, integrity and personal responsibility.

I think we can all agree that government's first obligation is to main- 23 tain order. We are a nation of laws, not looting. It has become clear that the riots were fueled by the vicious gangs that terrorize the inner cities. We are committed to breaking those gangs and restoring law and order. As James Q. Wilson has written, "Programs of economic restructuring will not work so long as gangs control the streets."

Some people say "law and order," are code words. Well, they are code 24 words. Code words for safety, getting control of the streets, and freedom from fear. And let's not forget that, in 1990, 84 percent of the crimes committed by blacks were committed against blacks.

We are for law and order. If a single mother raising her children in the 25 ghetto has to worry about drive-by shootings, drug deals, or whether her children will join gangs and die violently, her difficult task becomes impossible. We're for law and order because we can't expect children to learn in dangerous schools. We're for law and order because if property isn't protected, who will build businesses?

As one step on behalf of law and order—and on behalf of opportunity as well—the President has initiated the "Weed and Seed" program—to "weed out" criminals and "seed" neighborhoods with programs that address root causes of crime. And we have encouraged community-based policing, which gets the police on the street so they interact with citizens.   26

Safety is absolutely necessary. But it's not sufficient. Our urban strategy is to empower the poor by giving them control over their lives. To do that, our urban agenda includes: 27

—Fully funding the Home-ownership and Opportunity for People Everywhere program. HOPE—as we call it—will help public housing residents become home-owners. Subsidized housing all too often merely made rich investors richer. Home ownership will give the poor a stake in their neighborhoods, and a chance to build equity.

—Creating enterprise zones by slashing taxes in targeted areas, including a zero capital gains tax, to spur entrepreneurship, economic development, and job creation in inner cities.

—Instituting our education strategy, AMERICA 2000, to raise academic standards and to give the poor the same choices about how and where to educate their children as rich people.

—Promoting welfare reform to remove the penalties for marriage, create incentives for saving, and give communities greater control over how the programs are administered.

These programs are empowerment programs. They are based on the same principles as the Job Training Partnership Act, which aimed to help disadvantaged young people and dislocated workers to develop their skills to give them an opportunity to get ahead. Empowering the poor will strengthen families. And right now, the failure of our families is hurting America deeply. When families fail, society fails. The anarchy and lack of structure in our inner cities are testament to how quickly civilization falls apart when the family foundation cracks. Children need love and discipline. They need mothers and fathers. A welfare check is not a husband. The state is not a father. It is from parents that children learn how to behave in society; it is from parents above all that children come to understand values and themselves as men and women, mothers and fathers.   28

And for those concerned about children growing up in poverty, we should know this: marriage is probably the best anti-poverty program of all. Among families headed by married couples today, there is a poverty rate of 5.7 percent. But 33.4 percent of families headed by a single mother are in poverty today.   29

Nature abhors a vacuum. Where there are no mature, responsible men around to teach boys how to be good men, gangs serve in their place. In fact, gangs have become a surrogate family for much of a gen-   30 eration of inner-city boys. I recently visited with some former gang members in Albuquerque, New Mexico. In a private meeting, they told me why they had joined gangs. These teenage boys said that gangs gave them a sense of security. They made them feel wanted, and useful. They got support from their friends. And, they said, "It was like having a family." "Like family"—unfortunately, that says it all.

The system perpetuates itself as these young men father children   31
whom they have no intention of caring for, by women whose welfare checks support them. Teenage girls, mired in the same hopelessness, lack sufficient motive to say no to this trap.

Answers to our problems won't be easy.   32

We can start by dismantling a welfare system that encourages depen-   33
dency and subsidizes broken families. We can attach conditions—such as school attendance, or work—to welfare. We can limit the time a recipient gets benefits. We can stop penalizing marriage for welfare mothers. We can enforce child support payments.

Ultimately, however, marriage is a moral issue that requires cultural   34
consensus, and the use of social sanctions. Bearing babies irresponsibly is, simply, wrong. Failing to support children one has fathered is wrong. We must be unequivocal about this.

It doesn't help matters when prime time TV has Murphy Brown—a   35
character who supposedly epitomizes today's intelligent, highly paid, professional woman—mocking the importance of fathers, by bearing a child alone, and calling it just another "lifestyle choice."

I know it is not fashionable to talk about moral values, but we need to   36
do it. Even though our cultural leaders in Hollywood, network TV, the national newspapers routinely jeer at them, I think that most of us in this room know that some things are good, and other things are wrong. Now it's time to make the discussion public.

It's time to talk again about family, hard work, integrity and personal   37
responsibility. We cannot be embarrassed out of our belief that two parents, married to each other, are better in most cases for children than one. That honest work is better than hand-outs—or crime. That we are our brothers' keepers. That it's worth making an effort, even when the rewards aren't immediate.

So I think the time has come to renew our public commitment to our   38
Judeo-Christian values—in our churches and synagogues, our civic organizations and our schools. We are, as our children recite each morning, "one nation under God." That's a useful framework for acknowledging a duty and an authority higher than our own pleasures and personal ambitions.

If we lived more thoroughly by these values, we would live in a better   39
society. For the poor, renewing these values will give people the strength to help themselves by acquiring the tools to achieve self-sufficiency, a good education, job training, and property. Then they will move from permanent dependence to dignified independence.

Shelby Steele, in his great book, *The Content of Our Character,* writes   40

> Personal responsibility is the brick and mortar of power. The respon-
> sible person knows that the quality of his life is something that he will
> have to make inside the limits of his fate. . . . The quality of his life will
> pretty much reflect his efforts.

I believe that the Bush Administration's empowerment agenda will   41
help the poor gain that power, by creating opportunity, and letting people
make the choices that free citizens must make.

Though our hearts have been pained by the events in Los Angeles, we   42
should take this tragedy as an opportunity for self-examination and
progress. So let the national debate roar on. I, for one, will join it. The
president will lead it. The American people will participate in it. And as a
result, we will become an even stronger nation.

■

WHY I HATE "FAMILY VALUES"
(LET ME COUNT THE WAYS)

Katha Pollitt

*Writer Katha Pollitt argues that sitcom anchor Murphy Brown's decision to
have a child is defensible and unlikely to influence welfare recipients to follow suit. Pollitt pans conservative critics of Brown for using vague, contradictory, and outmoded notions of "family values" to coerce married parents
into remaining in unhappy marriages.*

Unlike many of the commentators who have made Murphy Brown the   1
most famous unmarried mother since Ingrid Bergman ran off with
Roberto Rossellini, I actually watched the notorious childbirth episode.
After reading my sleep-resistant 4-year-old her entire collection of Berenstain Bears books, television was all I was fit for. And that is how I know
that I belong to the cultural elite: Not only can I spell "potato" correctly,
and many other vegetables as well, I thought the show was a veritable
riot of family values. First of all, Murph is smart, warm, playful, decent
and rich: She'll be a great mom. Second, the dad is her ex-husband: The
kid is as close to legitimate as the scriptwriters could manage, given that
Murph is divorced. Third, her ex spurned *her,* not, as Dan Quayle implies,
the other way around. Fourth, she rejected abortion. On TV, women have
abortions only in docudramas, usually after being raped, drugged with
birth-defect-inducing chemicals or put into a coma. Finally, what does
Murph sing to the newborn? "You make me feel like a natural woman"!
Even on the most feminist sitcom in TV history (if you take points off
Kate and Allie for never so much as mentioning the word "gay"),
anatomy is destiny.

That a show as fluffy and genial as *Murphy Brown* has touched off a   2
national debate about "family values" speaks volumes—and not just
about the apparent inability of Dan Quayle to distinguish real life from a
sitcom. (And since when are TV writers part of the cultural elite, anyway?
I thought they were the crowd-pleasing lowbrows, and *intellectuals* were
the cultural elite.) The *Murphy Brown* debate, it turns out, isn't really
about Murphy Brown; it's about inner-city women, who will be encouraged to produce fatherless babies by Murph's example—the trickle-down
theory of values. (Do welfare moms watch *Murphy Brown?* I thought it
was supposed to be soap operas, as in "they just sit around all day
watching the soaps." Marriage is a major obsession on the soaps—but
never mind.) Everybody, it seems, understood this substitution immediately. After all, why get upset about Baby Boy Brown? Is there any doubt
that he will be safe, loved, well schooled, taken for checkups, taught to
respect the rights and feelings of others and treated to *The Berenstain
Bears Visit the Dentist* as often as his little heart desires? Unlike millions
of kids who live with both parents, he will never be physically or sexually
abused, watch his father beat his mother (domestic assault is the leading
cause of injury to women) or cower beneath the blankets while his parents scream at each other. And chances are excellent that he won't sexually assault a retarded girl with a miniature baseball bat, like those high
school athletes in posh Glen Ridge, New Jersey; or shoot his lover's
spouse, like Amy Fisher; or find himself on trial for rape, like William
Kennedy Smith—children of intact and prosperous families every one of
them. He'll probably go to Harvard and major in semiotics. Maybe that's
the problem. Just think, if Murph were married, like Dan Quayle's mom,
he could go to DePauw University and major in golf.

That there is something called "the family"—Papa Bear, Mama Bear,   3
Brother Bear and Sister Bear—that is the best setting for raising children,
and that it is in trouble because of a decline in "values," are bromides
accepted by commentators of all political stripes. The right blames a left-
wing cultural conspiracy: obscene rock lyrics, sex ed, abortion, prayerless
schools, working mothers, promiscuity, homosexuality, decline of respect
for authority and hard work, welfare and, of course, feminism. (On the
Chicago Tribune Op-Ed page, Allan Carlson, president of the ultracon-
servative Rockford Institute, found a previously overlooked villain: federal
housing subsidies. With all that square footage lying around, singles and
unhappy spouses could afford to live on their own.) The left blames the
ideology of postindustrial capitalism: consumerism, individualism, selfishness, alienation, lack of social supports for parents and children, atro-
phied communities, welfare and feminism. The center agonizes over teen
sex, welfare moms, crime and divorce, unsure what the causes are
beyond some sort of moral failure—probably related to feminism. Interesting how that word keeps coming up.

I used to wonder what family values are. As a matter of fact, I still do.   4
If abortion, according to the right, undermines family values, then single

motherhood (as the producers of *Murphy Brown* were quick to point out) must be in accord with them, no? Over on the left, if gender equality, love and sexual expressivity are desirable features of contemporary marriage, then isn't marriage bound to be unstable, given how hard those things are to achieve and maintain? Not really.

Just say no, says the right. Try counseling, says the left. Don't be so lazy, says the center. Indeed, in its guilt-mongering cover story "Legacy of Divorce: How the Fear of Failure Haunts the Children of Broken Marriages," *Newsweek* was unable to come up with any explanation for the high American divorce rate except that people just didn't try hard enough to stay married.

When left, right and center agree, watch out. They probably don't know what they're talking about. And so it is with "the family" and "family values." In the first place, these terms lump together distinct social phenomena that in reality have virtually nothing to do with one another. The handful of fortysomething professionals like Murphy Brown who elect to have a child without a male partner have little in common with the millions of middle- and working-class divorced mothers who find themselves in desperate financial straits because their husbands fail to pay court-awarded child support. And neither category has much in common with inner-city girls like those a teacher friend of mine told me about the other day: a 13-year-old and a 12-year-old, impregnated by boyfriends twice their age and determined to bear and keep the babies—to spite abusive parents, to confirm their parents' low opinion of them, to have someone to love who loves them in return.

Beyond that, appeals to "the family" and its "values" frame the discussion as one about morals instead of consequences. In real life, for example, teen sex—the subject of endless sermons—has little relation with teen childbearing. That sounds counterfactual, but it's true. Western European teens have sex about as early and as often as American ones, but are much less likely to have babies. Partly it's because there are far fewer European girls whose lives are as marked by hopelessness and brutality as those of my friend's students. And partly it's because European youth have much better access to sexual information, birth control and abortion. Or consider divorce. In real life, parents divorce for all kinds of reasons, not because they lack moral fiber and are heedless of their children's needs. Indeed, many divorce because they *do* consider their kids, and the poisonous effects of growing up in a household marked by violence, craziness, open verbal warfare or simple lovelessness.

Perhaps this is the place to say that I come to the family-values debate with a personal bias. I am recently separated myself. I think my husband and I would fall under *Newsweek*'s "didn't try harder" rubric, although we thought about splitting up for years, discussed it for almost a whole additional year and consulted no fewer than four therapists, including a marital counselor who advised us that marriage was one of modern mankind's only means of self-transcendence (religion and psychoanalysis were the others, which should have warned me) and admonished us that we risked a future of shallow relationships if we shirked our spiritual mission, not to mention the damage we would "certainly" inflict on our daughter. I thought he was a jackass—shallow relationships? *moi?* But he got to me. Because our marriage wasn't some flaming disaster—with broken dishes and hitting and strange hotel charges showing up on the MasterCard bill. It was just unhappy, in ways that weren't going to change. Still, I think both of us would have been willing to trudge on to spare our child suffering. That's what couples do in women's magazines; that's what the Clintons say they did. But we saw it wouldn't work: As our daughter got older, she would see right through us, the way kids do. And, worse, no matter how hard I tried to put on a happy face, I would wordlessly communicate to her—whose favorite fairy tale is "Cinderella," and whose favorite game is Wedding, complete with bath-towel bridal veil— my resentment and depression and cynicism about relations between the sexes.

The family-values types would doubtless say that my husband and I   9
made a selfish choice, which society should have impeded or even prevented. There's a growing sentiment in policy land to make divorce more difficult. In *When the Bough Breaks,* Sylvia Ann Hewlett argues that couples should be forced into therapy (funny how ready people are to believe that counseling, which even when voluntary takes years to modify garden-variety neuroses, can work wonders in months with resistant patients who hate each other). Christopher Lasch briefly supported a constitutional amendment forbidding divorce to couples with minor children, as if lack of a separation agreement would keep people living together (he's backed off that position, he told me recently). The Communitarians, who flood *The Nation*'s mailboxes with self-promoting worryfests, furrow their brows wondering "How can the family be saved without forcing women to stay at home or otherwise violating their rights?" (Good luck.) But I am still waiting for someone to explain why it would be better for my daughter to grow up in a joyless household than for her to live as she does now, with two reasonably cheerful parents living around the corner from each other, both committed to her support and cooperating, as they say on *Sesame Street,* in her care. We may not love each other, but we both love her. Maybe that's as much as parents can do for their children, and all that should be asked of them.

But, of course, civilized cooperation is exactly what many divorced   10
parents find they cannot manage. The statistics on deadbeat and vanishing dads are shocking—less than half pay child support promptly and in full, and around half seldom or never see their kids within a few years of marital breakup. Surely, some of this male abdication can be explained by the very thinness of the traditional paternal role worshiped by the preachers of "values"; it's little more than bread-winning, discipline and fishing trips. How many diapers, after all, has Dan Quayle changed? A

large percentage of American fathers have never changed a single one. Maybe the reason so many fathers fade away after divorce is that they were never really there to begin with.

It is true that people's ideas about marriage are not what they were in the 1950s—although those who look back at the fifties nostalgically forget both that many of those marriages were miserable and that the fifties were an atypical decade in more than a century of social change. Married women have been moving steadily into the work force since 1890; beginning even earlier, families have been getting smaller; divorce has been rising; sexual activity has been initiated even earlier and marriage delayed; companionate marriage has been increasingly accepted as desirable by all social classes and both sexes. It may be that these trends have reached a tipping point, at which they come to define a new norm. Few men expect to marry virgins, and children are hardly "stigmatized" by divorce, as they might have been a mere fifteen or twenty years ago. But if people want different things from family life—if women, as Arlie Hochschild pointed out in *The Second Shift,* cite as a major reason for separation the failure of their husbands to share domestic labor; if both sexes are less willing to resign themselves to a marriage devoid of sexual pleasure, intimacy or shared goals; if single women decide they want to be mothers; if teenagers want to sleep together—why shouldn't society adapt? Society is, after all, just us. Nor are these developments unique to the United States. All over the industrialized world, divorce rates are high, single women are having babies by choice, homosexuals are coming out of the closet and infidelity, always much more common than anyone wanted to recognize, is on the rise. Indeed, in some ways America is behind the rest of the West: We still go to church, unlike the British, the French and, now that Franco is out of the way, the Spanish. More religious than Spain! Imagine.   11

I'm not saying that these changes are without cost—in poverty, loneliness, insecurity and stress. The reasons for this suffering, however, lie not in moral collapse but in our failure to acknowledge and adjust to changing social relations.   12

We still act as if mothers stayed home with children, wives didn't need to work, and men earned a "family wage." We'd rather preach about teenage "promiscuity" than teach young people—especially young women—how to negotiate sexual issues responsibly. If my friend's students had been prepared for puberty by schools and discussion groups and health centers, the way Dutch young people are, they might not have ended up pregnant, victims of what is, after all, statutory rape. And if women earned a dollar for every dollar earned by men, divorce and single parenthood would not mean poverty. Nobody worries about single fathers raising children, after all; indeed, paternal custody is the latest legal fad.   13

What is the point of trying to put the new wine of modern personal   14
relations in the old bottles of the sexual double standard and indissoluble
marriage? For that is what most of the current discourse on "family
issues" amounts to. No matter how fallacious, the culture greets moralis-
tic approaches to these subjects with instant agreement. Judith Wallerstein's travesty of social science, *Second Chances,* asserts that children
are emotionally traumatized by divorce, and the fact that she had no
control group is simply ignored by an ecstatic press. As it happens, a
recent study in *Science* did use a control group. By following 17,000
children for four years, and comparing those whose parents split
with those whose parents stayed in troubled marriages, the researchers
found that the "divorce effect" disappeared entirely for boys and was
very small for girls. Not surprisingly, this study attracted absolutely no
attention.

Similarly, we are quick to blame poor unmarried mothers for all man-   15
ner of social problems—crime, unemployment, drops in reading scores,
teen suicide. The solution? Cut off all welfare for additional children.
Force teen mothers to live with their parents. Push women to marry in
order to attach them to a male income. (So much for love—talk about
marriage as legalized prostitution!)

New Jersey's new welfare reform law gives economic coercion a par-   16
ticularly bizarre twist. Welfare moms who marry can keep part of their
dole, but only if the man is *not* the father of their children. The logic is
that, married or not, Dad has a financial obligation to his kids, but Mr.
Just Got Into Town does not. If the law's inventors are right that welfare
policy can micromanage marital and reproductive choice, they have just
guaranteed that no poor woman will marry her children's father. This is
strengthening the family?

Charles Murray, of the American Enterprise Institute, thinks New Jer-   17
sey does not go far enough. Get rid of welfare entirely, he argued in *The
New York Times:* Mothers should marry or starve, and if they are foolish
enough to prefer the latter, their kids should be put up for adoption or
into orphanages. Mickey Kaus, who favors compulsory low-wage employment for the poor, likes orphanages too.

None of those punitive approaches will work. There is no evidence   18
that increased poverty decreases family size, and welfare moms aren't
likely to meet many men with family-sized incomes, or they'd probably be
married already, though maybe not for long. The men who impregnated
those seventh graders, for example, are much more likely to turn them
out as prostitutes than to lead them to the altar. For one thing, those
men may well be married themselves.

The fact is, the harm connected with the dissolution of "the family" is   19
not a problem of values—at least not individual values—it's a problem of
money. When the poor are abandoned to their fates, when there are no
jobs, people don't get to display "work ethic," don't feel good about
themselves and don't marry or stay married. The girls don't have any-

thing to postpone motherhood for; the boys have no economic prospects that would make them reasonable marriage partners. This was as true in the slums of eighteenth-century London as it is today in the urban slums of Latin America and Africa, as well as the United States. Or take divorce: The real harm of divorce is that it makes lots of women, and their children, poor. One reason, which has got a fair amount of attention recently, is the scandalously low level of child support, plus the tendency of courts to award a disproportionate share of the marital assets to the man. The other reason is that women earn much less than men, thanks to gender discrimination and the failure of the workplace to adapt to the needs of working mothers. Instead of moaning about "family values" we should be thinking about how to provide the poor with decent jobs and social services, and about how to insure economic justice for working women. And let marriage take care of itself.

Family values and the cult of the nuclear family is, at bottom, just   20
another way to bash women, especially poor women. If only they would get married and stay married, society's ills would vanish. Inner-city crime would disappear because fathers would communicate manly values to their sons, which would cause jobs to spring up like mushrooms after rain. Welfare would fade away. Children would do well in school. (Irene Impellizeri, anti-condom vice president of the New York City Board of Education, recently gave a speech attributing inner-city children's poor grades and high dropout rates to the failure of their families to provide "moral models," the way immigrant parents did in the good old days—a dangerous argument for her, in particular, to make; doesn't she know that Italian-American kids have dropout and failure rates only slightly lower than black and Latino teens?)

When pundits preach morality, I often find myself thinking of Samuel   21
Johnson, literature's greatest enemy of cant and fatuity. What would the eighteenth-century moralist make of our current obsession with marriage? "Sir," he replied to Boswell, who held that marriage was a natural state, "it is so far from being natural for a man and woman to live in the state of marriage that we find all the motives which they have for remaining in that connection, and the restraints which civilized society imposes to prevent separation, are hardly sufficient to keep them together." Dr. Johnson knew what he was talking about: He and his wife lived apart. And what would he think of our confusion of moral preachments with practical solutions to social problems? Remember his response to Mrs. Thrale's long and flowery speech on the cost of children's clothes. "Nay, madam," he said, "when you are declaiming, declaim; and when you are calculating, calculate."

Which is it going to be? Declamation, which feeds no children,   22
employs no jobless and reduces gender relations to an economic bargain? Or calculation, which accepts the fact that the Berenstain Bears, like Murphy Brown, are fiction. The people seem to be voting with their feet on "the family." It's time for our "values" to catch up.

ABOLISHING WELFARE WON'T STOP POVERTY, ILLEGITIMACY

Elija Anderson

Sociologist Elija Anderson argues against abolishing welfare as an answer to the problem of a growing "underclass." According to Anderson, the prospect of increased welfare benefits does not motivate poor women to have more children. Anderson instead attributes the growing number of single mothers to underlying economic problems.

Those who have been calling recently for an end to welfare, seeing this as a way of solving poverty and illegitimacy, are wrong. Eliminating the program would only make things much worse. As an ethnographer and sociologist who has worked in poor, inner-city neighborhoods, I welcome the debate and the search for solutions to these problems. But the proposals to abolish welfare outright espoused by such people as syndicated columnist Charles Krauthammer and Charles Murray are dangerously shortsighted. 1

Krauthammer, in fact, cites my research in one inner-city neighborhood in support of his thinking. Since welfare provides economic support to illegitimate babies and their mothers—a fact of inner-city life my research has indeed shown to be one consideration in the sexual game that leads to illegitimate births—he argues that eliminating welfare will eliminate the interest in having babies. This reasoning is seriously flawed precisely because it ignores all the other considerations bearing down on inner-city adolescents, thereby exaggerating the role played by welfare. 2

In "Sex Codes and Family Life Among Poor Inner-City Youths," a chapter in my book "Streetwise," I describe ethnographically the perspectives and experiences of young black men and women in one community. 3

I found that the lack of family-sustaining jobs denies many young men the possibility of forming an economically self-reliant family, the traditional American mark of manhood. Partially in response, the young men's peer groups emphasize sexual prowess as a sign of manhood, with babies as evidence. A sexual game emerges as girls are lured by the (usually older) boys' vague but convincing promises of love and marriage. When the girls submit, they often end up pregnant and abandoned. I also noted that these new mothers become eligible for a limited but steady welfare income that may allow them to establish their own households and at times attract other men who need money. But it is simplistic and wrongheaded to suggest that if you stop welfare, you will stop this behavior. A fundamental question is: Why do people behave in the ways I have described? 4

A significant part of the answer is: because of the unraveling of the economy in their communities, which results in hopelessness. The lack of responsibility shown by the men, the "wantonness," is exacerbated by 5 the very bad economic conditions—the exodus of jobs and the inability of people to get the jobs still available because of a lack of education, skills and training.

Illegitimacy is not caused by welfare, but it is, in part, an outgrowth of   6
the failure of the welfare system to achieve its purpose—to alleviate the human problems inherent in the vicissitudes of capitalism, enabling people temporarily (according to theory) displaced by changes in the economic marketplace to survive. Yet I see that what so many people in the inner city are up against are, in fact, the vicissitudes of the economy and an economy now global in scope that has left them behind.

The situation I describe in the "Sex Codes" chapter springs from alien-   7
ation and despair—which then creates nihilism. This is born of a lack of hope and the inability to form a positive view of the future. So many of the young men I got to know don't get married because they don't feel they can "play house." What they mean is they can't play the roles of men in families in the way they would like.

Their assumption is that men in middle- and upper-class families that   8
they see as models control their households. To be that upstanding husband and father, you need resources, you need money. Facing persistent discrimination, a lot of the men I interviewed believe they can't get the money, can't get the family-sustaining jobs. This has a profound impact on how they see their future.

As we move from a manufacturing to a service and high-tech econ-   9
omy, great numbers of inner-city poor people are not making an effective adjustment to the change. The service jobs they are able to obtain often don't pay them enough money to live, and so some of the most enterprising young people have opted for the underground economy of drugs and crime. One of the results is the social disorganization that contributes not only to increasing violence and alienation but also to a syndrome of abuse, in which people are bent on getting what they can out of other people—including sex and money—without any real concern for those they victimize.

Buffeted by the global economy, communities such as this one find   10
themselves with fewer and fewer dependable sources of capital. Welfare is one relatively small but reliable source. To eliminate welfare is to destroy an important source of capital in the community. If welfare suddenly ceased to exist, many people would be forced to look elsewhere for resources. Some would seek the low-paying jobs available, but the hard reality is that others would be driven to more desperate measures. The nihilism that you now see among inner-city people would only increase and spread further beyond the bounds of ghetto communities. Cities would become almost unlivable. Blacks would continue to be the primary victims, though; illegitimacy rates would rise, not diminish.

The welfare system is in need of an overhaul, but it does not follow   11
that we should throw meager income supports overboard. We need to maintain the support at the same time that we create opportunity for

independent income. The way to make real headway is to create jobs and job opportunities and build hope through education and job training.

When a sense of the future exists, we will see more responsible behav-   12
ior, sexual and otherwise. To take welfare away without replacing it with such opportunities would effectively remove a lifeline for the very poor but also what has become a safety valve protecting both inner-city communities and the rest of society from the consequences of steadily escalating frustration.

DAN QUAYLE WAS RIGHT

Barbara Dafoe Whitehead

Social scientist Barbara DaFoe Whitehead, responding to the furor created by Dan Quayle's critique of Murphy Brown, argues that the dissolution of the two-parent family has harmed many children, not to mention the very social fabric of the nation. Whitehead particularly laments the shift from a concern for children's welfare to a concern for adult happiness.

Divorce and out-of-wedlock childbirth are transforming the lives of   1
American children. In the postwar generation more than 80 percent of children grew up in a family with two biological parents who were married to each other. By 1980 only 50 percent could expect to spend their entire childhood in an intact family. If current trends continue, less than half of all children born today will live continuously with their own mother and father throughout childhood. Most American children will spend several years in a single-mother family. Some will eventually live in stepparent families, but because stepfamilies are more likely to break up than intact (by which I mean two-biological-parent) families, an increasing number of children will experience family breakup two or even three times during childhood.

According to a growing body of social-scientific evidence, children in   2
families disrupted by divorce and out-of-wedlock birth do worse than children in intact families on several measures of well-being. Children in single-parent families are six times as likely to be poor. They are also likely to stay poor longer. Twenty-two percent of children in one-parent families will experience poverty during childhood for seven years or more, as compared with only two percent of children in two-parent families. A 1988 survey by the National Center for Health Statistics found that children in single-parent families are two to three times as likely as children in two-parent families to have emotional and behavioral problems. They are also more likely to drop out of high school, to get pregnant as teenagers, to abuse drugs, and to be in trouble with the law. Compared with children in intact families, children from disrupted families are at a much higher risk for physical or sexual abuse.

Contrary to popular belief, many children do not "bounce back" after   3
divorce or remarriage. Difficulties that are associated with family breakup
often persist into adulthood. Children who grow up in single-parent or
stepparent families are less successful as adults, particularly in the two
domains of life—love and work—that are most essential to happiness.
Needless to say, not all children experience such negative effects. However, research shows that many children from disrupted families have a
harder time achieving intimacy in a relationship, forming a stable marriage, or even holding a steady job.

Despite this growing body of evidence, it is nearly impossible to dis-   4
cuss changes in family structure without provoking angry protest. Many
people see the discussion as no more than an attack on struggling single
mothers and their children: Why blame single mothers when they are
doing the very best they can? After all, the decision to end a marriage or
a relationship is wrenching, and few parents are indifferent to the painful
burden this decision imposes on their children. Many take the perilous
step toward single parenthood as a last resort, after their best efforts to
hold a marriage together have failed. Consequently, it can seem particularly cruel and unfeeling to remind parents of the hardships their children
might suffer as a result of family breakup. Other people believe that the
dramatic changes in family structure, though regrettable, are impossible
to reverse. Family breakup is an inevitable feature of American life, and
anyone who thinks otherwise is indulging in nostalgia or trying to turn
back the clock. Since these new family forms are here to stay, the reasoning goes, we must accord respect to single parents, not criticize
them. Typical is the view expressed by a Brooklyn woman in a recent letter to *The New York Times:* "Let's stop moralizing or blaming single parents and unwed mothers, and give them the respect they have earned
and the support they deserve."

Such views are not to be dismissed. Indeed, they help to explain why   5
family structure is such an explosive issue for Americans. The debate
about it is not simply about the social-scientific evidence, although that is
surely an important part of the discussion. It is also a debate over deeply
held and often conflicting values. How do we begin to reconcile our long-
standing belief in equality and diversity with an impressive body of evidence that suggests that not all family structures produce equal outcomes for children? How can we square traditional notions of public
support for dependent women and children with a belief in women's right
to pursue autonomy and independence in childbearing and child-rear-
ing? How do we uphold the freedom of adults to pursue individual happiness in their private relationships and at the same time respond to the
needs of children for stability, security, and permanence in their family
lives? What do we do when the interests of adults and children conflict?
These are the difficult issues at stake in the debate over family structure.

In the past these issues have turned out to be too difficult and too   6
politically risky for debate. In the mid-1960s Daniel Patrick Moynihan,

then an assistant secretary of labor, was denounced as a racist for calling attention to the relationship between the prevalence of black single-mother families and the lower socioeconomic standing of black children. For nearly twenty years the policy and research communities backed away from the entire issue. In 1980 the Carter Administration convened a historic White House Conference on Families, designed to address the growing problems of children and families in America. The result was a prolonged, publicly subsidized quarrel over the definition of "family." No President since has tried to hold a national family conference. Last year, at a time when the rate of out-of-wedlock births had reached a historic high, Vice President Dan Quayle was ridiculed for criticizing Murphy Brown. In short, every time the issue of family structure has been raised, the response has been first controversy, then retreat, and finally silence.

Yet it is also risky to ignore the issue of changing family structure. In   7 recent years the problems associated with family disruption have grown. Overall child well-being has declined, despite a decrease in the number of children per family, an increase in the educational level of parents, and historically high levels of public spending. After dropping in the 1960s and 1970s, the proportion of children in poverty has increased dramatically, from 15 percent in 1970 to 20 percent in 1990, while the percentage of adult Americans in poverty has remained roughly constant. The teen suicide rate has more than tripled. Juvenile crime has increased and become more violent. School performance has continued to decline. There are no signs that these trends are about to reverse themselves.

If we fail to come to terms with the relationship between family struc-   8 ture and declining child well-being, then it will be increasingly difficult to improve children's life prospects, no matter how many new programs the federal government funds. Nor will we be able to make progress in bettering school performance or reducing crime or improving the quality of the nation's future work force—all domestic problems closely connected to family break up. Worse, we may contribute to the problem by pursuing policies that actually increase family instability and breakup.

FROM DEATH TO DIVORCE

Across time and across cultures, family disruption has been regarded   9 as an event that threatens a child's well-being and even survival. This view is rooted in a fundamental biological fact: unlike the young of almost any other species, the human child is born in an abjectly helpless and immature state. Years of nurture and protection are needed before the child can achieve physical independence. Similarly, it takes years of interaction with at least one but ideally two or more adults for a child to develop into a socially competent adult. Children raised in virtual isolation from human beings, though physically intact, display few recognizably human behaviors. The social arrangement that has proved most successful in ensuring the physical survival and promoting the social development of the child is the family unit of the biological mother and father. Consequently, any event that permanently denies a child the presence and protection of a parent jeopardizes the life of the child.

The classic form of family disruption is the death of a parent. 10 Throughout history this has been one of the risks of childhood. Mothers frequently died in childbirth, and it was not unusual for both parents to die before the child was grown. As recently as the early decades of this century children commonly suffered the death of at least one parent. Almost a quarter of the children born in this country in 1900 lost one parent by the time they were fifteen years old. Many of these children lived with their widowed parent, often in a household with other close relatives. Others grew up in orphanages and foster homes.

The meaning of parental death, as it has been transmitted over time 11 and faithfully recorded in world literature and lore, is unambiguous and essentially unchanging. It is universally regarded as an untimely and tragic event. Death permanently severs the parent-child bond, disrupting forever one of the child's earliest and deepest human attachments. It also deprives a child of the presence and protection of an adult who has a biological stake in, as well as an emotional commitment to, the child's survival and well-being. In short, the death of a parent is the most extreme and severe loss a child can suffer.

Because a child is so vulnerable in a parent's absence, there has been 12 a common cultural response to the death of a parent: an outpouring of support from family, friends, and strangers alike. The surviving parent and child are united in their grief as well as their loss. Relatives and friends share in the loss and provide valuable emotional and financial assistance to the bereaved family. Other members of the community show sympathy for the child, and public assistance is available for those who need it. This cultural understanding of parental death has formed the basis for a tradition of public support to widows and their children. Indeed, as recently as the beginning of this century widows were the only mothers eligible for pensions in many states, and today widows with children receive more-generous welfare benefits from Survivors Insurance than do other single mothers with children who depend on Aid to Families With Dependent Children.

It has taken thousands upon thousands of years to reduce the threat 13 of parental death. Not until the middle of the twentieth century did parental death cease to be a commonplace event for children in the United States. By then advances in medicine had dramatically reduced mortality rates for men and women.

At the same time, other forms of family disruption—separation, 14 divorce, out-of-wedlock birth—were held in check by powerful religious, social, and legal sanctions. Divorce was widely regarded both as a deviant behavior, especially threatening to mothers and children, and as a personal lapse: "Divorce is the public acknowledgment of failure," a 1940s sociology textbook noted. Out-of-wedlock birth was stigmatized, and stigmatization is a powerful means of regulating behavior, as any smoker or overeater will testify. Sanctions against nonmarital childbirth discouraged behavior that hurt children and exacted compensatory behavior that helped them. Shotgun marriages and adoption, two common responses to nonmarital birth, carried a strong message about the risks of premarital sex and created an intact family for the child.

Consequently, children did not have to worry much about losing a parent through divorce or never having had one because of nonmarital birth. After a surge in divorces following the Second World War, the rate leveled off. Only 11 percent of children born in the 1950s would by the time they turned eighteen see their parents separate or divorce. Out-of-wedlock childbirth barely figured as a cause of family disruption. In the 1950s and early 1960s, five percent of the nation's births were out of wedlock. Blacks were more likely than whites to bear children outside marriage, but the majority of black children born in the twenty years after the Second World War were born to married couples. The rate of family disruption reached a historic low point during those years.   15

A new standard of family security and stability was established in postwar America. For the first time in history the vast majority of the nation's children could expect to live with married biological parents throughout childhood. Children might still suffer other forms of adversity—poverty, racial discrimination, lack of educational opportunity—but only a few would be deprived of the nurture and protection of a mother and a father. No longer did children have to be haunted by the classic fears vividly dramatized in folklore and fable—that their parents would die, that they would have to live with a stepparent and stepsiblings, or that they would be abandoned. These were the years when the nation confidently boarded up orphanages and closed foundling hospitals, certain that such institutions would never again be needed. In movie theaters across the country parents and children could watch the drama of parental separation and death in the great Disney classics, secure in the knowledge that such nightmare visions as the death of Bambi's mother and the wrenching separation of Dumbo from his mother were only make-believe.   16

In the 1960s the rate of family disruption suddenly began to rise. After inching up over the course of a century, the divorce rate soared. Throughout the 1950s and early 1960s the divorce rate held steady at fewer than ten divorces a year per 1,000 married couples. Then, beginning in about 1965, the rate increased sharply, peaking at twenty-three divorces per 1,000 marriages by 1979. (In 1974 divorce passed death as the leading cause of family breakup.) The rate has leveled off at about twenty-one divorces per 1,000 marriages—the figure for 1991. The out-of-wedlock birth rate also jumped. It went from five percent in 1960 to 27 percent in 1990. In 1990 close to 57 percent of births among black mothers were nonmarital, and about 17 percent among white mothers. Altogether, about one out of every four women who had a child in 1990 was not married. With rates of divorce and nonmarital birth so high, fam-   17 ily disruption is at its peak. Never before have so many children experienced family breakup caused by events other than death. Each year a million children go through divorce or separation and almost as many more are born out of wedlock.

Half of all marriages now end in divorce. Following divorce, many people enter new relationships. Some begin living together. Nearly half of all cohabiting couples have children in the household. Fifteen percent have new children together. Many cohabiting couples eventually get married. However, both cohabiting and remarried couples are more likely to break up than couples in first marriages. Even social scientists find it hard to keep pace with the complexity and velocity of such patterns. In the revised edition (1992) of his book *Marriage, Divorce, Remarriage,* the sociologist Andrew Cherlin ruefully comments: "If there were a truth-in-labeling law for books, the title of this edition should be something long and unwieldy like *Cohabitation, Marriage, Divorce, More Cohabitation, and Probably Remarriage.*"   18

Under such conditions growing up can be a turbulent experience. In many single-parent families children must come to terms with the parent's love life and romantic partners. Some children live with cohabiting couples, either their own unmarried parents or a biological parent and a live-in partner. Some children born to cohabiting parents see their parents break up. Others see their parents marry, but 56 percent of them (as compared with 31 percent of the children born to married parents) later see their parents' marriages fall apart. All told, about three quarters of children born to cohabiting couples will live in a single-parent home at least briefly. One of every four children growing up in the 1990s will eventually enter a stepfamily. According to one survey, nearly half of all children in stepparent families will see their parents divorce again by the time they reach their late teens. Since 80 percent of divorced fathers remarry, things get even more complicated when the romantic or marital history of the noncustodial parent, usually the father, is taken into account. Consequently, as it affects a significant number of children, family disruption is best understood not as a single event but as a string of disruptive events: separation, divorce, life in a single-parent family, life with a parent and live-in lover, the remarriage of one or both parents, life in one stepparent family combined with visits to another stepparent family; the breakup of one or both stepparent families. And so on. This is one reason why public schools have a hard time knowing whom to call in an emergency.   19

Given its dramatic impact on children's lives, one might reasonably expect that this historic level of family disruption would be viewed with alarm, even regarded as a national crisis. Yet this has not been the case. In recent years some people have argued that these trends pose a serious threat to children and to the nation as a whole, but they are dismissed as declinists, pessimists, or nostalgists, unwilling or unable to accept the new facts of life. The dominant view is that the changes in family structure are, on balance, positive.   20

There are several reasons why this is so, but the fundamental reason 21 is that at some point in the 1970s Americans changed their minds about the meaning of these disruptive behaviors. What had once been regarded as hostile to children's best interests was now considered essential to adults' happiness. In the 1950s most Americans believed that parents should stay in an unhappy marriage for the sake of the children. The assumption was that a divorce would damage the children, and the prospect of such damage gave divorce its meaning. By the mid-1970s a majority of Americans rejected that view. Popular advice literature reflected the shift. A book on divorce published in the mid-1940s tersely asserted: "Children are entitled to the affection and *association* of two parents, not one." Thirty years later another popular divorce book proclaimed just the opposite: "A two-parent home is not the only emotional structure within which a child can be happy and healthy. . . . The parents who take care of themselves will be best able to take care of their children." At about the same time, the long-standing taboo against out-of-wedlock childbirth also collapsed. By the mid-1970s three fourths of Americans said that it was not morally wrong for a woman to have a child outside marriage.

Once the social metric shifts from child well-being to adult well-being, 22 it is hard to see divorce and nonmarital birth in anything but a positive light. However distressing and difficult they may be, both of these behaviors can hold out the promise of greater adult choice, freedom, and happiness. For unhappy spouses, divorce offers a way to escape a troubled or even abusive relationship and make a fresh start. For single parents, remarriage is a second try at marital happiness as well as a chance for relief from the stress, loneliness, and economic hardship of raising a child alone. For some unmarried women, nonmarital birth is a way to beat the biological clock, avoid marrying the wrong man, and experience the pleasures of motherhood. Moreover, divorce and out-of-wedlock birth involve a measure of agency and choice; they are man- and woman-made events. To be sure, not everyone exercises choice in divorce or nonmarital birth. Men leave wives for younger women, teenage girls get pregnant accidentally—yet even these unhappy events reflect the expansion of the boundaries of freedom and choice.

This cultural shift helps explain what otherwise would be inexplicable: 23 the failure to see the rise in family disruption as a severe and troubling national problem. It explains why there is virtually no widespread public sentiment for restigmatizing either of these classically disruptive behaviors and no sense—no public consensus—that they can or should be avoided in the future. On the contrary, the prevailing opinion is that we should accept the changes in family structure as inevitable and devise new forms of public and private support for single-parent families.

With its affirmation of the liberating effects of divorce and nonmarital 24 childbirth, this opinion is a fixture of American popular culture today. Madison Avenue and Hollywood did not invent these behaviors, as their highly paid publicists are quick to point out, but they have played an influential role in defending and even celebrating divorce and unwed motherhood. More precisely, they have taken the raw material of demography and fashioned it into a powerful fantasy of individual renewal and rebirth. Consider, for example, the teaser for *People* magazine's cover story on Joan Lunden's divorce: "After the painful end of her 13-year marriage, the *Good Morning America* cohost is discovering a new life as a single mother—and as her own woman." *People* does not dwell on the anguish Lunden and her children might have experienced over the breakup of their family, or the difficulties of single motherhood, even for celebrity mothers. Instead, it celebrates Joan Lunden's steps toward independence and a better life. *People,* characteristically, focuses on her shopping: in the first weeks after her breakup Lunden leased "a brand-new six-bedroom, 8,000 square foot" house and then went to Bloomingdale's, where she scooped up sheets, pillows, a toaster, dishes, seven televisions, and roomfuls of fun furniture that was "totally unlike the serious traditional pieces she was giving up."

This is not just the view taken in supermarket magazines. Even the   25
conservative bastion of the greeting-card industry, Hallmark, offers a line of cards commemorating divorce as liberation. "Think of your former marriage as a record album," says one Contemporary card. "It was full of music—both happy and sad. But what's important now is . . . YOU! the recently released HOT, NEW, SINGLE! You're going to be at the TOP OF THE CHARTS!" Another card reads: "Getting divorced can be very healthy! Watch how it improves your circulation! Best of luck! . . ." Hallmark's hip Shoebox Greetings division depicts two female praying mantises. Mantis One: "It's tough being a single parent." Mantis Two: "Yeah . . . Maybe we shouldn't have eaten our husbands."

Divorce is a tired convention in Hollywood, but unwed parenthood is   26
very much in fashion: in the past year or so babies were born to Warren Beatty and Annette Bening, Jack Nicholson and Rebecca Broussard, and Eddie Murphy and Nicole Mitchell. *Vanity Fair* celebrated Jack Nicholson's fatherhood with a cover story (April, 1992) called "Happy Jack." What made Jack happy, it turned out, was no-fault fatherhood. He and Broussard, the twenty-nine-year-old mother of his children, lived in separate houses. Nicholson said, "It's an unusual arrangement, but the last twenty-five years or so have shown me that I'm not good at cohabitation. . . . I see Rebecca as much as any other person who is cohabiting. And *she* prefers it. I think most people would in a more honest and truthful world." As for more-permanent commitments, the man who is not good at cohabitation said: "I don't discuss marriage much with Rebecca. Those discussions are the very thing I'm trying to avoid. I'm after this immediate real thing. That's all I believe in." (Perhaps Nicholson should have had the discussion. Not long after the story appeared, Broussard broke off the relationship.)

As this story shows, unwed parenthood is thought of not only as a way   27
to find happiness but also as a way to exhibit such virtues as honesty and
courage. A similar argument was offered in defense of Murphy Brown's
unwed motherhood. Many of Murphy's fans were quick to point out that
Murphy suffered over her decision to bear a child out of wedlock. Faced
with an accidental pregnancy and a faithless love, she agonized over her
plight and, after much mental anguish, bravely decided to go ahead. In
short, having a baby without a husband represented a higher level of
maternal devotion and sacrifice than having a baby with a husband. Murphy was not just exercising her rights as a woman; she was exhibiting
true moral heroism.

On the night Murphy Brown became an unwed mother, 34 million   28
Americans tuned in, and CBS posted a 35 percent share of the audience.
The show did not stir significant protest at the grass roots and lost none
of its advertisers. The actress Candice Bergen subsequently appeared on
the cover of nearly every women's and news magazine in the country and
received an honorary degree at the University of Pennsylvania as well as
an Emmy award. The show's creator, Diane English, popped up in Hanes
stocking ads. Judged by conventional measures of approval, Murphy
Brown's motherhood was a hit at the box office.

Increasingly, the media depicts the married two-parent family as a   29
source of pathology. According to a spate of celebrity memoirs and interviews, the married-parent family harbors terrible secrets of abuse,
violence, and incest. A bumper sticker I saw in Amherst, Massachusetts,
read UNSPOKEN TRADITIONAL FAMILY VALUES: ABUSE, ALCOHOLISM, INCEST.
The pop therapist John Bradshaw explains away this generation's
problems with the dictum that 96 percent of families are dysfunctional,
made that way by the addicted society we live in. David Lynch creates
a new aesthetic of creepiness by juxtaposing scenes of traditional family
life with images of seduction and perversion. A Boston-area museum puts on an exhibit called "Goodbye to Apple Pie," featuring several
artists' visions of child abuse, including one mixed-media piece with
knives poking through a little girl's skirt. The piece is titled *Father
Knows Best.*

No one would claim that two-parent families are free from conflict,   30
violence, or abuse. However, the attempt to discredit the two-parent family can be understood as part of what Daniel Patrick Moynihan has
described as a larger effort to accommodate higher levels of social
deviance. "The amount of deviant behavior in American society has
increased beyond the levels the community can 'afford to recognize,'"
Moynihan argues. One response has been to normalize what was once
considered deviant behavior, such as out-of-wedlock birth. An accompanying response has been to detect deviance in what once stood as a
social norm, such as the married-couple family. Together these
responses reduce the acknowledged levels of deviance by eroding earlier
distinctions between the normal and the deviant.

Several recent studies describe family life in its postwar heyday as   31
the seedbed of alcoholism and abuse. According to Stephanie Coontz,
the author of the book *The Way We Never Were: American Families and
the Nostalgia Trap,* family life for married mothers in the 1950s consisted of "booze, bowling, bridge, and boredom." Coontz writes: "Few
would have guessed that radiant Marilyn Van Derbur, crowned Miss
America in 1958, had been sexually violated by her wealthy, respectable
father from the time she was five until she was eighteen, when she
moved away to college." Even the budget-stretching casserole comes
under attack as a sign of culinary dysfunction. According to one food
writer, this homely staple of postwar family life brings back images of "the
good mother of the 50's . . . locked in Ozzie and Harriet land, unable to
move past the canvas of a Corning Ware dish, the palette of a can of
Campbell's soup, the mushy dominion of which she was queen."

Nevertheless, the popular portrait of family life does not simply reflect   32
the views of a cultural elite, as some have argued. There is strong support at the grass roots for much of this view of family change. Survey
after survey shows that Americans are less inclined than they were a generation ago to value sexual fidelity, lifelong marriage, and parenthood as
worthwhile personal goals. Motherhood no longer defines adult womanhood, as everyone knows; equally important is the fact that fatherhood
has declined as a norm for men. In 1976 less than half as many fathers
as in 1957 said that providing for children was a life goal. The proportion
of working men who found marriage and children burdensome and
restrictive more than doubled in the same period. Fewer than half of all
adult Americans today regard the idea of sacrifice for others as a positive
moral virtue.

It is true that many adults benefit from divorce or remarriage. Accord-   33
ing to one study, nearly 80 percent of divorced women and 50 percent of
divorced men say they are better off out of the marriage. Half of divorced
adults in the same study report greater happiness. A competent self-help
book called *Divorce and New Beginnings* notes the advantages of single
parenthood: single parents can "develop their own interests, fulfill their
own needs, choose their own friends and engage in social activities of
their choice. Money, even if limited, can be spent as they see fit." Apparently, some women appreciate the opportunity to have children out of
wedlock. "The real world, however, does not always allow women who
are dedicated to their careers to devote the time and energy it takes to
find—or be found by—the perfect husband and father wanna-be," one
woman said in a letter to *The Washington Post.* A mother and chiroprac-
tor from Avon, Connecticut, explained her unwed maternity to an interviewer this way: "It is selfish, but this was something I needed to do for
me."

There is very little in contemporary popular culture to contradict this   34
optimistic view. But in a few small places another perspective may be

found. Several racks down from its divorce cards, Hallmark offers a line of cards for children—To Kids With Love. These cards come six to a pack. Each card in the pack has a slightly different message. According to the package, the "thinking of you" messages will let a special kid "know how much you care." Though Hallmark doesn't quite say so, it's clear these cards are aimed at divorced parents. "I'm sorry I'm not always there when you need me but I hope you know I'm always just a phone call away." Another card reads: "Even though your dad and I don't live together anymore, I know he's still a very special part of your life. And as much as I miss you when you're not with me, I'm still happy that you two can spend time together."

Hallmark's messages are grounded in a substantial body of well- 35
funded market research. Therefore it is worth reflecting on the divergence in sentiment between the divorce cards for adults and the divorce cards for kids. For grown-ups, divorce heralds new beginnings (A HOT NEW SINGLE). For children, divorce brings separation and loss ("I'm sorry I'm not always there when you need me").

An even more telling glimpse into the meaning of family disruption 36
can be found in the growing children's literature on family dissolution. Take, for example, the popular children's book *Dinosaurs Divorce: A Guide for Changing Families* (1986), by Laurene Krasny Brown and Marc Brown. This is a picture book, written for very young children. The book begins with a short glossary of "divorce words" and encourages children to "see if you can find them" in the story. The words include "family counselor," "separation agreement," "alimony," and "child custody." The book is illustrated with cartoonish drawings of green dinosaur parents who fight, drink too much, and break up. One panel shows the father dinosaur, suitcase in hand, getting into a yellow car.

The dinosaur children are offered simple, straightforward advice on 37
what to do about the divorce. *On custody decisions:* "When parents can't agree, lawyers and judges decide. Try to be honest if they ask you questions; it will help them make better decisions." *On selling the house:* "If you move, you may have to say good-bye to friends and familiar places. But soon your new home will feel like the place you really belong." *On the economic impact of divorce:* "Living with one parent almost always means there will be less money. Be prepared to give up some things." *On holidays:* "Divorce may mean twice as much celebrating at holiday times, but you may feel pulled apart." *On parents' new lovers:* "You may sometimes feel jealous and want your parent to yourself. Be polite to your parents' new friends, even if you don't like them at first." *On parents' remarriage:* "Not everyone loves his or her stepparents, but showing them respect is important."

These cards and books point to an uncomfortable and generally 38
unacknowledged fact: what contributes to a parent's happiness may detract from a child's happiness. All too often the adult quest for freedom, independence, and choice in family relationships conflicts with a

child's developmental needs for stability, constancy, harmony, and permanence in family life. In short, family disruption creates a deep division between parents' interests and the interests of children.

One of the worst consequences of these divided interests is a withdrawal of parental investment in children's well-being. As the Stanford economist Victor Fuchs has pointed out, the main source of social investment in children is private. The investment comes from the children's parents. But parents in disrupted families have less time, attention, and money to devote to their children. The single most important source of disinvestment has been the widespread withdrawal of financial support and involvement by fathers. Maternal investment, too, has declined, as women try to raise families on their own and work outside the home. Moreover, both mothers and fathers commonly respond to family breakup by investing more heavily in themselves and in their own personal and romantic lives.

Sometimes the tables are completely turned. Children are called upon to invest in the emotional well-being of their parents. Indeed, this seems to be the larger message of many of the children's books on divorce and remarriage. *Dinosaurs Divorce* asks children to be sympathetic, understanding, respectful, and polite to confused, unhappy parents. The sacrifice comes from the children: "Be prepared to give up some things." In the world of divorcing dinosaurs, the children rather than the grown-ups are the exemplars of patience, restraint, and good sense.

THREE SEVENTIES ASSUMPTIONS

As it first took shape in the 1970s, the optimistic view of family change rested on three bold new assumptions. At that time, because the emergence of the changes in family life was so recent, there was little hard evidence to confirm or dispute these assumptions. But this was an expansive moment in American life.

The first assumption was an economic one: that a woman could now afford to be a mother without also being a wife. There were ample grounds for believing this. Women's work-force participation had been gradually increasing in the postwar period, and by the beginning of the 1970s women were a strong presence in the workplace. What's more, even though there was still a substantial wage gap between men and women, women had made considerable progress in a relatively short time toward better-paying jobs and greater employment opportunities. More women than ever before could aspire to serious careers as business executives, doctors, lawyers, airline pilots, and politicians. This circumstance, combined with the increased availability of child care, meant that women could take on the responsibilities of a breadwinner, perhaps even a sole breadwinner. This was particularly true for middle-class women. According to a highly regarded 1977 study by the Carnegie Council on Children, "The greater availability of jobs for women means that more middle-class children today survive their parents' divorce without a catastrophic plunge into poverty."

Feminists, who had long argued that the path to greater equality for women lay in the world of work outside the home, endorsed this assumption. In fact, for many, economic independence was a stepping-stone toward freedom from both men and marriage. As women began to earn their own money, they were less dependent on men or marriage, and marriage diminished in importance. In Gloria Steinem's memorable words, "A woman without a man is like a fish without a bicycle." 43

This assumption also gained momentum as the meaning of work changed for women. Increasingly, work had an expressive as well as an economic dimension: being a working mother not only gave you an income but also made you more interesting and fulfilled than a stay-at-home mother. Consequently, the optimistic economic scenario was driven by a cultural imperative. Women would achieve financial independence because, culturally as well as economically, it was the right thing to do. 44

The second assumption was that family disruption would not cause lasting harm to children and could actually enrich their lives. *Creative Divorce: A New Opportunity for Personal Growth,* a popular book of the seventies, spoke confidently to this point: "Children can survive any family crisis without permanent damage—and grow as human beings in the process. . . ." Moreover, single-parent and stepparent families created a more extensive kinship network than the nuclear family. This network would envelop children in a web of warm and supportive relationships. "Belonging to a stepfamily means there are more people in your life," a children's book published in 1982 notes. "More sisters and brothers, including the step ones. More people you think of as grandparents and aunts and uncles. More cousins. More neighbors and friends. . . . Getting to know and like so many people (and having them like you) is one of the best parts of what being in a stepfamily`. . . . is all about." 45

The third assumption was that the new diversity in family structure would make America a better place. Just as the nation has been strengthened by the diversity of its ethnic and racial groups, so it would be strengthened by diverse family forms. The emergence of these brave new families was but the latest chapter in the saga of American pluralism. 46

Another version of the diversity argument stated that the real problem was not family disruption itself but the stigma still attached to these emergent family forms. This lingering stigma placed children at psychological risk, making them feel ashamed or different; as the ranks of single-parent and stepparent families grew, children would feel normal and good about themselves. 47

These assumptions continue to be appealing, because they accord with strongly held American beliefs in social progress. Americans see progress in the expansion of individual opportunities for choice, freedom, 48 and self-expression. Moreover, Americans identify progress with growing tolerance of diversity. Over the past half century, the pollster Daniel Yankelovich writes, the United States has steadily grown more open-minded and accepting of groups that were previously perceived as alien, untrustworthy, or unsuitable for public leadership or social esteem. One such group is the burgeoning number of single-parent and stepparent families.

In 1981 Sara McLanahan, now a sociologist at Princeton University's   49
Woodrow Wilson School, read a three-part series by Ken Auletta in *The New Yorker.* Later published as a book titled *The Underclass,* the series presented a vivid portrait of the drug addicts, welfare mothers, and school dropouts who took part in an education-and-training program in New York City. Many were the children of single mothers, and it was Auletta's clear implication that single-mother families were contributing to the growth of an underclass. McLanahan was taken aback by this notion. "It struck me as strange that he would be viewing single mothers at that level of pathology."

"I'd gone to graduate school in the days when the politically correct   50
argument was that single-parent families were just another alternative family form, and it was fine," McLanahan explains, as she recalls the state of social-scientific thinking in the 1970s. Several empirical studies that were then current supported an optimistic view of family change. (They used tiny samples, however, and did not track the well-being of children over time.)

One, *All Our Kin,* by Carol Stack, was required reading for thousands   51
of university students. It said that single mothers had strengths that had gone undetected and unappreciated by earlier researchers. The single-mother family, it suggested, is an economically resourceful and socially embedded institution. In the late 1970s McLanahan wrote a similar study that looked at a small sample of white single mothers and how they coped. "So I was very much of that tradition."

By the early 1980s, however, nearly two decades had passed since the   52
changes in family life had begun. During the intervening years a fuller body of empirical research had emerged: studies that used large samples, or followed families through time, or did both. Moreover, several of the studies offered a child's-eye view of family disruption. The National Survey on Children, conducted by the psychologist Nicholas Zill, had set out in 1976 to track a large sample of children aged seven to eleven. It also interviewed the children's parents and teachers. It surveyed its subjects again in 1981 and 1987. By the time of its third round of interviews the eleven-year-olds of 1976 were the twenty-two-year-olds of 1987. The California Children of Divorce Study, directed by Judith Wallerstein, a clinical psychologist, had also been going on for a decade. E. Mavis Hetherington, of the University of Virginia, was conducting a similar study of children from both intact and divorced families. For the first time it

was possible to test the optimistic view against a large and longitudinal body of evidence.

It was to this body of evidence that Sara McLanahan turned. When 53 she did, she found little to support the optimistic view of single motherhood. On the contrary. When she published her findings with Irwin Garfinkel in a 1986 book, *Single Mothers and Their Children,* her portrait of single motherhood proved to be as troubling in its own way as Auletta's.

One of the leading assumptions of the time was that single mother- 54 hood was economically viable. Even if single mothers did face economic trials, they wouldn't face them for long, it was argued, because they wouldn't remain single for long: single motherhood would be a brief phase of three to five years, followed by marriage. Single mothers would be economically resilient: if they experienced setbacks, they would recover quickly. It was also said that single mothers would be supported by informal networks of family, friends, neighbors, and other single mothers. As McLanahan shows in her study, the evidence demolishes all these claims.

For the vast majority of single mothers, the economic spectrum turns 55 out to be narrow, running between precarious and desperate. Half the single mothers in the United States live below the poverty line. (Currently, one out of ten married couples with children is poor.) Many others live on the edge of poverty. Even single mothers who are far from poor are likely to experience persistent economic insecurity. Divorce almost always brings a decline in the standard of living for the mother and children.

Moreover, the poverty experienced by single mothers is no more brief 56 than it is mild. A significant number of all single mothers never marry or remarry. Those who do, do so only after spending roughly six years, on average, as single parents. For black mothers the duration is much longer. Only 33 percent of African-American mothers had remarried within ten years of separation. Consequently, single motherhood is hardly a fleeting event for the mother, and it is likely to occupy a third of the child's childhood. Even the notion that single mothers are knit together in economically supportive networks is not borne out by the evidence. On the contrary, single parenthood forces many women to be on the move, in search of cheaper housing and better jobs. This need-driven restless mobility makes it more difficult for them to sustain supportive ties to family and friends, let alone other single mothers.

Single-mother families are vulnerable not just to poverty but to a par- 57 ticularly debilitating form of poverty: welfare dependency. The dependency takes two forms: First, single mothers, particularly unwed mothers, stay on welfare longer than other welfare recipients. Of those never-married mothers who receive welfare benefits, almost 40 percent remain on the rolls for ten years or longer. Second, welfare dependency tends to be passed on from one generation to the next. McLanahan says, "Evidence on intergenerational poverty indicates that, indeed, offspring from [single-mother] families are far more likely to be poor and to form mother-only families than are offspring who live with two parents most of their pre-adult life." Nor is the intergenerational impact of single motherhood limited to African-Americans, as many people seem to believe. Among white families, daughters of single parents are 53 percent more likely to marry as teenagers, 111 percent more likely to have children as teenagers, 164 percent more likely to have a premarital birth, and 92 percent more likely to dissolve their own marriages. All these intergenerational consequences of single motherhood increase the likelihood of chronic welfare dependency.

McLanahan cites three reasons why single-mother families are so vul-   58
nerable economically. For one thing, their earnings are low. Second, unless the mothers are widowed, they don't receive public subsidies large enough to lift them out of poverty. And finally, they do not get much support from family members—especially the fathers of their children. In 1982 single white mothers received an average of $1,246 in alimony and child support, black mothers an average of $322. Such payments accounted for about 10 percent of the income of single white mothers and for about 3.5 percent of the income of single black mothers. These amounts were dramatically smaller than the income of the father in a two-parent family and also smaller than the income from a second earner in a two-parent family. Roughly 60 percent of single white mothers and 80 percent of single black mothers received no support at all.

Until the mid-1980s, when stricter standards were put in place, child-   59
support awards were only about half to two-thirds what the current guidelines require. Accordingly, there is often a big difference in the living standards of divorced fathers and of divorced mothers with children. After divorce the average annual income of mothers and children is $13,500 for whites and $9,000 for nonwhites, as compared with $25,000 for white nonresident fathers and $13,600 for nonwhite nonresident fathers. Moreover, since child-support awards account for a smaller portion of the income of a high-earning father, the drop in living standards can be especially sharp for mothers who were married to upper-level managers and professionals.

Unwed mothers are unlikely to be awarded any child support at all,   60
partly because the paternity of their children may not have been established. According to one recent study, only 20 percent of unmarried mothers receive child support.

Even if single mothers escape poverty, economic uncertainty remains   61
a condition of life. Divorce brings a reduction in income and standard of living for the vast majority of single mothers. One study, for example, found that income for mothers and children declines on average about 30 percent, while fathers experience a 10 to 15 percent increase in income in the year following a separation. Things get even more difficult when fathers fail to meet their child-support obligations. As a result, many divorced mothers experience a wearing uncertainty about the fam-

ily budget; whether the check will come in or not; whether new sneakers can be bought this month or not; whether the electric bill will be paid on time or not. Uncertainty about money triggers other kinds of uncertainty. Mothers and children often have to move to cheaper housing after a divorce. One study shows that about 38 percent of divorced mothers and their children move during the first year after a divorce. Even several years later the rate of moves for single mothers is about a third higher than the rate for two-parent families. It is also common for a mother to change her job or increase her working hours or both following a divorce. Even the composition of the household is likely to change, with other adults, such as boyfriends or babysitters, moving in and out.

All this uncertainty can be devastating to children. Anyone who knows   62 children knows that they are deeply conservative creatures. They like things to stay the same. So pronounced is this tendency that certain children have been known to request the same peanut-butter-and-jelly sandwich for lunch for years on end. Children are particularly set in their ways when it comes to family, friends, neighborhoods, and schools. Yet when a family breaks up, all these things may change. The novelist Pat Conroy has observed that "each divorce is the death of a small civilization." No one feels this more acutely than children.

Sara McLanahan's investigation and others like it have helped to   63 establish a broad consensus on the economic impact of family disruption on children. Most social scientists now agree that single motherhood is an important and growing cause of poverty, and that children suffer as a result. (They continue to argue, however, about the relationship between family structure and such economic factors as income inequality, the loss of jobs in the inner city, and the growth of low-wage jobs.) By the mid-1980s, however, it was clear that the problem of family disruption was not confined to the urban underclass, nor was its sole impact economic. Divorce and out-of-wedlock childbirth were affecting middle- and upper-class children, and these more privileged children were suffering negative consequences as well. It appeared that the problems associated with family breakup were far deeper and far more widespread than anyone had previously imagined.

Judith Wallerstein is one of the pioneers in research on the long-term   64 psychological impact of family disruption on children. The California Children of Divorce Study, which she directs, remains the most enduring study of the long-term effects of divorce on children and their parents. Moreover, it represents the best-known effort to look at the impact of divorce on middle-class children. The California children entered the study without pathological family histories. Before divorce they lived in stable, protected homes. And although some of the children did experience economic insecurity as the result of divorce, they were generally free from the most severe forms of poverty associated with family breakup. Thus the study and the resulting book (which Wallerstein wrote with Sandra Blakeslee), *Second Chances: Men, Women, and Children a Decade after Divorce* (1989), provide new insight into the consequences of divorce which are not associated with extreme forms of economic or emotional deprivation.

When, in 1971, Wallerstein and her colleagues set out to conduct clin-   65
ical interviews with 131 children from the San Francisco area, they thought they were embarking on a short-term study. Most experts believed that divorce was like a bad cold. There was a phase of acute discomfort, and then a short recovery phase. According to the conventional wisdom, kids would be back on their feet in no time at all. Yet when Wallerstein met these children for a second interview more than a year later, she was amazed to discover that there had been no miraculous recovery. In fact, the children seemed to be doing worse.

The news that children did not "get over" divorce was not particularly   66
welcome at the time. Wallerstein recalls, "We got angry letters from therapists, parents, and lawyers saying we were undoubtedly wrong. They said children are really much better off being released from an unhappy marriage. Divorce, they said, is a liberating experience." One of the main results of the California study was to overturn this optimistic view. In Wallerstein's cautionary words, "Divorce is deceptive. Legally it is a single event, but psychologically it is a chain—sometimes a never-ending chain—of events, relocations, and radically shifting relationships strung through time, a process that forever changes the lives of the people involved."

Five years after divorce more than a third of the children experienced   67
moderate or severe depression. At ten years a significant number of the now young men and women appeared to be troubled, drifting, and underachieving. At fifteen years many of the thirtyish adults were struggling to establish strong love relationships of their own. In short, far from recovering from their parents' divorce, a significant percentage of these grownups were still suffering from its effects. In fact, according to Wallerstein, the long-term effects of divorce emerge at a time when young adults are trying to make their own decisions about love, marriage, and family. Not all children in the study suffered negative consequences. But Wallerstein's research presents a sobering picture of divorce. "The child of divorce faces many additional psychological burdens in addition to the normative tasks of growing up," she says.

Divorce not only makes it more difficult for young adults to establish   68
new relationships. It also weakens the oldest primary relationship: that between parent and child. According to Wallerstein, "Parent-child relationships are permanently altered by divorce in ways that our society has not anticipated." Not only do children experience a loss of parental attention at the onset of divorce, but they soon find that at every stage of their development their parents are not available in the same way they once were. "In a reasonably happy intact family," Wallerstein observes, "the child gravitates first to one parent and then to the other, using skills and

attributes from each in climbing the developmental ladder." In a divorced family, children find it "harder to find the needed parent at needed times." This may help explain why very young children suffer the most as the result of family disruption. Their opportunities to engage in this kind of ongoing process are the most truncated and compromised.

The father-child bond is severely, often irreparably, damaged in dis- 69 rupted families. In a situation without historical precedent, an astonishing and disheartening number of American fathers are failing to provide financial support to their children. Often, more than the father's support check is missing. Increasingly, children are bereft of any contact with their fathers. According to the National Survey of Children, in disrupted families only one child in six, on average, saw his or her father as often as once a week in the past year. Close to half did not see their father at all in the past year. As time goes on, contact becomes even more infrequent. Ten years after a marriage breaks up, more than two thirds of children report not having seen their father for a year. Not surprisingly, when asked to name the "adults you look up to and admire," only 20 percent of children in single-parent families named their father, as compared with 52 percent of children in two-parent families. A favorite complaint among Baby Boom Americans is that their fathers were emotionally remote guys who worked hard, came home at night to eat supper, and didn't have much to say to or do with the kids. But the current generation has a far worse father problem: many of their fathers are vanishing entirely.

Even for fathers who maintain regular contact, the pattern of father- 70 child relationships changes. The sociologists Andrew Cherlin and Frank Furstenberg, who have studied broken families, write that the fathers behave more like other relatives than like parents. Rather than helping with homework or carrying out a project with their children, nonresidential fathers are likely to take the kids shopping, to the movies, or out to dinner. Instead of providing steady advice and guidance, divorced fathers become "treat" dads.

Apparently—and paradoxically—it is the visiting relationship itself, 71 rather than the frequency of visits, that is the real source of the problem. According to Wallerstein, the few children in the California study who reported visiting with their fathers once or twice a week over a ten-year period still felt rejected. The need to schedule a special time to be with the child, the repeated leave-takings, and the lack of connection to the child's regular, daily schedule leaves many fathers adrift, frustrated, and confused. Wallerstein calls the visiting father a parent without portfolio.

The deterioration in father-child bonds is most severe among children 72 who experience divorce at an early age, according to a recent study. Nearly three quarters of the respondents, now young men and women, report having poor relationships with their fathers. Close to half have received psychological help, nearly a third have dropped out of high school, and about a quarter report having experienced high levels of problem behavior or emotional distress by the time they became young adults.

LONG-TERM EFFECTS

Since most children live with their mothers after divorce, one might   73
expect that the mother-child bond would remain unaltered and might
even be strengthened. Yet research shows that the mother-child bond is
also weakened as the result of divorce. Only half of the children who were
close to their mothers before a divorce remained equally close after the
divorce. Boys, particularly, had difficulties with their mothers. Moreover,
mother-child relationships deteriorated over time. Whereas teenagers in
disrupted families were no more likely than teenagers in intact families to
report poor relationships with their mothers, 30 percent of young adults
from disrupted families have poor relationships with their mothers, as
compared with 16 percent of young adults from intact families. Mother-
daughter relationships often deteriorate as the daughter reaches young
adulthood. The only group in society that derives any benefit from these
weakened parent-child ties is the therapeutic community. Young adults
from disrupted families are nearly twice as likely as those from intact
families to receive psychological help.

Some social scientists have criticized Judith Wallerstein's research   74
because her study is based on a small clinical sample and does not
include a control group of children from intact families. However, other
studies generally support and strengthen her findings. Nicholas Zill has
found similar long-term effects on children of divorce, reporting that
"effects of marital discord and family disruption are visible twelve to
twenty-two years later in poor relationships with parents, high levels of
problem behavior, and an increased likelihood of dropping out of high
school and receiving psychological help." Moreover, Zill's research also
found signs of distress in young women who seemed relatively well
adjusted in middle childhood and adolescence. Girls in single-parent
families are also at much greater risk for precocious sexuality, teenage
marriage, teenage pregnancy, nonmarital birth, and divorce than are girls
in two-parent families.

Zill's research shows that family disruption strongly affects school   75
achievement as well. Children in disrupted families are nearly twice as
likely as those in intact families to drop out of high school; among children who do drop out, those from disrupted families are less likely eventually to earn a diploma or a GED. Boys are at greater risk for dropping
out than girls, and are also more likely to exhibit aggressive, acting-out
behaviors. Other research confirms these findings. According to a study
by the National Association of Elementary School Principals, 33 percent
of two-parent elementary school students are ranked as high achievers,
as compared with 17 percent of single-parent students. The children in
single-parent families are also more likely to be truant or late or to have
disciplinary action taken against them. Even after controlling for race,
income, and religion, scholars find significant differences in educational
attainment between children who grow up in intact families and children
who do not. In his 1992 study *America's Smallest School: The Family,*

Paul Barton shows that the proportion of two-parent families varies widely from state to state and is related to variations in academic achievement. North Dakota, for example, scores highest on the math-proficiency test and second highest on the two-parent-family scale. The District of Columbia is second lowest on the math test and lowest in the nation on the two-parent-family scale.

Zill notes that "while coming from a disrupted family significantly   76 increases a young adult's risks of experiencing social, emotional or academic difficulties, it does not foreordain such difficulties. The majority of young people from disrupted families have successfully completed high school, do not currently display high levels of emotional distress or problem behavior, and enjoy reasonable relationships with their mothers." Nevertheless, a majority of these young adults do show maladjustment in their relationships with their fathers.

These findings underscore the importance of both a mother and a   77 father in fostering the emotional well-being of children. Obviously, not all children in two-parent families are free from emotional turmoil, but few are burdened with the troubles that accompany family breakup. Moreover, as the sociologist Amitai Etzioni explains in a new book, *The Spirit of Community*, two parents in an intact family make up what might be called a mutually supportive education coalition. When both parents are present, they can play different, even contradictory, roles. One parent may goad the child to achieve, while the other may encourage the child to take time out to daydream or toss a football around. One may emphasize taking intellectual risks, while the other may insist on following the teacher's guidelines. At the same time, the parents regularly exchange information about the child's school problems and achievements, and have a sense of the overall educational mission. However, Etzioni writes,

> The sequence of divorce followed by a succession of boy or girlfriends, a second marriage, and frequently another divorce and another turnover of partners often means a repeatedly disrupted educational coalition. Each change in participants involves a change in the educational agenda for the child. Each new partner cannot be expected to pick up the previous one's educational post and program. . . . As a result, changes in parenting partners mean, at best, a deep disruption in a child's education, though of course several disruptions cut deeper into the effectiveness of the educational coalition than just one.

THE BAD NEWS ABOUT STEPPARENTS

Perhaps the most striking, and potentially disturbing, new research   78 has to do with children in stepparent families. Until quite recently the optimistic assumption was that children saw their lives improve when they became part of a stepfamily. When Nicholas Zill and his colleagues began to study the effects of remarriage on children, their working hypothesis was that stepparent families would make up for the shortcomings of the single-parent family. Clearly, most children are better off economically when they are able to share in the income of two adults. When a second adult joins the household, there may be a reduction in the time and work pressures on the single parent.

The research overturns this optimistic assumption, however. In general the evidence suggests that remarriage neither reproduces nor restores the intact family structure, even when it brings more income and a second adult into the household. Quite the contrary. Indeed, children living with stepparents appear to be even more disadvantaged than children living in a stable single-parent family. Other difficulties seem to offset the advantages of extra income and an extra pair of hands. However much our modern sympathies reject the fairy-tale portrait of stepparents, the latest research confirms that the old stories are anthropologically quite accurate. Stepfamilies disrupt established loyalties, create new uncertainties, provoke deep anxieties, and sometimes threaten a child's physical safety as well as emotional security.

Parents and children have dramatically different interests in and expectations for a new marriage. For a single parent, remarriage brings new commitments, the hope of enduring love and happiness, and relief from stress and loneliness. For a child, the same event often provokes confused feelings of sadness, anger, and rejection. Nearly half the children in Wallerstein's study said they felt left out in their stepfamilies. The National Commission on Children, a bipartisan group headed by Senator John D. Rockefeller, of West Virginia, reported that children from stepfamilies were more likely to say they often felt lonely or blue than children from either single-parent or intact families. Children in stepfamilies were the most likely to report that they wanted more time with their mothers. When mothers remarry, daughters tend to have a harder time adjusting than sons. Evidently, boys often respond positively to a male presence in the household, while girls who have established close ties to their mother in a single-parent family often see the stepfather as a rival and an intruder. According to one study, boys in remarried families are less likely to drop out of school than boys in single-parent families, while the opposite is true for girls.

A large percentage of children do not even consider stepparents to be part of their families, according to the National Survey on Children. The NSC asked children, "When you think of your family, who do you include?" Only 10 percent of the children failed to mention a biological parent, but a third left out a stepparent. Even children who rarely saw their noncustodial parents almost always named them as family members. The weak sense of attachment is mutual. When parents were asked the same question, only one percent failed to mention a biological child, while 15 percent left out a stepchild. In the same study stepparents with both natural children and stepchildren said that it was harder for them to love their stepchildren than their biological children and that their chil-

79

80

81

dren would have been better off if they had grown up with two biological parents.

One of the most severe risks associated with stepparent-child ties is the risk of sexual abuse. As Judith Wallerstein explains, "The presence of a stepfather can raise the difficult issue of a thinner incest barrier." The incest taboo is strongly reinforced, Wallerstein says, by knowledge of paternity and by the experience of caring for a child since birth. A stepfather enters the family without either credential and plays a sexual role as the mother's husband. As a result, stepfathers can pose a sexual risk to the children, especially to daughters. According to a study by the Canadian researchers Martin Daly and Margo Wilson, preschool children in stepfamilies are forty times as likely as children in intact families to suffer physical or sexual abuse. (Most of the sexual abuse was committed by a third party, such as a neighbor, a stepfather's male friend, or another nonrelative.) Stepfathers discriminate in their abuse: they are far more likely to assault nonbiological children than their own natural children. 82

Sexual abuse represents the most extreme threat to children's well-being. Stepfamilies also seem less likely to make the kind of ordinary investments in the children that other families do. Although it is true that the stepfamily household has a higher income than the single-parent household, it does not follow that the additional income is reliably available to the children. To begin with, children's claim on stepparents' resources is shaky. Stepparents are not legally required to support stepchildren, so their financial support of these children is entirely voluntary. Moreover, since stepfamilies are far more likely to break up than intact families, particularly in the first five years, there is always the risk— far greater than the risk of unemployment in an intact family—that the second income will vanish with another divorce. The financial commitment to a child's education appears weaker in stepparent families, perhaps because the stepparent believes that the responsibility for educating the child rests with the biological parent. 83

Similarly, studies suggest that even though they may have the time, the parents in stepfamilies do not invest as much of it in their children as the parents in intact families or even single parents do. A 1991 survey by the National Commission on Children showed that the parents in stepfamilies were less likely to be involved in a child's school life, including involvement in extracurricular activities, than either intact-family parents or single parents. They were the least likely to report being involved in such time-consuming activities as coaching a child's team, accompanying class trips, or helping with school projects. According to McLanahan's research, children in stepparent families report lower educational aspirations on the part of their parents and lower levels of parental involvement with schoolwork. In short, it appears that family income and the number of adults in the household are not the only factors affecting children's well-being. 84

DIMINISHING INVESTMENTS

There are several reasons for this diminished interest and investment. 85
In the law, as in the children's eyes, stepparents are shadowy figures.
According to the legal scholar David Chambers, family law has pretty
much ignored stepparents. Chambers writes, "In the substantial majority
of states, stepparents, even when they live with a child, have no legal
obligation to contribute to the child's support; nor does a stepparent's
presence in the home alter the support obligations of a noncustodial parent. The stepparent also has . . . no authority to approve emergency
medical treatment or even to sign a permission slip. . . ." When a marriage breaks up, the stepparent has no continuing obligation to provide
for a stepchild, no matter how long or how much he or she has been
contributing to the support of the child. In short, Chambers says, stepparent relationships are based wholly on consent, subject to the inclination of the adult and the child. The only way a stepparent can acquire the
legal status of a parent is through adoption. Some researchers also point
to the cultural ambiguity of the stepparent's role as a source of diminished interest, while others insist that it is the absence of a blood tie that
weakens the bond between stepparent and child.

Whatever its causes, the diminished investment in children in both sin- 86
gle-parent and stepparent families has a significant impact on their life
chances. Take parental help with college costs. The parents in intact families are far more likely to contribute to children's college costs than are
those in disrupted families. Moreover, they are usually able to arrive at a
shared understanding of which children will go to college, where they will
go, how much the parents will contribute, and how much the children will
contribute. But when families break up, these informal understandings
can vanish. The issue of college tuition remains one of the most contested areas of parental support, especially for higher-income parents.

The law does not step in even when familial understandings break 87
down. In the 1980s many states lowered the age covered by child-
support agreements from twenty-one to eighteen, thus eliminating college as a cost associated with support for a minor child. Consequently,
the question of college tuition is typically not addressed in child-custody
agreements. Even in states where the courts do require parents to
contribute to college costs, the requirement may be in jeopardy. In a
recent decision in Pennsylvania the court overturned an earlier decision
ordering divorced parents to contribute to college tuition. This decision is
likely to inspire challenges in other states where courts have required parents to pay for college. Increasingly, help in paying for college is entirely
voluntary.

Judith Wallerstein has been analyzing the educational decisions of the 88
college-age men and women in her study. She reports that "a full 42 percent of these men and women from middle class families appeared to
have ended their educations without attempting college or had left

college before achieving a degree at either the two-year or the four-year level." A significant percentage of these young people have the ability to attend college. Typical of this group are Nick and Terry, sons of a college professor. They had been close to their father before the divorce, but their father remarried soon after the divorce and saw his sons only occasionally, even though he lived nearby. At age nineteen Nick had completed a few junior-college courses and was earning a living as a salesman. Terry, twenty-one, who had been tested as a gifted student, was doing blue-collar work irregularly.

Sixty-seven percent of the college-age students from disrupted families attended college, as compared with 85 percent of other students who attended the same high schools. Of those attending college, several had fathers who were financially capable of contributing to college costs but did not.   89

The withdrawal of support for college suggests that other customary forms of parental help-giving, too, may decline as the result of family breakup. For example, nearly a quarter of first-home purchases since 1980 have involved help from relatives, usually parents. The median amount of help is $5,000. It is hard to imagine that parents who refuse to contribute to college costs will offer help in buying first homes, or help in buying cars or health insurance for young adult family members. And although it is too soon to tell, family disruption may affect the generational transmission of wealth. Baby Boomers will inherit their parents' estates, some substantial, accumulated over a lifetime by parents who lived and saved together. To be sure, the postwar generation benefited from an expanding economy and a rising standard of living, but its ability to accumulate wealth also owed something to family stability. The lifetime assets, like the marriage itself, remained intact. It is unlikely that the children of disrupted families will be in so favorable a position.   90

Moreover, children from disrupted families may be less likely to help their aging parents. The sociologist Alice Rossi, who has studied intergenerational patterns of help-giving, says that adult obligation has its roots in early-childhood experience. Children who grow up in intact families experience higher levels of obligation to kin than children from broken families. Children's sense of obligation to a nonresidential father is particularly weak. Among adults with both parents living, those separated from their father during childhood are less likely than others to see the father regularly. Half of them see their father more than once a year, as compared with nine out of ten of those whose parents are still married. Apparently a kind of bitter justice is at work here. Fathers who do not support or see their young children may not be able to count on their adult children's support when they are old and need money, love, and attention.   91

In short, as Andrew Cherlin and Frank Furstenburg put it, "Through divorce and remarriage, individuals are related to more and more people, to each of whom they owe less and less." Moreover, as Nicholas Zill   92 argues, weaker parent-child attachments leave many children more strongly exposed to influences outside the family, such as peers, boyfriends or girlfriends, and the media. Although these outside forces can sometimes be helpful, common sense and research opinion argue against putting too much faith in peer groups or the media as surrogates for Mom and Dad.

POVERTY, CRIME, EDUCATION

Family disruption would be a serious problem even if it affected only individual children and families. But its impact is far broader. Indeed, it is not an exaggeration to characterize it as a central cause of many of our most vexing social problems. Consider three problems that most Americans believe rank among the nation's pressing concerns: poverty, crime, and declining school performance. 93

More than half of the increase in child poverty in the 1980s is attributable to changes in family structure, according to David Eggebeen and Daniel Lichter, of Pennsylvania State University. In fact, if family structure in the United States had remained relatively constant since 1960, the rate of child poverty would be a third lower than it is today. This does not bode well for the future. With more than half of today's children likely to live in single-parent families, poverty and associated welfare costs threaten to become even heavier burdens on the nation. 94

Crime in American cities has increased dramatically and grown more violent over recent decades. Much of this can be attributed to the rise in disrupted families. Nationally, more than 70 percent of all juveniles in state reform institutions come from fatherless homes. A number of scholarly studies find that even after the groups of subjects are controlled for income, boys from single-mother homes are significantly more likely than others to commit crimes and to wind up in the juvenile justice, court, and penitentiary systems. One such study summarizes the relationship between crime and one-parent families in this way: "The relationship is so strong that controlling for family configuration erases the relationship between race and crime and between low income and crime. This conclusion shows up time and again in the literature." The nation's mayors, as well as police officers, social workers, probation officers, and court officials, consistently point to family breakup as the most important source of rising rates of crime. 95

Terrible as poverty and crime are, they tend to be concentrated in inner cities and isolated from the everyday experience of many Americans. The same cannot be said of the problem of declining school performance. Nowhere has the impact of family breakup been more profound or widespread than in the nation's public schools. There is a strong consensus that the schools are failing in their historic mission to prepare every American child to be a good worker and a good citizen. And nearly everyone agrees that the schools must undergo dramatic 96 reform in order to reach that goal. In pursuit of that goal, moreover, we have suffered no shortage of bright ideas or pilot projects or bold experiments in school reform. But there is little evidence that measures such as curricular reform, school-based management, and school choice will address, let alone solve, the biggest problem schools face: the rising number of children who come from disrupted families.

The great educational tragedy of our time is that many American children are failing in school not because they are intellectually or physically impaired but because they are emotionally incapacitated. In schools across the nation principals report a dramatic rise in the aggressive, acting-out behavior characteristic of children, especially boys, who are living in single-parent families. The discipline problems in today's suburban schools—assaults on teachers, unprovoked attacks on other students, screaming outbursts in class—outstrip the problems that were evident in the toughest city schools a generation ago. Moreover, teachers find many children emotionally distracted, so upset and preoccupied by the explosive drama of their own family lives that they are unable to concentrate on such mundane matters as multiplication tables.

In response, many schools have turned to therapeutic remediation. A growing proportion of many school budgets is devoted to counseling and other psychological services. The curriculum is becoming more therapeutic: children are taking courses in self-esteem, conflict resolution, and aggression management. Parental advisory groups are conscientiously debating alternative approaches to traditional school discipline, ranging from teacher training in mediation to the introduction of metal detectors and security guards in the schools. Schools are increasingly becoming emergency rooms of the emotions, devoted not only to developing minds but also to repairing hearts. As a result, the mission of the school, along with the culture of the classroom, is slowly changing. What we are seeing, largely as a result of the new burdens of family disruption, is the psychologization of American education.

Taken together, the research presents a powerful challenge to the prevailing view of family change as social progress. Not a single one of the assumptions underlying that view can be sustained against the empirical evidence. Single-parent families are not able to do well economically on a mother's income. In fact, most teeter on the economic brink, and many fall into poverty and welfare dependency. Growing up in a disrupted family does not enrich a child's life or expand the number of adults committed to the child's well-being. In fact, disrupted families threaten the psychological well-being of children and diminish the investment of adult time and money in them. Family diversity in the form of increasing numbers of single-parent and stepparent families does not strengthen the social fabric. It dramatically weakens and undermines society, placing new burdens on schools, courts, prisons, and the welfare system. These new families are not an improvement on the nuclear family, nor are they even just as good, whether you look at outcomes for children or outcomes for society as a whole. In short, far from representing social progress, family change represents a stunning example of social regress.

THE TWO-PARENT ADVANTAGE

All this evidence gives rise to an obvious conclusion: growing up in an intact two-parent family is an important source of advantage for American children. Though far from perfect as a social institution, the intact family offers children greater security and better outcomes than its fast-growing alternatives: single-parent and stepparent families. Not only does the intact family protect the child from poverty and economic insecurity; it also provides greater noneconomic investments of parental time, attention, and emotional support over the entire life course. This does not mean that all two-parent families are better for children than all single-parent families. But in the face of the evidence it becomes increasingly difficult to sustain the proposition that all family structures produce equally good outcomes for children.   100

Curiously, many in the research community are hesitant to say that two-parent families generally promote better outcomes for children than single-parent families. Some argue that we need finer measures of the extent of the family-structure effect. As one scholar has noted, it is possible, by disaggregating the data in certain ways, to make family structure "go away" as an independent variable. Other researchers point to studies that show that children suffer psychological effects as a result of family conflict preceding family breakup. Consequently, they reason, it is the conflict rather than the structure of the family that is responsible for many of the problems associated with family disruption. Others, including Judith Wallerstein, caution against treating children in divorced families and children in intact families as separate populations, because doing so tends to exaggerate the differences between the two groups. "We have to take this family by family," Wallerstein says.   101

Some of the caution among researchers can also be attributed to ideological pressures. Privately, social scientists worry that their research may serve ideological causes that they themselves do not support, or that their work may be misinterpreted as an attempt to "tell people what to do." Some are fearful that they will be attacked by feminist colleagues, or, more generally, that their comments will be regarded as an effort to turn back the clock to the 1950s—a goal that has almost no constituency in the academy. Even more fundamental, it has become risky for anyone—scholar, politician, religious leader—to make normative statements today. This reflects not only the persistent drive toward "value neutrality" in the professions but also a deep confusion about the purposes of public discourse. The dominant view appears to be that social criticism, like criticism of individuals, is psychologically damaging. The worst thing you can do is to make people feel guilty or bad about themselves.   102

When one sets aside these constraints, however, the case against the   103
two-parent family is remarkably weak. It is true that disaggregating data
can make family structure less significant as a factor, just as disaggregating Hurricane Andrew into wind, rain, and tides can make it disappear as
a meteorological phenomenon. Nonetheless, research opinion as well as
common sense suggests that the effects of changes in family structure
are great enough to cause concern. Nicholas Zill argues that many of the
risk factors for children are doubled or more than doubled as the result
of family disruption. "In epidemiological terms," he writes, "the doubling
of a hazard is a substantial increase. . . . the increase in risk that dietary
cholesterol poses for cardiovascular disease, for example, is far less than
double, yet millions of Americans have altered their diets because of the
perceived hazard."

The argument that family conflict, rather than the breakup of parents,   104
is the cause of children's psychological distress is persuasive on its face.
Children who grow up in high-conflict families, whether the families stay
together or eventually split up, are undoubtedly at great psychological
risk. And surely no one would dispute that there must be societal measures available, including divorce, to remove children from families where
they are in danger. Yet only a minority of divorces grow out of pathological situations; much more common are divorces in families unscarred by
physical assault. Moreover, an equally compelling hypothesis is that family breakup generates its own conflict. Certainly, many families exhibit
more conflictual and even violent behavior as a consequence of divorce
than they did before divorce.

Finally, it is important to note that clinical insights are different from   105
sociological findings. Clinicians work with individual families, who cannot
and should not be defined by statistical aggregates. Appropriate to a clinical approach, moreover, is a focus on the internal dynamics of family
functioning and on the immense variability in human behavior. Nevertheless, there is enough empirical evidence to justify sociological statements
about the causes of declining child well-being and to demonstrate that
despite the plasticity of human response, there are some useful rules of
thumb to guide our thinking about and policies affecting the family.

For example, Sara McLanahan says, three structural constants are   106
commonly associated with intact families, even intact families who would
not win any "Family of the Year" awards. The first is economic. In intact
families, children share in the income of two adults. Indeed, as a number
of analysts have pointed out, the two-parent family is becoming more
rather than less necessary, because more and more families need two
incomes to sustain a middle-class standard of living.

McLanahan believes that most intact families also provide a stable   107
authority structure. Family breakup commonly upsets the established
boundaries of authority in a family. Children are often required to make
decisions or accept responsibilities once considered the province of parents. Moreover, children, even very young children, are often expected to

behave like mature adults, so that the grown-ups in the family can be free to deal with the emotional fallout of the failed relationship. In some instances family disruption creates a complete vacuum in authority; everyone invents his or her own rules. With lines of authority disrupted or absent, children find it much more difficult to engage in the normal kinds of testing behavior, the trial and error, the failing and succeeding, that define the developmental pathway toward character and competence. McLanahan says, "Children need to be the ones to challenge the rules. The parents need to set the boundaries and let the kids push the boundaries. The children shouldn't have to walk the straight and narrow at all times."

Finally, McLanahan holds that children in intact families benefit from   108
stability in what she neutrally terms "household personnel." Family disruption frequently brings new adults into the family, including stepparents, live-in boyfriends or girlfriends, and casual sexual partners. Like stepfathers, boyfriends can present a real threat to children's, particularly to daughters', security and well-being. But physical or sexual abuse represents only the most extreme such threat. Even the very best of boyfriends can disrupt and undermine a child's sense of peace and security, McLanahan says. "It's not as though you're going from an unhappy marriage to peacefulness. There can be a constant changing until the mother finds a suitable partner."

McLanahan's argument helps explain why children of widows tend to   109
do better than children of divorced or unmarried mothers. Widows differ from other single mothers in all three respects. They are economically more secure, because they receive more public assistance through Survivors Insurance, and possibly private insurance or other kinds of support from family members. Thus widows are less likely to leave the neighborhood in search of a new or better job and a cheaper house or apartment. Moreover, the death of a father is not likely to disrupt the authority structure radically. When a father dies, he is no longer physically present, but his death does not dethrone him as an authority figure in the child's life. On the contrary, his authority may be magnified through death. The mother can draw on the powerful memory of the departed father as a way of intensifying her parental authority: "Your father would have wanted it this way." Finally, since widows tend to be older than divorced mothers, their love life may be less distracting.

Regarding the two-parent family, the sociologist David Popenoe, who   110
has devoted much of his career to the study of families, both in the United States and in Scandinavia, makes this straightforward assertion:

> Social science research is almost never conclusive. There are always methodological difficulties and stones left unturned. Yet in three decades of work as a social scientist, I know of few other bodies of data in which the weight of evidence is so decisively on one side of the issue: on the whole, for children, two-parent families are preferable to single-parent and stepfamilies.

THE REGIME EFFECT

The rise in family disruption is not unique to American society. It is evi- 111
dent in virtually all advanced nations, including Japan, where it is also
shaped by the growing participation of women in the work force. Yet the
United States has made divorce easier and quicker than in any other
Western nation with the sole exception of Sweden—and the trend toward
solo motherhood has also been more pronounced in America. (Sweden
has an equally high rate of out-of-wedlock birth, but the majority of such
births are to cohabiting couples, a long-established pattern in Swedish
society.) More to the point, nowhere has family breakup been greeted by
a more triumphant rhetoric of renewal than in America.

What is striking about this rhetoric is how deeply it reflects classic 112
themes in American public life. It draws its language and imagery from
the nation's founding myth. It depicts family breakup as a drama of revolution and rebirth. The nuclear family represents the corrupt past, an
institution guilty of the abuse of power and the suppression of individual
freedom. Breaking up the family is like breaking away from Old World
tyranny. Liberated from the bonds of the family, the individual can
achieve independence and experience a new beginning, a fresh start, a
new birth of freedom. In short, family breakup recapitulates the American
experience.

This rhetoric is an example of what the University of Maryland political 113
philosopher William Galston has called the "regime effect." The founding
of the United States set in motion a new political order based to an
unprecedented degree on individual rights, personal choice, and egalitarian relationships. Since then these values have spread beyond their original domain of political relationships to define social relationships as well.
During the past twenty-five years these values have had a particularly profound impact on the family.

Increasingly, political principles of individual rights and choice shape 114
our understanding of family commitment and solidarity. Family relationships are viewed not as permanent or binding but as voluntary and easily
terminable. Moreover, under the sway of the regime effect the family
loses its central importance as an institution in the civil society, accom-
plishing certain social goals such as raising children and caring for its
members, and becomes a means to achieving greater individual happiness—a lifestyle choice. Thus, Galston says, what is happening to the
American family reflects the "unfolding logic of authoritative, deeply
American moral-political principles."

One benefit of the regime effect is to create greater equality in adult 115
family relationships. Husbands and wives, mothers and fathers, enjoy
relationships far more egalitarian than past relationships were, and most
Americans prefer it that way. But the political principles of the regime
effect can threaten another kind of family relationship—that between parent and child. Owing to their biological and developmental immaturity,
children are needy dependents. They are not able to express their

choices according to limited, easily terminable, voluntary agreements. They are not able to act as negotiators in family decisions, even those that most affect their own interests. As one writer has put it, "a newborn does not make a good 'partner.'" Correspondingly, the parental role is antithetical to the spirit of the regime. Parental investment in children involves a diminished investment in self, a willing deference to the needs and claims of the dependent child. Perhaps more than any other family relationship, the parent-child relationship—shaped as it is by patterns of dependency and deference—can be undermined and weakened by the principles of the regime.

More than a century and a half ago Alexis de Tocqueville made the   116
striking observation that an individualistic society depends on a communitarian institution like the family for its continued existence. The family cannot be constituted like the liberal state, nor can it be governed entirely by that state's principles. Yet the family serves as the seedbed for the virtues required by a liberal state. The family is responsible for teaching lessons of independence, self-restraint, responsibility, and right conduct, which are essential to a free, democratic society. If the family fails in these tasks, then the entire experiment in democratic self-rule is jeopardized.

To take one example: independence is basic to successful functioning   117
in American life. We assume that most people in America will be able to work, care for themselves and their families, think for themselves, and inculcate the same traits of independence and initiative in their children. We depend on families to teach people to do these things. The erosion of the two-parent family undermines the capacity of families to impart this knowledge; children of long-term welfare-dependent single parents are far more likely than others to be dependent themselves. Similarly, the children in disrupted families have a harder time forging bonds of trust with others and giving and getting help across the generations. This, too, may lead to greater dependency on the resources of the state.

Over the past two and a half decades Americans have been conduct-   118
ing what is tantamount to a vast natural experiment in family life. Many would argue that this experiment was necessary, worthwhile, and long overdue. The results of the experiment are coming in, and they are clear. Adults have benefited from the changes in family life in important ways, but the same cannot be said for children. Indeed, this is the first generation in the nation's history to do worse psychologically, socially, and economically than its parents. Most poignantly, in survey after survey the children of broken families confess deep longings for an intact family.

Nonetheless, as Galston is quick to point out, the regime effect is not   119
an irresistible undertow that will carry away the family. It is more like a swift current, against which it is possible to swim. People learn; societies can change, particularly when it becomes apparent that certain behaviors damage the social ecology, threaten the public order, and impose new burdens on core institutions. Whether Americans will act to overcome the legacy of family disruption is a crucial but as yet unanswered question.

☐ FOR CLASS DISCUSSION

1. Analyze and evaluate the disagreements among these writers concerning issues of illegitimacy, single parenthood, and welfare by applying the first set of guide questions from page 473. How do you account for the differing points of view? (Do the writers disagree about questions of truth? About definitions? About appropriate comparisons or analogies? About values, assumptions, and beliefs?)

2. Choose one of the arguments for closer analysis, applying the second set of guide questions on page 474.

OPTIONAL WRITING ASSIGNMENT   As the junior staffer for Senator Murk, you've been asked to help the Senator determine an appropriate response to Charles Murray's proposal that welfare benefits be eliminated for unwed mothers (see pages 26–32 for Murray's argument). In particular, the Senator has asked you to prepare a working paper that summarizes the arguments for and against Murray's proposal, evaluates these arguments, and sets forth recommendations for the stand that Senator Murk should take. Drawing on your reading of the Murray and Gilliam arguments (Gilliam's argument is on pp. 47–48) as well as the arguments in this section, write your working paper for Senator Murk.

Acknowledgments

Gordon F. Adams, "Math Petition." Reprinted by permission of the author.
Elijah Anderson, "Abolishing Welfare Won't Stop Poverty, Illegitimacy," *Seattle Times,* January 6, 1994. Reprinted by permission of the author.
Anonymous. "Reading, Writing and (Ugh!) You Know What," reprinted by permission from *Science '86,* May 1986, pp 7–8. Copyright © 1986 by the American Association for the Advancement of Science.
Paul Appelbaum, "Crazy in the Streets," *Commentary,* May 1987. Reprinted by permission of the author.
William Arnold, "Tarnished Image of Academy Awards Hasn't Dulled World's Appetite for this Flawed Farce," *Seattle Post-Intelligencer,* March 29, 1987. Reprinted with permission of the *Seattle Post-Intelligencer.*
Katherine T. Bartlett, "Some Factual Correctness About Political Correctness," *The Wall Street Journal,* June 6, 1991. Reprinted by permission of *The Wall Street Journal,* © 1991 Dow Jones & Company, Inc. All rights reserved worldwide.
Stephen Bean, "What Should Be Done About the Mentally Ill Homeless?" Reprinted by permission of the author.
Wallace A. Broecker, "Global Warming on Trial." Reprinted with permission from *Natural History,* April, 1992. Copyright by the American Museum of Natural History 1992.
Susan Brownmiller, "Pornography Hurts Women," from *Against Our Will: Men, Women and Rape,* 1975. Copyright © 1975 by Susan Brownmiller. Reprinted by permission of Simon & Schuster, Inc.
Martha Chamallas, "Universal Truth and Multiple Perspectives: Controversies on Sexual Harassment," *Et Cetera,* Fall 1992. Reprinted by permission of the International Society for General Semantics, Box 728, Concord, CA 94522.
Lynnea Clark, "Women Police Officers: Should Size and Strength Be Criteria for Patrol Duty?" Reprinted by permission of the author.
Susan Crawford, "A Wink Here, A Leer There: It's Costly," *The New York Times,* March 28, 1993. Copyright © 1993 by The New York Times Company. Reprinted by permission.
Richard J. Dennis, "The Economics of Legalizing Drugs," *The Atlantic,* November 1990. Copyright 1990 by Richard J. Dennis as first published in *The Atlantic.* Reprinted by permission of the author.
"Dissent on Warming," a policy statement circulated by the Science and Environment Policy Project and signed by 50 atmospheric scientists. From the *Bulletin of the Atomic Scientists,* June 1992. Copyright © 1992 by the Educational Foundation for Nuclear Science, 6042 S. Kimbark Ave., Chicago, IL 60637.
Dao Do, "Choose Life!" Reprinted by permission of the author.
Barbara Ehrenreich, "Teach Diversity With a Smile," *Time,* April 8, 1991. Copyright 1991 Time Inc. Reprinted by permission of Time Inc.

Victor Fuchs, "Why Married Mothers Work." Reprinted by permission of the publishers from *How We Live* by Victor Fuchs, Cambridge, Mass.: Harvard University Press. Copyright © 1983 by the President and Fellows of Harvard College.

Michael S. Gazzaniga, "The Federal Drugstore," an interview with Michael S. Gazzaniga, *National Review,* February 5, 1990. Copyright © 1990 by *National Review,* Inc., 150 East 35th Street, New York, NY 10016. Reprinted by permission.

Dorothy Gilliam, "Wrong Way to Reform Welfare," *The Washington Post,* December 12, 1993. © 1993 *The Washington Post.* Reprinted with permission.

Ellen Goodman, "Minneapolis Pornography Ordinance," from *The Boston Globe,* 1985. © 1994, The Boston Globe Company. Reprinted with permission.

Ellen Goodman, "We Have Children for All Sorts of Reasons and Now One Is Made To Save Her Sibling," from *The Seattle Times,* 1990. © 1994, The Boston Globe Company. Reprinted with permission.

Debra Goodwin, "Beauty Pageant Fallacies." Reprinted by permission of the author.

Garrett Hardin, "Lifeboat Ethics: The Case Against Helping the Poor," *Psychology Today,* September 1974. Reprinted by permission of the author.

Bill C. Healy, "The Mandatory Motorcycle-Helmet Law is Bad Law." Reprinted by permission of the author.

Nat Hentoff, "'Speech Codes' on the Campus," *Dissent,* Fall 1991. Reprinted by permission of the author.

Molly Ivins, "200 Million Guns—Let's Not Make It Any Worse," *Seattle Times,* January 3, 1994. By permission of Molly Ivins and Creators Syndicate.

Erica Jong, "Fear of Flirting," *The Washington Post,* December 6, 1992. Reprinted by permission of the author.

Karen Kartes, "A Proposal to Restructure the Washington State High School Dance and Drill Team Association Competition." Reprinted by permission of the author.

Martin Luther King, Jr., "Letter from Birmingham Jail," from *Why We Can't Wait* by Martin Luther King, Jr. Copyright © 1963, 1964 by Martin Luther King, Jr. Reprinted by permission of HarperCollins, Publishers, Inc.

David Kopel, "Many Good People Own Guns: Better Safe Than Sorry." From *Los Angeles Times,* November 21, 1993, and *Yakima Herald-Republic,* December 1993. Reprinted by permission of the author.

Jonathan Kozol, "Are the Homeless Crazy? *Harpers Magazine,* February 1992. Excerpted from *Rachel and Her Children,* Crown Publishers, 1988. Reprinted by permission of the author.

Charles Krauthammer, "How to Save the Homeless Mentally Ill," by Charles Krauthammer. From *The New Republic,* February 8, 1988. Copyright by Charles Krauthammer. Edited version reprinted by permission of the author.

H. Richard Lamb, "Will We Save the Homeless Mentally Ill?" *American Journal of Psychiatry,* Vol. 147, pp. 649–651, May 1990. Copyright 1990, the American Psychiatric Association. Reprinted by permission.

Ursula K. Le Guin, "The Ones Who Walk Away from Omelas," by Ursula Le Guin. Copyright © 1973, 1975 by Ursula K. Le Guin; reprinted by permission of the author and the author's agent, Virginia Kidd.

Jeremy Leggett, "Global Warming: The Worst Case," from the *Bulletin of the Atomic Scientists,* June 1992. Copyright © 1992 by the Educational Foundation for Nuclear Science, 6042 S. Kimbark Ave., Chicago, IL 60637.

John Leo, "At a cultural crossroads," *U.S. News & World Report,* December 20, 1993. Copyright John Leo 1993. Reprinted by permission of the author.

John Leo, "New Cultural Conscience Shifts Welfare Debate," *Seattle Times,* December 14, 1993. Reprinted by permission of Universal Press Syndicate. All rights reserved.

John Leo, "The Politics of Feelings," *U.S. News and World Report,* March 23, 1992. Reprinted by permission of U.S. News and World Report.

Michael Levin, "The Case for Torture," *Newsweek,* June 7, 1982. Reprinted by permission of the author.

Daniel Maguire, "Death by Choice: Who Should Decide?" from *Death by Choice* by Daniel Maguire. Copyright © 1973, 1974 by Daniel C. Maguire. Used by permission of Doubleday, a division of Bantam Doubleday Dell Publishing Group, Inc.

Judith Martin and Gunther Stent, "Say the Right Thing—Or Else; Attack Ideas not People," *The New York Times,* March 20, 1991. Copyright © 1991 by The New York Times Company. Reprinted by permission.

William F. May, "Rising to the Occasion of Our Death," *The Christian Century,* July 11–18, 1990.

James Q. Wilson, "Against the Legalization of Drugs," reprinted from *Commentary*, February 1990, by permission; all rights reserved; also by permission of the author.

Walter Wink, "Biting the Bullet: The Case for Legalizing Drugs," *The Christian Century*, August 8–15, 1990. Copyright 1990 Christian Century Foundation. Reprinted by permission from the August 8–15, 1990 issue of *The Christian Century*.

Index

A

Accidental criteria. *See* Criteria, accidental, necessary, and sufficient
Adams, Gordon (student), 16–21, 143–44
Ad hominem fallacy, 435–36
Analogy, 274–77. *See also* Resemblance arguments
  as source of disagreement, 42–43
  extended analogies, 275–76
  in causal arguments, 247–48
  undeveloped analogies, 273
Anderson, Elija, 721
APA (American Psychological Association) Documentation system, 405–20
Appeal to false authority (bandwagon fallacy), 434
Appeal to irrational premises fallacy, 433
Appeal to the person fallacy. *See Ad hominem* fallacy
Appelbaum, Paul S., 676
Argument
  clarification as goal of, 8–10
  different from persuasion, 3–5
  different from pseudo-argument, 90–93
  from cause/consequence, 198–99
  from principle/definition, 197–98
  from resemblance/analogy, 199–200
  initial definition of, 6–8
  logical structure of, 93–94, 98–117
  one-sided versus two-sided, 169–71
  process of, 13–21
  standard form of, 158–65
Argument to the people fallacy (stirring symbols), 432–33
Aristotelian definition, 211–13
Aristotle, 100, 141. *See also* Aristotelian definition
Arnold, William, 303–07
Assumptions
  lack of shared assumptions as cause of pseudo-argument, 91–93
  understanding of audience's assumptions, 140–47
  unstated assumptions. *See* Enthymeme
Attributive tags, 37–38, 402–403
Audience
  accomodation of, 166–83
  analysis of, 145–47
  moving your audience, 140–65
  respectful treatment of, 21–22, 166–83 *passim*
Audience-based reasons. *See* Reasons
Ayala, Abe and Mary, 52–58, 75–77

B

Backing. *See* Toulmin logic
Bandwagon fallacy. *See* Appeal to irrational premises fallacy
Bartlett, Katherine T., 547
Bean, Stephen (student), 64–65, 66–67, 72–74
Because clauses. *See also* Reasons
  because clauses as enthymemes, 100–02
  brainstorming pro/con because clauses, 69
  expanding because clauses into logical structures. *See* Toulmin logic
  stating reasons as because clauses, 94–96
Begging the question fallacy, 437–38
Believing/doubting game, 66–69
Bone-marrow transplant case. *See* Ayala, Abe and Mary
Broecker, Wallace S., 648
Brownmiller, Susan, 284–87
Bucalo, Patricia, 44–45

C

Caesarean section case, 11–12
Callicles, 8–11 *passim*, 22, 92, 140
Card catalog, 374–76
Causal arguments, 15, 195, 234–69
Cause/consequence, argument from. *See* Argument from cause/consequence
Chain of reasons. *See* Reasons, chain of
Chief Sealth, 152–53

Circular argument. *See* Begging the question fallacy
Citing sources, 390–92
Claim, 93. *See also* Toulmin logic
Clark, Lynnea (student), 372, 373, 388–90, 421–29
Clonethink, 453
Complex question fallacy, 438
Concession, 178–79
Conciliatory or Rogerian approach, 179–82
Concrete language for creating *pathos*, 151–52
Conditions of rebuttal. *See* Toulmin logic; Refutation
Consequences. *See also* Causal arguments
    in ethical theory, 356–59, 361–62
    problem of predicting and evaluating, 316–17
Constraints, 249
Contributing cause, 248
Correlation, 245–46, 439
Correlation for cause fallacy. *See Post hoc ergo propter hoc*
Cost, in evaluation arguments, 294–95
Crank letter, 21–22
Crawford, Susan, 641
Criteria, accidental, necessary, and sufficient, 211–12
Criteria, determination of in evaluation arguments, 295–97
Criteria-match structure in argument
    in definition arguments, 205–07, 210–14
    in evaluation arguments, 290–92
Cross-burning case, 12–13

D
Davis, Darlene H., 593
Definition
    arguments from. *See* Arguments from principle/definition
    Aristotelian, 211–13
    claims, 15
    difference between definition claims and resemblance claims, 271–73
    operational, 213–14
    as source of disagreement, 42
Definition arguments, 202–33
Delayed thesis arguments, 158–65
Dennis, Richard J., 569
"Dissent on Warming," 674
Do, Dao (student), 138–39
Documentation of sources, 404–20

E
Egothink, 453
Ehrenreich, Barbara, 550
Elbow, Peter, 66
Emotional appeals. *See Pathos*
Empirical measures in evaluation arguments, 294
Enthymeme, 100–02 *See also* Toulmin logic
Equivocation fallacy, 438

Ethical arguments, 196, 352–67
Ethos, 15, 86–87, 97, 140, 147–49, 149–50, 157, 164, 318
Evaluation arguments, 15, 196, 288–311
Evidence
    distinguishing fact from opinion in citing, 129
    examples, 113
    from interviews, surveys, and questionnaires, 120–22
    from personal experience, 118–20
    persuasive use of, 127–31
    from reading and research, 122–26
    refutation of, 176–78
    statistics, 114
    as support, 110–14
    testimony, 114
Examples
    in creation of *pathos*, 152–54
    as evidence, 113
Experts, what to do when they disagree, 125–27
Exploration and rehearsal
    as exploration tasks, 77–81
    as stage of writing process, 61–62
Expressive writing. *See* Exploration and rehearsal

F
Fact, 129, 195
Facts as source of disagreement, 41–42
Fallacies, informal, 430–43. *See also* names of specific fallacies
False analogy, 248, 441
False authority fallacy, 434
False dilemma fallacy, 438
Fanatics, 90–91
Forecasting structures, 96–97
Freewriting, 64–65
Fuchs, Victor, 246, 263–67

G
Gazzaniga, Michael S., 552
Gilliam, Dorothy, 47–49, 49–51
Global warming, 122–27
Goodman, Ellen, 56–58, 160–65
Goodwin, Debra (student), 309–11
Goodwin, Donald W., 593
Graphs, interpretation of, 445–49
Grounds. *See* Toulmin logic
Groups, working in, 452–71

H
Hardin, Garrett, 494
Hasty generalization fallacy, 244–45, 440–41
Healy, Bill C. (student), 307–09
Hentoff, Nat, 538
Heuristic strategies, 63. *See also* Toulmin logic; Principles/Consequences/Analogies strategy; Stock issues strategy
Hillocks, George, 205fn.

Hobbes, Thomas, 356
Homelessness, 13, 226–33, 339–51

I
Idea maps, 65–67
Immediate cause, 248
Index to periodicals and newspapers, 376–81
Induction, 244–45
Inference, 129
Informal fallacies. *See* Fallacies, informal
Issue questions
    different from information questions,
        88–90
    as origins of argument, 87–88
Ivins, Molly, 481

J
Johnson, Lyndon, 281–82
Jong, Erica, 633

K
Kant, Immanuel, 359–60, 362
Kartes, Karen (student), 318, 332–38
King, Martin Luther, Jr., 513
Kopel, Dave, 483
Kozol, Jonathan, 687
Krauthammer Charles, 223, 226–33

L
Le Guin, Ursula, 362–67
Leggett, Jeremy, 656
Leo, John, 46, 544
Levin, Michael, 395–97, 398–403 *passim*
Loaded language, 170
Logical fallacies. *See* Fallacies, informal
Logos, 15, 86–87, 98–117 passim, 140, 147–49,
    157
Lunt, Elwood, Jr. (fictional student), 456–57,
    461–62
Lynnea (student). *See* Clark, Lynnea

M
Maguire, Daniel C., 489
Maraldo, Pamela Jo, 45–46
Martin, Judith, 546
May, William F., 487
Metaphor, 154–56
Mill, John Stuart, 356–62 *passim*
Minot, Walter, 267–69
Mitigating circumstances, 293
MLA (Modern Language Association) docu-
    mentation system, 405–20
Monastersky, R., 670
Moral agruments. *See* Ethical arguments
Morgenson, Gretchen, 637
Munson, Naomi, 629
Murray, Charles, 26–32, 32–52 *passim*

N
Naive egoism as ethical theory, 354–56
Necessary cause, 249

Necessary criteria. *See* Criteria, accidental,
    necessary, and sufficient
Nelson, Sandra (student), 52, 58, 75–77
Non sequitur fallacy, 441–42
Note taking for research paper, 390

O
Occam's razor, 439
One-sided arguments, 169–70
Operational definitions, 213–14
Opposing views. *See* Refutation
Oversimplified cause fallacy, 248

P
Paraphrasing and quoting in research
    papers, 394–404
Pathos, 15, 86–87, 140, 147–49, 150–57, 164
Plagiarism, 403–04
Plato, 8–13 *passim*, 452, 533. *See also* Callicles;
    Socrates
Pollitt, Katha, 714
Post hoc ergo propter hoc fallacy, 244, 439
Precedence, argument from, 277–80. *See also*
    Resemblance arguments
Precipitating cause, 248
Premises. *See* Reasons
Presence, 314–16. *See also Pathos*
Principle, argument from, 197–98
Principle of charity, 170–71
Principle as an ethical theory, 357–59, 361–62
Proposal argument, 15, 312–51
Provincialism fallacy, 433

Q
Qualifier. *See* Toulmin logic
Quayle, Dan, 708
Quoting. *See* Paraphrasing and quoting in
    research papers

R
Ray, Dixy Lee, 672
Reading arguments
    analyzing why disputants disagree, 26,
        41–51
    as a believer, 26–38
    as a doubter, 26, 38–41
    evaluating the conflicting positions 26,
        51–52
    improving your reading process, 24–26
Reasons. *See also* Toulmin logic
    audience-based, 141–47
    chain of, 114–16
    as core of argument, 93–96
    defined, 93
    expressed as "because" clauses, 94–96
    support of, 108–17
    writer-based, 141–47
Rebuttal. *See* Refutation
Recency of data, 128
Red herring fallacy, 434
Refutation

Refutation (*continued*)
    conceding to opposing views, 178–79
    conciliatory or Rogerian approach,
        179–82
    rebutting opposing views, 171–78, 188–90
    refuting causal claims, 254–56
    refuting definitional claims, 221–23
    refuting evaluation claims, 301–02
    refuting evidence, 176–78
    refuting proposal claims, 329–31
    refuting resemblance claims, 280–83
    in standard form arguments, 158–65
    summarizing opposing views in 170–71
Remote cause, 248
Representativeness of data, 128
Research paper, 370–429
Research question, 371–74
Resemblance, argument from. *See* Argument
    from resemblance
Resemblance arguments, 195, 270–87
Rhetorical triangle, 86–88
Riger, Stephanie, 612
Robins, Lee N., 593
Rogerian argument, 179–82
Rogers, Carl, 26, 179
Rule of Justice, 209–210

S
Sagan, Carl, 242, 256–61
Self-announcing structures, 96–97
Singer, Peter, 504
Singer, S. Fred, 663
Single-parenthood issue, 26–52 *passim*
Sharry, Frank, 478
Skeptics, 90–91
Slanted language, 154–57
Slippery slope fallacy, 439–40
Socrates, 8–11 *passim*, 23, 92, 140
Sophistry, 8–11 *passim*, 140
Sources, incorporating into your argument,
    390–404
Standard form arguments, 158–65
Standards in evaluation arguments, 293
Starting points
    as exploratory tasks, 77–79
    as stage of writing process, 62
Stated reason. *See* Because clause;
    Enthymeme; Toulmin logic
Statistical traps, 444–51
Statistics, 114
Stein, Dan, 475
Stent, Gunther, 546
Stock issues strategy, 70, 322–24
Strawperson fallacy, 171, 436
Sufficiency of data, 128
Sufficient cause, 249
Sufficient criteria. *See* Criteria, accidental,
    necessary, and sufficient
Sullivan, Kathy (student), 219–21, 224–26
Summary writing, 32–39
    in research papers, 38, 392–94

T
Team-writing case, 166–83 *passim*
Testimony, 114. *See also* Evidence
Thesis statement. *See also* Claim; Working
        thesis statement
    as one-sentence summary of argument, 93
    placement of thesis, 96–97, 157–65
Three-step strategy
        (principle/consequence/resemblance),
        196–201, 321–22, 328
Torpey, Mary Lou (student), 243, 261–63
Torrey, E. Fuller, 701
Toulmin, Stephen, 102. *See also* Toulmin logic
Toulmin logic, 70, 102–17, 172–76 *passim*
    as a schema to determine a strategy of
        support, 108–110
    in causal arguments, 238–39
    in definition arguments, 206, 219–21
    in evaluation arguments, 291–92, 298–99
    in proposal arguments, 324
    in resemblance arguments, 273, 281
Tree diagrams, 70–75
Truth claims, 195
Truth in the modern world, 10–13
Two-sided arguments, 169–71

U
Unfolding structures, 96–97
Utilitarianism. *See* Mill, John Stuart

V
Vanderstaay, Steven, 691
Values as a source of disagreement, 43
Value claims, 196
Van Dusen, Lewis H., Jr., 000

W
Warrant. *See* Toulmin logic
Whitehead, Barbara Dafoe, 723
Wilson, James Q., 579
Wink, Walter, 563
Word choice. *See* Slanted lanuage
Working thesis statement, 95
Writing assignments
    analogy microtheme, 274
    analysis of the sources of disagreement in
        opposing arguments, 82
    analysis of a resemblance argument
    argument summary, 82
    conciliatory or Rogerian strategy, 188–90
    debate essay, 82–83
    evaluation of a controversial X, 290
    extended definition/borderline case, 205
    letter to instructor about yourself as a
        writer, 81–82
    microtheme drawing on newspaper story
        for data, 134–35
    microtheme supporting reason with per-
        sonal experience data, 132
    microtheme that uses evidence from
        research, 132–34

microtheme using statistical data, 135
multi-reasoned formal argument, 135–38
policy proposal as guest editorial,
    318–19
policy proposal as research paper,
    318–19
practical proposal addresssing a local
    problem, 318–19
precedence microtheme, 274

summarizing and refuting the opposition,
    185
surprising or disputed causes, 241
Writing processes, 61–62
    in causal arguments, 251–56
    in definition arguments, 215–23
    in evaluation arguments, 300–02
    in proposal arguments, 327–31
    strategies for improving, 62–64